Red Star over the Black Sea

# Red Star over the Black Sea

*Nâzım Hikmet and his Generation*

JAMES H. MEYER

Great Clarendon Street, Oxford, OX2 6DP,
United Kingdom

Oxford University Press is a department of the University of Oxford.
It furthers the University's objective of excellence in research, scholarship,
and education by publishing worldwide. Oxford is a registered trade mark of
Oxford University Press in the UK and in certain other countries

© James H. Meyer 2023

The moral rights of the author have been asserted

First Edition published in 2023

All rights reserved. No part of this publication may be reproduced, stored in
a retrieval system, or transmitted, in any form or by any means, without the
prior permission in writing of Oxford University Press, or as expressly permitted
by law, by licence or under terms agreed with the appropriate reprographics
rights organization. Enquiries concerning reproduction outside the scope of the
above should be sent to the Rights Department, Oxford University Press, at the
address above

You must not circulate this work in any other form
and you must impose this same condition on any acquirer

Published in the United States of America by Oxford University Press
198 Madison Avenue, New York, NY 10016, United States of America

British Library Cataloguing in Publication Data

Data available

Library of Congress Control Number: 2022945786

ISBN 978-0-19-287117-6

DOI: 10.1093/oso/9780192871176.001.0001

Printed in the UK by
Bell & Bain Ltd., Glasgow

*For Mom and Dad*

# Acknowledgments

There is no "I" in "history."

Well—okay, I guess technically there is. But writing a book is a team effort, even if the author alone is responsible for any mistakes, mischaracterizations, and other defects.

It begins with family. I write about border-crossers because I am one, having grown up with a deep and developing interest in foreign languages and seeing the world. This didn't come about by accident, but was rather ingrained in me by my parents, Dr. John F. and Nancy Meyer, who dragged me around Europe when I was a kid. My brother Jack encouraged me to see the world after my graduation from college and provided an example of what living abroad could be like. My sister Trish and brother-in-law Mark helped to make my trips back to Ann Arbor pleasant ones. Thank you for raising me in a home were I always felt loved, and where a youngest child could feel prompted to ask about the events that took place before he was born. And thank you, to my daughter Eszter, for making this world a more beautiful place.

Mentors, friends, and colleagues in academia have played vital roles in this book's conception. Many years ago, Norman Itzkowitz helped to steer me toward Brown University, for which I will always be grateful. While I was a doctoral student writing a dissertation on the pan-Turkists, Engin Akarlı once mentioned to me that a number of other individuals had "gone in the other direction" in the 1920s. I would recall this observation some twelve years later when, standing in a bookstore in the Istanbul district of Beşiktaş as a newly-minted associate professor, it occurred to me that I might explore the possibility of writing a book about Nâzım Hikmet.

Cristina Pop read this manuscript, and its many associated components, on occasions too numerous to estimate. Throughout this process, I always felt that she understood what I was trying to accomplish, and without her friendship and moral support this book would have been something different altogether. Bruce Grant has been an incredible source of encouragement, wisdom, and good cheer, reading this manuscript on multiple occasions and challenging me to take steps that ended up improving the quality of the work enormously. Brigid O'Keeffe time and again steered me toward scholarship that greatly improved this book, and as a discussant and co-panelist at various ASEEES conferences spoke to me on numerous occasions regarding how it could be made better. Orit Bashkin organized a workshop at the University of Chicago that, while ultimately canceled in March 2020, nevertheless spurred me toward writing a paper that became an important component of this book's argument. Mark Mazower was an important early mentor who helped me in the initial phases of this project. Charles King was kind enough to talk to me about publishing.

I am grateful to my colleagues at Montana State University. In particular I would like to acknowledge Prasanta Bandyopadhyay, Susan Cohen, Catherine Dunlop, Dan

viii ACKNOWLEDGMENTS

Flory, Maggie Greene, Hunter Hash, Kristen Intemann, Tim LeCain, Dale Martin, James Martin, Mary Murphy, Michael Reidy, Robert Rydell, Peter Schweppe, Billy Smith, Peter Tillack, Molly Todd, and Brett Walker. Outside of MSU a number of academic and non-academic friends likewise provided advice, assistance, and good company, including: Azat Akhunov, Pablo Coletes, Earl Flanagan, Destan Kandemir, Filiz Mirkelam, Mike Reynolds, James Ryan, Pınar Şenışık, James Sletten, Will Smiley, Judy Weissmann, Josh White, and Sufian Zhemukhov Very special thanks are due to İrfan Özdabak for reading through this entire manuscript with a keen eye—I greatly appreciate your help. Greg Merchant spent countless hours working on this book's images—thank you so much for this. I'd also like to express my gratitude to Gordon Dobie, who gave me my first job in Turkey in 1992, as well as to all of my teachers at Purdue, McGill, Princeton, and Brown universities.

Researching in multiple countries over the course of seven years is not cheap, so financing tends to be an important part of the process. A scholarship from the Fulbright US Scholar Program provided me with funding and first-rate logistical support during the course of nine months of research in Russia during the 2016–17 academic year. Research trips to Istanbul, Amsterdam, and Washington, DC, as well as a follow-up visit to Moscow in the summer of 2019, were generously supported through several grants awarded by Montana State University, including: a Scholarship and Creativity Grant, two Faculty Excellence Grants, and multiple Research Enhancement Awards. Montana State University also awarded me a full-year sabbatical, without which this book would have likely never been written in its present form. Thank you to the provost's office, the College of Letters and Science, and the Department of History and Philosophy for making this research possible. I am also much obliged to the Renne Library, especially its ILL department, as well as to Dave Michael. Thank you for the great amount of assistance you provided in connection with this book.

In Moscow, Joel Ericson, Director of the Fulbright Program in Russia, was an outstanding source of information and support, as was his office's wonderful staff. The Higher School of Economics, which served as my host institution in Moscow, provided me with both academic support and a terrific intellectual atmosphere. Albina Gasimova at HSE somehow managed to make my research year in Russia bureaucratically painless: Бик зур рәхмәт! During my Fulbright year I also got to know a number of younger scholars in Moscow who provided good company and sound advice relating to the Soviet archives, including: Betty Banks, Tyler Kirk, Nick Levy, and Mike Loader, among others. Friends from Moscow whom I met while researching this book, and who were nice enough to listen to me try to explain what I was seeking to accomplish, include Venera Gumirova, Nelly Elagina, and Ella Baranova.

The year in Moscow would not have been the same without Andrew Wiget and Olga Balalaeva, whose friendly company and elegant dinner parties I'll never forget. Andy, Olga, and Elena Diakova also intervened at an important moment to help make this book better—thank you so much for everything. I would also like to gratefully acknowledge Anna Stepanova, who granted me permission to work with Nâzım Hikmet's personal archive at RGALI; Yekaterina Simonova, who gave me access to the RGALI papers of Konstantin Simonov; and Gün Benderli, who was kind enough to speak with me on three occasions at her home in Budapest in June 2018. Thank you as well to the staffs of RGALI, RGASPI, and GARF, as well as of the Lenin Library in Moscow and the National Library in St. Petersburg.

In Istanbul, where I researched this book on numerous occasions over the past seven years, I am particularly thankful to the staff of the Prime Ministry Ottoman Archives (BOA), who also helped me to access the holdings of the Prime Ministry Republican Archives (BCA). Just outside Istanbul, in the town of Çatalca, I was assisted by the staff of the Aziz Nesin Vakfı (ANV), who went out of their way to provide me with the access that I needed. Erden Akbulut of TÜSTAV was kind and helpful in suggesting books I would need and giving me access to TÜSTAV's digital archives. The staff at Mimar Sinan University's cinema archives allowed me to watch difficult-to-find films. During the last days of ARIT's now-shuttered guesthouse in Arnavutköy, Gülden Güneri and Anthony Greenwood once again made staying in Istanbul feel that much sweeter.

The staff of the International Institute of Social History (IISH) in Amsterdam provided me with very efficient and helpful services in providing access to their extensive holdings relating to Nâzım Hikmet and the Turkish Communist Party. In College Park, MD, David Langbart of the National Archives and Records Administration assisted me immensely, providing me with detailed responses to my numerous queries.

At Oxford University Press, I would like to thank Cathryn Steele for her support of this project and patience with me—it's been a pleasure working with you. The two anonymous readers who provided peer reviews for this book helped to improve the quality of this work greatly—their attention to detail was so impressive and beneficial to the final product. Stephanie Ireland played an early role in this project's development, for which I am grateful. During the final production period, Saraswathi Ethiraju and Jo North both provided much-needed and highly appreciated editorial assistance. I would also like to thank the editors, staffs, and peer reviewers of the *Journal of the Ottoman and Turkish Studies Association* and *Middle Eastern Studies*, who published articles of mine that I later drew upon in writing this book. Thanks, finally, to the M7M team—I couldn't have done this without you.

I feel very fortunate to have had the chance to spend the last seven years thinking and writing about Nâzım Hikmet and his friends, classmates, and comrades on a daily basis. I've done my best to tell their stories well, and I'll remember this time with them fondly even as I move on to new things.

James H. Meyer

*The Borderlands Lodge*
*Belgrade, Montana*
*January, 2023*

# Contents

| | |
|---|---|
| *Illustrations and Maps* | xiii |
| *Abbreviations* | xv |
| *Notes on Transliteration and Names* | xvii |
| Prologue: Tears of Joy | 1 |
| Introduction: The Border-Crosser | 4 |
| 1. Child of the Imperial Borderlands | 18 |
| 2. On the Road to Ankara | 39 |
| 3. Up for Grabs in Anatolia | 62 |
| 4. First Soviet Steps | 88 |
| 5. In Revolutionary Russia | 105 |
| 6. Moscow-Istanbul-Moscow-Istanbul | 133 |
| 7. At Large in Istanbul | 158 |
| 8. Closing Doors | 184 |
| 9. Descending into Darkness | 212 |
| 10. Desperate Measures | 238 |
| 11. In Stalin's USSR | 258 |
| 12. A Kind of Freedom | 284 |
| 13. Final Frontiers | 314 |
| Epilogue: Afterlives | 339 |
| *Bibliography* | 353 |
| *Index* | 365 |

# Illustrations and Maps

## Illustrations

| | | |
|---|---|---|
| I.1 | Nâzım Hikmet | 6 |
| 1.1 | Nâzım with his mother Celile and younger sister Samiye | 20 |
| 2.1 | Şevket Süreyya in 1918 | 41 |
| 2.2 | Süleyman Nuri in 1920 | 51 |
| 2.3 | Vâlâ and Nâzım in their *kalpak*s | 60 |
| 5.1 | The Hotel Luxe | 107 |
| 5.2 | Fahri Reşid prior to and during his studies in Moscow | 114 |
| 5.3 | Fevziye Habibova | 118 |
| 5.4 | Alexander Senkevich | 119 |
| 5.5 | "International Literary Meeting" | 131 |
| 6.1 | Letter from Vâlâ to Semyon Brikke | 134 |
| 6.2 | The METLA Theater | 154 |
| 6.3 | Nâzım's letter to the Comintern | 156 |
| 7.1 | Nâzım and İsmail on *Cumhuriyet*'s front page | 159 |
| 7.2 | Zekeriya Sertel | 166 |
| 7.3 | Sabiha Sertel | 167 |
| 7.4 | Abdülhak Hamit's portrait crossed out in *Resimli Ay* | 171 |
| 8.1 | Münevver Andaç | 190 |
| 8.2 | Mara Kolarova | 202 |
| 10.1 | Nâzım and Münevver | 254 |
| 11.1 | All smiles for now: Nâzım arriving in Moscow, June 29, 1951 | 259 |
| 11.2 | Nâzım's arrival on the front page of *Scânteia*, June 21 | 261 |
| 11.3 | Buried in the middle: the smaller print of Nâzım's page 3 arrival in *Pravda* | 262 |
| 12.1 | In Peredelkino with Galina, 1954 | 287 |
| 12.2 | Nâzım and Vera | 296 |
| 13.1 | Nâzım, Vera, and Abidin Dino in Paris, 1962 | 329 |
| 14.1 | Meeting Fidel Castro in Cuba in 1978 | 347 |
| 14.2 | Nâzım Hikmet's tomb in Moscow | 349 |

## Maps

| | |
|---|---|
| 1.1 The Ottoman Balkans in 1912 | 19 |
| 2.1 Istanbul today | 40 |
| 2.2 Present-day map highlighting Zonguldak, İnebolu, Kastamonu, and Ankara | 56 |
| 3.1 Contemporary map of central and eastern Anatolia, with Ankara and Kars circled | 83 |
| 9.1 Northwestern Turkey and the Marmara Sea | 216 |

# Abbreviations

## Archives and Sources

| | |
|---|---|
| ANV | Aziz Nesin Foundation Archive |
| BCA | Prime Ministry Republican Archive |
| BOA | Prime Ministry Ottoman Archive |
| GARF | State Archive of the Russian Federation |
| IISH | International Institute of Social History |
| NARA | National Archive and Records Administration |
| RGALI | Russian State Archive of Literature and Art |
| RGASPI | Russian State Archive of Socio-Political History |

## Archival Citations

| | |
|---|---|
| f. | *fond* (collection) |
| op. | *opis'* (inventory) |
| d. | *delo* (file) |
| l. | *list* (leaf) |
| ob. | *Oborot* (verso) |
| s. | *sayfa* (page) |

# Notes on Transliteration and Names

I have followed the Library of Congress transliteration system from the Cyrillic alphabet to the Latin script. However, in certain cases I have retained the common English-language spelling of names. So, for example, I have written "Tolstoy" rather than "Tolstoi," and "Tulyakova" rather than "Tuliakova."

Surnames were not used in Turkey until 1935, so when introducing individuals prior to that year I put their later surname in parentheses: Şevket Süreyya (Aydemir), Mustafa Kemal (Atatürk).

Since 1929, Turkish has been written in the Latin script, so it is not transliterated in English-language texts. However, some letters in Turkish are pronounced quite differently from their English-language equivalent, including:

C is pronounced like the English J. So *Can* should be pronounced like "John."

Ç is pronounced like CH in English, so *Andaç* should be pronounced like "Andach."

Ş is pronounced like SH in English, so *Şevket* sounds like "Shevket."

Ğ is silent, so *Hacıoğlu* sounds like "Haji-oh-loo."

E is always pronounced, and rhymes with "say" or "jay," so *Celile* sounds like "Jay-lee-lay."

İ, i is pronounced like "ee" in English.

I, ı is pronounced like "le" in French.

There are no dipthongs in Turkish, so *Suphi* is pronounced "Soup-he."

Unless otherwise noted, all translations are my own.

Nikolai Nikolaevich was living in Lausanne. In the books he published there in Russian and in translation, he developed his long-standing notion of history as a second universe, erected by mankind in response to the phenomenon of death with the aid of the phenomena of time and memory.

Boris Pasternak, Doctor Zhivago

# Prologue

## Tears of Joy

It was an early Sunday morning—June 17, 1951—and Nâzım Hikmet was awakening into darkness.[1] Turkey's best-known poet was fleeing his country, heading north to Bulgaria. At forty-nine years of age, Nâzım was making one more reach beyond his grasp, seeking to escape from the prison that Turkey had become for him. His once reddish-blond locks were showing hints of grey and Nâzım's face was now creased with age, but still he was seeking to add chapters to his life. Nâzım Hikmet would remain trapped inside no longer.

As he would later recount to his debriefers in Romania, Nâzım had started this day well before dawn. Creeping out of his home on the Anatolian (or "Asian") side of Istanbul, he had walked down to the main road and flagged a taxi. Arriving at the prearranged spot, he exited the car and made his way down to the Bosphorus, the turquoise saltwater strait that divides Istanbul—and Turkey—between continental Europe and Asia.[2] The Bosphorus would this morning serve as the highway that Nâzım would take in his escape, just as he had done when he had fled British-occupied Istanbul at the age of nineteen. This time, Nâzım's brother-in-law Refik was spiriting him out of the country on a small Chris-Craft motorboat.

On the face of it, their plan was insane. The Black Sea is notorious for its rough waves and strong current. Yet Nâzım and Refik, the husband of Nâzım's younger half-sister Melda, were proposing something even more challenging than just riding the potentially treacherous seas on such a small craft. They were also hoping to somehow make their way past the patrols of Turkish navy and coast guard vessels and enter the territorial waters of the People's Republic of Bulgaria, some 130 miles away. The idea was for them to do an end-around past the Iron Curtain, enabling Nâzım to go and live as a free man, he hoped, in the USSR or elsewhere in the Eastern Bloc.

It wasn't going to be easy. In recent years, the Turkish–Bulgarian border had emerged as a potential Cold War flash point, with the two countries positioned in opposite camps across a burgeoning superpower divide. The frontier between Turkey and Bulgaria was now a death-zone for those attempting to cross illegally. For an idea

---

[1] "Hikmet" was not Nâzım's surname, as no one had an official family name in Turkey until 1935. Instead, his given name was "Nâzım Hikmet," with many of his friends simply calling him "Nâzım," a convention that I follow in this book. In 1935 Nâzım chose the surname "Ran," but is seldom referred to by this name. On the surname law, see Bernard Lewis, *The Emergence of Modern Turkey* (London: Oxford University Press, 1961), 289.

[2] Personal (*lichnyi*) file of Nâzım Hikmet, Russian State Archive of Socio-Political History (henceforth RGASPI), f. 495, op. 266, d. 47, Part I, ll. 17–23, here 22. June 26, 1951. "Statement of Nâzım Hikmet."

*Red Star over the Black Sea: Nâzım Hikmet and his Generation.* James H. Meyer, Oxford University Press. © James H. Meyer 2023.
DOI: 10.1093/oso/9780192871176.003.0001

of what could go wrong, Nâzım needed to look no further than at the example of his fellow leftist writer Sabahattin Ali. In March of 1948 the author of *Madonna in a Fur Coat* paid a guide to lead him from Kırklareli, Turkey to Burgaz, Bulgaria. Weeks passed, however, and Ali never showed up on the Bulgarian side of the border. On April 16, a Turkish shepherd discovered his decomposing body near the frontier. Someone had rained down blows upon the bespectacled novelist's head, crushing Sabahattin Ali's skull with a bat.

Riding the choppy tide of the Black Sea toward Bulgaria, Nâzım and Refik noticed that a ship had appeared in the distance. Getting closer, the brothers-in-law could see that it was a Romanian cargo vessel called the *Plekhanov*. As was the case with Bulgaria, Romania was an ally of the USSR, which meant that boarding the *Plekhanov* could conceivably be just as useful to Nâzım as traveling all the way into Bulgarian waters.

After a brief conversation, Nâzım and Refik decided to audible. Refik changed course and the Chris-Craft slowly approached the *Plekhanov*, with the brothers-in-law now waving excitedly at the ship's surprised crewmembers. Refik endeavored to steer closer to the ship while Nâzım shouted up several more times to the crew in Russian and French. The little motorboat was pummeled by the waves that were churned up by the much larger vessel.

They began to perceive signs of progress. The ship's crewmembers cut the *Plekhanov*'s engines, making it easier for them to hear what Nâzım was saying. But meanwhile, time was passing. If the ship's crew didn't take Nâzım, the brothers-in-law would still have a long journey ahead of them.[3]

But Nâzım was in luck, if that's how it can be described. The previous year, he had been the subject of an international, and largely Eastern Bloc-driven, campaign demanding his release from prison in Turkey. For this reason, Nâzım was relatively well-known in Eastern Europe. The crew of the *Plekhanov* recognized him, eventually, and came to realize what he wanted from them. After an extended delay while the ship's captain radioed back to Bucharest to explain that someone claiming to be the famous communist poet Nâzım Hikmet was asking to be let on board, at last a rope ladder was lowered down to the motorboat.[4]

Nâzım turned to Refik and kissed him farewell on both cheeks, Turkish-style.[5] The 49-year-old poet climbed the ladder up toward the deck of the cargo ship looming far above. Refik turned the Chris-Craft around and headed back toward Istanbul. He would never see his brother-in-law again.

*

[3] For Refik's account of this day, see Refik Erduran, *Gülerek: Gençlik Anılar* (İstanbul: Cem Yayınevi, 1987). Also see Saime Göksu and Edward Timms, *Romantic Communist: The Life and Work of Nâzım Hikmet* (London: Hurst and Company, 2nd edition, 2006), 251–252.
[4] Technically, the USSR and its Eastern Bloc satellites were "socialist" countries that were evolving toward communism. However, Nâzım and most of the others from his generation routinely described themselves specifically as communists, rather than socialists.
[5] Göksu and Timms, *Romantic Communist*, 252.

The next several days were busy ones for Nâzım. First, the *Plekhanov* transported him to the Black Sea port of Constanța, Romania. After two days in Constanța, Nâzım was taken to Bucharest, where he was visited by a doctor and finally given some fresh clothing to wear. He had only brought what he had been wearing during the escape, not wishing to attract extra attention should he and Refik be stopped by Turkish authorities.[6]

Nâzım's handlers in Bucharest could not help but notice that the Turkish poet had been deeply affected by the tumultuous events of the previous few days. He had left his wife, infant son, and all of his close friends and family behind in Istanbul, along with his in-progress writings. The new life that he was escaping into, moreover, was at this time still difficult to predict. Despite the fact that he had spent more than fourteen years in Turkish prisons, Nâzım's reputation in Moscow was far from sterling. His plight underscored the potential lethality of Cold War-era border-crossing. Could it be that Nâzım had escaped from a Turkish frying pan only to jump into a Stalinist fire?

In Bucharest, the officers responsible for looking after Nâzım had observed their charge's anxiety. "His nerves are always tense," read one report to Moscow, "and due to his agitation he is unable to hold back his tears." Nâzım, however, told his minders not to worry. The uncontrolled rivulets streaming down his cheeks were nothing more, he assured them, than "tears of joy."[7]

---

[6] RGASPI, f. 495, op. 266, d. 47, Part I, l. 30. "Note," June 21, 1951.
[7] RGASPI, f. 495, op. 266, d. 47, Part I, ll. 30–31. "Note," June 21, 1951.

# Introduction

## The Border-Crosser

Back when I was working as an English teacher in Istanbul in the 1990s, a private student of mine named Gökhan, the CEO of a small Turkish bank, was recounting his recent business trip to Moscow. We were sitting in the meeting room adjacent to Gökhan's office, looking out the windows onto Gezi Park.

I had a personal interest in Russia, having traveled around various parts of the ex-USSR in recent years, and had just begun to study Russian with a private tutor. Always happy to find a way to get my students talking, I began peppering Gökhan with questions about his visit. He told me that it hadn't been very exciting, as he had spent most of his time stuck inside offices, restaurants, taxis, and his hotel room.

With one exception, however: "Do you know Nâzım Hikmet?" he asked me.

"I know of him," I replied. Emphasis on the "of."

Gökhan took note of the gentle correction. "You know of him, Jim, yes," he began. In his dark, well-tailored suit and relaxed smile, Gökhan was an easy-going guy who looked to be in his early fifties. The bank was taking care of the cost of his lessons, and he was happy enough to sit and chat with me like this.

"I will tell you about Nâzım Hikmet," he continued. Clearing his throat, Gökhan—a banker who was no friend of communism—proceeded to speak movingly in his upper-intermediate English about Nâzım Hikmet and what the poet-communist still meant to him. Amid all of the meetings he'd attended during the course of his busy stay in Moscow, Gökhan had made one special trip for himself: a visit to Nâzım Hikmet's tomb in the Russian capital's famous Novodevichy Cemetery, where Chekhov, Bulgakov, Gogol, and many other well-known Russian and Soviet writers are buried.

Yes, I did know of Nâzım Hikmet. His name had come up in my classes whenever my students were asked to describe their "favorite" something or someone. Everyone knew who Nâzım was. His life story—that of a leftist poet who had resided in the USSR in his early twenties, then returned to celebrity, repression, and imprisonment in Turkey before fleeing back to the USSR in 1951—carried a larger-than-life reputation. There was, it seemed, something about Nâzım that radiated romance, a quality that was attractive even to people who might not otherwise read much, if at all.

But it was only when I sat in Gökhan's office that day, listening to this middle-aged banker wax nostalgically about his university years, that I began to realize something much more important than the highlights from Nâzım's life that I had often heard

*Red Star over the Black Sea: Nâzim Hikmet and his Generation.* James H. Meyer, Oxford University Press. © James H. Meyer 2023.
DOI: 10.1093/oso/9780192871176.003.0002

before: to a great many people Nâzım Hikmet remains, decades after his death, meaningful far beyond the parameters of his writing.

*

Ask anyone from Turkey who their country's most famous poet is, and chances are good that the first name you will hear is "Nâzım Hikmet." Nâzım, who was born in the Ottoman Empire in 1902 and died in the Soviet Union in 1963, is primarily known as a poet. Yet he also wrote plays, novels, short stories, screenplays, and newspaper columns over the course of a publishing career that spanned forty-five years. His most recent set of complete works runs to twenty-six volumes, only eight of which are dedicated to poetry.[1]

To this day, Nâzım Hikmet remains a subject of fascination in Turkey. Not just one, but two cultural centers in Istanbul bear his name.[2] All of his books are in print, and even new ones have emerged out of the woodwork in recent years, reproductions of his scribblings in long-ignored early notebooks.[3] In traditionally bookstore-heavy districts of Istanbul like Beyoğlu or *Sahaflar*—the famed book bazaar abutting the main campus of Istanbul University in Beyazit—no self-respecting bookseller has less than a shelf devoted to works by and about Turkey's most famous poet. His verse has been translated into dozens of languages, and he has been a favorite topic for biographers in Turkey and elsewhere. Literally hundreds of books have been published in Turkish relating, in some way, to Nâzım Hikmet's life story.[4] Only the country's founder, Mustafa Kemal Atatürk, has been the subject of more biographical attention.

Something else Nâzım has in common with Atatürk is the degree to which the images of both men have been thoroughly commercialized in Turkey.[5] In tourist districts across the country, it is easy to find refrigerator magnets, coffee cups, keychains, tote-bags, and other inexpensive trinkets bearing the communist icon's visage. To his admirers, Nâzım Hikmet is seen as something of a Turkish Che Guevara, only jollier, and coming in the form of a middle-aged man, a little chubby for his time, bearing what appears to be a cheerful yet thoughtful disposition (Figure I.1).

---

[1] The Yapı Kredi edition of Nâzım's collected works includes: eight books of poetry, five books of plays, six books of "writings" (*yazılar*) made up of mostly newspaper columns, four books of short stories, and three books of novels.

[2] Among several others in cities around the country, including Ankara, İzmir, Edirne, Bursa, and Antalya.

[3] Recently Yapı Kredi published a finely crafted seven-volume boxed set consisting of high-quality reproductions of Nâzım's notebooks called *Nâzım'ın Cep Defterlerinde Kavga, Aşk ve Şiir Notları (1937–1942)* (İstanbul: Yapı Kredi Yayınları, 2018).

[4] A search on Worldcat.org on January 12, 2022 yielded 337 books in Turkish with the words "Nâzım Hikmet" as the subject, and 565 such books total in 19 languages. These include two works in English: Göksu and Timms, *Romantic Communist*, and Mutlu Konuk Blasing, *Nâzım Hikmet: The Life and Times of Turkey's World Poet* (New York: Persea Books, 2013). Since I started researching this project in 2015, five more books on Nâzım Hikmet have been published: Oğuz Makal, *Beyaz Perdede ve Sahnede Nâzım Hikmet* (İstanbul: Kalkedon Yayımları, 2015); M. Melih Güneş, *Suyun Savkı: Leipzig'de Bir Aile ve Nâzım Hikmet* (İstanbul: Yapı Kredi Yayınları, 2017); Nâzım Hikmet, *Cep Defterlerinde Kavga, Aşk ve Şiir Notları (1937–1942)* (2018); Haluk Oral, *Nâzım Hikmet'in Yolculuğu* (İstanbul: Türkiye İş Bankası Yayınları, 2019); Gün Benderli, *Giderayak: Anılarımdaki Nâzım Hikmet* (İstanbul: İletişim, 2020).

[5] On the commodification of secular and Islamic identities in Turkey, see Yael Navaro-Yashin, "The Market of Identities: Secularism, Islamism, Commodities," in *Fragments of Culture: The Everyday of Modern Turkey*, ed. Deniz Kandiyoti and Ayşe Saktanber (New Brunswick, NJ: Rutgers University Press, 2002), 221–253.

**Figure I.1** Nâzım Hikmet

While Nâzım is well-known in Turkey, he is not universally beloved. During the Cold War, liking or disliking Nâzım Hikmet usually depended upon one's politics. Leftists, in particular, celebrated Nâzım as a brave dissident who spoke truth to power. Nâzım's critics, meanwhile, pointed to his communism, uncritical embrace of the Soviet Union, and non-participation in the Turkish War of Liberation (1919–23) as reasons to fault him.[6] In the wake of Nâzım's flight from Turkey in 1951, he was stripped of his Turkish citizenship and treated as an enemy of the state.[7]

One should not, however, get the impression that everyone in Turkey today is somehow obsessed with a long-deceased poet. In an increasingly post-literate world, Turkey is hardly unique in witnessing a decline in book-reading across the population at large. But even as people read fewer books, they still buy them, alongside postcards, posters, and other items stamped with the faces of their literary icons. Among an urban, bookstore-frequenting population in Turkey, Nâzım remains an enduringly relevant and well-regarded figure.

---

[6] "War of Liberation" is a literal translation of the Turkish "Kurtuluş savaşı."
[7] Original copies of his writings in newspapers and journals are today virtually impossible to find in the holdings of Turkish state libraries, as they appear to have been systematically purged in years past.

## Biographies of Nâzım

Even from beyond the grave, Nâzım continues to exert a formidable level of indirect control over the narratives that have developed regarding his life. One way in which this has occurred is through Nâzım's own writings. The Turkish humorist Aziz Nesin, who revered Nâzım, once observed that "[t]here are very many fabrications (*uydurmalar*) in the writings and reminiscences relating to Nâzım. Chief among them are the fabrications of Nâzım himself."[8]

In his later years, Nâzım became increasingly preoccupied with creating his own "official history" regarding his life.[9] This project of self-narration included, but was not limited to, the production of Nâzım's highly autobiographical "novel" *Life's Good, Brother*, which he completed shortly before his death in 1963 at the age of sixty-one.

Nâzım's generation of international communists—Turkish or otherwise—was particularly adept at the art of self-narration. They'd certainly had practice. In the 1920s and 1930s, these border-crossing communist internationals were frequently called upon by Moscow to produce self-narratives in the form of "party autobiographies." This often happened, for example, when an individual arrived in the Soviet Union from abroad, or when someone already living in the USSR was changing jobs or city of residence. Obliging their authors to frame past activities and associations in a particular light, party autobiographies were read by Comintern officials in Moscow, who would place them in an individual's file for future reference.[10]

From writing party autobiographies in the 1920s and 1930s, a great number of these communists would eventually graduate, in the 1960s and afterward, to producing books of memoirs.[11] These later autobiographical writings of aging communists constitute a fascinating sub-genre of Cold War-related primary source literature. While such published reminiscences can be useful to biographers—I draw upon them myself in this book—they need to be read in a critically-minded way, something that has not always been the case.[12]

Nâzım's border-crossing has, at times, also presented complications for his biographers, most of whom have researched him only in Turkey. As for his contemporaries, Nâzım moved far too often for anyone to have seen more than one part of

---

[8] Aziz Nesin, *Türkiye Şarkısı Nâzım* (İstanbul: Nesin Yayınevi, 2008), 12.

[9] Yet another characteristic Nazım shared with Ataturk.

[10] On party autobiographies and other forms of documentation in the USSR, see Brigitte Studer, *The Transnational World of the Cominternians* (New York: Palgrave Macmillan, 2015), 15–17, 74–77.

[11] Examples of memoirs of TKP members include: İsmail Bilen, *TKP MK Genel Sekreteri İsmail Bilen Kısa Biyografi* (İstanbul: TÜSTAV, 2004); Mara Kolarova-Bilen (trans. Cemal Kıral), *Kanatlı Gençlik* (İstanbul: TÜSTAV, 2003); Erden Akbulut (ed.), *Zeki Baştımar: Yaşam Öyküsü, Mektuplar, Yazılar* (İstanbul: TÜSTAV, second printing, 2018); Süleyman Nuri, *Çanakkale Siperlerinden TKP Yönetimine Uyanan Esirler* (İstanbul: TÜSTAV, 2002); Erden Akbulut (ed.), *Milli Azadlık Savaşı Anıları* (İstanbul: TÜSTAV, 2006); Gün Benderli, *Su Başında Durmuşuz* (İstanbul: Belge Uluslararası Yayıncılık, 2003); Benderli, *Giderayak*; Sevim Belli, *Boşuna mı Çiğnedik? Anılar* (İstanbul: Cadde Yayınları, 2006); Vartan İhmalyan, *Bir Yaşam Öyküsü* (İstanbul: Cem Yayınevi, 2012).

[12] See, for example, Ben MacIntyre's account of the life of the German communist Ursula Kuczynski (Werner). The book draws liberally, and uncritically, from Werner's latter-day novels, which MacIntyre describes as "essentially autobiographical." *Agent Sonya: Moscow's Most Daring Wartime Spy* (New York: Crown, 2020), 339.

his life up close.[13] Few of his friends from Turkey had first-hand knowledge about his experiences in the USSR, and hardly any of Nâzım's acquaintances from his later Soviet days had known him when he lived in Turkey.[14] By the same token, most people outside of prison were not familiar with Nâzım's day-to-day life behind bars, while his prison comrades had limited interactions with him beyond jail. The great majority of Nâzım's friends and acquaintances knew just one side of his multi-faceted life, and they relied upon Nâzım to fill in the blanks about the rest. The stories that Nâzım told them were then uncritically repeated in the memoirs and biographies that these friends would write in relation to Nâzım years later.[15] From there, they have since made their way into the biographical literature as well.

In addition to trying to be more critically-minded with respect to the manner in which I read the available source materials, another difference between this biography and previous ones relates to context. Whereas Nâzım's other biographers tend to discuss his life in terms of its uniqueness, I am more interested in what Nâzım Hikmet had in common with others from his time. When I first began researching this project in Moscow in 2016, I was struck by the degree to which the border-crossing lives of many Turkish Communist Party (TKP) members, well-known and obscure, resembled that of Nâzım. Gradually, I began to see Nâzım's biography less as an isolated case, and more like the story of a generation.

This book also situates Nâzım within a much more international milieu than is usually the case. Existing works on Nâzım Hikmet can be quite Turkey-centric, and often have little to say about the years Nâzım spent living abroad. The periods 1922–28 and 1951–63 are treated as black holes of a sort, unknowable save for Nâzım's own publications and a few well-worn anecdotes. Out of the approximately 1,500 pages devoted to Nâzım's life in Kemal Sülker's six-volume biography of Nâzım, only nine relate to the years 1951–63.[16] Nâzım's most recent English-language biography, meanwhile, provides just over five pages for the years 1922–28.[17] In this book, by

---

[13] The main sources for Nâzım's final years are the individuals who were closest to him in the USSR, including Vera Tulyakova-Hikmet, *Bahtiyar Ol Nâzım* (İstanbul: Yapı Kredi Yayınları, 2007); Rady Fish, *Nâzım'ın Çilesi* (trans. Güneş Bozkaya-Kollontay) (İstanbul: Gün Yayınları, 1969); and Ekber Babayev, *Nâzım Hikmet: Yaşamı ve Yapıtları* (İstanbul: Cem Yayınevi, 1976; 5th edition, İstanbul: Cumhuriyet Kitapları, 2011). Alexander Fevralski's accounts, meanwhile, relate mostly to Nâzım's literary production and interactions with well-known Soviet cultural figures. See Aleksandr Fevralski (trans. Ataol Behramoğlu), *Nâzım'dan Anılar* (İstanbul: Cem Yayınevi, 1979).

[14] Zekeriya Sertel, who was living in Hungary and East Germany in the 1950s and 1960s, met up with Nâzım at various points during these years, which he describes in *Hatırladıklarım* (İstanbul: Can Sanat Yayınları, 2015; first published, 1977); *Mavi Gözlü Dev* (İstanbul: Can Sanat Yayınları, 2015; first published, 1968); *Nâzım Hikmet'in Son Yılları* (İstanbul: Remzi Kitabevi, 3rd edition, 2001; first published, 1978). Yet Sertel's observations, too, often seem flawed when compared with other sorts of source material employed in the research of this book.

[15] Some of these individuals, such as Rady Fish and Ekber Babayev, would go on to write biographies of Nâzım based largely upon the stories Nâzım told them in the 1950s and 1960s.

[16] Kemal Sülker, *Nâzım Hikmet'in Gerçek Yaşamı*, vol. 6 (İstanbul: Yalçın Yayınları, 1989), 231–240. Ekber Babayev, who met Nâzım after his arrival in the Eastern Bloc in 1951 and knew him only in the USSR, devotes just 30 out of almost 400 pages to events taking place in Nâzım's life after 1951, *Nâzım Hikmet*, 359–388. Göksu and Timms' discussion of these years likewise draws mainly from published accounts and Nâzım's own writings. *Romantic Communist*, 257–289, 312–347.

[17] And only 17 pages on his activities between 1951 and 1963. Blasing, *Nâzım Hikmet*, 50–56, 201–217. Göksu and Timms' coverage of the early Moscow years 1922–24 comes out to 13 pages, half of which is devoted to reprints of Nâzım's poetry from the time. *Romantic Communist*, 40–53. Ten pages, meanwhile, are devoted to

contrast, Nâzım's international life and his crossing of borders—including those between freedom and imprisonment—lie at the very heart of the story.

Something else that is different about this biography of Nâzım relates to my treatment of his writing. This book does not set out specifically to interpret Nâzım's poetry. Instead, I look more carefully at matters like: changes taking place with respect to style, genre, and approach; his level of productivity; how much he was paid; where his works were published, and other more tangible points that I connect to Nâzım's ever-changing circles, his surroundings, and the crossing of frontiers.

While in these respects and others my approach and conclusions regarding Nâzım often differ from those of his previous biographers, I owe them a considerable debt of gratitude. Only because of their books was I able to write about Nâzım's life in the way that I have.[18]

## Sources and Voices

The story I tell takes place across frontiers, and it has been researched as such. Like Nâzım's other biographers, I draw from the memoirs and other published writings that have traditionally been used in discussing his life. However, an important methodological difference between this biography and earlier ones is that I juxtapose these published documents alongside thousands of pages of previously untapped archival materials and personal papers that I researched in Moscow, Istanbul, Amsterdam, and Washington, DC.

Archival sources are by no means perfect. In most cases, no single document constitutes a "silver bullet" that, on its own, proves or disproves anything complex. Party and state archival sources can, moreover, contradict one another, or prove otherwise incorrect when it comes to many of the specific details to which they refer. But even information that is "wrong" with regard to specific facts can still be useful. In the words of Luise White—in reference to the use of rumor and gossip in research—it is precisely "the inaccuracies in these stories [that] make them exceptionally reliable historical sources."[19] In-the-moment contradictions can at times feel more authentic, and less rehearsed, than some of the stories about Nâzım Hikmet that have been passed down over the years from one biography to the next.

The most important archive for researching this project was the Russian State Archive of Socio-Political History (RGASPI) in Moscow. This institution's collections include: the personal files of Turkish communists living in the USSR from the early

---

Göksu and Timms' discussion of Nâzım's time in Moscow between 1925 and 1928, ibid., 63–72. A recent Turkish-language biography devotes just four pages to Nâzım's early years in Moscow. Oral, *Nâzım Hikmet'in Yolculuğu*, 66–69.

[18] The biographies of Nâzım Hikmet that I relied upon most in writing this book were: Göksu and Timms, *Romantic Communist*; Sülker, *Nâzım Hikmet'in Gerçek Yaşamı*; Memet Fuat, *Nâzım Hikmet*; Ekber Babayev, *Nâzım Hikmet*; and Mutlu Konuk Blasing, *Nâzım Hikmet*.

[19] Luise White, *Speaking with Vampires: Rumor and History in Colonial Africa* (Berkeley, CA: University of California Press, 2000), 5.

1920s onward; records of early Bolshevik–Kemalist interactions, communications, and negotiations; and materials pertaining to bodies like the Comintern, the TKP, and Communist University of the Toilers of the East (KUTV).[20] This highly valuable storehouse of information has not been used in any of Nâzım's previous biographies, and has only recently begun to be employed by historians working on broader topics related to Turkish–Soviet relations and the TKP.[21]

A second institution that was critical to the writing of this book was the Russian State Archive of Literature and Art (RGALI), which holds materials from Nâzım's final years (1951–63) in Moscow. This is another valuable archive that has not been accessed by Nâzım's other biographers.[22] The Nâzım Hikmet personal *fond* at RGALI includes business papers, contracts, and hundreds of letters to Nâzım, 400 of which were written by Nâzım's fourth wife Münevver Andaç. Also of benefit to this book from this archive were the papers of Konstantin Simonov, as well as Nâzım-related material in the collections of the Writers' Union and the newspaper *Literaturnaia Gazeta*.

In Moscow, I also researched at the State Archive of the Russian Federation (GARF). While the materials at RGASPI relate to Nâzım's party life, and those at RGALI shine light upon his personal and business affairs, documents at GARF pertain mostly to Nâzım's relationship with the Soviet state. Materials that I read in this archive mostly concern the thorny question of Nâzım's citizenship, alongside other issues in connection with Nâzım's legal and administrative status in the USSR and the Eastern Bloc.

Unsurprisingly, these three Moscow-based archives have been especially helpful for researching the years that Nâzım lived in the USSR and Eastern Bloc (1922–28, 1951–63). At the same time, however, they also provide insights with respect to the years 1928–51, when Nâzım was in Turkey. During that 23-year period, party members and communist officials in Moscow continued to write about Nâzım. Archival materials from these times also discuss individuals from Nâzım's generation, his comrades in the TKP who were then still living in—or had recently returned to—the USSR.

Archives in Turkey were likewise important to the production of this book. In Istanbul I worked at the Prime Ministry Ottoman Archive (BOA) and the Turkish Republican Archive (BCA), reading through Latin and Arabic-script Turkish-language materials, most of which were produced by state organs.[23] While there was relatively little in these archives relating directly to Nâzım Hikmet, both the BOA and the BCA provided a great deal of information pertaining to larger-context questions.

---

[20] Nâzım Hikmet's personal file comes out to more than 350 pages, but this is just one of many files in RGASPI that relate to him.

[21] In addition to researching Nâzım Hikmet at RGASPI, I also looked at materials relating to approximately 150 other Turkish communists in Moscow, most of them students at KUTV in the 1920s.

[22] As far as I can tell, the only other individual to have looked through these materials is M. Melih Güneş. An architect, fan of Nâzım Hikmet, and friend of the Tulyakova family, Güneş has reproduced images of some of Nâzım's correspondence in *Hasretle: Nâzım Hikmet Mektupları* (İstanbul: Yapı Kredi Yayınları, 2007).

[23] Turkish was written in the Arabic script until 1928, when a law was passed banning the Arabic script after the start of the new year. Lewis, *Emergence of Modern Turkey*, 276–278. The BCA is actually housed in Ankara, but researchers at the BOA in Istanbul are able to directly search and read documents from the BCA, and vice versa.

These included: Russian–Ottoman, Turkish–Soviet, and Turkish–Bulgarian relations; the borders between these entities; and the people who crossed these frontiers.

I also researched at the Aziz Nesin Foundation archive (ANV) in the Istanbul suburb of Çatalca. This archive, which holds the private papers and correspondence of the Turkish writer Aziz Nesin (1915–95), includes a large collection of Nâzım-related materials, including eighty-eight of Nesin's hand-written Arabic-script copies of letters written to Nâzım by Münevver Andaç.[24] In Istanbul I additionally had the good fortune to benefit from the TÜSTAV archive, a wonderful resource for anyone interested in the history of the TKP.

The International Institute of Social History (IISH) in Amsterdam is a first-rate research site for anyone working on labor movements, leftist political organizations, and communist parties from the Eastern Bloc and beyond. In writing this book I drew upon the institute's letters, books, photographs, and sound recordings pertaining to Nâzım Hikmet, as well as scanned copies from certain collections of Moscow's RGASPI.[25]

A final site of my research for this project was the US National Archive and Records Administration (NARA) in Washington, DC.[26] At NARA I researched US diplomatic reports relating to Nâzım Hikmet's incarceration and release, Turkey's Cold War borders with the Eastern Bloc, and the individuals who sought to cross these borders.

All of this new, more archivally-based research does not simply add to what we know about Nâzım. It changes how we understand the story and significance of his life. While Nâzım was unusual in the sense that he would go on to become a famous poet, his experiences as a border-crosser paralleled those of many from his generation. This book tells their story.

## Border-Crossers

Born at the turn of the twentieth century and coming of age over the course of the final two decades of the late imperial era, the women and men of Nâzım's generation were the last of the Ottomans. While Nâzım and other Turkish communists were anti-imperial in their politics, they were nevertheless products of the empire in which they had been raised.

One of the ways in which this generation would differ from later ones was through their interactions with borders. The approaches of Nâzım's generation to politics, careers, and even their personal lives were dramatically influenced by their relationship with the frontier.

---

[24] Aziz Nesin wrote his personal notes in the Arabic script, to which he would have been exposed in his early education. In the Aziz Nesin Vakfı collection, there are copies of 88 of Münevver Andaç's letters with numbers ranging from 665 to 753, as well as two original letters.

[25] Digitized RGASPI materials researched in Amsterdam at IISH are cited in this book as RGASPI/IISH. Materials listed as RGASPI were researched in Moscow.

[26] NARA is headquartered in Washington, DC, but the research conducted for this project took place at NARA's reading room in College Park, Maryland.

Typically, Nâzım Hikmet's life is discussed in terms of his poetry and politics. While this book also examines these subjects, what interests me most about Nâzım is his border-crossing. In using the term "border-crossers," I am referring to people whose lives were indelibly shaped by their traversing of the frontier and experiences living abroad at a young age. What, I ask, do Nâzım's experiences, and those of his generation, tell us about changing attitudes in the twentieth century toward borders and the people who cross them?

Policymaking toward the border and border-crossers changed greatly in this part of the world during the transition from late empire to a post-imperial age. Border-crossers, meanwhile, adopted new strategies in response to shifting conditions. In the late imperial era—i.e., the time between the end of the Crimean War (1853–56) and the beginning of World War I—it was relatively easy to cross the Russian–Ottoman frontier. During those last years of empire, Nâzım and many of his friends, comrades, and contemporaries developed approaches to understanding the world that would serve them for decades, including a tendency to see frontiers as something flexible, and a source of opportunity.

This is not, however, how borders would always be understood. The end of fighting on the frontier brought, for a while, a revival of cross-border traffic in the 1920s. Nevertheless, by the end of the next decade it had become much more difficult to cross, legally or illegally, between Turkey and the USSR.[27] While it is true that "even under the most isolationist phases of the Stalin period" there remained certain types of cross-border interactions, overall the Turkish–Soviet frontier became subject to ever-stricter controls.[28]

Nâzım's plight—getting caught between the closing doors of two post-imperial states—was not an uncommon one for his generation. The individuals who populate this story make up three concentric rings. Nâzım's life is the center ring, with his friends, comrades, and classmates in a larger ring around him. The outermost ring consists of a broader population of late and post-imperial border-crossers. Collectively, the lives of all of these individuals tell us "something else, something larger" about the times in which they lived.[29]

The world that Nâzım and his contemporaries were born into was one of wide-open territories and malleable frontiers. In the wake of World War I, however, much changed along the border. A formerly vast world was gradually turning into one of closing doors.

---

[27] On emigration and immigration restrictions in the USSR over the decades, see Matthew A. Light, "What Does It Mean to Control Migration? Soviet Mobility Policies in Comparative Perspective," *Law & Social Inquiry*, vol. 37, no. 2 (Spring 2012), 395–429.

[28] For this quotation, see Michael David-Fox, "The Iron Curtain as Semipermeable Membrane," in *Cold War Crossings: International Travel and Exchange across the Soviet Bloc, 1940s–1960s*, ed. Patryk Babiracki and Kenyon Zimmer (College Station, TX: Texas A&M University Press, 2014), 14–39, here 16.

[29] In his account of late imperial Russia and the life of the "Mad Baron" Roman Fedorovich von Ungern-Sternberg, Willard Sunderland makes a distinction between biography and micro-history. The objective of the former, writes Sunderland, is "to tell a life story." The latter, however, endeavors "to explain something else, something larger." Willard Sunderland, *The Baron's Cloak: A History of the Russian Empire in War and Revolution*. (Ithaca and London: Cornell University Press, 2014), 8–9.

## From Empire to Republic

In a world of empires, size mattered. This was a fact of late imperial life that impacted both the heterogeneity of states and the nature of their frontiers. From the perspective of the individuals who ran empires, it was much more important to be large than racially, ethnically, or religiously homogeneous. This focus upon geographical breadth and growing populations is an important reason why both the Ottoman and Russian empires were so diverse with respect to religion and ethnicity.

By the end of the nineteenth century, less than 50 percent of Russia's population was ethnic Russian.[30] According to some estimates, there were more Muslims in Russia at the beginning of the twentieth century than there were in either the Ottoman Empire or Iran, the two largest independent Muslim states in the world at the time.[31] While political leaders in Istanbul or St. Petersburg may have preferred, in an ideal world, to rule over more ethnically or religiously homogeneous populations, they did not have much choice in the matter. If they wanted their states to expand, or even just maintain their size, they would have to tolerate the presence of a diverse set of communities within their frontiers.

Partly as a result of this diversity, government officials in both late imperial Russia and the Ottoman Empire approached the administration of their diverse subjects according to largely pragmatic—rather than ideological or nationalist—terms. This consistent—but not constant—pragmatism could also sometimes lead to discrepancies between the approaches of officials in the capital and those working on the ground in the borderlands.

At a time, for example, when Russian policymakers in St. Petersburg were obsessing over the alleged threats stemming from "pan-Turkism" and "pan-Islamism," local officials in the Crimea opened the door to Crimean Tatars to return to Russia following their previous immigration to the Ottoman Empire.[32] Such an approach to "return migrants" hardly constituted an expression of fear of an Islamic bogeyman, nor did it represent an isolated case.[33] Ultimately, it was more important to state officials in Russia and the Ottoman Empire to gain taxpayers, craftsmen, food-growers, soldiers, factory-workers, and other useful subjects, and doing so meant finding ways of managing difference, as opposed to resisting it.

---

[30] According to Russian census information from 1897. Andreas Kappeler, *The Russian Empire: A Multiethnic History* (Harlow: Pearson, 2001), 399.

[31] Robert Crews, "Empire and the Confessional State: Islam and Religious Politics in Nineteenth Century Russia," *American Historical Review*, vol. 108, no. 1 (February 2003), fn. 1. For Ottoman population figures, see Kemal H. Karpat, *Ottoman Population 1830–1914: Demographic and Social Characteristics* (Madison, WI: University of Wisconsin Press, 1985), 198.

[32] So long as they were willing to become Russian subjects again and, ostensibly, give up their Ottoman subjecthood—a condition that tsarist officials had no means of enforcing. This was following the Young Turk takeover in Istanbul in 1908. James H. Meyer, *Turks Across Empires: Marketing Muslim Identity in the Russian-Ottoman Borderlands, 1856–1914* (Oxford and New York: Oxford University Press, 2014), 33–34. Also see Prime Ministry Ottoman Archive (henceforth, BOA), HRH 576/41, s. 1–2.

[33] James H. Meyer, "Immigration, Return, and the Politics of Citizenship: Russian Muslims in the Ottoman Empire, 1860–1914," *International Journal of Middle East Studies*, vol. 39, no. 1 (2007), 9–26, esp. 21–23; Meyer, *Turks Across Empires*, 31–34.

14    RED STAR OVER THE BLACK SEA

In the first two decades of Nâzım Hikmet's life, merchants, migrants, pilgrims, teachers, students, activists, and other types of border-crossers traversed the frontier on numerous occasions—sometimes even holding the passports of both empires.[34] Others simply jumped the border illegally and found work on the other side. De facto dual subjecthood (or "citizenship") was a frequent occurrence, with individuals gaining subjecthood in one country without the other's bureaucracy knowing about it.[35] This was especially the case among Turkic-speaking Muslims, who made up the bulk of Russia's Muslim populations, and whose settlement in the Ottoman Empire was encouraged by authorities in Istanbul.[36]

Following the end of empire, however, the frontier was no longer seen by state authorities in the Republic of Turkey (established in 1923) or the USSR (1922) as a source of opportunity. Rather, borders—and the people who crossed them—came to be viewed as a menace. This change in attitude could be seen in many ways, including in the choice of capitals for these new countries. The imperial centers of Istanbul and St. Petersburg had been elegant port cities, facing water at various angles and situated not far from the frontier. They were replaced, by the empires' post-imperial successors, with inward-looking Moscow and Ankara, cities that were chosen precisely because of their relatively long distance from the border.

In looking at border-crossers, I draw upon a wide variety of historical literature that has examined the frontier in different ways.[37] For years, border-crossing between Russia and the Middle East was discussed mainly in terms of state-directed wartime actions, such as the mass expulsions of Muslims from regions like the Balkans, the Crimea, and the north Caucasus. These studies, like those relating to the Armenian

---

[34] Meyer, "Immigration, Return, and the Politics of Citizenship," 23–26; Meyer, *Turks Across Empires*, 27–28.

[35] "Subjecthood" and "citizenship" are quite different concepts, and "subjecthood" is the more suitable term when discussing empires. In this paragraph, I am simply referring to the question of which country's passport one holds. On matters pertaining to extra-territoriality vis-à-vis Russia and the Ottoman Empire, see Meyer, "Immigration, Return, and the Politics of Citizenship"; Meyer, *Turks Across Empires*, 34–36; Lâle Can, "The Protection Question: Central Asians and Extraterritoriality in the Late Ottoman Empire," *International Journal of Middle East Studies*, vol. 48, no. 4 (2016), 679–699. On subjecthood and citizenship, also see Will Smiley, "The Burdens of Subjecthood: The Ottoman State, Russian Fugitives, and Interimperial Law, 1774–1869," *International Journal of Middle East Studies*, vol. 46, no. 1 (2014), 73–93; Dina Rizk Khoury and Sergey Glebov, "Citizenship, Subjecthood, and Difference in the late Ottoman and Russian Empires," *Ab Imperio*, vol. 18, no. 1 (2017), 45–58. On Ottoman Jews and the issue of "citizenship," see Sarah Abrevaya Stein, *Extraterritorial Dreams: European Citizenship, Sephardi Jews, and the Ottoman Twentieth Century* (Chicago, IL: University of Chicago Press, 2016). On policies relating to citizenship in the Turkish Republic, see Kemal Kirişci, "Disaggregating Turkish Citizenship and Immigration Practices," *Middle Eastern Studies*, vol. 36, no. 3 (July 2000), 1–22.

[36] By "Turkic-speaking Muslims" I am referring to the ancestors of today's Azeris, Tatars, Kazaks, Kyrgyz, Uzbeks, Bashkirs, and other predominantly Turkic Muslim populations living in former Soviet space. Non-Turkic Muslim populations of Russia would include Chechens and other populations in the North Caucasus.

[37] An important early study on migration and return migration is Fouad Akram Khater's *Inventing Home: Emigration, Gender, and the Middle Class in Lebanon, 1870–1920* (Berkeley, CA: University of California Press, 2001). Other notable works on return migration include, from Khater: Ewa Morawska, "Return Migrations: Theoretical and Research Agendas," in *A Century of European Migrations, 1830–1930*, ed. Rudolph Vecoli and Suzanne M. Sinke (Urbana, IL: University of Illinois Press, 1991), 277–292; Walter D. Kamphoefner, "The Volume and Composition of German-American Return Migration," in *A Century of European Migrations*, 293–314; and Dino Cinel, *The National Integration of Italian Return Migration, 1870–1929* (New York: Cambridge University Press, 1991). An early book relating to trans-imperial people is E. Natalie Rothman, *Brokering Empire: Trans-Imperial Subjects between Venice and Istanbul* (Ithaca, NY: Cornell University Press, 2012).

deportations and genocide, were concerned primarily with establishing a record of these events and explaining how they unfolded.[38]

More recently, historians of Russia and the Middle East have begun looking at border-crossing in new ways. These works tend to be less state-centric, looking not only at government actions but also at the stories of border-crossers themselves. Rather than treating "migration" as if it were a simple, unidirectional act, these historians follow their subjects across the frontier, back and forth, often drawing from multiple archives in more than one country, examining issues like reverse migration, dual subjecthood, and extra-territorial sovereignty.[39] Others have looked at the construction of borders[40] or non-human border-crossers, such as disease.[41] Today, the late imperial border is discussed in ways that would not have been imaginable just two decades ago.

This book takes these discussions about borders and border-crossers deep into the twentieth century.[42] Existing works on late imperial border-crossers end with World War I. Biography, however, enables one to evade such traditional historical timelines.[43]

---

[38] Justin McCarthy, *Death and Exile: The Ethnic Cleansing of Ottoman Muslims, 1821–1922* (Princeton, NJ: Darwin Press, 1995); Alan Fisher, "Emigration of Muslims from the Russian Empire in the Years after the Crimean War," *Jahrbucher für Geschichte Osteuropas*, vol. 35, no. 3 (1987), 336–371; Mark Pinson, "Russian Policy and the Emigration of the Crimean Tatars to the Ottoman Empire, 1854–1862," *Güney-Doğu Araştırmaları Dergisi*, vol. 1 (1972), 38–41; Bedri Habiçoğlu, *Kafkasya'dan Anadolu'ya Göçler ve İskânları* (İstanbul: Nart Yayıncılık, 1993).

[39] On borders and border-crossing in Russia and the Middle East, see Khater, *Inventing Home*; Meyer, "Immigration, Return, and the Politics of Citizenship"; Meyer, *Turks Across Empires*; Smiley, "The Burdens of Subjecthood"; Will Smiley, "Freeing 'The Enslaved People of Islam': The Changing Meaning of Ottoman Subjecthood for Captives in the Russian Empire," *Journal of the Ottoman and Turkish Studies Association*, vol. 3, no. 2 (2016), 235–254; Will Smiley, *From Slaves to Prisoners of War: The Ottoman Empire, Russia, and International Law* (New York: Oxford University Press, 2018); Eileen Kane, *Russian Hajj: Empire and the Pilgrimage to Mecca* (Ithaca and London: Cornell University Press, 2015); Lâle Can, "Connecting People: A Central Asian Sufi Network in Turn-of-the-Century Istanbul," *Modern Asian Studies*, vol. 46, no. 2 (2012), 373–401; Can, "The Protection Question"; Lâle Can, *Spiritual Subjects: Central Asian Pilgrims and the Ottoman Hajj at the End of Empire* (Palo Alto, CA: Stanford University Press, 2020); Michael Christopher Low, "Unfurling the Flag of Extraterritoriality: Autonomy, Foreign Muslims, and the Capitulations in the Ottoman Hijaz," *Journal of the Ottoman and Turkish Studies Association*, vol. 3, no. 2 (2016), 293–323; David Gutman, "Travel Documents, Mobility Control, and the Ottoman State in an Age of Global Migration, 1880–1915," *Journal of the Ottoman and Turkish Studies Association*, vol. 3, no. 2 (2016), 347–368.

[40] Regarding the construction of the Ottoman–Iranian frontier, see Sabri Ateş, *Ottoman-Iranian Borderlands: Making a Boundary, 1843–1914* (Cambridge: Cambridge University Press, 2013). On modern border construction, also see Matthew H. Ellis, *Desert Borderland: The Making of Modern Egypt and Libya* (Stanford, CA: Stanford University Press, 2018). For recent theoretical discussions of the border and how it is discussed through narratives and images, see Johan Schimanski and Jopi Nyman (eds.), *Border Images, Border Narratives: The Political Aesthetics of Boundaries and Crossings* (Manchester: Manchester University Press, 2021).

[41] Andrew Robarts, *Migration and Disease in the Black Sea Region: Ottoman-Russian Relations in the Late Eighteenth and Early Nineteenth Centuries* (London: Bloomsbury Academic, 2016); Seçil Yılmaz, "Threats to Public Order and Health: Mobile Men as Syphilis Vectors in Late Ottoman Medical Discourse and Practice," *Journal of Middle East Women's Studies*, vol. 13, no. 2 (2017), 222–243.

[42] On Turkish–Soviet exchange in the early post-imperial decades, see Samuel J. Hirst, "Anti-Westernism on the European Periphery: The Meaning of Soviet-Turkish Convergence in the 1930s," *Slavic Review*, vol. 72, no. 1 (2013), 32–53; Samuel J. Hirst, "Comrades on Elephants: Economic Anti-Imperialism, Orientalism, and Soviet Diplomacy in Afghanistan," *Kritika*, vol. 22, no. 1 (2021), 13–40; Samuel J. Hirst and Onur İşçi, "Smokestacks and Pipelines: Russian-Turkish Relations and the Persistence of Economic Development," *Diplomatic History*, vol. 44, no. 5 (2020), 834–859; Onur İşçi, *Turkey and the Soviet Union during World War II* (London: I. B. Tauris, 2020).

[43] Other recent and semi-recent biographical studies that are thematically connected to this book include: Elizabeth McGuire, *Red at Heart: How Chinese Communists Fell in Love with the Russian Revolution* (New York: Oxford University Press, 2018); Christine Philliou, *Turkey: A Past against History* (Oakland, CA: University of California Press, 2021); Marci Shore, *Caviar and Ashes: A Warsaw Generation's Life and Death in Marxism,*

# RED STAR OVER THE BLACK SEA

Beginning with the final decades of empire and going all the way up to the last years of the Cold War, I tell a story about Nâzım Hikmet and his generation that transcends both borders and eras.

## Communist Internationals

How did foreign nationals end up living as communists in the Soviet Union? For a long time, studies relating to international communism focused mainly upon ideology and institutions like the Comintern or the various international parties.[44] In more recent years, however, a number of books and articles have been produced which look more closely at the human side of communist internationalism.[45] These works combine personal stories with broader analysis to explore larger questions relating to the Soviet Union, international communist movements, and networks of "communist internationals," i.e., communists who had crossed borders and lived abroad.[46]

Earlier histories focusing more specifically on the Turkish Communist Party likewise tended to look most closely at matters pertaining to institutions and ideology, rather than people. When individuals have been discussed in this literature, it has usually

---

*1918–1968* (New Haven, CT: Yale University Press, 2006). Also see Charles King's brief but inspired account of Nâzım's life in *Midnight at the Pera Palace: The Birth of Modern Istanbul* (New York and London: W. W. Norton, 2015), 217–232.

[44] On the Comintern as an international institution, see E. H. Carr, *Twilight of the Comintern, 1930–1935* (New York: Pantheon Books, 1982); Milorad M. Drachkovitch and Branko Lazic, *The Comintern* (Stanford, CA: Hoover Institution Publications, 1966); Kermit Eubank McKenzie, *Comintern and World Revolution, 1928–1943: The Shaping of Doctrine* (London: Columbia University Press, 1966); Kevin McDermott and Jeremy Agnew, *The Comintern: A History of International Communism from Lenin to Stalin* (New York: St. Martin's Press, 1997); Duncan Hallas, *The Comintern: A History of the Third International* (Ann Arbor, MI: Chicago Haymarket Books, 2016).

[45] Recent academic studies investigating the lived experiences of foreign communists in the 1920s and 1930s include: Robbie Aitken, "From Cameroon to Germany and Back via Moscow and Paris: The Political Career of Joseph Bilé (1892–1959), Performer, 'Negerarbeiter' and Comintern Activist," *Journal of Contemporary History*, vol. 43, no. 4 (October 2008), 597–616; Anna Belogurova, "The Civic World of International Communism: Taiwanese Communists and the Comintern (1921–1931)," *Modern Asian Studies*, vol. 46, no. 6 (November 2012), 1602–1632; Sandra Pujals, "A 'Soviet Caribbean': The Comintern, New York's Immigrant Community, and the Forging of Caribbean Visions, 1931–1936," *Russian History*, vol. 41, no. 2 (2014), 255–268; Studer, *Transnational World of the Cominternians*; Lisa Kirschenbaum, *International Communism and the Spanish Civil War: Solidarity and Suspicion* (Cambridge: Cambridge University Press, 2015); McGuire, *Red at Heart*; Masha Kirasirova, "The Eastern International: The 'Domestic East' and the 'Foreign East' in Soviet-Arab Relations, 1917–1968," PhD dissertation, New York University, 2014; Masha Kirasirova, "The East as a Category of Bolshevik Ideology and Comintern Administration: The Arab Section of the Communist University of the Toilers of the East," *Kritika: Explorations in Russian and Eurasian History*, vol. 18, no. 1 (2017), 7–34; Glennys Young, "To Russia with 'Spain': Spanish Exiles in the USSR and the *Longue Durée* of Soviet History," *Kritika: Explorations in Russian and Eurasian History*, vol. 15, no. 2 (Spring 2014), 395–419. Studies working on later periods include Elidor Mëhilli, *From Stalin to Mao: Albania and the Socialist World* (Ithaca and London: Cornell University Press, 2017); Rachel Applebaum, *Empire of Friends: Soviet Power and Socialist Internationalism in Cold War Czechoslovakia* (Ithaca and London: Cornell University Press, 2019). A recent non-scholarly account of Americans in Stalin's USSR is Tim Tzouliadis, *The Forsaken: An American Tragedy in Stalin's Russia* (New York: Penguin, 2008).

[46] This scholarship on communist border-crossers has a lot in common with the studies, cited in fns. 39–41, which look at the frontier in the late imperial era. However, there tends to be little cross-referencing between these two sets of historical literature.

been in the context of their party activities.[47] By looking more at communists—and less at communism per se—I aim to examine the complex lives of these individuals on a more human scale, one that also tells us something about the eras in which they lived. The women and men of the TKP were far more than simple repositories of ideology. As best I can, I have tried to reconstruct their vanished world.

\*

Long before Stalinism or the party's eventual domination in Eastern Europe by grumpy old bureaucrats, communism was sexy.[48] And so was Nâzım Hikmet. In seeking to rescue Nâzım "from the dreary bondage of myth, from the oppressive aftershock of cultural significance," my goal has been to breathe life back into a figure who has often been treated in one-dimensional terms.[49] The brash young poet who once endeavored to tear down the idols of Turkey's literary establishment has himself been transformed into one.

The first step in moving beyond this monument is to see how Nâzım fit in.

---

[47] Important studies on Turkish communism include Mete Tunçay, *Türkiye'de Sol Akımlar 1908–1925* (Ankara: Bilgi Yayınevi, 1967); George Harris, *The Origins of Communism in Turkey* (Stanford, CA: Hoover Institution Publications, 1967); Aclan Sayılgan, *Türkiye'de Sol Hareketler, 1871–1972* (İstanbul: Hareket Yayınları, 1968); Erik Zürcher and Mete Tunçay, *Socialism and Nationalism in the Ottoman Empire 1876–1923* (London: Bloomsbury Academic, 1994).

[48] This phrasing was inspired by Shore, *Caviar and Ashes*, 4.

[49] This quotation is from Peter Guralnick, *Last Train to Memphis: The Rise of Elvis Presley* (Boston: Little, Brown, 1994), xiii.

# 1

# Child of the Imperial Borderlands

Nâzım Hikmet's family was quintessentially Ottoman. An elite, if downwardly-mobile clan that boasted military leaders, scholars, and writers in its recent history, Nâzım's ethnically diverse bloodline mirrored the cosmopolitan makeup of the upper echelon of Ottoman society. Growing up initially in Salonica, and then in Aleppo and Istanbul, Nâzım was the product of three vibrant, cosmopolitan cities that provided the background to his earliest years.

## A Trans-Imperial Family

Mehmet Nâzım, whose parents would soon start calling him Nâzım Hikmet, is believed to have been born on January 15, 1902.[1] His hometown of Salonica, a port on the Aegean Sea, was home to large communities of Jews, Greeks, Turks, and Bulgarians, in addition to being a major transport and shipping hub. In Ottoman history, Salonica is also known as one of the major sites of re-settlement for Spanish Jews who were expelled during the Inquisition of 1492.[2] At the time of the annihilation of the Jewish population of Thessaloniki under the German occupation during World War II, roughly twenty percent of the city's population was Jewish.[3]

Salonica was not just an ethnically and religiously diverse city, it was also a cultural and political entrepôt (Map 1.1). A wide array of ideas and fashions circulated in town, with travelers arriving from a wealth of lands. Salonica was, moreover, the cradle of the 1908 Ottoman constitutional revolution, and during the first years of Young Turk rule the city became an early center of new ideologies like socialism and Turkism.

Nâzım's childhood household was cultured but tense. He was very close to his mother, Celile Hanım, from whom Nâzım had inherited his blue eyes as well as his creative interests in writing and painting (Figure 1.1).[4] From an early age, Nâzım would report to friends later in life, he was jealous of anyone else who had managed to

---

[1] While Nâzım's date of birth is typically listed as January 15, 1902, Memet Fuat, who was the son of Nâzım's third wife Piraye, writes that Nâzım was actually born in late 1901. *Nâzım Hikmet: Yaşamı, Ruhsal Yapısı, Davaları, Tartışmaları, Dünya Görüşü, Şiirinin Gelişmeleri* (İstanbul: Yapı Kredi Yayınları, 2015), 11. Nâzım himself alternately wrote "1901" and "1902" as his birthdate on the forms he provided to Communist University in Moscow in the spring of 1922. RGASPI, f. 495, op. 266, d. 47, Part I, ll. 152, 156, 157, 160.

[2] Ottoman Sultan Beyazit II invited these stateless people to come to the Ottoman Empire, where they re-settled primarily in Istanbul, Smyrna (today's İzmir), and Salonica.

[3] Mark Mazower, *Salonica: City of Ghosts* (New York: Vintage Books, 2004), 9. Thessaloniki is the present-day name of Salonica.

[4] "Hanım" is a term that typically follows a woman's first name in Turkish.

*Red Star over the Black Sea: Nâzim Hikmet and his Generation.* James H. Meyer, Oxford University Press. © James H. Meyer 2023.
DOI: 10.1093/oso/9780192871176.003.0003

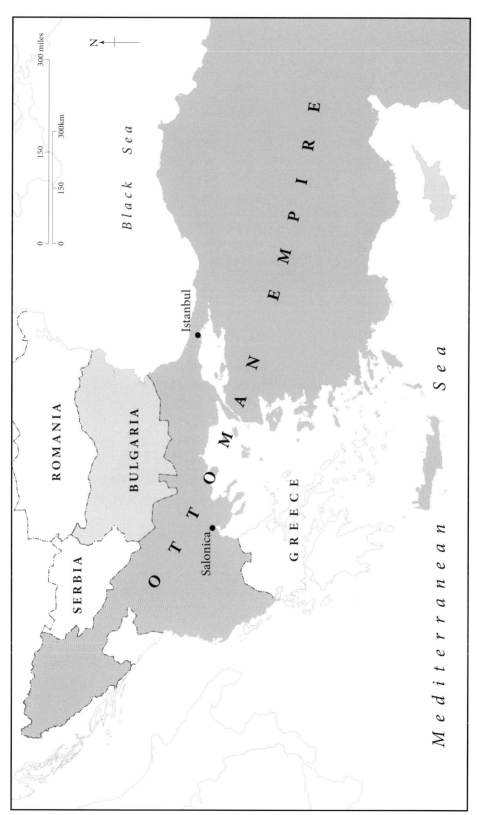

Map 1.1 The Ottoman Balkans in 1912

**Figure 1.1** Nâzım with his mother Celile (far left) and younger sister Samiye

hold his mother's attention. "She is the first woman I fell in love with," Nâzım would recall. "I was insanely jealous of my father. I'm no fan of Freud, but it's a fact: I was in love with my own mother."[5]

Celile Hanım was born in Salonica in 1880. According to some biographers, Nâzım's mother's family was of *dönme* origins—i.e., Jews who had converted to Islam, yet continued to observe Jewish holidays and rites alongside Islamic ones.[6] The daughter of an Ottoman official named Dilci Enver Pasha, Celile Hanım was the descendant of a number of well-traveled figures whose life stories, in some ways, presaged that of Nâzım.

Celile's maternal grandfather was a man named Constantine Borzhenski, a Polish nobleman who, after the failed rebellion against Austrian rule in 1848, sought exile in the Ottoman Empire. In Istanbul, Borzhenski converted to Islam and took on a new Muslim name: Mustafa Celalettin Pasha. He went on to become an Ottoman military commander and noteworthy Turkologist who, in 1870, published a book on Turkic civilizations called *Les Turcs: Anciens et Modernes*.

Nor was Borzhenski the only border-crossing relative on Nâzım's mother's side. Celile Hanım's paternal grandfather was one Karl Detroit, who was born in 1827 to a Huguenot family in Brandenburg. Raised in an orphanage, Karl Detroit took a job as a cabin-boy on a boat sailing from Hamburg to Istanbul, then jumped ship in the Ottoman capital, where he converted to Islam and adopted the name Mehmet Ali. He

---

[5] Ekber Babayev, *Ustam ve Ağabeyim Nâzım Hikmet* (İstanbul: Milliyet, 1997), 14. Taken from Blasing, *Nâzım Hikmet*, 31.

[6] See, for example, Blasing, *Nâzım Hikmet*, 27.

went on to become the protégé of Ali Pasha, one of the most important statesmen of the Ottoman nineteenth century.

Through the assistance of his powerful mentor, Mehmet Ali rose to the rank of general, earning the sobriquet "pasha" and serving as an Ottoman military commander in Bulgaria during the 1877–78 war against Russia. Mehmet Ali Pasha had four daughters, one of whom—Zekiye Hatice Hanım—married İsmail Fazıl Pasha, who would become Celile Hanım's uncle. İsmail Fazıl Pasha was an Ottoman officer and statesman who was an early supporter of Mustafa Kemal (Atatürk) during the War of Liberation, sitting in Mustafa Kemal's first parliament in Ankara.

İsmail Fazıl Pasha's son, the first cousin of Celile Hanım, was Ali Fuat (Cebesoy), who would go on to play a critical role in Ottoman military affairs during World War I. He later emerged as one of Mustafa Kemal's leading commanders during the Turkish War of Liberation. Nâzım's "uncle" (*dayı*) Ali Fuat Pasha would also serve as Mustafa Kemal's first ambassador to Soviet Russia, signing the Treaty of Moscow between Ankara and the Bolsheviks in March 1921.[7]

Without question, Celile Hanım's family, and thus Nâzım's, was unusual in certain respects. Not everyone had Polish, Huguenot, and possibly *dönme* roots in their family tree. At the same time, such a family background was hardly unheard of in the Ottoman capital. Religious and ethnic cosmopolitanism had long been features of the empire, which had for centuries absorbed both Christian and Jewish-born figures into its power structure and general population.[8] Since conversion to Islam was the primary marker of inclusion among Ottoman ruling circles, there were numerous outsiders—including some rather colorful renegades—who managed to create new lives for themselves by converting to Islam and finding employment as Ottoman advisors. Many went on to provide years of service to the Ottoman state.[9]

Nâzım's father, Hikmet Bey, also came from a well-known and respected family, albeit somewhat less illustrious than that of Celile Hanım.[10] Born in 1876, Hikmet Bey was a senior-level Ottoman civil servant who, like his own father, had held a number of positions across the empire. Hikmet Bey's father was Mehmet Nâzım Pasha, after whom Nâzım had been named. In the 1870s, Nâzım's paternal grandfather had been close to a number of well-known Ottoman figures, including the revered intellectuals and writers Namık Kemal and Ziya Pasha. Mehmet Nâzım Pasha was also known to be a supporter of Mithat Pasha, the constitutionalist statesman who, in

---

[7] On Nâzım Hikmet's family and childhood, see Sülker, *Nâzım Hikmet'in Gerçek Yaşamı*, vol. 1, 13–24; Göksu and Timms, *Romantic Communist*, 1–6; Memet Fuat, *Nâzım Hikmet*, 11–13; Blasing, *Nâzım Hikmet*, 26; Babayev, *Nâzım Hikmet*, 13–16.

[8] The Ottoman practice of converting Christian-born *devşirme* children from the Balkans resulted in large numbers of non-Muslim born rulers in the empire up through to the eighteenth century. Jewish conversion was less common, but there were still large numbers of *dönme*s and non-*dönme* Muslims in the empire with Jewish backgrounds. On *devşirme*s, see Stanford Shaw, *History of the Ottoman Empire and Modern Turkey*, vol. I (Cambridge: Cambridge University Press, 1976), 27–29. On *dönme*s, see Stanford Shaw and Ezel Kural Shaw, *History of the Ottoman Empire and Modern Turkey*, vol. II, (Cambridge: Cambridge University Press), 265.

[9] Heath Lowry traces the careers of several Christian Balkan nobles who made their way to the Ottoman state between the fifteenth and seventeenth centuries and established new lives for themselves as Muslim statesmen. *The Nature of the Early Ottoman State* (Albany: State University of New York Press, 2003), 115–130.

[10] As "Hanım" is a polite way of addressing women, "Bey" is a term for addressing men in Turkish, and likewise follows the first name.

1876, had obliged Sultan Abdülhamid II to accept a constitution and parliament as conditions for being placed on the throne.[11]

After Mithat Pasha's political downfall in 1877, Mehmet Nâzım Pasha was transferred to the province of Adana, in south-central Anatolia. This move was followed by a stint in provincial administration in Konya. Konya is the center of the Mevlevi brotherhood, and during his time there Mehmet Nâzım Pasha reputedly became a follower, or at least a keen observer, of Sufi traditions. While today the Mevlevi are known as the crowd-pleasing "whirling dervishes" performing as a folkloric troupe in Turkey, the Mevlevi sect is an Islamic brotherhood that has traditionally followed the teachings of the Sufi poet Mevlana Celalettin Rumi.

Later in life, Nâzım Hikmet would describe to his friend, the Soviet writer and translator Ekber Babayev, the close relationship that he developed with his grandfather, who would take young Nâzım to Mevlevi ceremonies. Nâzım's grandfather wrote and recited poetry, and is widely considered to have been an early model to his young grandson with respect to both his embrace of poetry and the power of his belief.[12]

Nâzım's father Hikmet Bey was working in the Ottoman government's employ in Salonica when he was first introduced to Celile Hanım. The two had quite different personalities, and their marriage is often described as difficult. Hikmet Bey was a bureaucrat whose career had culminated during the turbulent period spanning the rule of Abdülhamid II and the Young Turk Revolution of 1908. Celile Hanım, meanwhile, was an aspiring artist who organized soirées bringing together Ottoman creative and literary figures to her house. Something of a free-thinker, Celile Hanım was known to attend mixed social gatherings with her head uncovered, an unusual practice at the time for an urban middle-class woman of her generation. Celile Hanım was well-educated, a fluent speaker of French who was especially fond of the poetry of Lamartine. She is also remembered for encouraging the open expression of one's ideas, no matter how taboo they might appear.[13]

While Nâzım's childhood was in some ways quite happy, this was also an unstable time marked by the family's financial struggles, repeated uprooting, and searing personal loss. During the final years of Abdülhamid's reign, Nâzım's father began to attract the suspicions of officials in Istanbul. In 1905, Hikmet Bey was recalled from his post in Salonica and detained for twenty days. During this period, he was repeatedly interrogated and, eventually, forced to resign his position in the Foreign Ministry. Following these events, Hikmet Bey and the family moved to Aleppo, where they stayed for a while with Celile's relatives. Hikmet Bey, whose only work experience up to then had been in the Ottoman bureaucracy, set out to try his hand at a series of business ventures.

---

[11] Only to pay with his life in 1883, once Sultan Abdülhamid II had accumulated enough power to destroy his career. On Mehmet Nâzım Pasha, also see Fish, *Nâzım'ın Çilesi*, 17–18.

[12] Göksu and Timms, *Romantic Communist*, 5–6; also see Sülker, *Nâzım Hikmet'in Gerçek Yaşamı*, vol. 1, 20–21; Blasing, *Nâzım Hikmet*, 27–28.

[13] Göksu and Timms, *Romantic Communist*, 3.

Although the family was rich in what might be called "cultural capital," their fiscal conditions were highly unstable. Nâzım's parents, while unmistakably far better off than the majority of Ottoman subjects, struggled with a changing economy that witnessed, in the late nineteenth and early twentieth centuries, the emergence and growth of an entrepreneurial class in the empire.[14] At a time when private capital and business were proving to be increasingly dynamic fields in the Ottoman Empire's major cities, the men of Nâzım's bloodline had usually followed more traditional types of employment in the form of bureaucratic or military service. As the years passed, it became increasingly difficult for Nâzım's family to keep up with the standards of a newly rising bourgeoisie, with success now increasingly understood in economic terms like, for example, being able to send one's children to prestigious private schools.

In Aleppo, Hikmet Bey had invested heavily in the timber business, seeking to farm birch trees, but the venture ended in failure. A tragic blow then struck when Nâzım's younger brother, Ali İbrahim, died in infancy.[15] The family soon moved again, this time to Istanbul, where Nâzım's sister Samiye was born in 1907. At around this time Hikmet Bey launched another business, a dairy farm, which was also soon shuttered.[16] Somehow, Hikmet and Celile would have to find a way to educate Nâzım without descending further into financial ruin. They began to seek, through their remaining connections, assistance in placing Nâzım within one of the military academies.

## Socialists and Young Turks

If Nâzım's family circumstances were unstable throughout much of his youth, so too were the fortunes of the empire at large. Nâzım grew up during a period of Ottoman history that is well known for its political turmoil, intellectual ferment, and international crises. During the final years of Sultan Abdülhamid's reign, Nâzım's hometown of Salonica emerged as one of the most important centers of underground activity by the Committee of Union and Progress.

The Committee of Union and Progress (CUP) had been founded in 1889 as an umbrella group uniting a variety of opponents of the autocracy of Abdülhamid II. Some CUP members lived abroad, chiefly in Paris, where they published newspapers critical of Abdülhamid and the Ottoman government. Within the Ottoman Empire, meanwhile, CUP members created secret cells inside the military and government bureaucracy. CUP sympathizers typically described themselves as *İttihatçılar*, or "Unionists," but internationally would soon become better known as the Young Turks.[17]

---

[14] On the changing Ottoman economy during these years, see Fatma Müge Göçek, *Rise of the Bourgeoisie, Demise of Empire: Ottoman Westernization and Social Change* (New York: Oxford University Press, 1996).

[15] Sülker, *Nâzım Hikmet'in Gerçek Hayatı*, vol. 1, 40.

[16] On the family's time in Aleppo, see Sülker, *Nâzım Hikmet'in Gerçek Yaşamı*, vol. 1, 38–40; Göksu and Timms, *Romantic Communist*, 4.

[17] On the CUP during these years, see Şükrü Hanioğlu, *The Young Turks in Opposition* (New York: Oxford University Press, 1995).

In late spring of 1908, authorities in Istanbul caught wind of the existence of a conspiratorial cell that had formed among the Salonica-based officers leading the Third Ottoman Army. A team of investigators was sent from Istanbul to Salonica to find out what, if anything, was going on. Fearing disclosure, the conspiring officers in Salonica responded to Istanbul's move by choosing to go for broke, deciding to march on Istanbul immediately. Abdülhamid sought to impede the Third Army's progress toward the capital by summoning other forces to engage them. However, the soldiers sent by Abdülhamid refused to attack the other army.

Instead, the commanders of the two armies worked in tandem to force Abdülhamid to accept the CUP's demands that he bring back the Ottoman constitution and parliament, both of which he had suspended in 1878.[18] While Abdülhamid was initially allowed to retain his throne in a ceremonial role, in April 1909 he was removed altogether and replaced by his brother, Mehmet V, who became little more than a figurehead for the Young Turks.[19]

The Unionist, or Young Turk Revolution of 1908 that put an end to Abdülhamid's rule constituted one-third of a wave of constitutional-parliamentary uprisings taking place in the region during these years. In 1905, the seemingly stable regime of Tsar Nicholas II of Russia had been pushed to the point of overthrow amid a disastrous war in the Far East against Japan. Desperate to stabilize the situation and hang on to his throne, Nicholas had agreed to the creation of an elected parliament, or "Duma," and constitution.[20] In Iran, meanwhile, the autocratic government of Mozaffar ad-din Shah was similarly pushed, in 1905–6, to the brink of revolution on the heels of mass strikes and protests, prompting the Shah to likewise agree to the creation of a constitution and parliament.[21]

Now, with the successful uprising against Abdülhamid by the Young Turks in 1908, it appeared, at least to some observers, that constitutionalism and parliamentarianism were the wave of the future in this part of the world.[22] Looked at alongside Japan's trouncing of Russia in the 1904–1905 Russo-Japanese War, the concept of a "rising East" became increasingly fashionable in the cafés and political back rooms of cities like Istanbul, Kazan, Baku, and even Budapest.[23] In the intoxicating spirit of this time, anything seemed possible. Constitutionalism and parliamentarianism had come to be viewed as a magic bullet of sorts, a two-headed panacea that would somehow resolve the Ottoman Empire's many ills.

---

[18] As one of the conditions for his accession to the throne in 1876, Abdülhamid had agreed to introduce both a constitution and an elected parliament. Once he had consolidated his power, however, Abdülhamid unilaterally shut down these institutions.

[19] On the revolution overthrowing Abdülhamid II in 1908, see Shaw and Shaw, *History of the Ottoman Empire and Modern Turkey*, vol. II, 266–267.

[20] Although Nicholas II had agreed to promulgate a constitution for Russia, this was never done.

[21] The revolution in Iran was, in some ways, a consequence of events taking place in Russia at this time, as St. Petersburg had been the dominant power in Tehran.

[22] This was a particularly common view among the Russian-born Muslim activists who would end up establishing themselves in Istanbul after 1908, many of whom had witnessed the revolutions in Russia and Iran first-hand.

[23] On the views regarding a "rising East" among Hungarian Orientalists at this time, see Meyer, *Turks Across Empires*, 163; Tarık Demirkan, *Macar Turancıları* (İstanbul: Tarih Vakfı, 2000), 26.

With the overthrow of Abdülhamid II, Nâzım's father was given another chance at government service. Soon, he began working as a translator in the Young Turk government's press department. The higher salary associated with this position allowed Nâzım's parents to send him to the prestigious, and expensive, Galatasaray High School, where Hikmet Bey had also studied. At Galatasaray, Nâzım received a first-rate education in French, and was making the first steps toward a likely future career as an Ottoman diplomat or statesman, the positions of choice for many of the school's graduates. Nâzım commuted to Galatasaray from the family home in Kadıköy, located on the Anatolian side of the Bosphorus.[24]

During the years of Young Turk rule between 1908 and 1918, Istanbul developed into a center of trans-imperial Turkic-language publishing, attracting to the Ottoman capital individuals with experience in producing newspapers in Russia and Iran.[25] Prior to 1908, print media in the Ottoman Empire had been strictly controlled by the government, with newspapers producing little more than stolid reports surrounded by stacks of statistics. In the aftermath of the Young Turks coming to power, however, a wide array of ideas and opinion was permitted to circulate in the Ottoman press. Suddenly, any number of views, many of them influenced by developments taking place internationally, came into public prominence in the Ottoman Empire, and especially its urban centers.

After 1908, Nâzım's hometown of Salonica became the heart of socialist thought and activity in the Ottoman Empire. Almost immediately following the July revolution, an Ottoman Jew named Abraam Benaroya took advantage of newly-liberalized laws regarding the creation of social organizations, registering his Socialist Club with government authorities. The Socialist Club, based in Salonica, focused mainly upon advocating for the right to organize labor unions. Benaroya and his colleagues produced a newsletter, written in Ladino, the first language of many of the Ottoman Empire's Spanish-origin Jews, called *La Solidaridad Ouvradera*. When money was available, the Socialist Club additionally ran a Greek-Turkish translation.[26] Overall, however, socialist activity in the final years of the Ottoman Empire was rather sparse, and was limited mainly to Christians and Jews.

## Turkists and Pan-Turkists

Open any history of communism in Turkey, and typically the story focuses upon the theme of continuity from empire to republic, presenting the handful of socialist clubs and groups that were first created during the Young Turk era as the roots of Turkish

---

[24] Sülker, *Nâzım Hikmet'in Gerçek Yaşamı*, vol. 1, 43–44; Göksu and Timms, *Romantic Communist*, 3; Fish, *Nâzım'ın Çilesi*, 53.

[25] Both Russia and Iran included large numbers of subjects who spoke Turkic languages.

[26] Harris, *Origins of Communism in Turkey*, 18. Also see Mazower, *Salonica*, 269–270.

communism.[27] Looked at from the perspective of communists, rather than communism, however, it quickly becomes clear that there was relatively little overlap between Ottoman-era socialist organizations and the TKP of the 1920s. Rather, it was Turkist and pan-Turkist circles, not socialist or communist ones, from which future TKP members would most frequently be drawn.

Who were the Turkists? The term "Turkist" is applied to a broad collection of Ottoman-born writers based in Salonica and Istanbul during the Young Turk era. Ziya Gökalp (1876–1924) was the most influential and best-known figure from this group, and was the key force behind the creation of the Turkists' journal *Genç Kalemler* ("The Young Pens"), the first issue of which was published in Salonica in 1911. Turkists like Gökalp are best known for their calls to simplify the Ottoman language—especially in its literary form—by stripping Ottoman of its Arabic and Persian words and constructions and employing more Turkic ones. Working alongside writers and poets like Ömer Seyfettin, Ali Canip, and Aka Gündüz, Gökalp was sharply critical of what he saw as the flowery, Arabic-infused literary styles that had received official sanction during the decades of Abdülhamid's reign. The Turkists at *Genç Kalemler* argued that Ottoman writers needed to create a "new language" (*yeni lisan*) that would produce works in a more vernacular-sounding Turkish. At the heart of the Turkist argument was an explicit commitment to mend what they saw as the estrangement between Ottoman literature and the empire's reading public.

Gökalp had grown up in southeastern Anatolia, outside the city of Diyarbakır. He was relatively untrained in literature, having studied to become a veterinarian following his completion of secondary school. While living as a young man in Istanbul, however, Gökalp had become enamored of the literary and political debates surrounding him, developing increasingly close ties with underground Young Turk figures in the 1890s and early 1900s. After the Unionist takeover in Istanbul, he was given a job as the CUP's party inspector in Diyarbakır province, and then began working for the party in its stronghold of Salonica. According to Kemal Karpat, it was Gökalp's suggestion that *Genç Kalemler* be created, with financial backing from the CUP.[28]

Another well-known writer associated with Turkism was Halide Edip. Born into a privileged family in Istanbul in 1884, Halide Edip began studying English at an early age.[29] As was the case with Gökalp, she was a beneficiary of the changes that had been brought to Ottoman society by the revolution. She began writing a weekly column for the newspaper *Tanin*, an unusual occupation for an Ottoman woman, and soon after branched out into other literary forms. In 1909, Halide Edip published her first novel, *Seviyye Talip*, a tragic three-way love story that caused a sensation among the reading

---

[27] Harris, *Origins of Communism in Turkey*, 16–19; Tunçay, *Türkiye'de Sol Akımlar*, 19–64; Sayılgan, *Türkiye'de Sol Hareketler*, 28–98.

[28] Kemal Karpat, *The Politicization of Islam: Reconstructing Identity, State, Faith, and Community in the Late Ottoman State* (New York: Oxford University Press, 2001), 375–376.

[29] See Halide Edip (Sibel Erol, ed.), *House with Wisteria: Memoirs of Halide Edip* (Charlottesville, VA: Leopolis Press, 2003).

public of the Ottoman Empire. Three years later, she completed *The New Turan*, her most ambitious work to date, which brought a much more pronounced political tone to her writing. The term "Turan" was in vogue at this time in Istanbul, as it was the name given to the original homeland of the Turks in Central Asia. During the years immediately preceding World War I, the idea of Turan became an inspiration for a variety of writers and poets publishing in Turkish.

The attraction of Turan to the Turkists was both cultural and political. While "Turan" was thought of in terms of a geographical location in Central Asia, Edip and other Turkist writers were primarily focused upon developments taking place within the present-day borders of the Ottoman Empire. For Edip and others, Turan and Turkism meant more than just using more Turkic-origin words in one's poetry. The idea of Turan also informed an aesthetic based upon simplicity, austerity, and the pre-Islamic history of the Turks, views which would go on to influence successive generations of Turkish intellectuals and writers.[30]

The pan-Turkists, while often conflated with the Turkists, were different in some important ways. Whereas the Turkists were writers and poets who had been born in the Ottoman Empire and were mainly interested in matters relating to Ottoman literature and politics, the pan-Turkists were activists and intellectuals from Turkic-speaking areas of Russia—in particular, the Volga-Ural region, the Crimea, and the southern Caucasus. Several of the pan-Turkists had held high-profile positions within Muslim community leadership politics in Russia in the wake of the Revolution of 1905, only to re-locate to Istanbul in the face of a counter-revolution that began in 1907.

The best-known pan-Turkist was Yusuf Akçura, a border-crosser who spent much of his life on the road.[31] Born in 1876, Akçura was a Tatar from the central Russian city of Simbirsk (today's Ulyanovsk), growing up just a few doors down the street from the childhood home of V. I. Ulyanov (Lenin).[32] The scion of the wealthy and established Akchurin family, Yusuf Akçura—as he would become known in the Ottoman Empire and Turkey—carried himself with a scholarly air.[33] His writing and speeches often digressed into arcane topics, his tone pedantic. In early adulthood the bespectacled Yusuf began to sport a meticulously trimmed mustache and beard.

When Akçura was two years old his father, a well-known merchant who had suffered business reversals in recent years, died in what has been described as a sudden and "unnatural" manner. In 1883, the seven-year-old Yusuf and his widowed mother left Russia for Istanbul, settling in the somewhat blighted neighborhood of

---

[30] On the Turkists, see Karpat, *The Politicization of Islam*, 374–388; Meyer, *Turks Across Empires*, 158–163.

[31] In fact, the "pan-Turkist" phase of the careers of both Akçura and Ağaoğlu was quite short, and for most of their lives they described the communities to which they belonged in quite different terms. Meyer, *Turks Across Empires*, 138–142.

[32] Lenin was born six years before Akçura.

[33] On the Akchurins, see Nail Tairov, *Akchuriny* (Kazan: Tatarskoe knizhnoe izdatel'stvo, 2002); Meyer, *Turks Across Empires*, 42.

Aksaray.[34] A bright and energetic student, Yusuf was later accepted into Istanbul's prestigious Kuleli military academy and War College ("Harbiye"). This would have been a badge of honor for any student in the empire, let alone an immigrant from Russia who had grown up speaking Volga Tatar at home.

In 1896, the 20-year-old Akçura was implicated as an alleged member of a revolutionary organization made up of students at the War College. Akçura and some eighty-three other defendants, who seem to have been mostly interested in holding wide-ranging discussions about politics and philosophy, were found guilty of having conspired against the Sultan. They were exiled to the distant Ottoman province of Fezzan, in today's Libya.[35] In exile, Akçura was appointed to an administrative position, a means through which prisoners with talent and an education could work their way back into the good graces of the Sultan.

Instead, Akçura decided to escape. In 1899, Yusuf and his friend and fellow student-prisoner Ahmet Ferit (Tek) fled for Tunisia. Making their way up to the north African coastline, the two boarded a ship to Marseille, and from there traveled to Paris. Akçura would go on to study for four years at L'École des Sciences Politiques, better known today as *Sciences Po*. His education and living expenses were likely defrayed by his wealthy relatives in Russia, with whom Yusuf and his mother had long since kept in touch.[36]

Following the completion of his studies in Paris, and with a return to the Ottoman Empire still off limits to him, Yusuf went back to Russia in 1903.[37] Akçura's family connections in the land of his birth helped him find a job working as a history teacher at one of the more prestigious "new method" (*usul-u cedid* or "jadidist") schools in Kazan. These schools, championed by the well-known Muslim educational reformer İsmail Gasprinskii (1851–1914), emphasized the teaching of literacy in both Russian and a simplified Ottoman Turkish variant that Gasprinskii had dubbed "Turki" (or "Turkic").[38] Gasprinskii, who was fifteen years older than Akçura, also happened to be a relative of Yusuf by marriage.

Gasprinskii would also emerge, in 1904–5, as a key figure in the formation of the "Muslim Union" (*Musul'manskii soiuz*) of Russia, also known as "İttifak."[39] This development took place in the context of steadily increasing political upheaval in Russia, during which time "unions" (*soiuzy*) were being formed as a means of further-ing the political demands of individuals representing a wide array of communities, trades, and professions in the empire. İttifak was, at the time of its founding, a "big tent"

---

[34] On Akçura's background, see François Georgeon, *Aux Origines du Nationalisme Turc: Yusuf Akçura, 1876-1935* (Paris: ADPF, 1980), 12–15; Karpat, *The Politicization of Islam*, 388–389; Meyer, *Turks Across Empires*, 42.

[35] Georgeon, *Aux Origines du Nationalisme Turc*, 15; Meyer, *Turks Across Empires*, 44.

[36] On Yusuf and his mother returning to Russia for stays long and short, see Meyer, *Turks Across Empires*, 43.

[37] Karpat, *The Politicization of Islam*, 388–396; Meyer, *Turks Across Empires*, 43–45.

[38] On Gasprinskii, see Edward J. Lazzerini, "İsmail Bey Gasprinskii and Muslim Modernism in Russia, 1878-1914," unpublished dissertation, The University of Washington, 1973. Meyer, *Turks Across Empires*, 2–5, 12–13, 20–21, 86–86, and elsewhere. On jadidism in Russia, also see James H. Meyer, "The Economics of Muslim Cultural Reform: Money, Power, and Muslim Communities in Late Imperial Russia," in *Asiatic Russia: Imperial Power in Regional and International Contexts*, ed. Uyama Tomohiko (London: Routledge, 2012), 252–270.

[39] The term was a translation of "soiuz," or "union."

organization that attracted the support of Russian Muslims from a variety of political and social backgrounds.[40]

Akçura also became involved with İttifak, but came to play quite a divisive role within the movement. In particular, the move to remake İttifak into a political party with its own platform—an undertaking for which Akçura was largely responsible—proved disastrous. Akçura's platform, which many Muslims opposed, had the effect of splintering İttifak, contributing to the party's dismal performance in later elections to the third and fourth dumas.[41] By the time of the 1908 Young Turk revolution, both İttifak and Akçura's reputation within Muslim political circles in Russia were in tatters.

Another Russian-born Muslim closely associated with pan-Turkism was Ahmet Ağaoğlu. Like Yusuf Akçura, Ağaoğlu was a late imperial border-crosser who had lived in a variety of locales. He had attended university in St. Petersburg, an unusual occurrence for a Muslim from the southern Caucasus at this time. From St. Petersburg, Ağaoğlu had moved on to study in Paris, where he lived between 1888 and 1894, before eventually returning to the southern Caucasus.[42] For a while, Ağaoğlu wrote for the Baku-based Russian-language newspaper *Kaspii*, which was geared toward a Muslim readership. As was the case for Akçura and many other Muslim intellectuals in Russia, the Revolution of 1905 created new opportunities for Ağaoğlu, who became editor of the recently established Baku-based newspaper *Hayat*. During these years Ağaoğlu also became a leading voice in Muslim political organization in the Caucasus.

Changes, however, were coming to Russia, and not all of them were welcome to the empire's would-be reformers. In June 1907, Chairman of the Council of Ministers Pyotr Stolypin launched a political crackdown, drafting a new electoral law which disenfranchised large portions of the empire—including Muslim communities in Central Asia and the north Caucasus. One consequence of this action was the creation of a much more conservative parliament dominated by large landowners. Over the months to follow, thousands of suspected political criminals were arrested in Russia, with more than one thousand executed. Hundreds of newspapers were closed.[43] Politically active Muslims in Russia were among those targeted by tsarist police at this time.[44]

The closing down of political opportunities in Russia coincided with the opening up of possibilities in the Ottoman Empire. This was due to the reintroduction of constitutional and parliamentary rule following the Young Turk overthrow of Sultan

---

[40] On İttifak, see Meyer, *Turks Across Empires*, 84–87, 89–102. My conclusions regarding this movement differ from older studies of Russian Muslims, which see İttifak primarily through the lens of nationalism. See Serge Zenkovsky, *Pan-Turkism and Islam in Russia* (Cambridge, MA: Harvard University Press, 1960), 40–53, 117–118; Azade-Ayşe Rorlich, *The Volga Tatars: A Profile in National Resistance* (Stanford: Hoover Institution Press, 1986), 111–118; Jacob Landau, *Pan-Turkism: From Irredentism to Cooperation* (Bloomington: Indiana University Press, 1995), 11–12.

[41] Meyer, *Turks Across Empires*, 124–128.

[42] On Ahmet Ağaoğlu, see Ada Holly Shissler, *Between Two Empires: Ahmet Ağaoğlu and the New Turkey* (London: I. B. Tauris, 2003); Karpat, *The Politicization of Islam*, 305, 376–378, 382, 395; Meyer, *Turks Across Empires*, 2–6, 9–16, 20–21, 45–47, 122–123, 169–170, and elsewhere.

[43] Nicholas V. Riasanovsky and Mark D. Steinberg, *A History of Russia* (New York: Oxford University Press, 2011), 410–411.

[44] Meyer, *Turks Across Empires*, 127.

Abdülhamid II in 1908. Muslim activists from Turkic-speaking regions of Russia began arriving in Istanbul at this time, often bringing with them their experiences relating to the operation of Turkic-language newspapers and journals in Russia. These individuals possessed skills regarding a medium that was only beginning to develop in the Ottoman Empire.

Akçura moved back to Istanbul in late 1908. Initially, he planned to stay just temporarily, working as a correspondent in the Ottoman capital for the Orenburg (Russia)-based Turkic-language newspaper *Vakit*.[45] Not long thereafter, Ahmet Ağaoğlu similarly left Russia, arriving in the Ottoman Empire in early 1909. While both Akçura and Ağaoğlu were initially more interested in maintaining their reading audiences in Russia, they eventually began focusing upon Ottoman-based projects and in 1912 set up the journal *Türk Yurdu* ("Turkic Homeland").

At around this same time, Akçura and Ağaoğlu were responsible for a much more ambitious venture, the opening of a chain of lodges called the *Türk Ocakları* ("The Turkic Hearths"), which were designed to bring together Ottoman and Russian-born individuals with a broader interest in the Turkic world. The money to finance these operations has usually been described as having come from Russia, via the estate of Mahmut Bey Hüseyinov, a Muslim millionaire who had supported various philanthropic causes in the past. An alternate theory is that the CUP contributed the money to create the Hearths, using the Hüseyinov story as a cover.[46] By 1914, at least sixteen branches of the Turkic Hearths had opened, totaling more than 3,000 members.[47]

*Türk Yurdu* received the literary contributions of dozens of talented Turkic writers from Russia who were now living in Istanbul. Ali Hüseyinzade, an activist from the southern Caucasus in Russia who had worked alongside Ahmet Ağaoğlu on a number of Muslim community-related projects during 1905–7, would go on to contribute essays to *Türk Yurdu* and became a key collaborator of Akçura and Ağaoğlu in the years to come. Mehmet Emin Resulzade, another activist from the southern Caucasus who had previously helped to operate Turkic-language newspapers in Baku and Tehran, was also contributing articles to *Türk Yurdu* at this time. Following the Russian Empire's collapse in 1917, Resulzade would briefly become president of the Azerbaijan Democratic Republic.[48]

What did the pan-Turkists want? Traditionally, historians of the Russian and Ottoman empires assumed that Akçura, Ağaoğlu, and other Russian-born Muslim activists in Istanbul at this time were seeking to somehow bring together all the world's "Turks," including Turkic communities in Russia, into a common state.[49] However,

---

[45] According to letters Akçura sent to his friend Fatih Kerimi at this time. Meyer, *Turks Across Empires*, 153.

[46] Karpat, *The Politicization of Islam*, 377.

[47] Landau, *Pan-Turkism*, 42; İsmail Karaer, *Türk Ocakları (1912–1931)* (Ankara: Türk Yurdu Neşriyatı, 1992), 13–14.

[48] Ali Haydar Bayat, *Hüseyinzade Ali Bey* (Ankara: Atatürk Yüksek Kurumu, 1998); Meyer, *Turks Across Empires*, esp. 151–156, 166–178. On Resulzade, see Meyer, *Turks Across Empires*, 156, 173–174.

[49] For more traditional portrayals of the pan-Turkists, see Zenkovsky, *Pan-Turkism and Islam in Russia*, 106–112; Landau, *Pan-Turkism*, 29–55; Rorlich, *The Volga Tatars*, 178–179; Robert P. Geraci, *Window on the*

such a view does not give much credit to the intelligence and sophistication of the pan-Turkists, who well understood that Ottoman statesmen were having enough trouble simply trying to keep their empire afloat, let alone expand into territories deep inside Russia. Indeed, the political agendas and identity-based rhetoric of the pan-Turkists shifted alongside their locations. While still in Russia, figures like Akçura, Ağaoğlu, and Hüseyinzade had viewed their communities primarily as "Russian Muslims," "Tatars," or "Caucasian Muslims." Only after establishing themselves in Istanbul under the Young Turk regime did any of them begin to speak of a "Turkic World."[50]

The Turkist and pan-Turkist circles that were formed in Istanbul during the early years of Young Turk rule constituted an important intellectual foundation for many of the individuals who would later become involved in the TKP in the early 1920s. At first glance this might seem counter-intuitive, as nationally oriented worldviews like Turkism and pan-Turkism are typically considered the ideological antithesis of communism. People, however, unlike ideologies, are bound to change over time.[51] Overwhelmingly, it was Turkism and pan-Turkism, and not late Ottoman-era socialist movements, that proved to be the most important source for the creation of Turkish communists in the early 1920s.

## The Formation of a Young Poet

Nâzım Hikmet's early years were marked by a series of catastrophes in both his personal life and in the empire more generally. With Istanbul in a state of tumult following the overthrow of Sultan Abdülhamid II, the Ottoman Empire's neighbors and rivals moved in quickly to wrest control of Ottoman territory. In October 1908, leaders of the principality of Bulgaria, which had held autonomous status in the Ottoman Empire since the Congress of Berlin in 1878, declared its outright independence. One day later, Austria-Hungary annexed the Ottoman territory of Bosnia-Herzegovina.[52] In September 1911, Italy began its invasion of Ottoman Libya, which concluded just over a year later with the Ottoman withdrawal from the region.

In October 1912, an even more devastating blow was struck when the Ottoman Empire was attacked by the combined forces of Greece, Serbia, and Bulgaria. The First Balkan War, as it would come to be known, lasted seven months and marked the retreat of the Ottomans from almost all of the empire's remaining holdings in southeastern Europe, including Salonica. These losses were mitigated somewhat the

---

*East: National and Imperial Identities in Late Tsarist Russia* (Ithaca and London: Cornell University Press, 2001), 279.

[50] Meyer, *Turks Across Empires*, 138–144, 158–161. On Akçura's "Three Types of Policy," see idem., 134–138. My conclusions differ from those of Jacob Landau, who argues that Akçura was "a dedicated pan-Turkist throughout his life." *Pan-Turkism*, 43.

[51] Harris notes the connections between Turkish communist circles in the 1920s and Young Turk-era pan-Turkist circles, attributing them to Akçura's alleged interest in "social reform." *Origins of Communism in Turkey*, 29.

[52] Austrian control over Bosnia-Herzegovina had been a de facto condition ever since the Congress of Berlin.

following year when the victorious allies, unable to agree upon a division of their spoils, attacked one another. In setting off the Second Balkan War, the three erstwhile partners enabled the Ottomans to retake Edirne, which the empire had lost the previous year. Together, however, the First and Second Balkan Wars brought terrible consequences for the Muslim populations of southeastern Europe, resulting in the re-settlement of over 400,000 Muslim refugees within the remaining territories of the empire.[53]

Homeless immigrants from the Balkans flooded into Istanbul's mosques and other public buildings that were utilized as temporary shelters. The instability caused by the Balkan Wars created economic hardship for countless more Ottoman subjects, and middle-class families such as Nâzım's were also affected. In 1914 Nâzım's parents withdrew him from Galatasaray, with its high tuition fees, and enrolled him in a state school located in the district of Nişantaşı.[54]

Serious domestic political problems had also been developing in the Ottoman Empire since the parliamentary elections of 1912, which had been marred by violence and allegations of widespread voter fraud. These elections had resulted in an official victory for the Young Turks—269 out of 275 seats—that was met with disbelief and indignation among the opposition and public at large. In response, a group of non-CUP officers, aligning themselves with the political opposition, forced the creation of the so-called "Great Cabinet," which included no one from the CUP.

On January 23, 1913, chaos gripped Istanbul when senior CUP leader Enver Pasha and a group of co-conspirators burst into a meeting of the cabinet and opened fire. The attack left several wounded and killed the Minister of War, Nâzım Pasha. In the aftermath of this coup d'état, the Young Turk "triumvirate" of Enver Pasha, Cemal Pasha, and Talat Pasha would form the core group responsible for high-level Ottoman government decision-making.[55]

The political and foreign policy crises buffeting the empire formed the background for much of Nâzım's early poetry. Nâzım was just ten years of age when the First Balkan War broke out in 1912. As the fighting progressed, he began writing small pieces that reflected the patriotic tone surrounding the war in the Ottoman Empire.

"Cry of the Motherland" (*Feryad-ı Vatan*), which Nâzım wrote in 1913, is typical of his poetry from this time.[56] The work resembles other elegies that were composed during these years in the Ottoman Empire, following the fashionably bellicose style of Gökalp and others.[57]

> It was still a misty morning
> all sides were enveloped in smoke

---

[53] Justin McCarthy's figures indicate a total of 413,922 refugees officially re-settled at this time. *Death and Exile*, 161–163.

[54] Sülker, *Nâzım Hikmet'in Gerçek Yaşamı*, vol. 1, 46–47; Göksu and Timms, *Romantic Communist*, 6; Blasing, *Nâzım Hikmet*, 31.

[55] Shaw and Shaw, *History of the Ottoman Empire and Modern Turkey*, vol. II, 294–296.

[56] For Sülker's take on this poem, see *Nâzım Hikmet'in Gerçek Yaşamı*, vol. 1, 63.

[57] Such as Gökalp's 1912 poem "A Soldier's Prayer."

in the distance came a voice oh please for goodness' sake!
Hear the cry of the motherland
Listen and tell your conscience
The torn heart of your motherland
is counting on you.[58]

*Mehmet Çavuşa!* ("To Sergeant Mehmet!"), which was written in March 1915, is another example of the nationalistic overtones of Nâzım's adolescent poetry. The poem begins with a similar call to action in defense of the "*vatan*," or motherland.

O hero for the motherland
you treated your life with scorn
attacking like a lion
you shot down all the cowards

This poem then continues with a series of lines promising the inevitable return of "the Turk" to greatness:

Again the great name of the Turk
Will be imparted as far as the eye can see
Again the Turk's flag
Will tear down fortresses
Again the Turk's ship
Will traverse the oceans[59]

Nâzım's family did not escape its own tragedy during the war years. A brother of Celile Hanım, Mehmet Ali, was killed in the Battle of Gallipoli in July 1915. Nâzım dedicated several poems to his memory, again returning to the militaristic and nationalistic themes that marked many of his works from these years.[60]

"My Uncle," which was one of the more typical poems from this series, begins with these lines:

Uncle! Uncle! He was the great hero
He's the one who makes
my noble Turkish breast swell[61]

One more poem which similarly emulates the aggressively patriotic style of Gökalp, Mehmet Emin (Yurdakul), and other Turkist poets of the day was "To my Race"

---

[58] "Feryad-ı Vatan," Yapı Kredi edition of Nâzım Hikmet's collected works (*Şiirler* Vol. 8), 11.

[59] "Mehmet Çavuşa!" Yapı Kredi edition of Nâzım Hikmet's collected works (*Şiirler* Vol. 8), 14.

[60] Other poems about Nâzım's uncle were "Şehit Dayıma," "A Mon Oncle," "Şehit Dayıma Mabat," Yapı Kredi edition of Nâzım Hikmet's collected works (*Şiirler* Vol. 8), 17–19.

[61] "Benim Dayım," Yapı Kredi edition of Nâzım Hikmet's collected works (*Şiirler* Vol. 8), 17.

("Irkıma"). Like most of Nâzım's war-inspired work from these years, "To my Race" is a short, celebratory ballad.

> Oh, my race at one time you
> were the heirs of the conquerors
> who made Europe tremble
> and conquered Istanbul.[62]

The poem concludes by asking:

> Why should Europe try to challenge you today
> Why should that nest of ignorance teach you anything?

All in all, it's a far cry from the communist internationalism that Nâzım would later embrace in Moscow. With respect to these poems and others, Nâzım's early verse was, unsurprisingly for an adolescent, not terribly original. Nevertheless, these works do provide some insight into young Nâzım's approach to poetry.

To begin, he took his work seriously. Nâzım followed the styles that were then fashionable in Istanbul and sought to write in a manner that he had encountered in literary circles. The writing and reciting of verse, moreover, constituted an important "glue" which served to cement several of Nâzım's early friendships. Nâzım and a schoolmate named Vâlâ (Nureddin) would ride the ferries together between the European and Anatolian sides of the Bosphorus, trying to out-do one another in the composition of patriotic lyrics. Poetry became a means of passing the time and sharing confidences.

The rhythms of life were determined by the school year and one's own imagination. In the summers Nâzım and Vâlâ went to the beach and mixed socially with girls and boys they knew, many of whom were similarly the offspring of elite government-bureaucratic-military families.[63] The two young friends followed domestic and world events carefully. Perhaps they even imagined themselves, like Pierre or Prince Andrei in *War and Peace*, as the future saviors of their empire.[64]

The outbreak of World War I had a galvanizing impact on Nâzım. In December 1914, he enrolled in the Ottoman Naval Academy. This decision was made in the early months of the war, when optimism surrounding the conflict was still running high. Finding a spot for Nâzım in the academy had constituted a coup of sorts for the family, as it would ensure that he would receive an excellent education at little expense.

---

[62] "Irkıma," Yapı Kredi edition of Nâzım Hikmet's collected works (*Şiirler* Vol. 8), 16.

[63] Fish mentions a young Greek girl named Marika, supposedly a servant in Nâzım Pasha's house, with whom Nâzım allegedly had his first date at age 17. *Nâzım'ın Çilesi*, 190. A young Nâzım was also friends with Suat Derviş, who would later become a well-known writer in Turkey. Göksu and Timms, *Romantic Communist*, 14.

[64] On Nâzım's early poems, also see Sülker, *Nâzım Hikmet'in Gerçek Yaşamı*, vol. 1, 59–74, 95–96.

Hikmet Bey had called in favors: Nâzım's place in the academy had been secured by none other than Minister of the Navy himself, "triumvirate" member Cemal Pasha.[65]

In Nâzım's home life, meanwhile, matters were rapidly deteriorating. Celile and Hikmet's marriage had long been strained by repeated financial upheaval and their distinctly different personalities. Now the two had decided to divorce, and the circumstances surrounding his parents' breakup were intensely unpleasant for Nâzım. One of his teachers and mentors, the celebrated poet Yahya Kemal, had taken to visiting Celile Hanım frequently, and was rumored to be carrying on an affair with her.[66] Yahya Kemal was, in some respects, a friend of the family who was on good terms with Nâzım's paternal grandfather, Nâzım Pasha. According to some accounts, Yahya Kemal and Celile Hanım planned to marry, but the poet changed his mind at the last moment and opted against the union.[67]

Yahya Kemal had previously demonstrated an interest in young Nâzım's poetry. He had once invited Nâzım over to his house on the Bosphorus, where the elder poet had shown the boy his library and played chess with him before asking Nâzım to recite some of his verse. Nâzım had been elated that his teacher had shown interest in his work, a sensation that was bitterly punctured once Nâzım learned of the reputed relationship between his teacher and his mother.[68] Yahya Kemal's involvement with Celile Hanım reportedly began in 1916, with Celile Hanım and Hikmet Bey finalizing their divorce in 1919.[69]

The 16-year-old was devastated upon getting the news of his parents' impending breakup. In 1918 Nâzım wrote a blistering letter to his mother, begging her not to leave.

> Mother,
> I'm leaving, perhaps forever…because from what I've heard—or rather from what people are saying—you and father will divorce. If you divorce, I assure you that you will never see me or Samiye again. I implore you with all my soul to be patient…If you divorce, goodbye forever. If you don't, then I kiss your beautiful cheeks and hands.[70]

Nâzım was attempting to punish his mother by not only withholding his own love, but also that of his younger sister, should Celile not give in to his threats. It was not the last time Nâzım would seek to manipulate the women in his life in such a manner.

---

[65] Blasing, *Nâzım Hikmet*, 31. On Nâzım's admission to the Naval Academy, see Sülker, *Nâzım Hikmet'in Gerçek Yaşamı*, vol. 1, 50–51.

[66] On Nâzım's misery as a result of this affair, see Sülker, *Nâzım Hikmet'in Gerçek Yaşamı*, vol. 1, 24–25.

[67] Syed Tanvir Wasti writes that Yahya Kemal "got cold feet at the eleventh hour." *An Introduction to Late Ottoman Turkish Poetry 1839–1922* (Berkeley, CA: Computers and Structures, Inc., 2012), 188.

[68] On Nâzım's interactions with Yahya Kemal, see Fish, *Nâzım'ın Çilesi*, 62–64, 71. Also see Sülker, *Nâzım Hikmet'in Gerçek Yaşamı*, vol. 1, 24–36; Blasing, *Nâzım Hikmet*, 31–32.

[69] Göksu and Timms, *Romantic Communist*, 13.     [70] Blasing, *Nâzım Hikmet*, 32.

36  RED STAR OVER THE BLACK SEA

Shortly after Hikmet Bey's divorce from Celile, Nâzım's father remarried. His new bride was some twenty-four years younger than he was.[71] Celile, meanwhile, would soon leave Istanbul altogether, traveling to Paris, where she would study painting.[72] While Celile's emancipation is something that Nâzım would later embrace, at the time that these events were taking place he was terribly scandalized.

## Poetry under Occupation

Nâzım continued to write. His first published poem, "Are They Still Weeping Among the Cypresses," appeared in the journal *Yeni Mecmua* in September 1918 under the name Mehmet Nâzım. This was a love poem, one that was put into print with the assistance of none other than Yahya Kemal, who had first been shown the work by Celile Hanım.

Starting in l918, Nâzım had drawn close to the Syllabist poets Faruk Nafiz (Çamlıbel) and Yusuf Ziya (Ortaç). The "Five Syllabists" (*5 hececiler*), of whom Faruk Nafiz and Yusuf Ziya constituted forty percent, were known for their employment of personal, often romantic motifs in their work.[73] Istanbul-based newspapers like *Alemdar* and *Ümid* provided outlets for the Syllabists, and Nâzım published several of his early works in each. From 1919 to the end of 1920, he placed eleven of his poems in *Alemdar*, where Yusuf Ziya was one of the editors, and another eleven in *Ümid*. Thirteen more of Nâzım's poems, meanwhile, were published in a series of books (called "The First Book," "The Second Book," etc.) that Nâzım's school friend Vâlâ had published. The eight-volume collection, called the *Yeni Edebiyat Neşriyatı* ("New Literature Publishing"), was put together by the well-known *Tanin* publishing group in Istanbul in 1920.[74] In total, Nâzım had succeeded in publishing thirty-four poems by the end of 1920.[75] Not bad for an eighteen-year-old.

He was on his way. In November 1920, Nâzım gave a reading at Istanbul's Apollon Theater as part of a concert featuring Turkish classical music.[76] Gradually, and through hard work, the young poet was developing a reputation within the rather insular context of Istanbul's literary circles of the time.[77] For an unknown young writer like Nâzım, the attention he had begun to receive must have been gratifying,

---

[71] Ibid., 32.    [72] Sülker, *Nâzım Hikmet'in Gerçek Yaşamı*, vol. 1, 36; Blasing, *Nâzım Hikmet*, 32.

[73] Faruk Nafiz and Yusuf Ziya were two of the "Five Syllabists." The other three were Enis Behiç (Koryürek), Halit Fahri (Ozansoy), and Orhan Seyfi (Orhon). Emin Karaca, *Sevdalınız Komünisttir: Nâzım Hikmet'in Siyasal Yaşamı* (İstanbul: Destek Yayınevi, 5th edition, 2010), 14.

[74] This was the same publishing group that Halide Edip and other Turkist figures had worked with. On Vâlâ publishing "The First Book" and its successors, see Göksu and Timms, *Romantic Communist*, 14. On Vâlâ's brochures, see Vâ-Nû (Vâlâ Nureddin), *Bu Dünyadan Nâzım Geçti* (İstanbul: Remzi Kitabevi, 1965), 59.

[75] Several other poems were published in Istanbul in early 1921, but written prior to Nâzım and Vâlâ's departure on January 1, 1921. The Yapı Kredi edition of Nâzım's collected works includes seventy-five unpublished poems from the years 1913–20, and fifty-one published poems between 1919 and 1921 (*Şiirler* Vol. 8), 6–7.

[76] Göksu and Timms, *Romantic Communist*, 15.

[77] On Nâzım's literary production in Istanbul at this time, see Sülker, *Nâzım Hikmet'in Gerçek Yaşamı*, vol. 1, 91–93. Also see Asım Bezirci, "Toplumcu Şiirimiz içinde Nâzım Hikmet," *Gelecek* (May 1971), 36–41, here 36. Accessed via papers of Kemal Sülker, IISH, 210, "1930 üstüne."

especially since it came at a time when his relations with his family, and his mother in particular, had become quite strained.

Already his style had begun to evolve away from the belligerent patriotism of his earliest works. The "cry for the motherland" tone of national lamentation that had characterized much of his wartime writing was now largely gone. It had been replaced by the steady rhythm of the Syllabists' influence. During these later teenage years, Nâzım's poetry usually invoked at least one of the following three themes, all of which were common among the Syllabists' work: (a) human beings, their emotions, interactions, relationships, and major life events (especially dying); (b) dreams, fantastical phenomena, ghosts, and legends; and (c) the natural environment, such as mountains, the sea, wind, rain, weather, shadows, and trees.

While Nâzım was working extensively with such "romantic" tropes, his poetry at this time was neither personal nor revealing. Instead, Nâzım appears to have used the drama of his storytelling as a means of obfuscating his private experiences. In some works, especially those which evoke women as their subjects, a certain rage comes through at times. Such is the case, for example, in the poem "Like Everybody."

The poem is a denunciation of someone who has broken the speaker's heart. Here are the work's last four lines:

> I've totally forgotten you, I'm sure
> I'm now taking an oath against the past
> There isn't even anger for you in my heart
> I think that now you too are like everybody[78]

This work, the first version of which was written in 1918, is often thought to have been written with an ex-girlfriend in mind. But is it not possible—given his letter to Celile Hanım from that same year—that Nâzım was thinking of another woman when he wrote these lines?

Following the Ottoman Empire's defeat in World War I, Istanbul was under foreign occupation. There was, however, very little that was overtly political in either Nâzım's published or unpublished poetry from 1918 to 1920. In contrast to his earlier works, only a handful of Nâzım's poems from these years even refer to the events of the real world. One unpublished poem, called "Armistice Nights," bemoans the fate of Nâzım's "broken" homeland.[79] Nâzım also composed three short works that seem to have originally been devised to fit into a larger project called "Immigrants" (*Muhacirler*). The series was left unfinished and was not published during his lifetime.[80]

With these exceptions, Nâzım's poetry during his last two years in Istanbul was dominated by works that, while technically interesting and well executed, were not

---

[78] Nâzım Hikmet, "Bence Sen de Şimdi Herkes Gibisin," Yapı Kredi edition of Nâzım Hikmet's collected works (*Şiirler* Vol. 8), 23. This poem would, in 1920, be published as "Herkes Gibi," albeit in a somewhat modified form.

[79] Yapı Kredi edition of Nâzım Hikmet's collected works (*Şiirler* Vol. 8), "Mütareke Geceleri," 36.

[80] Ibid., "Muhacirler'den bazı parçalar," 52–53.

about anything that was very specific to Nâzım or his life. He was clearly a talented young poet but had not yet found his voice or subject matter.

In 1919, the year of his parents' divorce, Nâzım developed a severe inflammation of the lungs and chest cavity. He missed several months of school during the course of a hospital stay and convalescence at home with Hikmet Bey. Although he made a full recovery, Nâzım's lungs were deemed too weak for him to continue serving. He was released from the hospital and allowed to return home on May 17, 1920. One year later, he would officially be discharged from his service duties with the Navy. By that time, however, Nâzım would already be long gone from Istanbul.[81]

*

He was a child of the late Ottoman era, with a long family lineage of border-crossing. On Nâzım's mother's side of the family, there had been repeated instances of individuals leaving their homeland and pursuing a career in another country. On his father's side, there was a history of political disfavor and exile.

Nâzım's poetic style changed over time. Initially, he had embraced the jingoistic tone that the Turkists had popularized during the Balkan Wars and World War I. His writing had then turned less political and more romantic, in the style of the Syllabists. Along with his friend Vâlâ, Nâzım had been actively involved in Istanbul's poetry scene, and his work was starting to garner attention. He was studiously following standards and models created by other poets, but his verse was still quite derivative.

Taking to the road would change all that.

---

[81] Sülker, *Nâzım Hikmet'in Gerçek Yaşamı*, vol. 1, 52–56; Göksu and Timms, *Romantic Communist*, 12–13; Blasing, *Nâzım Hikmet*, 32–33; Memet Fuat, *Nâzım Hikmet*, 15.

# 2

# On the Road to Ankara

Late in the afternoon of December 31, 1920, Nâzım Hikmet met up with Vâlâ Nureddin, his friend from Galatasaray high school. The two had rendezvoused at a tavern next to the Galata Bridge, the legendary crossing over the Golden Horn. Having ordered their refreshments, the boys looked ahead.[1] They were about to take their first steps on the way to Ankara, where Nâzım and Vâlâ planned to join the resistance movement of Mustafa Kemal (Atatürk). They were nineteen years old.

Istanbul opens onto water upon multiple fronts (Map 2.1). Between the European side of the city and its Asian suburbs runs the Bosphorus Strait. This waterway connects the Black Sea—the mouth of which lies approximately twenty miles north of the city—to the inland Marmara Sea. On the western side of the Marmara Sea the Dardanelle Strait flows into the Aegean Sea. The European side of Istanbul is further divided by the Golden Horn, an inlet separating the palace-and-government quarter of Sultanahmet in the south from the entertainment districts of Taksim and Beyoğlu (or "Pera") to the north.

For those who have spent much time in Istanbul, the cry of seagulls and the salty smell of the breeze form a common background to one's daily routine or commute. Water is the means through which many people—like Nâzım's ancestor Karl Detroit—first arrive in the city.

The waterways surrounding Istanbul can also provide a convenient means of escape. At this time of Istanbul's occupation by the British, many of the city's best-known writers and intellectuals, along with a much larger contingent of young women and men looking to somehow assist the Kemalist government, had already set out for Ankara. And it was by water that Nâzım and Vâlâ were now seeking to join their numbers.

## Sudden Salvation

On a March morning in 1917, Şevket Süreyya (Aydemir) was perched on top of a hill just to the south of Kars. He was sitting at the point where the steppelands of eastern Anatolia begin to give way to the snowy peaks of the Caucasus mountains. Dug into the outcrop of a mountain at an altitude of over 9,000 feet, Şevket Süreyya was

---

[1] In Turkish, unmarried young males are typically referred to as "boys" (*erkekler*), and I follow this convention with regard to Nâzım and Vâlâ.

*Red Star over the Black Sea: Nâzim Hikmet and his Generation.* James H. Meyer, Oxford University Press. © James H. Meyer 2023.
DOI: 10.1093/oso/9780192871176.003.0004

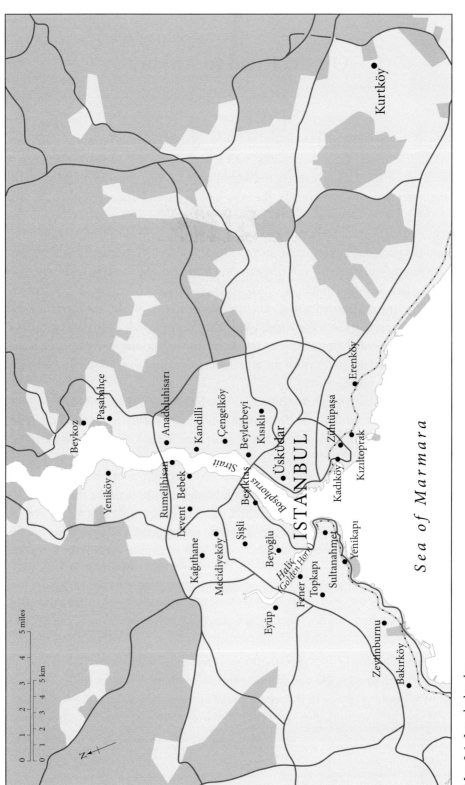

Map 2.1 Istanbul today

**Figure 2.1** Şevket Süreyya in 1918

commanding a team of machine gunners whose sights were trained upon the Russian soldiers holding tight to the hills across from them.[2]

A thin, thoughtful, elegant-looking 20-year-old officer, Şevket was—like Nâzım and Vâlâ—a product of the Ottoman Empire's western borderlands (Figure 2.1).[3] He was a native of Edirne, the former imperial capital that the Ottomans had managed to reclaim in 1913, and which today is situated just a few miles from the Bulgarian and Greek borders. Şevket had grown up alongside Muslim refugees from the Balkans, people who had fled to the Ottomans' last remaining European possessions in the nineteenth and early twentieth centuries. An ardent pan-Turkist, Şevket Süreyya dreamed of liberating the Turkic-Muslim "prisoner nations" he thought of as "occupied" by Russia.[4] Şevket had been fighting in the Ottoman Army for two years and was currently based not far from where his older brother had perished a couple of years earlier during the course of Enver Pasha's disastrous Sarıkamış campaign.[5]

Suddenly, Şevket and his men noticed a fast-growing collection of Russian soldiers assembling on the hill below them. Tempted to sound the order to attack, he

---

[2] Şevket S. Aydemir, *Suyu Arayan Adam* (İstanbul: Remzi Kitabevi, 1987), 96.
[3] Şevket Süreyya was an *asteğmen*, which was the lowest officer rank in the Ottoman Army. Halil İbrahim Göktürk, *Bilinmeyen Yönleriyle Şevket Süreyya Aydemir* (İstanbul: Arı Matbaası, 1977), 41.
[4] Şevket Süreyya's mother, who was his first teacher and a particularly important influence on his early life, was, like Nâzım's grandfather, a follower of the Mevlevis. Göktürk, *Bilinmeyen Yönleriyle Şevket Süreyya Aydemir*, 14–15. Also see William Allister MacLeod, "Şevket Süreyya Aydemir, Modern Turkish Biographer," PhD dissertation, University of Michigan, Department of Near Eastern Studies, 1984, 50.
[5] A military fiasco that had resulted in the deaths of more than 90,000 Ottoman soldiers.

nevertheless held back, sensing that something unusual was afoot. The Russians in this procession were yelling loudly, practically cheering, but what Şevket heard did not sound like battle cries. Responsible for the lives of his men, he was just twenty years old and unsure of what to do.

Şevket called his commanding officers to ask for guidance, but there was no response. A decision had to be made quickly, and Şevket was the one who needed to make it. Jumping out of his foxhole, he beckoned to a sergeant named Halil. The two slowly made their way down the hill to take a closer look at the Russian troops below. Gazing down upon the advancing soldiers, Şevket perceived that they were walking with their arms linked to one another and did not appear to be carrying weapons.

A Russian officer—blond, blue-eyed, perhaps around forty years of age—was among the first to approach the two battle-tested Ottoman soldiers. In the officer's hands was a large loaf of bread, which he handed to Şevket and Sergeant Halil with a smile. Alongside the bread was a small heap of salt. From a childhood spent in the Ottoman Balkans, Şevket knew enough about Slavic traditions to understand that this was a gesture of peace.[6]

For Şevket, Halil, and tens of thousands of others fighting on the Ottoman–Russian front, sudden salvation had come in the form of events taking place 1,800 miles to the north, in the Russian capital of Petrograd.[7] The revolution had begun on Women's Day, March 8, 1917. Large numbers of celebrants joined forces with protesters—mostly women—who had been demonstrating against the material privations brought on by the war.

At first, relatively little effort was made to put down the protests with force, as security officials did not consider the women a threat. Over the course of the days that followed, however, the number of marchers ballooned to more than 200,000 workers—one half of the industrial workforce of Petrograd.[8] Eventually, soldiers and police cut the center of the capital off from the rest of the city in order to prevent more protesters from joining. The move backfired, however, as it only contributed to the multiplication of protests outside the city center. Before long, large swaths of Petrograd were out of the government's control.

On March 16, Nicholas II made the stunning decision to abdicate the throne in his own name and that of his twelve-year-old son Alexei. When the former tsar's brother, then living in Warsaw, refused to accept the crown, the 304-year history of the Romanov dynasty came to an end—all during the course of just eight days of protest.[9] The Russian Empire would soon be gone, replaced by the Russian Republic.

---

[6] Aydemir, *Suyu Arayan Adam*, 96–97. Also see Göktürk, *Bilinmeyen Yönleriyle Şevket Süreyya Aydemir*, 43; MacLeod, "Şevket Süreyya Aydemir," 60.

[7] In 1914, the name of the Russian imperial capital of St. Petersburg had been changed to the less German-sounding Petrograd.

[8] Ronald Grigor Suny, *The Soviet Experiment: Russia, the USSR, and the Successor States* (New York: Oxford University Press, 2011), 48.

[9] As Russia at this time employed the Julian calendar, which was fourteen days behind the Gregorian one used in the West, these events would come to be known as "the February Revolution."

## Scrambling for POWs

In Istanbul, too, there was now a sense that sudden salvation might yet be obtained. Ottoman forces, along with their Central Power allies Austria and Germany, had for months been on the brink of not just defeat, but collapse. At the beginning of 1917, the Ottomans were in desperate straits, having lost over 100,000 men fighting the Russians on the Caucasus front. Still more casualties had been sustained in the empire's Arab provinces, the Balkans, and on the Aegean coast. But now, it was hoped, the implosion of Russia would allow the Ottomans to somehow snatch victory out of the jaws of what had only recently seemed a certain and devastating defeat.

In the late summer of 1917, Yusuf Akçura was living in Istanbul. He had spent the war years in the Ottoman capital, continuing with his work on *Türk Yurdu* and playing an active role in the conferences and lectures that were still regularly held in the Turkic Hearths. Akçura was also, as the Young Turk leadership knew, an expert on Russia, someone with many contacts among the Muslim communities of Istanbul's adversary to the north.

Akçura had never joined the Committee of Union and Progress, but his friends Ahmet Ağaoğlu and Ali Hüseyinzade had long-standing connections with the Young Turks.[10] During the course of the war, all three of these Russian-born Muslim activists had been involved in propaganda campaigns on behalf of the Ottoman government and against Russia. In 1915, the trio had created the "Committee for the Defense of the Rights of Turko-Tatar Muslims in Russia," and one year later Akçura gave a speech criticizing Petrograd at a meeting of the "Congress of Oppressed Peoples" in neutral Switzerland.[11] Now that the tsarist regime had been toppled, the possibility that some of these "Turko-Tatar Muslims in Russia" could achieve political independence had become more realistic.

In order to translate Russian imperial collapse into victory, the Ottomans needed more than just a peace deal. They needed men. This manpower shortage was particularly acute in the empire's Arab provinces, as British and French troops were occupying much of the Ottoman Empire's territories in what is today Syria, Jordan, and Israel. Istanbul's hold on the empire's last remaining Balkan possessions, meanwhile, was threatened by Greece's entry into the conflict in July 1917. During the final two years of the war, the dearth of fighting men had become so severe that Ottoman authorities had begun to send captured deserters back to the front.[12] At times, only a few thousand Ottoman soldiers were left to defend key regions from the advancing British

---

[10] According to Şükrü Hanioğlu, Ali Hüseyinzade was one of the founders of the CUP. *The Young Turks in Opposition*, 266, n. 13.

[11] See Michael Reynolds, *Shattering Empires: The Clash and Collapse of the Ottoman and Russian Empires, 1908–1918* (New York: Cambridge University Press, 2001), 129.

[12] Mehmet Beşikçi argues that desertion from the Ottoman armed forces developed into a "major social problem requiring measures on the part of not only the military but also state authority on the entire home front." *The Ottoman Mobilization of Manpower in the First World War: Between Voluntarism and Resistance* (Leiden: Brill, 2012), 31. On Ottoman deserters, also see Reynolds, *Shattering Empires*, 102–106.

44    RED STAR OVER THE BLACK SEA

armies. Estimates of the number of Ottoman POWs held in Russia alone range between 40,000 and 60,000.[13]

Following the October Revolution in Russia, Ottoman officials in Istanbul pored over Lenin's early pronouncements relating to POWs held on Russian territory.[14] The idea to enlist Akçura or one of the other Russian-born pan-Turkist intellectuals had first been floated in the months immediately following the February Revolution. The head of the Ottoman mission in Budapest, one Hikmet Bey, had suggested sending Yusuf Akçura, Ahmet Ağaoğlu, and Ali Bey Hüseyinzade to Russia as a means of inciting Russia's Muslims to rebel.[15]

With Red Cross/Red Crescent-related conferences set to take place in neutral Denmark and Sweden in October and November 1917, Akçura was sent from Istanbul to Copenhagen. Alongside him were Rauf (Orbay), the Ottoman Minister of the Navy, Chief of the General Staff Seyfi Bey, and İzzet Bey, a Red Crescent official responsible for the repatriation of POWs.[16] The four left Istanbul in September 1917, traveling overland via allied and non-combatant countries: Bulgaria, Austria-Hungary, Germany, and Denmark. Akçura stayed in Copenhagen and Stockholm until the middle of December, working on Red Crescent-related activities involving the shipment of food, money, and Ottoman-language reading materials to POWs in Russia.[17]

In the aftermath of imperial Russia's collapse, the Central Powers concluded an armistice with the Bolsheviks on December 15, 1917. Akçura then received orders from Istanbul to immediately travel to Berlin, where he joined the Ottoman committee at the Bolshevik–Ottoman peace talks.[18] On January 13, 1918, Akçura arrived in Russia, beginning a stay that would last more than a year. For six months, he lived in Moscow, which in March 1918 became the capital of Soviet Russia. At the end of July, Akçura traveled eastward to Kazan. He spent two weeks there before continuing onward to Simbirsk, his hometown. For the next five months Yusuf Akçura remained in the Volga-Ural region of central Russia, traveling back and forth between Simbirsk, Samara, and Ufa.

Unable to travel to Siberia due to the general breakdown of political order there and the nearby presence of "White" (i.e., anti-Bolshevik) Russian forces, Akçura returned to Moscow at the beginning of January 1919. A month later, he would leave

---

[13] While Akçura himself put the number at 60,000, Celal Metin estimates that the actual figure was closer to 40,000, "Yusuf Akçura ve I. Dünya Savaşında Rusya'daki Türk Esirleri," *Modern Türklük Araştırma Dergisi*, vol. 2, no. 3 (September 2005), 31–52, here 39.

[14] An early translation of Lenin's comments on POWs, from November 1917, can be found in BOA, DH.EUM.5. Şb 84/57.

[15] BOA, DH KMS 44-1/50, from Meyer, *Turks Across Empires*, 171. This was not Nâzım Hikmet's father.

[16] The Red Crescent shared a long-standing relationship with Akçura's Turkic Hearths, and the current director of the Ottoman Red Crescent, Adnan Bey, was the husband of Halide Edip. On Akçura's activities with the Red Crescent, also see Murat Uluğtekin and M. Gül Uluğtekin, *Osmanlı'dan Cumhuriyet'e Hilal-i Ahmer İcraat Raporları, 1914–1928* (Ankara: Türk Kızılayı Derneği, 2013), 35, 95. Also see Taylan Esin, "Hilal-i Ahmer, Esirler ve Yusuf Akçura," *Toplumsal Tarih Dergisi*, no. 291 (March 2013), 22–29.

[17] Mesut Çapa, *Kızılay (Hilal-i Ahmer) Cemiyeti (1914–1925)* (Ankara: Türkiye Kızılay Derneği Yayınları, 2010), 114. On Ottoman POWs and their care, also see Yücel Yanıkdağı, *Healing the Nation: Prisoners of War, Medicine and Nationalism in Turkey 1914–1939* (Edinburgh: Edinburgh University Press, 2013).

[18] Metin, "Yusuf Akçura," 41.

Russia, and begin the long trip back to Istanbul, which he finally reached in August.[19] He would never again return to the land of his birth.

## In Occupied Istanbul

Following his demobilization, Şevket Süreyya stopped in Istanbul en route home to Edirne. Noting that the Ottoman capital was filled with foreign occupation troops at this time, his later memoirs recorded a bitter scene:

> When we arrived at the Bosphorus, the first thing that caught our attention was the sight of enemy ships in front of Istanbul…The Galata quay was filled with drunken French sailors, their berets tilted at an angle, and black soldiers. Indeed, for these sailor boys, who were staggering back and forth, harassing those they encountered, the term "soldier" could not even be used.

> Along with a friend I decided to go to a restaurant. But later we realized this was a mistake. We got out of there as soon as we had finished. We were wearing Circassian cloaks, with pistols tucked into our belts, dressed as if we were still officers on the front lines. But our clothes, in this restaurant jammed full of foreign soldiers, immediately attracted attention…The mumbling and murmuring increased. But we got out of there as quickly as possible. For the first time we were encountering this enmity, this enemy occupation, on our own soil. We realized that we were no longer the rulers of this place.[20]

The main leaders of the Young Turk government—the "triumvirate" of Enver, Talat, and Cemal—had fled Istanbul on a German submarine ahead of the arrival of British troops. Rumors quickly began to swirl regarding the possibility of impending trials for members of the CUP and the Unionist government. On January 2, 1919, the British began arresting Unionist leaders. Official courts, designed for trying former Young Turk officials on charges of war crimes perpetrated against the empire's Armenian population, were set up on April 28.

The creation of these courts took place just two weeks before the Greek Navy landed in the western Anatolian city of İzmir. The allies had given Athens permission to enter the area in order to "restore order." This was in response to reports alleging Muslim attacks against Ottoman Greeks living on the Ottoman Aegean coastline. Shortly after landing in early May, however, Greek armed forces began advancing steadily in an eastward direction. It soon became clear that the goal of the Greek government was nothing less than the annexation of large portions of western Anatolia.

---

[19] Ibid., 48–52.     [20] Aydemir, *Suyu Arayan Adam*, 121.

On May 16, 1919, five days after the Greek landing in İzmir, Mustafa Kemal Pasha sailed out of Istanbul. Kemal, who had emerged as one of the few Ottoman generals without a defeat to his name, had resigned his commission at the conclusion of World War I and become a civilian. At the end of April, however, Kemal had been appointed by the Sultan to work as an inspector of Ottoman troops in Anatolia, where he was supposed to begin the process of demobilizing the remains of the Ottoman Army.

Kemal, who was himself a former Unionist, instead began to organize resistance against the Greek Army. After the Ottoman government signed the Treaty of Sèvres in August 1920, Kemal called for volunteers to fight against the terms of the agreement.[21] His goal was to somehow salvage, in Anatolia, a postwar independent Muslim state. He chose Ankara as his capital, and called for volunteers to come join his cause.

Within Nâzım's family and social circles a number of individuals had already taken up residence in Ankara. Most notable was Nâzım's uncle Ali Fuat Pasha (Cebesoy), a highly respected military commander in the Ottoman Army. Ali Fuat Pasha had been appointed, in September 1920, general commander of Mustafa Kemal's Ankara-based forces. Ali Fuat's father, the retired Ottoman general İsmail Fazıl Pasha, had likewise joined Kemal in Ankara, where the 65-year-old elder statesman was now serving in parliament.[22] Also in Ankara at this time was a love interest of Nâzım's named Nüzhet, who was staying with her older sister and politically connected brother-in-law, Muhittin Bey (Birgen).

The siren-song of resistance was intoxicating. On a late May afternoon in 1920, an estimated 200,000 people jammed into the main square of the Istanbul district of Sultanahmet. They were there to protest the city's occupation and the peace terms that had been imposed upon the Ottoman government. Halide Edip was one of the featured speakers that day, while Nâzım and Vâlâ were among those in attendance. "I am going to fight," pledged Halide Edip to the enthralled crowd, "until my people regain their freedom." The Istanbul-based journal *Büyük Mecmua*, published by the husband-and-wife team of Zekeriya and Sabiha Sertel, had likewise sought to galvanize its readers, covering the May 15 issue of the journal entirely in black.[23]

Nâzım and Vâlâ left the event in Sultanahmet feeling utterly transfixed, and soon resolved to head to Ankara themselves.[24] In addition to the important sense of purpose that resistance to the occupation had undoubtedly raised within them, the boys also had other reasons for wishing to light out for Anatolia. For Nâzım, the breakup of his household and the departure of his mother for France may well have contributed to his desire for a change of scenery. Vâlâ, meanwhile, had experienced painful

---

[21] This treaty, which was later superseded by the Treaty of Lausanne, envisioned a postwar rump-state Ottoman Empire based along the southern littoral of the Black Sea. Anatolia was to be divided up by the victorious powers in much the same way that the Ottoman Empire's former Arab provinces were. The government in Greece was to be the primary beneficiary of this re-drawing of the map.

[22] For a list of Nâzım's relatives in Ankara at this time, see Memet Fuat, *Nâzım Hikmet*, 28.

[23] Göksu and Timms, *Romantic Communist*, 9–11. Also see Korhan Atay, *Serteller* (İstanbul: İlestişim, 2021), 115–116.

[24] Memet Fuat, *Nâzım Hikmet*, 23. Nevertheless, it would still take them an additional seven months before they would actually go through with this plan.

setbacks of his own in recent years, following the death of his father in 1913 and the straitened financial conditions which had haunted his family ever since.

The two friends hatched a plan. They would set off for Ankara alongside two older boys they knew, the Syllabist poets Yusuf Ziya and Faruk Nafiz, with the four agreeing to surreptitiously leave town together on New Year's Day, 1921. Nâzım and Vâlâ had been issued travel permits on the recommendation of Halide Edip, whose husband Adnan was now working as the Minister of Internal Affairs in Kemal's Ankara government.[25] The permits were good for Anatolia, but first Nâzım and Vâlâ would have to find a way of getting out of Istanbul, as the British occupation forces were determined to prevent young men from making their way to Mustafa Kemal's rebel headquarters.

From the tavern where they had met up, Nâzım and Vâlâ headed over to Sultanahmet, spending the night at a hotel. The next morning, the two friends walked down the hill to Sirkeci, where they joined Yusuf Ziya and Faruk Nafiz. The four boarded a small boat that would take them up the Bosphorus and over to the Black Sea port of Zonguldak. The vessel they were taking was called *Yeni Dünya*, the "New World."[26]

## Mustafa Suphi: From Pan-Turkism to the TKP

While Nâzım and Vâlâ were making plans to travel to Ankara, in Bolshevik-controlled Baku the leaders of the newly-formed Turkish Communist Party (TKP) were plotting their next move. The TKP had been founded in September 1920 in an Azeri city that had only the slightest of historical ties to the Ottoman Empire.[27] Leading the Baku-based TKP was an Ottoman-born former pan-Turkist and civilian POW in Russia by the name of Mustafa Suphi.[28]

Originally from Giresun, on the eastern Black Sea coast, Mustafa Suphi was born in 1882 into the family of an Ottoman civil servant and his wife. As was the case with Nâzım and Vâlâ, Suphi's father's work had taken the family to a series of posts around the empire, including Jerusalem, Damascus, and Istanbul—where Mustafa was a student at Galatasaray high school. In 1905, Suphi traveled to Paris to study at *Sciences Po*, the same elite institution from which Yusuf Akçura had graduated two years earlier. Returning to Istanbul in 1908 in the wake of the Young Turk takeover, Suphi soon became involved in the city's burgeoning print media sector.[29] Photographs from the

---

[25] According to Blasing, Edip "spoke in favor of Nâzım," so that her husband would issue the permits to Nâzım and Vâlâ. *Nâzım Hikmet*, 37.

[26] Göksu and Timms, *Romantic Communist*, 15; Vâ-Nû, *Bu Dünyadan Nâzım Geçti*, 64. Also see Sülker, *Nâzım Hikmet'in Gerçek Yaşamı*, vol. 1, 77; Babayev, *Nâzım Hikmet*, 48–49; Fish, *Nâzım'ın Çilesi*, 195; Memet Fuat, *Nâzım Hikmet*, 25.

[27] Baku had briefly been an Ottoman territory in the late sixteenth and early seventeenth centuries.

[28] On Suphi, also see Paul Dumont, "Bolchevisme et Orient (Le parti communiste turc de Mustafa Suphi, 1918–1921)," *Cahiers du monde russe et soviétique*, vol. 18, no. 4 (1977), 377–409; Sayılgan, *Türkiye'de Sol Hareketler*, 148–154; Turhan Feyzioğlu, *Türk Ocağından Türk Komünist Parti'sine Mustafa Suphi* (İstanbul: Ozan Yayıncılık, 2007); İnan Kahramanoğlu, *Mustafa Suphi* (İstanbul: İleri Yayınları, 2008); King, *Midnight at the Pera Palace*, 225–227; Göksu and Timms, *Romantic Communist*, 28–31, 34.

[29] Dumont, "Bolchevisme et Orient," 378–379.

time reveal a handsome clean-cut man with thinning hair, mustache, and a youthful face.

During the early years of Young Turk rule, Suphi wrote for a number of newspapers that were part of the Turkist and pan-Turkist scene, including *Tanin*, the Young Turk-affiliated paper that also served as Halide Edip's publisher.[30] While Suphi was an active supporter of the CUP during his first few years back in Istanbul, he later helped to establish a new political party, separate from the Young Turks. Founded on July 5, 1912, the National Constitution Party's other early backers included Yusuf Akçura and Ahmet Ferit. Also in 1912, Suphi became one of the editors of a newspaper called *İfham*, which had similarly evolved out of Istanbul's Turkist and pan-Turkist circles of the time.[31]

On June 13, 1913, Suphi's life would change forever. The Ottoman Grand Vizier, Mahmut Şevket Pasha, was assassinated on Beyazit Square in Istanbul.[32] The murder took place in the context of an ongoing and increasingly acrimonious political showdown between the Young Turks and their political opponents. The Committee of Union and Progress used the assassination as a pretext for systematically dismantling the political opposition in the empire. Istanbul was placed under martial law, and sixteen leaders of the opposition Liberal Union party were sentenced to death due to their alleged involvement.[33] Hundreds more were implicated in the murder and given lesser penalties. Within the wide net that was cast in punishing the political rivals of the CUP for Mahmut Şevket Pasha's death, Suphi was exiled to the Black Sea city of Sinop, where he arrived at the end of 1913.

On May 24, 1914, Suphi participated in a mass escape, making his way across the Black Sea to the Crimea.[34] For Suphi, going to the Crimea was not simply a means of achieving his freedom. It also constituted a pilgrimage of sorts. The Crimean peninsula was, after all, home to the Crimean Tatars, one of the "brother" Turkic nations toward which pan-Turkists like Suphi felt considerable affinity. Moreover, İsmail Gasprinskii lived in the Crimea, in the town of Akmescit outside Simferopol. Hero to a generation of Turkic-speaking supporters of cultural reform in Russia, Gasprinskii was also a beloved figure in the eyes of self-styled Turkists and pan-Turkists in the Ottoman Empire. Gasprinskii was, moreover, a friend and in-law of Yusuf Akçura, who had been an associate of Suphi in Istanbul.

Suphi stayed in the Crimea throughout the late spring and early summer, writing a few pieces for Gasprinskii's newspaper *Tercüman* at this time.[35] At the beginning of July 1914, Suphi left the Crimea to travel to the southern Caucasus. He spent approximately one month in Baku, publishing articles in the Turkic-language newspapers

---

[30] As well as some of Nâzım Hikmet's early adolescent writings.
[31] On Suphi's childhood, education, and early career see Hamit Erdem, *Mustafa Suphi* (İstanbul: Sel, 3rd edition, revised and updated, 2010), 17–21.
[32] The position of Grand Vizier was somewhat akin to that of a prime minister.
[33] Shaw and Shaw, *History of the Ottoman Empire and Modern Turkey*, vol. II, 295–296.
[34] Harris, *Origins of Communism in Turkey*, 52; Erdem, *Mustafa Suphi*, 43.
[35] Erdem, *Mustafa Suphi*, 44.

*Basiret* and *İkbal*.[36] Toward the third week of August, Suphi arrived in Batumi, where he began writing for an Ottoman Turkish-language newspaper. From Batumi, Suphi may well have entertained the idea of crossing back into Anatolia undetected. During an era in which passports bore no photographs, traversing the frontier with fraudulent documents was hardly uncommon.[37]

In November 1914, following mutual declarations of war between Russia and the Ottoman Empire, Mustafa Suphi was arrested by tsarist authorities as a civilian POW. He was then transported, alongside 975 other prisoners, to the province of Kaluga, in western Russia—not far from the border of today's Ukraine and Belarus. Three years later, with the signing of a formal armistice between the Bolsheviks and the Ottomans, Suphi became a free man. But instead of returning to what was still the Ottoman Empire, Suphi headed to Moscow.[38]

Mustafa Suphi was taking his first steps toward starting a new career in the growing field of international communism. In June 1918, he and nineteen other former Ottoman POWs met in Kazan and established an organization of Turkish communists.[39] Over the next two years, Suphi would take on various party-organizational projects on behalf of the Bolsheviks in places like Kazan, Samara, Ufa, the Crimea, and Turkestan, all regions with significant populations of Turkic-speaking Muslims.[40]

On April 28, 1920, the Azerbaijani Soviet Socialist Republic was created. This was a satellite of Moscow that was created after the Bolsheviks overthrew the nationalist Müsavat government that had existed in Baku since May 1918.[41] Not long after the Red Army's arrival, Mustafa Suphi appeared in the Azeri capital, where he soon began working toward the creation of a Turkish party.

POWs were the initial target audience for the TKP's recruiting efforts. According to a June 1920 report by one L. Borsh, a Bolshevik operative based in the Kuban region of southern Russia, there was an abundance of former Ottoman POWs who had expressed interest in joining what Borsh described as the "Turkish Red Party." Borsh then wrote that there were "1000–1200" Turkish POW volunteers in Rostov-on-Don alone, and that an additional "400 to 500" could be found in various locations in the Caucasus. Borsh recommended sending them all down to Baku immediately.[42]

Funding for the new party came from Moscow. A document from Moscow dated August 22, 1920 indicates that the Bolshevik *Orgbiuro* agreed to give 1,290,000 rubles

---

[36] Ibid., 45. Ahmet Ağaoğlu was connected to both of these newspapers prior to his departure for Istanbul.

[37] Meyer, "Immigration, Return, and the Politics of Citizenship," 18–23.　　[38] Erdem, *Mustafa Suphi*, 58.

[39] Harris, *Origins of Communism in Turkey*, 53–54. On these events also see Erdem, *Mustafa Suphi*, 76–80; Dumont, "Bolchevisme et Orient," 382.

[40] Dumont, "Bolchevisme et Orient," 380. On Suphi's early activities, also see Mete Tunçay, "Sunuş," in *Haziran-Eylül 1920 Türkiye İştirakiyun Teşkilatı*, ed. Banu İşlet and Cemile Moralıoğlu Kesim (İstanbul: TÜSTAV, 2008), 9; Erdem, *Mustafa Suphi*, 72–73. For a report written by Suphi on his Bolshevik activities in Russia in 1919, see Prime Ministry Republican Archive (henceforth, BCA), 930-2-0-0/1-2-1. "Reports relating to Mustafa Suphi's travels in Mocow, Kazan, Samara, Turkestan, and the Volga-Ural Region," s. 5–6, 17–19.

[41] And join the USSR upon its establishment in 1922.

[42] "Report to the Central Bureau for Turkish Communist Organization." L. Borsh, June 25, 1920, RGASPI/ IISH, f. 495, op. 181, d. 18, ll. 35–36-ob.

"to the Turkish communists," i.e. Suphi, at this time.[43] The Baku-based TKP then began a recruitment campaign prioritizing Ottoman POWs. In September 1920, Baku would host the Congress of the Peoples of the East, which attracted more than 1,300 delegates from both the former Russian Empire and abroad. The first meeting of the TKP was timed to coincide with the congress and began shortly after it concluded.[44]

Ottoman POWs joined up with the Bolsheviks for a variety of reasons. Without question, some newly-minted Turkish communists were genuinely committed to communism from an ideological perspective. Others, meanwhile, were individuals who needed the support of an organization during a time of chaos. In the words of Şevket Süreyya Aydemir, many of the people attending the Baku Congress and joining the TKP were simply looking for "road money" to take them home, or at least put a roof over their head for the time being.[45]

Where else, after all, were Ottoman POWs supposed to go? The main routes that most would have to take in order to go back to their homes—via either the Caucasus by land or by ship from the Crimea or Odessa—were cut off by the civil war raging around Russia at this time. Moreover, the situation in Anatolia, where the fighting would not come to an end until 1923, was not necessarily any better than that of Russia. For many ex-Ottoman POWs it therefore made sense, in practical terms, to sign up with the Bolsheviks for now and then see what would happen.

As the year 1920 wound to a close, Suphi became increasingly interested in taking his party to Anatolia. He and Mustafa Kemal's key advisor General Kâzım Karabekir, commander of the eastern front for the Ankara government, maintained a regular correspondence with one another. While most of official Ankara was suspicious of Suphi and the TKP, Karabekir nevertheless went out of his way to reassure Suphi, emphasizing that he was looking forward to meeting the TKP leader in person.

This was a big opportunity for Mustafa Suphi. Recognition from the Ankara government could make an enormous difference for the party. Responding favorably to Karabekir's encouraging telegraphs, Suphi and fourteen other members of the Baku-based TKP's central committee set out for Ankara in December 1920.

## Mission to Constantinople

Nestor Lakoba was traveling eastward across Anatolia, his destination Istanbul. A native of Abkhazia, a Russian imperial outpost on the eastern littoral of the Black Sea,

---

[43] These and other BCA documents beginning with the classification number "930" were transferred to the BCA from archives in the former USSR. See BCA 930-1-0-0/1-1-1, s. 3, "General expenditures for the meeting of Turkish Communists," August 22, 1920; BCA 930-1-0-0/1-2-1, "According to the Caucasus Communist Party, the Turkish Communist Party's budget will be 1,290,000 rubles," August 22, 1920; BCA 930-1-0-0/1-3-1, "On Azerbaijan," August 28, 1920; and BCA 930-1-0-0/1-8-1, "The Azerbaijan Communist Party," October 2, 1922. On early organization, see BCA 930-1-0-0/1-13-1 "Correspondence between the Turkish Communist Party and the Council for Propaganda and Activities of the Peoples of the East," December 12, 1920.

[44] On the congress and the opening meeting of the TKP, see Harris, *Origins of Communism in Turkey*, 61–63; Dumont, "Bolchevisme et Orient," 391–392.

[45] Aydemir, *Suyu Arayan Adam*, 169–170.

**Figure 2.2** Süleyman Nuri in 1920

Lakoba had played an active role in the consolidation of Bolshevik rule in Abkhazia and Batumi during the period 1918–20. In the second half of December in 1920, he would arrive in Istanbul on a delicate mission. Lakoba was part of a team of party members from the Caucasus, headed by his friend and political partner Efrem Eshba, that was charged with the task of making contact with Turkish communists in Istanbul and Anatolia.[46]

Prior to their departure from Bolshevik-controlled territory, Lakoba and his traveling companions had made their way to Baku, where they met up with a young Turkish communist by the name of Süleyman Nuri (Figure 2.2). Born in Istanbul in 1895, Süleyman Nuri had been a soldier in the Ottoman Army when he was captured by Russian troops in the Caucasus. After spending six months in a POW camp in Sarıkamış, Nuri was transferred to Nargin, an island prison in the Caspian Sea off the coast of Baku.[47] There he had spent another half-year.

After he was freed in early 1918, Süleyman Nuri bounced around for some time in the former territories of the Russian Empire. Between March and October 1918, he worked on a ship called the *Emmanuel Nobel*, and then made his way to Central Asia,

---

[46] On Lakoba's trip to Istanbul, also see Timothy Blauvelt, *Clientelism and Nationality in an Early Soviet Fiefdom: The Trials of Nestor Lakoba* (New York: Routledge, 2021), 32, 37 (fn. 84); V. V. Novikov, "On logichen v svoikh orientatsiyakh," *Kavkazskii sbornik*, vol. 8, no. 40 (2014), 288–325.

[47] RGASPI, f. 544, op. 3, d. 46, ll. 104–117, here 104–106. Report by N. Lakoba (in Sukhumi) to the Council for Propaganda and Activities of the Peoples of the East, May 8, 1921.

where Nuri was employed in a number of different capacities. In Krasnovodsk (today's Turkmenbashi, in Turkmenistan), he was arrested by British agents, and spent three months in yet another POW camp. Upon his release, Süleyman Nuri returned to Baku, falling in with local Bolsheviks during the course of their invasion of the Caucasus in 1920. In September 1920, Nuri attended the Bolshevik-organized Congress of the Peoples of the East in Baku.[48] Immediately after the congress ended, Süleyman Nuri became one of the TKP's first members.

Meeting with Nestor Lakoba in Baku in December 1920, Süleyman Nuri provided his interlocutor with a list bearing the names of known Turkish communists in Istanbul. These were the individuals with whom Lakoba would try to rendezvous upon arriving in the Ottoman capital. In Lakoba's report, Süleyman Nuri is described as "a member of the Central Committee of the Turkish Communist Party." The Abkhaz-born Bolshevik noted laconically that Süleyman Nuri "had the modesty to say that he has his doubts regarding the existence of a 'big time' (*gromkikh*) communist organization in Turkey."[49]

Following his interview with Nuri in Baku, Lakoba made his way to Istanbul. According to the report he would write at the conclusion of his mission, Lakoba arrived in the occupied capital on December 17, 1920 and would stay for one month and ten days.[50] Searching for communists in an urban haystack, Lakoba went about his business tracking down the names that Süleyman Nuri had given him. One of the first people on Lakoba's list was Dr. Şefik Hüsnü (Deymer).

Şefik Hüsnü was born in Salonica in 1887 to a *dönme* family, and was one of the rare examples of an early Turkish communist who had come to the party through prewar socialism.[51] He had first become interested in Marx and communism while living in Paris, where he had been a medical student between 1905 and 1912. Returning to the Ottoman Empire during the First Balkan War, Şefik Hüsnü had worked as a volunteer in a Red Crescent hospital. Following the war's conclusion, he set up a private medical practice.

It was at around this time that Şefik Hüsnü married Leokadia, a Polish woman that he had apparently met during his years in Paris. With the onset of World War I, he served in Çanakkale, working again as a military doctor amid the carnage of the year-long British naval siege of Gallipoli. Following Şefik Hüsnü's demobilization from the army at the end of 1918, he returned to his wife and medical practice in Istanbul. He also began taking on a more public role in politics. In 1919, Şefik Hüsnü established the Worker and Peasant Socialist Party of Turkey, a legal organization under the British occupation.[52]

As Şefik Hüsnü had been at the top of Lakoba's list of people to see in Istanbul, the Bolshevik agent was perplexed to learn that the party leader was taking a vacation in Italy at this time. Incredibly, to the hardened communist Lakoba, the second person

---

[48] Nuri, *Uyanan Esirler*, 6.    [49] RGASPI, f. 544, op. 3, d. 46, l. 104.

[50] RGASPI, f. 544, op. 3, d. 46, l. 104.

[51] Some documents list Şefik Hüsnü's year of birth as 1890. On Şefik Hüsnü, also see Mazower, *Salonica*, 271.

[52] RGASPI, f. 495, op. 266, d. 38, l. 43. "Spravka" from April 13, 1941. Signed by Vladimirov. Personal file of Şefik Hüsnü.

on his list, the artist Namık İsmail (Yeğenoğlu), had also begged off meeting, as he too would soon be heading to Italy. "And so," Nestor Lakoba deadpanned in his letter to Moscow, with "the leaders of Constantinople's communists 'vacationing' in Italy," it was quickly becoming obvious that he would have to find other people to talk to.[53]

One Turkish communist that Lakoba did manage to have a conversation with was Sadık Ahi, a member of Şefik Hüsnü's newly formed party. Ahi had spent the war years as a student in Germany. He and his friends had been inspired by the short-lived Spartakist uprising of January 1919, which they had witnessed first-hand.[54] Ahi estimated, in his meeting with Lakoba, that most of the 200–250 Turks who had been part of Ahi's group in Germany had returned to their homeland as communists.[55] In Istanbul, Ahi's political collaborators included his fellow "Germans" Vehbi (Sarıdal), Nurullah Esat (Sümer), İlhami Nafiz (Pamir), and Vedat Nedim (Tör).[56]

Like many other Turks who were turning toward communism at this time, some of these "German" or "Spartakist" Turkish communists had first cut their teeth politically within pan-Turkist circles.[57] Such was the case, for example, with Ethem Nejat. Prior to traveling to Germany in 1918 as a representative of the Ottoman Ministry of Education, Ethem Nejat had been a member of the Turkic Hearths and had published in *Türk Yurdu*.[58] In Germany, however, he would change his political stripes to communism.[59] After returning to Istanbul in 1919, Ethem Nejat made his way across Anatolia and the Caucasus to Baku, where he had joined up with the TKP of Mustafa Suphi.[60]

Sadık Ahi promised Lakoba that he would write him a report detailing the prospects for recruiting communists in Turkey. In his later missive to Moscow, however, Lakoba noted that he had never received any such document. Nevertheless, Lakoba had gotten word that, in the middle of January 1921, Ahi and four other Turkish Spartakists had set off for Ankara to have a first-hand look at Mustafa Kemal's capital.[61]


## Escape to Anatolia


At the dock in Sirkeci, the policeman that was helping Nâzım, Vâlâ, and their friends sneak out of Istanbul tried to break the news to them gently. "Don't be alarmed, but

---

[53] RGASPI, f. 544, op. 3, d. 46, ll. 104–117, here 105.
[54] RGASPI, f. 544, op, 3, d. 46, ll. 104–117, here 106. This word is often spelled "Spartacist," but I prefer "Spartakist" because it is closer to the Turkish and Russian versions of this word.
[55] RGASPI, f. 544, op, 3, d. 46, ll. 104–117, here 105.     [56] Memet Fuat, *Nâzım Hikmet*, 26.
[57] "German" is my term for these students. They do not appear to have described themselves by this name.
[58] Hüseyin Tuncer, *Türk Yurdu Bibliyografyası (1911–1992)* (İzmir: Akademi Kitabevi, 1993), 223.
[59] Another "German" with a background in pan-Turkist circles was Nihat Nuri "the Electrician," who had been involved with the Turkic Hearths in Germany prior to the Spartakist uprising. RGASPI, f. 495, op. 266, d. 86, l. 35. Personal file of Nihat Nuri Elektrikçi.
[60] According to Harris, there were "several thousand students and skilled laborers whom the Young Turks had sent to Germany during the war." *Origins of Communism in Turkey*, 36. On Ethem Nejat, see Erden Akbulut and Mete Tunçay (eds.), *İstanbul Komünist Grubu'ndan (Aydınlık Çevresi) Türkiye Komünist Partisi'ne 1919–1926, I Cilt 1919–1923* (İstanbul: TÜSTAV, 2012), 373–374. On the Turkish communists who had studied in Germany, also see Emel Akal, *Moskova-Ankara-Londra Üçgeninde İştirakiyuncular, Komünistler ve Paşa Hazretleri* (İstanbul: İletişim, 2013), 103, 439–440.
[61] RGASPI, f. 544, op. 3, d. 46, ll. 104–117, here 106.

there's some danger. Once you get to Kız Kulesi, officers from the occupation forces are going to board the ship. In recent days the heat has been turning up."[62]

The papers that Nâzım and Vâlâ were carrying identified them as traveling egg merchants. However, the policeman was concerned that, should the boys actually have to talk to the occupation authorities, it would quickly become clear that these two 19-year-old sons of privilege didn't know the slightest thing about the egg business. Therefore, their helper advised, it would be better to simply hide somewhere on the boat, such as among the many sacks of cotton that the *Yeni Dünya* was transporting.

Nâzım and Vâlâ took the man's advice. Buried deep under the sacks of cotton, the boys held their breath and listened. In Vâlâ's later retelling, they heard the footsteps of the occupation-authority police walking by and later disembarking the ship. The *Yeni Dünya* pulled away, continuing its journey northward toward the Black Sea, and suddenly Nâzım and Vâlâ realized that they had escaped.[63]

Vâlâ Nureddin, who would later go by the pen name Vâ-Nû, was Nâzım's closest friend at this time. His background was, in some ways, quite similar to that of Nâzım. Born in 1901 in Salonica, Vâlâ was the son of an Ottoman civil servant who would later become the governor of Beirut. Skinnier than Nâzım, with floppy short black hair and round-lensed glasses, Vâlâ was also an aspiring poet.

Vâlâ's adolescent years had been challenging. His father had died when Vâlâ was twelve years old, and his mother was left nearly penniless with four children to raise on her own. At age sixteen, Vâlâ was sent to Vienna to study banking, the recipient of a government scholarship.[64] After graduating in 1919, he had returned to Istanbul to work in the Ottoman Ministry of Finance, a job that he despised. As Vâlâ would later recall in his memoirs, it was at this time that he began to dream of the freedom that a writing career could afford him.[65]

Back in Istanbul after his years in Vienna, Vâlâ had reconnected with Nâzım, his old friend from Galatasaray. The boys soon began spending most of their free time together, writing and reciting verse and becoming fierce partisans of the Syllabist style. Poetry, and the circle of new friends that it brought to Vâlâ, soon formed the heart of his renewed life. Borrowing money from his mother, Vâlâ set up a small poetry journal that featured his own works and those of his friend Nâzım, among others.[66]

The two older boys that Nâzım and Vâlâ were traveling with, Yusuf Ziya and Faruk Nafiz, were twenty-five and twenty-two years old, respectively. They were Nâzım and Vâlâ's "big brothers" (in Turkish "*ağabey*" or, colloquially, "*abi*"), more accomplished as writers and poets than their younger traveling companions. Yusuf and Faruk had

---

[62] Kız Kulesi (the "maiden's tower") is a small man-made island in the middle of the Bosphorus just to the north of Sirkeci.

[63] Vâ-Nû, *Bu Dünyadan Nâzım Geçti*, 54–55, 61; Sülker, *Nâzım Hikmet'in Gerçek Yaşamı*, vol. 1, 80–81; Göksu and Timms, *Romantic Communist*, 17–19.

[64] According to Vâlâ's paperwork at KUTV in Moscow from 1922, he had a 16-year-old brother and two sisters, one who was 18 and another who was 12. RGASPI, f. 495, op. 266, d. 152, l. 2. Personal file of Vâlâ Nureddin.

[65] Vâ-Nû, *Bu Dünyadan Nâzım Geçti*, 56. Also see RGASPI, f. 495, op. 266, d. 152, ll. 14–15.

[66] Vâ-Nû, *Bu Dünyadan Nâzım Geçti*, 56–60.

been participants in the Young Turk-era intellectual public sphere, writing for news-papers and publishing their poetry, something that likely impressed Nâzım and Vâlâ as well.

The four poet-travelers reached Zonguldak the day after they had set out from Istanbul (Map 2.2). Approaching the city's docks from the sea, they noticed an assem-bled group of young people waiting at the pier. A welcoming party had been arranged, coming out to greet the *Yeni Dünya* on small rowboats. Much to Nâzım and Vâlâ's surprise, it turned out that this gesture had been prepared on behalf of none other than the four poets themselves. A banquet had even been set up in their honor. The festivities had been organized, the boys would later learn, by one Ragıp Bey, a wealthy local supporter of the Ankara cause.[67]

That night, after the banquet had ended, a storm hit Zonguldak. The next day's onward travel to İnebolu, located about 150 miles to the east, would prove a rough ride. Upon arriving in İnebolu, Yusuf Ziya reminded the others to kiss the ground when disembarking, a tradition that had recently become fashionable among the freedom-fighters arriving by boat from Istanbul.

Their affectionate interactions with İnebolu's shoreline notwithstanding, the four friends were given a somewhat brusque reception. Instead of a welcoming committee in the manner of Zonguldak, their boat was met by a military commissar and two civil officials. The four poets were taken directly to the closest police station. On the way there, the commissar explained, somewhat cryptically, that he was just following "orders from Ankara." The boys would later learn that there was concern in Kemal's capital about the possibility of spies and saboteurs infiltrating the movement. Everyone arriving in İnebolu had to be thoroughly vetted before receiving permission to continue onward to Ankara.[68]

While waiting to begin the next leg of their journey, Nâzım, Vâlâ, Yusuf Ziya, and Faruk Nafiz spent their days and nights getting acquainted with İnebolu. There was a teahouse frequented by the town's younger set, and Nâzım and Vâlâ spent hours there reading newspapers and trading gossip with fellow travelers and locals. In the even-ings, the teahouse grew crowded and intimate. The four visitors took turns reciting their works, helping to break the chill of the town's blustery winter nights. Despite the somewhat severe treatment they had been given at the harbor, the boys were again fêted in the style of minor celebrities. The most popular of the four poets, according to Vâlâ's later recollections, was Nâzım, whose fiery nationalistic verse routinely received the most energetic applause.[69]

They waited for fifteen days in İnebolu, but in the end the news they received was disappointing: Yusuf Ziya and Faruk Nafiz were ordered to return to Istanbul. Apparently, the two had been flagged as security risks due to their past associations.

---

[67] Ibid., 62–63. According to Sülker, it took them 75 hours to get from Istanbul to İnebolu. *Nâzım Hikmet'in Gerçek Yaşamı*, vol. 1, 88. Also see Memet Fuat, *Nâzım Hikmet*, 25.

[68] Vâ-Nû, *Bu Dünyadan Nâzım Geçti*, 62–64; Sülker, *Nâzım Hikmet'in Gerçek Yaşamı*, vol. 1, 80–83; Fish, *Nâzım'ın Çilesi*, 199–200; Göksu and Timms, *Romantic Communist*, 17–19.

[69] Vâ-Nû, *Bu Dünyadan Nâzım Geçti*, 74; Sülker, *Nâzım Hikmet'in Gerçek Yaşamı*, vol. 1, 82.

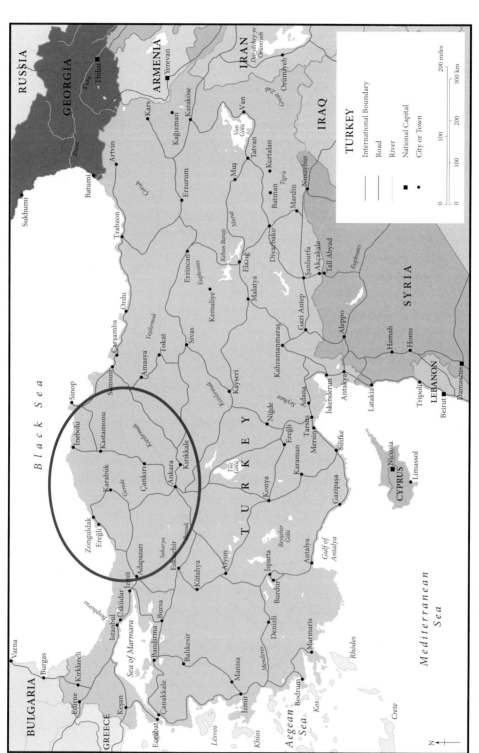

Map 2.2 Present-day map highlighting Zonguldak, İnebolu, Kastamonu, and Ankara

Yusuf Ziya had previously worked for the newspaper *Alemdar*, which had been critical of the erstwhile Young Turks who made up the bulk of Mustafa Kemal's inner circle. Faruk Nafiz, meanwhile, had once received a medal from Damat Ferit Pasha, a politician who had been the Ottoman signatory to the Treaty of Sèvres.[70] The services of Faruk Nafiz and Yusuf Ziya would therefore not be desired in Ankara.[71]

Nâzım and Vâlâ, on the other hand, were not only given permission to proceed, but were also supplied with money for their expenses. Their happiness at receiving this funding was tempered, however, by the boys' sadness—perhaps fear—stemming from the loss of their elder companions. Nâzım and Vâlâ, two "Istanbul children," were totally out of their element in rural Anatolia.[72] They had thought that their two *abi*s, or "older brothers," would look after them on this trip, but now Nâzım and Vâlâ were on their own.

The boys walked down to the shoreline and stared out to the west, climbing a hill to get a better look at the departing vessel. Below them was a small cluster of houses not far from the water. In the distance, Vâlâ could hear a donkey braying. They watched the boat for some time longer as it carried their friends away.[73]

## Walking in the Wind

In the absence of their older traveling companions, Nâzım and Vâlâ rebounded quickly. The very same day that Yusuf Ziya and Faruk Nafiz were shipped back to Istanbul, the boys made friends with a new group of travelers.

Having decided to treat themselves by spending some of their road money, Nâzım and Vâlâ walked over to the large coffeehouse next to the pier and bought dinner.[74] While they were eating the boys noticed a group of young men sitting nearby, people they had seen a few times around town. The group was easy to spot because their leader always wore a long red scarf around his thin neck. This was Sadık Ahi.

After his meeting with Nestor Lakoba in Istanbul, Sadık Ahi had made good on his pledge to set off for Ankara. He was traveling alongside a collection of his fellow "German" Spartakists, including Vehbi (Sarıdal) and Nafi Atuf (Kansu), among others.[75] Sadık and his friends had, like Nâzım and Vâlâ, been hanging out in town, waiting to be cleared for onward travel to Ankara. Talking loudly at the teahouse, Ahi

---

[70] And was now therefore considered a traitor in Kemalist circles.

[71] Nâzım writes about this incident in *Life's Good, Brother*, when the book's main character, based on Nâzım, is informed in İnebolu that his two friends had been sent back to Istanbul on orders from Ankara. "They were sent back because they couldn't be trusted." *Life's Good, Brother: A Novel* (trans. Mutlu Konuk Blasing) (New York: Persea Books, 2013), 50.

[72] "İstanbul çocuğu," or "Istanbul child" is a term used to refer to an urbanized resident of the city, i.e., an individual who might feel somewhat out of place in more rustic settings.

[73] Fish, *Nâzım'ın Çilesi*, 195.

[74] The money had been sent by Adnan (Adıvar), Halide Edip's husband and an important official in Ankara. Sülker, *Nâzım Hikmet'in Gerçek Yaşamı*, vol. 1, 88; Fish, *Nâzım'ın Çilesi*, 204.

[75] Vâ-Nû, *Bu Dünyadan Nâzım Geçti*, 71–72. Vedat Nedim (Tör) may have also joined this traveling party. On the Spartakists, see Göksu and Timms, *Romantic Communist*, 20–21.

and company soon attracted the attention of Nâzım and Vâlâ, who eventually joined the older boys at their table.

At the time that Nâzım and Vâlâ met Ahi and the other Spartakists, the boys still held, in Vâlâ's later words, quite nationalistic political views. In his later memoirs from this journey, Vâlâ described Nâzım as having been "a dyed-in-the-wool nationalist" at this time.[76] Their intellectual heroes were Turkists like Ziya Gökalp and Halide Edip, and Nâzım's earliest poetry had emulated the aggressively nationalistic style that was then in vogue.

Eagerly, Nâzım and Vâlâ explained their literary and political interests to Ahi and his companions. To the boys' embarrassment and dismay, however, Ahi and his friends soon began teasing their younger colleagues about these views. Far from celebrating the boy-poets in the manner to which they had become accustomed, Ahi and the other Spartakists deemed Nâzım and Vâlâ's nationalism a sign of naïveté and ignorance. Vâlâ, in his memoirs, remembered the experience as a humiliating one, at least initially.

Rather than get angry or storm out, however, Vâlâ and Nâzım appear to have almost enjoyed the intellectual dressing-down they were receiving. Realizing that the older boys had something to teach them, and perhaps hoping to join forces with their interlocutors for the rest of the way to Ankara, Nâzım and Vâlâ kept coming back to the Spartakists for more punishment in the days to come.

Although the boys were now free to leave town and continue their journey, Nâzım and Vâlâ decided to postpone their departure for a while. After all, what was the hurry? They had plenty of money, and they were now beginning to enjoy themselves again after the hasty dispatch of their older friends. For the next several days, Nâzım and Vâlâ spent nearly all of their time with the Spartakists, drinking tea in the enormous but sparsely decorated room that Ahi and his confederates had rented on the edge of town. In Vâlâ's reminiscences, the boys followed the Spartakists through the streets of İnebolu, over the hills and along the shoreline outside of town, engaging in hours-long conversations amid the relentless gusts of a January Black Sea wind.

Eventually, the Spartakists received permission for onward travel to Ankara. They immediately rented a wagon and left town without the boys. Nâzım and Vâlâ, who had hung around İnebolu for as long as the Spartakists were still there, remained in town for two more days. By the time they were ready to leave town, however, snow had begun to fall. The boys were told by locals that the roads would be muddy and unsuitable for wheeled vehicles, and that it would be best for them to travel on foot. They were also warned to not go alone, as there were bandits in the hills. Nâzım and Vâlâ heeded this advice and joined up with a larger party of travelers who were setting out to make the journey together.[77]

---

[76] Vâ-Nû, *Bu Dünyadan Nâzım Geçti*, 67–68. Also see Sülker, *Nâzım Hikmet'in Gerçek Yaşamı*, vol. 1, 83–84; Babayev, *Nâzım Hikmet*, 50–51; Fish, *Nâzım'ın Çilesi*, 197, 206.

[77] Vâ-Nû refers to the "young soldiers and civilians" with whom they walked from İnebolu in *Bu Dünyadan Nâzım Geçti*, 97–98. Rady Fish mentions that Nâzım and Vâlâ walked with another ten individuals, some of whom had fought in World War I. *Nâzım'ın Çilesi*, 209.

In Vâlâ's memoirs, Nâzım is presented as almost childlike, barely capable of looking after himself. Vâlâ wrote that Nâzım had even turned over his money to Vâlâ to hold on his behalf, lest Nâzım lose it or waste it on some trifle. "From that day forward and for years I was his money-manager," Vâlâ wrote. "In all of our travels…in Anatolia, the Caucasus, in Russia," Vâlâ would hold the cash.

> When standing in front of a store window, if he really craved a kebab, halva, cake or something like that, he would stand and look at me with a bashful and hesitant expression. I understood. He loved sweets. I'd take him inside and get him something to eat.[78]

Vâlâ's memoirs, which were written in the late 1950s, gently tease Nâzım on occasion. Such is the case, for example, with Vâlâ's story about Nâzım setting out to buy a new hat. No longer in temperate Istanbul, the boys needed heavier clothing to make it through the harsh Anatolian winter. Vâlâ, as he would later record, convinced Nâzım to get himself a *kalpak*, the type of headwear that Mustafa Kemal was making popular at the time. Up until then, Nâzım had always worn a fez, "a rather decadent thing" that was associated primarily with urban life, and therefore unsuitable for the rough country they would now be encountering.[79]

According to Vâlâ, Nâzım immediately went out and bought a strange-looking *kalpak* that was as tall "as the headwear worn by whirling dervishes."[80] This creation was decorated on top with red flowers and silver ribbons, which Nâzım had reluctantly shown off to Vâlâ after making the purchase (Figure 2.3). In response to Vâlâ's teasing, Nâzım gave his new headwear a solid punch from the inside, producing a momentary flurry of red-and-silver ornamentation.[81]

Ankara was 200 miles to the south of İnebolu. It was a hard walk, and mostly uphill at first. Yet in that first day they still managed to cover almost twenty miles. Walking through forests that covered the mountains lying inland from Anatolia's Black Sea coastline, Nâzım and Vâlâ's party trekked for hours without encountering any other people or dwellings. Finally, in a barren location on the edge of a cliff, the traveling party came across a small village that had a few places to stay.

The boys were exhausted. At the first place they stopped, Vâlâ sat down briefly on a small bench while Nâzım went inside to ask about finding a place to sleep. There was nothing available, but Nâzım and Vâlâ were told to go try their luck at an inn located just fifty feet down the road. According to Vâlâ's later recollection of the journey, walking those last fifty feet after having already sat down was harder than anything else he had done that day. Vâlâ felt certain he would not be able to walk the next morning.

---

[78] Vâ-Nû, *Bu Dünyadan Nâzım Geçti*, 79. Nâzım's inability to look after himself is a common theme in Vâlâ's memoirs.

[79] In 1925, Mustafa Kemal would ban the fez outright in Turkey, deeming the headwear to be too Oriental-looking and incompatible with his plans for the country's cultural Europeanization.

[80] Vâ-Nû, *Bu Dünyadan Nâzım Geçti*, 79.   [81] Ibid., 79–80.

**Figure 2.3** Vâlâ and Nâzım in their *kalpak*s

The boys would surprise themselves, however, with their own fortitude. When the two friends woke up in the morning, they breakfasted on some eggs they bought in the village and found that they had the strength to go forward. Once again, the entire day was spent walking, but the boys noticed that, once this second day of trekking through steep, difficult terrain had passed, they felt less tired than they had the previous evening. And then, on the third day, they were barely tired at all, reaching Kastamonu by nightfall. Distance-wise, Nâzım and Vâlâ had covered just over a quarter of the way between İnebolu and Ankara, but the most topographically challenging part of the trek was now behind them.[82]

As Kastamonu was the largest town they would encounter until Ankara, Nâzım and Vâlâ decided to spend a few days resting up before continuing their journey. During the course of their stay, they were befriended by some young locals who gave them moonshine *rakı* and took them to a brothel on the edge of town. According to Vâlâ's later account, he and Nâzım drank the *rakı* but stayed away from the women. The ladies, wrote Vâlâ, invited the boys up to their rooms, but Nâzım and Vâlâ begged off,

---

[82] Ibid., 85.

claiming to be too tired. Ever mindful of not hurting anyone's feelings, the two young poets promised to come back at their earliest convenience.[83]

During the course of the six days they spent walking from Kastamonu to Ankara, Nâzım and Vâlâ saw living conditions that shocked them. On one occasion, the sun was just about to set and the boys were afraid they would find no shelter. Suddenly, they smelled burning dung, a sure sign that they were approaching an inhabited area. Try as they might, however, Nâzım and Vâlâ could not find the source of the smell.

They asked the mule-driver they were traveling with how much farther it would be until they reached the next village.

"This is it," came the reply.

Vâlâ and Nâzım were baffled. No house was in sight.

"The village is beneath us," explained the mule-driver.

Sure enough, the boys discovered that the villagers lived in the caves that ran through the hill that Nâzım and Vâlâ were at that moment standing upon. The mule-driver yelled out below to explain that company had arrived, pushing open a wooden door that led underground. Straight into Nâzım and Vâlâ's faces came a plume of black smoke. The two friends quickly found a place to lie down and, exhausted, fell right to sleep. They awoke the next morning refreshed, if jarred somewhat by the sight of one another's soot-smeared expressions.[84]

That day, Nâzım and Vâlâ walked to Çankırı, a final travelers' outpost located just ninety miles to the northeast of Ankara. There they again encountered the Spartakists, who were resting up and reprovisioning after their own trip down from İnebolu. Nâzım and Vâlâ spent two days hanging out with Ahi and the others in Çankırı, sitting in coffeehouses and picking up their conversations where they had left off. The boys and the Spartakists then traveled together the rest of the way into Ankara.[85]

*

Only a few weeks had passed, but the boys were arriving in the Kemalist capital in a very different frame of mind from that with which they had departed Istanbul. Already, it felt like they were in a new world entirely.

---

[83] Ibid., 85–86. In *Life's Good*, Nâzım writes that it was fear of syphilis that discouraged the travelers from partaking, 53. Also see Fish, *Nâzım'ın Çilesi*, 160.

[84] Vâ-Nû, *Bu Dünyadan Nâzım Geçti*, 95–96.    [85] Ibid., 97–99.

# 3

# Up for Grabs in Anatolia

The war had ended, but Şevket Süreyya was hardly at peace. Back home in Edirne, Şevket had trouble fitting back into his old life. He thought a lot about politics, and in particular the continuing allied occupation of the Ottoman Empire. He was angry and at a loss for what to do with himself, and had started meeting up with others who shared his political concerns. Şevket would later dismiss these days as a time of all talk and no action, an experience which left him feeling even more powerless. He found a job working at a teacher-training school, but remained unfulfilled. Having seen a bit of the world, he wanted to see more. Not long after coming back home from the war, Şevket Süreyya was looking for a way out again.

He soon found one. The new nationalist government in Azerbaijan, which had declared independence in May 1918, was looking for teachers. In Baku, *Türk Yurdu* alumni Ahmet Ağaoğlu and Mehmet Emin Resulzade now held important positions in the new administration. Resulzade was the head of state, and Ağaoğlu was, in these pre-Bolshevik days, a member of the Azeri national parliament.

The Müsavat government that Ağaoğlu and Resulzade were serving was looking to reform education in Azerbaijan by importing Turkish teachers from the Ottoman Empire.[1] Since the middle of the nineteenth century, most Ottoman state schools had employed the sort of literacy-based education favored by Muslim supporters of educational reform in late imperial Russia.[2] Now that imperial-era Muslim community activist figures like Ağaoğlu and Resulzade had risen to positions of power in Baku, they turned to graduates of Ottoman educational institutions to shape the language skills of what they envisioned to be the first generation of students of an independent Azerbaijan.

The idea of working as a Turkish language teacher in Azerbaijan appealed strongly to Şevket Süreyya, who jumped at the chance to leave Edirne. To Şevket, Azerbaijan represented an opportunity to finally see part of "Turan," which he understood as a continuum including Turkic-speaking territories from the Balkans to Central Asia. Still a devoted pan-Turkist, Şevket Süreyya believed that all of the world's "Turks"—i.e., populations that are now known by national terms like "Azeris," "Tatars," and "Bashkirs," to name just a few—should support one another.

---

[1] On the presence of Russian-Muslim activists in the Müsavat government in Baku, also see Meyer, *Turks Across Empires*, 173–174.

[2] On education in the Ottoman Empire, see Benjamin Fortna, *Imperial Classroom: Islam, the State, and Education in the Late Ottoman Empire* (New York: Oxford University Press, 2002), 9–10, 12; Karpat, *The Politicization of Islam*, 98–100; Meyer, *Turks Across Empires*, 109–110.

*Red Star over the Black Sea: Nâzim Hikmet and his Generation.* James H. Meyer, Oxford University Press. © James H. Meyer 2023.
DOI: 10.1093/oso/9780192871176.003.0005

Turks, thought Şevket Süreyya, ought to be fighting on behalf of Azerbaijan, whose independence and territorial integrity had been thrown into doubt by a war that had broken out with local Armenian communities in Nagorno-Karabakh. Şevket saw Azerbaijan, where most of the predominantly Shiite Muslim population spoke a language similar to Turkish, as a "brother" Turkic nation making a bid for freedom. Feeling unable to facilitate meaningful change in Edirne, Şevket decided to go someplace where he perhaps could make more of a difference.

In 1919, he set out by ship for Batumi, gateway to the Caucasus.

*

The end of the war had not brought the clean, decisive conclusion that the leaders of the Entente powers had hoped for. To the contrary, from the western ranges of Anatolia and the Balkans to the eastern edges of the Caucasus, the future was far from clear. A litany of actors were vying for power. For some, it was their first time on stage. Others were hoping for a second act.

## Searching for Second Chances

This was the wide-open context in which Nâzım and Vâlâ began making their way across Anatolia and the Caucasus in early 1921. The individuals and groups that the boys would meet and spend time with during the months they spent on the road were the flotsam and jetsam of dissolving armies, societies, and empires. Men and women seeking to make some sense out of the present, or perhaps just achieve a modicum of protection for themselves, signed up with movements promising a more hopeful future.

At the same time that the nationalist Müsavat Party was seeking to consolidate Azerbaijan's political independence in Baku, Mustafa Kemal and a growing list of supporters had established themselves in Ankara. They, too, were searching for second chances, as many of the figures in Mustafa Kemal's coterie had held positions of authority in Istanbul during the Unionist era, making them vulnerable to arrest by the British. For Mustafa Kemal and the Ankara government, the war against the occupation was not simply a struggle for the motherland, sultan, or caliphate—all of which were invoked by Kemal and his associates in their efforts to inspire others to join the uprising. As far as Mustafa Kemal Pasha and his leadership circle were concerned, the battle they were undertaking was also a matter of personal survival.

Many ex-Unionists had followed Mustafa Kemal to Ankara, but the former Young Turk leaders—i.e., the triumvirate of Enver, Talat, and Cemal pashas—were currently seeking out their own second chances abroad. Initially, the three had fled to Germany, where Enver and Talat had held meetings with the German communist Karl Radek, a confidant of Lenin who had accompanied the future Soviet leader to Russia in his famous sealed railway car in 1917. Shortly after meeting with Radek, Enver traveled to Moscow while Talat and Cemal remained in Germany. Cemal Pasha would later move to Moscow as well.

In his meetings with Lenin in Moscow, Enver had presented himself as a leader of the Turkish resistance against the imperialist Entente occupation. He wanted support from the Bolsheviks and, initially, there were signs that he might find success in obtaining their assistance. In September 1920, People's Commissar for Foreign Affairs Georgii Chicherin submitted a proposal to the Politburo calling for 10 million German marks to be provided to Enver to buy guns in Germany for Turkish fighters in Anatolia.[3] This money was, notably, never actually provided, but the Bolsheviks continued to maintain contacts with Enver for as long as he might prove useful. In the summer of 1921, Enver moved from Moscow to Batumi, just across the border from Kemalist-held territory.[4]

Even as the Bolsheviks carried on negotiations with Enver, they were simultaneously engaged in far more substantial talks with Mustafa Kemal's Ankara-based government. Since late July 1920, when Kemal had responded favorably to the Bolsheviks' suggestion that they hold negotiations, Ankara and Moscow had been moving more closely toward one another. Ankara's chief negotiator of what would eventually become the Treaty of Moscow (March 1921) was Kemal's emissary to Soviet Russia, Ali Fuat (Cebesoy).

Ali Fuat Pasha also happened to be an "uncle" of Nâzım Hikmet, as he was the first cousin of Nâzım's mother, Celile Hanım. Born in 1882 in Salonica, Ali Fuat had been a high-ranking Ottoman military commander in the Balkan Wars and World War I. Following the Ottoman defeat, he became one of the first officers to join up with Mustafa Kemal's resistance movement. In November 1920, Ali Fuat was appointed the Ankara government's first ambassador to Moscow, a position of considerable importance.[5]

Moscow carried on negotiations with Enver and Mustafa Kemal pashas simultaneously, as the Bolsheviks did not initially know who, if either of these two individuals, would ultimately come out on top in Anatolia. Bolshevik leaders were hoping to block further French and British expansion into the region, so it made sense for them to support whichever movement appeared to have the best chance of succeeding, regardless of their Marxist bona fides. Meanwhile, Moscow's practice of simultaneously supporting multiple would-be Turkish leaders—Enver, Mustafa Kemal, and TKP leader Mustafa Suphi—also contributed to the creation of certain tensions in Anatolia.[6]

Ankara was keen to maintain good relations with Moscow, and, for a while, Kemal's government tolerated the Baku-based TKP. With respect to the opening of

---

[3] Samuel Hirst, "Eurasia's Discontent: Soviet and Turkish Anti-Westernism in the Interwar Period," PhD dissertation, Department of History, University of Pennsylvania, 2012, 24, 110. On Enver Pasha and the Bolsheviks, also see Paul Dumont, "La fascination du bolchevisme: Enver pacha et le parti des soviets populaires, 1919–1922," *Cahiers du Monde russe et soviétique*, vol. 16, no. 2 (1975), 141–166.

[4] Shaw and Shaw, *History of the Ottoman Empire and Modern Turkey*, vol. II, 354.

[5] Ali Fuat Cebesoy, *Moskova Hatıraları* (İstanbul: Vatan Neşriyatı, 1955). On Ali Fuat Pasha, also see Ayfer Özçelik, *Ali Fuat Cebesoy* (Ankara: Akçağ, 1993).

[6] Samuel Hirst points out that the Bolsheviks were also supporting Circassian Ethem, the leader of the so-called "Green Army," which "frequently changed sides." "Eurasia's Discontent," 110. On the Green Army, also see Harris, *Origins of Communism in Turkey*, 69–71.

communist parties in Anatolia, however, the Kemalist government took a significantly different stand.[7]

In June 1920, the first Turkish Communist Party—formed three months ahead of Suphi's Baku-based organization—had been created in Ankara by Şerif Manatov and Salih Hacıoğlu.[8] Manatov was a young Russian-born Bolshevik—a Bashkir by nationality—who had a background in pan-Turkist circles. During the Young Turk era, Manatov had lived in Istanbul, where he had become a member of the Turkic Hearths.[9]

In late 1918 Manatov, who at some point had returned to Russia, came back to Anatolia and began to organize politically.[10] Manatov had worked for the "Muslim Bureau" in Moscow, an organization dedicated to winning over Muslim support for the Bolshevik cause. The Muslim Bureau was initially concerned with "domestic" Muslims, i.e., those living in the territories of the former Romanov Empire.[11] Now, however, figures such as Manatov, Mustafa Suphi, and other early Muslim Bolsheviks had become increasingly visible in projects devoted to recruiting Muslims living in other countries as well.[12]

Manatov's partner in establishing the new Anatolian-based TKP was Salih Hacıoğlu. Hacıoğlu was born in a village outside the Black Sea city of Trabzon in 1880, and had graduated from the military veterinary institute in Istanbul in 1904. Since then, he had been working as an animal doctor for the Ottoman Army. A recent convert to communism, Hacıoğlu had up until the end of the war been a supporter of the Young Turk government in Istanbul.[13]

The Turkish Communist Party that Manatov and Hacıoğlu formed did not last long.[14] In August 1920, the party was closed, just two months after it was established. Manatov was detained and then deported to Soviet Russia. Salih Hacıoğlu was arrested and sentenced to fifteen years in prison, although he would be amnestied after having spent ten and a half months behind bars.[15]

Two months after closing the TKP in Ankara, the Kemalist establishment organized, in October 1920, a "Turkish Communist Party" of their own. This organization,

---

[7] Also see Harris, *Origins of Communism in Turkey*, 85–86.

[8] Alongside two other individuals: one was identified as "Nuri," but this does not appear to have been Süleyman Nuri. The other was Vakkas Ferid. See Hirst, "Eurasia's Discontent," 146, fn. 415. On Vakkas Ferid, also see Emel Akal, *Mustafa Kemal, İttihat Terakki ve Bolşevizm* (İstanbul: İletişim, 2012), 110.

[9] Akal, *Moskova-Ankara-Londra Üçgeninde*, 87.

[10] Emel Akal argues that, because "there was no sign that an Anatolian-based communist party could be formed" in 1918, Manatov must not have been sent, but rather arrived in Anatolia on his own initiative. *Moskova-Ankara-Londra Üçgeninde*, 90–91.

[11] Manatov, in his capacity as a member of the Muslim Bureau, worked closely with Joseph Stalin, who directed the Bolsheviks' policies toward nationalities at this time. See RGASPI, f. 558, op. 1, d. 4384, l. 1, "Telegram from the People's Commissariat for Nationalities to the Executive Committee of the Orenburg Soviet of Worker and Soldier Deputies," February 6, 1918; RGASPI, f. 558, op. 1, d. 5311, l. 1. "In the Moscow Committee of the Party (Bolsheviks)," May 1918.

[12] Harris, *Origins of Communism in Turkey*, 53, 61.

[13] RGASPI, personal file of Gadzhiev Salikh Süleyman (Salih Hacıoğlu) f. 495, op. 266, d. 98, ll. 7, 39–40. A second, much smaller, file on Salih Hacıoğlu can be found in RGASPI, f. 495, op. 266, d. 116, "Salikh." Also see Akbulut and Tunçay (eds.), *İstanbul Komünist Grubu'ndan*, 402–403.

[14] On this party, see Akal, *Moskova-Ankara-Londra Üçgeninde*, 119–120.

[15] RGASPI, f. 495, op. 266, d. 98, l. 39.

unlike Suphi's TKP in Baku or the party that Manatov and Hacıoğlu had formed, was controlled by the authorities in Ankara. Members of the new party included İsmet (İnönü) Pasha, one of Kemal's closest allies, alongside numerous other military and political figures associated with Mustafa Kemal's government.

Why would the Ankara government establish its own TKP, let alone allow senior government officials to join? The creation of this "official" communist party took place about one month after the formation of Suphi's TKP in Baku. In founding an official communist party dominated by Mustafa Kemal's lieutenants, Ankara was sending a clear message to Moscow, as well as to local communists: there was no need in Anatolia for an independent communist movement.[16]

## The Bolshevik Eastern Strategy

The creation of Suphi's TKP comprised one example of what I describe as the "Bolshevik eastern strategy." This strategy would serve as the context through which Nâzım and his friends, as well as thousands of other communists, first found a home in the USSR in the early 1920s. It constituted a form of recruitment directed by Moscow and aimed at potential communists among "eastern" populations, both domestic and foreign.[17]

For the Bolsheviks, the domestic east inside the USSR and the foreign one outside it made up two separate, but largely overlapping, entities. Bolshevik recruitment of "eastern" populations reached an early new height with the holding of the Congress of Peoples of the East in Baku in September 1920. Among the 1,891 delegates to the congress, the largest two contingents were "Turks" (235) and "Persians" (192).[18] At a time when communism was still little understood outside of Russia—and even within it—the Congress of Peoples of the East attracted a wide array of second chance-seekers. As was the case with Mustafa Kemal and his coterie in Ankara, many of the individuals attending the Baku Congress were opponents of British and French imperialism, rather than necessarily proponents of communism.

One of the speakers at the Baku Congress was none other than Enver Pasha.[19] He was no communist, but like Mustafa Kemal, Enver Pasha was willing to play at being one if that could help bring funding from Moscow. Watching Enver's speech that day was Şevket Süreyya, who noted the odd atmosphere that enveloped the room when

---

[16] Samuel Hirst views the creation of a Kemalist-backed Communist Party in more ideological terms, presenting it as a genuine reflection of communism's "attraction" to the Ankara elite of this time. "Eurasia's Discontent," 132–134, here 132.

[17] This is a concept that is at the heart of Masha Kirasirova's work on Arab students at KUTV. "The Eastern International"; Kirasirova, "The East as a Category of Bolshevik Ideology and Comintern Administration." Also see James H. Meyer, "Children of Trans-Empire: Nâzım Hikmet and the First Generation of Turkish Students at Moscow's Communist University of the East," *Journal of the Ottoman and Turkish Studies Association*, vol. 5, no. 2 (Fall 2018), 195–218, here 198, 208–217.

[18] From among 1,275 attendees who completed the questionnaire regarding their nationality. John Riddell (ed.), *To See the Dawn: Baku, 1920 – First Congress of the Peoples of the East* (New York: Pathfinder Press, 1993), 274.

[19] For Ahmet Cevat Emre's account of Enver's speech, see Akbulut (ed.), *Milli Azadlık Savaşı Anıları*, 59–60.

the former Young Turk leader took the podium. "While he was reading his speech, there was an indecisive air blowing regarding whether to applaud or not," wrote Şevket years later. "It was a sad and painful sight, a broken, indecisive man, so out of place in such an environment."[20]

The first meeting of the Turkish Communist Party was held immediately after the Congress of Peoples of the East. There were 125 delegates at the TKP's inaugural session. In his memoirs, Şevket underscored the contrast he saw between the meeting's pretensions and the reality on the ground in Anatolia.

> If one looked at the crowd in the room, at the delegates taking the stage and speaking in the name of every province in Turkey, and at the speeches they gave, it would have made sense to say that Turkey was now a communist country. But upon closer inspection it could be seen that the people in this crowd in fact did not represent any place or any organization. Among them all there was no common connection. Every one of them had a different understanding of what communism was. Making up much of the crowd, in fact, were Turkish prisoners of war who had been left stranded in Russia after the revolution and were just looking for a way to get home.[21]

Despite Şevket Süreyya Aydemir's later mockery of this first TKP meeting, clearly some force was propelling him toward communism. And he was hardly alone.

## Mustafa Suphi's Last Ride

Throughout the winter of 1920–21, Nâzım Hikmet's uncle Ali Fuat Pasha was engaged in negotiations with officials from the People's Commissariat for Foreign Affairs in Moscow.[22] As these discussions intensified, it became increasingly clear that the potential value to the Bolsheviks of a has-been like Enver Pasha or a never-was like Mustafa Suphi would be minimal. Mustafa Kemal, by contrast, was leading a genuine movement in Ankara, one that Moscow could work with.

The Treaty of Moscow, which Ali Fuat signed on behalf of the Ankara government on March 16, 1921, constituted an adjustment of the Brest-Litovsk treaty that the Bolsheviks had signed with the Ottoman government three years earlier. Brest-Litovsk had transferred the provinces of Kars, Ardahan, and Batumi—all of which had been lost to Russia in 1878—back to the Ottoman Empire. The treaty that Ali Fuat negotiated, meanwhile, revised this agreement. The provinces of Kars and Ardahan would still be ceded—now to Ankara, rather than to the government in Istanbul—but Batumi would remain under Moscow's control.[23]

---

[20] Aydemir, *Suyu Arayan Adam*, 165. Göktürk, *Bilinmeyen Yönleriyle Şevket Süreyya Aydemir*, 76.

[21] Aydemir, *Suyu Arayan Adam*, 169–170. On early Bolshevik recruitment of Ottoman POWs and appeals by POWs to join up with the Bolsheviks, see RGASPI/IISH, f. 495, op. 181, dd. 20, 42, 89, 94, 97, 112, and elsewhere.

[22] This would later be renamed the Ministry of Foreign Affairs.

[23] On Batumi between Russia and the Ottoman Empire, see Mustafa Sarı, *Türkiye-Kafkasya İlişkilerinde Batum (1917–1921)* (Ankara: Türk Tarih Kurumu, 2014).

68    RED STAR OVER THE BLACK SEA

What Ankara gave up in territory nevertheless yielded important dividends in terms of financial and military assistance. In the months leading up to the treaty, the Politburo approved several shipments of weapons and gold to Ankara. Unlike the money that had been promised to Enver Pasha, these funds and munitions were actually delivered. In total, Moscow would send about eleven million gold rubles to Mustafa Kemal's government. The first shipment of gold was approved in June 1920, and the last in late February 1921.[24] The final check having cleared and the last weapon accounted for, Ali Fuat Pasha put his name to the treaty and renounced, in the name of the Ankara government, any claim to Batumi.[25]

While relations between Moscow and Ankara grew warmer, the relative importance to the Bolsheviks of Enver Pasha and Mustafa Suphi diminished. Seven months after Ali Fuat Pasha signed the Treaty of Moscow, Enver Pasha pulled up stakes in Batumi. He had been dispatched by Moscow to help quell a Muslim anti-communist rebellion in Central Asia. Soon after, however, Enver himself would join the revolt, leading an unlikely counter-revolution against his former paymasters. He was killed in August 1922 in a battle against Red Army forces outside Dushanbe. Enver was forty-one years old at the time of his death.

In the wake of Moscow's new treaty with Ankara, Mustafa Suphi had also become expendable.[26] In the second half of 1920, Suphi had received several encouraging telegrams from General Kâzım Karabekir in Ankara. Karabekir, who was in fact one of the most religious and conservative members of Mustafa Kemal's inner circle, sought to give Suphi the impression that the Ankara government was communist-leaning.

At a time when Ankara was invoking Islam and the Sultan-Caliph in efforts to attract Anatolian Muslims to its cause, Kâzım Karabekir demonstrated a willingness to similarly speak the Bolsheviks' language, at least for as long as the promised money and guns from Soviet Russia were still pending.[27] In late July 1920, Karabekir—addressing Suphi as "Dear Comrade"—identified himself as "a long-time opponent of capital" and stressed that "since its very first days I have been a supporter of Bolshevism." The general went on to describe the parliament in Ankara as one "chosen by the workers and peasants of the country."[28] Subsequent communications from Kâzım Karabekir were likewise warm and seemingly pro-communist, such as when the two discussed the possibility of Ankara sending representatives to the Baku Congress.[29]

---

[24]  Hirst, "Eurasia's Discontent," 106–107.

[25]  My view of this treaty differs from that of Hirst, who sees Ankara–Moscow relations more in terms of "ideological affinity" than "momentary expedience." "Eurasia's Discontent," 132.

[26]  Harris, *Origins of Communism in Turkey*, 89.

[27]  On Mustafa Kemal's simultaneous appeals to both Islam and communism, see M. Şükrü Hanioğlu, *Atatürk: An Intellectual Biography* (Princeton: Princeton University Press, 2011), 103-109.

[28]  RGASPI/IISH, f. 495, op. 181, d. 15, ll. 3–4. Letter from Kâzım Karabekir to Mustafa Suphi, July 23, 1920.

[29]  RGASPI/IISH, f. 495, op. 181, d. 15, l. 9. Letter from Kâzım Karabekir to Mustafa Suphi, undated but apparently from late July or August of 1920.

Kâzım Karabekir's efforts to charm Suphi and the TKP were successful. In a party report written on October 12, 1920, Mustafa Suphi depicted Kâzım, rather optimistically, as a friend of communism.

> Between Mustafa Kemal and Kâzım Karabekir there is some disagreement. Thanks to Karabekir's closer connection to Russia, the latter shows a better understanding and more sympathetic feeling toward communism. The disagreement between Mustafa Kemal and Kâzım Karabekir has taken on an oppositional character.[30]

In December 1920, Mustafa Suphi, Ethem Nejat, and thirteen other members of the TKP Central Committee set out for Ankara. Because the road to the Kemalist capital was considered unsafe, Suphi and his cohort elected to travel westward along the Black Sea coastline until Trabzon, then take a boat to Kastamonu. From there they would head south to Ankara.

Trabzon had been on edge for some time.[31] The city had been occupied by Russian troops during World War I, and even following the war's conclusion it was not always clear in which country the Black Sea port would eventually land. Suphi's connections with Russians, no matter what their politics, were bound to generate a wary reception. The Soviet Consul in Trabzon had noted that his staff was "subject to harassment" in the days leading up to Suphi's arrival, and that the consulate was not in a position to offer protection to the TKP traveling party.[32]

Arriving in Trabzon, Suphi's group found the conditions to be even worse than they had expected. They were met by "an angry crowd," which greeted the committee members with chants of "We don't want it!" (*istemiyoruz!*). Suphi and the Central Committee had been "strongly forbidden from going out on the street" in Trabzon by the Consul in the interest of their own safety.[33]

The precise circumstances surrounding what transpired next are to some extent unclear. In the words of one account, "in the middle of the night" of January 28, a mob formed outside the house where Suphi and the other fourteen committee members were staying. Somehow the fifteen were "induced or compelled" to leave their residence and were then marched down to the shoreline and obliged to board a boat captained by one Yahya the boatman.[34]

Yahya pulled out from the pier in the direction of Batumi. Once they were on the open seas, he approached a second boat filled with men carrying guns. These men then boarded Yahya's boat and proceeded to shoot the trapped TKP committee members and dump their wounded and dying bodies into the sea. All fifteen perished,

---

[30] RGASPI, f. 544, op. 3, d. 9, ll. 41–48-ob, here 46-ob. Report by Mustafa Suphi and Ethem Nejad, October 12, 1920.

[31] RGASPI, f. 544, op. 3, d. 23, ll. 26–26-ob. Report by G. Astakhov, undated, but likely from December 1920.

[32] Harris, *Origins of Communism in Turkey*, 90–91. Also see Dumont, "Bolchevisme et Orient," 396–397.

[33] Harris, *Origins of Communism in Turkey*, 91. Also see RGASPI, f. 544, op. 3, d. 53, ll. 4–4-ob. Report by Mehmet Tair in Tuapse to the Presidium of the Council for Propaganda and Activities of the Peoples of the East, February 16, 1921.

[34] RGASPI, f. 544, op. 3, d. 53, ll. 4–4-ob. Report from Mehmet Tair, Tuapse, February 16, 1921.

either from their wounds or by drowning.[35] According to a party report written on February 4, 1921, one week after the murders Suphi's Russian widow Mariam was still being held "under detention in the home of Yahya the boatman."[36] Yahya was eventually arrested, but then was acquitted and released from jail.[37] He was later killed "under mysterious circumstances."[38]

Was Yahya acting on someone else's behalf? Given the level of organization involved, it certainly seems likely. There were quite a few individuals who would have been glad to be rid of Suphi and his entourage. In particular, the Ankara government is frequently cited as a possible culprit in the mass slaying.[39] The thinking in this regard is that liquidating Suphi's TKP was one of Ankara's unofficial conditions for signing the treaty with Moscow. Mustafa Kemal himself had, after all, already created an Anatolian-based Communist Party of his own. Did Suphi and his comrades really believe that Kemal desired a second one?

Suphi also had enemies within the TKP, and the final months of his life were punctuated by a series of denunciations and counter-allegations pertaining to his alleged corruption. One of Suphi's biggest critics was Süleyman Nuri, the ex-POW agitator who had met with Nestor Lakoba prior to the latter's mission to Constantinople in late 1920. On February 2, 1921—just a few days after the murders in Trabzon—Süleyman Nuri wrote a letter from Yerevan denouncing Suphi to a Bolshevik official by the name of Otarbekov. In this letter—which makes no mention of Suphi's murder and refers to the TKP leader in the present tense—Nuri alleged that "Suphi, upon his departure from Baku, purchased diamonds and other precious stones worth seven million" rubles.[40] Nuri also charged that Suphi had spent half a million rubles of party money on a coat for his wife, and claimed that he had found a witness named Hasan Cevat who was "prepared to testify" against the TKP leader.[41] In a separate report written during this period, Nuri further criticized Suphi for having attempted to establish a "personal dictatorship" over TKP activities.[42]

Another letter, meanwhile, signed by one "Mahdi," similarly alleged that Suphi was guilty of corruption. Sent to the Russian mission in Ankara, this undated letter claimed that Suphi had sent one and a half million rubles to Istanbul, and then spent

---

[35] Also see Erdem, *Mustafa Suphi*, 238–239.

[36] RGASPI, f. 544, op. 3, d. 53, l. 23. Report from Mehmet Tair to the Presidium of the Council for Propaganda and Activities of the Peoples of the East, Tuapse, February 4, 1921.

[37] On Yahya's acquittal, see Harris, *Origins of Communism in Turkey*, 94.    [38] Ibid., 91.

[39] Harris has written that "Ankara may have authorized" the destruction of the TKP leadership "as a convenient way to be rid of a potentially dangerous competitor," before ultimately concluding that it was "most likely" that Yahya the boatman—an ardent supporter of Enver Pasha—"took matters into his own hands." Ibid., 91. This explanation does not, however, account for where the boatload of gunmen who killed the fifteen had come from.

[40] According to Emel Akal, news of the murders in Trabzon did not reach Baku until February 14. *Moskova-Ankara-Londra Üçgeninde*, 497.

[41] RGASPI, f. 544, op. 3, d. 53, l. 1. Letter from Süleyman Nuri to Otarbekov. Also see f. 544, op. 3, d. 46, ll. 85–87, letter from Süleyman Nuri to the Council for Propaganda and Activities of the Peoples of the East, February 18, 1921. From Hirst, "Eurasia's Discontent," 111, fn. 324.

[42] RGASPI, f. 544, op. 3, d. 46, ll. 210–214. Report by Süleyman Nuri, undated but apparently from early February 1921.

two million rubles on his wedding in Baku. Suphi, alleged "Mahdi," was "now in the possession of one and a half million in foreign money."[43]

Someone else who was on bad terms with Mustafa Suphi was Abid Alimov. A Muslim from late imperial Russian Azerbaijan, Alimov had been an officer in the Russian Army prior to the October Revolution.[44] Beginning in late 1919, he had worked with Suphi in Moscow, traveling with him to Tashkent before eventually returning to Baku. Alimov was an important figure in the TKP's efforts to recruit ex-Ottoman POWs, having served as the director of the party's "military branch" in its earliest days.[45]

In late December, 1920, Alimov had been the subject of an unsigned denunciation claiming that he was spending party money on personal goods and engaging in activity that was "harmful for our party."[46] Documents from TKP files produced at this time indicate that various conflicts had been taking place between Alimov and Mustafa Suphi throughout December 1920 and January 1921, with Suphi seeking to have Alimov transferred to the Crimea.[47] But Alimov—who would, in February 1921, team up with Süleyman Nuri to denounce a Suphi ally named Kayserili İsmail Hakkı—did not leave.[48]

Was Suphi really corrupt? In the aftermath of the murders, letters supposedly written by Suphi's wife Mariam were found that appeared to support the charges.[49] Addressed to "Mama, Tonya, Shura, Varya, and Sashenka," these letters make frequent reference to the great deals that Mariam was allegedly able to find for herself in Anatolia. "In Turkey," goes one passage from these letters, "diamonds are very cheap, for example three or four karats for seven gold liras." Elsewhere, the letter-writer exclaims her enthusiasm for having just purchased "an enormous emerald for 14 liras."[50]

Among the remaining fragments of the Baku-based TKP, there appeared to be little doubt regarding who was behind the massacre in Trabzon. In a letter written on August 31, 1921 to Lenin and Comintern head Grigory Zinoviev—a copy of which was also sent to Süleyman Nuri—İsmail Kadirov, who identified himself as the

---

[43] Suphi's confederate Kayserili İsmail Hakkı was also denounced in Mahdi's letter, which claimed that he "sent so-called propagandists to Turkey and under this pretext steals a lot of money." RGASPI, f. 544, op. 3, d. 53, l. 18. Letter to the Russian mission in Ankara, from "Mahdi," undated.

[44] Akbulut and Tunçay (eds.), *İstanbul Komünist Grubu'ndan*, 365. Vâlâ Nureddin wrote that Alimov's father was a Kazan Tatar. *Bu Dünyadan Nâzım Geçti*, 355.

[45] Akbulut and Tunçay (eds.), *İstanbul Komünist Grubu'ndan*, 365.

[46] RGASPI/IISH, f. 495, op. 181, d. 147, l. 24–26-ob, here 26-ob. Note from the TKP Foreign Bureau denouncing Abid Alimov, undated, but apparently from late December 1920 or early January 1921.

[47] RGASPI/IISH, f. 495, op. 181, d. 147, l. L. 3. "Note to the Presidium of the TKP Foreign Bureau," Mustafa Suphi, January 7, 1921.

[48] Alimov and Nuri alleged that İsmail Hakkı had used five gold liras of party money on improper expenses. RGASPI/IISH, f. 544, op. 3, d. 53, ll. 19–19-ob. Report to the Presidium of the Council for Propaganda and Activities of the Peoples of the East, February 23, 1921.

[49] Suphi's wife is sometimes referred to as "Maria" in TKP-related writings.

[50] Mariam also noted that Süleyman Nuri's wife "had come to Baku in September" to sign up for university classes. "She was neither pretty nor young," observed Suphi's soon-to-be widow. RGASPI, f. 544, op. 3, d. 53, ll. 21–22. Also see f. 544, op. 3, d. 46, ll. 37–37-ob.

Vice-Executive Secretary of the TKP in Baku, lamented that his "honest comrades," as he described Suphi and the others, "were murdered at the hands of the KEMALISTS."[51]

Claims of Ankara's alleged culpability in the murders notwithstanding, Moscow was more interested in collaborating with Mustafa Kemal than avenging the murders. If officials in Moscow were upset about the Central Committee's killings, or thought that Ankara was behind them, they did not go out of their way to convey this to Mustafa Kemal's government. Indeed, in the weeks and months immediately following the murders, relations between Moscow and Ankara continued to strengthen. Months would pass before Suphi's death was even reported in Soviet newspapers.[52]

There were contrasting notions in Baku and Moscow regarding how best to move forward with the party. One idea, floated during the course of a TKP meeting in March 1921, was to create a new Central Committee led by Süleyman Nuri.[53] In his letter to Lenin and Zinoviev, İsmail Kadirov had described Süleyman Nuri as the TKP's "delegate" to the Comintern in Moscow. There was a hope that the TKP, which had "ceased its activities and broken apart" in the aftermath of the murders in Trabzon, would somehow be reconstituted in Baku.[54]

But the Baku-based TKP would not be revived, and Süleyman Nuri would not become its leader. Rather, the party's focus now shifted toward Istanbul. Şefik Hüsnü, one of the Turkish communists who had been vacationing in Italy when Nestor Lakoba had come calling in December 1920, re-established the TKP under his own leadership. He had already created, in 1919, the Worker and Peasant Socialist Party of Turkey, with the permission of British authorities. In 1922, while still living under the occupation and again with official consent, Şefik Hüsnü changed the organization's name to the Turkish Communist Party (*Türkiye Komünist Partisi*). This party became the successor to Suphi's liquidated movement, yet it was also in some ways a brand-new organization. Şefik Hüsnü's TKP membership number was "No. 1."[55]

Not long after Suphi's murder, the "organizational bureau" of the TKP in Baku received the following note from a woman identifying herself as Anna Kapitanovna Ershovskaia.

> I am the mother of the wife of the deceased Mustafa Suphi. I am requesting assistance as I am in extreme need at present. My daughter served on your behalf while suffering from tuberculosis, and now requires food and time at a *dacha*. For this reason, I am requesting material assistance.[56]

---

[51] RGASPI/IISH, f. 495, op. 181, d. 307, l. 23. Letter from İsmail Kadirov to Lenin, Zinoviev, and Süleyman Nuri, August 31, 1921. The all-caps appear in the original.

[52] Dumont, "Bolchevisme et Orient," 399.

[53] This proposal also envisioned an enhanced role for Abid Alimov. RGASPI, f. 544, op. 3, d. 46, l. 37. "Supplement to the report on the Foreign Bureau of the TKP," March 19, 1921.

[54] Quotation from RGASPI/IISH, f. 495, op. 181, d. 307, l. 23. Letter from İsmail Kadirov to Lenin, Zinoviev, and Süleyman Nuri, August 31, 1921.

[55] RGASPI, Şefik Hüsnü personal file, f. 495, op. 266, d. 38, l. 127. Personnel form for the Executive Committee of the Comintern, 1926.

[56] RGASPI/IISH, f. 495, op. 181, d. 177, ll. 107–107-ob. Letter to the TKP Organizational Bureau from Anna Kapitanovna Ershovskaia, undated, but apparently from early 1921.

## Ankara Circles

At home with a sick daughter and a three-and-a-half-year-old grandson with no father, Anna Kapitanovna was in desperate straits. There's no indication, however, that anyone from the party ever followed up on her request. The TKP's days in Baku were, in any event, themselves already numbered.

## Ankara Circles

Ankara was, in January 1921, still a very small town. Photographs from the time reveal a sparse, dusty little settlement with a scattering of houses clinging to the hill leading up to an eighth-century castle. The community of supporters who had followed Mustafa Kemal to this outpost was, in a similar manner, grafted onto the existing population, as opposed to really blending in with it.

Sitting in the coffeehouses surrounding the small building where Mustafa Kemal's first parliament was held, Nâzım and Vâlâ would regularly bump into well-known politicians, officers, and others who to this day are written about in standard Turkish history textbooks. The boys were just nineteen years old, but they were not without connections. For Nâzım and Vâlâ, arriving in the Kemalist capital was less a jump into the unknown than an entrée into an extended family reunion.

The boys were living at a place called the Stone Inn, occupying a couple of rooms above a stable.[57] Upon moving in, Nâzım and Vâlâ's first order of business was to stop by the press directorate, which was led by an acquaintance of theirs, Muhittin Bey. Muhittin Bey, who was born in 1885, had been the managing editor of the pro-Young Turk newspaper *Tanin*. He was also the older brother-in-law of a woman named Nüzhet, with whom Nâzım had been carrying on a relationship in Istanbul.

Nüzhet was two years older than Nâzım. She had first met him in 1915 in Nişantaşı, the leafy neighborhood on the European side of Istanbul where he had been enrolled for a while in a state school. Nüzhet had been orphaned at the age of eleven and since then had been living with her older sister and her sister's husband, Muhittin Bey.[58] Whether or not Muhittin knew about his younger sister-in-law's involvement with Nâzım is not clear. Either way, from Vâlâ's later account it appears that the boys expected to be warmly received by him, and they were.

However, Muhittin did not have any work to give them at the press office, and asked Nâzım and Vâlâ if they would mind accepting an appointment from the Education Ministry instead. The boys agreed—it sounds like they had little choice—and headed over to the ministry to look into their work prospects. Instead of being journalists, they would now become teachers.

---

[57] Blasing writes that it was an "uncle" who had paid the bill, probably a reference to Ali Fuat Pasha or his father. *Nâzım Hikmet*, 42.

[58] Sülker, *Nâzım Hikmet'in Gerçek Yaşamı*, vol. 1, 100, 143–144, 178; Göksu and Timms, *Romantic Communist*, 14. On Nüzhet also see Memet Fuat (ed.), *A'dan Z'ye Nâzım Hikmet* (İstanbul: Yapı Kredi Yayınları, 2002), 253. Arın Dilligil Bayraktaroğlu has written "not an academic study, but rather a historical novel" based on the life of Nüzhet Berkin, *Nüzhet: Nâzım Hikmet'in "Minnacık" Kadını* (İstanbul: Remzi, 2022), 7.

Muhittin also assigned the boys a special task. He asked them to compose a poem about the "national struggle," telling the boys that he would get it published if at all possible. Excited by this possibility, Nâzım and Vâlâ eagerly set to work, returning later to Muhittin's office to show off what they had produced.

The poem was harshly critical of those who were sitting out the war effort. In its closing lines, it rhetorically asks:

> And have you, too, joined up with
> that sell-out of a minister, that sell-out of a Sultan?
> Have you, too, joined up with those sell-out slaves?
> Have you, too, sold out? Have you, too, sold out?[59]

According to Vâlâ's later account, Muhittin Bey loved the poem, rubbing Nâzım and Vâlâ on the shoulders and addressing them as "Lions!" (*arslanlar*), a term of affection. Muhittin then ordered the printing of thousands of copies of the poem for distribution—Vâlâ later estimated that between ten and twenty thousand leaflets were eventually produced. Coming at a time when paper was an expensive luxury for the cash-strapped Ankara government, the decision to print so many copies of the poem ended up turning into a minor scandal, and Muhittin Bey was severely criticized on the floor of parliament for his poor judgment.

The poem's contents also proved controversial. The official line of the Kemalist government at this time was that they were working to rescue the Sultan, whom the Kemalists still publicly described as a prisoner of the British. For a publication authorized by the Ankara government to call the Sultan a "sell-out" was quite dangerous, since he was a revered figure among many of the Anatolian Muslims that the Kemalists were attempting to win over to their side.[60] For Nâzım, this was the first, but hardly the last occasion in which something he wrote would get him into trouble with Kemalist authorities.

In the wake of the parliamentary outcry surrounding the boys' poem, Muhittin Bey lost interest in maintaining further contact with his young protégés.[61] While Muhittin Bey's home had become a lively base of discussion and dining in Ankara—even the Spartakists were welcome guests there—the boys were shut out. For Nâzım, this state of affairs also cut off his possibilities for meeting up with Nüzhet. Unlike Istanbul, Ankara was a small town. If he could not visit Nüzhet at Muhittin Bey's home, he would not be able to see her at all.

Within Ankara officialdom, however, Muhittin Bey was hardly the boys' only contact. Having been directed to go to the Education Ministry to receive their appointments as teachers, Nâzım and Vâlâ were delighted to find themselves

---

[59] The word for "Sultan" that was used in this verse was "Hünkâr." Vâ-Nû, *Bu Dünyadan Nâzım Geçti*, 100. Also see Babayev, *Nâzım Hikmet*, 63; Fish, *Nâzım'ın Çilesi*, 216.

[60] On this episode, see Vâ-Nû, *Bu Dünyadan Nâzım Geçti*, 101–102; Sülker, *Nâzım Hikmet'in Gerçek Yaşamı*, vol. 1, 104, 125; Blasing, *Nâzım Hikmet*, 44.

[61] Fish, *Nâzım'ın Çilesi*, 217.

face-to-face with one Kâzım Nami Bey, a close friend of Vâlâ's late father, who greeted the boys warmly. Sensing an advantage, it seems, Nâzım and Vâlâ soon began making demands of him. Vâlâ informed Kâzım Nami Bey straight out that he and Nâzım had no intention of "being sent to some treeless region" in the middle of nowhere. Nâzım then chimed in to say that the two of them had to be sent to the same place, otherwise they would refuse their appointments.

Kâzım Nami Bey shuffled through his papers for a while and found two suitable locations that each needed two teachers. The boys were given a choice. The first was Elaziz (today's Elâzığ), in southeastern Anatolia. Elaziz fit Vâlâ's stipulation that they be sent someplace "with trees," as it was located in the Euphrates River basin. Their other option was Bolu, a smallish town that was relatively close to Istanbul.[62] Kâzım Nami Bey gave his young charges a day to think things over. After some discussion—Nâzım and Vâlâ were largely ambivalent about which of the two towns they would pick—they eventually gave word that they had chosen Bolu.[63]

Much of the rest of the time that Nâzım and Vâlâ spent in Ankara involved hanging out at the Kuyulu Café, their favorite spot among the ring of establishments that had sprung up across the street from the parliament building.[64] Before too long, the boys were caught up in the café's chatty late-night atmosphere, arguing politics and exchanging the latest war gossip over tea. They befriended folks like "Patriot Hilmi," an older gentleman who had allegedly earned his nickname by shooting himself in response to the news that Edirne, the former Ottoman capital, had fallen in 1912. Patriot Hilmi frequently held court at the café, anchoring a circle that included Nâzım, Vâlâ, and a number of other young admirers, regaling his listeners with tales of the adventures that he and his boon companion, Külhanbey Celal, had experienced in Paris during their student days.[65]

One night, Patriot Hilmi announced to those assembled that none other than Külhanbey Celal himself would soon be visiting Ankara. A ripple of excitement ran through the group as the news circulated. Upon arriving in the Kemalist capital, Külhanbey Celal invited Vâlâ and Nâzım to take several long walks with him, something the boys considered to be a real honor. Külhanbey Celal asked them to tell him everything they thought about politics, the future, and their friends at the Kuyulu Café, they were to hold back on nothing. The three talked for hours. Years later, Vâlâ claimed, he would learn that Külhanbey Celal had actually been an undercover policeman.[66]

Most of all, Nâzım and Vâlâ spent their time in Ankara hanging out with Sadık Ahi and his band of Spartakists. The boys even moved in with the group for a while when they were short of money.[67] Although the Spartakists now showed their young

---

[62] About 150 miles. Closer proximity facilitated communications with the boys' families in Istanbul. On Nâzım's sister Samiye sending care packages to Nâzım, see Vâ-Nû, *Bu Dünyadan Nâzım Geçti*, 132.

[63] Ibid., 103; Sülker, *Nâzım Hikmet'in Gerçek Yaşamı*, vol. 1, 106–107.

[64] On Nâzım and Vâlâ's time in Ankara, also see Göksu and Timms, *Romantic Communist*, 22–23.

[65] "Külhanbey" is a slang term that translates roughly to "thug."

[66] Vâ-Nû, *Bu Dünyadan Nâzım Geçti*, 115; Sülker, *Nâzım Hikmet'in Gerçek Yaşamı*, vol. 1, 108.

[67] Vâ-Nû, *Bu Dünyadan Nâzım Geçti*, 104; Also see Göksu and Timms, *Romantic Communist*, 17.

colleagues a little more respect than before, their conversations continued to be largely one-sided, with Nâzım and Vâlâ both still playing the role of pupil. Even as the boys rubbed shoulders with important, well-known individuals during their stay in Ankara, it was the Spartakists who had made the greatest impression upon them.

Thus far, Nâzım and Vâlâ had not seen any of Nâzım's relatives in Ankara. Nâzım's "uncle," Ali Fuat Pasha, was traveling at this time in connection with his diplomatic duties.[68] However, Ali Fuat Pasha's father, İsmail Fazıl Pasha, was in town and serving in the Ankara government's parliament.[69] For some time, İsmail Fazıl Pasha had been sending messages to the boys via a friend of his, the poet Samih Rıfat, whom Nâzım and Vâlâ often bumped into at the Kuyulu Café. In these messages, İsmail Fazıl Pasha had repeatedly invited the boys to come pay him a visit soon.

One day, Nâzım and Vâlâ were standing on the street in front of a restaurant, wishing, as Vâlâ later recalled, they had enough money to go inside to get something to eat. Suddenly, Vâlâ felt a hand on his shoulder. He turned around to see a smiling, elderly gentleman. It was Hüsnü Pasha, another old friend of Vâlâ's father. It turned out that Hüsnü Pasha was sharing a large residence with İsmail Fazıl Pasha on the outskirts of town. He chastised the boys genially for having not yet visited Nâzım's great uncle. Hüsnü Pasha then pulled out twenty-five liras—which Vâlâ described as enough money for two people to live on for two to three weeks at that time—and gave it to the boys. The three agreed upon a day when Nâzım and Vâlâ would go visit the two pashas at their residence.

The boys duly went out to see the two pashas shortly thereafter, picking up Samih Rıfat at the Kuyulu Café en route. At İsmail Fazıl Pasha's place, Nâzım and Vâlâ ate, drank, and recited poetry for their hosts. After listening to Nâzım and Vâlâ read for a while, İsmail Fazıl Pasha stood up and told his young guests to keep the next day open.

The next day, Nâzım and Vâlâ went to parliament with İsmail Fazıl Pasha. They were led into a large room situated just off from the building's entrance. According to Vâlâ's subsequent account, the first thing they saw was Mustafa Kemal Pasha's silhouette. The figure initially walked toward İsmail Fazıl Pasha, sharing a few words in confidence with the elderly parliamentarian. Then the two began to slowly approach Nâzım and Vâlâ, with İsmail Fazıl Pasha introducing the young men to the leader of the Ankara government. Mustafa Kemal Pasha extended his hand to the boys. In Vâlâ's later recollection, Kemal's touch felt "as delicate as a woman's."[70]

Vâlâ wondered if he should kiss Kemal's hand and press it to his forehead, a manner of showing respect to one's elders in Turkey. He decided against the gesture, reasoning that it was not a very military way of behaving. Besides, Vâlâ thought to himself, even if he had kissed Kemal Pasha's hand, Nâzım—who did not believe in such

---

[68] Nâzım referred to Ali Fuat Pasha as "*dayım*" or "my uncle."
[69] Given Nâzım's ties to Ali Fuat Pasha and İsmail Fazıl Pasha, I would disagree with Charles King's observation that Nâzım had "no real military connections" in the Kemalist capital. *Midnight at the Pera Palace*, 222. The boys were well-connected.
[70] Vâ-Nû, *Bu Dünyadan Nâzım Geçti*, 110.

behavior—would have likely refused to do so, inevitably causing a scandal. Better to just shake hands and move on.

Mustafa Kemal and the young poets traded small talk for a few minutes. The leader asked the boys about their trip from Istanbul and what their impressions were of Ankara. Kemal then proceeded to give Nâzım and Vâlâ some unsolicited advice about how to write poetry. "Some poets," intoned the future president of Turkey, "try to be modern by writing poems that have no subject. My advice to you is to write poems with a purpose" (*gaye*). Kemal looked as if he had more to say, but at this moment he was interrupted by an advisor bearing a telegram. After reading the note, he bade the others farewell and departed from the room.[71]

As had been the case in Zonguldak and İnebolu, the boys enjoyed the sense of community they found in Ankara. Only now it was all much bigger. Everything felt much more urgent. Settling in for some time in the Kemalist capital and getting to know the different circles of people there, Nâzım and Vâlâ were intoxicated by the conversation, ideas, and the exciting atmosphere that surrounded them. Sometimes, in a manner perhaps not so uncommon at age nineteen, the two friends spoke and acted as if the fate of the world hinged upon how their discussions were resolved.

But they couldn't stay in Ankara forever. Having been appointed to teach at a school in Bolu, Nâzım and Vâlâ soon packed up their belongings and again headed out back onto the road.

## Starting Out in Bolu

Once again, they were walking. The distance between Ankara and Bolu was "only" 115 miles, much less ground than they had covered during their previous trek. Nâzım and Vâlâ hired a mule-driver in Ankara, and the three began heading north through the mountains via Kızılcahamam, where they stopped to sleep the first night. From Kızılcahamam the travelers pushed forward, spending nights in Çınarlıhan and Gerede en route.

The journey was a tiring one. Nâzım fell ill in Gerede, complaining of an intense headache. He then lost all strength. Vâlâ carried his friend on his back for much of the last day of their trip. Finally, the two arrived in Bolu in the middle of the night, stopping at an inn. As Vâlâ would recount, their "terrible" room was unheated and barely furnished, but it would do for the time being. More tired than they had ever been in their lives, the boys threw their bags into a corner and fell fast asleep on the floor.[72]

They awoke the next morning to the sound of wheels and hooves upon the cobblestone street below. Nâzım and Vâlâ had slept well and, feeling revived, the two

---

[71] Vâ-Nû, *Bu Dünyadan Nâzım Geçti*, 110. Also see Sülker, *Nâzım Hikmet'in Gerçek Yaşamı*, vol. 1, 108–111; Babayev, *Nâzım Hikmet*, 64–65; Fish, *Nâzım'ın Çilesi*, 222.

[72] Vâ-Nû, *Bu Dünyadan Nâzım Geçti*, 124. Also see Fish, *Nâzım'ın Çilesi*, 54, 222. On Nâzım and Vâlâ's time in Bolu, also see Göksu and Timms, *Romantic Communist*, 24–27.

friends headed out into the streets to look for breakfast. Asking around with regard to where they might find a coffeehouse, Nâzım and Vâlâ were pointed in the direction of the Beyler, a place that would become a staple of their time in Bolu.

Making their way inside, Nâzım and Vâlâ were surprised to find that some of the other café patrons appeared to recognize them, welcoming the boys with honorifics normally employed in Turkish for teachers. It turned out that the crowd inside the Beyler coffeehouse included a table-full of Nâzım and Vâlâ's fellow instructors. Knowing that two new teachers were due to arrive any day, they had recognized Nâzım and Vâlâ as their likely new colleagues and greeted them as such.[73]

The teachers made a point of filling their new friends in on the gossip relating to the school. One point they all emphasized was that the school was divided into two warring factions. The school's "reformers," Nâzım and Vâlâ were told, were battling with the so-called "reactionaries." The reformers were mostly the younger teachers whom Nâzım and Vâlâ had met at the Beyler. The reactionaries, meanwhile, were led by the school director, Hilmi Bey, and his sidekick, the religious instructor Ziyaeddin Effendi.

Vâlâ and Nâzım, in the former's later retelling, immediately pronounced themselves to be on the side of reform. So, when they were led into Hilmi Bey's office, the boys ignored the efforts of the school director to be friendly to them. Nâzım responded to Hilmi Bey's questions with only short, brusque replies, until the director steered the conversation toward a rather sensitive topic: the young poet's beloved sideburns. He wanted Nâzım to shave them.

Nâzım hit the roof. Launching into a spirited defense of "personal freedom" (*şahsi hürriyet*), Nâzım raised his voice at his new boss.[74] At this point, some of the other teachers had begun filing into the room, their faces bearing perplexed looks. Hilmi Bey backed off—he had not been looking for a fight—but Nâzım refused to be mollified. "I'll show them," he muttered to himself as he exited the room with Vâlâ. Nâzım punctuated his words with a quick punch into the interior of his *kalpak*, launching a small burst of flowers and ribbons into the air.[75]

As time passed, Nâzım and Vâlâ found themselves reassessing the alliances they had made on their first day in town. The so-called "reactionaries" had turned out to be quite friendly. Hilmi Bey, the allegedly dictatorial old school director, had not only backed down with respect to Nâzım's sideburns, but also had proven to be very helpful with respect to a variety of matters. He had, for example, assisted the boys in finding a decent place to live, convincing the father of one of the school's students to rent Nâzım and Vâlâ a large house in town at a very favorable price.

After some weeks in Bolu, moreover, Nâzım and Vâlâ began to tire of the group of younger teachers that they had originally befriended. There were about ten people in this circle, all of them male, and their interests were quite different from those of the boys. Whenever Nâzım and Vâlâ met up with this group at the Beyler or at somebody's house, the other teachers liked to entertain themselves by telling silly jokes or vulgar

---

[73] Vâ-Nû, *Bu Dünyadan Nâzım Geçti*, 126–127.      [74] Ibid., 128.      [75] Ibid., 129.

stories. Nâzım and Vâlâ, on the other hand, wanted to discuss literature and politics, but found no audience for that among this crowd. The boys were looking for someone, in Vâlâ's later recollections, that they could learn from. They missed the sort of intellectual community that they had found in Ankara.[76]

## Drifting Eastward

Bolu was not so bad, but the boys were beginning to think that life was elsewhere. After an adolescence spent in Istanbul, and more recent stints on the road and in Ankara, adjusting to the norms of a small Anatolian town was not so easy.

Part of the problem, as Vâlâ later remembered, was that the boys longed for the company of women. In Istanbul there had been opportunities for them to interact with the opposite sex, but in a small town like Bolu such possibilities constituted little more than fantasy. Nâzım and Vâlâ got so desperate that they had fallen into the habit of walking past the house of two sisters that were rumored to be good-looking, on the off-chance of catching a glimpse of a silhouette in a window. Not once did they even see the girls' faces.[77]

As time passed, Nâzım and Vâlâ began to think about trying to find a way out. In Vâlâ's reminiscences, it all started with a message Nâzım received from his girlfriend. One day, Nâzım and Vâlâ were sitting at home when the mailman delivered a postcard from Nüzhet. She was writing from Kastamonu, just south of the Black Sea coast, where she and her sister and brother-in-law were staying on the way to Tbilisi. Georgia had recently come under Bolshevik control, so this news came as something of a surprise to the boys. Was Muhittin Bey heading to Tbilisi as part of some sort of government mission, they wondered, or was this a private venture?[78]

Nâzım—ever the artist—picked up a pencil and sketched a rough map of eastern Anatolia and the Caucasus, then put it up on the wall. He and Vâlâ took a step back and looked over Nâzım's handiwork. If Nüzhet and her family were traveling through Kastamonu on their way to Tbilisi, that meant they were probably going by sea via Batumi.[79] Bolu was about 500 miles from Batumi, and 850 miles from Tbilisi—not a close distance by any means. A journey to Georgia would be doable, however, if the boys could travel to Batumi by boat. Suddenly, Nâzım and Vâlâ —who were not particularly enamored with either Bolu or the people they had met there so far— began to think of possibilities beyond the frontier. All of a sudden, they felt less trapped somehow.

One day not long after Nüzhet's postcard arrived, Nâzım and Vâlâ were drinking tea at the Beyler when some of their younger colleagues from the school came up to them with news. Once classes ended for the summer, a teachers' congress was going to be taking place in Ankara. Nâzım and Vâlâ's colleagues had held a meeting—which

---

[76] Ibid., 129–131.　　[77] Ibid., 154.　　[78] Ibid., 154–155.　　[79] Ibid., 158.

the boys had skipped—to decide whom they would send to represent their school. "Congratulations, Vâlâ Bey!" exclaimed the teachers. "Nobody opposed you."

Vâlâ thanked the other teachers for their support, but their congratulatory sentiments were hardly welcome. Outside of urban areas, the law did not carry much weight in the region at this time. The hills, Vâlâ would later recall, were filled with criminals. He wondered if he might be pressing his luck a bit too far by taking yet another trip to and from Ankara. Moreover, Vâlâ had not yet even been paid for his work in Bolu. He and Nâzım had been getting by on Nâzım's thirty liras per month while Vâlâ's salary, which was supposed to have been provided out of a separate fund from the Ankara government's Ministry of Education, had not yet materialized. So why should he have to be the one to attend this congress?

When Vâlâ raised these objections, his colleagues maintained their sunny attitude. "But that's the best part!" they exclaimed. "Once you're at the congress, you'll have the chance to talk to people at the ministry and get your salary." Vâlâ had to admit they had a point. He decided to go to the congress, if for no better reason than to try to recover his money.[80]

That very afternoon, an even more fateful development would transpire. After hanging out for a bit longer at the Beyler, Nâzım and Vâlâ joined up with some of the other teachers to attend a murder trial that was taking place at the local courthouse. The proceedings, Vâlâ later recalled, were spellbinding. Nâzım and Vâlâ were particularly impressed by the power and intelligence displayed by the articulate young chief magistrate, one Ziya Hilmi, who appeared to be not much older than the boys.

Later that day, after Nâzım and Vâlâ returned to the Beyler to break down all that they had seen, Ziya Hilmi himself walked into the coffeehouse. The magistrate was greeted like a celebrity. The moment he stepped through the door, all conversation ceased, and most of those seated stood up to show their respect for him. Ziya Hilmi motioned to everyone that they should sit down, then headed over to the table next to the one where Nâzım and Vâlâ were seated.

The boys struck up a conversation with him.[81] It was as if Nâzım and Vâlâ were back in İnebolu with the Spartakists. Ziya Hilmi and the boys quickly delved into a deep conversation that lasted for hours. They jumped eagerly from one topic to another, but mainly focused upon the fields of politics and literature—Nâzım and Vâlâ's two favorite subjects.

Nâzım and Vâlâ felt increasingly ignorant in the face of what was quickly becoming Ziya Hilmi's second dazzling verbal performance of the day. Upon learning that Nâzım and Vâlâ were poets, Ziya Hilmi recited some of his favorite lines of Ottoman *divan* verse, then launched into a discourse about French literature and his own personal favorite, Baudelaire. From there, the magistrate only picked up steam, shifting his focus to history—the French Revolution, and then the Russian Revolution

---

[80] Ibid., 158. A similar episode appears in Nâzım's *Life's Good, Brother*, only in this account the entire teaching staff had been working without salary, 65.

[81] Vâ-Nû, *Bu Dünyadan Nâzım Geçti*, 160. On Nâzım and Vâlâ's early encounters with Ziya Hilmi, also see Sülker, *Nâzım Hikmet'in Gerçek Yaşamı*, vol. 1, 112–113.

of 1905—before segueing into an overview of current events and the divisions that had opened up recently between Lenin and the Marxist theorist Karl Kautsky. The boys sat there, in Vâlâ's later retelling of the events, looking back and forth at one another as if to ask: "how does he know all of this?"

Something else that reminded Nâzım and Vâlâ of their interactions with Sadık Ahi was Ziya Hilmi's evident interest in communism. Comparing the historical significance of the Bolshevik takeover in Russia with that of the French Revolution, Ziya Hilmi told the boys that, while they had all missed out on the storming of the Bastille, the same sort of epoch-defining event was taking place at that very moment in a country right next door to them.[82]

The three began meeting up on a regular basis. Over the months to follow, Ziya Hilmi would provide Nâzım and Vâlâ with the intellectual sustenance that they had thus far been missing in Bolu. One day, when Nâzım, Vâlâ, and Ziya Hilmi were sitting around talking about developments in Russia, Nâzım looked up at Ziya Hilmi and, perhaps in an effort to impress the judge, casually mentioned to him that he and Vâlâ were "going to Tbilisi this summer. From there, we'll see what's going on inside Russia. We'll travel a bit and have a look around."

For the first time, the boys perceived a slight crack in Ziya Hilmi's usually quite cool demeanor. This sort of declaration was clearly not something that he had been expecting from them. Looking back at Nâzım, Ziya Hilmi asked him: "You mean this summer you're going to just pick up and head to Russia?"

"Yes," answered Nâzım and Vâlâ, now in unison.

"Well if that's the case," responded Ziya Hilmi, having regained his composure, "then I'm going with you."[83]


## Batumi Bound

The school year had come to an end and the summer of 1921 began.[84] Freed from their teaching obligations, Nâzım and Vâlâ moved out of their place in town. They were now sharing a house outside Bolu that Ziya Hilmi had rented for the summer. The three had even pooled their resources to purchase a horse. This had been another one of the magistrate's ideas.[85]

They divided up the chores. Ziya Hilmi did the cooking. Nâzım and Vâlâ, who appear to have thus far subsisted mainly on eggs, jam, bread, and tea, were put in charge of cleaning. The three friends, in Vâlâ's later remembrance, spent long hours locked in discussion, arguing about politics, literature, and the fate of the world.

---

[82] Vâ-Nû, *Bu Dünyadan Nâzım Geçti*, 161. In *Life's Good, Brother*, one of the main character's friends is a magistrate named Yusuf, who appears to be based in large part upon Ziya Hilmi, 68–69.

[83] Sülker, *Nâzım Hikmet'in Gerçek Yaşamı*, vol. 1, 119; Babayev, *Nâzım Hikmet*, 67; Fish, *Nâzım'ın Çilesi*, 234.

[84] This is at variance with Sülker's timeline, which places them in Ankara and leaving for Bolu on September 4, 1921. *Nâzım Hikmet'in Gerçek Yaşamı*, vol. 1, 144.

[85] Fish, *Nâzım'ın Çilesi*, 244.

To the north, a dynastic monarchy, the bitterest rival of the Ottoman Empire, had been overthrown by what appeared to be a dynamic and exciting new force. And now it seemed that similar developments might be taking place in Anatolia. "In those days," recalled Vâlâ, "we were going to solve all of the world's problems, right there in our kitchen."[86]

The boys had a number of alternatives available to them, or at least it seemed that way at the time. Vâlâ, a speaker of German, had at times suggested to Nâzım that they go to Berlin, home of the Spartakist revolution that had so inspired Sadık Ahi and his friends. Celile Hanım, meanwhile, had invited Nâzım to Paris, where she was then living.[87] Nâzım and Vâlâ could also have decided to push on to Kars, where Turkish teachers were in great demand. Georgia was one possibility among several. Nothing was written in stone.

Before setting off, the boys decided that Vâlâ should still go to Ankara to participate in the teachers' congress. In addition to trying to get his salary from the Ministry of Education, Vâlâ would likewise have the chance to explain to ministry officials why he and Nâzım were leaving their positions in Bolu. He hoped to set up a back-up plan for himself and Nâzım in case they ended up needing jobs.

Why would Kars make sense as an option? The city and surrounding province had, after a period of more than forty years of Russian rule, recently been ceded by the Bolsheviks to the Kemalist government.[88] Located more than 700 miles to the east of Bolu, Kars could be reached in two ways (Map 3.1). Traveling by land through eastern Anatolia was arduous, obliging one to venture through long stretches of lawless country. By sea via Batumi, however, the trip could be undertaken much more easily, and would involve transiting most of the way through Georgia. For Nâzım and Vâlâ, demonstrating an interest in teaching in Kars provided an iron-clad excuse for requiring permits to cross the border and travel into Georgia.[89] Kars, meanwhile, could provide a possible place for them to land should nothing work out in Tbilisi.

The trip from Bolu to Ankara was perilous. As he and Nâzım had done during their earlier treks, Vâlâ traveled as part of a constellation of wayfarers, reasoning that there would be strength in numbers should they encounter any bandits. Some of his traveling companions, Vâlâ later claimed, broke off from the main group and were murdered by thieves. Vâlâ and the others pushed on.

On the outskirts of Ankara, Vâlâ's group came across a different kind of threat. It was not bandits that people living in the capital's hinterlands feared, but the Greek Army. The summer of 1921 marked a pivotal moment for Mustafa Kemal's movement. The Ankara government had been pushed to the brink of destruction, as Greek forces had taken Kütahya and Eskişehir in the Marmara region of western Anatolia. Throughout the month of August, the Greek Army progressed steadily eastward, coming within thirty miles of Ankara. Vâlâ later recalled that he could hear cannon

---

[86] Vâ-Nû, *Bu Dünyadan Nâzım Geçti*, 165.    [87] Memet Fuat, *Nâzım Hikmet*, 36.

[88] The Bolsheviks had previously ceded this territory to the Ottoman government in the Brest-Litovsk Treaty.

[89] Vâ-Nû, *Bu Dünyadan Nâzım Geçti*, 186. Ahmet, the hero of Nâzım Hikmet's *Life's Good, Brother* similarly obtains permission to travel through Georgia by stating his intention of going to Kars. *Life's Good, Brother*, 70–71.

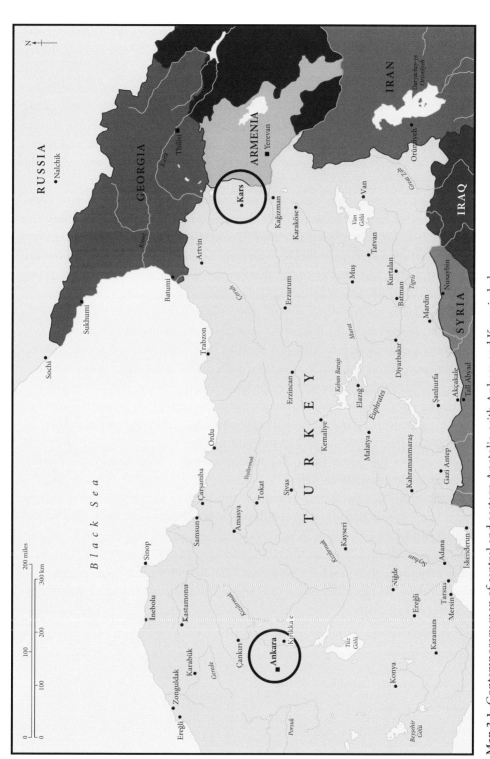

Map 3.1 Contemporary map of central and eastern Anatolia, with Ankara and Kars circled

firing outside Mudurnu, one of the few direct references to the fighting that he makes in his memoirs.[90]

The chaotic scene outside Ankara notwithstanding—or perhaps because of it—Vâlâ's life in the Kemalist capital carried on in much the same fashion as it had during his previous stay. Sadık Ahi was no longer around, but Vâlâ did spend a lot of time with the other Spartakists, especially Vehbi (Sarıdal). Upon learning that Vâlâ and Nâzım were planning to visit Tbilisi, Vehbi mentioned the name of a friend of his, Budu Mdivani, a Georgian communist who had previously been stationed in Ankara as a Georgian government representative. Vehbi told Vâlâ that, should he and Nâzım ever need help in Tbilisi, they should contact Mdivani, who was now working in the Georgian capital.[91]

In addition to meeting up with Vehbi and some of the other Spartakists in town, Vâlâ also carried on what he would later characterize as epic conversations with two of the most important intellectuals from Unionist-era Istanbul, Ziya Gökalp and Mehmet Akif (Ersoy). Gökalp had been an early hero of the boys, a poet, writer, and proponent of the Turkist aesthetic that would inspire a generation of young intellectuals.[92] In his later account Vâlâ describes meeting Gökalp by chance one afternoon at the Kuyulu Café, where they engaged in a wide-ranging all-night discussion about politics, the Bolsheviks, and literature, among other subjects.[93]

Another day at the Kuyulu, Vâlâ met Mehmet Akif, the influential Young Turk-era poet, writer, and journal editor associated with both Turkism and Islamism. Akif, whose verse would later be adopted as the lyrics to Turkey's national anthem, offered Vâlâ advice on writing that was strikingly similar to that which Mustafa Kemal had provided: write with a purpose. As Vâlâ later observed, the advice may have been the same, but the purpose that each had in mind was different. For one, it was Turkish nationalism. For the other, Islam. For Nâzım, surmised Vâlâ, that purpose would prove to be something else entirely.[94]

It did not take Vâlâ much time to finish his business in Ankara. He met again with Kâzım Nami Bey at the Ministry of Education and explained to him that he and Nâzım could no longer remain in Bolu. Vâlâ claimed, falsely, that he and Nâzım had made enemies of some local reactionaries, and now feared for their lives. Instead of staying on at their current school, suggested Vâlâ, he and Nâzım could travel to Kars and teach there. Kâzım Nami Bey agreed with Vâlâ, and even promised to help with the matter of Vâlâ's salary.[95] At the end of August, Vâlâ returned to Bolu with 300 liras in his pocket.[96]

---

[90] Vâ-Nû, *Bu Dünyadan Nâzım Geçti*, 182–183.

[91] Ibid., 199. On Mdivani, also see Göksu and Timms, *Romantic Communist*, 21–22, 30, 34; Sülker, *Nâzım Hikmet'in Gerçek Yaşamı*, vol. 1, 132.

[92] Karpat describes Akif as an "activist nationalist-Islamist poet." *The Politicization of Islam*, 201.

[93] Vâ-Nû, *Bu Dünyadan Nâzım Geçti*, 184.

[94] Ibid., 111. On Vâlâ's meeting with Akif, also see ibid., 191–196.

[95] Ibid., 185–186. Vâlâ notes that he and Nâzım only received money for work they had already done in Bolu, and none for the trip to Kars. 194–195.

[96] Ibid., 207.

Nâzım, Vâlâ, and Ziya Hilmi were ready to roll. Their immediate destination was the little Black Sea town of Akçakoca, from which they would travel by sea to Zonguldak. From there, the three would continue eastward by boat to Trabzon, and then Batumi. The initial leg of their trip would be the most dangerous, taking them through remote trails and isolated forests.[97] But what mattered most of all right now was that they were getting out of Bolu and back onto the open road.

## Farewell to Anatolia

"Waiter! Bring over some more of that lion's milk! I think the gentlemen's glasses are empty!"[98]

"Boy, bring these gentlemen some fresh plates. They need some more *mezes*.[99] Show them what's on the menu. Fish, chicken, whatever, just ask them what they want."

The boys looked at Ziya Hilmi and asked him one more time. "Ziya Hilmi, are you sure they don't use money" in the Soviet Union?

The magistrate ruled in the affirmative, and that was all they needed to know.

"Waiter, boy! Bring over some of those kebabs!"

"Coming right up, sir!"

During the course of the war in Anatolia, there was a prohibition in Kemalist-held territory against the sale of alcohol. The ban did not, however, stop some entrepreneurial individuals from distilling and selling their own moonshine. While Nâzım and Vâlâ had, thus far in their journey, usually displayed rather sober-minded and thrifty behavior, the trip from Bolu up to Zonguldak would prove an exception.

According to Vâlâ's later account, one that mirrors a story in Nâzım's semi-autobiographical *Life's Good, Brother*, the boys were under the impression that the Bolsheviks had banned the use of money altogether. Sadık Ahi had, apparently, been the original source of this erroneous information, which Ziya Hilmi had later confirmed. The windfall from Ankara, meanwhile, was burning a hole in the boys' pockets. Fueled, perhaps, by a sense of liberation upon bidding farewell to drab Bolu, Nâzım and Vâlâ were in no mood to investigate the matter any further.[100]

In Akçakoca, the boys decided to splash out some extra liras for their boat tickets to Zonguldak.

"What do you say, Nâzım?" asked Vâlâ. "Shall we get a berth in first class?"

"Is there no luxury class, Vâlâ?"[101]

---

[97] Ibid., 207–208.

[98] "Lion's milk" is a slang expression for *rakı*, the aniseed-flavored liquor that turns a milky white when mixed with water.

[99] *Mezes* are Turkish appetizers.

[100] On Sadık Ahi telling the boys about money not being used in Soviet Russia, see Vâ-Nû, *Bu Dünyadan Nâzım Geçti*, 199. On Ziya Hilmi providing them with the same information, see ibid., 208–209. Nâzım provides an account of something like this happening in *Life's Good, Brother*, 29. Also see Fish, *Nâzım'ın Çilesi*, 240–241; İbrahim Balaban, *Nâzım Hikmet'le Yedi Yıl* (İstanbul: Berfin Yayınları, 2003), 84.

[101] Vâ-Nû, *Bu Dünyadan Nâzım Geçti*, 209–210.

The party lasted as far as Zonguldak, where finally the boys were disabused of their misinformation. Money was indeed still in use under the Bolsheviks, and the Turkish Lira was a prized currency, particularly in a border-town like Batumi. They counted out their remaining funds. Out of the 300 liras they had started off with in Bolu, just 130 remained.[102]

From Zonguldak Nâzım, Vâlâ, and Ziya Hilmi took a boat to Trabzon, their last stop before entering Bolshevik territory. Here Nâzım and Vâlâ received their paperwork to travel through Georgia en route to Kars. It was at this point, however, that Ziya Hilmi presented the boys with some devastating news: he had decided against continuing onward to Georgia with them, at least for the time being. "You two have the excuse of teaching in Kars," he told them. "For you, asking for a travel permit would make sense to anyone. But I'm a member of the judiciary. What's my excuse? Why don't the two of you go ahead without me, and I'll try to catch up later."[103]

Perhaps Ziya Hilmi had simply changed his mind about the wisdom, or feasibility, of his leaving Anatolia. Or maybe he had never been that serious about going abroad in the first place. In any case, Ziya Hilmi would now be heading back to Bolu, his share of the adventure over.

The news that Ziya Hilmi was not going to cross the border with them evoked mixed emotions for the boys. Nâzım and Ziya Hilmi had not been getting along well lately. At times, Vâlâ later noted, Nâzım seemed jealous of Vâlâ's friendship with the magistrate, while Ziya Hilmi tended to treat Nâzım with a certain intellectual disdain.

For Vâlâ, however, the prospect of losing their group's "leader" was truly frightening. He had liked Ziya Hilmi and was angry that their group was losing its oldest and most experienced member. Vâlâ wrote later that he was afraid that he would now be stuck "in a foreign country with very little money and a traveling companion with no common sense."[104]

Feelings were raw. Nâzım and Vâlâ bade Ziya Hilmi farewell without shaking hands.[105] As had been the case when they had lost Yusuf Ziya and Faruk Nafiz in İnebolu, the boys once again found themselves left to their own devices.

*

Nâzım and Vâlâ sat drinking tea, glumly playing backgammon near the port in Trabzon. In Ziya Hilmi's absence, the frustration that the two had been feeling toward one another redoubled.

Everything appeared to be going wrong. First, they had wasted most of their money on trifles, and now their friend had left them on bad terms. They were, moreover, about to cross a border into a country that neither of them knew much about, where they didn't speak any of the local languages. Neither Nâzım nor Vâlâ had any real

---

[102] Ibid., 212.

[103] Ibid., 217; Memet Fuat, *Nâzım Hikmet*, 39.    [104] Vâ-Nû, *Bu Dünyadan Nâzım Geçti*, 219.

[105] Only years later would either of them hear about him again, by which point Ziya Hilmi had allegedly become involved in trafficking heroin. Vâ-Nû, *Bu Dünyadan Nâzım Geçti*, 220–221; Sertel, *Hatırladıklarım*, 149–150.

connections at all in Georgia, other than the faint hope that somehow, somewhere, they could find Muhittin Bey and Nüzhet. About eight months had passed since they had departed Istanbul, but it seemed like they had never been as alone as they were right now.

On the backgammon board, meanwhile, the antagonism that had been building between Nâzım and Vâlâ since Bolu finally came to a head.

"Double sixes!" cried out Vâlâ, rolling the dice. It was double sixes. If Nâzım rolled a one, Vâlâ would gammon him.

"Roll a one!" yelled Vâlâ while Nâzım was rolling. Nâzım rolled a one.

Infuriated by Vâlâ's obnoxious behavior, Nâzım lost his composure. He stood up, reared back, and slapped his friend across the face.

The coffeehouse went silent, and the boys—themselves shocked by the rapid escalation of their hostilities—quickly regained their composure. Realizing that all eyes were upon them, Nâzım and Vâlâ settled down quietly into another game. A short while later they got up, left the café, and began heading toward the port.

Something about stepping onto the boat seemed to boost their spirits, however. Once again, the boys were heading off into a new world. They were beginning to feel excited, despite all that had happened that day. "When we got on the boat," wrote Vâlâ, "I was so eager and happy, there was no need anymore for Nâzım and I to shake hands and make peace. We started getting along again as if nothing had happened."[106]

Friends once more, Nâzım and Vâlâ settled in for their passage to Batumi.

---

[106] Vâ-Nû, *Bu Dünyadan Nâzım Geçti*, 219.

# 4

# First Soviet Steps

Their boat pulled into the port in Batumi on a late September morning in 1921.[1] Looking out from the ship's deck on a clear day, the boys would have seen a lush, almost tropical landscape, with large, bright green mountains hemming the city in from behind. Officially, they were entering the Soviet Socialist Republic of Georgia. As far as Nâzım and Vâlâ were concerned, however, they had just set foot in the land of communism.[2] Eight months after first encountering the Spartakists in İnebolu, Nâzım and Vâlâ were going to see what communism looked like first-hand.

Vâlâ's memoirs emphasize how strange everything struck them that day. Everywhere they went, they encountered confusing new phenomena. At customs, for example, they were asked to describe their "social origins." This concept was highly important in Bolshevik society, but totally foreign to Nâzım and Vâlâ. The term refers to one's class background, i.e., whether one derives from "workers," "peasants," or "intellectuals." Nâzım and Vâlâ were not used to seeing or describing themselves in such a manner.

Vâlâ was asked the question first, and in response confessed that he didn't understand what the officer wanted to know. The customs agent then told him to simply state his father's profession.

"Provincial governor," he calmly replied.

"Governor, what???"

"He was the governor of Beirut," added Vâlâ. "He's deceased now."

Having made their way through the customs area, Nâzım and the late Beirut governor's son took their initial steps into Georgia. The first person who approached them was a Turkish guy.

"Hey, are you Turkish?" asked the man, who was carrying a length of rope wound up in a spiral. "Welcome to Batumi. I'm Turkish, too."

Nâzım and Vâlâ were genuinely relieved to have found someone who spoke their language. But what did he want with them?

"You're foreigners here," continued the man. "You won't find a place to stay on your own. I'll carry your bags and can take you to a hotel."

The boys weren't sure what to do. The thought occurred to them that their interlocutor might want money in exchange for his services. Nâzım and Vâlâ barely had enough for their own expenses, let alone hiring others to carry their bags for

---

[1] Sülker writes that it was September 30, *Nâzım Hikmet'in Gerçek Yaşamı*, vol. 1, 127.
[2] This phrasing inspired by John W. Meyer, *No Turning Back: On the Loose in China and Tibet* (Ann Arbor, MI: The Neither/Nor Press, 1991), 14.

*Red Star over the Black Sea: Nâzım Hikmet and his Generation.* James H. Meyer, Oxford University Press. © James H. Meyer 2023.
DOI: 10.1093/oso/9780192871176.003.0006

them. On the other hand, the two reasoned, this was a Turkish-speaker who could help them find a place to stay. Maybe it would be worthwhile to give him a little money in exchange for his assistance.

Vâlâ wanted to hire the fellow, if only because he had claimed that he would find them a good, inexpensive hotel. Nâzım, however, responded by saying that he could only accept half of the man's offer. "He can take us to the cheapest place to stay. But given that we've come to a communist country, let's stop exploiting people. We won't let him carry our bags."

"You're right," concurred Vâlâ. "From now on, let's stop exploiting the proletariat."

Glancing back and forth at the boys, Nâzım and Vâlâ's newfound comrade couldn't help smiling. "Okay," he wondered aloud to them, "but then how am I supposed to earn any money?"[3]

## From Batumi to Tbilisi

Walking around Batumi felt like a dream that day. After dropping off their bags, Nâzım and Vâlâ decided to explore the town and get their first taste of communism. Wandering aimlessly among the palm trees and tropical plants which lined the big city park the boys had stumbled across, they quickly got lost.

Having been prepared to find a revolutionary republic in the throes of upheaval, the boys were stunned by how ordinary everything appeared. For example, as they were walking Nâzım and Vâlâ saw a beautiful little church—but hadn't the Spartakists told them that religion had been outlawed? And what about that couple over there, strolling hand in hand, with a baby in tow? Didn't Sadık Ahi say that the traditional family patriarchy had come to an end under communism?

"That's what he said," confirmed Nâzım.

But it sure didn't look that way, at least insofar as Nâzım and Vâlâ could tell. In fact, everywhere the boys turned, they saw something that seemed relaxed, comfortable, and... quite normal. Having arrived in Georgia thinking of their surroundings mainly in political and ideological terms, this juxtaposition of everyday life alongside what Nâzım and Vâlâ had been told about communism was jarring.[4]

From an old lady in the park, they bought some little black grapes wrapped in paper cartons. Carrying their snacks, Nâzım and Vâlâ walked along the rocky shoreline for a while before stumbling across something that definitely did feel out of the ordinary: a nude beach. Astonished by their surroundings as they ran a gauntlet of naked flesh, the two young friends glanced back at one another in wonder. "Women and girls," recounted Vâlâ breathlessly almost forty years later, "were walking around with their breasts and every organ exposed."[5]

---

[3] Vâ-Nû, *Bu Dünyadan Nâzım Geçti*, 226–227.

[4] Ibid., 225. On Nâzım and Vâlâ traveling to Batumi, also see Sülker, *Nâzım Hikmet'in Gerçek Yaşamı*, vol. 1, 127–130; Göksu and Timms, *Romantic Communist*, 32–33.

[5] Vâ-Nû, *Bu Dünyadan Nâzım Geçti*, 229. On Nâzım and Vâlâ's first impressions of Batumi, also see Sülker, *Nâzım Hikmet'in Gerçek Yaşamı*, vol. 1, 128–129.

90 RED STAR OVER THE BLACK SEA

In *Life's Good, Brother*, Nâzım described something similar in presenting the experiences of his fictional hero, Ahmet:

> In 1922, midsummer, men and women lay side by side on the Batumi beach, face down or on their backs—all completely naked. I mean, no bathing suits or anything, just stark naked.[6]

"Are we in a dream?" Vâlâ remembered asking himself.[7] Or was this really communism?

Despite their rather positive first impressions of Batumi, the boys were concerned about money. After paying for their hotel room for the night, they had a total of twenty-six liras remaining. Nâzım and Vâlâ therefore decided that it would be best to continue traveling as soon as possible to Tbilisi, where they hoped to find Muhittin Bey and Nüzhet. The easiest way to get there was by train, but the boys had been warned that it might be difficult to obtain tickets. One of the desk clerks at their hotel had told them that, in order to secure a place in line, they would need to arrive at the station hours ahead of time.

He was right. When the boys showed up at the train station the next morning, they found a line "more than a kilometer long," stretching far beyond the large building's doors. Slowly, and by subtly cutting in front of people "in the Turkish style," Nâzım and Vâlâ made it to the ticket window some eight hours later.[8] The bad news, however, was that the train they wanted was sold out. They would have to come back the next day.[9]

At this point, Vâlâ lost his temper. He wrote later that he could not remember "having ever been so angry in my life, kicking and stomping my feet, my fists clenched." This time, however, it was Nâzım who kept his cool. According to Vâlâ's later reminiscences, Nâzım managed to calm Vâlâ down, urging his friend to focus on the matter at hand. In order to be sure about getting tickets the next day, the two quickly decided to spend the night in the station sleeping in front of the sales window. The following morning, they were the first in line, and later that day they boarded a train for Tbilisi.[10]

Traveling day and night, the boys took in the sights, sounds, and smells of the crowded train, which ambled past mountain peaks of more than 9,000 feet. Some of Nâzım and Vâlâ's fellow passengers shared food and wine with them, while others passed the time singing songs. Years later, Vâlâ would recall the large number of attractive women on board. He tried to listen in on their conversations, observing that it sounded as if they were "speaking with letters that came right from their throats."[11] The train finally pulled into Tbilisi the next morning.[12]

---

[6] Nâzım Hikmet, *Life's Good, Brother*, 28–29. Blasing's translation renders the city as "Batum," but I have changed it to "Batumi" here to make it consistent with other references.

[7] Vâ-Nû, *Bu Dünyadan Nâzım Geçti*, 229.      [8] "*Alaturka hilelerle.*" Ibid., 231.

[9] Ibid., 231. Sülker writes that the boys spent "several" ("*bir kaç*") days in Batumi before going to Tbilisi. *Nâzım Hikmet'in Gerçek Yaşamı*, vol. 1, 130.

[10] On Batumi, also see Memet Fuat, *Nâzım Hikmet*, 43.

[11] Vâ-Nû, *Bu Dünyadan Nâzım Geçti*, 232–233. Vâlâ here is referring to Georgian, which he remembers as sounding different from how it was spoken in Batumi and elsewhere in Adjara.

[12] Sülker, *Nâzım Hikmet'in Gerçek Yaşamı*, vol. 1, 130–131.

While they were still in Batumi, Nâzım and Vâlâ had met a few Turks who claimed to know Muhittin Bey. Everybody had said the same thing: look for him at the Orient Hotel. Disembarking at Tbilisi's main train station, Nâzım and Vâlâ went straight to the Orient. The hotel was easy to find, as it was an imposing building located right in the heart of the city center. The boys, Vâlâ later recalled, felt a bit uncomfortable walking into such a fancy place in their grimy, travel-worn clothes, so they took a minute to straighten their hair and clean up their faces before entering.

"Parlez-vous Français?" ventured Vâlâ, addressing the receptionist. Receiving a response in the affirmative, Vâlâ quickly explained that he and Nâzım were looking for Muhittin Bey.

"Muhittin Bey has left the hotel," came the abrupt reply. The words tumbled down upon Nâzım and Vâlâ like a collapsing wall. Their worst fears had been realized. From further questioning, the boys apprehended that Muhittin Bey had recently departed for Moscow, and that Nüzhet had gone with him.[13]

Just as it had begun to appear that all hope had been lost, the receptionist added that Muhittin Bey had not left permanently, and that his wife and mother were still staying at the Orient.[14] This was good news. Vâlâ and Nâzım begged for the ladies to be called in their room. Agreeing to the request, the receptionist reported that they were in. While they had never met Vâlâ before, the women knew Nâzım and invited the boys to come up and visit them in their rooms.

Upstairs, the women treated Nâzım and Vâlâ to breakfast and a round of questions. Why had they come to Tbilisi? How much money did they have? Where were they staying? After hearing the boys' answers, it became clear to the women that their guests were in need of assistance. Muhittin Bey's wife, Melâhat Hanım, offered to let Nâzım and Vâlâ stay with them. The women would share the bedroom, and Nâzım and Vâlâ could sleep on the couch and armchair in the sitting room.[15]

The problem with this arrangement was that the hotel had a standing rule against non-paying visitors staying in guests' rooms beyond midnight. Sure enough, just before twelve o'clock there was a knock at the door of the suite. The boys were told that they would have to go. With their bags still at the left-luggage room of the train station, Nâzım and Vâlâ walked out into the nearly empty streets without any idea of what to do or where to go.

They approached a few people on the street and tried, in various languages, to ask about cheap hotels in the area. No one understood them. Eventually, Nâzım and Vâlâ noticed that one fellow had been following them ever since they had left the Orient. Half-suspecting he was a plain-clothes policeman, they decided to ask him if he knew of a decent place to stay. It turned out that he did, directing Nâzım and Vâlâ to a clean,

---

[13] Why Muhittin and Nüzhet were traveling together to Moscow is unclear.

[14] Vâlâ actually writes that this was Muhittin's mother-in-law, but as Nüzhet was an orphan and Muhittin was married to her older sister, it does not seem possible that Muhittin would have a mother-in-law. *Bu Dünyadan Nâzım Geçti*, 233–234.

[15] Ibid., 232–234; Sülker, *Nâzım Hikmet'in Gerçek Yaşamı*, vol. 1, 131.

but quite expensive, inn. By the time they had paid for their room, Nâzım and Vâlâ had just nine liras left. But at least they had a bed for the night.[16]

After breakfast the following morning, the boys were at a loss for what to do. They wandered the streets for a while, walking underneath the graceful wrought-iron balconies typical of the architecture of the southern Caucasus. Eventually, Nâzım and Vâlâ headed over to the Orient to see if Melâhat Hanım could do anything about their plight.

As the boys entered the Orient's ornate foyer, the receptionist hurried up to them with unexpected news. He told Nâzım and Vâlâ that Polikarp "Budu" Mdivani, one of the most important politicians in Georgia, wanted to see them immediately. Vâlâ remembered the name, as Spartakist Vehbi had mentioned it to him back when the two had met up at the Kuyulu Café in Ankara. Vehbi, Vâlâ recalled, had told him that if he ever found himself stranded in Tbilisi, he should get in touch with Mdivani—and now Mdivani was making contact with them! The boys' luck appeared to be changing.

The receptionist led Nâzım and Vâlâ to Mdivani's living quarters, which were located about two hundred yards down the street from the hotel. The boys went upstairs, where they were ushered into a large room. Mdivani entered shortly after they did. He told Nâzım and Vâlâ that he knew who they were and why they were in Tbilisi.[17] This must have come as news to Nâzım and Vâlâ, who themselves had only the vaguest notion of what they were doing in Georgia.

At this moment, Vâlâ came close to ruining their unexpected good fortune by needlessly launching into an elaborate lie. The maneuver was something that Spartakist Vehbi had suggested he try back when they were at the Kuyulu. Following Vehbi's advice, Vâlâ "reminded" the Georgian politician that they had once met at Muhittin Bey's house in Ankara. "That day," began Vâlâ, "Sadık Ahi Bey was there, Servet Bey was there, Vehbi Bey was there…"

Vâlâ's clumsy trick, however, was quickly shot down by Mdivani, who interrupted him by saying: "I have never seen either of you before in my life. Yes, I did in fact go frequently to Muhittin Bey's house. I know Sadık, Servet, and Vehbi. But if I were to see either of you passing in the street, I wouldn't recognize you."

Nâzım rescued the moment, however, by changing the subject. Discreetly shifting away from the failed ruse, Nâzım explained to Mdivani that he and Vâlâ were poets who had come to Tbilisi because they were curious about the revolution. They did not know anyone in town, and had been unable to find Muhittin Bey, their only contact. They were willing to work hard, explained Nâzım, to overcome their difficulties.[18]

"I know," responded Mdivani cryptically. "That's what everyone has told me. But my train is about to depart—I'm on my way to Moscow. When I get back, our mutual friend Muhittin Bey will have already returned. We'll look after you." With these words, Mdivani escorted Nâzım and Vâlâ back to the Orient, scene of their previous

---

[16] Vâ-Nû, *Bu Dünyadan Nâzım Geçti*, 235; Sülker, *Nâzım Hikmet'in Gerçek Yaşamı*, vol. 1, 130.
[17] Vâ-Nû, *Bu Dünyadan Nâzım Geçti*, 199; Sülker, *Nâzım Hikmet'in Gerçek Yaşamı*, vol. 1, 131–133.
[18] Vâ-Nû, *Bu Dünyadan Nâzım Geçti*, 237.

eviction. Mdivani explained to the hotel manager that the two young travelers would be staying free of charge in a room reserved for guests of the Georgian government. Instructions were issued to supply Nâzım and Vâlâ with vouchers in order to dine without cost at the hotel restaurant.

After checking in to their new abode, Nâzım and Vâlâ returned to the train station and retrieved their bags. The boys took a taxi back to the Orient with their things, draining still more of their remaining funds. But who needed money now? Perhaps Sadık Ahi and Ziya Hilmi had been right all along. As long as you knew the right people, maybe you really didn't need money under communism, after all.

## Another Shift in the Wind

Upon getting back to the Orient, Nâzım and Vâlâ paid Melâhat Hanım a visit to spread the good news. At first Melâhat and her mother-in-law did not believe them— maybe the boys had misunderstood Mdivani? But then, as the four were chatting in Melâhat Hanım's suite, there was a knock at the door. The hotel manager was looking for Nâzım and Vâlâ so that he could give them their meal vouchers. After the man had left, Melâhat Hanım and her mother-in-law could barely contain their laughter. "Why, aren't you two the devils? The devils!" Melâhat Hanım cried out, slapping their knees jocularly. Then the four of them, vouchers in hand, headed downstairs for lunch, "two ladies and their knights" alongside them.[19]

Walking toward their table in the hotel restaurant that morning, Nâzım and Vâlâ looked around at the other diners. Among the scattered customers seated in the room was a group of about ten Turks who nodded hello to Melâhat Hanım as she passed by. At the head of the table was an intense-looking bearded man who caught the boys' attention. Melâhat Hanım knew him, and proceeded to introduce Nâzım and Vâlâ to Ahmet Cevat (Emre).

Born in Ottoman Crete in 1879, Ahmet Cevat had studied at the Istanbul-based military academies of Kuleli and Harbiye.[20] It was during his time at the latter institution that Ahmet Cevat—like a young Yusuf Akçura—had been arrested and tried for political crimes, resulting in his exile to Fezzan, in Ottoman-held Libya.[21] Again like Akçura, Ahmet Cevat would later escape to Europe, where he began what would become a brilliant career as a student and teacher of foreign languages. At the time that he met Nâzım and Vâlâ, Ahmet Cevat could speak, in addition to Turkish: Russian, French, Greek, English, Italian, Arabic, and Persian.[22] Like many other early TKP members, his intellectual background had been in the Turkist and pan-Turkist

---

[19] Ibid., 240–241.    [20] The Harbiye academy would later be transferred to Ankara.
[21] It is not clear if Ahmet Cevat was one of the students arrested alongside Akçura, but the timing of Ahmet Cevat's arrest makes it seem likely. Georgeon, *Aux Origines du Nationalisme Turc*, 15. According to one source, Ahmet Cevat and Yusuf Akçura had published a newspaper called *Hatıra* together in Fezzan. Akbulut (ed.), *Milli Azadlık Savaşı Anıları*, 45.
[22] RGASPI, f. 532, op. 12, d. 1406, ll. 5–6. 1922. Ahmet Cevat's KUTV employee file.

print media of Young Turk-era Istanbul, where he had written for newspapers like *Şura-yı Ümmet* and *Siper-i Saika*, both of which were a part of these circles.[23]

Ahmet Cevat had originally been drawn to the postwar Caucasus by a combination of pan-Turkist sympathies and personal opportunity. At the beginning of 1920, he had left his wife and four children in Istanbul in order to seek his fortune in the Azerbaijan Democratic Republic, which was at that time still independent and under the political domination of Müsavat-affiliated republican nationalists like Mehmet Emin Resulzade and Ahmet Ağaoğlu. In Baku, Ahmet Cevat had worked as a member of the Azeri government's language commission, which sought to replace the Arabic Azerbaijani alphabet with a Latin one.[24] Following the Bolshevik takeover of Azerbaijan in April 1920, Ahmet Cevat had remained in the Caucasus, where he attended, in Baku, the Congress of the Peoples of the East in September 1920. He then signed up with the TKP at the party's inaugural meeting several days later.

Why would a pan-Turkist like Ahmet Cevat join up with the communists? The path from pan-Turkism to communism does not necessarily make a lot of sense when looked at strictly from an ideological perspective. But with the routing of the nationalist government in Baku in the spring of 1920, the Bolsheviks quickly became the only game in town. While in ideological terms, pan-Turkism and communism were diametrically opposed to one another, in a more practical sense there was some overlap between them. The fact that pan-Turkists and communists viewed the world in ideological terms was itself something that bound them together, separating both groups from dynastically centered views of political organization. Also important was the fact that both pan-Turkism and communism looked beyond borders. With pan-Turkism appearing increasingly bankrupt in the wake of the Young Turks' collapse in Istanbul and the fall of the nationalist government in Baku, communism made sense as an alternative ideology to many former pan-Turkists.

The morning that Nâzım and Vâlâ met Ahmet Cevat at the Orient Hotel restaurant, there were several other early TKP members at his table.[25] One was Zinetullah Nevşirvanov. A Tatar from a village outside Ufa, capital of today's Republic of Bashkortostan in Russia, Nevşirvanov had moved to Istanbul to study prior to the outbreak of World War I. During this time, he had traveled mainly in pan-Turkist circles, publishing several articles in Yusuf Akçura's *Türk Yurdu* between 1915 and 1917.[26] In August 1920, Nevşirvanov set off for Anatolia. His party paperwork indicates that he was working "as a secret TKP member" at this time, but it is unclear what exactly he was doing there.[27]

---

[23] Ertan Temuçin, "Ahmet Cevat Emre ve Kemalizm'de Öncü Bir Dergi: *Muhit*," *Kebikeç*, vol. 5 (1997), 17–34, here 19. On Ahmet Cevat, also see RGASPI, f. 495, op. 65a, d. 9377. Ahmet Cevat, personal file.

[24] This project to change the Azeri alphabet was later shelved under the Bolsheviks, then revived in 1929.

[25] On Nâzım and Vâlâ's early days in Georgia, see Memet Fuat, *Nâzım Hikmet*, 43. Abid Alimov was one of those in Ahmet Cevat's party. Vâ-Nû, *Bu Dünyadan Nâzım Geçti*, 242. Sülker, *Nâzım Hikmet'in Gerçek Yaşamı*, vol. 1, 133–134. According to Sülker, Nâzım and Vâlâ met Kayserili İsmail Hakkı, his wife Rahime, Zinetullah Nevşirvanov, Aynühayat, "Sergeant Kadri," and one Abdurrahman Hoca.

[26] For a list of these articles, see Tuncer, *Türk Yurdu Bibliyografyası (1911–1992)*, 336.

[27] Akbulut and Tunçay (eds.), *İstanbul Komünist Grubu'ndan*, 416–417. Akal, *Moskova-Ankara-Londra Üçgeninde*, 121.

Joining Nevşirvanov at the Hotel Orient that morning was his wife, Cemile Nevşirvanova. An Ottoman-born daughter of Crimean Tatar immigrants, Cemile had studied for one year at a teachers' training school in Istanbul before heading to Ankara in 1920. There she and her husband had joined Manatov and Hacıoğlu's TKP. Following the closure of the party, Cemile and Zinetullah had made their way to the Caucasus, where they had become members of Mustafa Suphi's Baku-based organization.

Cemile Nevşirvanova's younger sister Rahime was also part of the group of Turkish communists staying at the Orient.[28] Born in 1900, Rahime was four years younger than her sister. Like Cemile, Rahime had graduated from a teacher-training institute in Istanbul before making her way out to Georgia, via Ankara, along with her sister and brother-in-law.[29] In Baku, Rahime had married Kayserili İsmail Hakkı ("İsmail Hakkı from Kayseri"), a former Ottoman soldier and POW in Russia who had become one of the earliest members of the TKP.[30] Rahime's later paperwork from Moscow identifies her as "Rahime Hakkı," a Crimean Tatar born in Istanbul.[31] Decades later, Vâlâ Nureddin would recall Rahime's short hair and bangs, unusual for Turkish women at this time.[32]

With precious few liras left to spend and little obvious purpose in Tbilisi, Nâzım and Vâlâ spent much of their time sitting in the Orient's restaurant and exploring the city's winding streets. The boys soon developed a good rapport with the scholarly Ahmet Cevat, whose interests in literature and politics aligned with their own. While Ahmet Cevat was more than twenty years older than the boys, Nâzım and Vâlâ nevertheless felt that they had much more in common with him than they did with any of the younger communists in his retinue. "Nâzım and I," wrote Vâlâ years later, "were flying among the intellectual heights. We were into poetry and the theories of pure socialism. We looked down on this entire group...We turned up our noses at them. Only with Ahmet Cevat did we form a friendship."[33]

Once again, the boys had found themselves an intellectual mentor, someone who could take the place previously occupied by Syllabists, Spartakists, and Ziya Hilmi. Although Nâzım and Vâlâ were not especially taken with their elder companion's poetry, they respected Ahmet Cevat's intellect and education. Nâzım and Vâlâ knew, moreover, that he had much to teach them about one subject in particular: communism. Here, after all, was a fellow intellectual who had actually spent time with the martyred hero Mustafa Suphi, not to mention the transition to Bolshevism that had taken place in the Caucasus the previous year. If anyone could school the boys on the theories and practices of communism, it was Ahmet Cevat.

One day, Ahmet Cevat mentioned to the boys that he and the other Turkish communists at the Orient would soon be leaving for Batumi, where they were setting

---

[28] *Milli Azadlık Savaşı Anıları*, 96.
[29] RGASPI, f. 495, op. 266, d. 134, ll. 1–7–ob. Personal file of Rahime Hakkı.
[30] According to Vâlâ's memoirs from the early 1960s, Kayserili İsmail Hakkı had been "40–45" years old in 1921, *Bu Dünyadan Nâzım Geçti*, 242. See RGASPI, f. 495, op. 266, d. 102, l. 31. Personal file of İsmail Hakkı.
[31] RGASPI, f. 495, op. 266, d. 134, l. 5. Personal file of Rahime Hakkı. On Kayserili İsmail Hakkı, also see Akbulut (ed.), *Milli Azadlık Savaşı Anıları*, 56–57.
[32] Vâ-Nû, *Bu Dünyadan Nâzım Geçti*, 242.     [33] Vâ-Nû, *Bu Dünyadan Nâzım Geçti*, 243.

up a local edition of the Turkish-language communist newspaper *Yeni Dünya*.[34] He suggested that Nâzım and Vâlâ join them, and even offered to lend them money for their train tickets. Ahmet Cevat added that he could find the boys a free place to stay in Batumi at the Hotel de France, where he and the other communists already had rooms.[35]

Stranded in a foreign city with no money, Nâzım and Vâlâ would have found Ahmet Cevat's offer hard to refuse no matter what. But it was not mere desperation that brought Nâzım and Vâlâ back to Batumi to write for *Yeni Dünya*. They genuinely liked their older comrade, and realized that, by going to Batumi with him and the others, they could find a way to both provide for themselves and finally learn something about communism. Wasn't that at least one of the reasons why they had come to Georgia in the first place? Now they would no longer be tourists in the land of Bolshevism, but actual residents.

Batumi had experienced many changes over the course of the previous half-century. The city and the province that shared its name had been part of the Ottoman Empire for more than 300 years. Following the Russian-Ottoman War of 1877–78, however, the Sublime Porte had ceded the territory, alongside the provinces of Ardahan and Kars, to Russia. Since 1917, Batumi had been a part of no fewer than seven states: the Russian Empire, the Russian Republic, the Transcaucasian Commissariat, the Transcaucasian Democratic Federative Republic, the Ottoman Empire, the Democratic Republic of Georgia, and the Georgian Soviet Socialist Republic.

The city had an unsavory reputation in Ankara at this time. In these early years following the end of World War I, Batumi was filled with a large population of refugees from Anatolia and the Caucasus, who were now sharing the city's streets with Young Turk political exiles, communist agents, and ex-Ottoman POWs. In the words of a report written for the Ankara government's cabinet in August 1922, Batumi was teeming with marauding young men, "some of whom are Turks who have fled military service" who were "wandering around like bums."[36] The Treaty of Moscow that Kemal's government had signed with the Bolsheviks notwithstanding, there was a sense of uncertainty and unpredictability in the air in Batumi, as no one could predict with certainty in which country the city would ultimately wind up. Also adding to the somewhat spirited feeling in town, perhaps, was the fact that one could drink alcohol legally there.[37]

Nâzım and Vâlâ were given a room at the Hotel de France. It is not clear when exactly they moved back to Batumi with Ahmet Cevat, but it appears to have been late September 1921. To help the boys earn extra money, Ahmet Cevat found them work

---

[34] Named after Mustafa Suphi's first Turkish-language communist newspaper. "Yeni Dünya" was, coincidentally, also the name of the boat Nâzım and Vâlâ had taken from Istanbul at the outset of their journey.

[35] Sülker, *Nâzım Hikmet'in Gerçek Yaşamı*, vol. 1, 134; Memet Fuat, *Nâzım Hikmet*, 42–43; Fish, *Nâzım'ın Çilesi*, 124.

[36] "*Serseri.*" BCA 30-10-0-0/55-371-8. "On the amnesty and return of Turkish citizens, most of whom are deserters from the army, from various places in the Caucasus, starting with Batumi." August 26, 1922.

[37] Alcohol was still forbidden as a wartime measure in territories controlled by the Ankara government at this time.

as tutors for an Azeri family that was hoping to re-settle in Anatolia. With a little change now in their pockets, Nâzım and Vâlâ spent their evenings enjoying Batumi's warm, tropical air, drinking *rakı*, and meeting up with communists, exiled Young Turks, and the local Turkish-speaking population. Enver Pasha's uncle, Halil Pasha, had a house in Batumi which had become a center of Unionist socializing during these months. Enver Pasha himself had been in Batumi over the summer, although Nâzım and Vâlâ do not appear to have met him.[38]

The Bolsheviks had only recently taken Georgia, in February 1921, and Nâzım and Vâlâ were part of the first wave of Turkish-language Bolshevik propagandizers to appear in the region. The boys were drawing ever closer to the party. On December 2, 1921, Nâzım and Vâlâ were each listed as "candidates" for membership in the Batumi cell of the TKP.[39]

## A Search for Embeddedness

When Şevket Süreyya had first arrived in Azerbaijan in 1919, he had felt exhilarated. Here he had the chance, thought Şevket, to provide a genuine service to the community, as well as for the Turkic world more generally. In Baku, however, he had grown to feel only disdain for the other Turks he had seen, indolent types who wasted their time hanging out at the Çanakkale coffeehouse. Surrounded by the sea breeze, and the smacking of pips and rolling of dice from the establishment's much-used backgammon boards, Şevket Süreyya had come to the conclusion that most of those other teachers had somehow lost their way.

He vowed to be different. Early on in Baku, Şevket had visited the offices of the Azeri Ministry of Education and requested to be appointed to a school far from the capital. They gave him a position in Nuha, today's Şeki, in the far northwest of the country. Arriving in Nuha with the mountains looming far above him, Şevket Süreyya had finally made it to the real Turan.[40]

It was a stretch, of course. Technically speaking, "Turan" was usually thought of in terms of Central Asia, as Şevket Süreyya well knew. But to the newly-arrived Turkish teacher from Edirne, Azerbaijan represented reclaimed Turkic land, territory that had been taken back from the Russians. Just as Nâzım and Vâlâ had initially searched for an idealized communism in Batumi, Şevket Süreyya had, in those early days under the nationalist Müsavat government, thought of Azerbaijan mainly in ideological terms as a pan-Turkic entity. Yet, as had also been the case with Nâzım and Vâlâ on their first day in Georgia, the reality of life in Turan would ultimately prove quite disorienting to Şevket.

---

[38] Vâ-Nû, *Bu Dünyadan Nâzım Geçti*, 251, 256, 261, 263–264. Ahmet Cevat writes about Nâzım and Vâlâ visiting Halil in Batumi, Akbulut (ed.), *Milli Azadlık Savaşı Anıları*, 61–62.
[39] RGASPI/IISH, f. 495, op. 181, d. 188, l. 18. "Protocol No. 12." Meeting of the Batumi cell of the TKP, December 2, 1921.
[40] Aydemir, *Suyu Arayan Adam*, 124.

This time of Şevket Süreyya's life was particularly intense with feeling. Working in Nuha as the local teacher, he had begun a secret love affair with a woman named Sitare. Şevket had also become a soldier again, commanding a group of men in fighting that had broken out between Muslims and Armenians in Nagorno-Karabakh. As a veteran of World War I, Şevket Süreyya was a valued presence. But even as he was living out what once had been his pan-Turkist fantasy—leading his brother "Turks" into battle against their enemies—Şevket Süreyya was growing increasingly disillusioned with his life in Azerbaijan.

His pan-Turkism died in Turan. Whereas young men like Şevket had, in the years prior to and during World War I, eagerly bought into the idea that all "Turks" from the Balkans to Central Asia were part of one nation, the reality of living in Azerbaijan had disabused him of this notion. In what was supposedly part of the greater "Turan" of his youthful dreams, Şevket came to the conclusion that the people around him cared nothing for the pan-Turkic identity to which he had ascribed so much importance. Instead, the Azeris that Şevket Süreyya had met usually viewed themselves and others in much more parochial terms, specifically as either Sunni or Shiite Muslims.[41] The idea of somehow tying together the various Turkic peoples of the former Ottoman and Russian empires into a single community began to strike him as a preposterous fantasy.[42] As Şevket Süreyya Aydemir would later record in his memoirs, this realization brought upon a period of philosophical re-evaluation and personal uproar (hengâme).[43]

Returning to Nuha from the fighting, Şevket Süreyya received the news that Baku had fallen to Bolshevik forces. It was April 1920, and the days of the Azerbaijan Democratic Republic were numbered. By the end of the month, the nationalist government would be thoroughly routed and the Azerbaijan Soviet Socialist Republic erected in its place. The new government was under the political domination of Moscow, with which Azerbaijan would formally be politically reunited when the Soviet Union was created in 1922.[44]

One day, not long after getting back to Nuha, Şevket Süreyya was waiting for Sitare to visit him when he heard footsteps approaching. Turning around in the expectation of greeting his lover at the door, Şevket instead found himself face-to-face with a young man. The intruder had tousled hair and was completely covered with the dirt and grime of the battlefield. He carried a gun and stood staring at Şevket Süreyya with a mocking expression. Throwing his filthy cloak down onto the carpet in front of him, the man looked up at Şevket and announced, "I'm going to stay here, too."

Tongue-tied, and perhaps trying to make some kind of connection with this strange new presence, Şevket Süreyya asked him: "Were you in the war as well?" The intruder responded by saying "I was a fisherman in Astrakhan. Then I got drafted. They sent

---

[41] Ibid., 125.  [42] Ibid., 130–131.  [43] Ibid., 186–187.

[44] Starting in 1922 Azerbaijan, Armenia, and Georgia would collectively constitute the Transcaucasian Socialist Federative Soviet Republic, which was a republic of the USSR. In 1936, the three entities each became Soviet republics in their own right.

me to the German front. I joined the party once the revolution broke out." From that point forward, Şevket Süreyya took to calling the man "the Astrakhan Fisherman."[45]

The Astrakhan Fisherman and his colleagues were the first communist unit to make their way to Nuha, over which they quickly went about establishing administrative control. Posters were hung demanding that the city's families, businesses, and inns turn over their valuables. By the end of the day, the town's new rulers had confiscated a pile of expensive carpets alongside gold and silver objects and coins, all of which lay stacked together in front of the Bolsheviks' new headquarters in town. Those who were found to have hidden their possessions from the Astrakhan Fisherman's gang were put on trial as speculators or spies.[46]

What Şevket Süreyya was witnessing first-hand in Nuha was part of a larger process of Bolshevization that took place more generally in Azerbaijan in the spring and summer of 1920. The Bolsheviks saw the southern Caucasus as crucial to exporting their revolution to the Muslim populations of Asia and Africa. Bordering Turkey and Iran, Azerbaijan was emerging as Moscow's window on the Middle East.

According to paperwork that Şevket would fill out in Moscow in 1922, he had formally joined the TKP in Azerbaijan on December 19, 1920. These forms also indicate that Şevket had served as a member of the district committee of the Azerbaijan Communist Party (or "AKP") in Nuha.[47] This would have made him a colleague of the Astrakhan Fisherman, rather than his antagonist. Yet Şevket soon left town all the same, making his way to Batumi, which he reached in September 1921. The former pan-Turkist, disillusioned by the lack of "unity" he had seen in Azerbaijan, was gradually shifting his gaze from one ideal to another.[48]

Şevket Süreyya's newfound allegiance to communism did not, moreover, constitute the only way in which he was taking on new commitments at this time. Having left Sitare behind in Nuha, Şevket decided that it was time to get married. Shortly after arriving in Batumi, he heard about a young woman named Leman, whose family had recently arrived in the region as refugees from İzmir. The two were quickly betrothed. At the time of their wedding, Şevket Süreyya was twenty-three years old and Leman fifteen or sixteen.[49] As Şevket would note in his account from many years later, upon arriving in Batumi "I married the first Turkish girl I came across."[50]

## Making a "Social Family"

Upon first moving back to Batumi with Ahmet Cevat and his Turkish communist crew, Nâzım and Vâlâ had lived for a while at the Hotel de France alongside the rest of

---

[45] Aydemir, *Suyu Arayan Adam*, 148.    [46] Ibid., 153–154.

[47] RGASPI, f. 532, op. 12, d. 60, l. 1. Şevket Süreyya employee file, KUTV, 1922.

[48] On Aydemir writing about joining the TKP in Batumi, see *Suyu Arayan Adam*, 186–187.

[49] Paperwork that Leman filled out in Moscow in September of 1922 lists her age as sixteen, some several months after she had married Şevket Süreyya. RGASPI, Leman Aidemirova (Aydemir) university file, f. 532, op. 11, d. 171, l. 4. On another document her date of birth is listed as 1905. Ibid., l. 6.

[50] Aydemir, *Suyu Arayan Adam*, 186. In contrast to the pages Aydemir would later devote to Sitare, his memoirs never mention Leman's name again.

their comrades. After a series of break-ins at the hotel, however, the boys began staying with a man named Ali Rıza, the typesetter at *Yeni Dünya*.[51] Ali Rıza had recently begun to occupy a villa that had previously been owned by a "Scandinavian banker" who had left Batumi after the revolution. Setting up camp on two couches in the Scandinavian banker's former sitting room, Nâzım and Vâlâ spent their days writing for *Yeni Dünya* at the Hotel de France. Their evenings, meanwhile, were filled with chatter about politics in the late-night cafés of Batumi.

One evening in late September or early October 1921, Nâzım and Vâlâ were sitting at home, looking out at the fountain and the flowers in the Scandinavian banker's garden. In front of them suddenly appeared a young man with a brightly colored handkerchief and several pencils stuffed into the breast pocket of his suit jacket. The visitor had an agitated way of walking, and peered at the boys through a pair of bright, arresting blue eyes. Şevket Süreyya had arrived.[52]

Şevket was older and more experienced than Nâzım and Vâlâ, but was still very much a part of their generation. Whereas Ahmet Cevat had seemed more like an avuncular figure, Şevket was their *ağabey*, or "big brother." Years later, Vâlâ would identify Şevket Süreyya as having been the "leader" (*başkan*) of their group.[53] As was the case with his newfound friends Nâzım and Vâlâ, Şevket had little patience for most of the communists he had gotten to know in the Caucasus. He also shared his new friends' love of poetry. The three young men, often joined by Ahmet Cevat, began spending most of their free time together, roaming the streets and parks of Batumi, carrying on conversations that drew upon the usual mix of personal, political, and literary themes.

Nâzım's girlfriend Nüzhet traveled back to Tbilisi from Moscow with Muhittin Bey toward the end of 1921. Not long thereafter, she visited Batumi. Nüzhet wanted to return to Istanbul to study, and was coming to Batumi in order to obtain travel documents for the journey back. She ended up staying in Batumi for a total of fifteen days, during which time her relationship with Nâzım began to show signs of new life. He reportedly begged her to remain in Georgia with him, but she did not. Yet Nüzhet was unable to go to Istanbul either, as she could not obtain the necessary paperwork. So, she returned to Tbilisi to resume living with her sister and brother-in-law, the future of her relationship with Nâzım still unclear.[54]

In his memoirs, Vâlâ would use the term "social family" to refer to the group that he, Nâzım, Şevket Süreyya, Leman, and Ahmet Cevat had formed in Batumi at this time. This term has been employed in a number of Nâzım's biographies to describe the series of loose-knit "families" that Nâzım would construct around himself over the course of his life.[55] In Batumi, Nâzım, Vâlâ, and Ahmet Cevat—who had since moved

---

[51] Göksu and Timms, *Romantic Communist*, 36.     [52] Göktürk, *Bilinmeyen Yönleriyle*, 86.

[53] Vâ-Nû, *Bu Dünyadan Nâzım Geçti*, 325. For Şevket Süreyya Aydemir's recounting of his interactions with Nâzım Hikmet and experiences in Russia, see *Suyu Arayan Adam*, 194–198, 202–205, 206–218.

[54] According to Sülker, Nüzhet and her family spent fifteen days in Batumi, but then Nüzhet had to spend another few days in town due to a bureaucratic snafu. *Nâzım Hikmet'in Gerçek Yaşamı*, vol. 1, 145–146. Also see Göksu and Timms, *Romantic Communist*, 35.

[55] On the "social family," see Vâ-Nû, *Bu Dünyadan Nâzım Geçti*, 271–272, 276–277; Göksu and Timms, *Romantic Communist*, 34; Blasing, *Nâzım Hikmet*, 51.

into the Scandinavian banker's house as well—divided up the housework, while Şevket Süreyya and Leman lived in a room of their own, frequently joining their friends for meals and conversation. Ahmet Cevat was responsible for most of the cooking at home, making soups and the occasional meat-based meal. Vâlâ helped out with simple food preparation like slicing potatoes, his personal specialty.[56] Nâzım did not know how to cook but sometimes peeled vegetables. He usually washed the dishes and did basic cleaning.[57]

Poetry still constituted one of the most important bonds connecting Nâzım and Vâlâ. While traveling across Anatolia, the boys had collaborated on several songs and marching chants. Their poem "A First Look at Inner Anatolia" (February 17, 1921) is one such example, a paean to the adventure and wildness of the places they had seen. It is an attractive, optimistic image, one that was soon published in the Kemalist newspaper *Anadolu'da Yeni Gün*. The poem's final lines sum up its spirit well:

> What a beautiful place this is: it's winter up in the high mountains
> On the road, it's autumn, in its stream it's spring,
> In its golden sun there is also the heat of summer.[58]

Other poems that Nâzım and Vâlâ composed together at this time similarly extolled the freedom of the road. In "Travel Bug" (*Dolaşmak Arzusu*), Nâzım and Vâlâ crafted an ode to pursuing distant horizons, with the "perfectly clear night" awakening within the two travelers "a need to hurtle ourselves forward."[59] "Road Türkü" (*Yol Türküsü*), meanwhile, is a tune the boys would sing as they marched forward over the course of long days on the Anatolian steppe. It likewise celebrated the spirit of their journey:

> We don't want a palace, or a *hamam*, or an inn
> Wherever the sun sets, that's where we'll lie.
>
> If we're over here in the morning, then in the evening we're
> over there.[60]

One of the better-known works from Batumi that is credited to both Nâzım Hikmet and Vâlâ Nureddin is "For the Fifteen." It is an elegy for Mustafa Suphi and the other TKP Central Committee members murdered in Trabzon in late January 1921. This poem is more hortative than nuanced, but it reflects the enthusiasm, albeit at times jarring, that Nâzım and Vâlâ were feeling for communism.

> Old world, bow down before the new one!
> Instead of taking some of our comrades from us,
> Whatever you may do, we will achieve our goal![61]

---

[56] For Aydemir's account of events in the Caucasus at this time, see *Suyu Arayan Adam*, 185–191.
[57] Sülker, *Nâzım Hikmet'in Gerçek Yaşamı*, vol. 1, 135.
[58] Yapı Kredi edition of Nâzım Hikmet's collected works (*Şiirler* Vol. 8), 111.  [59] Ibid., 121.
[60] Ibid., 112.  [61] This is the third of four stanzas. Ibid., 122.

No longer jingoistic in the form of his earlier works, or derivatively romantic in the style of his Syllabist-inspired verse, Nâzım's writing had now come to celebrate communism, and the independent life of adventure that he and Vâlâ had been leading on the road. While Nâzım's best poetry was yet to be written, the travels he was currently undertaking with Vâlâ had already begun to widen his range.

## Destination Moscow

The social family may have been rich when it came to fellowship, but the gang was nevertheless low on funds. So, in the early months of 1922, Ahmet Cevat asked Vâlâ to do him a favor. While working in Baku under the pre-Soviet nationalist regime, Ahmet Cevat had supported himself by selling Ottoman books and carpets. However, in the aftermath of the Bolshevik takeover in Azerbaijan, several of Ahmet Cevat's most valuable items had been confiscated by the police. He now wanted Vâlâ to travel to Baku, sell some books, and see if he could retrieve Ahmet Cevat's carpets from police custody.

Ahmet Cevat's explanation for why he could not go himself was a bit dubious sounding. He had insisted, according to Vâlâ's later recollection, that it would be irresponsible for him to leave their "social family" without a leader. Consequently, Ahmet Cevat wanted either Nâzım or Vâlâ to make the trip for him. As there was a general consensus within the family that Nâzım could not be trusted to carry money, Vâlâ agreed to undertake the mission. Ahmet Cevat gave Vâlâ the books he wanted him to sell, told him with whom to get in touch in Baku, and explained to his young friend how to exchange gold on Baku's black market.[62] Vâlâ, who had absolutely no experience with any of these matters, then set off with Ahmet Cevat's gold, books, and best wishes.

Arriving in Baku, Vâlâ began to carry out his list of errands. He duly visited the Ankara government's representative to Baku, Memduh Şevket Bey, seeking assistance in getting Ahmet Cevat's carpets back from the Azeri police. Vâlâ then went to the Azeri Ministry of Education in an effort to sell Ahmet Cevat's books. But in neither of these undertakings did Vâlâ feel like he had much prospect for success, and soon he found himself doubting the general direction of his life. What was he doing in the Caucasus, anyway? Maybe, Vâlâ began to think, it would make more sense to start heading back to Istanbul.[63]

Meanwhile, Vâlâ was living out a minor drama in the dormitory where he was staying in Baku. Feeling a bit paranoid due to the nature of the jobs he was carrying out for Ahmet Cevat, Vâlâ had become convinced that his roommate was an Azeri government agent ready to arrest him for his involvement in these schemes. Upon first meeting this roommate, Vâlâ had identified himself as a poet. A couple of days later, the roommate had abruptly invited Vâlâ to give a talk at an international congress

---

[62] Vâ-Nû, *Bu Dünyadan Nâzım Geçti*, 289.   [63] Ibid., 294.

taking place the next day. Apparently, the congress was in need of an extra speaker. Would Vâlâ like to come and talk about literature?[64]

Unsure if this was a genuine offer or else some kind of trap, Vâlâ considered it unwise to refuse. The congress, however, proved to be legitimate. Attending with his roommate the next day, Vâlâ gave a talk "in front of thousands." Much to his surprise, he proved to be something of a hit. In fact, Vâlâ was so well-received that he was immediately invited to participate in another conference that the roommate was helping to organize in Tbilisi. Again, Vâlâ agreed to go with him, although it is not entirely clear whether he was doing so out of a sense of obligation, or simply because he had enjoyed the warm reception he had received after his first talk. The meeting in Tbilisi was going to be held at Vâlâ's old stomping grounds, the Orient Hotel.[65]

Just as Vâlâ was entering the Orient's foyer, he saw Nâzım! Vâlâ quickly noticed, moreover, that his friend was not alone. The whole social family was there, collected in the hotel's entranceway. What was going on? Were they headed to Baku?

"What business do we have in Baku?" responded Nâzım cheerfully. "We're going to Moscow. We're going to attend school in Moscow. Didn't you know?"[66]

Vâlâ did not know, so Nâzım filled him in. While Vâlâ had been away, Ahmet Cevat had been offered a Turkish-language teaching position at a university recently opened in Moscow: Communist University of the Toilers of the East, known by its Russian initials KUTV.[67] Even better, Ahmet Cevat had been asked to find others—native Turkish speakers—who would be willing to study at the newly-founded school. So, explained Nâzım, all of them would be traveling up to Moscow together.[68]

Had they been planning on leaving for Moscow without Vâlâ? In his memoirs, Vâlâ Nureddin confessed to having wondered about this, and he asked his old friend if it could possibly have been the case. Nâzım assured him that he would have traveled personally to Baku to find Vâlâ had they not been able to make contact with him from Tbilisi. Feeling somewhat mollified by this information, Vâlâ rejoined his traveling companions as they set their compasses northward.

*

Nâzım and Vâlâ had never drawn up a master plan for their travels. Instead, they had seemingly stumbled from one opportunity to the next. Their decision to travel from Batumi to Moscow was similarly a product of improvisation. Just a few days before bumping into the rest of the social family in the lobby of the Hotel Orient, Vâlâ had been thinking about returning to Istanbul. Now, he and the others were headed in the opposite direction. Had any one of a dozen or so developments worked out differently

---

[64] Vâ-Nû, *Bu Dünyadan Nâzım Geçti*, 291.    [65] Ibid., 292.

[66] Ibid., 296. Also see Memet Fuat, *Nâzım Hikmet*, 44. Ahmet Cevat, "1920 Moskova'sında Türk Komünistler," in Akbulut (ed.), *Milli Azadlık Savaşı Anıları*, 63–64.

[67] See Sülker's take on this, *Nâzım Hikmet'in Gerçek Yaşamı*, vol. 1, 135–137.

[68] Ahmet Cevat's paperwork at KUTV describes him as working as a lecturer in the Turkish sector of the university, teaching courses on economic geography, the history of the workers' movement, and the history of Turkey. RGASPI, f. 532, op. 12, d. 1406, ll. 4, 7. Other sources indicate that Ahmet Cevat also worked as a professor of Turkish at the Oriental Institute at Moscow University. Göksu and Timms, *Romantic Communist*, 37; Vâ-Nû, *Bu Dünyadan Nâzım Geçti*, 346.

on their journey through Anatolia and the Caucasus, Nâzım and Vâlâ's travels—and indeed their lives—may well have followed a quite different trajectory.

On the other hand, the re-location to Moscow of the social family was not simply a matter of chance. There were currents below the surface that had, almost imperceptibly, been driving Nâzım and Vâlâ eastward ever since they had left Istanbul. Sadık Ahi and his friends had not been random travelers who just happened to be interested in communism. Rather, they were members of Şefik Hüsnü's Worker and Peasant Socialist Party, and just a few weeks earlier Ahi had met with a Soviet emissary about recruiting Turks to the party. In Batumi, meanwhile, Nâzım and Vâlâ had found jobs and a place to stay precisely because they were young "easterners" who were interested in communism. And now, it was an opportunity from Communist University of the East in Moscow that was carrying them still further into Bolshevik territory. It wasn't only a shifting wind that had led Nâzım and Vâlâ down this path, but also Bolshevik recruitment.

Boys no longer, Nâzım and Vâlâ were now stepping into adulthood to the tune of a 1,235-mile trip northward.

Moscow was waiting.

# 5

# In Revolutionary Russia

It was springtime in Moscow, 1922, and Nâzım and his friends were registering for classes at the Communist University of the Toilers of the East. The forms that Nâzım and the others filled out were a couple of pages long and relatively straightforward, focusing mainly upon family history and the recent past.[1] "What is your family's social background?" they asked. "Did you participate in the civil war and, if so, in what capacity?" "What is your party background?"

"Do you write?" asked the questionnaire. "If so, then what?"

"I write everything," responded Nâzım.

"What is your street address in Moscow?"

*Gde ia zhivu*, Nâzım wrote. "Where I live."[2]

*

Nâzım's comment may have sounded a little glib, but it also contained a kernel of truth. After more than a year of traveling, including stays in Ankara, Bolu, and Batumi, home for Nâzım and Vâlâ perhaps really was wherever they happened to find themselves at the moment. It had been a long time since they'd had a fixed address. Moscow would finally provide them with one.

While Nâzım's years in Moscow in the 1920s are typically discussed in terms of his interactions with well-known cultural personages like Vladimir Mayakovsky and Vsevolod Meyerhold, in fact Nâzım spent little time with such exalted figures.[3] By far the most influential individuals in Nâzım's life in the Soviet capital were the people he knew from school, worked with in the TKP, and spent time with socially. At first glance it might seem like Nâzım and his bourgeois traveling companions had relatively little in common with their more working-class comrades at KUTV. In fact, they fit in with this broader community of students in certain unanticipated ways.

---

[1] Someone else likely wrote in the responses for him, as Nâzım indicates on this form that he knew no Russian at this time.

[2] Meyer, "Children of Trans-Empire," 195. RGASPI, f. 495, op. 266, d. 47, Part I, l. 157-ob. Student questionnaire, Nâzım Hikmet, KUTV.

[3] For example, Fevralski (trans. Ataol Behramoğlu), *Nâzım'dan Anılar*, 10–13, 63–68, and elsewhere. Virtually the entirety of Göksu and Timms' account of Nâzım's early years in Moscow is devoted to exploring these connections. *Romantic Communist*, 46–52. This is also the case with Blasing, *Nâzım Hikmet*, 50–55.

---

*Red Star over the Black Sea: Nâzım Hikmet and his Generation.* James H. Meyer, Oxford University Press. © James H. Meyer 2023.
DOI: 10.1093/oso/9780192871176.003.0007

## Early Days in the Bolshevik Capital

The ride up from Batumi had been a grim one. Traveling very slowly, "at the speed of a caravan from the Middle Ages," Nâzım, Vâlâ, Şevket, Leman, and Ahmet Cevat wound their way through former battlefields in the Caucasus, Ukraine, and the Volga River valley.[4] Surrounding their often-stalled train, in places, were scenes of utter devastation. Photographs from the era reveal crowds of stunned and weakened refugees seeking shelter in railway stations.

It took Nâzım and the others eleven days, riding multiple trains, to reach their destination. Stopping off at one railroad station after another, the travelers stayed at inns and schools while waiting for the next train forward. The stations were unbearably crowded. Civil war and the threat of starvation had forced hundreds of thousands onto the roads and rails in search of a means of survival. Inching their way through the burnt out remains of central Russia, the five friends pressed onward.

They finally arrived in Moscow in late spring of 1922.[5] From the train station, the traveling companions headed directly to the Hotel Luxe, where rooms had been arranged for them. Originally constructed in 1911, the Luxe's building had previously housed the Hotel Frantsiia. Following the October Revolution, the Frantsiia had been nationalized, and now the Luxe was used mainly to house foreign communists visiting the Soviet capital for stays both long and short. (Figure 5.1).

Located on Tverskaia Street, the broad boulevard extending north from the Kremlin, the Hotel Luxe was well known in Moscow for providing Bolshevik-class comfort in a downtown location. The hotel included a cafeteria for which Nâzım and his traveling companions were provided vouchers, a matter of critical importance in food-scarce Moscow. Vâlâ later wrote that he had made quick use of the modern bathtub at the Luxe, divesting himself of the web of fleas that had been infesting his clothes for much of the last 1,300 miles of travel.[6]

In the early 1920s, the Luxe had an exciting international vibe of the sort that many of its one-time guests would remember fondly in their memoirs.[7] Nâzım and his friends, who spoke French and German among other languages, similarly got a thrill from the sheer cosmopolitanism of the legendary hotel-residence. "Amid the conversations taking place at mealtimes," wrote Şevket Süreyya years later, "you could

---

[4] Aydemir, *Suyu Arayan Adam*, 194; Vâ-Nû, *Bu Dünyadan Nâzım Geçti*, 307–309.

[5] Leman's paperwork is dated March 24, 1922. RGASPI, f. 532, op. 11, d. 171, l. 2. Also in Leman's file is a copy of a note from the Eastern Section of the Comintern requesting that Nâzım Hikmet, Vâlâ Nureddin, Şevket Süreyya Aydemir, and Leman Aydemir be granted admission into KUTV, dated April 24, 1922. Nâzım's file indicates that he was first registered as a student at KUTV in May 1922. RGASPI, f. 495, op. 266, d. 47, Part I, l. 157.

[6] Vâ-Nû, *Bu Dünyadan Nâzım Geçti*, 310.

[7] See, from Studer, Ruth von Mayenburg, *Hotel Lux. Das Absteigequartier der Weltrevolution* (Munich: Piper, 1991). On the Hotel Luxe (often written "Lux"), see Studer, *Transnational World of the Cominternians*, 67, 69; McGuire, *Red at Heart*, 30, 143, 177, 180, 216, 227, 252; Brigid O'Keeffe, *Esperanto and Languages of Internationalism in Revolutionary Russia* (London: Bloomsbury Academic, 2021), 116.

**Figure 5.1** The Hotel Luxe

hear all of the languages of the world."[8] Vâlâ observed drily that there were people at KUTV from "seventy-two and a half nations."[9]

Staying at the Luxe also gave the friends a chance to rub elbows with well-known Bolsheviks.[10] Şevket would later note that at the Luxe "it was possible to see practically all of the revolution's leaders," including Bolshevik luminaries like Karl Radek, Nikolai Bukharin, Lev Kamenev, and Grigory Zinoviev, the head of the Comintern.[11] If only Sadık Ahi and the rest of the Spartakists could see them now.

Despite the excitement aroused among Nâzım and his friends by the international flavor of their surroundings, the state of the KUTV campus was somewhat dispiriting. Şevket Süreyya, the only one among the younger members of their group to have received actual training to work as a teacher, thought the campus felt "abandoned" and "cold." He started to wonder if he had made the wrong choice in traveling up to Moscow with the others. Maybe, Şevket thought, it would be a better idea to just turn around and head back to the Caucasus with Leman.[12]

Moscow was, moreover, ill-equipped to handle the influx of new mouths to feed. During this time in Russia, cities were hit especially hard by famine, and even in the capital there were dire food shortages. After having spent about a month in Moscow

---

[8] Vâ-Nû, *Bu Dünyadan Nâzım Geçti*, 310; Aydemir, *Suyu Arayan Adam*, 198. Nâzım makes similar observations in his semi-autobiographical account in *Life's Good, Brother*.
[9] Vâ-Nû, *Bu Dünyadan Nâzım Geçti*, 349. Brigid O'Keeffe has described Moscow in the 1920s as a "Bolshevik tower of Babel." *Esperanto and Languages of Internationalism*, esp. 81–111.
[10] On KUTV and the Soviet literary sphere, see Rossen Djagalov, *From Internationalism to Postcolonialism: Literature and Cinema Between the Second and Third Worlds* (Montreal: McGill-Queen's University Press, 2020), 43–52. On Nâzım Hikmet at KUTV, see ibid., 28, 36, 43.
[11] Quotation is from Aydemir, *Suyu Arayan Adam*, 198. Also see Vâ-Nû, *Bu Dünyadan Nâzım Geçti*, 310.
[12] Aydemir, *Suyu Arayan Adam*, 199.

at the Luxe, Nâzım, Vâlâ, Şevket, and Leman were informed that they would have to go to a youth summer camp in Udel'naia, a village located about fifteen miles to the southeast of the capital.[13] Ahmet Cevat would stay in Moscow, preparing for the upcoming school year.

Nâzım did not like this idea one bit. "We didn't come here to stay in some village," he sniffed. "Life is in Moscow."[14]

But so was death. Nâzım's objections notwithstanding, the four had no choice in the matter. They bade farewell to Ahmet Cevat and were soon on their way to camp.

## Camp Life

On the ride down to Udel'naia, the four friends were impressed by the contrast between Moscow and its surrounding countryside. Their camp was located deep within what Şevket described as an "infinite forest."[15] The vastness of their physical surroundings was a little intimidating. "If the forests in other countries are pools," wrote Vâlâ years later, "this was a sea."[16] All hailing from urban areas, the four friends had limited experience with such an environment. Riding out to camp in a food provision truck from the local train station, they had initially passed a number of little houses inhabited by locals. Eventually, as the four penetrated deeper into the forest, human dwellings became fewer in number. It was dark and late at night by the time they reached the campsite.[17]

At first they saw no one, not even a light in a window. The camp itself was a modest-looking enterprise. There were a few tents scattered about and some wooden sheds, but no people around. It felt like the camp had been abandoned just before the four friends had arrived. Where was everybody?

Then, in the distance, they saw a light, and began to perceive snippets of voices. Approaching on foot, the four friends heard more and more of what sounded like an indeterminate number of young people carrying on several—no, dozens—of conversations simultaneously. They came to a clearing in the woods, and there they saw groups of women and men, perhaps a hundred or so in all, sitting around a crackling bonfire.

Everywhere one turned, it seemed, a different scene was being acted out. Şevket watched as a baby-faced shirtless man launched into a heated denunciation of the English Workers' Party. Nâzım sat down to join a group that was chatting by the fire. Young people sang Tatar folk melodies from somewhere deeper in the forest. Someone, out in the darkness, was strumming a mandolin.[18]

It turned out that life at a Soviet summer camp wasn't so bad, after all. Udel'naia introduced the four friends to many novel experiences. Nâzım and Vâlâ took on jobs the likes of which they had never before held, such as cutting wood, preparing food

---

[13] Vâ-Nû, *Bu Dünyadan Nâzım Geçti*, 335–336.      [14] Ibid., 318.

[15] Aydemir, *Suyu Arayan Adam*, 210.      [16] Vâ-Nû, *Bu Dünyadan Nâzım Geçti*, 336.

[17] On Udel'naia, also see Sülker, *Nâzım Hikmet'in Gerçek Yaşamı*, vol. 1, 136–137; Göksu and Timms, *Romantic Communist*, 40–41.

[18] Aydemir, *Suyu Arayan Adam*, 200.

for their fellow campers, and helping to look after the homeless street children who had been adopted by the camp. They worked hard to improve their language skills as well, with Vâlâ later writing that "with all of our strength we began studying Russian."[19] According to an account later written by Ahmet Cevat Emre, Nâzım and Vâlâ also experienced their first Russian-language romances at Udel'naia. In Ahmet Cevat's recollection, two sisters, bearing the names Sofia and Grunya, shared a small cottage not far from the camp. Nâzım, recalled Ahmet Cevat, became Sofia's lover, while Vâlâ spent his nights with Grunya.[20]

Almost every day, Nâzım, Vâlâ, and Şevket would take long hikes through the woods, with Şevket later recalling that his first lesson in the forest involved learning which plants and roots were edible. For these urbanites, the camp's rustic setting constituted a dazzling experience. "It felt," wrote Şevket later, "like we were the first people ever to lay eyes upon the green fields, blue lakes, and little rivers that we encountered." After a while, the three began camping out together overnight, talking late into the evening about the experiences of their young lives.[21]

At the end of summer, the camp at Udel'naia dispersed and the four friends made their way back to Moscow and KUTV. The administrators at the university had used the past couple of months to make improvements to the campus and its classrooms. Şevket Süreyya, who had been quite skeptical of the university's facilities when he had first arrived in Moscow, was pleasantly surprised by how much better the place looked now. "We found that the school had changed considerably," he later wrote. "The building had been cleaned up and repaired. The old jam jars that had served as teacups in the cafeteria had been removed, and on the tables there were now forks, spoons, and plates."[22] All things considered, he concluded, it was not a bad start.

## Communist University

What kind of school was Communist University of the Toilers of the East? Located on Mokhovaia Street, just a fifteen-minute walk from the Hotel Luxe in central Moscow, KUTV had opened its doors in the spring of 1921.[23] The school was one of a series of internationally focused institutions established in Moscow and elsewhere in the USSR in the 1920s. In addition to KUTV, these schools included: Communist University of the National Minorities of the West (or "KUNMZ," which also opened in 1921), Sun Yat-sen Communist University (1925), and the International Lenin School (1926).[24]

---

[19] Vâ-Nû, *Bu Dünyadan Nâzım Geçti*, 336–337.

[20] Ahmet Cevat, whose account is reprinted in Sülker, refers to Sofia by her first name and patronymic, "Sofia Is'hakovna." Sülker, *Nâzım Hikmet'in Gerçek Yaşamı*, vol. 1, 136. Vâ-Nû, meanwhile, refers to a certain "Sofia İsk" as a later acquaintance of theirs in Moscow. Vâ-Nû, *Bu Dünyadan Nâzım Geçti*, 375; Göksu and Timms, *Romantic Communist*, 41.

[21] Aydemir, *Suyu Arayan Adam*, 201–203.    [22] Ibid., 214.

[23] On the early set-up of KUTV and its leading officials, see Heather Winter Ashby, "Third World Activists and the Communist University of the Toilers of the East," Dissertation, University of Southern California, 2014, 65–78.

[24] On KUTV, also see Irina Filatova, "Indoctrination or Scholarship? Education of Africans at the Communist University of the Toilers of the East in the Soviet Union, 1923–1937," *Paedagogica Historica*, vol. 35, no. 1 (1999),

The organization of the "eastern" KUTV and the "western" KUNMZ fell under the purview of the Comintern. Formally established in 1919, the Comintern was a Moscow-based institution that played a critical role in international communist organization.[25] Starting in pre-revolutionary times, there had been a series of meetings, dubbed "communist internationals," that had brought together communists from various countries. Following the Bolshevik takeover in Russia, the Comintern was transformed into a more permanent institution responsible for maintaining connections between Moscow and Communist Party organizations in other countries.[26]

The Comintern was also involved in more quotidian tasks relating to the daily lives of international communists living in the USSR. Staff from the Comintern could help, for example, if a foreign communist needed assistance finding accommodation or employment. Until its dissolution in 1943, the Comintern employed thousands of individuals. During the organization's bureaucratic heyday in the early 1930s, more than 500 people worked for the Comintern in Moscow alone.[27]

Why create two separate universities for "eastern" (KUTV) and "western" (KUNMZ) students? The reasoning behind this division was both theoretical and practical. In theoretical terms, the splitting of the world into "western" and "eastern" populations was a very old practice, in Russia and elsewhere, one that had survived into the Soviet era.[28] Easterners and westerners came from separate civilizations and learned differently, it was believed, so why not offer them separate educations?[29]

There were also more practical reasons behind this institutional division. The Bolsheviks viewed the types of issues facing revolutionaries in the East and West as distinct from one another. "Western" communists, they reasoned, were more likely to come from industrialized societies that were considered ripe for communist revolution due to their more advanced stage of economic and social development. "Eastern" communists, on the other hand, more frequently came from colonized

---

41–66, here 44; Lana Ravandi-Fadai, "'Red Mecca'—The Communist University for Laborers of the East (KUTV): Iranian Scholars and Students in Moscow in the 1920s and 1930s," *Iranian Studies*, vol. 48, no. 5 (2015), 713–727; Kirasirova, "The Eastern International"; Kirasirova, "The East as a Category of Bolshevik Ideology and Comintern Administration"; Ashby, "Third World Activists and the Communist University of the Toilers of the East"; Meyer, "Children of Trans-Empire," 198, 208–217. On the International Lenin School, see Studer, *Transnational World of the Cominternians*, 23, 34, 36, 42, 53, 64, 77, 79–80, 91, 98–124, 133, 139. On Sun Yat-sen University, see Miin-ling Yu, "Sun Yat-sen University in Moscow, 1925–1930," PhD dissertation, New York University, 1995; McGuire, *Red at Heart*, 116–135. On KUTV from a literary-cultural perspective, see Katerina Clark, *Eurasia Without Borders: The Dream of a Leftist Literary Commons, 1919–1943* (Cambridge, MA: The Belknap Press of Harvard University Press, 2021), 59–64.

[25] On the establishment of the Comintern, see Studer, *Transnational World of the Cominternians*, 22–23.

[26] I use the term "communist internationals" to refer to people. The most important new study on the Comintern is Studer's *Transnational World of the Cominternians*. For more traditional studies on the Comintern as an international institution, see Carr, *Twilight of the Comintern*; Drachkovitch and Lazic, *The Comintern*; McKenzie, *Comintern and World Revolution*; McDermott and Agnew, *The Comintern*; Hallas, *The Comintern*.

[27] Studer, *Transnational World of the Cominternians*, 25. The Comintern also ran the Hotel Luxe, which employed, as of 1924, 73 staff and administrative personnel. "Report," RGASPI, f. 495, op. 18, d. 331, l. 40.

[28] On the conceptual division of the world into "eastern" and "western" socio-cultural spheres, see Edward Said's classic volume *Orientalism* (New York: Vintage Books, 1979).

[29] On the creation of a Soviet "east," see Terry Martin, *The Affirmative Action Empire* (Ithaca, NY: Cornell University Press, 2001), 126–129; Kirasirova, "The Eastern International"; Kirasirova, "The 'East' as a Category of Bolshevik Ideology."

populations, where anti-imperialism and agricultural questions were considered to be of more practical benefit for revolutionary training.[30] Segregated national populations of communists studied at different universities in Moscow, with African Americans and black South Africans attending the "eastern" KUTV, whereas their white co-nationals enrolled at other schools.[31]

KUNMZ was primarily responsible for working with foreign students from the USSR's "near-abroad," countries on the western borderlands which had gained their independence from Russia following the revolutions of 1917.[32] Originally, KUNMZ was supposed to consist of departments teaching in nine languages, four of which—Latvian, Estonian, Lithuanian, and Polish—were spoken in countries which had, until recently, been part of the Russian Empire. The other five anticipated languages of instruction at KUNMZ were German, "Jewish" (Yiddish), Hungarian, "Yugoslavian" (Serbo-Croatian), and Czech. The last three of these, which were all spoken primarily in regions that had never been a part of Russia, were later scrapped in favor of Finnish and Romanian, two languages which were spoken in former Russian imperial territories.[33] The goal, here and elsewhere, was to employ KUNMZ as a means of making contact with young communists from regions of the former Russian Empire that had not (yet) been re-incorporated into the Soviet Union.

KUTV and KUNMZ were not exclusively, or even predominantly, populated by foreign students. In the 1920s, the total number of students enrolled at KUTV and KUNMZ typically ranged between 600 and 1,000 per university.[34] Internal documents at KUNMZ routinely referred to the university's students as hailing from both "the western regions of the RSFSR" and "the west" more generally.[35] "[I]n some sectors," one report noted, "students coming from abroad make up the majority" of the overall number of enrollees, an indication that in the other sectors Soviet students outnumbered their foreign classmates.[36]

In a similar manner, KUTV was home to both Soviet and foreign students, with the numbers in the "Foreign Group" (*ingruppa*) at KUTV usually ranging between 200

---

[30] See Filatova, "Indoctrination or Scholarship?," 44.

[31] On African Americans and black Africans at KUTV, see Woodford McClellan, "Africans and Black Americans in the Comintern Schools, 1925–1934," *The International Journal of African Historical Studies*, vol. 26, no. 2 (1993), 371–390; Aitken, "From Cameroon to Germany and Back via Moscow and Paris."

[32] On KUNMZ, see Studer, *Transnational World of the Cominternians*, 30, 42, 64, 66–67, 90–107, 113, 120, 129–130, 139; Zev Katz, "Party-Political Education in Soviet Russia 1918–1935," *Soviet Studies*, vol. 7, no. 3 (1956), 237–247; Michael David Fox, *Revolution of the Mind: Higher Learning among the Bolsheviks, 1918–1929* (Ithaca, NY: Cornell University Press, 1999), 61–62.

[33] Finland was a former territory of Russia, and Romania had recently gained a significant share of Russian imperial territory, Bessarabia, parts of which would be re-incorporated into the USSR after World War II.

[34] Kirasirova notes that there were 622 students at KUTV at the end of its first year. "The 'East' as a Category of Bolshevik Ideology," 14. Ravandi-Fadai cites RGASPI sources indicating a "total number of students" of 713 in 1921, 930 in 1922, and 1,015 in 1924, "'Red Mecca'," 720. At KUNMZ, there were 800 at the Moscow branch, and 315 at a separate KUNMZ branch in Leningrad. RGASPI, f. 529, op. 1, d. 19, l. 2. "Bulletin from the First Semester."

[35] The RSFSR was the Russian Soviet Federative Socialist Republic, i.e. the Russian union republic inside the USSR.

[36] See correspondence from Vice-Rector, KUNMZ. RGASPI, f. 529, op. 1, d. 3, l. 36. June 10, 1922. On the experiences of Chinese students at KUTV, also see McGuire, *Red at Heart*, 67–88.

and 300 per year.[37] However, not all of the students listed in these reports were necessarily in Moscow, or even the Soviet Union. In December 1924, for example, out of a total number of 294 KUTV Foreign Group students, thirty-two Turks were counted. Only sixteen of these students, however, were actually living within the borders of the USSR at the time.[38]

When Nâzım and his friends arrived in Moscow, there was not yet a Turkish sector at KUTV. Five language sectors were then available: Russian, French, English, Chinese, and Korean, with Nâzım and Vâlâ opting to study in the French one.[39] In the 1924–25 academic year, KUTV opened several new sectors, including one for Turkish, alongside Greek, Malayan, Japanese, and Persian.[40] From this point forward, there were usually between ten and fifteen Turkish students on campus at KUTV at any given time.[41]

A typical course of study at KUTV or KUNMZ usually lasted about two years, with students receiving an education in subjects both theoretical and applied.[42] Nâzım's university papers indicate that he took courses on Leninism and Historical Materialism, in addition to more traditional ones like Geography, Geology, Physics, and Chemistry.[43] Life at KUTV was not all work and no play, however. Students were taken on a variety of excursions in and around Moscow, visiting factories, the Ethnographical Museum, the zoo, and other sites.[44]

No one received letter or numerical grades. Rather, students were provided with performance evaluations. A short note, often just a word like "good," "average," or "weak," was typically written directly onto the student's file, next to a list of classes taken. At the end of the semester, students received party references (*kharakteristiki*) that were one to three sentences in length. A good reference would say something like "an active, disciplined, and fully mature comrade. Mastered coursework in a fully

[37] In a report dated December 1, 1924, a total of 292 students from the Foreign Group are listed. RGASPI, f. 532, op. 1, d. 12, l. 25. "List of Students in the Foreign Group." In June 1926, there were 260 students in the Foreign Group. RGASPI, f. 532, op. 1, d. 44, l. 4. "Composition of the Foreign Group by Nationality," June 15, 1926. In March 1927, there were 289 students in the Foreign Group. RGASPI, f. 532, op. 1, d. 44, l. 2. "Composition of the Foreign Group," which also listed one "Amerikanets."

[38] RGASPI, f. 532, op. 1, d. 12, ll. 44–52, here l. 53. "List of students from the KUTV foreign group," December 15, 1924. On the early organization of students at KUTV, also see Ashby, "Third World Activists and the Communist University of the Toilers of the East," 84–89.

[39] Vâ-Nû, *Bu Dünyadan Nâzım Geçti*, 344.

[40] See the sector-by-sector breakdown of students for February 1925, RGASPI, f. 532, op. 1, d. 25, l. 5. "List of cells in the foreign group by nationality, February 1925." Greece was considered part of the "East" at this time.

[41] In the spring of 1925, there were discussions to accept 12–15 Turks for the upcoming school year. RGASPI, f. 532, op. 1, d. 21, ll. 6, 45. "Recommended composition of students for the upcoming year," April 24, 1925. As of January 1, 1927, 12 students enrolled in the program were Turks. RGASPI, f. 532, op. 1, d. 44, l. 1. "Information on students in the foreign group of KUTV," January 1927. For the 1926–27 school year, there was an allotment for a total of 20 Turkish students at KUTV, 12 of whom would be in the first year of the program. RGASPI, f. 17, op. 3, d. 653, l. 145. In October 1931, there were 13 Turkish students at KUTV. RGASPI, f. 532, op. 1, d. 455, l. 1. "List of Turkish students," October 15, 1921.

[42] Some stayed longer, or else began working as teachers, and there was also a graduate program. Filatova writes that the "normal course" was 20 months. "Indoctrination or Scholarship?," 47.

[43] For Nâzım's courses, see RGASPI, f. 495, op. 266, d. 47, Part I, l. 150-ob. On coursework at KUTV more generally, see Ashby, "Third World Activists and the Communist University of the Toilers of the East," 93–95.

[44] RGASPI, f. 532, op. 1, d. 5, l. 38. Report from the "Department of Excursions," KUTV, undated but likely produced in 1924.

satisfactory manner." A less enthusiastic one stated "Not very mature with respect to party-oriented relations toward comrades," or "immature party member, not very active."[45]

The material conditions associated with studying in Moscow at this time could be challenging. Breakfast usually consisted of little more than "boiling water, perhaps with a little sugar," and later in the day students were provided small allotments of potatoes, soup, and occasionally "a tiny piece of meat or dried fish."[46] In early 1928, the African Americans Carl Jones and Roy Farmer complained to KUTV authorities about worms in the dessert they'd been given in the cafeteria. Jones and Farmer also bemoaned the state of the school's "stinking" toilets, which, they noted, were "deplorable beyond description and a menace to the general health of the student body."[47]

In 1927, KUTV created a special division, the *Spetsgruppa*. This section of the university, unlike others at KUTV, was reserved specifically for "highly qualified party workers" interested in learning how "to apply in practice the methods of Marxism-Leninism in the revolutionary struggle."[48] Those who completed this training were sent back to their home country pseudonymously to work underground for the party.[49]

Most of the individuals studying at KUTV did not, however, go into such cloak-and-dagger careers. Many, in fact, would end up staying in the Soviet Union, where they found jobs, settled down, and often became Soviet citizens. Turkish alumni of KUTV who remained in the USSR after graduation were usually sent to areas of the country with Turkic-Muslim populations, such as the Volga-Ural region, Central Asia, and, especially, Azerbaijan. Students who were considered promising were groomed by university and Comintern officials to enter leadership positions within their national parties.

This was what the TKP had in mind for Nâzım and his friends.

## Children of Trans-Empire

Who were Nâzım's classmates at KUTV, and how had they ended up at the university? Nâzım's fellow Turks at KUTV had typically arrived in Moscow via one of three main

---

[45] RGASPI, f. 532, op. 1, d. 40, l. 5. "Protocol," May 14, 1927.

[46] McGuire, *Red at Heart*, 67.

[47] RGASPI, f. 532, op. 1, d. 67, l. 10. Letter of complaint from Carl Jones and Roy Farmer, January 1928. "Logical and reasonable complaints compiled and presented by students of House 15A of KUTV—also a number of suggestions regarded helpful." Also see RGASPI, f. 495, op. 30, d. 539, l. 9, in which Jones and Farmer note the "poorly heated rooms" in their dormitory; Kirasirova, "The Eastern International," 134–135.

[48] RGASPI, f. 495, op. 30, d. 539, l. 25. "Conditions for admission to the special sector of KUTV," June 12, 1928; f. 495, op. 18, d. 607, l. 33. Also see RGASPI, f. 532, op. 1, d. 65, ll. 10, 14.

[49] In the 1930s, students in the *Spetsgruppa* were employing aliases, whereas those in other sectors tended to use their own names. See the list of Turkish students, with separate columns for their real names and their KUTV names, from November 20, 1932. RGASPI, f. 532, op. 1, d. 455, l. 3. "List of students."

channels. Interestingly, all three were based primarily upon connections with Russia that had preceded the October Revolution.[50]

The largest cohort of Turks at KUTV was made up of former Ottoman soldiers, almost all of whom were ex-POWs who had been held at prison camps in Russia during World War I. Repatriating Ottoman POWs had been important enough for the Ottoman government to send Yusuf Akçura across central Europe and Russia in 1917–18, and the Bolsheviks likewise placed considerable value upon these individuals. Rather than return to Anatolia, many Ottoman POWs had ended up in Baku, where they joined the TKP of Mustafa Suphi. Following the murders of Suphi and the rest of the TKP Central Committee in January 1921, these ex-POWs began making their way to Moscow to study at KUTV.

A fairly typical case was that of Fahri Reşid (Figure 5.2). A former soldier who began serving in the Ottoman Army in 1916, Fahri was later captured and imprisoned in Russia. Upon being freed by the Bolsheviks, he joined the Red Army and took part in the invasion of the Caucasus.[51] Once the fighting was over, Fahri became a member of Mustafa Suphi's TKP in Baku. He worked the POW camps as an agitator, giving speeches on behalf of the Bolsheviks in an effort to convince other ex-Ottoman soldiers to sign up with the TKP.[52] In 1922, Fahri Reşid arrived at KUTV, joining a large contingent of former Ottoman POWs at the school.[53]

**Figure 5.2** Fahri Reşid prior to and during his studies in Moscow

---

[50] Meyer, "Children of Trans-Empire," 211–214.
[51] Fahri had fought against Denikin's army as part of his Red Army experience. RGASPI, f. 495, op. 266, d. 136, ll. 1, 3, 6. Personal file of Fahri Reşid.
[52] RGASPI, f. 495, op. 266, d. 136, ll. 4–6. Also see f. 495, op. 266, d. 320B, ll. 153–154.
[53] Some of the other former officers, soldiers, and POWs at KUTV included: İbrahim Ahmetov, RGASPI, f. 495, op. 266, d. 130, ll. 6, 10; Mehmet Baytarzade, f. 495, op. 266, d. 64; Ahmet Ziya, RGASPI, f. 495, op. 266, d. 129. Also see files of Hasan İspirzade, RGASPI, f. 495, op. 266, d. 320B, ll. 125–126; Nadzhiev Masrur, RGASPI, f. 495, op. 266, d. 131; Süleyman Nuri, RGASPI, f. 495, op. 266, d. 117; Ali Hüsrev Tekin, RGASPI, f. 495, op. 266, d. 156, l. 8; Niyazi Ethem, RGASPI, f. 495, op. 266, d. 137; Nihat Nusret Mustafa, RGASPI, f. 495, op. 266, d. 240, l. 9; Yahya Muhammedov, RGASPI, f. 495, op. 266, d. 145; Reşid Şadi, RGASPI, f. 495, op. 266, d. 169; RGASPI, f. 495, op. 266, d. 28, personal file of Halil Mehmedoğlu, who fought in the Ottoman Army between 1914 and 1920,

Noureddin Kadirov was not an ex-POW, but rather an Ottoman deserter with a checkered past. He was born in 1899 in Bursa and orphaned at a young age. When he was thirteen, Noureddin had accidentally shot and killed one of his classmates when playing with his uncle's gun, but owing to his young age he had spent just two months in prison. In 1916 Noureddin was drafted into the Ottoman Army. Three years later, while posted to Kars, he deserted. Noureddin first headed to Batumi in search of work, then traveled to Baku before returning to Batumi, where he was arrested by Georgian authorities. Noureddin was then liberated by the Bolsheviks when they took Batumi in March 1921, and it was at this time that he signed up with them. In 1922, Noureddin arrived in Moscow to study at KUTV. [54]

While there were numerous ex-soldiers among the ranks of Turkish students at KUTV in the early years, most of them did not stay long. Trapped in the chaos of civil war-era Russia with no means of their own to get back home, many of these individuals had joined the TKP primarily as a means of survival. Although a few would stay on and live out their lives in the USSR, the great majority of the ex-POWs disappeared from KUTV's classrolls once the fighting had ceased in Anatolia and the Republic of Turkey was created in October 1923.

Another commonly seen trait among TKP students at KUTV was a family background in the Ottoman borderlands. This was particularly the case with respect to the eastern borderlands of the Ottoman Empire, such as the Black Sea cities of Trabzon and Rize, which were in close proximity to the Russian frontier. During the final decades of empire, it had been common for individuals living on one side of the border to have family members or a job on the other. Crossing the frontier for periods both short and long was not an unusual experience.[55]

One individual with a background of this sort was Trabzon-born Ali Yazıcı. "Due to some kind of conflict," explained a later report written by Şefik Hüsnü, Yazıcı "was obliged to escape" to Russia prior to the outbreak of World War I—and there he had stayed. After the war ended, Yazıcı signed up with Mustafa Suphi's Turkish communists, becoming a party member in Baku in 1920. Two years after that, Yazıcı made his way to Moscow to begin his studies at KUTV.[56]

Fırıncı Ahmet ("Ahmet the Baker") was born in 1901 in a village outside Hopa, about twenty miles south of Batumi. At the time of Ahmet's birth, Hopa was part of the Russian Empire. With the region scheduled to be turned over to Kemal's Ankara government, however, Ahmet had, in 1921, relocated north to Sukhumi, Abkhazia, where he began working with an uncle. In 1923, the Baker returned to Hopa, which by this time had become part of Turkey, and shortly thereafter he was conscripted into the Turkish Army. Following his discharge from the service in 1925, Ahmet once

---

and would stay on in the USSR after that, although he would not begin studying at KUTV until 1937. Also see Meyer, "Children of Trans-Empire," 211–212.

[54] RGASPI, f. 495, op. 266, d. 76, ll. 30–32. Personal file of Noureddin Kadirov.

[55] This form of "immigration and return" had hardly been uncommon on the Russian–Ottoman frontier of the late nineteenth and early twentieth centuries. See Meyer, "Immigration, Return, and the Politics of Citizenship," 21–26; Meyer, *Turks Across Empires*, 21–34.

[56] RGASPI, f. 495, op. 266, d. 72, ll. 1–2. Personal file of Ali Yazıcı.

more moved to the USSR, where he again worked for some time in Sukhumi. He then returned to Turkey, this time moving to Istanbul and finding employment in a café in the district of Ortaköy. In 1926, Ahmet the Baker joined the TKP, which sent him once again back to Russia the following year to study in Moscow.[57] While Ahmet's path to Moscow might seem a rather circuitous one, numerous other individuals had similarly spent their early lives traversing the Russian–Ottoman frontier in this way before moving on to KUTV.[58]

There were also quite a few TKP members at KUTV who hailed from the western borderlands of the Ottoman Empire. Nâzım and his friends were all in this category, having grown up in Salonica and Istanbul (Nâzım and Vâlâ), Edirne (Şevket Süreyya), Crete (Ahmet Cevat), and İzmir (Leman). While there were not as many TKP members from the western borderlands as from the Russian–Ottoman frontier region to the east, both borderland areas contributed far more TKP members to KUTV than did interior regions like central and eastern Anatolia.[59]

A third characteristic that was frequently seen in the backgrounds of early TKP members at KUTV was a personal family history of migrating from Russia to the Ottoman Empire. This was particularly the case among Crimean Tatars. Many Crimean Tatars had, in the late nineteenth and early twentieth centuries, left the Crimea for the Ottoman Empire, only to return to their homeland later on as either Ottoman or Russian subjects—or sometimes even both.[60] Whereas this form of return migration had come to an end with the outbreak of World War I, in the early 1920s a new generation of Ottoman-born Crimean Tatar offspring, whose parents had left Russia for the Ottoman Empire years earlier, was now "returning," as communists, to a Russia they had never before seen.

The "return" to Soviet Russia of Ottoman-born Crimean Tatars was a move that at least some individuals within the early Bolshevik state supported. Officials in Moscow had instructed, in late September 1922, that local party directors in the Crimea should "not delay the long-term repatriation of Crimean Tatars who are Turkish citizens" back into the Crimea.[61] During these years immediately following the revolution, the border was open and foreigners were welcome in the USSR.

---

[57] RGASPI, f. 495, op. 266, d. 37, ll. 18–19. Personal file of Ahmet Fırıncı.

[58] Some of the other TKP members at KUTV from the Russian–Ottoman borderlands included: Zeki Baştımar, İsmail Bilen, Hüseyin Kara Ahmedoğlu (Trabzon), RGASPI, f. 495, op. 266, d. 78; Mahmut Şevket (Trabzon), RGASPI, f. 495, op. 266, d. 111, l. 1-ob; Hamdi Şamilov (Trabzon); RGASPI, f. 495, op. 266, d. 150; Abdullah İsa (Trabzon), RGASPI, f. 495, op. 266, d. 320b, ll. 2–5; Hasan İspirzade (Trabzon), RGASPI, f. 495, op. 266, d. 320b, ll. 125–126; Tahsin Kulağazade (Trabzon), RGASPI, f. 495, op. 266, d. 320b, ll. 147–148-ob; Şükrü Martel (Rize), RGASPI, f. 495, op. 266, d. 80; Kara Mehmet (Rize), RGASPI, f. 495, op. 266, d. 78; Sabri Dervişev (Rize), RGASPI, f. 495, op. 266, d. 99; Safet (Trabzon), RGASPI, f. 495, op. 266, d. 132.

[59] Some of the other TKP members at KUTV from the Ottoman Empire's western borderlands included: Nihat Nuri "the Electrician" (Edirne), RGASPI, f. 495, op. 266, d. 86, l. 3; Mahir ("not far from Shipka," Bulgaria), f. 495, op. 266, d. 82, ll. 19, 24; Mehmet Şevket (Edirne), f. 495, op. 266, d. 83; Hamid Ahmed (Dedeağaç, today's Alexandroupolis), RGASPI, f. 495, op. 266, d. 179; Fakhrov (Manastır, today's Bitola), f. 495, op. 266, d. 156, l. 157; Faruk Kafadar (origins unknown, speaker of Turkish and Bulgarian), f. 495, op. 266, d. 77, ll. 1–2.

[60] This phenomenon is discussed in detail in Meyer, *Turks Across Empires*, 30–34. Also see Meyer, "Immigration, Return, and the Politics of Citizenship."

[61] RGASPI, f. 17, op. 3, d. 314, resolution by Lev Karakhan, September 28, 1922.

This was a policy toward the frontier that attracted people like İbrahim Krimskii. A Crimean Tatar born in Varna, Bulgaria, the 20-year-old Krimskii had made his way from Varna to the Crimea, and then to Moscow, following the conclusion of World War I.[62] İbrahim's tenure at KUTV would be marked by his repeated efforts, during the years 1923–25, to obtain permission to relocate to the Crimea for purposes relating to both work and rest.[63] At KUTV, İbrahim would encounter several other Ottoman-born Crimean Tatars who had similarly come "home" to the Soviet Union during these years.[64]

At a time when men far outnumbered women at the university more generally, there were several Ottoman-born Crimean Tatar women studying at KUTV in the 1920s.[65] The Crimean Tatar Cemile Nevşirvanova, whom Nâzım and Vâlâ had first met at the Orient Hotel in Tbilisi, began studying at KUTV at the same time as Nâzım and Vâlâ. She had come with her husband Zinetullah, who was also studying at the university. Cemile's goal, at least insofar as she explained it in her student paperwork, was to promote "revolution among the women of the east."[66] Her younger sister Rahime also came to Moscow at this time, noting in her KUTV paperwork that she wished to "participate in the women's movement."[67]

Aynühayat Voinova was another Crimean Tatar who, as she stated on her KUTV registration forms, was "born in Turkey." She too had been part of Ahmet Cevat's retinue at the Hotel Orient, where she had first met Nâzım and Vâlâ.[68] At age thirty-nine, Aynühayat was without question one of the oldest students at KUTV, and surely stood out as part of a class that was overwhelmingly male and in their early twenties.[69] Like many other Crimean Tatars, Aynühayat had made her way "back" to her ancestral homeland via communism. She had initially found work in the Crimea as an instructor in the *zhenotdel*, the branch of the Communist Party responsible for recruiting women to the ranks of the Bolsheviks.[70] In 1923, she left for Moscow to begin her studies at KUTV.[71]

Also studying at KUTV at this time was Fevziye Habibova, who was born in Istanbul in 1900 (Figure 5.3). Habibova may or may not have been a Crimean Tatar,

---

[62] Personal file of İbrahim Krimskii. RGASPI, f. 495, op. 266, d. 320B, assorted personal files, ll. 127–131.

[63] When he was in the Crimea, İbrahim sought to be allowed to stay there. RGASPI, f. 495, op. 266, d. 320B, ll. 133, 134–135, 138–139, 142, 144–146. Personal file of İbrahim Krimskii.

[64] Some of the other Crimean Tatars at KUTV included Hüsni, RGASPI, f. 495, op. 266, d. 174, ll. 15, 20; Süleyman Şevki, RGASPI, f. 495, op. 266, d. 320B, ll. 155–156-ob; Zeki Ahmet, RGASPI, f. 495, op. 266, d. 320B, assorted personal files, ll. 103–104-ob. Also see Meyer, "Children of Trans-Empire," esp. 213–215.

[65] For example, of the 292 students enrolled in the university's Foreign Group in December 1925, just fourteen were women. RGASPI, f. 532, op. 1, d. 12, l. 25. On women in the Comintern more generally, see Studer, *Transnational World of the Cominternians*, 40–58.

[66] Personal file of Cemile Nevşirvanova, RGASPI, f. 495, op. 266, d. 88. Also see Akbulut (ed.), *Milli Azadlık Savaşı Anıları*, 95–102.

[67] RGASPI, f. 495, op. 266, d. 134. Personal file of Rahime Hakkı.

[68] Vâ-Nû, *Bu Dünyadan Nâzım Geçti*, 242.

[69] Of the 292 students enrolled in the foreign group at KUTV in December 1924, only 18 were older than thirty, whereas 165 were between the ages of twenty-one and twenty-five. RGASPI, f. 532, op. 1, d. 12, l. 25.

[70] RGASPI, f. 495, op. 266, d. 320b, ll. 90–102, esp. ll. 90–95-ob; 99–102; also see RGASPI, f. 532, op. 2, 164, l. 15-ob. Personal files of Aynühayat Voinova.

[71] According to Vâlâ, he and Nâzım had met a woman named Aynühayat who had been "somebody's wife," and had been part of the group that the boys had first met at the Orient. Vâ-Nû, *Bu Dünyadan Nâzım Geçti*, 242.

**Figure 5.3** Fevziye Habibova

but she does appear to have been of Russian Muslim origins.[72] After attending a teacher-training college during the British occupation, Fevziye had set out for Ankara to volunteer for Mustafa Kemal's forces. She had, according to her Comintern file, worked for some time as a nurse in the war against the Greeks.[73] In Ankara, Fevziye had become involved in the TKP, and in 1922 she had left for Moscow on the recommendation of the party.

At around the beginning of April 1924, she became pregnant—party paperwork from December of that year indicates that Fevziye was drawing rations in accordance with her eighth month of pregnancy. In March 1925, Fevziye died in a Moscow hospital. No cause of death is listed, nor is there any indication of what happened to her child.[74]

Not all of the TKP "returnees" at KUTV were of Turkic-Muslim origins. Alexander Senkevich was the grandson of a Polish soldier—and Russian subject—who had reportedly received sanctuary in the Ottoman Empire after killing a tsarist officer (Figure 5.4).[75] Alexander's grandfather had then settled in Istanbul, where he would later marry an Ottoman Greek woman. Their son, Alexander's father, received Russian subjecthood as a youth through his father.[76]

---

[72] Habibova's student registration forms indicate that she could speak, read, and write Russian upon first arriving at the university. She identified her Istanbul-based father's surname as "Habibov." RGASPI, f. 495, op. 266, d. 135, l. 3-ob. Personal file of Fevziye Habibova.

[73] RGASPI, f. 495, op. 266, d. 135, l. 3-ob.

[74] RGASPI, f. 495, op. 266, d. 135, l. 17. Also see the collection of personal files, RGASPI, f. 495, op. 266, d. 320b, ll. 157–158-ob.

[75] During the Russian-Ottoman war of 1877–78. See Alexander Senkevich's party autobiography. Alexander Senkevich personal file, RGASPI, f. 495, op. 266, d. 118, l. 134.

[76] The practice of the Russian imperial government of distributing Russian passports to subjects of the Ottoman Empire was part of a policy in St. Petersburg to establish direct diplomatic connections with people residing in the Ottoman Empire. See Meyer, *Turks Across Empires*, 34–35; Can, *Spiritual Subjects*, 97–98. This approach to foreign policymaking can also be seen in more recent cases of the Russian Federation distributing passports to citizens of Ukraine and Georgia. See Eric Lohr, "What Can Passports Tell Us about Putin's Intentions?," *The Washington Post*, March 4, 2014.

**Figure 5.4** Alexander Senkevich

Born in 1907 in the Istanbul suburb of San Stefano, Alexander was similarly a subject of both the Russian and Ottoman empires. He had also benefited from the free education which he was eligible to receive, by dint of his Russian subjecthood, at the Russian School of Istanbul. Classes at the school came to an end, however, with the outbreak of war between the two empires. Only in 1920 was Alexander able to resume his studies at the school, which was now under the control of anti-communist "White" Russians of Istanbul.

During his time at the Russian school, "Sasha" Senkevich made friends in the Komsomol, a youth-oriented component of the Communist Party. He took to organizing various activities for the group, such as helping to establish their soccer team. Alexander's diligence eventually caught the attention of Şefik Hüsnü and others in the TKP, and in December 1924 Alexander was sent to Moscow, where he began his studies at KUTV in January of the new year.[77]

While it might be tempting to assume that human mobility followed the path of ideology, in many cases the opposite appears to have taken place. Ex-POWs stranded on Russian territory found it practical to join up with the Bolsheviks. So too did individuals who had grown up traveling back and forth between Russia and the Ottoman Empire, or whose parents had previously emigrated from Russia. While their reasons for moving to the USSR were doubtless complex and variegated, it is nevertheless striking how many of these individuals had first arrived in Russia for reasons other

---

[77] RGASPI, f. 495, op. 266, d. 118, ll. 72–76, here 74. Alexander Senkevich party autobiography.

than communism, or else had some sort of connection to Russia that preceded the October Revolution.

In this respect, Nâzım and his friends had something in common with many of their Turkish classmates at KUTV, as their conversion to communism had likewise followed, rather than preceded, their arrival in the USSR. Ahmet Cevat and Şevket Süreyya had arrived in the Caucasus as pan-Turkists, then became communists in the months following the Bolshevik takeover of Azerbaijan. Nâzım and Vâlâ, meanwhile, had been interested in seeing what communism looked like prior to first traveling to Batumi, but had only become communists after the TKP had given them jobs and a place to live.

None of this means that Nâzım, his friends, or the other students at KUTV were not genuine in their embrace of communism, but it does suggest that ideology was not always the determining factor guiding their decisions. For most of the Turks at KUTV, including Nâzım and his friends, geographical re-location had come first, with their shift toward communism taking place only later.[78] The choices that these women and men made were not always ideological ones, even if they were usually articulated in such terms in their party and Comintern paperwork, or in their later memoirs and reminiscences.

## Faces Around Campus

While there was no Turkish sector at KUTV when Nâzım and Vâlâ arrived in 1922, there were plenty of other Turks on campus. Nâzım and his friends knew these individuals from the Hotel Luxe and their classes, as well as through the political discussion groups, or "cells" (*kruzhki*), that were organized at the university according to nationality.[79]

One person at KUTV who would go on to play an important role in the life of Nâzım Hikmet and many other TKP members was İsmail Bilen. Bilen was born in 1902 in the eastern Black Sea city of Rize. When he was six years old, he had moved with his family to the hardscrabble district of Kasımpaşa, Istanbul. At age sixteen, he completed his studies at a technical high school, and for the next four years, until 1922, İsmail had worked as a mechanic in a motorboat factory.

It was during these years that the teenaged İsmail's life would change forever. Some of the mechanics who worked at the factory had begun to talk to their younger colleague about communism. They had spent the war years in Germany, and like the "Germans" who had formed the core of Sadık Ahi's Spartakist crowd, the experiences of İsmail's new friends had turned them on to communism.

---

[78] In a similar manner, the pan-Turkists of the late imperial era had embraced pan-Turkism only after they had arrived in Young Turk-era Istanbul. Meyer, *Turks Across Empires*, 158–161.

[79] Summaries of the Turkish cell meetings involving Nâzım and other Turkish students at KUTV can be found in RGASPI, f. 532, op. 2, d. 165, ll. 2–12; f. 532, op. 2, d. 166; f. 532, op. 2, d. 167.

At the heart of this communist circle at İsmail's factory was a fellow called "Baba Mehmet." Baba Mehmet had been working in Russia when World War I broke out. Arrested as a civilian POW, he had spent the war years in a prison camp. After the Bolshevik takeover in Petrograd he had joined up with the party. According to İsmail's later telling, none other than Mustafa Suphi himself had sent Baba Mehmet back to Turkey to recruit new communists.

Thin-faced and already in possession of a receding hairline, the 20-year-old İsmail joined the TKP in 1922. At first, according to a party autobiography he would write years later, young İsmail had worked mostly as an errand-boy for the party, "delivering literature, taking people around, but mainly working as a courier."[80] His hard work paid off, however, and before long he began to attract the attention of the party leadership. One day, Şefik Hüsnü took İsmail aside and told him that a man by the name of Kalakov was arriving that day from Moscow. Kalakov worked for the Comintern and was looking to recruit young Turks to go study at a university in Russia. Did İsmail want to go?[81]

Just months after officially joining the party, İsmail Bilen was on his way to Moscow. Whereas a university education had not been in the cards for him in Turkey, in the Soviet Union he would thrive. At the end of his first year of studies, İsmail's party report was glowing. He was described as "mature," someone who "behaved like a good Bolshevik. The most active, the best-prepared and strongest member of his group." In short, İsmail was "a great comrade."[82]

His life changed in other ways, too. A few years after İsmail came to Moscow, he married a Turkish communist named Sabiha Mesrure. A photograph from her Comintern file reveals a young woman with wavy, long black hair wearing a necktie held in place by a hammer-and-sickle tie pin. Mesrure was born in Istanbul in 1902 and had come to study at KUTV in 1925. She was, moreover, one of only a handful of Turkish sector students selected to study in the *Spetsgruppa*, and one of very few women overall.[83] Using the code name "Rosa," the trilingual Sabiha Mesrure would return to Turkey to work underground in 1927.[84]

Mehmet Husametdin, aka Aziz, was born in 1902 in the town of Silivri, located on the Marmara Sea to the west of Istanbul.[85] The same age as Nâzım, Vâlâ, and İsmail, Aziz had jet-black hair, bright eyes, and a boyish face. He had headed out to Ankara in 1921 to join the war effort, eventually finding work in a munitions factory. That same year, according to his party paperwork, Aziz became involved in the TKP. After

---

[80] RGASPI, f. 495, op. 266, d. 12, Part I, ll. 117–123, here l. 117. Personal file of İsmail Bilen. "Autobiography," July 16, 1937.

[81] RGASPI, f. 495, op. 266, d. 12, Part I, ll. 117–123, here l. 118. Personal file of İsmail Bilen. "Autobiography," July 16, 1937.

[82] RGASPI, f. 532, op. 2, d. 164, ll. 9–11, here 9. "Meeting of the Turkish Cell." Undated, but likely from late 1924.

[83] RGASPI, f. 495, op. 266, d. 155, ll. 2–6. Personal file of Mesrure.

[84] In addition to knowing Russian (albeit "poorly" in her early days in Moscow) and Turkish (her native language), Mesrure is described as knowing Greek "well." RGASPI, f. 495, op. 266, d. 155, l. 2. Personal file of Sabiha Mesrure, KUTV student questionnaire from April 1925. On her return to Istanbul, also see RGASPI, f. 495, op. 266, d. 118, l. 43.

[85] In Russian-language party records, Aziz is usually referred to as "Azis."

organizing for the party in Adapazarı and İzmir, Aziz was sent in 1924 to KUTV, where he stayed until 1926. Upon completing his studies in Moscow, Aziz returned to Turkey to work for the party.[86]

Also studying at KUTV at this time was Zeki Baştımar. Zeki was born in Trabzon in 1905. At the age of twelve he had gone to Istanbul to study, returning to his hometown in 1922 in order to attend a teacher-training school. Whereas İsmail and Aziz were laborers, working in factories from their teenage years onward, young Zeki was a poet. Writing verse while studying at school, Zeki also began to show an interest in politics, setting up an unofficial communist club at his school. At the end of 1925, Zeki joined the TKP. The following year, he too would head off to Moscow and KUTV.[87]

One of the more well-traveled figures at KUTV during this time was a Turkish language instructor by the name of Muhammad Ağa Shahtakhtinskii. The scion of a wealthy Muslim family from imperial-era Tbilisi, Shahtakhtinskii had studied at the Sorbonne and in Leipzig. Upon returning to the Caucasus after his years of European schooling, Shahtakhtinskii had become, in 1902, the editor of the state-owned *Şark-i Rus* ("the Russian East"), one of the first newspapers in Russia to be published in a Turkic language.[88] In 1906, Shahtakhtinskii was elected to the first Russian Duma.[89]

In the wake of the Stolypin "counter-revolution" that took place in Russia in June 1907, Shahtakhtinskii re-located to the Ottoman capital in the manner of many other Turkic Muslim activists, writers, and intellectuals from Russia. In Young Turk-era Istanbul, however, he became the center of controversy.[90] Having attended several meetings organized by politically minded Russian Muslim students in Istanbul, Shahtakhtinskii was discovered to have sent written reports describing these gatherings to the Russian Embassy. In fact, Shahtakhtinskii's reports emphasized the degree to which the students' meetings were politically harmless to Russian state interests. Nevertheless, he was detained by Ottoman authorities on suspicion of espionage and deported in 1912 back to Russia, where he would spend the war years in Petrograd.[91]

In late 1920, Shahtakhtinskii resurfaced in the Caucasus, and found a place for himself as a Russian-Turkish translator working for the Bolsheviks.[92] There he partnered for some time with Süleyman Nuri, whose correspondence and speeches

---

[86] RGASPI, f. 495, op. 266, d. 3, personal file of Mehmet Husametdin (Aziz), ll. 12–14, 19, 35.

[87] RGASPI, f. 495, op. 266, d. 30, l. 165. Personal file of Zeki Baştımar.

[88] On *Şark-i Rus* also see Alexandre Bennigsen and Chantal Lemercier-Quelquejay, *La Presse et le Mouvement Nationale chez les Musulmans de Russie avant 1920* (Paris: Mouton & Co., 1960), 45.

[89] M. F. Usal, *Birinci, ikinci, ve üçüncü duma'da Müslüman deputatlar* (Kazan: Tipografiia I. N. Kharitonova, 1909), 187.

[90] On Shahtakhtinskii, also see Reynolds, *Shattering Empires*, 92, 94; Meyer, *Turks Across Empires*, 166–167.

[91] Shahtakhtinskii's autobiographical statement to KUTV, written on September 5, 1922, notes that he "wrote for some Russian newspapers in Constantinople" before returning to Russia, where he set up in Petrograd. RGASPI, f. 532, op. 12, d. 5609, l. 6.

[92] In October 1920, Shahtakhtinskii's name first appeared in a translated document See RGASPI, f. 544, op 3, d. 19. l. 16-ob.

Shahtakhtinskii translated into Russian.[93] From the Caucasus, he had then made his way to Moscow, where the nearly 60-year-old Shahtakhtinskii began working, in February 1922, as a language teacher at KUTV.[94]

Not everyone was necessarily cut out for life at the new university. Şükrü Martel was never supposed to have been sent to Moscow in the first place. Born in 1901 in a village outside Mersin, on the Mediterranean coast, Şükrü had bounced around various factory jobs in Ankara and Adana before winding up in İzmir in 1926. There he had made the acquaintance of local communists and began attending TKP meetings. According to a later report by Şefik Hüsnü, Şükrü Martel had been sent to Moscow "by mistake" in late 1926, just one day after he had formally joined the party.[95] By all accounts, Şükrü did not fit in well at the university. Owing to what others described as his "very nervous character" and what Şükrü himself called an "illness," Martel was expelled from KUTV just weeks after matriculating. Nevertheless, he remained in the Soviet Union, where he later found work in a factory.[96]

## Friends, Kinsmen, and Lovers

Nâzım and Vâlâ were well regarded by their instructors at KUTV, and TKP officials were more than satisfied with their progress. In Nâzım's surviving transcripts, he is described as someone who "prepares himself for his work in class and in his discussion group (*kruzhok*), works well, [and] has a talent for literature." Shorter grading forms rate Nâzım's performance as "good," or at the very least "above average."[97]

Vâlâ also received warm feedback from his instructors, who noted that he "works well," and lauded him for his "maturity," "discipline," "seriousness," and "energy." He was, however, described as having never appeared at his classes on "The Agricultural Question" or "Historical Materialism."[98] Nevertheless, alongside Nâzım and İsmail Bilen, Vâlâ was considered one of the top TKP-member students at the university. In his second year at KUTV, Vâlâ found a job in the Comintern—a plum position for an up-and-comer interested in party-oriented office work. He also began teaching classes at the university in October 1922, lecturing to Azeri students.[99] Both Nâzım and Vâlâ joined the TKP officially in 1924.[100]

---

[93] On January 18, 1921, Shahtakhtinskii translated a speech that Süleyman Nuri had allegedly given at the Congress of the Peoples of the East. RGASPI, f. 544, op. 3. d. 46, ll. 63–66, 222–222-ob. He was recorded as the translator of a letter from Süleyman Nuri about Mustafa Suphi, February 18, 1921. RGASPI, f. 544. op. 3. d. 9, ll. 96–102.

[94] According to his KUTV paperwork, Shahtakhtinskii was born on March 21, 1862. RGASPI, f. 532, op. 12, d. 5609, l. 12. As of May 21, 1923, he was still employed at KUTV, but after that his trail goes cold. See ibid., l. 11. "Verification" (*udostoverenie*), May 21, 1923.

[95] "Par suite d'une erreur." See personal file of Şükrü Martel, RGASPI, f. 495, op. 266, d. 80, ll. 6, 22.

[96] RGASPI, f. 495, op. 266, d. 80, l. 22.      [97] RGASPI, f. 495, op. 266, d. 47, Part 1, ll. 150-ob–151.

[98] Vâlâ Nureddin personal file, RGASPI, f. 495, op. 266, d. 152, l. 8-ob.

[99] Vâlâ Nureddin KUTV file, RGASPI, f. 532, op. 12, d. 3576, ll. 1–3.

[100] For Vâlâ's reference and on his working in the Comintern, see RGASPI, f. 532, op. 2, d. 164, l. 9. "Meeting of the Turkish Cell." On Vâlâ joining the Communist Party in 1924, see RGASPI, f. 532, op. 12, d. 3576, l. 6. According to Şefik Hüsnü, Nâzım had been a member of the TKP "since 1924." RGASPI, f. 495, op. 266, d. 47, Part 1, l. 146.

Şevket and Leman also took classes at KUTV.[101] Şevket, who had already studied at a teacher-training school in Edirne, would soon go on to teach at KUTV, serving as an instructor starting at the end of 1923.[102] According to Vâlâ's memoirs, Şevket Süreyya was a popular and respected teacher at the school.[103] Leman, meanwhile, is listed as having been enrolled as a student at the university in 1922–23.[104] In her initial university paperwork, 16-year-old Leman described her future employment plans as likely taking place "in the cultural-educational sector."[105] In Moscow, Şevket and Leman were living at the Hotel Luxe, room 179.[106] Her permanent place of residence is indicated in this paperwork as "City of Batumi, Turkey."[107]

Vâlâ Nureddin would later identify Şevket as the most serious of the three friends with respect to his command of theoretical communism. A war veteran who was now married, Şevket Süreyya was already a grown man. "Nâzım and I," Vâlâ would later record in his account of these times, "both respected Şevket Süreyya very much," noting that their older friend held a certain authority over them.[108] Şevket, meanwhile, was less charitable in his later description of Nâzım, at least insofar as Nâzım's understanding of communism was concerned. In his reminiscences from the late 1950s, Şevket would observe that Nâzım preferred the thrill of revolution to more practical matters relating to organization.

Nâzım, in Şevket Süreyya's estimation, was not above grandstanding politically before having considered an issue. He could also be quite insulting, remembered Şevket, who claimed that Nâzım had referred to him as a "peasant." "Yes, a peasant," Nâzım had allegedly said, "and what, after all, is the peasant class? A relic from the Middle Ages. A static, frozen presence, tied to the land. A brake on all revolution."[109]

Nâzım, Vâlâ, and Şevket usually preferred the company of fellow literary-minded intellectual types to hanging out with the other Turks at KUTV.[110] One of Nâzım's new friends at the university was a student from China named Emi Siao. Siao was born in Hunan province in 1896, and had left home at age fourteen with his brother Yu to study in the provincial capital of Changsha. One of their classmates there was Mao Zedong, who became Yu's best friend. Yu, Mao, Emi, and about twenty others then headed to Beijing after they had completed their studies.

In May 1920, Emi Siao boarded a ship for Paris. He spent his early months working to improve his French at a school in Fontainebleau. He then lived outside Paris with a group of Chinese students, finding a job in a factory.[111] One day while visiting French

---

[101] There is relatively little KUTV paperwork pertaining to Şevket Süreyya and Leman, likely a consequence of Şevket's later falling out with the party. Şevket's file contains little more than a photograph, on the back of which is written "traitor or spy." See Aydemir personal file, RGASPI, f. 495, op. 266, d. 151.

[102] Şevket Süreyya KUTV student file, RGASPI, f. 532, op. 12, d. 60, l. 3.

[103] Vâ-Nû, *Bu Dünyadan Nâzım Geçti*, 344.

[104] University student file of Leman Aidemirova (Aydemir), RGASPI, f. 532, op. 11, d. 171, ll. 1–8. Göksu and Timms write that Nüzhet was also a KUTV student, but I was unable to locate a student file in her name at RGASPI. *Romantic Communist*, 43.

[105] RGASPI, f. 532, op. 11, d. 171, ll. 2–4, here 2.

[106] See Şevket Süreyya's KUTV paperwork, f. 532, op. 12, d. 60, l. 2.

[107] RGASPI, f. 532, op. 11, d. 171, ll. 1–6, here 5.    [108] Vâ-Nû, *Bu Dünyadan Nâzım Geçti*, 325.

[109] Aydemir, *Suyu Arayan Adam*, 204.    [110] Vâ-Nû, *Bu Dünyadan Nâzım Geçti*, 241–242.

[111] McGuire, *Red at Heart*, 19–30. On Emi Siao, also see Djagalov, *From Internationalism to Postcolonialism*, 50.

Communist Party headquarters, Emi heard about a new university opening in Moscow for "eastern" students. Short of money and "thinking that at the very least he could get back to China through Siberia," Emi boarded a train to Moscow at the end of 1922. Not long after that, he began his studies at KUTV.[112]

Another friend of Nâzım and Vâlâ's from this time was Zafer Hasan. A Muslim from India, Zafer had previously studied in England, where he had become involved in anti-colonial politics. From there he had made his way to the Soviet Union and KUTV. Following the conclusion of his studies in Moscow, Hasan would end up in Turkey, where he married a Turkish woman and became a citizen. Taking the surname Aybek, Zafer later joined the armed forces in Turkey, serving as a military instructor in Afghanistan.[113]

Vâlâ and Nâzım also consorted with individuals whose background would most certainly have raised eyebrows in official quarters. Such was the case with Reşit Kaplan, a former minister in the Müsavat government in Baku. After the overthrow of the Azerbaijan Democratic Republic in April 1920, Kaplan had briefly been detained by Bolshevik authorities. He was, however, allowed to remain in the country, and shortly thereafter he had moved to Moscow. Kaplan would eventually fall victim to the mass purges taking place under Stalin in the late 1930s. He was arrested and executed in 1937.

At Kaplan's apartment in Moscow, Nâzım and Vâlâ became friendly with several individuals who had previously been associated with the Young Turk regime. One such figure was Doctor Nâzım, who had been a highly influential personality within the Committee of Union and Progress and the Young Turk government. Tried in absentia by the British in 1920, Doctor Nâzım had been sentenced to death for his role in the 1915 genocide of Ottoman Armenians. Like much of the rest of the Young Turk leadership, however, he had fled Istanbul ahead of the occupying armies, heading first to Germany and then the Soviet Union. Later in 1922, Doctor Nâzım would make his way back to Anatolia. In 1926, he was arrested by Turkish authorities on charges of participating in an alleged assassination plot against Mustafa Kemal, and on August 26 of that year he was executed.[114]

An even more notorious Young Turk official with whom Nâzım and Vâlâ spent time during their early days in Moscow was Cemal Pasha. One of the "triumvirate" of Young Turks alongside Enver and Talat pashas, Cemal Pasha had likewise begun a period of exile in Russia and elsewhere after fleeing Istanbul. He, too, had been sentenced to death in absentia during the period of British occupation, on charges of

---

[112] McGuire, *Red at Heart*, 29. On Emi and Nâzım, see Sülker, *Nâzım Hikmet'in Gerçek Yaşamı*, vol. 1, 192–193; Göksu and Timms, *Romantic Communist*, 43–44; Fish, *Nâzım'ın Çilesi*, 20.

[113] He retired as an artillery captain in 1946. On Zafer Hasan, see Göksu and Timms, *Romantic Communist*, 44; Syed Tanvir Wasti, "The Political Aspirations of Indian Muslims and the Ottoman Nexus," *Middle Eastern Studies*, vol. 42, no. 5 (2006), 709–722, esp. 719, fn. 28. On Aybek's later service in Afghanistan, see BCA, 30-18-1-2/73-30-5, from April 14, 1937.

[114] Vâ-Nû, *Bu Dünyadan Nâzım Geçti*, 357. On Unionists in Moscow at this time, also see Aydemir, *Suyu Arayan Adam*, 228–231.

having committed war crimes. Cemal Pasha had, however, proven himself useful to the Soviets, helping them establish ties with the Emir of Afghanistan, Amanullah.[115]

Cemal Pasha also happened to be an old friend of the fathers of both Nâzım and Vâlâ. According to Vâlâ, he and Nâzım were invited to dinner at the luxurious house in Moscow where Cemal Pasha had been staying as a guest of the Bolshevik government. At one point in the evening, with Nâzım holding forth and lecturing the rest of the table on politics, Cemal Pasha interjected to tell him: "if I still had my old position, I would have you hanged right now, but underneath the gallows I would be in tears." According to Vâlâ, Nâzım's response was "the difference between you and me, my pasha, is that I would have had you hanged, too, but then wouldn't have cried about it."[116]

Vâlâ would later recall that Nâzım had also met up with his uncle, Ali Fuat Pasha, while the latter was serving as the Ankara government's ambassador to Moscow.[117] Ali Fuat Pasha had stayed on in his position in Moscow until late June 1922, within a month or so after Nâzım and his friends had arrived from the Caucasus.[118] One reason for these meetings may have been financial, as some sources indicate that Celile was sending money to Nâzım in Moscow through the Turkish Embassy at this time.[119]

Some of the Turkish students at KUTV thought that Nâzım and his friends did not belong at the university. One of the earliest of Nâzım's detractors was Ali Yazıcı. On June 1, 1923, Yazıcı sent a letter to the rector of KUTV, complaining about Nâzım's presence at the school. Nâzım, wrote Yazıcı, was a product of "the highest class of aristocrats of Turkey." Additionally, he was untrustworthy. Nâzım had, charged Yazıcı, "received letters via the Turkish Embassy, and about this did not once notify the school."

Something else that was concerning about Nâzım was the fact that he was suspiciously well-connected. "In my opinion," Yazıcı continued, Nâzım had "found ways of gaining influence" by use of his university contacts, "and there is no organization or person in Moscow that he does not know." Yazıcı went on to note that Nâzım "is informed about everything, of which we, communists, in our own secret correspondence do not speak."[120] Despite the alarmist rhetoric, there appears to have been no follow up resulting from Yazıcı's complaint. Nâzım was, after all, on good terms with university officials and TKP head Şefik Hüsnü. He and his friends were considered possible future leaders of the party, whereas Yazıcı was a relatively minor figure.

During his early years in Moscow, Nâzım continued to maintain a long-distance relationship with Nüzhet. Before leaving Batumi, he had written to Nüzhet asking her

---

[115] Soviet Commissar for Foreign Affairs Georgii Chicherin gave Cemal Pasha credit for a treaty signed between Soviet Russia and Afghanistan in 1921. Hirst, "Eurasia's Discontent," 125.

[116] Vâ-Nû, *Bu Dünyadan Nâzım Geçti*, 357. On Cemal and Enver pashas in Russia, also see Akal, *Moskova-Ankara-Londra Üçgeninde*, 167–170. Cemal Pasha was later assassinated in Tbilisi.

[117] Vâ-Nû, *Bu Dünyadan Nâzım Geçti*, 191.  [118] Cebesoy, *Moskova Hatıraları*, 347.

[119] Göktürk, *Bilinmeyen Yönleriyle*, 93–94.  [120] RGASPI, f. 82, op. 2, d. 1330, ll. 88–89.

to join him at KUTV. She had opted to stay on with her sister and brother-in-law in Tbilisi, but the letters and invitations from Nâzım continued. Eventually, Nüzhet decided to take him up on his offer. At the end of 1922, she made the long trip up to Moscow.[121]

As Nüzhet would explain decades later in an interview, she arrived in Moscow to find Nâzım at the center of a large social circle. Within this crowd of male and female friends from the university, Nâzım stood out as a "leader," in Nüzhet's eyes, not only due to his "intriguing, active, and lively" personality, but also because of the poetry that he was writing at the time. Nüzhet would later describe her life in Moscow with Nâzım in quite idyllic—perhaps somewhat idealized—terms, with Nâzım busying himself in his writing and the two of them strolling through the streets of the Bolshevik capital, discussing literature and ideas.

One day, according to Nüzhet, Nâzım suddenly asked her to marry him. She was not expecting a proposal, and at first gave no reply. A day or two later, however, he brought up the idea again, and asked her for an answer. Nüzhet's response was short and simple: "Okay," she said. "Let's get married."[122]

The consequences of sex, within or outside the confines of marriage, had been greatly liberalized in the early days of the USSR. In 1920, Russia became the first country in Europe to legalize abortion.[123] Meanwhile, getting married—or divorced—was now a relatively hassle-free process, involving little more than changing one's registration status.[124] In housing-starved Moscow of the early 1920s, moreover, marriage brought certain practical advantages, as Nâzım was able to move out of the room he had been living in with Vâlâ and receive a private one that he and Nüzhet could share.[125] Vâlâ, too, would get married in Moscow, to a Soviet-born woman named Anna with whom he would soon father a daughter.[126]

Toward the end of 1923, Nüzhet left Moscow. The reasons behind her departure have been the subject of speculation among Nâzım's biographers. Mutlu Konuk Blasing has suggested that Nüzhet did not enjoy the fast-paced lifestyle that Nâzım had become accustomed to in Moscow.[127] Kemal Sülker, meanwhile, describes Nüzhet's relationship with Nâzım as a tempestuous one, with Nâzım "quickly growing angry and upset" with her, particularly when he felt she was paying too much attention to other men.[128]

Despite the occasionally turbulent nature of their relationship, Nüzhet did not plan to leave Moscow permanently. She intended to return to the Bolshevik capital after visiting her sister and Muhittin Bey in Baku, where they had recently moved from

---

[121] Sülker, *Nâzım Hikmet'in Gerçek Yaşamı*, vol. 1, 146, 177–186. Also see Fish, *Nâzım'ın Çilesi*, 236–237.

[122] Sülker, *Nâzım Hikmet'in Gerçek Yaşamı*, vol. 1, 178–181.    [123] Suny, *The Soviet Experiment*, 203–204.

[124] On changes occurring with respect to marriage and divorce in the USSR, also see Vladimir Shlapentokh, *Love, Marriage, and Friendship in the Soviet Union: Ideals and Practices* (New York: Praeger, 1984), esp. 20–24. Nâzım describes himself as "married" on student registration forms he filled out that are dated September 19, 1923. RGASPI, f. 495, op. 266, d. 47, Part 1, 152.

[125] Sülker, *Nâzım Hikmet'in Gerçek Yaşamı*, vol. 1, 147; Göksu and Timms, *Romantic* Communist, 43.

[126] Vâ-Nû , *Bu Dünyadan Nâzım Geçti*, 397.    [127] Blasing, *Nâzım Hikmet*, 54.

[128] Sülker, *Nâzım Hikmet'in Gerçek Yaşamı*, vol. 1, 189–190. Also see Zekeriya Sertel, *Mavi Gözlü Dev*, 44–45.

## 128 RED STAR OVER THE BLACK SEA

Tbilisi. However, Muhittin Bey, who was working as a history professor at Baku University, was accused by the Cheka, or secret police, of "spreading pan-Turkist propaganda." Along with her older sister and Muhittin Bey, Nüzhet would soon leave the Soviet Union for Turkey.[129]

## Seizing the Future

In what ways did Nâzım develop his writing style while he was in Moscow? His time in the Soviet capital coincided with an era in which many of the USSR's greatest artists, musicians, and writers were seeking to out-do one another in pushing the boundaries of experimentation. In these early years of the revolution, Moscow was one of the most creatively wide-open cities in the world. Nâzım was quick to sense the opportunity that such an environment provided, and soon joined in. In the process of doing so, he altered the style of his poetry entirely.

In response to evolving fashions, conditions, and locations, Nâzım's poetic range had already progressed considerably over the years. The Gökalp-inspired works from his younger days had given way to the Syllabist romantic themes that Nâzım would embrace during the period of British occupation in Istanbul. In Anatolia and the Caucasus, too, Nâzım's writing had reflected the experiences that he and Vâlâ were going through at the time, with the two friends collaborating in the composition of a series of patriotic-sounding *türkü*s to march by. In Batumi, meanwhile, they had written more obviously political poems about Mustafa Suphi alongside paeans to their life on the road. Everywhere he went, Nâzım had developed his verse in some way.

And now, in Moscow, Nâzım changed his style again. The most obvious difference was that he had abandoned the strict forms of rhyme and meter that had constituted a key feature of his writing in Istanbul, Anatolia, and the Caucasus. Instead, Nâzım's verse from these early Moscow years reflected the work of Russian Futurist writers, Vladimir Mayakovsky and Sergei Yesenin in particular. While Nâzım would insist, for the rest of his life, that he had already started writing in his new, revolutionary style before he had ever heard of Mayakovsky, this seems implausible.[130] Even if this claim is true, it is clear that Russian Futurism—and Mayakovsky—had a profound influence upon Nâzım's writing at this time.[131] Whether or not Nâzım realized he was emulating the great Russian Futurist, that's exactly what he was doing.

It was while he was spending the summer at the Soviet summer camp Udel'naia that Nâzım wrote "We Believe!..." (İnandık!...), one of his first Futurist poems. The poem describes an airplane, "our plane," which, the narrator emphasizes, "we believe" can fly. But will it?

---

[129] Sülker, *Nâzım Hikmet'in Gerçek Yaşamı*, vol. 1, 182.

[130] On Nâzım and Mayakovsky, see Babayev, *Nâzım Hikmet*, 83–85; Göksu and Timms, *Romantic Communist*, 46–47; Memet Fuat, *Nâzım Hikmet*, 48–49, 53; Balaban, *Nâzım Hikmet'le Yedi Yıl*, 88; Clark, *Eurasia Without Borders*, 48–59.

[131] On Nâzım's poetry changing in Moscow, see Clark, *Eurasia Without Borders*, 51–57.

"We Believe!…" was not meant to be crooned while gazing into a lover's eyes, nor was it a song to march by. Rather, this was verse that was written to be read out loud to an audience of the already-converted. The tempo of "We Believe!…" changes repeatedly, never settling into a comfortable or predictable speed, like an airplane that is struggling to ascend. The poem concludes with a round of short, rapid-fire, bursting declarations.

> It's impossible that it won't fly!…
> It will fly
> It'll fly!!!
> We believe this in the language of numbers!
> We believe!
> We believe with our brain!…[132]

"We Believe!…" owed a considerable debt to the Russian Futurists, and Nâzım's conjuring of an airplane is typical of the valorization of technological progress that was common in Futurist writing.

This focus upon mechanically powered modernization can be seen in several examples of Nâzım's early Moscow work, such as his 1923 poem, "Machine-ization" ("*Makinalaşmak*").[133] The data-driven narrator of "Machine-ization" recites all of the key numbers in his life.[134]

> I live in a four-story wooden house
> My room is on the fourth floor.
> Across from my window
> there is a 20-story "concrete-army" apartment building.
> Twenty elevators work nonstop
> From roof to ground floor
> Ground floor to roof.

In transforming himself into a machine, the narrator expresses a wish to "machine-ize."

> However I
> am the man who wants to place a turbine on his belly
> and screw a couple of propellers onto his backside.

---

[132] Yapı Kredi edition of Nâzım Hikmet's collected works (*Şiirler* Vol. 8), 153.

[133] This poem's title is often translated as "Mechanize" or "Mechanization" ("makineleşmek" in modern Turkish). To my ear, however, the word "makinalaşmak," which does not exist in modern Turkish, sounds more like "becoming a machine," a meaning that is borne out in the poem's content. I therefore translate the title of this poem as "machine-ization."

[134] On Nâzım's poems during these years, also see Sülker, *Nâzım Hikmet'in Gerçek Yaşamı*, vol. 1, 151.

The narrator in this poem compares society to a modern apartment building with elevators ("Every night / I climb 80 wooden steps"), concluding that "machine-ization" constitutes the best means of going forward. Descending the stairs of the apartment building, the poem mimics the sounds of a lift:

> vizzzzz…
> I'm coming down…
> the cleaning lady
> Says "you're crazy" to me.
> She doesn't know that I—silly fool!
> I want to
> machine-ize.[135]

Another example of Nâzım's new Moscow-influenced style can be found in his 1922 poem "Us—Soon Enough" ("*Yakından—Biz*"). Written in commemoration of the fifth anniversary of the October Revolution, this poem similarly reflects Nâzım's newfound approach to writing in its opening lines:

> 1
> 2
> 3
> 4
> 5
> On top of five red flags five of them five
> Si-ix…
> Get ready!
> We're kicking off the sixth…[136]

Nâzım's new style attracted attention in Moscow. On March 8, 1923, a celebration for Women's Day was held at the Polytechnic Museum. Nâzım and Ahmet Cevat, along with several other members of the Comintern—i.e., foreign communists—helped to mark the occasion by reading their work. Headlining the evening was Mayakovsky, who recited three of his poems (Figure 5.5).[137]

Precisely because he was a foreigner, an "eastern" Turk, Nâzım had been provided with opportunities in Moscow that likely would not have been available to him then in Istanbul. More importantly, he was introduced to new poetic forms and approaches that differed greatly from what he had known previously. Nâzım made the most of the chances he was given. His poetry grew substantially as a result.

---

[135] Yapı Kredi edition of Nâzım Hikmet's collected works (*Şiirler* Vol. 8), 172. [136] Ibid., 163.
[137] Göksu and Timms, *Romantic Communist*, 46; Babayev, *Nâzım Hikmet*, 92–93. Also see "International Literary Meeting," *Pravda*, March 11, 1923, Number 55. According to Katerina Clark, Nâzım and Mayakovsky also shared the stage on January 15, 1923. *Eurasia Without Borders*, 48.

## Интернациональный литературный митинг.

8-го марта в Политехническом музее под председательством тов. Брика состоялся интернациональный митинг на тему «Революция в литература», устроенный студентами П. М. Г. У. по примеру международного митинга искусств, организованного театром Вс. Мейерхольда.

Выступали члены Коминтерна.

Тов. Эшли (Англия), сообщая об английской литературе,—сказал, что английские поэты не могут слагать песни побед освобожденного труда, как поэты Советской России, пока Англия—капиталистическая страна. Английские поэты могут пока писать боевые гимны или сатиру на господствующие классы. Тов. Эшли прочел несколько своих стихотворений.

Тов. Мадьяр (Венгрия) очертил положение революционной венгерской литературы, лишь недавно начавшей возрождаться после хортиевского террора.

Тов. Ахмед-Джевад (Турция) сообщил о националистической революционной литературе и о недавно зародившейся поэзии турецкого пролетариата, после чего молодой турецкий поэт-футурист тов. Назым прочел свои стихи, произведшие чрезвычайно сильное впечатление на аудиторию своей звуковой стороной.

Тов. Малакка (Остров Ява) продемонстрировал несколько малайских стихотворений и песен.

Из русских поэтов выступали т.т. Маяковский («Париж», «Левый марш», «III Интернационал»), Каменский (отрывки из «Паровозной обедни» и «Стеньки Разина») и Крученых («Богохульная поэма и «Утешение»).

В заключение группой студентов комм. универс. труд. Востока была продемонстрирована коллективная декламация на турецком языке.

Figure 5.5 "International Literary Meeting"

At the same time, Nâzım had yet to come up with a style that was really his own. Back in Istanbul, he had gone from mimicking the work of the best-known Turkists to doing the same with the Syllabists. Now in Moscow, this eager student of poetry was seeking to master the style of the Russian Futurists. While his own approach to poetry was not yet formed, Nâzım was familiarizing himself with the literary building blocks, the components of style and experience, that he would later draw upon in fashioning an original literary voice.

In March 1925 Vâlâ was filling out paperwork relating to his job as an instructor at KUTV. The form he was completing asked him to list his employment history. The 23-year-old explained that he had already held a number of positions in his young life, including: "accountant," "teacher," and "journalist." But "[m]ore than anything else," concluded Vâlâ, "I have worked as a professional revolutionary."[138]

Gainfully employed and possessing a diverse and exciting cadre of international friends and comrades, Nâzım and Vâlâ felt free in Moscow to indulge themselves

---

[138] RGASPI, f. 532, op. 12, d. 3576, l. 5-ob. March 21, 1925. Vâlâ Nureddin employee file.

intellectually, socially, culturally, and sexually in a city that seemed wide-open to them. It was a time of penetrable frontiers and more open minds.

Permeability on the Turkish–Soviet border in the early 1920s mirrored that of society within each of these countries. Flexibility on the frontier coincided with the circulation in Moscow of more expansive and diverse concepts relating to politics, revolution, social mores, art, literature, and even what it meant to be a "communist" or a "Bolshevik." In Turkey, meanwhile, the years prior to 1925 would likewise mark the freest period of political debate in the Kemalist era.

It wouldn't last, however. Along the Turkish–Soviet border, changes would soon be coming, just as they would inside the two countries.

# 6

# Moscow-Istanbul-Moscow-Istanbul

Vâlâ's letter was urgent. He was writing to a Comintern official named Semyon Brikke on behalf of Nâzım and a mission endangered (Figure 6.1).[1] Nâzım had, according to Vâlâ, departed Moscow on June 28 alongside Fahri Reşid, Mustafa Osman, and İsmail İbrahim.[2] The goal of their Comintern-sponsored journey, noted Vâlâ, was to undertake "clandestine work" in Turkey.[3] However, the four travelers still had not arrived at their destination. They were out of money and stranded in Odessa.

In his missive to Brikke, Vâlâ quoted directly from a letter that Nâzım had sent to him from Odessa.[4] It was thoroughly indignant in tone. Describing the funding that he and his three fellow travelers had received for the trip as "miserable," Nâzım had gone on to list what he perceived as the inadequacies surrounding their mission's organization. The first problem, wrote Nâzım, related to the tickets they'd been given for the trip down to Odessa. "The Comintern official charged with purchasing our tickets," complained Nâzım, "did not buy ones for an express train." The fact that the four had been obliged to take local trains all the way down to the Black Sea had, he claimed, "abnormally prolonged the duration of our trip."

Upon arriving in Odessa, continued Nâzım, the four travelers had encountered still more unpleasant surprises. They had asked a local Gubkom (provincial committee) official for assistance in covering the costs of their meals and lodging in Odessa, but had been rebuffed. Nâzım explained that he had been "stunned to be informed" that the letter from the Moscow office that they had presented in Odessa had stated that the four had already been outfitted with "all of their needs." The Gubkom office in Odessa had therefore deemed unnecessary any further financing for the travelers.

Due to these pecuniary difficulties, the foursome's travel plans had been delayed. Now, they had to make a quick decision regarding which of two ships they would take to Istanbul. The first would depart for Greece in two days, but would only dock in

---

[1] The dates provided by Nâzım's biographers regarding his departure from Moscow vary. According to Sülker, Nâzım left Moscow in October 1924. *Nâzım Hikmet'in Gerçek Yaşamı*, vol. 1, 200. Babayev, as well as Göksu and Timms, write that Nâzım left in December. *Romantic Communist*, 53; Babayev, *Nâzım Hikmet*, 117. Vâlâ's letter clearly states that Nâzım and his party left Moscow on June 28, but does not mention when they arrived in Odessa.

[2] "İsmail İbrahim" (or "İbrahimov") was one of İsmail Bilen's aliases, but it is unclear if Vâlâ was referring to Bilen, whose paperwork indicates that he remained in Moscow until 1926.

[3] Letter from Vâlâ Nureddin to Semyon Brikke. RGASPI/IISH, f. 495, op. 181, d. 327, ll. 90–91. Also see personal file of Fahri Reşid. RGASPI, f. 495, op. 266, d. 136, l. 10.

[4] Vâlâ noted in his letter to Brikke, which was written in French, that he was translating Nâzım's words, which presumably had been written to Vâlâ in Turkish.

*Red Star over the Black Sea: Nâzım Hikmet and his Generation.* James H. Meyer, Oxford University Press. © James H. Meyer 2023.
DOI: 10.1093/oso/9780192871176.003.0008

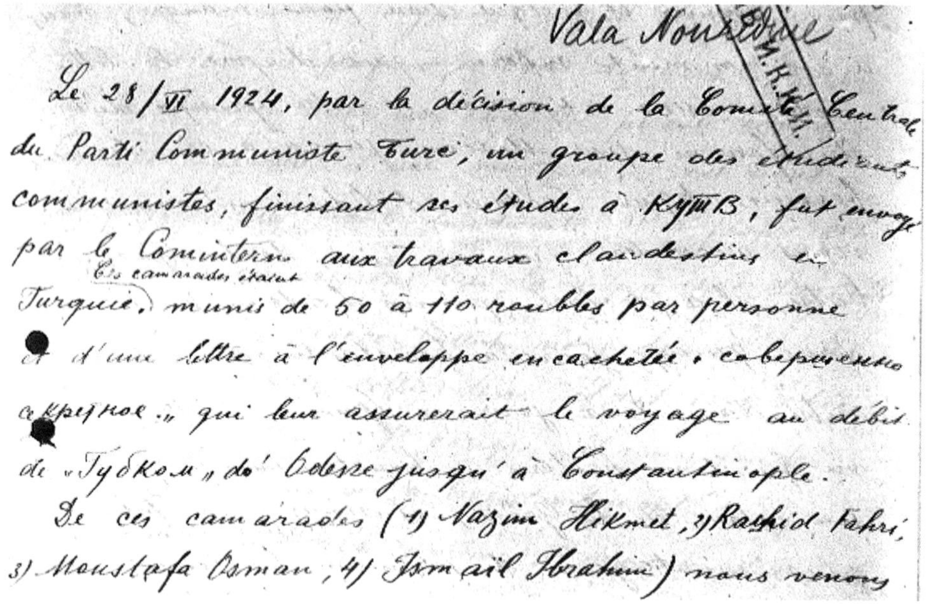

Vala Nourëddine

Le 28/VI 1924, par la décision de la Comité Central du Parti Communiste Turc, un groupe des étudiants communistes, finissant ses études à КУТВ, fut envoyé par le Comintern aux travaux clandestins en Turquie, (Ces camarades étaient) munis de 50 à 110 roubles par personne et d'une lettre à l'enveloppe cachetée « совершенно секретное » qui leur assurerait le voyage au débit de « Тубком » de Odesse jusqu'à Constantinople.

De ces camarades (1) Nazim Hikmet, 2) Rachid Fahri, 3) Moustafa Osman, 4) Ismaïl Ibrahim) nous venons

**Figure 6.1** Letter from Vâlâ to Semyon Brikke

Istanbul on its return trip to Odessa. The second option was a ship scheduled to leave Odessa thirteen days after the first one. Despite its circumlocutory route, the first ship would get them to Istanbul sooner. However, employing logic that might have struck Brikke as equally circuitous, Nâzım noted that he and the others were inclined to wait for the second boat. This was because they would have to spend a longer period of time at sea with the first ship and feared that food prices would be inflated on board. For this reason, they had decided to go with the second option and wait in Odessa for another two weeks.

Perhaps not coincidentally, taking the second ship would give Brikke time to set the travelers up with an influx of cash. Nâzım confessed that he and his companions had, "little by little," spent everything that the Comintern had given them for the trip. A shortage of funds could, he pointed out, end up compromising the mission, because they would need to buy new clothes upon getting to Istanbul. Otherwise, he predicted, "it wouldn't be too hard for the [Turkish] police to discover us" in their apparently attention-grabbing garb from Moscow.

Lest anyone think he was simply being soft, Nâzım invoked his experience and background to Brikke, albeit in somewhat fabricated terms.

> All of us, we were all soldiers once. All of us lived in Russia during the period of War Communism.[5] But none of us has ever lived in such miserable conditions.

[5] "War Communism" is the name given to the period between July 1918 and March 1921, during the time of civil war in Russia. Suny, *The Soviet Experiment*, 74.

While Nâzım had not, in fact, ever been a soldier, he did apparently know a thing or two about suffering. He and his comrades were, he reported to Brikke, sleeping "on the floor of a room that smells like a mosque's toilet."[6]

*

Officially, Nâzım was taking this trip for party purposes. He was going to attend, in Istanbul, the January 1925 congress of the TKP—which was still a legal party in Turkey at this time. The plan was for Nâzım to stay on in Turkey after the congress ended. Viewed in Moscow as an up-and-comer with the potential to achieve a future leadership position, Nâzım was now given the opportunity to prove his party mettle.

His return to Istanbul had been requested specifically by the party leadership. The previous April, Şefik Hüsnü—head of the TKP in Turkey—had written to Moscow asking that some of the Turkish students at KUTV be sent to Istanbul immediately. "We insist above all," Şefik Hüsnü had written, "upon the immediate return of Nâzım Hikmet, for whom we have great need here."[7]

But now, the triumphant trip home was turning into a fiasco before the four travelers had even had the chance to cross the border. These complications would prove a harbinger of difficulties to come during the course of a return to Istanbul that would prove challenging and painful for Nâzım in more ways than one.

## Returning to a New Land

Having either been on the road or living in the Soviet Union for most of the past four years, Nâzım was now "returning" to the Republic of Turkey, a newly established country that he had never before set foot in. At the time of Nâzım's voyage back to Istanbul, relations between Turkey and the USSR were still quite good, and the border between the two countries was relatively open. With so many ex-POWs and immigrants continuing to enter Turkey from the USSR and the Balkans, crossing the frontier was still quite easy.

The year before, in October 1923, Mustafa Kemal had proclaimed the foundation of the Turkish Republic. Slowly but surely, the young Turkish state had begun the long and painful process of recovering from over a decade of war and destruction. Back when Nâzım and Vâlâ had set out for Ankara in January 1921, Mustafa Kemal's government had consisted of little more than a parliament, a few scattered buildings,

---

[6] Letter from Vâlâ Nureddin to Comrade Brikke. RGASPI/IISH, f. 495, op. 181, d. 327, ll. 90–91. Sülker states that Nâzım got back to Istanbul in October 1924. *Nâzım Hikmet'in Gerçek Yaşamı*, vol. 1, 209. Göksu and Timms write that Nâzım arrived in December of that year. *Romantic Communist*, 55.

[7] RGASPI/IISH, f. 495, op. 181, d. 327, ll. 19–20. Letter from Şefik Hüsnü to the Comintern offices in Moscow, April 15, 1924. Şefik Hüsnü had also requested, "in order of preference," that "Şevki, the brothers Sadi and Fahri, comrade Fevziye, Sabri Ethem Niazi, Mustafa Osman, Yusuf Ahmet, and Hassan Sadri" also be sent to Turkey.

and a fledgling volunteer army. Since that time, the people who lived in the country that was now called Turkey had undergone a bitter trial by fire.

Politically, much had changed. In March 1924, the last caliph—Abdül Mecit—was stripped of his title and sent into exile. Mustafa Kemal and his political allies had created the People's Party, which would later come to be known as the Republican People's Party (*Cumhuriyet Halk Partisi*, or CHP). This political organization, through parliament, had declared Mustafa Kemal the party's leader and president in 1923.

In some ways, however, the domestic political situation in Turkey was still quite fluid. In November 1924, an opposition party, called the Progressive Republican Party, was established by Rauf (Orbay), Adnan (Adıvar, husband of Halide Edip), Kâzım Karabekir, and Nâzım's uncle Ali Fuat Pasha.[8] These four individuals had all been loyal supporters of Kemal during the War of Liberation, and they had all held important positions in the Ankara government.[9] Other political parties, like the TKP, similarly remained open as legal organizations. The TKP-sponsored newspaper *Aydınlık* ("Enlightenment") was published and distributed openly.[10]

Something that had changed considerably in recent years was the demographic makeup of what was now the Republic of Turkey. As had been the case in the aftermath of the Crimean War (1853–56), the Ottoman-Russian War of 1877–78, and the Balkan Wars of 1912 and 1913, hundreds of thousands of Muslims had fled or were expelled from the Balkans and the former Russian Empire at this time. They came to Turkey to start their lives over again.

Already, the Republic of Turkey was a nation of immigrants. According to Kemal Karpat's estimate, over the period 1856 to 1914 the number of Muslims coming to the lands of what would become the Turkish Republic numbered about five million.[11] Meanwhile, the Muslim population of the entire Ottoman Empire in 1912 was approximately 14 million.[12] Between 1921 and 1926, an additional 812,771 Muslim immigrants were officially recorded as having arrived in Turkey.[13] This in a country with a population of approximately 12 to 13 million in the early 1920s.[14]

The demands made upon incoming border-crossers by state authorities had changed over the years.[15] In imperial times, Muslims arriving in the Ottoman Empire

---

[8] Ali Fuat had previously served as second-in-command of the parliament, given the title of "*ikinci başkan*," after Mustafa Kemal. He was the parliamentary leader, or "*başkan*," when Mustafa Kemal was out of Ankara. BCA: 30-10-0-0/2-9-6, July 23, 1923.

[9] For a discussion of these issues in the context of Nâzım's life, see Göksu and Timms, *Romantic Communist*, 54.

[10] On *Aydınlık*, see Tunçay, *Türkiye'de Sol Akımlar*, 177–183.

[11] Karpat writes that "the total number of Muslim immigrants from the Crimea, the Caucasus, and the Balkans who had settled in Anatolia (and to some extent in Syria and Iraq) by 1908 was about 5 million." Karpat, *Ottoman Population, 1830–1914*, 55.

[12] Crews, "Empire and the Confessional State," fn. 1.    [13] McCarthy, *Death and Exile*, 164.

[14] In Istanbul alone, an estimated 116,692 refugees were officially registered between 1923 and 1930. BCA, 272-0-0-11/24-131-2, "List of immigrants and refugees re-settled in Istanbul," January 7, 1930.

[15] Muslims continued to enter Turkey from Russia during these years. See, for example, BCA, 272-0-0-12/42-52-2, "The re-settlement in Artvin of Azapzade Derviş and other refugees from the Caucasus who fled to Turkey following a Russian attack," August 3, 1924; BCA 272-0-0-12/41-48-29, "On speeding up the response to the orders relating to immigrants from Russia who have been re-settled in the three provinces (vilayat-ı selaseye)," May 15, 1924; BCA 272-0-0-12/41-46-19, "Sending requested funds to immigrants coming

were expected to become "Ottoman." This meant, in practical terms, conforming to a system that conferred both privileges and obligations upon the empire's subjects.[16] Now, however, Turkish state officials wanted something more ideological from incoming migrants. Muslim refugees, many of whom were not ethnically Turkish, were now expected to see themselves as ethnic "Turks," a term that state officials applied to virtually every Muslim in the country.

The new republic's secularism notwithstanding, religion would become the basis of what it took to be "Turk," much more than one's actual ethnicity. For Kurds, Arabs, Laz, Slavs, Circassians, Chechens, Tatars, and other non-Turkish Muslims living in Anatolia and eastern Thrace, the government's new slogan was "Happy is s/he who calls her/himself a Turk" (*Ne mutlu Türküm diyene*). Just *call* yourself a Turk, the message seemed to be imploring, or else be prepared to meet with some unhappiness.[17]

Incoming Muslims were now expected to see themselves in a fundamentally new way: as citizens whose Turkish ethnicity made them, in theory, equal partners in the nation-state of Turkey.[18] The more pragmatic manner in which Russian and Ottoman state officials, and border-crossers themselves, had viewed the frontier and subjecthood in the late imperial era was now giving way to a much more ideological and rigid understanding of belonging.

## Navigating Turkey

Amid the broader mass of POWs and refugees flowing into Turkey in the early-to-mid 1920s, it was not so difficult for four students from Communist University of the East to slip back in. Şefik Hüsnü had even suggested as such, writing that KUTV graduates who lacked the legal paperwork required to enter Turkey should "present themselves to authorities as prisoners of war."[19] In Vâlâ's letter to Brikke, no concern is expressed regarding the potential for any sort of problem relating to crossing the border, and it appears that Nâzım and his fellow travelers did not experience any difficulties.

Nâzım spent his early months back in Istanbul involved mainly with party work. In January 1925, he attended an assembly of the Turkish Communist Party in Istanbul. Of particular importance at this congress were discussions relating to the party's Turkey-based publishing efforts. At a meeting of the Comintern in Moscow in June and July 1924, *Aydınlık* had been criticized for being too supportive of the Kemalist government's state capitalism. The TKP-published newspaper was, moreover,

---

from Russia to Kars to help with agricultural production," March 30, 1924; BCA 272-0-0-11/22-113-28, "The re-settlement in Van and neighboring villages Turkish immigrants from Russia," December 26, 1926.

[16] On this point, also see Can, *Spiritual Subjects*, 15.

[17] Meyer, *Turks Across Empires*, 181.

[18] On differences in approach to subjecthood and citizenship among Ottoman and Turkish officials, see Kirişci, "Disaggregating Turkish Citizenship and Immigration Practices," 3–4.

[19] RGASPI/IISH, f. 495, op. 181, d. 327, ll. 19–20. Letter from Şefik Hüsnü to the Comintern offices in Moscow, April 15, 1924.

characterized by its detractors as too intellectual, holding little appeal to anyone beyond a collection of left-wing teachers, lawyers, and students who already supported the party.[20]

In the aftermath of the January TKP congress, an effort was undertaken within the party to improve its publications. Şevket Süreyya, who along with Leman had already returned to Istanbul, began working with Nâzım to boost the quality of the TKP's newspapers.[21] Alongside *Aydınlık*, the party began publishing a second newspaper called *Orak-Çekiç* ("Hammer and Sickle"), which was intended to appeal to a broader audience.[22] Nâzım penned a number of articles and poems for *Aydınlık* at this time, sometimes under the pseudonym "Ahmet."[23]

Working with Nâzım and Şevket Süreyya in the production and distribution of these newspapers were Vedat Nedim (Tör) and Salih Hacıoğlu. Vedat was, like Nâzım and Vâlâ, an old Galatasaray student. Having spent the war years studying at a university in Berlin, Vedat Nedim was another "German" who had first been turned on to communism by the Spartakist revolution.[24] Unlike most of the other younger TKP officials who were rising up the party ranks at this time, Vedat Nedim had never lived in the Soviet Union or studied at KUTV.[25] He would later become one of the party's leaders, chosen to be the TKP's General Secretary at the 1926 party congress in Vienna.[26]

Hacıoğlu, meanwhile, had been one of the early organizers of the Ankara-based Turkish Communist Party, which he had created in 1920 with Şerif Manatov. In 1921, Hacıoğlu had been arrested by Turkish authorities and sentenced to fifteen years behind bars. He was released in November of the following year after having spent ten and a half months in prison. From 1923 to 1925 Salih Hacıoğlu had worked in the office of a French railroad company, but was subsequently fired, reportedly due to his political activities on behalf of the TKP.[27]

Nâzım received good reviews from party higher-ups for the work he was doing in Istanbul. In 1925, the head of the Eastern Section of the Comintern, Fyodor Petrov, received a letter from Istanbul praising Nâzım's work. "Among the comrades who have arrived," noted the letter's author (most likely Şefik Hüsnü), "particular activity has

---

[20] On these events, see Göksu and Timms, *Romantic Communist*, 55–56.

[21] Şevket's university paperwork indicates that he was on the teaching staff until May 1924. RGASPI, f. 532, op. 12, d. 10, l. 3. His memoirs state that he returned to Istanbul in 1923. *Suyu Arayan Adam*, 301.

[22] On *Orak-Çekiç*, see Tunçay, *Türkiye'de Sol Akımlar*, 183–187.

[23] Nâzım would later use the name "Ahmet" for the protagonist in *Life's Good, Brother*.

[24] Göksu and Timms, *Romantic Communist*, 56. Sülker discusses Nâzım's *Aydınlık* writings in *Nâzım Hikmet'in Gerçek Yaşamı*, vol. 1, 155–160.

[25] Vedat Nedim had worked in Istanbul for the Arcos ("Arkos") trading company, which was owned by the Soviet government. Akbulut and Tunçay (eds.), *İstanbul Komünist Grubu'ndan*, 413. On Arcos, see George Harris, *The Communists and the Kadro Movement: Shaping Ideology in Ataturk's Turkey* (Piscataway, NJ: Gorgias Press, 2010), 69–70.

[26] Akbulut and Tunçay (eds.), *İstanbul Komünist Grubu'ndan*, 413. On the conference in Vienna, also see Sinan Dervişoğlu, trans., *Türkiye Komünist Partisi 1926 Viyana Konferansı* (İstanbul: TÜSTAV, 2004); Sülker, *Nâzım Hikmet'in Gerçek Yaşamı*, vol. 2, 8.

[27] RGASPI, f. 495, op. 266, d. 98, l. 7. "Spravka." Regarding Şefik Hüsnü and *Aydınlık*, see Göksu and Timms, *Romantic Communist*, 55. On Şevket Süreyya and *Aydınlık*, see Aydemir, *Suyu Arayan Adam*, 305–306. Also see Sülker, *Nâzım Hikmet'in Gerçek Yaşamı*, vol. 2, 157–160, 205–206.

been exhibited by comrade Nâzım." Nâzım, the letter went on to observe, "is a great rising star in Turkish literature," an attribute that could be of use to the party. "He is much loved in workers' meetings," this letter went on to add. "The bourgeois press writes about him and his talent. I have also heard him talked about in diplomatic circles, which have connections with the Turkish cultural world." Nâzım, the letter concluded, "promises much."[28]

While Nâzım was clearly making a good impression with his party work, his personal life was going through a difficult period. For Nâzım, returning to Istanbul meant confronting a family situation that was far different from that which he had previously known. Hikmet Bey was now living with his new wife Cavide, whom he had married in 1924, and Nâzım's younger sister Samiye. Nâzım, too, at this time moved into his father's house in Kadıköy.

Nâzım's father, who had for years worked as a diplomat and Ottoman Foreign Ministry official, was now managing a movie theater, the Süreyya Cinema on Kadıköy's Bahariye Caddesi.[29] The Süreyya was an elegant establishment at a time when such places catered to an upscale clientele. Nevertheless, Hikmet Bey's career path since the fall of the Young Turks was a telling reflection of the broader transitions taking place inside Turkey at this time. For generations, the men of Nâzım's bloodline had served the Ottoman state. Now, Hikmet Bey was selling movie tickets.

Hikmet Bey's post-Ottoman employment raises an interesting question: had the Ottoman order not been overthrown amid the political rise of the Ankara government, would Nâzım still have pursued this path toward communism? Or was communism more attractive to him now precisely because the traditional career route for the men in his family—service to the empire—had evaporated?

In the meantime, there were also matters of the heart to contend with. Nâzım hoped to revive his relationship with Nüzhet, and he tracked her down shortly after getting back to Istanbul. Nüzhet had left Moscow officially married to Nâzım, at least according to Soviet law, but the future of their relationship was far from assured. After she had come back to Istanbul at the end of 1923, Nüzhet had drawn increasingly close to Nâzım's family, Hikmet Bey in particular.[30] She had also met with Celile Hanım who, visiting from Paris, had called upon Nüzhet at the young woman's home. According to an interview that Nüzhet Berkin gave to Kemal Sülker in the late 1970s, Celile Hanım had provided her blessing to the young couple's union, imploring Nüzhet to take good care of her son.

However, Nüzhet's thoughts regarding her potential future with Nâzım had begun to change. Prior to Nâzım's return, Nüzhet had taken the advice of her doctor and gone on an extended trip to Europe, spending six months at a sanatorium in the Tatras Mountains on the border of Poland and Czechoslovakia. By the time she returned to

---

[28] Letter written from Istanbul to Petrov at the Comintern, dated February 5, 1925. RGASPI, f. 495, op. 266, d. 47, Part I, l. 139.

[29] Or "avenue." Göksu and Timms, *Romantic Communist*, 55. Sülker, *Nâzım Hikmet'in Gerçek Yaşamı*, vol. 2, 201–202.

[30] Nüzhet had also paid a visit to Nâzım's maternal grandfather, Nâzım Pasha.

Istanbul, Nüzhet no longer wanted to continue her relationship with Nâzım. She yearned for a quieter, more peaceful life for herself.[31]

When Nâzım returned to Istanbul in late 1924, Nüzhet gave him the bad news. According to Nüzhet's later account, Nâzım responded with denial. "He didn't fall completely into hopelessness," Nüzhet Berkin would later note, "he told me a number of times that everything was going to be okay, that if I wanted we could have an official wedding in Turkey." It was only after an incident at a theater, when Nâzım bumped into Nüzhet while she was out with another man, that Nâzım gave up his efforts to reconcile.[32] "Unfortunately," Nüzhet later observed, "I never had the chance to apologize to him."[33]

After four years of travel and adventure, during which time Nâzım had followed Nüzhet to Ankara and Tbilisi, and Nüzhet had visited Nâzım in Batumi and Moscow, Nâzım's last pilgrimage to this first serious romantic love of his had ended in heartbreak. According to Nüzhet, no paperwork was needed to dissolve their Soviet marriage, which had never been reported to Turkish authorities in the first place.[34]

Soon, Nâzım would have other problems to worry about. In February 1925, what would become known as the Sheikh Sait rebellion began. This rebellion, which took place in southeast Anatolia, is sometimes described as a Kurdish nationalist revolt. Only half of this description is accurate. While most of those who were rebelling were indeed of Kurdish ethnicity, this was not a specifically nationalist movement.[35] Sheikh Sait was a tribal leader whose power had derived from many of the pre-Republican aspects of Anatolian life that Mustafa Kemal's regime was looking to replace with centralized state power. The revolt lasted until the end of March, and was met by the deployment of over 25,000 Turkish soldiers. Ankara ordered aerial bombardments, in the form of six planes from the Turkish Air Force against an estimated 15,000 rebels. The revolt came to an end with Sait's capture. Along with forty-six of his followers, Sheikh Sait was sentenced to death on June 29. They were executed the next day.[36]

The rebellion proved to be a catalyst—or pretext—for a major crackdown on politics in Turkey. The government declared martial law and parliament passed the Law for the Maintenance of Public Order. This legislation established "independence tribunals" (*İstiklal Mahkemeleri*) that put thousands of individuals on trial and placed a stranglehold over the Turkish press. Dozens of newspapers were shut down. The Progressive Republican Party and all other opposition parties, including the TKP, were banned. Heroes from the War of Liberation like Kâzım Karabekir were put on

---

[31] At least this is how Nüzhet Berkin would describe her priorities at the time when she was interviewed more than a half-century later. Kemal Sülker, *Nâzım Hikmet'in Bilinmeyen İki Şiir Defteri* (İstanbul: Yazko, 1980), 24–25.

[32] Sülker, *Bilinmeyen İki Şiir Defteri*, 25.

[33] Ibid., 26. From Göksu and Timms, *Romantic Communist*, 52.

[34] Göksu and Timms, *Romantic Communist*, 54; Sülker, *Nâzım Hikmet'in Gerçek Yaşamı*, vol. 1, 183.

[35] Rather, the rebellion appears to have been inspired by a set of disparate issues, including the secularism of the new regime and the centralizing nature of its policies.

[36] Lewis, *Emergence of Modern Turkey*, 266; Shaw and Shaw, *History of the Ottoman Empire and Republic of Turkey*, vol. II, 380.

trial for treason.[37] Less than two years after the Republic of Turkey's creation, Mustafa Kemal was well on his way to becoming a dictator.

For a communist belonging to a now-illegal party, it was time to flee. According to Kemal Sülker, Nâzım had already left for İzmir prior to the Sheikh Sait rebellion.[38] In Sülker's biography, Nâzım's departure is described as having taken place mainly for personal reasons, rather than political ones. Nâzım, writes Sülker, was suffering from his own "internal" problems, a reference to his depression following the breakup with Nüzhet. This prompted "his father, sister, and separately-living mother all in one voice" to plead with him to go stay with relatives in İzmir. The idea was for Nâzım to stay at the home of Rahmi Bey, a former provincial governor and Unionist.[39]

According to party and Comintern reports in Moscow, however, Nâzım "worked underground in İzmir until the arrest of communists and the destruction (*razgrom*) of the party," allegedly operating an illegal printing press.[40] In Şefik Hüsnü's account, Nâzım "worked for a period of six months" for the TKP in Turkey, with his assignments including "party (illegal) work in the provinces," an apparent reference to İzmir.[41]

In the aftermath of the Sheikh Sait rebellion, both *Aydınlık* and *Orak-Çekiç* were closed by Turkish authorities. After the TKP organized May Day demonstrations in defiance of a ban on such activity, the police carried out raids on the homes of various individuals associated with the party. It was at this time that Şevket Süreyya was arrested and sent to Ankara to await trial. He was later sentenced to ten years in prison.[42]

The moves made by the Kemalist government to wipe out independent political action in Turkey only became bolder in the years to follow. In 1926, a plot to assassinate Mustafa Kemal was allegedly uncovered, leading to the arrests of dozens of individuals, including many formerly high-ranking officials, in an implausibly wide-ranging conspiracy. Among those arrested was Nâzım's uncle, Ali Fuat Pasha.[43] From this point forward, the relatively open period of Turkish political life that had existed between 1923 and 1925 came to an end. It would only resume after the conclusion of World War II.[44]

---

[37] Shaw and Shaw, *History of the Ottoman Empire and Republic of Turkey*, vol. II, 381. Nearly 7,500 people were arrested and put on trial under the Independence Tribunals. Erik Zürcher, *Turkey: A Modern History* (New York: I. B. Tauris, 3rd edition, 2014), 173.

[38] Sülker, *Nâzım Hikmet'in Gerçek Yaşamı*, vol. 1, 213.

[39] Ibid., 211–212.

[40] RGASPI, f. 82, op. 2, d. 1330, l. 64. This information is from a "Spravka" from June 1951. Göksu and Timms, *Romantic Communist*, 62, citing Tunçay. This is also how Nâzım depicts the İzmir-based activities of "Ahmet," the protagonist of *Life's Good, Brother*.

[41] RGASPI, Nâzım Hikmet personal file, f. 495, op. 266, d. 47, Part 1, l. 145. September 16, 1926, letter from Ferdi [Şefik Hüsnü] to the bureau for the acceptance of foreigners into the VKP (b), the official Communist Party of the USSR.

[42] Aydemir, *Suyu Arayan Adam*, 317.

[43] Ali Fuat Pasha was ultimately acquitted and released from prison. He would remain out of politics until 1931.

[44] On these events, also see Göksu and Timms, *Romantic Communist*, 62; Harris, *Origins of Communism in Turkey*, 136.

In August 1925, Nâzım showed up at the home where his mother was staying in Istanbul, wearing a sailor's uniform and carrying a fake ID card. After a final goodbye with Celile Hanım, Nâzım left the city clandestinely, ultimately taking a boat back to the USSR.[45] For neither the first time nor the last, Nâzım was fleeing Istanbul.

Among the individual TKP members who were associated with *Aydınlık*, only Şefik Hüsnü and Nâzım managed to evade the authorities.[46] Writing from Berlin to Moscow, Şefik Hüsnü celebrated the news of Nâzım's successful flight, reporting that he had "learned with great pleasure that our young poet Nâzım Hikmet was able to escape from Turkey."[47] Not long thereafter, Nâzım was tried in absentia and sentenced to fifteen years in prison.[48]

## New Voices for New Readers

Depending on where he placed his writing, the style of Nâzım's verse varied. The poems he had published in TKP-owned newspapers, for example, were much more traditional than the Futurist-inspired work that he had produced in Moscow. In works like *Destan* ("Epic"), which was published in *Orak-Çekiç* in January 1925, and *Onbeşlerin Kitâbesi* ("Epitaph for the Fifteen"), which first appeared in *Aydınlık* in February, Nâzım fell back on a creative—yet not particularly revolutionary—use of rhyme reminiscent of his earlier, pre-Moscow, writing.

These and other works that Nâzım published in TKP-produced organs in 1925 were more self-consciously political pieces than Nâzım's other writings had thus far been. Gone were the strange, jostling fonts and the valorization of the machine typical of his Mayakovsky-inspired verse. Now, Nâzım was returning to the more hortatory style that had characterized his published poetry in Batumi.

In "Epitaph for the Fifteen," Nâzım wrote:

> We engraved the names of the Fifteen
> On marble that was scarlet with blood!...
> Our eyes are a steel mirror,
> For those who want to see
> a picture of the Fifteen...[49]

---

[45] Blasing, *Nâzım Hikmet*, 59. At this time illegal crossings between Turkey and the Soviet Union were still rather common.

[46] On the arrests of TKP members at this time, see Göksu and Timms, *Romantic Communist*, 62; Harris, *Origins of Communism in Turkey*, 137.

[47] RGASPI/IISH, f. 495, op. 181, d. 331, ll. 7–18, esp. l. 18. Letter dated August 22, 1925, from Şefik Hüsnü in Berlin to Petrov at the Comintern in Moscow.

[48] On the trial, see Sülker, *Nâzım Hikmet'in Gerçek Yaşamı*, vol. 1, 246–250.

[49] Yapı Kredi edition of Nâzım Hikmet's collected works (*Şiirler* Vol. 8), 124. Originally published in *Aydınlık*, February 1925.

His style took different forms according to his readership. The poetry that Nâzım published in *Aydınlık* and *Orak-Çekiç* was overtly political, while the two works of his that appeared during this time on the pages of the Istanbul literary journal *Akbaba* were much more complex. *Akbaba*, after all, was not owned by the TKP, and the journal's editor was someone with whom Nâzım shared a literary, rather than political, connection: Yusuf Ziya (Ortaç), who had been one of the Syllabists with whom Nâzım and Vâlâ had traveled from Istanbul to İnebolu in January 1921.

Nâzım's "The Mountain Air" (*Dağların Havası*), which was first published in *Akbaba*, is a particularly ambitious work, one that reveals the more aesthetically diverse background of Nâzım's recent past.[50] In this poem, Nâzım demonstrates a simple phrasing and vocabulary, accompanied by clever rhyming. But there is also growth, showing off some of the characteristics that he had picked up in the USSR, such as altering the shape of the work as it appeared on the page. The poem is a romance, but stands in stark contrast to the "romantic" style that Nâzım had employed in his late adolescence. It details the first meeting and developing relationship of two characters, Leman and Süreyya.

While the heroes of this story share the names of Nâzım's two friends, the real focus of the poem can be found in its details. A long train ride, the visit to a suitor's home village, looking after a lover who has fallen ill—the small observations and snippets of dialogue that make this romance seem so much more real than the flights-of-fancy of Nâzım's Syllabist years. "The Mountain Air" anticipates—through its length, use of storytelling, and employment of dialogue—some of Nâzım's poetry from years later, including *Human Landscapes from My Country*. As would also be the case with *Human Landscapes*, Nâzım described "The Mountain Air" as a "novel in verse" (*manzum roman*).

In one scene, Süreyya stops a driver and forces Leman to make a decision on the spot regarding her future with him.

> The village teacher cried out in a booming voice: driver!
> A sturdy fellow came forth, cracking his whip...
> —From here how much is it to Gözi?
> —Five liras!
> —Isn't that a bit much?...
> —We'll get you there right away...
> After he stopped the wagon he turned to Leman:
> —Have you changed your mind about becoming my friend?
>    Make up your mind quickly, we don't have much time honey...
>    Tell me, are you coming with me?
> —I'm coming...[51]

---

[50] The literal translation of this title would be "The Air of the Mountains."
[51] Yapı Kredi edition of Nâzım Hikmet's collected works (*Şiirler* Vol. 8), 125–146, here 132. Originally published in *Akbaba*, March 5–April 2, 1341 (1925).

A second poem Nâzım published at this time in *Akbaba* was "The Pearl." Like "The Mountain Air," this poem was longer and much more complex than the pieces that Nâzım was then producing for TKP-owned newspapers. At the same time, the two works were also quite different from both his earlier Istanbul writings and his Moscow poems. Leaving Moscow, Nâzım's poetry had become somewhat more traditional in appearance than it had been during his Futurist heyday, but in returning to Istanbul he did not simply revert to his pre-Moscow style. With every border crossed, Nâzım acquired new tools and techniques.

Nâzım spent over six months in Turkey in 1925, the first time he had been in the country since its creation. Already, however, it was clear that he no longer fit in completely with his old stomping grounds. Nüzhet had broken up with him, and now the government in Ankara was forcing Turkish leftists to choose between Kemalism and communism.

To Nâzım, the decision was an easy one. Once again, he began to make his way northward.

## The Second Stint

On a late summer's evening in 1925, Vâlâ was sitting in the forest of Udel'naia with his wife and infant daughter. Looking up, he later recalled, he saw a figure emerging from the trees. It was Nâzım. A little over a year had passed since the two friends had seen one another.[52]

Had Nâzım once again fled his home, or was he now running back to it? Nâzım Hikmet's second stint in Moscow, which began in the summer of 1925 and ended in July 1928, took place in a much more independent fashion than had been the case with his first stay. Whereas Nâzım's original move to the Soviet capital in 1922 had been in the capacity of one of Ahmet Cevat's protégés, now he was arriving as his own man. Moving into a room on Tverskoi Boulevard in a building located across the street from the TASS news agency headquarters, Nâzım quickly found employment at KUTV as an instructor.[53] On September 8, he signed a contract with the university to work as an associate lecturer (*nauchnyi sotrudnik*) for the upcoming year, a job that he would hold until his return to Turkey. Nâzım's university records also indicate that he was occasionally paid for translation work at this time.[54] All in all, Nâzım did well financially in the USSR, with the poet later remarking that both his economic and personal worries had vanished upon his return to Moscow.[55]

---

[52] Vâ-Nû writes that Nâzım arrived in Udel'naia in August. *Bu Dünyadan Nâzım Geçti*, 398. According to Sülker, Nâzım arrived on June 20, 1925. *Nâzım Hikmet'in Gerçek Yaşamı*, vol. 1, 226. Göksu and Timms write that Nâzım was back in the USSR 'by September' 1925. *Romantic Communist*, 63.

[53] Fish, *Nâzım'ın Çilesi*, 156.

[54] Nâzım Hikmet KUTV file, RGASPI, f. 532, op. 12, d. 5335, l. 1. This paperwork indicates that Nâzım took up teaching duties at KUTV on September 1, 1925. On teachers at KUTV in its early years, also see Ashby, "Third World Activists and the Communist University of the Toilers of the East," 90–93.

[55] Sülker, *Nâzım Hikmet'in Gerçek Yaşamı*, vol. 1, 229.

During this second stint in Moscow Nâzım also became involved in his first serious relationship with a Soviet woman. She was a young doctor by the name of Yelena Yurchenko, a Ukrainian whom Nâzım sometimes referred to as "Dr. Lena." Nâzım had apparently been introduced to her at the Hotel Luxe. Lena was an anarchist whom Nâzım described as having a notably expressive face. Following another bureaucratic ceremony—marriages could still be formed and dissolved quite simply in the USSR at this time—the young couple moved into a room together. Nâzım wrote to both his mother and father about Lena, and her place in Nâzım's life was well known within his family.[56]

He had a good job, a new wife, and a private room to stay in. It was nice to be back home.

## The Opposition

Both the political and the cultural winds in Moscow were shifting. Following the conclusion of the Russian Civil War in 1921, divisions within the Bolshevik leadership became more pronounced, a trend that only intensified after Lenin's death in January 1924. As Stalin would not emerge as the USSR's paramount leader until the end of the decade, the second half of the 1920s was marked by repeated power struggles among the Soviet Union's warring leadership factions. These splits began to occur not only within the political heights of the Kremlin, but also among local state and party institutions across the USSR.

Inside the Turkish community at KUTV, too, new divisions opened up during these years—something that was becoming increasingly common among students of a variety of nationalities at the university more generally.[57] In 1924–25, Nâzım and individuals seen as his allies—the friends with whom he had originally come up from Batumi, as well as Şefik Hüsnü and İsmail Bilen—came under attack from a self-styled "opposition" movement made up of students in the Turkish sector at KUTV. Süleyman Nuri, the ex-POW and erstwhile critic of Mustafa Suphi who had once counseled Nestor Lakoba regarding his mission to Istanbul, was at the heart of this opposition and appears to have been the group's leader.

Following the mass murder in Trabzon of the TKP Central Committee, it had looked as if Süleyman Nuri might step into the role of new TKP leader or become the Baku-based party's representative to the Comintern. By 1922, however, Şefik Hüsnü had been recognized by Moscow as the head of an Istanbul-based TKP, and Süleyman Nuri was left out in the cold. After a spell working as an instructor at a

---

[56] A photograph of Nâzım and Yelena together was published in the May 1929 issue of *Resimli Ay*, 35. The photo bears the caption "Nâzım and his wife Lena." On Nâzım marrying Lena, also see Göksu and Timms, *Romantic Communist*, 71; Sülker, *Nâzım Hikmet'in Gerçek Yaşamı*, vol. 1, 232–234.

[57] On splits taking place within national groupings at the university, see Ashby, "Third World Activists and the Communist University of the Toilers of the East," 119–123.

party school in Baku in the early 1920s, Süleyman Nuri had traveled to Moscow to study at KUTV.[58]

Tensions within the Turkish cell at KUTV were hardly a new phenomenon. Nâzım and Vâlâ had a strained relationship with a number of the other Turkish communists they had encountered dating back to their days at the Orient Hotel in Tbilisi. At KUTV, too, there had been some run-ins, such as in August 1924, when Vâlâ had been part of a commission that voted to suspend four Turkish students—Hüsni, Server, Hamid, and Mazlum—from KUTV for one year.[59] About one month later, Vâlâ and Aziz Husametdin were involved in an incident with one of these students, a young man named Server.

Server's personal file indicates that he had begun studying at KUTV in the spring of 1924.[60] He was of military background, likely an ex-POW, and considered by university officials to be among the "weaker" students in the Turkish sector.[61] According to a letter of complaint that Server wrote to KUTV officials in September 1924, problems had started when Vâlâ entered Server's room one morning to insist that Server attend a tutorial session. As Server explained in his letter, he "had not yet eaten breakfast," and told Vâlâ as such. Vâlâ, Server said, then stormed out of the room in anger. A short time later, Aziz Husametdin entered Server's quarters, asking him "in the tone and manner of a supervisor," why Server had missed the lesson. Vâlâ and Aziz, argued Server, had behaved inappropriately, in response to something as minor as his "only missing a lesson."[62]

In his letter of complaint regarding this incident, Server played down the importance of his own behavior. His battles with Vâlâ and Aziz, he explained, were just symptoms of a broader problem at KUTV, which Server described as the "emergence of two mutually-opposed camps" among the Turks at KUTV.[63]

Server's explanations did him little good, however. In 1925, he was "sent away from the school due to indiscipline," and began working in a factory in Azerbaijan.[64] According to his personal file, following his expulsion from KUTV Server "went mad in 1925–26" and was committed to an insane asylum.[65]

---

[58] According to a book of memoirs that his daughter would publish decades later, Süleyman Nuri spent the years 1921–22 working as a teacher in a party school in Baku. The book does not discuss his experiences at KUTV. "Süleyman Nuri'nin Biyografisi," *Uyanan Esirler*, 6.

[59] RGASPI, f. 543, op. 2, d. 2, l. 2. "Minutes of the Meeting of the Party Commission of the Foreign Group from August 22, 1924."

[60] RGASPI, f. 495, op. 266, d. 106, l. 2. Personal file of Server.

[61] One file, from August 1924, refers to him as "having been raised in the school of the armed forces." RGASPI, f. 532, op. 2, d. 2, l. 2. The same KUTV report that had put Vâlâ and İsmail Bilen at the top of the list among the "better prepared" Turkish students on campus in early 1925 had found Server to be among the "weaker" ones. RGASPI, f. 532, op. 1, d. 25, l. 56. "List of Students at KUTV-Turks." Undated but apparently from February 1925.

[62] RGASPI, f. 532, op. 2, d. 164, l. 5. Letter from Server, September 23, 1924.

[63] Backing up Server in his letter of complaint were five other Turkish students, including Mazlum and Hamid, both of whom had been kicked out of school alongside Server, as well as Ferid, Selim, and Şinasi.

[64] For this quotation, see RGASPI, f. 495, op. 266, d. 106, l. 2. On the original decision to expel Server, see RGASPI, f. 532, op. 2, d. 2, l. 2, from August 29, 1924. For the letter signed by Server, and co-signed by Mazlum, Ferid, Hamid, Selim, and Şinası, see RGASPI, f. 532, op. 2, d. 164, l. 5. Regarding Server's eventual expulsion, see l. 15-ob of this file.

[65] RGASPI, f. 495, op. 266, d. 106, l. 2. Personal file of Server.

Evidence of conflict between Nâzım's "bourgeois" circle and other TKP members at KUTV can also be seen in Ahmet Cevat's later recollections from these times. In an account first published in 1965, Ahmet Cevat Emre claimed that Cemile Nevşirvanova had written a letter to Semyon Brikke at the Comintern, denouncing Ahmet Cevat as a "speculator," an apparent reference to his book-and-carpet business in the Caucasus. At some point in late 1924, Ahmet Cevat was evicted from the Luxe.[66] Shortly thereafter, he was told to depart Moscow, and the USSR, permanently. According to his KUTV employee paperwork, Ahmet Cevat left his job officially on November 1, 1924.[67]

Another echo from the conflicts taking place between Nâzım's circle and its critics can be found in the so-called "Four-Year Report on the Turkish Cell," which was produced anonymously by one or more of the Turkish students at KUTV. This report is undated, but appears to have been written sometime in 1925, when Nâzım, Şevket Süreyya, and Ahmet Cevat were all in Turkey. The report's stated purpose was to trace the history of Turkish students at KUTV, and it begins in a relatively benign manner by providing brief descriptions of the various TKP members who had arrived at KUTV in its earliest years. Soon, however, the tone of the report shifts noticeably toward a sustained attack against Nâzım, Vâlâ, Şevket Süreyya, and Ahmet Cevat.

Ahmet Cevat is described in the "Four-Year Report" as the heart of the TKP's problems. He was, the report argues, the "intellectual leader" of the party's bourgeois faction. A "revolutionary of the old type who of course didn't know how to organize because he didn't work in a party, but rather on his own," Ahmet Cevat had "stitched together this group around himself and now they have started to realize their future plans." According to the author(s) of the report, the plan of Ahmet Cevat and his bourgeois confederates was to create a party leadership in Turkey through their network of friends. "In ordinary language," the report continues, "they have set up and are creating an organization based upon personal sympathies."[68]

Şevket Süreyya and Nâzım are singled out in the "Four-Year Report" for having made "mistakes" in their dealings with the party. Şevket Süreyya had, according to the report, revealed "decentralizing tendencies," an apparent reference to a willingness, on his part, to organize independently.[69]

"This group," concluded the report, referring to Şevket Süreyya, Nâzım, Vâlâ, and Ahmet Cevat:

seriously considers itself called upon to organize the Turkish communist movement. Previously it was not possible to foresee the danger of the formation of a similar type

---

[66] Ahmet Cevat, in Akbulut (ed.), *Milli Azadlık Savaşı Anıları*, 73. Also see Göksu and Timms, *Romantic Communist*, 53.

[67] Göksu and Timms, *Romantic Communist*, 53. Regarding the KUTV paperwork, see Ahmet Cevat's employee file at KUTV, RGASPI, f. 532, op. 12, d. 1406, l. 9.

[68] RGASPI, f. 532, op. 2, d. 164, l. 14-ob. "Four-Year Report on the Turkish Cell." This report is undated but appears to have been produced in 1925. From Hirst, "Eurasia's Discontent," 202, fn. 558.

[69] On Comintern criticism of Şevket Süreyya in this report, see RGASPI, f. 532, op. 2, d. 164, l. 14-ob. Also see Hirst, "Eurasia's Discontent," 202.

148  RED STAR OVER THE BLACK SEA

of rotten idea of an organization. It appeared only toward the summer of 1924, after the work of comrade Aydemir in Turkey.[70]

The "Four-Year Report" would not be the last such expression of dissatisfaction with Nâzım and other "bourgeois" TKP members. In November 1925, another written complaint about the cadres surrounding Nâzım Hikmet was produced. This time, it was an eight-page letter signed by thirteen TKP members, and was addressed personally to Stalin, Bukharin, Zinoviev, and Comintern Eastern Section head Fyodor Petrov.[71] As was the case with the "Four-Year Report," the introductory paragraphs of this letter assumed an innocuous tone. The document was blandly titled the "declaration on the current situation" of the TKP.

On page 2 of the document, however, the knives came out:

The group that runs the Central Committee (Nâzım, Şefik, Sadreddin Celal, Cevat and company) represents nothing more than the legal editorial board of a legal journal (*Aydınlık*) that has recently been closed. The board itself embraces the chauvinism of solitary literary figures who are in no way connected to the proletarian masses, and who have arisen from sleeping with the exploiters (pashas, generals, merchants, nobles, speculators, etc....) <u>with whom up to this day they have not broken off connections</u>.[72]

The signatories of this letter also charged that "some of these leaders have long been discredited by commercial speculation (Cevat and his students), and by their connections and direct relations with government and bourgeois circles, their rich parents, and, in general, the milieu of exploitation." This "criminal, petit-bourgeois clique," charged the letter, "has carried out no organizational work among the proletarian masses, youth, workers, peasants, or army."[73]

There had apparently been some previous efforts, among the letter's signatories, to get Comintern officials to intervene in the matter of the party's leadership, but without success. This letter maintained, for example, that "it was in the month of July of this year" that its senders had brought up their concerns, "one after the other," to officials in the Eastern Section of the Comintern, which oversaw the Turkish party. In response to their pleas to the Comintern, however, the self-styled "opposition" members had "invariably encountered an attitude of untroubled formality, alternating with threats."[74]

---

[70]  RGASPI, f. 532, op. 2, d. 164, l. 14-ob.

[71]  "Declaration on the current situation of the Turkish Communist Party." RGASPI/IISH, f. 495, op. 181, d. 333, ll. 16–23. The letter is stamped November 18, 1925, an indication of when it was received. On these materials, also see Erden Akbulut (ed.), *Komintern Belgelerinde Nâzım Hikmet* (İstanbul: TÜSTAV, 2002), 49–64.

[72]  Underlining in original. RGASPI/IISH, f. 495, op. 181, d. 333, l. 17. Nâzım was not on the Central Committee of the TKP at this time, although in this letter and elsewhere he is described as a Central Committee member.

[73]  RGASPI/IISH, f. 495, op. 181, d. 333, ll. 18–19.

[74]  RGASPI/IISH, f. 495, op. 181, d. 333, l. 20. This is either a reference to the "Four-Year Report," or a different complaint.

While Şefik Hüsnü, "who has named himself the president of the party," was subjected to withering criticism in this letter, so too were his younger protégés.[75] The self-described "opposition" group's letter argued that Nâzım, Vâlâ, Şevket, and Ahmet Cevat were all unworthy of their status within the party, and that they even had blood on their hands. "The noble hands of the current members of the Central Committee," which the letter-writers identified as including Nâzım, Şefik Hüsnü, Ahmet Cevat, "and Company," "have been rendered scarlet with the working-class blood of our dear comrades who have died or have committed suicide."[76] The petition demanded that the TKP convoke a conference, at which point the opposition would press for the "reorganization of the party."[77]

Who was behind this? Subsequent party-produced paperwork would repeatedly identify Süleyman Nuri as the ringleader of this opposition. Nuri had, in the words of a report that would be written in 1927, "waged war against the leaders and the leading comrades of the Turkish Communist Party," including Şefik Hüsnü and Nâzım.[78] Moreover, the writing style of this letter—with its innocuous title and bland introductory remarks, followed by the fiercest of denunciations—was reminiscent of both the "Four-Year Report" and Süleyman Nuri's earlier written attacks on Mustafa Suphi.

The thirteen TKP members who signed the opposition's letter came from a variety of backgrounds.[79] Two of the signatories were Crimean Tatar women, Aynühayat Voinova and Rahime Nevşirvanova, who were joined by the Crimean Tatar İbrahim Krimskii and the Romanian-born George Ginzberg, aka Rolland.[80] Hilmi Rıza, an ally of Süleyman Nuri from their Baku days, also signed the letter.[81] Individuals mentioned in the letter as supporters, but who were outside of Moscow and unable to sign it, were Zinetullah Nevşirvanov in Tbilisi, "İdris in Baku," "Akif in Baku," one Bedross Torossian in Yerevan, and the Ottoman deserter Noureddin Kadirov in Baku.[82]

The letter-writers' stated objective was to reverse the decision, made in the aftermath of the murders of Suphi and the Central Committee, to recognize Şefik Hüsnü's party in Istanbul as the new TKP. Interestingly, given Süleyman Nuri's role in denouncing Suphi in 1921, the letter signed by these thirteen opposition members valorized the now-martyred TKP leader, pointing out that their letter's signatories included "collaborators of Comrade Suphi."[83]

---

[75] RGASPI/IISH, f. 495, op. 181, d. 333, l. 19.

[76] "Et Cie." RGASPI/IISH, f. 495, op. 181, d. 333, l. 18.

[77] RGASPI/IISH, f. 495, op. 181, d. 333, ll. 19, 21.

[78] RGASPI, f. 495, op. 266, d. 117, l. 52, personal file of Süleyman Nuri. "Spravka" on Süleyman Nuri from October 4, 1927. Also see ibid., l. 55, Letter from the Tsentral'naia kontrol'naia komissia, Russian Communist Party (Bolshevik), to the Eastern Department, Comintern. April 19, 1926. Also see ibid., l. 45, letter from Belov, March 24, 1943; l. 46, letter from Marat (İsmail Bilen), March 1943.

[79] The full list of signatories included Hilmi, Hamid, Liami Hicran, Faruk Kafadar, Aynühayat Voinova, Krimskii, Rahime, Sharif, Abdurrahman, Liami, Rolland, Süleyman Nuri, and Kerim.

[80] Rolland, i.e. George Ginzberg, had become active in the TKP in the early 1920s, at a time when he was living in Istanbul. See RGASPI, f. 495, op. 266, d. 93. Personal file of Rolland.

[81] On Hilmi and Süleyman Nuri, see RGASPI, f. 544, op. 3, d. 53, l. 19. Letter from Abid Alimov, February 23, 1921.

[82] See RGASPI/IISH, f. 495, op. 181, d. 333, ll. 21–23.　　　[83] RGASPI/IISH, f. 495, op. 181, d. 333, l. 21.

An "annex" attached to the opposition group's letter provided two lists: one was made up of individuals associated with the "Central Committee," and the other listed those who were partisans of the "opposition."[84] Underscoring the centrality of social background to the argument behind the letter, each "Central Committee" member's occupation, or that of their father, was listed, as were those of the individuals in the "opposition."

The titles and backgrounds of the committee members' fathers were quite exaggerated, to say the least, owing perhaps to the fact that the letter and annex were written in French. The "Central Committee," according to the "annex," included: Şefik Hüsnü ("son of a noble merchant"), Nâzım Hikmet ("son of General Hikmet Pasha"), Vâlâ ("son of General Nureddin Pasha"), Şevket Süreyya ("son of a general"), and Ahmet Cevat ("speculator, former professor of religion").[85] An additional ten TKP members were described in the opposition's "annex" as "partisans of the Central Committee," including İsmail Bilen ("former smuggler, son of a teacher at the Institute of Naval Studies"), his friend and political partner Aziz Husametdin, and İsmail's wife Mesrure ("a dark personality, woman").[86]

A short paragraph relating to Nuri in this "annex" emphasizes his shared history with Mustafa Suphi. In a brief blurb which was almost certainly penned by Süleyman Nuri himself, Nuri was described as having been "a close collaborator of S.U.B.H.I."[87] While Süleyman Nuri had repeatedly denounced Suphi in 1921, now that Suphi was dead he had become a useful figure with whom to associate oneself.

Meanwhile, the "annex" listed twenty-three individuals associated with the opposition and described the punishments they had allegedly received for having come out against Şefik Hüsnü. Ten comrades had been "distanced" from party work, and in most cases were dispatched to Turkic-speaking areas of the USSR like Azerbaijan, Kazan, and Central Asia.[88] Several had returned to Turkey, eventually dropping out of party activities altogether.[89]

Others had met more tragic ends. According to the "annex," Vâlâ's breakfast-savoring nemesis Server had been exiled to Yekaterinburg, where he had "<u>died of</u>

---

[84] RGASPI/IISH, f. 495, op. 181, d. 333, ll. 24–27. "Annex."

[85] RGASPI/IISH, f. 495, op. 181, d. 333, l. 28. This French-language document uniformly translates the term "pasha" as "general." The "Central Committee" is described in this document as consisting of: Nâzım, Sadreddin Celal (Antel), Vâlâ, Fahri Reşid, Şevket Süreyya, Şefik Hüsnü, Hüseyin Said, Ahmet Cevat, "Doktor Cevdet," Halim. RGASPI/IISH, f. 495, op. 181, d. 333, ll. 24–25.

[86] RGASPI/IISH, f. 495, op. 181, d. 333, l. 28. Supporters of the leadership were listed as Cem, Orhan, Sadık, Mesrure, İsmail Bilen, Mehmet Baytar, Şakır, Aziz, Faik, and Hakkı. "Hakkı" is likely not a reference to Kayserili İsmail Hakkı, but rather another individual by the same name. See İsmail Hakkı personal file, RGASPI, f. 495, op. 266, d. 102.

[87] RGASPI/IISH, f. 495, op. 181, d. 333, l. 27. The document, written in French—which was the *lingua franca* among some Turkish communists and their Soviet colleagues—uses the French spelling of Suphi's name.

[88] RGASPI/IISH, f. 495, op. 181, d. 333, ll. 26–27. Including Kâzım, Nevşirvanov, Idris, Noureddin, Süleyman Nuri, Rolland, Aynühayat, Vedros, Saalim, and Joseph. "Joseph" was likely Weintraub ("Vaintraub"), f. 495, op. 266, d. 67.

[89] The full list of opposition figures listed: Mahir, Hamid, Abdurrahman, Salım, Mazlum, Ecevit, Raif, Arıf, Feyzi, Şinasi, Reşid, Server, Niyazi, Hamdi, Kerim, Ferit, Doctor Selim, Hilmi, Faruk, İbrahim Krimskii, Akif, İsa Abdullah, Hassan, Yanni, Yorgi, Dina, Nico, "and six other Greek workers." RGASPI/IISH, f. 495, op. 181, d. 333, ll. 29–31.

cold."[90] Niyazi was exiled to Baku, "where he killed himself in protest." A TKP member in Moscow by the name of "Dr. Selim" had apparently "gone mad" as a result of his "persecutions."[91] Aynühayat Voinova was expelled from the university and sent to Samarkand, Uzbekistan.[92] Rolland was ejected from the party, as was İbrahim Krimskii. The Varna-born Krimskii, who had long sought permission to live and work in the Crimea, was issued orders on December 21, 1925 to report to Leningrad. There he would await further instructions regarding his eventual transfer to the northwest region of the USSR.[93]

Another student who sided with Süleyman Nuri at this time was a 22-year-old Bulgarian-born Turk named Mahir.[94] "When I arrived at the university," wrote Mahir some thirteen years later in a party autobiography, "there was a split within the Turkish sector. In one group there was a majority of 'alien elements,' as far as social class was concerned, like Vâlâ Nureddin...I was a member of the second group." According to Mahir, after the oppositionists held a meeting that was uncovered by KUTV authorities, "they decided to kick us out of the university and send us to various cities of the USSR." Mahir was dispatched to Kharkov, an industrial city in eastern Ukraine.[95]

In the relatively small world of the Turkish sector at KUTV, Nâzım and his friends were considered by university officials and Şefik Hüsnü alike to be highly important components for the TKP's future. Even their detractors recognized that Nâzım and his friends were up-and-coming members of the party. As the "Four Year Report" had noted, in reference to Şefik Hüsnü and his young "bourgeois" cohort, "the leadership of the party in Turkey is now in their hands."[96]

Süleyman Nuri was expelled from KUTV in late 1925. His reputation within the party now eviscerated, Nuri attempted to enroll in the International Lenin School (ILS). Upon learning of Nuri's background at KUTV, however, school officials at the ILS rejected his application.[97] Eventually, Nuri was accepted into an engineering school in Leningrad, from which he would graduate in 1927 or 1928. From there, he would be sent to work in Baku.[98]

The self-styled "opposition" was no more, and the Comintern leadership in Moscow had made it clear where their sympathies lay: with Şefik Hüsnü, Nâzım Hikmet, İsmail

---

[90] Underlining in original. This information differs from the material in Server's personal file, which indicates that he was living in a mental asylum in Azerbaijan. RGASPI, f. 495, op. 266, d. 106, l. 2.

[91] RGASPI/IISH, f. 495, op. 181, d. 333, ll. 25–26. Weintraub ("Joseph") was also sent away from KUTV due to his involvement in "group conflicts," RGASPI, f. 495, op. 266, d. 67, l. 16.

[92] On Aynühayat Voinova, also see RGASPI, f. 495, op. 266, d. 320b, ll. 92, 102.

[93] RGASPI, f. 495, op. 266, d. 320b, l. 145.

[94] RGASPI, f. 495, op. 266, d. 82, l. 25. Personal file of Mahir.

[95] Today known as Kharkiv. RGASPI, f. 495, op. 266, d. 82, ll. 11, 19. Letter from Mahir Ahmet to Georgi Dimitrov, September 5, 1937.

[96] RGASPI, f. 532, op. 2, d. 164, l. 14-ob. "Four-Year Report, Turkish Cell." The report mentions that Nâzım had returned to Turkey, an indication that the "Four-Year Report" was composed in the second half of 1924 or early 1925.

[97] RGASPI, f. 495, op. 266, d. 117, ll. 51–52. Personal file of Süleyman Nuri.

[98] According to a party "spravka" from March 24, 1943, Nuri graduated in 1927. RGASPI, f. 495, op. 266, d. 117, l. 45, "Spravka." The biography at the beginning of Nuri's *Uyanan Esirler* lists the date of his graduation as June 11, 1928, p. 6.

Bilen, and their "bourgeois" comrades. Süleyman Nuri would not soon forget what had happened to him. Nor would he let go of his resentment toward those who had taken over his party.

Nâzım exited the contretemps with Nuri's group in a stronger position than ever. He went on, in May 1926, to take part in the Vienna conference of the TKP, where he was formally chosen to sit on the TKP Central Committee.[99] In a letter written in 1927, Şefik Hüsnü placed Nâzım among possible designated successors, should the TKP leader himself be arrested.[100]

## Back to the Future

Nâzım's new Moscow writing from the years 1925–28 picked up, in certain ways, where he had left off after departing in 1924. Whereas the poems Nâzım had published in Turkey—both in the TKP's publications and in *Akbaba*—had differed considerably from Nâzım's early Moscow works, now that Nâzım had returned to the Soviet capital his verse had similarly resumed the Futurist-inspired style of his earlier years.

Such was the case with "Oil's Response" (*Neftin Cevabı*). Nâzım wrote this poem on the road from Moscow to Baku in 1927. On the one hand, it is a very Futurist-sounding work in its valorization of the immense industrial project of developing the oil fields of Azerbaijan. On the other hand, there is real humanity behind the work, which also displays a sense of humor.

> I'm in a city in whose houses live giants!
> We called from below ground to the giants of this city
> We built with our hands the homes of the giants
> And now the giants
> > waking
> > > from their deep sleep
> one by one
> > wandering
> > > I too, in this city's streets
> > > have come to knock on the doors of its houses...
> > > I've got a question for the oil.
> > > And I came to get an answer!
> > > Listen, oil!
> > > Listen to me from seven stories below ground
> > > You know that we
> > > by the sweat of our brow

---

[99] One document says that Nâzım was on the TKP Central Committee between 1927 and 1932. Nâzım Hikmet's personal file, RGASPI, f. 495, op. 266, d. 47, Part I, l. 141. "Spravka" from August 3, 1951.

[100] RGASPI/IISH, f. 495, op. 181, d. 338, ll. 33–36, esp. 35. Letter undated but classified under materials produced between January and November, 1927.

and our deceased master[101]
with his eyes that do not die
want to create a new world![102]

"Moscow-Tokyo-Moscow" similarly retains the experimentalism of Nâzım's earlier stay in the Soviet capital. In a manner that Nâzım embraced in the early 1920s, but which he had avoided in most of his poetry from Turkey in 1924–25, he re-arranged the spacing of the words on the page as a means of conveying both meaning and reading style. This poem ends with the cheer:

> Moscow
>> is a place
>> that is veee-ry far
>> from Tokyo
>
> Where is Moscow
>>> Where is Turkey!
>
> But look at
>> the work that has been born
>> in ten years:
> We've brought it to within three days of Tokyo![103]

Something new to Nâzım's second stint was the large number of theater-related projects that he began to work on. In 1920 in Istanbul, Nâzım had written a one-act play called "By the Hearth" (*Ocak Başında*), but otherwise he had not produced much for the stage. Finding himself surrounded by the works of directors like Meyerhold and Stanislavsky, Nâzım had become more interested in this genre during his earlier stay in Moscow.[104] Now, he further deepened his involvement in both the writing and staging of highly experimental dramatic performances.

Of particular importance to Nâzım's theater work at this time was the Riga-born Nikolai Ekk, who worked at the Meyerhold Theater and taught classes at KUTV. Together, Nâzım and Ekk set up a new theater called "METLA" (Figure 6.2).[105] "METLA" stood for, in Russian, "Moscow's Only Leninist Theatre Studio," an acronym which doubled as the Russian word for "broom." In keeping with the spirit with which revolutionary cultural forms were still publicly embraced in Moscow in 1925, Nâzım

---

[101] The Turkish word *usta* means "master" in the sense, for example, of a skilled tradesman.

[102] "Neft" is the Russian word for "oil." Yapı Kredi edition of Nâzım Hikmet's collected works, (*Şiirler* Vol. 8), 217–219, here 217.

[103] "Moskova-Tokyo-Moskova," ibid., 188–190, here 190.

[104] Göksu and Timms, *Romantic Communist*, 50.

[105] See Nikolai Ekk's personnel file from KUTV, RGASPI, f. 495, op. 65a, d. 8603. On METLA, also see Antonina Karlovna Svercheskaia, *Izvestnyi i neizvestnyi Nâzım: Materialy i biografii* (Moscow: Institut vostoko-vedenia RAN, 2001), 34–52; Clark, *Eurasia Without Borders*, 70. On Ekk, see McGuire, *Red at Heart*, 81; Göksu and Timms, *Romantic Communist*, 46, 65–68.

**Figure 6.2** The METLA Theater

and Ekk proposed to "sweep away" the traditional elements in theater and replace them with new forms of agitational production.[106]

METLA opened on September 19, 1926, with an exposition of several one-act works relating to World War I and the October Revolution. Using actors from the Meyerhold Theater and KUTV, Nâzım and Ekk encouraged their performers to improvise their roles and even change characters mid-production.[107] Documentary film footage was often shot against a screen in the background, behind the actors onstage.[108] While METLA closed down in March 1927, theater would continue to constitute an important genre in Nâzım's writing.[109]

In 1928, Nâzım's book *Güneşi İçenlerin Türküsü* ("The *Türkü* for those who Drink up the Sun") was published in Baku by *Azerneshr*, a state-owned publisher of Azeri-language Arabic-script books. The book, which was just over one hundred pages, was a mix of works, including a broad sampling of poems Nâzım had composed during his first stay in Moscow. This publication was a clear expression of experimental urban culture, something that would become increasingly rare in non-Russian language publications in the USSR in the years to come. By the mid-1930s, non-Russian cultural production in the USSR—especially when it came to "eastern" populations—would

---

[106] Vâlâ and Nâzım gave themselves nicknames at this time. Vâlâ became Vâ-Nû, Nâzım was Nun-Ha. Nâzım used this name, which derived from his Arabic-script initials, when putting on plays in the second half of the 1920s. Fish, *Nâzım'ın Çilesi*, 132.

[107] Ibid., 135–136. On Nâzım's plays during his second stint in Moscow, also see Makal, *Beyaz Perdede ve Sahnede Nâzım Hikmet*, 176–180.

[108] Göksu and Timms, *Romantic Communist*, 66–67; Fish, *Nâzım'ın Çilesi*, 132.

[109] The great Turkish theater and film director, Muhsin (Ertuğrul) spent approximately two years in Moscow in the 1920s and would later credit Nâzım with helping him gain access to the theater world of the Soviet capital. Hirst, "Eurasia's Discontent," 43, fn. 110. On Nâzım assisting Muhsin in making contacts in Moscow, see Sülker, *Nâzım Hikmet'in Gerçek Yaşamı*, vol. 1, 231; Fish, *Nâzım'ın Çilesi*, 143.

be largely confined to folkloric and rural models of expression, with Russian becoming the predominant language of Soviet "high" culture.[110]

During the late 1920s, Soviet cultural policymaking was becoming increasingly politicized. Whereas the earliest years of the revolution had been more wide-open with respect to literature and the arts, now the mood in Moscow was shifting in a substantially more conservative direction. The "cultural revolution" that had been championed during the USSR's earliest days had opened up space for radical experimentation. Now, however, influential figures within the party had begun to embrace more dogmatic and militant forms of cultural production. While Socialist Realism, with its emphasis on using art as propaganda, would not achieve a hegemonic position in the USSR until the 1930s, already in the late 1920s debates about culture were becoming deeply embedded within the politics of the era.[111]

Katerina Clark has observed that Nâzım's writing "continually interrogates the border between East and West," pointing to Nâzım's mockery of the Orientalist writer Pierre Loti's stereotypes of "the East."[112] While I agree with this statement, I would modify it to say that it is not only the "border between East and West" that is so closely bound up with Nâzım's verse, but rather borders in general—and that this would remain a feature of Nâzım's poetry for most of the rest of his life.

## Exit Strategies

One day in Moscow in the late summer of 1926 Nâzım received a postcard from Vâlâ Nureddin, who had returned to Istanbul approximately one year earlier. Since that time, Nâzım's old high school friend had been bouncing around between jobs, doing mostly journalism and translation work. It was in the latter role that Vâlâ was now returning, albeit briefly, to the USSR. The erstwhile communist who had once described himself as a "professional revolutionary" was now making plans to visit Leningrad with a delegation from the Istanbul Chamber of Commerce.[113]

Soon after receiving Vâlâ's card, Nâzım put himself on a train to Leningrad, where he met up with his friend on September 17. The two discussed the possibility of an amnesty being declared in Turkey. This would allow Nâzım to return to Istanbul without having to worry about serving his fifteen-year prison sentence from 1925. Nâzım then went back to Moscow and contacted the Turkish Embassy in order to

---

[110] This is an element of Bolshevik nationality policymaking that tends to be ignored in Martin's *Affirmative Action Empire*, which provides a more quantitative, rather than qualitative, approach to cultural production in languages other than Russian.

[111] Göksu and Timms, *Romantic Communist*, 63. Also see Suny, *The Soviet Experiment*, 237.

[112] Katerina Clark, "European and Russian Cultural Interactions with Turkey: 1910s–1930s," *Comparative Studies of South Asia, Africa, and the Middle East*, vol. 33, no. 2 (2013), 201–213, here 209.

[113] Vâlâ was to serve as their interpreter. Sülker, *Nâzım Hikmet'in Gerçek Yaşamı*, vol. 1, 236, 252. The amnesty was called in commemoration of the fifth-year anniversary of the founding of the Turkish Republic. Also see Vâ-Nû, *Bu Dünyadan Nâzım Geçti*, 407.

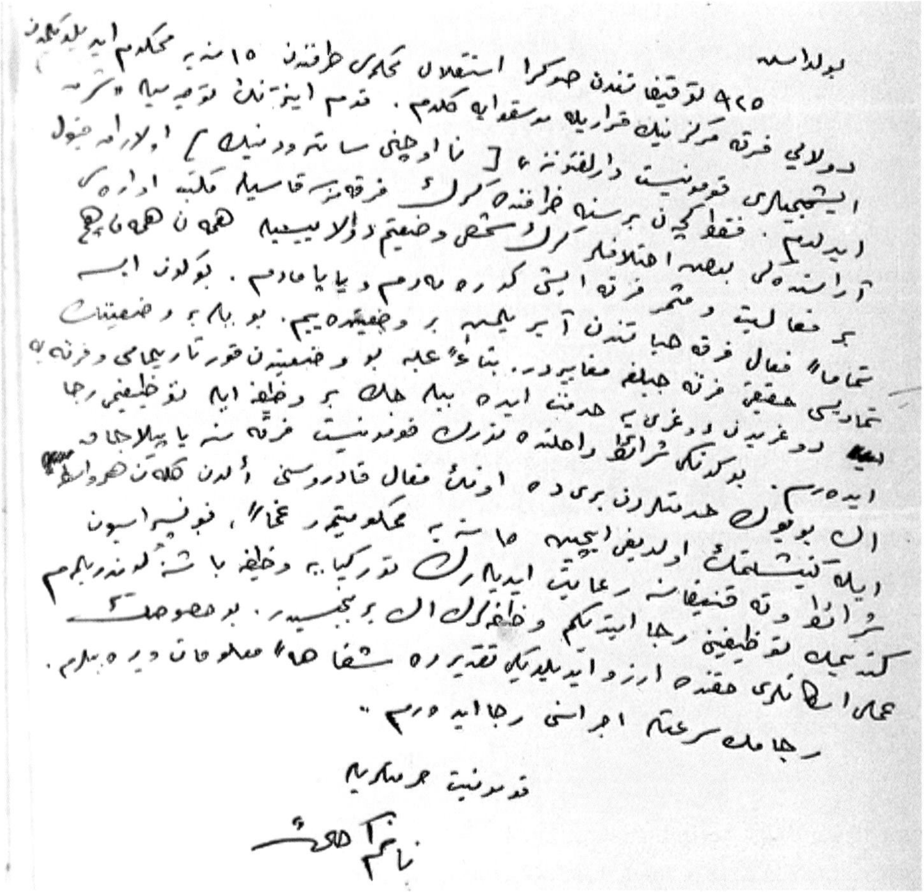

156   RED STAR OVER THE BLACK SEA

**Figure 6.3** Nâzım's letter to the Comintern

start the process of obtaining a Turkish passport. A general amnesty was declared in Turkey just one month later, at the end of October 1926.[114]

It was around this time that Nâzım wrote a letter to Comintern officials, telling them of his desire to return to Turkey (Figure 6.3). In this note, Nâzım explained that he was hungry for action. "Over the past year," he wrote, "I have not seen or experienced any activity or party work." "As for today," Nâzım lamented, "my situation is completely distanced from the life of party activity." In a tone of apparent, or perhaps performative, frustration, he emphasized that he needed to go where the important work was to be done—Turkey. In Nâzım's words, the point of his return would be to carry out undercover "conspiratorial" work on behalf of the now-outlawed TKP.[115]

Why leave the USSR at all? It was not really the custom at KUTV, at least among the Turkish students, for individuals with political ambitions to remain forever in the

[114] In conjunction with the Republican Day holiday of October 29. Sülker, *Nâzım Hikmet'in Gerçek Yaşamı*, vol. 1, 236–237.

[115] "Konspirasyon-i şerait." RGASPI/IISH, f. 495, op. 181, 335, l. 8. Letter from Nâzım Hikmet to the "3rd International," i.e., the Comintern's offices in Moscow. Undated but apparently from 1926 or 1927. On this document, also see Akbulut (ed.), *Komintern Belgelerinde Nâzım Hikmet*, 75–77.

USSR unless they had to. KUTV graduates who did not foresee a future in either politics or espionage were found jobs, usually industrial ones, in the Soviet Union, while those—like Nâzım—who were being groomed for leadership positions went back to their home country. Nâzım was now almost twenty-seven years old. If he was ever going to do something for the party in Turkey, now would be the time.

In his letter to the Comintern, Nâzım also hinted at some of the recent rifts in the TKP at KUTV. He explained that his desire to return to Turkey was due to "both conflicts (*ihtilaflar*) taking place within the party organization at KUTV, as well as for personal reasons." Nâzım went out of his way to emphasize the potential benefit to the party of his transfer to Istanbul, writing that his "greatest services" in Turkey would come in the form of his ability to recruit new party members. Somewhat disingenuously, Nâzım made a point of noting that he was making the decision to go back to Istanbul "despite my fifteen-year sentence," without mentioning that he fully expected the punishment to be commuted.[116] Indeed, it was due precisely to this amnesty that Nâzım now wanted to return to Turkey.

*

After a frustrating year of dealing with the Turkish Embassy in Moscow, Nâzım still had not received the paperwork he needed to return to Turkey legally. According to some accounts, he had hoped to take Dr. Lena with him, but neither one of them could obtain the permission required from Soviet and Turkish authorities to allow her to go. The border was growing increasingly difficult to cross.[117]

Nâzım made arrangements to return to Turkey illegally, traveling alongside İsmail Bilen. In the early summer of 1928, the two comrades set off on their journey, taking the train from Moscow down to Rostov-on-Don, in the south of Russia. From Rostov they went to Baku, where Nâzım and İsmail rested for a week. Heading westward from Azerbaijan, they made their way to Batumi.[118]

He had come of age in the USSR. Long gone was the stumbling, semi-competent man-child who couldn't be trusted to carry his own money. Not only had Nâzım managed to survive in Moscow, he had thrived. He had completed the two-year program of study at KUTV, held a number of jobs, learned a new language, published books, gotten to know people from all over the world, rubbed shoulders with famous Soviet cultural and political figures, and been married—twice. He had lived in an exciting, multilingual, international city where he felt that history was unfolding before his very eyes. Nâzım was also considered a rising star in the TKP, a veritable shoo-in for more senior leadership positions in the future.

Now Nâzım was once again returning "home" to a country where he had spent just six months of his life.

---

[116] Materials relating to the Turkish Communist Party, RGASPI/IISH, f. 495, op. 181, d. 335, l. 8.

[117] Sülker, *Nâzım Hikmet'in Gerçek Yaşamı*, vol. 1, 228–229, 234. Fish, *Nâzım'ın Çilesi*, 297.

[118] Sülker, *Nâzım Hikmet'in Gerçek Yaşamı*, vol. 1, 240; Göksu and Timms, *Romantic Communist*, 73; Memet Fuat, *Nâzım Hikmet*, 74. Bilen had just returned to the Soviet Union from Turkey, where he had been working for the party. RGASPI, f. 495, op. 266, d. 12, Part I, l. 80. "Spravka" from July 1941.

# 7
# At Large in Istanbul

Nâzım was back in Istanbul, and he was in the news. On Friday, October 5, 1928, the front page of the Istanbul daily *Cumhuriyet* featured two pictures of him (Figure 7.1). In the foreground was a small oval bearing his portrait, in which Nâzım is well-dressed and looking directly at the reader. Above the portrait is a photograph taken the day before. In it, Nâzım can be seen marching alongside İsmail Bilen, the two of them prodded forward by a police officer. Once again, Nâzım is staring straight into the camera, while İsmail Bilen lurks in the background, his face obscured by the shadows of his flat cap.

İsmail Bilen had been living in Turkey since 1926, when he had returned from the Soviet Union. At that time he had initially been appointed the provincial head of the underground TKP operation in Adana, in South-Central Anatolia. Later he moved to Istanbul, where, according to TKP paperwork, İsmail served as Secretary-General of the TKP in 1927–28. In 1928, he had crossed the border illegally back to the Soviet Union, returning to Turkey with Nâzım Hikmet later in the year.[1]

In July 1928, Nâzım and İsmail were arrested on the Turkish side of the frontier, outside Hopa, and charged with trying to enter Turkey illegally.[2] They spent two months in jail in Hopa before being sent to a prison in Rize. After two to three more weeks in Rize, Nâzım and İsmail Bilen were transferred to Istanbul, the moment captured on the front page of *Cumhuriyet*.[3]

The *Cumhuriyet* article was about Nâzım specifically—İsmail was no more than an afterthought, which the enigmatic and secretive Bilen surely preferred. The news item that ran in the paper came under a banner stating: "The poet says he is interested in communism from a literary perspective." The tone of the newspaper's coverage of Nâzım—no author is listed for the article—is sympathetic and credulous. The sub-headline of the piece read "Nâzım Hikmet Bey wants to put out a literary journal called 'Sol Cihan' ('Left World')." Two-thirds of the piece was devoted to simply reprinting Nâzım's own words.

"I am not a member of a secret organization," Nâzım declared, falsely. "I am interested in Marxism and Communism only from a literary perspective. In Russia, I was solely involved with literature."[4]

---

[1] On İsmail Bilen's activities during these years, see "Spravka," RGASPI, f. 495, op. 266, d. 12, Part I, l. 48. From May 28, 1948. Also see ll. 80, 113, 118.
[2] On Nâzım's return to Turkey, see Göksu and Timms, *Romantic Communist*, 70; Babayev, *Nâzım Hikmet*, 137.
[3] Memet Fuat, *Nâzım Hikmet*, 77.
[4] *Cumhuriyet*, October 5 (Teşrinevvel), 1928, 1. Also see Sülker, *Nâzım Hikmet'in Gerçek Yaşamı*, vol. 1, 269–270 for more on this brief interview.

*Red Star over the Black Sea: Nâzım Hikmet and his Generation.* James H. Meyer, Oxford University Press. © James H. Meyer 2023.
DOI: 10.1093/oso/9780192871176.003.0009

**Figure 7.1** Nâzım and İsmail on *Cumhuriyet*'s front page

None of this was true, of course. Nâzım was a member of a party that had been illegal in Turkey for three years, and he had returned to Turkey specifically—if his earlier letter to the Comintern is to be believed—in order to undertake "conspiratorial" organizing activities on behalf of the party.

It was time to get to work.

## Back "Home"

Before Nâzım could move back in with his family in Istanbul, he first needed to settle a series of legal issues stemming from both his 1925 conviction and his more recent arrest on the frontier. Nâzım had been sentenced to fifteen years in prison in 1925, but this was thrown out due to the amnesty from the following year. As for the arrest at the border, Nâzım's punishment was three months behind bars. Because he had already been imprisoned for a period longer than that, Nâzım was released immediately following the conclusion of his last hearing on December 23, 1928.[5]

After leaving detention, Nâzım moved into his father's crowded house, which now also included two young twin children, Metin and Melda.[6] Twenty-seven years old and newly released from prison, Nâzım had no money and few prospects of employment. The only real job he'd had in recent years had been in Moscow at a place called "Communist University." It is unclear how Hikmet Bey's young wife Cavide responded to her adult stepson's arrival.[7]

During these early months in Istanbul, Nâzım waited for news relating to his Soviet spouse, Dr. Lena Yurchenko. According to a much later account, Dr. Lena had accompanied Nâzım and his "comrade-communists" to Odessa. She could not, however, obtain the papers necessary for continuing onward to Turkey.[8]

After Nâzım returned to Istanbul, he and Dr. Lena continued to correspond for some time. With Nâzım now out of prison in Turkey, Lena had apparently not yet given up on getting her papers to join him in Istanbul. The odds, however, did not look good.

In a postcard that Lena sent to Nâzım dated May 29, 1929, she wrote:

My Dear Nâzım
I am happy to have your letter…Please write more frequently, this long silence has cost me dear…How do they explain the refusal to grant a visa? My regards to your father, uncle, Samiye…If you have no time, ask somebody else to write. Please send me a Turkish textbook and a kilo of coffee….I miss you very much my love…It will soon be a year since we parted. I miss you so much that sometimes it seems that the door will open and I will see you. I've lost all hope that this will happen.
Lots of kisses, Lena.[9]

This was the last Nâzım would hear from Lena. For neither the first time nor the last, the Turkish–Soviet frontier would come between Nâzım and someone he loved.[10]

---

[5] Göksu and Timms, *Romantic Communist*, 76.    [6] Memet Fuat, *A'dan Z'ye Nâzım Hikmet*, 170–171.
[7] According to Memet Fuat, Cavide Hanım was 24 years younger than Hikmet Bey. *A'dan Z'ye Nâzım Hikmet*, 343.
[8] Tulyakova-Hikmet, *Bahtiyar Ol Nâzım*, 253. It is unclear why Nâzım would have first traveled to Odessa, as he ended up crossing the border at Batumi-Hopa.
[9] This translation is taken from Göksu and Timms, *Romantic Communist*, 72.
[10] On Lena also see Sülker, *Nâzım Hikmet'in Gerçek Yaşamı*, vol. 1, 197–198; Memet Fuat, *Nâzım Hikmet*, 80.

Nâzım had gone from living independently, producing his own plays, and sharing a bed with Dr. Lena to having no job, earning no money, and staying with his father's second family. He was cut off from much of what had defined and shaped him over the previous six years. In Moscow, Nâzım had been special just because of who he was—an "eastern" foreigner interested in communism. In Istanbul, on the other hand, he was left more to his own devices.

## Party Trouble

Back "home" in Istanbul, it was not so easy for Nâzım to find a place for himself. The late Ottoman world that he had been trained to one day play a role in leading had been brought to a decisive end and he could no longer count on past connections. Back in Ankara in 1921, Nâzım and Vâlâ had found numerous relatives and friends of the family working in important positions, people who ended up helping in a variety of ways. The two 19-year-olds had occupied positions of privilege, and were able to make demands upon government officials and then abandon their jobs in Bolu without feeling much apparent concern for the consequences.

Nâzım no longer had the influential ties that had previously been his birthright. His uncle had been released from detention in relation to the alleged 1926 assassination plot, but Ali Fuat Pasha's political career was dormant for now. Nâzım had, moreover, indelibly damaged his standing in Turkey by leaving Anatolia during a time that was now recognized as one of "national" struggle. Having sat out the war, Nâzım was in no position to expect to be brought into elite Kemalist circles.

At the time of Nâzım's return to Istanbul, the TKP's organization was in dire need of new blood. On October 25, 1927, party General Secretary Vedat Nedim was arrested by Turkish authorities. In detention, he had given up a long list of names and addresses.[11] This information led to the arrest or trials in absentia of fifty-four alleged TKP members. Since the arrests, most of the party's high-ranking members had either been put in prison or were on the run. Efforts to reorganize the party were badly hampered by police raids unfolding in cities across the country.[12]

Sometime after returning to Istanbul, Nâzım began to hold meetings and recruit fellow TKP members in an effort to create a new TKP Central Committee. Şevket Süreyya, who was released in late 1926 after one-and-a-half years behind bars, may also have been involved in these undertakings.[13] While in his memoirs from the late 1950s Şevket Süreyya Aydemir gives the impression that he had cut his ties with the TKP following his release from prison, archival evidence from Moscow suggests otherwise.[14]

---

[11] Vedat Nedim became general secretary of the TKP after Şefik Hüsnü fled the country in 1925 following the crackdown prompted by the Sheikh Sait rebellion.

[12] Göksu and Timms, *Romantic Communist*, 79.    [13] Aydemir, *Suyu Arayan Adam*, 342–343.

[14] Şevket Süreyya Aydemir wrote that, upon being released from prison, he realized that the "Moscow-based Comintern, with its manner, behavior, and indoctrination had now lost all of its attributes of logic and leadership." *Suyu Arayan Adam*, 344.

Şevket and Nâzım continued to write, in coded messages, to one another while Nâzım was in Moscow. A 1927 letter from Şevket to Nâzım begins with the observation that "the return of the little one" needed to be "postponed." Şevket Süreyya's use of ellipsis in a number of places in the letter, and the nicknames he employed for the individuals they discussed, seems to have been designed to conceal the letter's meaning from the watchful eyes of authorities in Turkey, the Soviet Union, or perhaps both countries.[15]

Comintern paperwork alleges that, in 1928, Şevket Süreyya sent a letter from Turkey to the Comintern offices in Moscow. This would have been considered a serious breach of hierarchy, as a regular party member like Şevket Süreyya should not have been attempting to establish a direct line of communication with the Comintern in the first place. The courier employed by Şevket Süreyya was, according to these documents, Salih Hacıoğlu.[16]

Using Hacıoğlu to establish contact with the Comintern would have made sense to Şevket and Nâzım for a couple of reasons. First, they both knew Hacıoğlu personally, having worked with him on *Aydınlık* and *Orak-Çekiç* in 1925. More importantly, Hacıoğlu and his wife Sabiha Sünbül were already planning to immigrate to the USSR. Having been jailed on repeated occasions in Turkey, most recently in 1927, the 42-year-old Hacıoğlu and 32-year-old Sünbül began taking steps to leave Turkey permanently.

Despite Hacıoğlu's illustrious past as an early Turkish communist, he and Sabiha Sünbül were not welcomed with open arms in Moscow. Instead, Hacıoğlu ran afoul of expectations that foreign visitors arrive only after receiving the consent of party authorities—something that he had not done. This infraction, combined with the fact that Hacıoğlu had attempted to deliver to the Comintern an unsanctioned letter from Şevket Süreyya, led to Salih's expulsion from the party "on grounds of opportunism, in coming to the USSR on his own volition and passing on letters to the Comintern."[17]

Salih Hacıoğlu's wife, Sabiha Sünbül, had accompanied her husband in immigrating to the Soviet Union. Born in 1896 in a village called Vasket in Erzincan province in eastern Anatolia, Sabiha had married her first husband Ömer and relocated to Ankara at the age of 21. A daughter was born in 1916, but Ömer died in 1923, after which time Sabiha moved to Istanbul. As a 32-year-old widow with a 12-year-old daughter, Sabiha married Salih Hacıoğlu in 1928. That same year, all three members of the newly established family set off for a new life in the USSR.[18]

While Salih was expelled from the party as a result of his infractions, the family was allowed to remain in the Soviet Union.[19] They moved to Azerbaijan, where Salih

---

[15] RGASPI/IISH, f. 495, op. 181, d. 249, ll. 17–18. Letter from Şevket Süreyya to Nâzım Hikmet, April 10, 1927.

[16] RGASPI, f. 495, op. 266, d. 98, ll. 7–8, "Spravka," January 18, 1957. Also see ibid., ll. 42-ob, 59, 60, 66, and elsewhere.

[17] RGASPI, f. 495, op. 266, d. 98, ll. 7–8. "Spravka."

[18] On Hacıoğlu and Sünbül's daughter, see RGASPI, f. 495, op. 266, d. 98, l. 1-ob.

[19] RGASPI, f. 495, op. 266, d. 98, l. 59. "Spravka," October 23, 1940.

worked as a veterinarian and Sabiha was employed as a laboratory technician in his clinic.[20]

Thanks to Nâzım's efforts to create a new Central Committee in Istanbul, he quickly went from being Şefik Hüsnü's young protégé to an enemy of the party's leaders. A furious letter from the Comintern addressed "to all members of the TKP" described Nâzım as a member of the "opposition."[21]

"The IKKI," the letter began, employing the Russian initials for the Comintern, "does not and cannot recognize, and will not recognize, this group of renegades." Nâzım, Vâlâ, Şevket Süreyya, and Ahmet Cevat were "simply renegades, sell-outs to the police," argued the letter, which denounced the "opportunists" in typical fashion:[22]

> Opportunist-liquidators like the poet Nâzım Hikmet (employed in the good graces by the police and Kemalist justice) who, in the wake of their hypocritical submission to the party ran away during the purge of 1927—all of them are Menshevik elements, serving the interests of the bourgeoisie, who are for the moment still in the communist movement.[23]

According to TKP paperwork, a total of forty-five individuals, including Nâzım Hikmet and Zeki Baştımar, were expelled from the party in connection with Nâzım's leadership bid.[24] Different sets of documents in the archives suggest varying years for Nâzım's expulsion, and the biographical literature on Nâzım similarly differs with respect to this question.[25] It seems most likely, however, that Nâzım's takeover attempt occurred sometime in 1929, not long after his release from jail, although the groundwork may have begun in 1928 with Şevket Süreyya's letter to the Comintern.[26] Formal expulsion from the party occurred later, but regardless of when Nâzım was actually ejected from the TKP, his active participation in party work came to an end in 1929.[27]

---

[20] RGASPI, f. 495, op. 266, d. 98, ll. 7–8, "Spravka," January 18, 1957, and elsewhere. Memet Fuat writes that Nâzım was expelled after holding a secret meeting at Zeki Baştımar's Istanbul house in February 1932 (*Nâzım Hikmet*, 81). However, Zeki Baştımar's party file indicates that he fell in with the opposition in 1929. By 1932, Baştımar was already on record as having renounced his "mistakes." RGASPI, personal file of Zeki Baştımar, f. 495, op. 266, d. 30, l. 173.

[21] RGASPI, f. 82, op. 2, d. 1330, l. 113. "Informational report about Nâzım Hikmet," September 8, 1951, ll. 112–115, quoting documents from December 1930, 114. Also see f. 495, op. 266, d. 47, Part I, l. 132.

[22] Nâzım Hikmet's personal file, RGASPI, f. 495, op. 266, d. 47, Part I, ll. 135–140, here 137. "Documents from the Comintern Archive from 1925–1939." For a reproduction of this report from 1951, also see RGASPI, f. 82, op. 2, d. 1330, ll. 113, 120.

[23] RGASPI, f. 82, op. 2, d. 1330, l. 120. Also see RGASPI, f. 495, op. 266, d. 98, l. 59. "Spravka," October 23, 1940; İsmail Hakkı personal file, f. 495, op. 266, d. 102, ll. 1–5.

[24] RGASPI, f. 495, op. 266, d. 47, Part I, l. 141. Nâzım Hikmet personal file.

[25] Göksu and Timms imply that Nâzım's leadership quest began in 1929 and culminated three years later. *Romantic Communist*, 79–80. For a similar account, see Akbulut and Tunçay (eds.), *İstanbul Komünist Grubu'ndan*, 392. Blasing, citing Akgül, writes that Nâzım was expelled in 1930. *Nâzım Hikmet*, 66–67.

[26] The more reliable-seeming reports in Nâzım's Comintern and party paperwork usually put the date at 1929. See, for example, RGASPI, f. 495, op. 266, d. 47; Part I, ll. 85, 86, 96, 97, 135; Part II, ll. 23, 124. Individuals who were associated with Nâzım's takeover attempt, such as Zeki Baştımar, were similarly expelled in 1929, a further indication that this is when the attempt took place. RGASPI, f. 495, op. 266, d. 30, l. 173.

[27] In the words of a Kremlin archivist examining Nâzım's party history in 1951, "in the Comintern archive there are materials that indicate that Nâzım Hikmet was expelled from the party in 1927, 1929, and 1930," with still other documents stating he had been removed from the party in 1934. RGASPI, f. 82, op. 2, d. 1330, l. 121, September 21, 1951.

164    RED STAR OVER THE BLACK SEA

Throughout the 1930s, Nâzım's name would be hissed alongside those of Şevket Süreyya, Vedat Nedim, Vâlâ Nureddin, and Ahmet Cevat as a traitor to the party. TKP and Comintern paperwork from these years frequently describe Nâzım as a "Trotskyite," an increasingly devastating characterization to make of someone in the 1930s.[28] In the wake of Leon Trotsky's political defeat and deportation from the Soviet Union in 1929, any connection with the disgraced former hero of the revolution would potentially have serious consequences in years to come.[29]

As the years passed, Nâzım and the other individuals associated with his efforts to create a new party organization in Istanbul came to be known collectively as the "Nâzımist opposition." Zeki Baştımar, for instance, would claim in 1936 that he had, years earlier, been a member of "the Nâzımist (Nazymovskoi) opposition, without knowing or understanding its provocative and anti-party character."[30] Other so-called former members of the "Nâzımist opposition" included the former KUTV students Hüseyin Abdullahoğlu[31] and Ahmet Nuri Fırıncı ("the Baker"), who were each described as such on paperwork from the 1930s.[32]

Former confederates of Nâzım would denounce him for much of the decade to come.[33] In July 1932, a Turkish communist named Sakov Beki, who had studied at KUTV when Nâzım was in Moscow for his second stint at the university, told Comintern authorities that he had previously been enticed by Nâzım to join a "Trotskyite-Police opposition" group that the poet had allegedly been running.[34] Another erstwhile collaborator of Nâzım, Kara Mehmet, would later accuse the poet of gangster-style tactics, alleging in July 1932 that Nâzım had assigned him the task of breaking the "leg, arm, etc." of someone who "needed to be away from his post for a little while."[35] In a September 17, 1933 "Report on Failures, Provocations, and Conspiracies in the TKP," Nâzım is identified as "the leader of the Trotskyite-Police Opposition."[36]

---

[28] RGASPI, f. 82, op. 2, d. 1330, ll. 64, 88, 113, 120, 121, 122. Leon Trotsky lived in exile on an island in Turkey's Marmara Sea between 1929 and 1933, but appears to have had no contact with Turkish communist figures.

[29] In July 1932, the Central Committee of the TKP in Turkey sent a letter to the Comintern in Moscow observing that "Nâzım...is no longer a revolutionary, his revolutionary spirit has been extinguished." RGASPI, f. 82, op. 2, 1330, ll. 114, 122–123, July 27, 1932. Copy, part of compilation reports from 1951.

[30] Zeki Baştımar personal file, RGASPI, f. 495, op. 266, d. 30, l. 167. "Autobiography," from April 3, 1936.

[31] Abdullahoğlu had been a Turkish student at KUTV in 1927. Personal file of Hüseyin Abdullahoğlu, RGASPI, f. 495, op. 266, d. 320a, l. 2. Report written by "Miller," August 1933.

[32] Personal file of Ahmet Fırıncı, RGASPI, f. 495, op. 266, d. 37, l. 4. Ahmet had studied at KUTV in 1928. "Spravka" from 1934.

[33] Also see "Report on failures, provocations, and conspiracies within the Communist Party of Turkey," a document which can be found in numerous personal files at RGASPI. Nâzım is cited in this document, and the document would be used as a reference source for future denunciations of him. See, for example, RGASPI, f. 495, op. 266, d. 102, ll. 1–5.

[34] RGASPI, f. 82, op. 2, d. 1330, l. 122. Also see f. 495, op. 266, d. 47, Part I, l. 137.

[35] Personal file of Khadmi (aka Kara Mehmet), RGASPI, f. 495, op. 266, d. 78, ll. 4–5. "Autobiography" from July 15, 1932.

[36] In the same report, Vâlâ Nureddin is described as "a freelance agent" of the Turkish police. Nâzım Hikmet personal file, RGASPI, f. 495, op. 266, d. 47, Part I, l. 99. The original date for this document, September 17, 1933, is referred to in RGASPI, f. 495, op. 266, d. 47, Part 2, l. 124. Also see Nâzım Hikmet personal file, f. 495, op. 266, d. 47, Part I, ll. 100–104. Numerous copies of this report can be found in Nâzım's file as well as in the files of others. Also see f. 495, op. 266, d. 47, Part I, ll. 107–111; personal file of İsmail Hakkı, f. 495, op. 266, d. 102, ll. 1–5.

Some of the people who were associated with Nâzım's leadership bid would later own up to their "mistakes," as they learned to call them, and were allowed back into the party. Zeki Baştımar was one such example. Expelled from the TKP for his involvement with Nâzım's undertakings, Baştımar then served in the Turkish Army for two years. Upon leaving the service in 1931, he renewed his contacts with the TKP. In early 1932, according to a party report, "having acknowledged his mistakes, and provided help to the party in the battle against the opposition," Zeki was accepted by the TKP "once again into our ranks."[37]

Shortly after rejoining the party, Baştımar was arrested in Istanbul alongside a fellow party member named "Wilda."[38] The two were on the Unkapanı Bridge, crossing over the Golden Horn, when a former KUTV student-turned-police-informant named İbrahim Faik recognized Zeki.[39] Faik and a policeman had, in fact, been looking for two other communists at the time, but when Faik saw Zeki—whom he had known in Moscow—he decided to change tack. They tailed Zeki and Wilda to the district of Fatih, where the two TKP members stopped at a well-known stand selling *boza*, a popular millet-based wintertime drink.[40]

Upon finishing their refreshments, Zeki and Wilda were arrested. No prison time came out of the *boza* bust, but it was enough to convince Baştımar that it was time for him to leave Turkey. In February 1934, "with the permission of the party," Zeki returned to the Soviet Union.[41]

Had Nâzım also admitted his errors and shown some humility, he too would have likely found a road back into the good graces of Moscow. The shrill tone of TKP rhetoric surrounding Nâzım in the 1930s notwithstanding, his crimes against the party were not so egregious or unprecedented. Attempting to set up a Central Committee of one's own at a time of overall confusion within the TKP's organization was simply not that big a deal. The fact that Nâzım did not return to the party for another two decades, while others did, is an indication that staying out of the TKP was likely Nâzım's own choice.

## Meet the Sertels

Nâzım met up with Vâlâ Nureddin quite a bit during these early days back in Istanbul. Vâlâ was writing for the Istanbul newspaper *Akşam*. Newly married, he was well down the path of distancing himself from the TKP, as well as from the wife and daughter that he had left behind in the Soviet Union.

---

[37] RGASPI, f. 495, op. 266, d. 30, l. 173, July 23, 1935.   [38] Likely an alias.
[39] Alexander Senkevich would likewise identify Faik as a police informer and "provocateur" in his party autobiography from 1934. RGASPI, f. 495, op. 266, d. 118, l. 48. İsmail Bilen makes a similar observation about Faik in his party autobiography from 1937. RGASPI, f. 495, op. 266, d. 12, Part I, l. 120.
[40] This information came about in a trial which took place later, with İbrahim Faik testifying. The report came from one "Feridov" in Turkey, from December 4, 1933, and was translated from Turkish into Russian by the Comintern official Galdzhian. RGASPI, f. 495, op. 266, d. 30, l. 153.
[41] Zeki Baştımar personal file, RGASPI, f. 495, op. 266, d. 30, l. 167. "Autobiography," from April 3, 1936.

Vâlâ tried to find work for Nâzım, but the recently imprisoned poet was not easily employable. For the mainstream press, hiring Nâzım would have been construed as a political statement of the sort that most publishers were not willing to make.[42] Nâzım's problematic curriculum vitae notwithstanding, Vâlâ had an idea. He decided to introduce Nâzım to Sabiha and Zekeriya Sertel, friends of Vâlâ who published a journal called *Resimli Ay* ("Illustrated Monthly").[43] The Sertels were themselves leftists, and Vâlâ knew that they would not hold Nâzım's background against him. In connecting Nâzım with the Sertels, Vâlâ was not only helping his old friend get a much-needed job, but was also putting into motion what would become two of the most important friendships of Nâzım's life.

One day in the early months of 1929, Zekeriya Sertel (Figure 7.2) was sitting in his office at *Resimli Ay* when an unknown figure walked through the door. "Tall, with curly blondish hair, blue eyes and blond eyebrows," observed Zekeriya, "he was a very attractive and likeable young man."[44] Nâzım was accompanied by Vâlâ.

The three sat down and started talking. In Zekeriya's recollections from almost fifty years later, Nâzım looked bashfully to the floor while Vâlâ was praising his writing. Zekeriya took a liking to Vâlâ's modest friend, and hired him on the spot.[45] Originally,

**Figure 7.2** Zekeriya Sertel

[42] On the Sertels, also see James D. Ryan, "The Republic of Others: Opponents of Kemalism in Turkey's Single Party Era, 1919–1950," PhD dissertation, University of Pennsylvania, 2017; Atay, *Serteller*; Philliou, *A Past against History*, 189–190, 191, 192, 195.

[43] Sabiha Sertel's memoirs, *Roman Gibi*, have been translated into English as *The Struggle for Modern Turkey: Justice, Activism and a Revolutionary Female Journalist*, trans. David Selim Sayers and Evrim Emir-Sayers, ed. Tia O'Brien and Nur Deriş (London and New York: I. B. Tauris, 2019).

[44] Zekeriya Sertel, *Hatırladıklarım*, 147–148. Zekeriya Sertel writes that this first meeting took place in 1927, but this is not correct. On this meeting, also see Atay, *Serteller*, 182. On the Sertels and Nâzım, also see Yıldız Sertel, *Annem Sabiha Sertel Kimdi Neler Yazdı?* (İstanbul: Yapı Kredi Yayınları, 1993), 98–103; Yıldız Sertel, *Nâzım Hikmet ile Serteller: İdeolojileri, Yaşamlarında Bilinmeyenler* (İstanbul: Everest Yayımları, 2008).

[45] Zekeriya Sertel, *Hatırladıklarım*, 149–150.

the understanding was that Nâzım would work as a proofreader for *Resimli Ay*, but soon he began writing for the magazine as well.[46]

Who were the Sertels? Like Nâzım, Sabiha and Zekeriya were both children of the Ottoman borderlands. Sabiha (Figure 7.3) was from Salonica, and had been born into a *dönme* family in 1897.[47] Zekeriya was seven years older than Sabiha, hailing from Sturmica, in today's North Macedonia. In 1913, Zekeriya received a stipend from the Ottoman government to study at the Sorbonne. This educational scholarship to Paris, however, was cut short due to war. Returning to Istanbul, Zekeriya came to know of Sabiha through the assistance of an older woman Zekeriya knew who had recommended the match to him. They were wed in 1915.[48]

The Sertels had been well-connected then. Not long after Zekeriya and Sabiha had announced their engagement, Zekeriya was visited by the well-known Young Turk ideologue and future convicted war criminal Doctor Nâzım, with whom Nâzım Hikmet and Vâlâ would later meet up in Moscow. According to Zekeriya's memoirs, Doctor Nâzım saw the upcoming wedding primarily in larger, political terms. "You might not be aware of this," he said to Zekeriya, "but you're helping to lead the way toward the union of two communities. You're dealing a death-blow to the *dönme*s as a

**Figure 7.3** Sabiha Sertel

[46] Sabiha Sertel, *The Struggle for Modern Turkey*, 73.
[47] On Sabiha Sertel's childhood, see Yıldız Sertel, *Annem*, 15–79.
[48] On Sabiha's marriage to Zekeriya Sertel, see ibid., 65–68.

caste. We need to treat this event properly and celebrate the union of *dönme*s with Turks. We need to treat this as a national and historical event."[49]

Widely publicized in the Young Turk press, the wedding ceremony included a number of powerful Unionist figures. Sabiha's "representative" (*vekil*) was Talat Pasha, a member of the "triumvirate," and one of the most powerful men in the empire's political hierarchy.[50] Zekeriya's was Tevfik Rüştü (Aras), another high-ranking Young Turk figure who would go on to become Minister of Foreign Affairs in the Turkish Republic. All of the expenses for the wedding were paid for by the Committee of Union and Progress.[51]

Like many individuals who would later be associated with the TKP, Zekeriya had come to leftist politics via Turkist and pan-Turkist circles.[52] During the Unionist years, he had frequented the Turkic Hearths, the clubs that the pan-Turkist intellectuals Yusuf Akçura and Ahmet Ağaoğlu had created in 1912. In the years immediately following his wedding, moreover, Zekeriya's connections to the Young Turks would continue to work in his favor.

In particular, Zekeriya's friendship with Halide Edib proved helpful during the postwar occupation of Istanbul. His previous work in the Ottoman press had brought Zekeriya to the attention of the British authorities, who detained him for seven days. Following his release from custody, Zekeriya received news from Edip that he had been selected to receive a grant from Ankara to study at Columbia University.[53] In late November 1919, Zekeriya and Sabiha set sail for New York, where they would remain until 1923.[54]

While Zekeriya studied at Columbia University's School of Journalism, both he and Sabiha were active in raising money and awareness for the Kemalist cause, an arrangement which may well have been part of the reason behind their grant's existence in the first place.[55] Sabiha collected funds in American cities, such as Detroit, where communities of Ottoman Muslims resided, raising money on behalf of the Ankara government. Zekeriya, meanwhile, published articles about the movement in the *New York Times* and *Current History*, outlining Mustafa Kemal's goals and the progress of the war.[56]

---

[49] Zekeriya Sertel, *Hatırladıklarım*, 78–79.

[50] The representative performed a role similar to that of a witness.

[51] Zekeriya Sertel, *Hatırladıklarım*, 78–79. On these years, also see Sabiha Sertel, *The Struggle for Modern Turkey*, 19–22.

[52] Zekeriya Sertel sympathized with the TKP and would later work on TKP-oriented endeavors, but never officially joined the party.

[53] Sertel does not elaborate on how he received the documents needed to travel to, live, and study in the United States on a grant from a government that was not yet recognized by Washington.

[54] "Biographical and Historical Timeline" from Sabiha Sertel, *The Struggle for Modern Turkey*, xxx–xxxi; Zekeriya Sertel, *Hatırladıklarım*, 92.

[55] On the Sertels' studies at Columbia, see Ryan, "The Republic of Others," 47–48. Also see Yıldız Sertel, *Annem*, 98–103.

[56] Zekeriya Sertel, *Hatırladıklarım*, 97–98; Atay, *Serteller*, 126–127; Sabiha Sertel, *The Struggle for Modern Turkey*, 23–25, 28–32, and elsewhere. See M. Zekeria, "The Turkish Government at Angora," *Current History*, vol. 16, no. 1 (1922), 73–75; M. Zekeria, "The New Turkish Caliph," *Current History*, vol. 17, no. 4 (1923), 669–671; M. Zekeria, "Solving Greco-Turkish Blood Feuds by Migration," *Current History*, vol. 17, no. 6 (1923), 939–942. Another article written by Zekeriya early on was "The Posthumous Memoirs of Mehmed Talat Pasha," *Current History*, vol. 15, no. 2 (1921), 287–295.

One of Zekeriya's articles was a fast-paced account of Halide Edip that he published in the *New York Times*. Its breathless headline presented the subject of the story as a combination of Joan of Arc and Annie Oakley:

TURKEY'S FIERY "JOAN OF ARC"
HER DOUBLE ROLE AS LEADER
PEN AND GUN HER WEAPONS
Stirs Up People Through Novels and at Mass Meetings
EXPERT SHOT AND RIDER
How Halide Hanum Escaped from Constantinople and
Joined Army in Anatolia.[57]

In the summer of 1923, Sabiha and Zekeriya returned to Istanbul. The intellectual mood there was far different from that of the city they had left behind three years earlier.[58] So were their political circumstances. Relatively well connected during the Unionist period, Zekeriya and Sabiha soon discovered that a number of their former mentors were now in the opposition, or else out of politics altogether.[59] At the same time, the creation of the Turkish Republic in October 1923 provided potential opportunities for people with the Sertels' skills and background. Sabiha and Zekeriya set out to stake their claim in the new arena of Turkish print media.

After working at the Istanbul daily *Cumhuriyet* for a year, Zekeriya set up, with Sabiha, a new, American-style journal of their own: *Resimli Ay*.[60] Like many journals not controlled directly by Mustafa Kemal's Republican People's Party, *Resimli Ay* had been shut down in the aftermath of the Sheikh Sait rebellion in 1925. Zekeriya Sertel was sentenced by an "Independence Tribunal" to three years' exile in Sinop, on the Black Sea. He was allowed to return to Istanbul in 1927, at which point the Sertels were given permission to re-open *Resimli Ay*.[61]

At the time of Nâzım's arrival at *Resimli Ay*, the journal's audience was made up largely of urban, educated, middle-class women. Aside from some rather safe exposés pointing out backwardness in Turkey's villages, the news in *Resimli Ay* was not particularly radical or critical of the regime. If anything, *Resimli Ay* was helping the Kemalist government carry out its self-defined mission of "modernizing" urban Turkish women by encouraging them to more closely follow European models of beauty and fashion. The journal's cover illustrations usually featured women displaying the "modern" style, wearing western-looking clothes and leaving their hair left partially uncovered.[62]

---

[57] M. Zekeria, *The New York Times*, November 26, 1922. The article begins as follows: "A dim pale feminine figure is emerging from the bloody shadows of the battlefield of the Greco-Turkish war. This is Halide Hanum…"
[58] Zekeriya Sertel, *Hatırladıklarım*, 105.
[59] Such as Halide Edip, who would become a critic of the regime.
[60] Sülker, *Nâzım Hikmet'in Gerçek Yaşamı*, vol. 2, 18–19.
[61] Sabiha Sertel states, in her memoirs from the 1960s, that Zekeriya was released "toward the middle of 1925, after one and a half years." *The Struggle for Modern Turkey*, 69. However, it appears that Zekeriya returned to Istanbul in 1927. On his exile, also see Zekeriya Sertel, *Hatırladıklarım*, 139–145.
[62] On *Resimli Ay* also see Nuran Özlük, *Siyasetten Edebiyata Türk Basınında Dergiler (1883–1957)* (İstanbul: Başlık Yayın Grubu, 2011), esp. 69–108.

## 170 RED STAR OVER THE BLACK SEA

Soon, however, with Nâzım's arrival, *Resimli Ay* would find itself locked in battle with several of the country's best-known writers.

## Trashing the Idols

Originally, Nâzım had been hired to do technical work relating to the design and layout of *Resimli Ay*. Soon, however, he began playing a much more significant role in shaping the journal's direction and producing its content. Largely as a result of Nâzım's contributions, *Resimli Ay* would become embroiled in a series of battles that were fought across the literary mastheads of Istanbul newspapers.

The title of the series was "We're Smashing the Idols" ("Putları Yıkıyoruz"). Written exclusively by Nâzım, "Smashing the Idols" consisted of the young poet choosing one well-known Turkish literary figure after another to take down in the most insulting manner possible. In his first shot across the bow of the Turkish literary establishment, Nâzım chose Abdülhak Hamit (1852–1937), an elderly figure whose most productive days were already decades behind him. At a time when younger poets in Turkey may well have shared Nâzım's frustrations regarding an elder generation of writers, Nâzım went after the *Tanzimat*-era legend with both guns blazing.

In a piece published in *Resimli Ay*'s June 1929 issue, Nâzım used his essay on Abdülhak Hamit as a means of attacking the older generation for not writing in a manner that was sufficiently "national" (*milli*). He understood the term "national" not simply in a narrow ethno-national sense, but rather as the degree to which writers captured the spirt of their people and times. It was an interesting perspective coming from someone who had spent most of the 1920s outside of the country.

Abdülhak Hamit, argued Nâzım, was a relic of the past (Figure 7.4). Nâzım mocked the older poet's style, claiming that one needed to know Ottoman Turkish in order to understand it. At times himself slipping into a particularly dense form of writing that may have been an imitation—or an internalization—of Abdülhak Hamit's prose, Nâzım summed up the 77-year-old poet: "for his era, Hamit Bey was a new, solid Ottoman poet, and that's all."[63]

In the July 1929 issue of *Resimli Ay*, Nâzım produced another installment of the "Smashing the Idols" series. This time, it was Mehmet Emin (Yurdakul) whose writing Nâzım critiqued. Mehmet Emin had been an important figure in Turkist and pan-Turkist circles during the Young Turk years, and had also been an old friend of Zekeriya Sertel from the Turkic Hearths. Mehmet Emin Bey was younger than Abdülhak Hamit, but still, the 60-year-old's most creative years were well in the past. In his piece, Nâzım characterized Mehmet Emin's Turkish as "elementary" (*ibtidai*). As had been the case with the attack on Abdülhak Hamit, the illustrations accompanying Nâzım's articles were gratuitously insulting, with the word "cancel" (*iptal*) stamped across Mehmet Emin's face.[64]

---

[63] Yapı Kredi edition of Nâzım Hikmet's collected works (*Yazılar* Vol. 1), 18.
[64] Translation taken from Göksu and Timms, *Romantic Communist*, 88.

**Figure 7.4** Abdülhak Hamit's portrait crossed out in *Resimli Ay*

Nâzım's attacks on the literary establishment were not entirely uninvited. On May 14, 1929, Yakup Kadri (Karaosmanoğlu) had published an article in the Istanbul daily *Milliyet* called "Poetry in the New Society," in which he had sharply criticized the works of Nâzım Hikmet, among others. Writing that Nâzım's poems "bring to mind in no way Beethoven's sonatas," but rather constituted a "fanfare" of sound, Yakup Kadri Bey argued that Nâzım's works "have no place in contemporary Turkish society," as Turkey was "not yet developed enough" to be receptive to this kind of experimental verse.[65] The implication, as would often be the case with critics of Nâzım's writing, was that his style was too foreign for Turkish audiences. This was the context in which Nâzım, in his "Smashing the Idols" series, would make the argument that poetry had to be "national" in a manner that Turkey's literary elders were not.[66]

Is it a coincidence that Yahya Kemal, the well-known Unionist-era poet who had carried on an affair with Celile Hanım, was also a high-profile example of a late Ottoman-era poet whose best days were behind him? In his "Smashing the Idols" series, Nâzım never once mentioned the name of his former teacher, who at this point

---

[65] Sülker, *Nâzım Hikmet'in Gerçek Yaşamı*, vol. 2, 39.
[66] On the "Smashing the Idols" series, also see Sabiha Sertel, *The Struggle for Modern Turkey*, 101–102.

172    RED STAR OVER THE BLACK SEA

was working abroad as a diplomat for the Kemalist government.[67] Nevertheless, Yahya Kemal's career trajectory did have something in common with Nâzım's targets: all of them had peaked at some point during the final decades of the Ottoman Empire's existence. By thus "canceling" this generation of writers, it may well have been the case that Nâzım was acting out not only a literary fantasy, but also a personal one.

This form of bare-knuckled public taunting was hardly unusual in Moscow of the early 1920s, where Nâzım had cut his teeth as a young poet. It was not, however, the kind of behavior that one frequently saw in Turkey, where more deference was expected from younger writers. The literary establishment-types that Nâzım was publicly attacking, moreover, were powerful individuals even outside of the cultural circles in which they are now primarily remembered. At a time when the Turkish political and cultural worlds overlapped to a far greater degree than they do today, it was not uncommon for writers, professors, artists, and other culturally elite figures to serve in government posts. Mehmet Emin Bey, for example, had been a member of parliament since 1923, and Yakup Kadri would serve in Ankara as a parliamentarian between 1931 and 1935.[68] They were joined in criticizing Nâzım by Hamdullah Suphi (Tanrıöver), a former Minister of Education, who charged Nâzım and the Sertels with attempting to introduce to Turkey "the idols of the Bolshevik religion!"[69]

Nâzım had earned *Resimli Ay* some powerful enemies. On the day after Hamdullah Suphi's denunciation of Nâzım appeared in print, the offices of *Resimli Ay* were attacked by a group of approximately thirty so-called "nationalists." The police stood by without intervening as the mob sacked the building, and the next day another anti-communist demonstration was held at one of the Turkic Hearths.[70] İrfan Emin, who served as a lawyer for Nâzım in the years to follow, would later connect Nâzım's take-downs of these politically connected writers to his subsequent persecution in Turkey, observing that Nâzım's problems all stemmed from the fact that he had "attacked the literary big-shots (*anaçlar*), and the gods want their sacrifice."[71]

## Early Trials

With Nâzım earning himself so much notoriety within the Turkish cultural world, it was only a matter of time before some of this acrimony spilled over into the Turkish political universe. During the course of a series of arrests of Turkish communists taking place in May and June 1929, Nâzım was detained by the police in Istanbul. His friend from KUTV İsmail Bilen was also among those arrested, on charges of disseminating

---

[67] Yahya Kemal (Beyatlı) held a number of foreign diplomatic positions in the 1920s and 1930s, including in Poland, Portugal, and Spain.

[68] On the barbs traded by Nâzım, Yakup Kadri, and Hamdullah Suphi, see Sülker, *Nâzım Hikmet'in Gerçek Yaşamı*, vol. 2, 90–100, 106–107, 120–123; Sülker, *Nâzım Hikmet'in Gerçek Yaşamı*, vol. 3, 105–106.

[69] Hamdullah Suphi's comments appeared in the July 7, 1929 edition of the newspaper *İkdam*. Göksu and Timms, *Romantic Communist*, 89.

[70] Göksu and Timms, *Romantic Communist*, 90; Zekeriya Sertel, *Mavi Gözlü Dev*, 190.

[71] Sülker, *Nâzım Hikmet'in Gerçek Yaşamı*, vol. 2, 49.

communist propaganda. In a trial that began in late June and ended on July 16, Nâzım was ultimately released without receiving a sentence, but İsmail Bilen was given four years and six months behind bars.[72]

Nâzım's legal problems, however, were only just beginning. Following the July 1929 publication, in *Resimli Ay*, of Nâzım's poem "The City that Lost its Voice," he was again summoned to court. In a trial that began on August 16, 1929, Nâzım was accused of having used his poetry as a means of disseminating communist ideas. "The City that Lost its Voice" had been published during the course of a taxi drivers' strike, and prosecutors argued that the poem was an agitational work designed to keep strikers on the picket lines. Nâzım would not be intimidated, however, and he used the proceedings as an opportunity to make a public defense of himself. On March 24, 1930, Nâzım—in a courtroom filled with supporters—was acquitted.[73]

In December 1929, the editor of *Resimli Ay*, Behçet Bey, was arrested.[74] The charge was "insulting Turkishness," an accusation that has long since been employed in Turkey as a means of silencing opposition. The offending story was "Savulun Geliyorum," a translation of an English-language article called "The Psychology of the Leader." Nâzım was the one who changed the article's title at the last moment. The literal translation of the piece's Turkish version, "Get out of my way, I'm coming through," was perceived by the prosecutor as critical of the Turkish government and Mustafa Kemal in particular.[75] Sabiha Sertel would later express relief at being sentenced, alongside Behçet Bey, to only two months behind bars for this infraction. These sentences were later overturned on appeal.[76]

In the early morning of May 1, 1931, Nâzım was arrested again. This time, he was rounded up alongside numerous other communists as part of police efforts to crack down pre-emptively against leftist rallies on May Day. Nâzım's trial, which began on May 5, was well attended, again with many friends and supporters present.[77] The Turkish media was there, too.

With much of the country's attention focused upon him, Nâzım framed his defense around the issue of freedom of thought.

"Communism," he argued:

is a belief like any other political or economic theory. I cannot possibly break the law by believing in communism. I have never encouraged the dominance of one class over another.[78]

---

[72] Ibid., 32. Also see Sayılgan, *Türkiye'de Sol Hareketler*, 206–207. On Bilen's imprisonment, see RGASPI, f. 495, op. 266, d. 12, Part I, l. 48, "Spravka" from May 28, 1948.

[73] Göksu and Timms, *Romantic Communist*, 110.

[74] The article was published in *Resimli Ay*, no. 10 (1929), 5.

[75] Atay, *Serteller*, 200–201. For a copy of the charges, see BCA 30-10-0-0/36-214-16, "The undertaking of legal proceedings against Behçet, the general editor of *Resimli Ay*, for insulting Turkishness" ("Türklüğe hakaret"), December 29, 1929.

[76] Sabiha Sertel, *The Struggle for Modern Turkey*, 93–94.

[77] Sülker, *Nâzım Hikmet'in Gerçek Yaşamı*, vol. 2, 185–186.

[78] Göksu and Timms, *Romantic Communist*, 111.

Again, Nâzım was acquitted, on May 10, 1931, "amid cheers in the crowded courtroom."[79]

Even as Nâzım came under increased legal scrutiny, the personal trials that he began to suffer at this time were even more painful. One stormy night in April 1930, Nâzım was walking down İstiklâl Caddesi in the entertainment district of Beyoğlu. Looking for something with which to shield his head from the rain, Nâzım bought a French magazine with a picture of Vladimir Mayakovsky on the cover. He then walked into Tünel, the funicular station used for transporting passengers up and down the steep hill to Karaköy, where Nâzım opened the magazine and received an awful blow: Mayakovsky was dead, having apparently shot himself through the heart in his Moscow apartment. While Nâzım and Mayakovsky had not been particularly close personally, the Soviet poet had nevertheless played an enormous role in Nâzım's literary development.[80] According to Kemal Sülker's account, Nâzım rode the ferry to the city's Asian side unable to get one thought out of his head: why did he do it?[81]

The blows continued to rain down. In March 1932, Nâzım's father Hikmet Bey was bitten by a dog and received an inoculation against rabies. Nâzım's father had, however, also been given a tetanus shot recently. According to Sülker and other biographers, doctors told Nâzım that the two vaccinations, when taken in combination, had created a toxic reaction in the 56-year-old's bloodstream. Hikmet Bey was dead.[82]

On March 18, 1933, Nâzım was detained yet again.[83] This time he was charged with spreading communist propaganda in his new book, *Gece Gelen Telgraf* ("Night Telegraph"). The book, first published in November 1932, had been banned on March 5. In an effort to avoid a repeat of Nâzım's previous pattern of giving speeches in court in defense of liberty, his trial was held behind closed doors. No press was allowed in attendance. Even Nâzım, the defendant, was banned from the proceedings. He was transferred to prison on June 1, 1933, with the trial still going on. Unsurprisingly, given the manner in which the legal process was conducted, Nâzım was found guilty this time. He was sentenced to six months behind bars.[84]

While Nâzım was facing charges of propagandizing communism through *Gece Gelen Telgraf*, he was also accused of defamation of character. This charge stemmed from an incident relating to his father's demise the previous year. With Hikmet Bey lying on his deathbed, his boss at the movie theater, Süreyya Pasha, had rushed to the sick man's bedside. Nâzım got the impression that the cinema owner had come simply to interrogate Hikmet Bey about alleged shortfalls in the movie theater's books. After Hikmet Bey's death, Nâzım wrote a poem about the incident.[85]

The poem was called "An Experiment in Satire" ("Hiciv Vadisinde Bir Tecrübe-i Kalemiye"). Important to note is the fact that this poem was a part of *Gece Gelen*

---

[79] Quotation from ibid., 111. Also see Sülker, *Nâzım Hikmet'in Gerçek Yaşamı*, vol. 2, 190.

[80] Bengt Jangfeldt's thorough biography of Mayakovsky mentions Nâzım Hikmet just once, describing him as an "unusual guest" at a Mayakovsky party in Moscow on December 30, 1929. Nâzım had, in fact, left the USSR some 14 months earlier. *Mayakovsky: A Biography* (Chicago: University of Chicago Press, 2014), 472.

[81] Sülker, *Nâzım Hikmet'in Gerçek Yaşamı*, vol. 2, 162–163.

[82] On Hikmet Bey's death, see ibid., 203; Göksu and Timms, *Romantic Communist*, 103.

[83] Göksu and Timms, *Romantic Communist*, 103.     [84] Ibid., 111–112.     [85] Ibid., 103.

*Telgraf*, which was already under legal attack. Under Turkish law, defamation of character was a criminal, rather than a civil, offense. So, when Süreyya Pasha complained to the police about Nâzım's account of the incident, the charge was added to Nâzım's offenses and a second trial begun. Nâzım was found guilty, tacking another year onto the six-month term that he had been sentenced to in the other proceeding.[86]

If these two trials were not enough, Nâzım was also included, alongside twenty-three other Turkish Communist Party members, in a third legal process that had begun with a series of pre-May Day arrests in late April 1933. He was charged with "forming an illegal organization" and "attempting to overthrow the government," with the latter offense including a possible death penalty.[87] Between this trial—in which Nâzım was also found guilty—and the other two, he was sentenced to a total of five years in prison, a term that was immediately commuted to two.[88]

Nâzım also had to pay a 200 lira fine, as well as an additional 500 liras in compensation to Süreyya Pasha.[89] These were significant sums, easily a month's salary for someone earning a good living at that time in Turkey.[90] For Nâzım, who had been making do with a meager salary at *Resimli Ay*, the financial cost of these fines was almost as onerous as his deprivation of liberty.

He had come back from Moscow looking for a fight. Now, however, the battle had been brought to him.

## Letters to Piraye

Despite the difficulties Nâzım experienced during these early years back in Turkey, there were also some better times. In 1929, a young woman named Piraye, a friend of Nâzım's younger sister Samiye, began frequenting Hikmet Bey's family house in Kadıköy.[91] The 23-year-old Piraye was married when she first met Nâzım. She and her husband—the actor, pianist, novelist, and film director Vedat Örfi (Bengü)—had two children, daughter Suzan and a son named Memet Fuat.[92]

---

[86] Sülker, *Nâzım Hikmet'in Gerçek Yaşamı*, vol. 2, 205–206, 208.

[87] Göksu and Timms, *Romantic Communist*, 112.

[88] Memet Fuat (ed.), *Piraye'ye Mektuplar* (İstanbul: Yapı Kredi Yayınları, 2012), 53, letter # 36. Letter from Nâzım to Piraye, February 3, 1934. Also see Göksu and Timms, *Romantic Communist*, 112.

[89] Aydın Aydemir, *Nâzım: Gençlik ve Mapusane Yılları* (İstanbul: Broy Yayınları, 1986), 183. From Göksu and Timms, *Romantic Communist*, 112. Also see Sülker, *Nâzım Hikmet'in Gerçek Yaşamı*, vol. 2, 231–232.

[90] In 1933, a foreign professor teaching at Istanbul University could expect to earn a monthly salary of around 550 Turkish liras, while the salary of a representative to the Turkish parliament in Ankara was 500 Turkish liras per month. Regarding the former, see Pelin Arslan, "1933–1950 Yılları Arasında Türkiye'ye Gelen Alman İktisatçılar: Gerhard Kessler'in Türkiye'de Sosyal Politikaların Gelişimine Katkıları," MA thesis, Maltepe University, 2019, 352. On the salaries of Turkish parliamentarians in 1933, see *T.C. Resmi Gazete*, May 21, 1930, law number 1613.

[91] Göksu and Timms, *Romantic Communist*, 100–102, here 101. Also see Memet Fuat, *Nâzım Hikmet*, 95.

[92] Memet Fuat's name was actually "Mehmet," but he later began writing it as "Memet," a convention I follow here. Suzan was older and appears to have lived separately. *Nâzım Hikmet'in Gerçek Yaşamı*, vol. 2, 160; Göksu and Timms, *Romantic Communist*, 101. According to Memet Fuat, Piraye was born on December 23, 1906. *Gölgede Kalan Yıllar* (İstanbul: Adam Yayınları, 1997), 22.

176    RED STAR OVER THE BLACK SEA

After the birth of Memet Fuat in 1926, Vedat Örfi Bey moved to Paris. He left Piraye and their children in the care of his father, who lived in the district of Erenköy on the Anatolian side of the city. At the time that Nâzım met her, Piraye had recently moved out of her father-in-law's residence and into her mother's house in Kadıköy. There she had met and become friends with Samiye. Samiye introduced Piraye to her older brother and, after some time, Nâzım and Piraye began to see one another romantically in 1930.

Following Hikmet Bey's death in March 1932, Nâzım suggested to Piraye that they combine their two households. Securing a seven-bedroom "ramshackle" villa located across the street from Piraye's father-in-law, Nâzım was joined by Samiye, her husband Seyda (Yaltırım), Piraye, Memet Fuat, Piraye's mother Nurhayat, sister Fahamet, and Fahamet's husband.[93] Soon, another sister of Piraye, Selma, also joined them. Piraye and Memet Fuat, as well as this more extended collection of individuals, now formed the heart of Nâzım's new "social family." This peaceful time, marked by chickens roaming around the pine trees and vegetable gardens of the villa's grounds, would last for just one year, ending with his arrest in March 1933.[94]

Nâzım would ultimately spend fourteen months in prison, starting on June 1. During this time, he and Piraye corresponded regularly. Nâzım's letters survive and have been published in a book edited by Memet Fuat.[95] The first of these sixty-three letters is dated June 1, 1933, and the last is from July 29, 1934.

Nâzım frequently expressed optimism about his chances of being released early. "Maybe you read about this in the papers," wrote Nâzım to Piraye in mid-June of 1933. "They write that there is going to be a general amnesty soon......but will we be able to benefit from it?"[96] On the one hand, his predictions of imminent release were likely intended to reassure Piraye. At the same time, the idea of Nâzım being let out early was not unrealistic. Turkish authorities had, after 1925, demonstrated a tendency to punish political crimes with heavy sentences initially, followed by commutation. This had been Nâzım's own experience as well, so why shouldn't he have thought it possible that his current sentence would be reduced?

He looked to his uncle, Ali Fuat Pasha, as a possible source of assistance. In a letter to Piraye from late June, Nâzım noted—with a whiff of impatience—that "our uncle, Ali Fuat Pasha, was a [parliamentary] representative for Konya. They could get a reference from him quite easily."[97] Nevertheless, Nâzım continued to express confidence as time passed. "I think I'll be freed," predicted Nâzım in late December 1933.[98] In mid-January 1934, he wrote that he hoped to be released in February.[99]

---

[93] This was Vedat Örfi's father. According to Memet Fuat, Piraye divorced Vedat Örfi on September 3, 1932. *A'dan Z'ye Nâzım Hikmet*, 351. It is unclear if the proximity of their villa to Vedat Örfi's father was simply a coincidence, or if it was part of the settlement of the divorce.

[94] On this "ramshackle" house, see Göksu and Timms, *Romantic Communist*, 100–102, here 102. On Nâzım and Piraye's courtship, also see Memet Fuat, *Nâzım Hikmet*, 95–97.

[95] Piraye's letters to Nâzım have not been published, and apparently have not survived.

[96] *Piraye'ye Mektuplar*, 16. Letter # 5 from Nâzım to Piraye, June 12, 1933.

[97] Ibid., 20. Letter # 8 from Nâzım to Piraye, June 28, 1933.

[98] Ibid., 45. Letter # 30 from Nâzım to Piraye, December 21, 1933.

[99] Ibid., 51. Letter # 34 from Nâzım to Piraye, January 14, 1934.

Sitting in prison on trumped up charges rarely brings out the best in a person, and Nâzım could be quite cutting in his interactions with Piraye. He frequently chastised her for not showing him adequate attention or writing him enough. If a letter from Piraye did come, he still needled her: "Finally, a letter of yours has arrived," he sniffed.[100] At other times he complained that Piraye's correspondence was too short. "Look at how long my letters are," he declared, "and look at how small yours are."[101] When Piraye responded by observing that their letters were more or less the same length, Nâzım countered by remarking that her handwriting was bigger than his, so her letters were actually shorter.[102]

He complained about feeling unloved and ill-treated, a theme he would return to at various points over the course of their relationship. Piraye, claimed Nâzım, knew nothing about writing love letters. In response, she had apparently confessed to being unsure how to write to Nâzım in the way that he wanted. She asked him to show her an example. "Send me a love letter, you tell me," Nâzım snarled. "What have I been sending you so far, mostly?" He also decried her lack of passion, observing that she did not show him enough affection. "You have never told me once," admonished Nâzım, "while looking into my eyes, 'I love you.'"[103]

Money was a never-ending concern. Even without having to worry about support-ing his wife and stepchildren, Nâzım would have been hard-pressed to finance his own life behind bars. In a report for the Comintern from January 20, 1935, a TKP member going by the name of "George" wrote that Turkish prisons only provided "one kilo of bread per day, 100 grams of soap per month," and "one trip per month to the *hamam* (Turkish bath)."[104] It was not uncommon for inmates to establish work-shops devoted to carpentry, textile-making, and other forms of small-scale manufac-turing, legally selling their wares to contacts within prison and outside.

At first glance, it may seem like a contradiction. Nâzım had been expelled from the TKP, yet he would end up spending more than a year in prison due to the fact that he refused to renounce communism. For Nâzım, however, the issue was much bigger than simple membership in the Communist Party. It was a question of freedom of thought and expression.

In the meantime he waited, and so did his family, for some kind of good news to come about an early release.

---

[100]  Ibid., 67. Letter # 49 from Nâzım to Piraye, April 17, 1934, and elsewhere.
[101]  Ibid., 19. Letter # 7 from Nâzım to Piraye, June 23, 1933.
[102]  Ibid., 21. Letter # 9 from Nâzım to Piraye, July 2, 1933. On Nâzım's complaints about Piraye's infrequent letters, see ibid., 19 (# 8), 29–30 (# 17), 32 (# 20), 41 (# 27), 43 (# 29), 49 (# 32), 61 (# 44), 63 (# 45), 63–64 (# 46), 67 (# 49), and elsewhere.
[103]  Ibid., 32. Letter # 20 from Nâzım to Piraye, October 15, 1933.
[104]  "George" described a typical schedule at a Turkish prison: "6–7 get up, bathe; 7–8 gymnastics and get the tea ready; 8–9 tea, read the newspaper; 9–12 prepare meals, walk around, play, read, laundry, repairs. etc.; 12–13 lunch, dishes, relaxing, 13–17 walk around in the garden, read, play backgammon, do laundry and other jobs; 17–19 prepare dinner, read books or newspapers; 20–21 talk or read; 21–6 sleep." RGASPI, f. 495, op. 11, d. 373. ll. 6–10, here ll. 7, 10. Report on prison conditions in Turkey, January 19, 1935.

## A Star is Born

During the course of Nâzım's first five years back in Turkey, his writing style changed again. It now reflected a composite set of elements. There were still many aspects of his poetry that came from his experiences in the Soviet Union, but there were also newer components that he had developed since then.

Nâzım's first book of poetry to be published in Turkey, *835 Lines*, came out in an initial run of 3,000 copies in early 1929.[105] All of the poems in this volume were written during the years 1923–28, and generally reflect the more revolutionary style that Nâzım had developed when living in Moscow. These works draw upon previously underemployed—from an Ottoman or Turkish perspective—techniques, like making onomatopoeic sounds in a new version of "Machine-ization" (*Makinalaşmak*), with a "trrrum, trrrum, trrrum!" and a "trak tiki tak." He used varying font sizes, bold print, and irregular capitalization and spacing, so that he could draw attention, say, to a word like CRAZY.

Later in 1929, Nâzım published "Gioconda and Siao" (*Jokund ile Si-Ya-U*).[106] This book consists of a single long poem which tells the story of the Mona Lisa traversing the globe in search of Nâzım's friend from KUTV, Emi Siao. The poem's speaker, one Nâzım Hikmet, explains to the reader that he has inside information regarding the disappearance from the Louvre of the *Mona Lisa*, i.e., "La Gioconda." The poem then provides excerpts from the diary of "Gioconda," in which she writes about the boredom associated with spending all of her days inside the museum.

The tedium of her existence is only relieved when the young Siao begins to visit. Gioconda promptly falls in love with him. Following Siao's arrest and deportation from France, however, "Nâzım Hikmet" assists Gioconda in escaping from the Louvre and flies her to the Indian Ocean. There, he drops Gioconda off onto a British ship bound for Shanghai. Gioconda ultimately succeeds in finding Siao in China, only to witness his execution. Seeking revenge, she strangles a British officer. Tried in a French military court, Da Vinci's masterpiece is sentenced to be destroyed. The poem "draws to a close with Gioconda laughing as she burns."[107]

> A voice:
> "All right, the lighter.
> Burn, Gioconda, burn…."
> A silhouette advances,

---

[105] Babayev, *Nâzım Hikmet*, 154. A review of *835 Lines* appeared in the May 1929 issue of *Resimli Ay* as a "recently released book," 35.

[106] The book was dedicated "to the memory of my friend Si-Ya-U (Siao), whose head was cut off in Shanghai." Emi Siao had not, however, been executed in China, and would even live to see Nâzım again. Göksu and Timms, *Romantic Communist*, 266; Blasing, *Nâzım Hikmet*, 260 (fn. 60). Also see McGuire, *Red at Heart*, 183–184.

[107] This quotation is from Alice Xiang. "Re-Worlding the *Mona Lisa*: Nâzım Hikmet's Modernist Diplomacy," *Journal of Modern Literature*, vol. 41, no. 2 (2018), 1–22, here 3. On the poem's summary, see ibid., 2–3. Regarding "Gioconda and Siao," also see Clark, "European and Russian Cultural Interactions with Turkey," esp. 208–210; Clark, *Eurasia Without Borders*, 65–70.

A flash…

They lit the lighter

And set Gioconda on fire.

The flames painted Gioconda red.

She laughed with a smile that came from her heart.

Gioconda burned laughing…

Art, Shmart, Masterpiece, Shmasterpiece, And So On,
   And So Forth,
    Immortality, Eternity—
         H-E-E-E-E-E-E-E-E-E-Y…

### "HERE ENDS MY TALE'S CONTENDING, THE REST IS LIES UNENDING…"

THE END[108]

"Gioconda and Siao" constitutes some of Nâzım's most experimental work from this time, and clearly bears the mark of his experiences in the USSR.[109] What Nâzım brought to this poem was, crucially, his own brand of border-crossing.[110] During a time when Nâzım was particularly active with respect to the crossing of frontiers, he wedded Mayakovsky's Russian Futurism with his own experiences in the Soviet Union to produce a work in Turkey that describes events taking place in Paris, the Indian Ocean, and China.[111]

In 1930, Nâzım published two more volumes of poetry: *3 Coming Up* (*Varan 3*) and *1+1=1*. *Varan 3* consisted of twenty-four poems, most of them older, Futurist-inspired works written during the years 1922–29. *1+1=1*, meanwhile, was a thin volume for which Nâzım collaborated alongside a young colleague named Nail Çakırhan. Nâzım contributed four poems to the book, mostly from his time in the Soviet Union.[112]

Nâzım's next book of poetry was *The City that Lost its Voice* (*Sesini Kaybeden Şehir*), which came out in 1931. While this book, too, included some older works from Nâzım's days in the USSR, most of the poems from this volume were written in 1930, i.e., after Nâzım had begun living in Turkey again. In *The City that Lost its Voice*, Nâzım's style is noticeably more traditional than was the case with his Futurist-inspired works from the 1920s. While Nâzım was by no means returning to his occupation-era Syllabist style, he was nevertheless sensitive to the different reading

---

[108] This translation is from Randy Blasing and Mutlu Konuk, *Poems of Nâzım Hikmet: Revised and Expanded* (New York: Persea Books, 1994), 31. Bolding in original.

[109] On *835 Lines* see Babayev, *Nâzım Hikmet*, 151. Mayakovsky also had a poem called "A Cloud in Trousers" which refers to the "Gioconde," i.e., the *Mona Lisa*.

[110] On Nâzım Hikmet's "interrogation" of the border between East and West, see Clark, "European and Russian Cultural Interactions with Turkey," 209.

[111] On this point, see Xiang, "Re-Worlding the *Mona Lisa*," 19. Xiang further connects the border-crossing content of "Gioconda" to Nâzım's flight to the Eastern Bloc in 1951.

[112] Nâzım's poems in this volume included "Meşin Kaplı Kitap" from 1921, "Cevap" (1925), "Sükût" (1929), and "İzmir'den Akdeniz'e Dökülen…" (undated). Çakırhan, writing as "Nail V.," contributed three poems to the volume: "Yeni Sanatın Akını," "Kadavra," and "Dışarımı Dışarı!"

tastes of his variegated audience. His new poems from Turkey were made up mostly of free-verse, but of a less self-consciously revolutionary variety.

Such was the case, for example, with "Farewell" ("Veda"), which began:

> So long
>> my friends
>>> so long!
>> I carry you
>>> in my soul
>>>> and my struggle in my head.
>> So long
>>> my friends
>>>> so long…[113]

The remainder of "Farewell" is similarly subdued, with relatively few expressions of the mayhem that was common in Nâzım's earlier works. It is a simpler style and tone that can also be detected in Nâzım's other works from this time.

In another poem from this volume, "Optimism" ("Nikbinlik"), Nâzım likewise scales back his earlier experimentation, drawing instead upon relatively conventional forms of rhythm and pacing:

> We're gonna see good days ahead, friends
> sunny days
>> we
>> will see…
> We will ride the motorboats out onto the blueness
> onto the shimmering blueness
>> we
>> will ride…[114]

By this time Nâzım had, for the most part, finally set down the Futurist suitcases that he had brought back with him from Moscow.[115] The blaring, bold fonts, the ALL-CAPS, and other features of his Futurist-style works were gradually abandoned in these new Turkish publications.

But his poetry was still developing. While the words on the page may have looked more like what he had been writing in Istanbul in 1920, the themes that Nâzım was now addressing in the 1930s were much more mature, measured, and original.

---

[113] Yapı Kredi edition of Nâzım Hikmet's collected works (*Şiirler* Vol. 1), 186.

[114] This is the first third of the poem. Ibid., 190.

[115] But not entirely. In 1932, Nâzım published *Benerci Kendini Niçin Öldürdü?* ("Why Did Banerjee Kill Himself?"), which was reminiscent of his more experimental works from Moscow. Meanwhile, *Gece Gelen Telgraf* ("Night Telegraph"), also from 1932, mostly featured a more traditional style that was typical of his Istanbul-based writings in the early 1930s.

His Soviet-era poetic cacophony had irritated Turkey's literary elite back in 1929, but in many ways his new writings from Turkey posed a much more serious challenge to that generation. As Nâzım's verse began to shed some of its eccentricity, it acquired more depth and power.

Meanwhile, Nâzım was reaching new audiences. In 1930, he recorded a vinyl album of himself reading selections of his own verse. In 1932, a book of Nâzım's poetry was published in Russian translation in Moscow, his recent divorce from the TKP notwithstanding.[116] In the United States, Nâzım received a brief but enthusiastic write-up in the January–February 1932 edition of a literary journal called *The Bookman*.

Nermine Mouvafac, an Istanbul-born 1928 graduate of the Women's College at Brown University, showed a journalist's eye for detail in making the case for Nâzım's greatness:

> The corner shop at the lower end of Bab'ali, the Avenue of the Sublime Porte, sells His Master's Voice gramophones, and just outside taxis stand and hoot. A little further up there are dingy eating-places, their windows containing rows of sheep-heads hideously grinning and festoons of eggs and lemons, with here and there a tomato for color. Then the bookshops begin...
>
> Against this setting may be seen almost any day a tall young man with impressive shoulders and equally impressive strides, a strong chin, clear blue eyes and fair hair, usually wearing the cloth cap which in his mind is a symbol of the proletariat. He is Nâzım Hikmet, communist poet, perhaps the only poet of the new generation who will leave a lasting mark.[117]

Nâzım had made quite an impression upon her. Years later Nermine would recall that, after interviewing him in Istanbul on July 10, 1930, she recorded in her diary: "I have met a MAN!"[118]

While Nâzım is known primarily as a poet, starting in the 1930s he also began to write more frequently in other genres. These included short stories, novels, plays, screenplays, and newspaper columns. Theater was particularly important to Nâzım, an interest that was, to a large degree, a carry-over from his second stint in the Soviet Union. In 1932, he published two new plays: *House of Death* (*Bir Ölü Evi*) and *The Skull* (*Kafatası*).

The conditions for putting on theatrical productions were considerably more rudimentary in Istanbul of the 1930s than they had been in Moscow in the 1920s. In the Soviet Union, staging a play had, to a large extent, meant obtaining the building space and other supplies from party-supported agencies, then finding volunteers to take

---

[116] *Stikhi* (Moscow: "Federatsiia," 1932). This book featured translations of Nâzım's verse by E. Bagrinstkii, N. Dement'ev, and V. Bugaevskii.

[117] Nermine Mouvafac, "A Poet of the New Turkey," *The New Bookman*, vol. 74, no. 5 (1932), 508–515, here 508–509. From Göksu and Timms, *Romantic Communist*, 82–83. On Mouvafac, also see "Life at the Women's College," *Brown Alumni Monthly*, vol. 28, no. 6 (Providence, RI, January 1928).

[118] Göksu and Timms, *Romantic Communist*, 82.

part in the production. In Istanbul, however, it was far more difficult and expensive to produce something. *The Skull*, which Nâzım had begun to write during his second stint in Moscow, appeared on stage in Istanbul in March 1932.[119] While Göksu and Timms describe the audience's reception of the play as "rapturous," it closed after just five performances.[120]

In need of a means to feed his family and finding it increasingly difficult to publish under his own name, Nâzım began to pseudonymously write short (200–300 word) newspaper columns. Starting in September 1930, he published, under the names "Orhan Selim" and "Ben" ("Me"), eighty-one columns for the Istanbul newspaper *Yeni Gün*.[121] In December 1930, he produced another seventeen pieces for a newspaper called *Hür Adam*.

These and other small columns that Nâzım wrote for *Akşam*, *Halk Dostu*, *Tan*, *Resimli Perşembe*, and *Yarım Ay* pertained to music, art, writing, and other topics that were not overtly political.

He worked on other types of publications as well. In 1931, Nâzım translated a total of thirty-eight short stories into Turkish from French and Russian. In 1932, he produced a book of original short stories called *The Adventure of the Forest Dwarves* (*Orman Cücelerinin Sergüzeşti*).

As if all of the above were not enough, Nâzım was also employed in a number of cinema-related projects during these years. Films that Nâzım Hikmet worked on in the early 1930s included *Cici Berber* (*The Cute Barber*), *Düğün Gecesi* (*Wedding Night*), *Fena Yol* (*The Bad Way*), *Karım beni Aldatırsa* (*If my Wife Deceives Me*), *Naşit Dolandırıcı* (*Naşit the Con-Artist*), and *Söz Bir Allah Bir* (*I'm a Man of My Word*). Nâzım wore a variety of hats in these ventures, helping with everything from writing screenplays to producing the voice-overs.

Some of these movies were quite light in their subject matter, and were perhaps more attractive to Nâzım as sources of income than as artistic accomplishments.[122] Others were more ambitious.[123] Nâzım worked on several films directed by Muhsin Ertuğrul, who today is considered the "father" of Turkish cinema.[124] Nâzım's friendship with Ertuğrul went back to Moscow, which Muhsin Bey had visited during the

---

[119] Makal, *Beyaz Perdede ve Sahnede Nâzım Hikmet*, 83–84. Also see Sülker, *Nâzım Hikmet'in Gerçek Yaşamı*, vol. 2, 179–180.

[120] Göksu and Timms, *Romantic Communist*, 116. Also see Sülker, *Nâzım Hikmet'in Gerçek Yaşamı*, vol. 2, 197. Memet Fuat writes that Nâzım directed both his plays and those of others for the municipal theater in the 1930s. *Gölgede Kalan Yıllar*, 302.

[121] Yapı Kredi edition of Nâzım Hikmet's collected works (*Yazılar* Vol. 2), 99–228.

[122] Makal, *Beyaz Perdede ve Sahnede Nâzım Hikmet*, 90–106.

[123] Nâzım frequently instructed Piraye to get in touch with İpek Films in order to retrieve some of the money that Nâzım had earned through his writing. See, for example, *Piraye'ye Mektuplar*, 22–23; letter # 10 from Nâzım to Piraye, July 5, 1933; 56, letter # 39 from Nâzım to Piraye, February 22, 1934; 57–58; letter # 40 from Nâzım to Piraye, February 24, 1934; 59–60, letter # 42 from Nâzım to Piraye; 74, letter # 56 from Nâzım to Piraye, June 6, 1934.

[124] Including *Wedding Night*, *If My Wife Deceives Me*, and *I'm a Man of My Word*. Makal, *Beyaz Perdede ve Sahnede Nâzım Hikmet*, 256. On Nâzım's films, also see Orhan Ünser, "Nâzım Hikmet'in sinema çalışmaları: Ali Baba," *Antrakt*, vol. 33 (1996), 23–25.

course of a two-year stay in the USSR between 1925 and 1927.[125] Among the films that Nâzım played some role in creating was Ertuğrul's *A Nation Awakens* (*Bir Millet Uyanıyor*). Shot in 1932, it tells the story of the Turkish War of Liberation, and today is remembered as one of the most important films from this early era of Turkish cinematography.

Great writers develop their style over time, and Nâzım was no exception. Having crossed borders and lived abroad, he had exposed himself to a variety of different literary approaches. Nâzım was now long since past the point of trying to "find" a poetic voice. Rather, he had begun to create one of his own.

⋆

As anyone who has lived abroad for years knows, the worst form of culture shock is typically that which arises upon returning "home." The effect can be disorienting, especially if certain aspects of life begin to seem more difficult than they had been abroad. In Moscow, Nâzım had never experienced any trouble finding good employment, interesting friends, or a suitable place to live. In Istanbul, however, he struggled to establish himself, even as his fame as a poet continued to grow.

Like it or not, Nâzım would have to live with this. The doors had already started to close behind him.

---

[125] Hirst, "Eurasia's Discontent," 43. On Muhsin Ertuğrul's experiences in the USSR, see his memoirs *Benden Sonra Tufan Olmasın* (İstanbul: Remzi Kitabevi, 2007), 355–396; Makal, *Beyaz Perdede ve Sahnede Nâzım Hikmet*, 46–48.

# 8

# Closing Doors

Zehra Hasan Galip Kızı traversed a frontier for the first time when she was still an infant. She had been born in Kavala in 1915, just a couple of years after the Ottoman port city was annexed by Greece during the Second Balkan War. In 1916, Zehra and her family were evacuated by Greek authorities to Salonica ahead of the advancing Bulgarian Army. From there, they followed a circuitous route as refugees, moving on to Varna, Soğuk Pınar, and the Dobruja region of Bulgaria before making their way back to Kavala at the end of the war.[1] In the aftermath, however, of the population exchange mandated by the peace treaty signed between Greece and the Ankara government in 1923, Muslim families like Zehra's were obliged to leave Greece for Turkey. So, the family crossed a border once more.

Zehra and her parents were re-settled in Tokat, a port city on the Black Sea coast. Growing up amid grinding poverty and an intermittent education cut short by the need to earn money for her family, Zehra would soon leave this town, too. Her parents had decided to try their luck in Istanbul, but life in the big city would prove no easier. Not long after their arrival in town, her father suddenly passed away, in 1932. Seventeen-year-old Zehra became the family's chief breadwinner, taking care of both mother and sister.[2]

Then she met a young man named Mustafa. Mustafa was deeply interested in politics, as were most of his friends. He introduced Zehra to some of the people he knew, and these new acquaintances lent her books about Marx and Lenin. Together with Mustafa, Zehra began to attend meetings of young Turkish communists. Meanwhile, she and Mustafa drew closer.

One day while they were taking a stroll together, Mustafa asked Zehra an unexpected question. If, for some reason, the party wanted to send him to another country, would she be willing to go with him? Could she leave her mother behind?

"I'll go," she replied.[3]

On June 1, 1934, Zehra and Mustafa boarded a ferry to Hopa, the last Turkish town before Batumi and the USSR. They checked into a hotel, where they were later visited by a comrade from the party. This was the scout who would help the young couple cross the border into the Soviet Union. The next day, he led them deep into the forest north of town, where they met up with a group of five other would-be crossers. Once

---

[1] As Turkish-speaking Muslims living in a region only recently conquered by Greece, Zehra's family may have considered themselves safer in Bulgaria, which was an ally of the Ottoman Empire in World War I.

[2] RGASPI, f. 495, op. 266, d. 208, ll. 16–23-ob, here ll. 16–17. Party Autobiography, undated, but apparently from 1935. Personal file of Zehra Hasan Galip Kızı.

[3] RGASPI, 495, op. 266, d. 208, ll. 15–23-ob. Here, l. 22, personal file of Zehra Hasan Galip Kızı.

*Red Star over the Black Sea: Nâzim Hikmet and his Generation.* James H. Meyer, Oxford University Press. © James H. Meyer 2023.
DOI: 10.1093/oso/9780192871176.003.0010

darkness had fallen, they made their way down to the shoreline, where a small vessel was waiting for them.[4]

*

Zehra was part of a vanishing breed. From the late 1920s onward, the Turkish–Soviet frontier had become increasingly difficult to cross. Whereas Nâzım and others from his generation had easily made their way back and forth across the frontier in the previous decade, both legal and illegal migration between Turkey and the USSR had, in the 1930s, turned into a much more challenging undertaking.

For Zehra, the risk seemed worth it, at least insofar as she would later indicate in her party autobiography. Now living in Moscow, she had begun, in February 1935, studying at KUTV, and noted that "since March 8, 1934, I have been married to Comrade Peres," an apparent reference to Mustafa.

Life was good. "In our family relations," Zehra observed, "we have experienced no incompatibilities." They had a four-month-old daughter named Ayten.[5] A sepia-drenched photograph in Zehra's Comintern personal file shows a young woman wearing a jacket, scarf, and beret.[6] She had just turned twenty years old.

## Tightening the Screws

The final years of the 1930s marked the onset of a particularly violent and unstable period in modern European history. The Rome-Berlin pact of 1936 was only the first step in the emerging Axis alliance that would bring Italy, Germany, and Japan together alongside a host of smaller collaborators.

This time is also known for the show trials and purges which dominated the Soviet political arena in the latter half of the 1930s. In the immediate aftermath of Lenin's death in 1924, a coalition of Politburo members, including but not limited to Joseph Stalin, had assumed control of the party. Since the second half of the 1920s, Stalin had been consolidating his position, drawing upon newer cadres whose recruitment had, in many cases, been personally overseen by Stalin himself. The Moscow Trials of 1936 and 1937 were, in some ways, the Soviet leader's declaration of war against other old Bolsheviks who, at least in Stalin's mind, had become his rivals for power.

The American philosopher Sidney Hook, who had broken with the American Communist Party a few years before the Moscow Trials began, would later describe them in these terms:

> The charges against the defendants were mind-boggling. They had allegedly plotted and carried out the assassination of Kirov on December 1, 1934 and planned the assassination of Stalin and his leading associates—all under the direct instructions of

---

[4] RGASPI, 495, op. 266, d. 208, l. 23.    [5] RGASPI, 495, op. 266, d. 208, l. 5.

[6] RGASPI, 495, op. 266, d. 208, ll. 23–25.

Trotsky. This, despite their well-known Marxist convictions concerning the untenability of terrorism as an agency of social change. Further, they had conspired with Fascist powers, notably Hitler's Germany and Imperial Japan, to dismember the Soviet Union, in exchange for the material services rendered by the Gestapo...

Despite the enormity of these offenses, all the defendants in the dock confessed to them with eagerness and at times went beyond the excoriations of the prosecutor in defaming themselves. This spectacular exercise in self-incrimination, unaccompanied by any expression of defiance or asseveration of basic principles, was unprecedented in the history of any previous Bolshevik political trial.[7]

The first of the Moscow show trials, which took place in August 1936, ended with the execution of all sixteen of those accused. Included among those who were shot at this time were well-known and once-powerful figures like former Comintern head Grigory Zinoviev.[8] A subsequent trial focused upon the alleged treason of the German communist Karl Radek, whom Şevket Süreyya had once been so excited to catch a glimpse of at the Hotel Luxe.[9] Among seventeen communists put on trial in 1937, thirteen were found guilty and executed, while Radek and three others were sentenced to forced labor in prison camps. In 1939, Radek was murdered in the camp where he was serving out his term.

The year 1937 marked the height of the purges.[10] It was in this year that roughly half of the USSR's 60,000-strong officer corps were pushed out of their positions under charges of disloyalty. Fifteen of sixteen army commanders were executed, as were 136 of 199 division commanders. Among the 1,966 delegates to the Seventeenth Communist Party Congress in 1934, 1,108 would be arrested in the coming years, and during the years 1937–38 alone the *official* number of individuals executed in the USSR was 681,692. By the end of the 1930s, 1,360,000 Soviet citizens were in labor camps, within which 90,595 Soviets died in 1938. Estimates for the total number of state-sponsored murders in the 1930s—including those from famines resulting from forced collectivization and other forms of state violence—range between 10 and 11 million.[11] This in a country with a total population of about 160 million in 1937.

While Turkey did not experience anything close to the level of mass terror taking place in the Soviet Union in the 1930s, the political climate in Ankara was likewise becoming more authoritarian and reliant upon force. The first major blow that the Kemalist regime struck against the country's political freedoms had taken place in 1925, as a pretext for fighting the Sheikh Sait rebellion. Since that time, there had been less and less room for political debate in parliament and in the Turkish press at large. While Mustafa Kemal Atatürk is often remembered as a modernizer who dragged Turkey into the twentieth century, his means of doing so depended, in large part,

---

[7] Sidney Hook, *Out of Step: An Unquiet Life in the 20th Century* (New York: Carroll & Graf, 1987), 222–223.
[8] Zinoviev was chair of the Communist International between 1919 and 1926.
[9] Aydemir, *Suyu Arayan Adam*, 198.
[10] On the year 1937 and the Soviet purges, see Karl Schlögel, *Moscow 1937* (Cambridge: Polity Press, 2012).
[11] Suny, *The Soviet Experiment*, 282, 285–287; Schlögel, *Moscow 1937*, 1.

upon the threat and employment of state violence against enemies both real and invented.

In the aftermath of the uncovering of a so-called plot to assassinate Mustafa Kemal in 1926, many of the country's best-known intellectuals and writers had been arrested.[12] In all, nineteen individuals were hanged in trials taking place in İzmir and Ankara, despite the fact that prosecutors "produced no evidence linking [the accused] to the assassination attempt."[13]

Increasing state violence in both Turkey and the Soviet Union took place in the context of a tightening frontier.[14] Making one's way across the Ottoman–Russian frontier had once been relatively easy, but now such undertakings had become exceedingly dangerous.[15] Meanwhile, Turkish and Soviet officials worked together to shore up the border and crack down upon smuggling and other forms of illegal crossing.[16] Throughout the 1930s, measures were adopted in each country to place more controls upon both legal and illegal migration between the two states.[17]

Soviet troops employed deadly force and other strong-arm tactics as a means of preventing individuals from crossing the border. In 1930, Moscow closed access for Soviet Muslims wishing to travel to Mecca on the hajj.[18] In the fall of 1933, Turkish government officials recorded that a group of 24 households, containing a total of 115 refugees, was shot at by Soviet soldiers as they attempted to flee into Turkey. The Muslim villagers had been seeking to cross the Aras River, which marked the border between the two countries.[19]

The development of the Turkish–Soviet border that took place in the 1930s was not an isolated phenomenon. The tightening of the frontier followed patterns of state behavior that were taking place more generally at this time in Europe and the Middle East.[20] Whereas in the late imperial era Russian and Ottoman officials had seen the

---

[12] Including Nâzım's uncle, Ali Fuat Pasha.    [13] These are the words of Mango, *Atatürk*, 451.

[14] Tim Tzouliadis describes similar issues facing Americans living in the USSR in the late 1930s, amid borders that were now "sealed tight." *The Forsaken*, 80.

[15] Étienne Forestier-Peyrat writes that revolts taking place on the Soviet side of the border in 1929–31—relating to unveiling campaigns in Muslim communities—contributed to increased efforts among Muslims in the USSR to cross illegally into Turkey. "Dans les forêts d'Adjarie…: Franchir la frontière turco-soviétique, 1922–1937," *Diasporas*, vol. 23–24 (2014), 164–184, here 176–177.

[16] BCA, 30-18-1-1/28-15-18. "Determining the individuals to attend a conference on the prevention of smuggling, and for the signing of agreements with the Transcaucasian Socialist Federative Soviet Republic and the Russian Soviet Republic regarding pastures and the crossing of the frontier," March 11, 1928; BCA 30-18-1-2/25-1-10, "On the re-settlement to other locations of 24 individuals living near the Russian border who engaged in theft and smuggling," January 3, 1932. On Turkish-Soviet treaties in the mid-to-late 1920s regulating the border, also see Leonard Shapiro, *Soviet Treaty Series, vol. I, 1917–1928* (Washington, DC: The Georgetown University Press, 1950), esp. 164, 324, 367, 368, 379, 398.

[17] Forestier-Peyrat, "Dans les forêts d'Adjarie," 181–183. Andrey Shlyakhter similarly finds that, while the border was relatively open in the early 1920s, it tightened considerably from the mid-1920s onward. "Smuggler States: Poland, Latvia, Estonia, and Contraband Trade across the Soviet Frontier, 1919–1925," PhD dissertation, University of Chicago, Department of History, 2020.

[18] Kane, *Russian Hajj*, 182.

[19] One of the villagers, İsa Mustafaoğlu, was killed in the encounter, while another was injured. BCA, 30-10-0-0/116-810-1, "115 refugees from the Russian village of Şitli were subjected to fire from Russian soldiers as they attempted to cross the Aras River," October 10, 1933.

[20] On frontier and nationhood in the nineteenth and twentieth centuries, see Firoozeh Kashani-Sabet, *Frontier Fictions: Shaping the Iranian Nation, 1804–1946* (Princeton, NJ: Princeton University Press, 1999); Ateş, *Ottoman-Iranian Borderlands*; Ellis, *Desert Borderland*.

frontier—and the people who crossed it—as a source of opportunity, by the 1930s authorities in Turkey, the USSR, and much of the rest of the world had come to regard porous borders as a sign of weakness.

The border was not yet entirely closed, but it saw much less traffic than had been the case in previous years. In the 1930s, some Muslims continued to enter Turkey from the USSR, but this now occurred most frequently on an individual, rather than mass, basis.[21] The much larger demographic shifts that had immediately followed the conclusion of the fighting in the region in the early 1920s had, by the early 1930s, mostly come to an end. The number of ex-Ottoman POWs crossing the frontier into Turkey had also diminished greatly by this time into a mere trickle.

In both Turkey and the Soviet Union, hardening attitudes toward the frontier could also be seen in the manner in which border-crossers were treated by state authorities. Individual border-crossers from both the political left and the right felt pressure from Ankara during these years. When relations with the USSR were good, former pan-Turkists in Turkey, many of whom were now critics of the Soviet Union, were silenced in an effort to placate Moscow.[22] Meanwhile, crackdowns on the illegal TKP became a regular feature of Turkish political life in the late 1920s and 1930s. On the Soviet side of the frontier, it was now expected that even party members arriving from Turkey and other countries receive permission to enter the USSR prior to showing up at the frontier. Emphasizing that one had arrived "with party permission" became a common trope among party autobiographies and other forms of TKP and Comintern paperwork in the 1930s.[23]

In the USSR, foreign organizations were closed in large numbers in the second half of the decade, depriving foreign communists of contacts, and making them even more dependent upon the Comintern and their national party's organization in Moscow.[24] Communist University of the Toilers of the East was shuttered in 1938, following the arrest of "the majority" of the school's faculty.[25] While both Soviet and foreign communists were targeted in the purges, the extraordinarily xenophobic nature of these activities all but guaranteed that foreign cadres in the USSR would be decimated during these years.[26]

---

[21] Some former Russian subjects who converted to Islam were also granted Turkish citizenship. See, for example, BCA, 30-18-1-2/29-49-18, "The granting of citizenship to Andriya Danilof, also known as the convert Abdullah Rüşdü, a subject of tsarist Russia who immigrated to Turkey and married a Turkish woman in Samsun," June 30, 1932; BCA 30-18-1-2/31-68-9, "The granting of citizenship to the convert Emin Enis, originally a subject of Russia who came to Turkey and settled in Istanbul," October 7, 1932, among others.

[22] On the erstwhile pan-Turkists in the Turkish Republic, see Meyer, *Turks Across Empires*, 174–175.

[23] See, for example, "spravkas" on Rasim Şakir, RGASPI, f. 495, op. 266, d. 92, l. 24; Aram Pehlivanyan, f. 595, op. 266, d. 307, l. 16; Zeki Baştımar, RGASPI, f. 495, op. 266, d. 30, l. 167; and Yıldız Sertel, f. 595, op. 266, d. 274, ll. 1–3 (here, 3), among others.

[24] Studer, *Transnational World of the Cominternians*, 135. The year 1938 also witnessed "the death of Esperanto" in the Soviet Union, marking the demise of one of the late imperial era's most ambitious transnational projects. O'Keeffe, *Esperanto and Languages of Internationalism*, 181–192.

[25] Ravandi-Fadai, "Red Mecca," 723.

[26] On foreign communists and the purges, see Studer, *Transnational World of the Cominternians*, 73–86, 108–120, 138–149. Tzouliadis observes that during the purges "anyone who had been outside the borders of the USSR in any capacity whatsoever became an immediate suspect." *The Forsaken*, 90.

Citizenship, too, had become a much more contentious matter since the end of empire. In the 1930s, Soviet officials sought to more clearly define the legal and administrative borders separating Soviet citizens from foreigners.[27] Whereas dual subjecthood had been a common feature of life among late imperial border-crossers, in the post-imperial era dual citizenship came to be seen in Moscow as a likely sign of disloyalty. The Soviet government repeatedly strengthened its citizenship laws in the 1930s and adopted, in 1936, a new constitution which more clearly delineated the legal distinctions between Soviet citizens and non-Soviet residents.[28] Throughout the 1930s, foreign-born communists living in the USSR came to live under increasing suspicion, and international communists were systematically targeted.[29]

All of this marked, however, only a taste of what was to come. Soon, with the outbreak of war in Europe, the Turkish–Soviet frontier would become more tightly sealed than ever. For the erstwhile children of trans-empire who constituted Nâzım's generation, there was now little room left in which to maneuver.


## Back in the Arena

In August 1934, Nâzım was released. He had spent fourteen months in Bursa prison, and almost three months in detention prior to that.[30] While this was less than the two-year sentence he had received, it was still time lost. He wasted little time in getting back to work, once again producing columns for the newspapers *Tan* and *Akşam* under the pseudonym "Orhan Selim." Most of these pieces were short prose sketches about daily life, characters the author had run across, and other general commentary. Even with these relatively low-key writings, however, Nâzım managed to draw the ire of the well-known intellectual and writer Peyami Safa.

In a column published in the newspaper *Tan* on June 7, 1935, Nâzım had criticized so-called "coffeehouse intellectuals" in Turkey who, Nâzım alleged, preferred chatting with one another to engaging in political activity. Safa, who also wrote for *Tan*, shot back at "Orhan Selim" with a piece on June 23 called "Herd Man," criticizing those who followed collective ideologies like communism. Safa later left *Tan*, began writing for the newspaper *Hafta*, and went on to spar with "Orhan Selim" for a period of several months.[31]

According to Memet Fuat, Nâzım and Piraye were married in Kadıköy on January 31, 1935.[32] Although Nâzım seems to have remained committed to the idea of

---

[27] Studer, *Transnational World of the Cominternians*, 131.

[28] Ibid., 130, 135–143. Also see David-Fox, "The Iron Curtain as Semipermeable Membrane," 15.

[29] On stepped-up arrests and purges of foreigners in the Soviet Union in the middle-to-late 1930s, see Studer, *The Transnational World of the Cominternians*, 140–143.

[30] On Nâzım's release, see Babayev, *Nâzım Hikmet*, 184; Göksu and Timms, *Romantic Communist*, 104; Fish, *Nâzım'ın Çilesi*, 315.

[31] Göksu and Timms, *Romantic Communist*, 118–120. On Nâzım's feud with Peyami Safa, also see Ergün Göze, *Peyami Safa Nâzım Hikmet Kavgası* (Ankara: Selçuk Yayınları, 1981).

[32] In a civil ceremony at the state office for weddings, which would have been the norm at this time. Memet Fuat, *A'dan Z'ye Nâzım Hikmet*, 353.

carrying on a family relationship with Piraye and her children, this apparently did not stop him from pursuing liaisons with others. Over the decades that have passed since Nâzım's death, he has been linked to a variety of women from these years, including the opera singer Semiha Berksoy (1910–2004). In 1985, Berksoy published a book of memoirs in which she described a love affair with Nâzım beginning in the mid-1930s and continuing into the early 1940s, even meeting up with Nâzım for conjugal visits while he was in Bursa prison. The sexual element of their relationship apparently came to an end when Berksoy married another man.[33]

Another reputed lover of Nâzım in the 1930s was Cahit Uçuk. Uçuk (1909–2004) was a young writer who first met Nâzım in 1935. She had enjoyed one of Nâzım's articles in *Akşam*, which he had written under the moniker "Orhan Selim." Uçuk wrote to the paper, explaining how the topic of Nâzım's piece, called "The Scent of the Sun," had brought back memories of her childhood in an Anatolian village. Nâzım appreciated the note, and published it in *Akşam* alongside a warm response. Already, Uçuk was a minor figure within Istanbul literary circles, and she and Nâzım had a number of friends in common. Their relationship is said to have lasted a few months.[34]

In 1935, Nâzım also began to spend more time with Münevver Andaç (Figure 8.1). Münevver was Nâzım's 18-year-old first cousin, the daughter of Celile's brother Mustafa, who had married a French woman by the name of Gabrielle Taron. Münevver was born in February 1917. Following the end of World War I, Gabrielle had taken Münevver and her sister Leyla to Paris. Münevver's father had died when the girls

**Figure 8.1** Münevver Andaç

[33] Füsun Özbilgen, *Sana Tütün ve Tespih Yolluyorum: Semiha Berksoy'un Anıları Nâzım Hikmet ve Fikret Muallâ ile Mektuplaşmaları* (İstanbul: Broy Yayınları, 1985), 57–65, 147–155.
[34] Göksu and Timms, *Romantic Communist*, 108–109.

were still young, and the two of them were raised in a mainly French-speaking environment.[35]

"Madame Gabrielle," as she is known in Nâzım's biographies, died in 1926, after which point nine-year-old Münevver matriculated at a French-language boarding school in Italy. She later reportedly attended classes for some time at a university in Marseilles. In 1935, Münevver returned to Istanbul, where she studied law and taught French.[36] Back in Turkey, she rolled her r's French-style. Like Nâzım in Moscow, Münevver stood out.

In an interview that Münevver gave in 1996, she described her relationship with Nâzım as "turbulent." "He was a married man," she is quoted as saying in apparent reference to these earlier years, "so it was very difficult."[37] Whether or not the connection was physical at this time is unclear, but an emotional "flirtation" between the two does seem to have begun to develop.[38] This early form of their relationship, whatever it entailed, continued until 1938, when Nâzım would go on trial again.[39] The fact that they were first cousins would not have raised eyebrows, as consanguineous marriages were not uncommon in Turkey.[40]

## The View from Moscow

In the aftermath of Nâzım's thwarted effort to create a new TKP Central Committee, İsmail Bilen had risen up through the ranks of the party ladder. In 1929, not long after his return to Turkey with Nâzım, Bilen had been arrested, and he remained behind bars until 1933. While still in prison, İsmail was elected to the Central Committee of the TKP. From 1933 to 1937 he continued to live in Turkey, working for the party.[41]

Bilen is usually described in the memoirs of other TKP members in quite unflattering terms. He is presented as overbearing, secretive, and conspiratorial in a rather over-the-top manner, someone who never gave up on the black leather jacket ethos of Bolshevism's earliest days.[42] During a conversation with me in Budapest in

---

[35] Ibid., 190–191. Also see Memet Fuat, *A'dan Z'ye Nâzım Hikmet*, 239.

[36] Göksu and Timms, *Romantic Communist*, 191–193. Also see Sülker, *Nâzım Hikmet'in Gerçek Yaşamı*, vol. 1, 15; Fish, *Nâzım'ın Çilesi*, 293–295.

[37] Göksu and Timms, *Romantic Communist*, 191.    [38] In the words of Göksu and Timms. Ibid., 109.

[39] Ibid., 191. However, Memet Fuat writes that Münevver visited Nâzım and Piraye's house in 1936 or 1937. Nâzım was not at home, and Piraye hosted Münevver, who looked as uncomfortable "as if she were in an exam." *Gölgede Kalan Yıllar*, 272–273.

[40] Nor are they today. A 2016 study in Turkey found rates of consanguineous marriage within the sampled population to be 18.5 percent, and of these 57.8 percent were first cousin marriages. Sena Kaplan, Gül Pınar, Bekir Kaplan, and Fılız Aslantekin, "The Prevalence of Consanguineous Marriages and Affecting Factors in Turkey: A National Survey," *Journal of Biosocial Sciences*, vol. 48, no. 5 (September 2016), 616–630.

[41] İsmail had made a visit back to the USSR in 1935 "for several months." RGASPI, f. 495, op. 266, d. 12, Part I, l. 113. "Spravka" on Bilen, written by Galdzhian, from June 1937. Other materials suggest that this return to the USSR occurred in 1934.

[42] See, for example, Zekeriya Sertel, *Nâzım Hikmet'in Son Yılları*, 182–184; Gün Benderli, *Su Başında Durmuşuz*, 41, 206–210, 219, 222–225, and elsewhere; Benderli, *Giderayak*, 76–80. On İsmail Bilen in the eyes of other Turks in the Eastern Bloc, also see Yıldız Sertel, *Nâzım Hikmet ile Serteller*, 135–138, 167–171; İhmalyan, *Bir Yaşam Öyküsü*, 304–305, 307; Hayk Açıkgöz, *Anadolulu bir Komünistin Anıları* (İstanbul: Belge Yayınları, 2006), 423–425, 435, 443–444, 484–486, 554–557, 582–645, and elsewhere.

2018, Gün Benderli (previously "Togay"), who worked with İsmail for years in TKP politics, remarked that Bilen could be a friendly, talkative, and even quite charming individual in a social setting. However, he was "180 degrees different" with respect to his political life.[43] İsmail knew how to compartmentalize.

Like many communists who crossed borders illegally and worked underground for the party, İsmail Bilen had lived under a variety of assumed names over the years. While it was hardly uncommon for Turkish communists to work with aliases, İsmail outdid most of his comrades when it came to picking new names. For İsmail these included: "İsmail Bilen," "İsmail İbrahimov," "İbrahimov Bilen," "Laz İsmail," "Bostancı," "Liubomir," "İskender Mustafa," and "Yazykov."[44] In the wake of his release from prison in 1933, Bilen adopted yet another *nom de guerre*: "Marat."[45]

Marat, i.e., İsmail Bilen, shared an adversarial relationship with Alexander Senkevich, the Istanbul-born grandson of a Polish officer from tsarist Russia. Senkevich had known İsmail since their early days at KUTV. Party paperwork indicates that Senkevich had studied in the regular two-year program at the university starting in January 1925, leaving Moscow in May 1927.[46]

Back in Istanbul in the late 1920s, Alexander Senkevich had begun working for the now-illegal TKP. In 1929, he was arrested in Turkey and sentenced to three years and four months in prison. Released in December 1932, Alexander was again detained in April 1933. After being held for a month, he was released, then fled to the Soviet Union, making his way back to Moscow in May.[47]

Not long after returning to the Soviet capital, Senkevich wrote a party autobiography accounting for his activities in Turkey. Such documents were often asked of individuals who had just arrived in the USSR from abroad, yet Senkevich's statement stood out for several reasons. It was, for one thing, eighteen pages long, easily twice as large as even the more extensive of such documents.[48] Also unusual about Senkevich's autobiography was that he said very little about himself. Instead, he devoted most of his report to commenting upon the activities and perceived political reliability of other Turkish communists, individuals with whom he had interacted in Istanbul. Altogether in this "autobiography," Senkevich delivered information on forty-two fellow party members.

Something else strange about this document is that it began with a discussion of a relatively minor figure who had not been associated with the party for years: Sabiha Mesrure. Mesrure, aka "Rosa," had been İsmail Bilen's wife.[49] After finishing her

---

[43] Conversation with the author, Budapest, June 2, 2018.

[44] According to the opening page on Bilen's party file. RGASPI, f. 495, op. 266, d. 12, Part I.

[45] The first instance I have encountered of İsmail Bilen calling himself, or being called by others, by the name "Marat" was in a TKP report produced by Fisher on March 14, 1931. RGASPI, f. 495, op. 266, d. 12, Part I, ll. 146–147.

[46] RGALI, f. 495, op. 266, d. 118, l. 6. "Spravka" on Alexander Senkevich. No date, but apparently written around 1936.

[47] RGALI, f. 495, op. 266, d. 118, l. 6.

[48] Some of which came to 10–12 pages. However, most TKP party autobiographies were 1–5 pages long.

[49] Senkevich personal file, RGASPI, f. 495, op. 266, d. 118, ll. 36–53. Here, l. 36. "Autobiography," February 15, 1934.

training with the *Spetsgruppa*, Rosa had returned to Istanbul in 1927 to work under-ground for the now-banned party. At the beginning of 1928, however, she was arrested by Turkish police. Under detention, Mesrure gave up the names of several comrades. "Rosa" would never again return to the party.[50]

In his party autobiography, Senkevich sounded oddly defensive in explaining his interactions with Mesrure:

> Until the beginning of 1928, she [Mesrure] and I worked together. She was detained during a wave of arrests but was released soon afterward. After her release we met up again a few times, but these meetings were strictly of a friendly nature.[51]

In writing about Sabiha Mesrure in this manner, Senkevich may well have simply been trying to distance himself from someone who was now in political disgrace. Nevertheless, this was an unusual way for a communist in the USSR to describe interactions with a comrade of the opposite sex.

It is unclear whether Senkevich's friendship with Mesrure played a role in the souring of his relationship with İsmail. Nevertheless, the two had clashed on a number of occasions in the early 1930s.[52] This, at any rate, is how Senkevich characterized his dealings with Bilen in his party autobiography.[53] Alongside other points, Alexander criticized Bilen for having failed to cut his ties to Nâzım Hikmet more quickly. Writing that İsmail was "one of the best comrades of [Nâzım] and supported him very well," Senkevich noted that this was an ongoing issue. İsmail, claimed Alexander, had "only recently distanced himself" from Nâzım.[54]

Senkevich's autobiography also alluded to what he described as a power struggle taking place between his "faction" and that of İsmail Bilen and Aziz Husametdin.[55] Senkevich wrote that he had criticized İsmail and Aziz's ideas regarding the direction of the party.[56] According to Senkevich, he and "a pretty good collection of comrades" had met up and "adopted a resolution" against İsmail and Aziz. "Of course, Aziz and İsmail were not pleased by our speeches, and they started to criticize us sharply."[57]

Senkevich submitted his autobiography to party officials in Moscow in February 1934. At this time, İsmail was still working underground for the TKP in Turkey.[58] In 1935, İsmail became the General Secretary of the TKP's Istanbul-based underground

---

[50] RGASPI, f. 495, op. 266, d. 12, Part I, l. 93. Letter from Ivanova, December 25, 1937.

[51] RGASPI, f. 495, op. 266, d. 118, ll. 36–53, here l. 43.

[52] Senkevich personal file, RGASPI, f. 495, op. 266, d. 118, ll. 36–53. Here, l. 40. "Autobiography," February 15, 1934. Senkevich brought up Mesrure two more times in the "Autobiography," an effort, perhaps, to remind his readers of İsmail's connection to the party traitor.

[53] Senkevich also criticized TKP members, like Boz İsmail, whom he called a "partisan of İsmail and Aziz." "İsmail" in this case is a reference to İsmail Bilen. Senkevich also said that Boz İsmail was "politically unhealthy" and "played one of the main roles among the provocateurs" who had been damaging the Turkish party in the late 1920s. RGASPI, f. 495, op. 266, d. 118, l. 45.

[54] RGASPI, f. 495, op. 266, d. 118, l. 41.      [55] RGASPI, f. 495, op. 266, d. 118, l. 40.

[56] RGASPI, f. 495, op. 266, d. 118, l. 41.      [57] RGASPI, f. 495, op. 266, d. 118, l. 39.

[58] İsmail would, however, reportedly make a quick trip to Moscow in April 1934 in order to "settle our internal party issues." RGASPI, f. 495, op. 266, d. 12, Part I, ll. 48, 123. This may, however, be a reference to İsmail's 1935 trip.

## 194 RED STAR OVER THE BLACK SEA

organization.[59] That same year, he visited Moscow "for several months" in order to receive an unspecified "treatment" (*lechenie*), before returning once again to Istanbul.[60] Bilen would stay in Turkey for the next two years.

### Marat's Return

On April 22, 1937, İsmail Bilen illegally crossed the border from Turkey into the USSR, where he was arrested by Soviet border guards.[61] İsmail freely acknowledged to his captors that he had traversed the frontier unlawfully. He insisted, however, that he had received "permission from the TKP and the Comintern" to do so.[62] Claiming that he had *carte blanche* to cross illegally into the USSR if ever he needed to, Bilen encouraged the border police to get in touch with the Comintern. He was given a brief trial and was sentenced to five years in a Soviet prison.[63]

In Moscow, meanwhile, there was a movement afoot to replace Şefik Hüsnü as TKP representative to the Comintern, a position he had held for the past two years. Following the Sheikh Sait rebellion and subsequent crackdown in Turkey, Şefik Hüsnü had escaped to Europe, spending the next ten years in Poland and Germany.[64] In 1935, he had come to Moscow, where he took up the reins as head of the TKP in the USSR.

The job of party representative to the Comintern was an important one. It brought real power in a manner that İsmail's previous positions in the TKP—all of them based in Turkey—had not. The head of the TKP apparatus in Moscow had a tangible impact upon the lives of TKP members in the USSR, playing a crucial role in determining where they would work and live. During a time of political purging, moreover, being on good terms with the party representative could mean the difference between life and death.

Şefik Hüsnü was not, however, held in high esteem by Comintern officials. In a report from September 1936, he is derided by one Galdzhian as "the worst organizer," and someone who "suffers from liberalism." Galdzhian, who is identified in Comintern paperwork as an officer responsible for "cadres," or personnel, blasted Şefik Hüsnü for running a loose ship in Istanbul prior to coming in Moscow. There had not been enough discipline in Istanbul back in the 1920s, argued Galdzhian, and this was why Şefik Hüsnü's leadership had been challenged. "He brought the fractionalists upon

---

[59] RGASPI, f. 495, op. 266, d. 12, Part I, l. 113. "Spravka" on Bilen, written by Galdzhian, from June 1937. Other materials indicate that this return to the USSR occurred in 1934.

[60] Sometimes it is written that this treatment took place in 1934–35. RGASPI, f. 495, op. 266, d. 12, Part 1, l. 48. "Spravka" from May 28, 1948.

[61] Perhaps a reflection of stepped-up border protections taking place at this time. RGASPI, f. 495, op. 266, d. 12, Part II, l. 179.

[62] On this investigation, see RGASPI, f. 495, op. 266, d. 12, Part I, ll. 106–110; f. 495, op. 266, d. 38, ll. 70–72. For the party autobiography that Bilen wrote in Moscow in July 1937, see ll. 117–123.

[63] RGASPI, f. 495, op. 266, d. 12, Part I, l. 113. "Spravka" regarding Bilen, June 1937. Written by Galdzhian.

[64] Şefik Hüsnü's wife was Polish. Şefik Hüsnü personal file, RGASPI, f. 495, op. 266, d. 38, l. 87. "Spravka," September 3, 1936.

himself," Galdzhian complained, referring to Nâzım Hikmet and others seeking to establish their own party committees.[65]

Meanwhile, Galdzhian's Comintern colleague, one Comrade Poliachek, kept up the attack on Şefik Hüsnü with a devastating biographical review. On April 4, 1937, he listed several names: "Şevket Süreyya, Vedat Nedim, Ahmet Cevat, Vâlâ Nureddin, Nâzım Hikmet." "All of these people," he wrote, "were friends and protégés of [Şefik Hüsnü]."[66]

Shortly thereafter, Galdzhian wrote a letter to a more senior-level Comintern official, Alikhanov, charging that Şefik Hüsnü was "too lazy in his work, and is lacking in elementary organizational skills."[67] Galdzhian wanted Şefik Hüsnü replaced, and he had two suggestions for a new representative. "Marat [İsmail Bilen] and Sidki [Reşat Fuat Baraner] will immediately become the leaders of the party," wrote Galdzhian on April 14.[68] A Comintern "spravka," or biographical reference-report, later indicated that "in the Spring of 1937" the decision had already been made to issue Şefik Hüsnü with a reprimand due to his sloppy organization.[69]

İsmail Bilen would not stay behind bars for long. In a note Galdzhian would write on July 2, the Comintern official emphasized that "Turkish law does not severely punish illegal border crossing," and that jail sentences in Turkey related to such infractions ranged "between two days to three months, maximum."[70] Whether it was due to the intervention of Galdzhian, or of someone else in the Comintern, İsmail was released shortly after his arrest. He then traveled to Moscow, where—despite the fact that he had literally just been let out of a Soviet prison—İsmail was given Şefik Hüsnü's job as TKP representative to the Comintern.[71]

Marat had arrived. Şefik Hüsnü, meanwhile, soon left Moscow for Istanbul. It would be the last time that he would make that journey. Before long, Şefik Hüsnü—TKP member No. 1—was out of the party altogether.[72]

Another noteworthy incident that took place at this time related to Reşat Fuat Baraner. Known as "Sidki," Baraner had been identified by Galdzhian as someone who, alongside İsmail Bilen, would assume a leadership position in the TKP once Şefik Hüsnü was out of the way. In February 1937, however, Baraner was arrested when he attempted to cross the border into Turkey from the USSR.

[65] "This, despite the fact that Şefik Hüsnü had himself left Istanbul in 1925. "Autobiographical report on Şefik Hüsnü," by Galdzhian, September 3, 1936. RGASPI, f. 495, op. 266, d. 38, ll. 87–88. Personal file of Şefik Hüsnü. For the quotation at the end of the paragraph, see l. 88.

[66] RGASPI, f. 495, op. 266, d. 38, ll. 83–84.

[67] RGASPI, f. 495, op. 266, d. 38, ll. 78–82. Quotation from l. 82. "About Ferdi." "Ferdi" was an alias of Şefik Hüsnü. April 14, 1937.

[68] The letter from Galdzhian was written on April 14. Also see RGASPI, f. 495, op. 266, d. 12, Part I, l. 113. "Spravka" from June 1937.

[69] A "spravka" is a brief report describing an individual's party-related history. RGASPI, f. 495, op. 266, d. 38, ll. 42–44, here 43. "Spravka" from April 13, 1941. Signed by Vladimirov.

[70] RGASPI, f. 495, op. 266, d. 12, Part I, l. 111. July 2, 1937. Galdzhian, "About Comrade Marat."

[71] Also see RGASPI, f. 495, op. 266, d. 38, ll. 42–44, 60–61, ll. 123–124. Also see Akbulut and Tunçay (eds.), İstanbul Komünist Grubu'ndan, 408–409.

[72] According to party records, Şefik Hüsnü would begin organizing on behalf of the legal Socialist Worker and Peasant Party of Turkey following the reintroduction of multi-party elections in 1946. This party would later be closed and Şefik Hüsnü and other organizers would be arrested and given prison sentences. RGASPI, f. 495, op. 266, d. 38, l. 3, reproduction of TASS bulletin from October 13, 1948.

## 196 RED STAR OVER THE BLACK SEA

In the aftermath of Baraner's arrest, Bilen was criticized for having withheld crucial information that could have helped Baraner stay out of police hands.[73] In the words—written in June 1937—of a Comintern commission consisting of comrades Pik, Belov, and Galdzhian:

> [Bilen] knew well the danger threatening Comrade Sidki [Baraner]. From a letter by Ferdi [Şefik Hüsnü][74] from January 10, [Bilen] knew that Sidki was thinking of returning soon to come in-country. But he never concretely—meaning through a decision of the Politburo of the party—managed with all of his means to get in touch with Moscow about the fact that Sidki shouldn't go in-country.[75]

İsmail's "mistake," wrote the committee members, was in assuming that Sidki would stay in Moscow. For this infraction of party discipline, which had resulted in the elimination of a possible rival for the TKP leadership position in Moscow, İsmail was given a reprimand.[76] Sidki, meanwhile, ended up spending the next several months behind bars in Turkey. By the time Baraner was released from prison, İsmail Bilen—Marat—had already consolidated his position in Moscow.[77]

### Last Man Standing

By the time Nâzım had returned to Turkey in late 1928, all of the old comrades with whom he had first traveled to Moscow—Vâlâ, Ahmet Cevat, Şevket Süreyya and Leman—had left the party. Şevket Süreyya had worked for some time as a teacher, and in 1932 became one of the founders and leading contributors to the journal *Kadro*. This publication constituted a political and intellectual experiment: a journal focusing upon a non-Soviet, Turkish brand of communism. The journal was closed down in 1935.[78] Later, Aydemir would be appointed to various positions within the state bureaucracy.[79] By the late 1930s, Şevket Süreyya had become an establishment figure in Kemalist Turkey.

Vâlâ, meanwhile, was working as a journalist, writing for *Akşam*. His revolutionary bravado of previous years notwithstanding, Vâlâ no longer had time for or interest in the Communist Party or the USSR.[80] Instead, he had begun, in the late 1920s, to

---

[73] Belov is described in Georgi Dimitrov's diary as an official working in connection with the personnel division of the Comintern. Rüstem Aziz (trans.), *Georgi Dimitrov: Günlük 2* (İstanbul: TÜSTAV, 2004), 245.

[74] "Ferdi" was Şefik Hüsnü's alias.    [75] RGASPI, f. 495, op. 266, d. 38, l. 67. Personal file of Şefik Hüsnü.

[76] RGASPI, f. 495, op. 266, d. 38, ll. 65–69. "Work of the Commission Investigating the Arrest of Comrade Sidki." June 13, 1937.

[77] Reşat Fuat Baraner's personal file indicates that he was arrested in February 1937, and that he "spent 1937–38 behind bars." RGASPI, f. 495, op. 266, d. 2, l. 26.

[78] Harris, *Origins of Communism in Turkey*, 147. On *Kadro*, also see ibid., 143–146; MacLeod, "Şevket Süreyya Aydemir," 101–107; Sülker, *Nâzım Hikmet'in Gerçek Yaşamı*, vol. 2, 250.

[79] On later positions that Şevket Süreyya would hold in Turkey, also see BCA, 30-18-01/02-124-100-10, from February 9, 1951.

[80] Vâlâ's departure following his siring of a daughter was not an unusual occurrence among the foreign students in the USSR. On "Sino-Soviet love children," see McGuire, *Red at Heart*, 226–253.

establish himself as one of the early producers of "pulp" fiction in Turkey. In 1928, he published *The Woodsman and Catherine* ("Baltacı ile Katerina"), a ribald and fantastical take on an old story.[81] In the 1930s, Vâlâ was supplementing his income by writing "romance, adventure, and murder novels" like *Little Declarations* (1933) and *Who was the Killer?* (1934). During this time, Vâlâ and Nâzım drifted apart due to a variety of issues, some of them relating to politics. The two would eventually go years without speaking.[82]

Ahmet Cevat Emre had also joined the Kemalist establishment, leading the commission overseeing Turkey's transition from the Arabic script to the Latin alphabet in 1929. He had served on a similar body in Azerbaijan under the pre-communist Müsavat government. In the late 1930s, Ahmet Cevat Emre would sit as a member of the Turkish parliament, serving as a representative from Çanakkale.[83]

Nâzım was the last man standing. According to an article written by Şevket Süreyya Aydemir some three decades later, Nâzım had been given the opportunity, in the second half of the 1930s, to mend his relations with Ankara. Şevket wrote that he had arranged for Nâzım to have dinner with Şükrü Kaya, the Turkish Minister of the Interior, and Şükrü Sökmensüer, the Chief of State Security. In Aydemir's later account of this meal, which took place in July 1937, Nâzım spent much of the night lecturing his dining companions on capitalism, imperialism, and world revolution.[84] Nothing came of the evening. The story indicates that, even at this late date, there were still opportunities for Nâzım to join the cultural establishment of Turkey, if he so desired. What Nâzım needed to do, however, was renounce communism, and that he would not do.

Why didn't Nâzım just back down? The TKP had, after all, long since cut ties with him. For all Nâzım knew, he would never again set foot in the USSR. Yet there he was, suffering through one trial after another, in defense of a political system whose local representatives now considered him a "renegade."

He didn't back down because he didn't think he had to or ought to. As far as Nâzım was concerned, he wasn't just defending communism. He was standing up for his right to believe in it.


## Purging the Ranks

The purges taking place in the Soviet Union in the late 1930s were directed against a broad cross-section of the USSR's many communities, domestic and foreign alike.[85]

---

[81] Nergis Ertürk traces some of the ways in which Vâlâ's writings in Turkey reflect his previous experiences in the USSR. "Vâlâ Nureddin's Comic Materialism and the Sexual Revolution: Writing across Turkey and the Soviet Union," *Comparative Literature*, vol. 73, no. 3 (2021), 299–319.

[82] From the early 1930s until the late 1940s the two friends would not speak to one another. Blasing, *Nâzım Hikmet*, 96.

[83] On Ahmet Cevat, also see Temuçin, "Ahmet Cevat Emre ve Kemalizm'de Öncü Bir Dergi."

[84] Karaca, *Sevdalınız Komünisttir*, 179; Göksu and Timms, *Romantic Communist*, 135–136; Blasing, *Nâzım Hikmet*, 102.

[85] Among the "eastern" domestic communists who were arrested and executed at this time were figures like Mustafa Suphi's former political partner Mirsaid Sultan-Galiev, as well as older Muslim cultural reformers who

The Comintern was intimately involved with these activities, which often began with expulsion from the party and a loss of "bread and board," i.e., the ability for someone to make a living or find accommodation. The next step was "life behind bars at best."[86] In August 1936, the cadre department reported to Comintern head Georgi Dimitrov that it had sent information regarding approximately 3,000 individuals to the NKVD, forerunner to the MGB and KGB.[87]

Dimitrov was already a well-known figure in communist history. Living in Germany in 1933, the Bulgarian had earned international acclaim following his arrest in connection with the Reichstag fire. During the course his trial, Dimitrov had famously defended himself in court, winning an acquittal and becoming a communist legend in the process. He was soon expelled from Germany, whence he then departed for the Soviet Union.

Not long after his arrival in the USSR in 1934, Dimitrov was chosen to become the General Secretary of the Comintern. The job had many practical dimensions, such as providing accommodation, employment, and other forms of assistance to foreign communists in the USSR. During the purge years, international communists who found themselves under suspicion or arrest often contacted Dimitrov, as well as their own party's representative to the Comintern, in desperate efforts to extricate themselves from the charges made against them.

Why had it become so important, in the spring 1937, to replace Şefik Hüsnü with İsmail Bilen as TKP representative in Moscow? It is possible that Şefik Hüsnü's alleged "laziness" and "liberalism" was the Comintern's way of alluding to an unwillingness to participate in purge-related arrests. This might explain why Şefik Hüsnü left the USSR immediately after he was removed from his position, and his subsequent departure from TKP activities altogether.

Şefik Hüsnü had been removed from his job in Moscow amid an investigation that was then taking place in relation to Şükrü Martel. Martel was the hapless TKP member from 1920s-era KUTV who had been sent to the USSR "by mistake" one day after joining the party in Turkey. He had been expelled from the university in 1927, not long after he had arrived in Moscow. Nevertheless, this accidental border-crosser had still managed to persevere. Following his expulsion from the university, Martel had stayed on in the USSR, bouncing around from one region to another and picking up different jobs along the way.

Martel displayed a penchant for getting into and out of trouble. After leaving KUTV, he had found work in a factory and, despite his checkered past, was even allowed to join the Communist Party of the Soviet Union (CPSU). In December 1934, however, Martel was banished from the party on charges of "fraudulently presenting himself as a specialist in agriculture" and misspending government money. In the trial

---

had achieved prominence in late imperial Russia, such as Fatih Kerimi. Meyer, *Turks Across Empires*, 178. Mirsaid Sultan-Galiev, one of the original Muslim communists in the USSR, was arrested in 1937 and shot in 1940. See Bulat Faizrakhmanovich, *Neizvestnyi Sultan Galiev* (Kazan: Tatarskoe knizhnoe izd-vo, 2002).

[86] Studer, *Transnational World of the Cominternians*, 138.  [87] Ibid., 86.

that ensued, however, Martel was acquitted on all charges. He was then able to resurrect his career, and his party membership was reinstated in 1936.[88]

Martel's difficulties resumed, however, in early 1937. In March of that year, Şefik Hüsnü had written an unflattering description of him, apparently in response to a query from the Comintern. "We don't consider him useful," Şefik Hüsnü had concluded in this note. "We don't know the details of his life in the USSR over the course of the past ten years. We don't believe it useful to prolong his stay here."[89]

Not long thereafter, Martel was arrested by the NKVD. This prompted Martel's wife Anna to write a letter to Şefik Hüsnü, who was still TKP representative to the Comintern at this time, pleading with him to intervene on Martel's behalf.

> In the name of his children, he asks me to ask you. I am certain of your love toward him and that you won't toss him aside like some kind of good-for-nothing. He doesn't deserve this.[90]

It was bad timing for the Martels. Şefik Hüsnü did not have a high opinion of Martel, but by now his views were of little matter. Soon, Şefik Hüsnü was en route, via France, back to Istanbul.[91] And Şükrü Martel was on his way to a labor camp.

Nail Çakırhan, the young communist poet with whom Nâzım co-authored *1+1=1* in 1931, was living in Moscow at this time.[92] In memoirs that Çakırhan would write years later, he states that Martel had gone to İsmail Bilen looking for help, but was rebuffed and sent to Siberia instead.[93]

> [Şükrü Martel] goes to the Comintern and finds İsmail. "I don't want to go," he says. İsmail says "I can't do anything." Martel was then sent to exile in Siberia. He spent 18 years there.[94]

Martel was, in fact, released in 1939. However, he was arrested again in 1941, and would not be heard from again until 1956.[95]

Another TKP member who was arrested at this time was Kara Mehmet. Kara Mehmet had been an acquaintance of Nâzım Hikmet in the 1920s and had joined up

---

[88] Personal file of Şükrü Martel, RGASPI, f. 495, op. 266, d. 80, ll. 6, 6-ob. "Spravka," from August 3, 1944.

[89] RGASPI, f. 495, op. 266, d. 80, l. 22.    [90] RGASPI, f. 495, op. 266, d. 80, ll. 18–19. August 4, 1937.

[91] Şefik Hüsnü "returned to Turkey in 1937 via France." Akbulut and Tunçay (eds.), *İstanbul Komünist Grubu'ndan*, 409.

[92] Prior to returning to Turkey later in 1937.

[93] In September 1956, a request was made by the office of the district *prokuror*, or "district attorney's" office, to look into Martel's party file. Given the timing, this might be a sign that Martel was being considered for restitution. RGASPI, f. 495, op. 266, d. 80, l. 8. Letter from Martynov, September 7, 1956.

[94] Nail Çakırhan, *Anılar* (İstanbul: TÜSTAV, 2008), 99–100. Sources vary with regard to how long Martel spent in prison camps. Hayk Açıkgöz would later write that Martel had spent 25 years in Siberia. Açıkgöz, *Anadolulu bir Ermeni Komünistin Anıları*, 555. For a summary of Martel's activities, see RGASPI, f. 495, op. 266, d. 80, l. 6, "Spravka," August 3, 1944.

[95] For Martel's file at RGASPI, see f. 495, op. 266, d. 80, l. 6, "Spravka," August 3, 1944; l. 8, "Spravka," September 7, 1956.

with Nâzım's "opposition" in 1929. Expelled from the party because of his support for Nâzım, Kara Mehmet was, two years later, reinstated to the party's ranks. He had renounced the mistakes of his past, denouncing Nâzım upon rejoining the party. In 1937, however, Kara Mehmet was arrested on charges of having helped people exit the USSR illegally.[96] His file comes to an abrupt end shortly after his arrest.

Ahmet Kaya was also arrested at this time. A native of Bulgaria who had immigrated in the early 1920s to what would become Turkey, Ahmet had come to the USSR in 1933 to study at KUTV. He did not finish his studies, however, and upon leaving school Ahmet moved to the city of Kirov, in Azerbaijan, to work in industry.[97] In 1938, Kaya was arrested by the NKVD on charges of "provocation."

Bewildered and confused, Ahmet wrote an urgent letter to İsmail Bilen, explaining that he had been held for months without the ability to communicate with others. He wanted the Comintern, and the TKP leadership in the USSR, to know where he was, and to follow up on information that he was providing them that would prove his innocence. There is no indication that he ever received a response. The letter he wrote to İsmail Bilen marks the last page in his file.[98]

Several of the TKP members who were arrested during these years had been part of Süleyman Nuri's "opposition" movement in 1925. İsmail Bilen had been on Nâzım's side during the conflict at KUTV, and had been described in the opposition's letter and "annex" as a supporter of the "bourgeois" Central Committee. With İsmail Bilen now in charge of the TKP's offices in Moscow, a number of the individuals who had risen up against Nâzım, İsmail, and the others in 1925 would find themselves facing investigation and arrest.

Mahir Ahmet had been one of the thirteen opposition members signing the initial letter criticizing Şefik Hüsnü and his protégés back in 1925. After getting kicked out of school and the party, Mahir had remained in the USSR, moving between a series of jobs in the field of agriculture. By the late 1930s, he had begun working as a lecturer at a Kirov (Azerbaijan)-based agricultural institute called ASKHI.

Mahir's problems began in mid-July 1938. Attending a mandatory ten-day training course related to his job, Mahir had left the meetings early to return to his family's dacha. Now, wrote Mahir in a letter to Comintern head Georgi Dimitrov, he feared that this relatively minor offense would be used as a pretext to punish him. As would be the case with many other international communists caught up in the purges, Mahir attributed his problems to the fact that he was a foreigner. "In the opinion of our party organization," complained Mahir to Dimitrov, "it is never possible for a foreigner to be a communist." Soviet authorities, Mahir claimed, saw him simply as "a spy, an

---

[96] It was common for foreigners in the purge-era USSR to be arrested for more foreign-specific types of crimes, such as espionage or illegal emigration. For Kara Mehmet's file, see RGASPI, Khadmi (aka Kara Mehmet), f. 495, op. 266, d. 78, l. 4. On the purge years and Arab communists in the USSR, see Kirasirova, "The Eastern International," 224–232. On Americans arrested and executed in the Soviet Union during the purge years, see Tzouliadis, The Forsaken, 93–121.

[97] Kirov is now known as Ganje.

[98] RGASPI, f. 495, op. 266, d. 61, ll. 34–34-ob. Personal file of Ahmet Kaya, aka Alekseev-Grigoriev.

intelligence officer, and saboteur for the Turkish government." "Probably," he surmised, "they will arrest me within days."[99]

Asked to comment on Mahir, İsmail Bilen made direct reference to Mahir's involvement in Nuri's opposition from thirteen years before. Writing on May 5, 1938, Bilen noted that other members of Süleyman Nuri's old group had also been recently arrested by the NKVD:

> Mahir Ahmedov, while a student at KUTV, in 1924–25 participated in an anti-party opposition against the Central Committee of the TKP and the leadership of KUTV, although he was not active in this opposition.
>
> As would later come to light, this opposition was employed by Trotskyites—for example, Süleyman Nuri, one of the leaders of the opposition—who were connected to Lominadze.[100]
>
> Many members of this opposition have since become provocateurs and agents of the Turkish police. For example, Fazıl, Mazlum, Raif, and others—and some of the participants of the opposition have been arrested by the organs of the NKVD—for example, Rolland.
>
> Mahir Ahmedov was also connected to Ali Yazıcı, who clearly did not participate in the anti-party opposition, but who encouraged them. Yazıcı, too, has been arrested by the NKVD.[101]

On May 5 1938, eight months after he had mailed off his pleas to İsmail Bilen and Georgi Dimitrov, Mahir's file comes to an end.[102] The file of Rolland, who had been "arrested by Soviet organs as a suspicious element," also comes to an abrupt end at this point.[103] Süleyman Nuri himself, meanwhile, made the rather prudent decision to leave the USSR for Turkey in April 1937—at just around the time that İsmail Bilen was coming back to the Soviet Union. Nuri would not return to the USSR for more than two decades.

## Mara & Sasha

Not long after İsmail returned to Moscow in 1937, Alexander Senkevich was informed that he would be transferred to a job working in a factory in Mariupol, on the Azov

---

[99] RGASPI, f. 495, op. 266, d. 82, ll. 19–23, here ll. 21–22. Letter from Mahir to Georgii Dimitrov, September 5, 1937. Mahir is sometimes referred to as "Mahir Ahmedov."

[100] Vissarion Lominadze, an early Bolshevik from Georgia, had shot himself in 1935 ahead of his apparent arrest.

[101] Mahir Ahmet was also known as "Mahir Ahmedov." Vissarion Lominadze (1897–1935) was a Georgian revolutionary then in disgrace following his opposition to Stalin. For İsmail Bilen's note on Mahir, see RGASPI, f. 495, op. 266, d. 82, ll. 1–2.

[102] Report written by Bilen on May 5, 1938. RGASPI, f. 495, op. 266, d. 82, ll. 1–2. For other TKP members disappearing in the USSR in the late 1930s, see RGASPI, f. 495, op. 266, d. 309; f. 495, op. 266, d. 78, ll. 4–5.

[103] RGASPI, f. 495, op. 266, d. 93, l. 1. Someone else who had been involved in Süleyman Nuri's "opposition" against the Central Committee in 1925 was Osman "Sarı" Mustafa. Osman's file includes a note from 1940, stating that he had been "[e]xpelled from the party. Suspected spy." RGASPI, f. 495, op. 266, d. 145, l. 1.

Sea in southeast Ukraine.[104] It is unclear at whose initiative this took place. The timing may not have been entirely coincidental, given Senkevich's adversarial history with Bilen.

Getting ready for his move down to Mariupol, Senkevich was back in his room at the Hotel Luxe. He decided to pay a visit to a woman he knew as "Stanka," who also lived at the Luxe. "Stanka" was Mara Kolarova (Figure 8.2), a Bulgarian communist from Sliven.

Born in 1912, Mara had worked in a textile factory as a young woman, at which point she had become increasingly involved in labor politics, joining the Bulgarian Communist Party in 1932.[105] Three years later, Mara was arrested while striking at her factory, and spent five months in prison as a result. While behind bars, Mara fell ill and was transferred to a hospital. From there, according to Mara's party file, she escaped.[106]

Kolarova's sacrifices for the movement notwithstanding, she was expelled from the Bulgarian party because of her so-called "erratic" behavior vis-à-vis the Bulgarian police.[107] She would later claim that the party had nevertheless given her permission to flee to the USSR in order to avoid prison.[108] In May 1936, and armed with a fake

**Figure 8.2** Mara Kolarova

[104] RGASPI, f. 495, op. 266, d. 118, l. 109.
[105] Kolarova writes in her memoirs that she was born in 1912. Documents in her Comintern file state that she was born in 1914. See Kolarova-Bilen, *Kanatlı Gençlik*, 9.
[106] Mara Todorovna Kolarova personal file. RGASPI, f. 495, op. 195, d. 303, ll. 1, 3, 29, 53; Kolarova-Bilen, *Kanatlı Gençlik*, 9–10.
[107] RGASPI, f. 495, op. 195, d. 303, l. 53, "Spravka," June 11, 1942.
[108] "Spravka," June 11, 1942. Personal file of Mara Kolarova, RGASPI, f. 495, op. 195, d. 303, l. 53.

passport, Mara Kolarova fled Bulgaria. Traveling via Varna, Bucharest, Brno, and Prague, she finally arrived in Moscow in June 1936.[109] Mara was five months pregnant at the time.

In October 1936, Mara gave birth to a daughter, whom she named Maya.[110] The two of them lived together in a room at the Luxe. As she was not a party member, Mara was concerned about her long-term prospects for staying in the Soviet Union. She was worried that she might have to return to Bulgaria, and maybe even face jail time there.[111] Then, Mara's daughter fell ill. In March 1937, Maya died.[112]

It was at around this time that Kolarova had first made the acquaintance of Alexander Senkevich. In memoirs that she would later write, Kolarova described "Sasha" as friendly and funny, always willing to be of assistance. He had helped her out, she later noted, during the hard times that followed the death of her daughter.

In a moment of inspiration, their relationship transformed into something more consequential. According to Kolarova's later telling, one night at the Luxe Senkevich showed up at her room and informed her that he would soon be leaving for Mariupol.

Sasha had something to tell her. He did not know how he would survive, Kolarova recalled him saying, without being able to spend his time with her.

> "I love you very much, Stanka![113] Be my wife…Come on, let's go to Mariupol together!"
>
> "Why not, Sasha…," I said. "During this difficult time, now it's my turn to help you. I hope that together things will be better."[114]

Following their decision at the Hotel Luxe to make a go of things together, Alexander Senkevich and Mara Kolarova arrived in Mariupol toward the end of 1937.[115] Before much time had passed, however, Kolarova's lingering health problems forced the two to return to Moscow. Back in the capital, Kolarova was given a job at the International Red Aid Society (MOPR), while Senkevich began working as a typesetter for a publishing house specializing in foreign language literature.[116]

Kolarova and Senkevich's living conditions in Moscow were, however, quite pitiful, consisting of a "summer room" in an apartment they shared with others. This arrangement was fine when the weather was warm, but with the arrival of autumn the room, which had no heat, became unbearably frigid.[117] Sasha and Mara reached out to the TKP for help with their finances and accommodation. This meant appealing to Senkevich's former adversary, İsmail Bilen.

---

[109] Kolarova-Bilen, *Kanatlı Gençlik*, 29.

[110] Ibid., 46. In a party autobiography that Kolarova wrote on May 23, 1941, she stated that her child was born in December 1936. RGASPI, f. 496, op. 195, d. 303, ll. 56–60, here l. 58. "Avtobiografiia."

[111] Kolarova-Bilen, *Kanatlı Gençlik*, 50–51.   [112] Ibid., 46, 48.

[113] "Stanka Vasileva" was Mara Kolarova's alias.   [114] Kolarova-Bilen, *Kanatlı Gençlik*, 48.

[115] RGASPI, f. 495, op. 266, d. 118, l. 113.

[116] RGASPI, f. 495, op. 266, d. 118, l. 94. Letter about Senkevich by Guliaev, a Comintern official, and addressed to the publishing house where Senkevich was employed. November 5, 1940.

[117] RGASPI, f. 495, op. 266, d. 118, l. 113. "Statement" (*zaiavlenie*) to Marat (İsmail Bilen). October 16, 1939.

In a series of letters to Bilen, Senkevich repeatedly asked for assistance in finding a warmer place to live. İsmail does appear to have put some effort into helping Senkevich at this time, but worked slowly. In mid-December 1939, some two months after Senkevich's initial request, the Comintern issued a directive to the Red Aid Society, asking them to look into finding the hapless couple an apartment somewhere "on the outskirts of Moscow."[118] Nothing, however, seems to have come of the proposal.

Amid Sasha and Mara's difficulties in Moscow, an ominous development was taking place further south. On December 16, 1937, Alexander Senkevich's older brother, Lefter Senkevich, was arrested by the NKVD. Lefter had emigrated from Turkey in 1928, settling in Odessa.[119] On April 28, 1938, Alexander contacted İsmail in relation to a party-related letter he needed İsmail to write on his behalf. Toward the end of this message, Senkevich noted that he had recently learned of his brother's arrest, "the reason for which is unknown." Alexander informed İsmail at this time that, as far as he was concerned, Lefter "is no longer a brother to me."[120]

Living at the mercy of someone with whom he had once clashed, "Sasha" Senkevich was in an unenviable position. İsmail now held the power in their relations, and he was determined to use it.

## Rehabilitating the Prodigal Son

If İsmail Bilen remembered his adversaries from KUTV, he had similarly not forgotten his friends. In his party autobiography, written shortly after he returned to the USSR in 1937, Bilen went out of his way to say positive things about someone who for years had been the target of nothing but vitriol within the TKP: Nâzım Hikmet.

In reference to their trip back together from the USSR to Turkey in 1928, İsmail noted that "at trial and in prison, Nâzım handled himself well."[121] While such an observation hardly constituted a full-throated endorsement of Nâzım, Bilen's comments struck a starkly different tone from virtually everything else that had been written about Nâzım in TKP and Comintern paperwork since the early 1930s.

Galdzhian, the Comintern official who had played a key role in replacing Şefik Hüsnü as TKP representative with İsmail Bilen, similarly began to offer conciliatory words about Nâzım Hikmet. In a report that Galdzhian wrote about Bilen in 1937, the Comintern official observed that Bilen and Nâzım had been arrested together on the Turkish border in 1928. "Nâzım Hikmet had a strong influence as a poet," observed Galdzhian. "Turkish society raised a great uproar in response to Nâzım's arrest."[122]

---

[118] RGASPI, f. 495, op. 266, d. 118, l. 110. December 16, 1939.

[119] Personal file of Lefter Senkevich. RGASPI, f. 495, op. 266, d. 87.

[120] RGASPI, f. 495, op. 266, d. 118, l. 114. Letter from Alexander Senkevich to Marat [İsmail Bilen], April 28, 1938.

[121] RGASPI, f. 495, op. 266, d. 12, Part I, ll. 117–123, here l. 121. Bilen's party autobiography from June 24, 1937.

[122] This was apparently a reference to Nâzım's arrest and detention in Turkey at the end of 1936. RGASPI, f. 495, op. 266, d. 12, Part I, l. 111. Galdzhian, "About Comrade Marat." July 2, 1937.

As was the case with Bilen's comments about Nâzım, this was hardly earth-shattering praise. Nevertheless, these observations marked a real shift from the manner in which Nâzım had been discussed in recent years, while also acknowledging Nâzım's potential usefulness to the party.

This revised view of Nâzım may have had something to do with recent political writing that he had been involved with in Turkey. In 1936, Nâzım participated in the production of two pamphlets that had likely involved the TKP.[123] The first of these was called "German Fascism and Racism." Consisting of excerpts from the writings of the European communist intellectuals Theodor Balk, B. M. Bernadiner, and Ernst Henri, this booklet contained the sort of boilerplate political discourses regarding European foreign policymaking that the Soviet government had been emphasizing for much of the 1930s.[124]

Also in 1936, Nâzım lent his name to the publication of a booklet called "Soviet Democracy" (*Sovyet Demokrasisi*). This document was produced to commemorate the "Stalin Constitution" that was adopted in the USSR that year. As was the case with "German Fascism and Racism," "Soviet Democracy" reflected the party-line views of the Kremlin during this era of high Stalinism. The title of the brochure was one that would be familiar to anyone in communist circles at this time, as the concept of "Soviet Democracy," in contradistinction to the "bourgeois democracy" of the West, had long been a rhetorical reference point in the USSR.

The term "Soviet Democracy" was disseminated broadly by, among others, Soviet Foreign Minister Vyacheslav Molotov, whose *La démocratie soviétique* had been published in Paris by an organization called "the friends of the Soviet Union" in 1935.[125] During the years 1936–38, pro-Moscow publications bearing the title "Soviet Democracy" were produced in numerous countries and languages.[126] Like "German Fascism and Racism," "Soviet Democracy" was taken almost entirely from other sources—in this case, the new Soviet constitution. Nâzım is credited with a brief preface, but most of this volume's contents appear to have been translated into Turkish from pro-Soviet (or Soviet-sponsored) publications in other countries.

Not long after the appearance of these two brochures, Nâzım was arrested again by Turkish authorities, on December 30, 1936.[127] He had been sitting in a café on Taksim Square when he was approached by a plainclothes police officer who informed Nâzım that he was being detained on suspicions of "inciting communism." Alongside twelve other defendants, Nâzım was held until April 17, 1937. The trial came to an end on June 21 with an acquittal.[128]

---

[123] On these two brochures, also see Sülker, *Nâzım Hikmet'in Gerçek Yaşamı*, vol. 3, 73.

[124] Nâzım Hikmet, "Alman Faşizmi ve Irkçılığı" (İstanbul: Kader Basımevi), 1936.

[125] Vyacheslav Molotov, *La démocratie soviétique* (Paris: Bureau d'éditions: les Amis de l'Union soviétique, 1935).

[126] See, for example, Pat Sloan, *Soviet Democracy* (London: Gollancz, 1937); André Ribard, *Les conquêtes de la démocratie soviétique* (Paris: Bureau d'éditions, 1937); and Sirio Rosado Fernández, *La democracia soviética* (Madrid: Asociación de Amigos de la Unión Soviética, 1938).

[127] Sülker, *Nâzım Hikmet'in Gerçek Yaşamı*, vol. 4, 141.

[128] The defendants also included Hikmet Kıvılcımlı. Ibid., 149.

While it is not clear how close Nâzım actually came to rejoining the TKP during the years 1936–37, it does seem evident that the new TKP representative in Moscow had a much more positive view of the poet. In May 1938, İsmail Bilen wrote the following about Nâzım in a reference-report (*kharakteristika*), the first which had been written about the poet-communist in years:

> Despite the fact that Nâzım participated in the opposition, he at no time and in no place ever came out against the USSR. To the contrary, he always openly defended the Soviet Union. For example, he wrote many poems about the Soviet Union. His last brochure, "Soviet Democracy" in its portrait of Comrade Stalin, was a strong blow against the agents of fascism in Turkey. Nâzım Hikmet actively participated in the creation of the national front in Turkey. He frequently took on all tasks. In 1937 he was arrested for his anti-fascist activities in Turkey. He is now in detention as a result of his defense of the Spanish Republic, that is, for his call to the Turkish nation to help Spain.[129]

The very fact that a *kharakteristika* had been prepared regarding Nâzım is noteworthy. With the exception of the occasional denunciation, Nâzım's file had largely lain dormant for almost a decade. It would have been unusual, moreover, for a party representative in Moscow to be asked to provide a *kharakteristika* about someone whose connection to the party was not under review for some reason.[130]

In documents produced after Nâzım had returned to the USSR in 1951, there are indications that some sort of reconciliation had taken place between Nâzım and the TKP in the mid-1930s. In June 1951, a "spravka" pertaining to Nâzım alleged that, with regard to Nâzım's expulsion from the TKP, "the Politburo of the TKP reversed this decision in 1935."[131] Another "spravka" from 1955, probably basing its information upon the preceding document, makes the same claim,[132] as does a third from 1961.[133] While it does not appear that Nâzım rejoined the TKP at this time—no documents I've seen from the 1930s indicate as such—it does seem possible that an unofficial reconnection had occurred, if only on a personal basis between Nâzım and İsmail Bilen, who had known each other since their days at KUTV in the early 1920s.

---

[129] "Kharakteristika," May 1938. RGASPI, f. 495, op. 266, d. 47, Part I, l. ll. 135–140, here 138. Also see ibid., ll. 81, 90, 136, "Materials from the Comintern Archive Relating to Nâzım Hikmet from 1925 to 1939." The same document can be found in RGASPI, f. 82, op. 2, d. 1330, ll. 112–115.

[130] Other now-disgraced ex-communists like Vâlâ, Sevket, Ahmet Cevat, and Vedat Nedim, who had likewise been out of the party for years, did not, for example, have reports written about them at this time.

[131] At this time, Nâzım had escaped from Turkey and was in Romania, awaiting a decision from Moscow, as I discuss in Chapter 11. See RGASPI, f. 82, op. 2, d. 1330, l. 64. "Spravka" on Nâzım Hikmet from June, 1951.

[132] "Spravka" signed by F. Voloshin. Nâzım Hikmet personal file, RGASPI, f. 495, op. 266, d. 47, Part II, l. 57. August 23, 1955.

[133] Nâzım Hikmet personal file. RGASPI, f. 495, op. 266, d. 47, Part II, ll. 23–24, 125. "Spravka" from 1961. All three of the documents attesting to an alleged "reversal" of Nâzım's expulsion were produced decades after the event supposedly took place.

## A Tale of Two Futurists

Nâzım's return to Istanbul in the late 1920s had come at a crucial moment in the history of Turkish letters. With the establishment of the Turkish Republic, a new literature was also being created, not to mention a new alphabet and a rapidly changing language.[134] Everybody knew that poetry would be different going forward, but what would it look and sound like?

His travels with Vâlâ and cosmopolitan existence in Moscow had brought Nâzım back to Istanbul with wits as sharp as a razor. He and Vâlâ had not only learned something about Russian Futurism, but also the world. Now, Nâzım was eager to make a contribution in Turkey—or at least have his voice heard. For a poet with dreams of immortality, the sense of possibility that the future of Turkish verse appeared to provide at this time must have been thrilling. No wonder Nâzım had been so eager to demolish the country's literary idols.

Nâzım was not, however, the only Futurist in town. One young Turkish poet who had likewise discovered Futurism through his international travels was Ercümend Behzad (Lav). Born in 1903 in Istanbul, Ercümend Behzad shared several points in common with Nâzım. Like Nâzım, Ercümend had lived abroad during an important part of his early adulthood, studying the violin at the Stern Music Conservatory in Berlin between 1921 and 1925. In his poetry, too, Ercümend's interests and approach overlapped with those of Nâzım. Like Nâzım, Ercümend Behzad frequently introduced elements of cinema, or stagecraft, into his writing, and both poets had been involved in theater in the 1920s. Ercümend had even acted in three of Muhsin Ertuğrul's films: *Ankara Post*, *A Nation Awakens*, and *If My Wife Deceives Me*, the latter two of which Nâzım had also worked on.[135] In 1931, Ercümend Behzad published a book of poetry called *S.O.S.*, followed by *Chaos* in 1934.

Behzad valorized, in a manner not unlike "Machine-ization" and other poems that Nâzım wrote in the late 1920s, modern technology and science. He also sought, like Nâzım, to allow the page to come alive through the creative employment of font and spacing.

In the opening lines to *S.O.S.*, for example, Behzad writes:

> The sleepiness of sleepiness in space
>
> Not
>
> a
>
> soul
>
> It opens
>
> unravels
>
> the mouth of darkness

---

[134] On changes taking place to the Turkish language during these and following years, see Geoffrey Lewis, *The Turkish Language Reform: A Catastrophic Success* (Oxford: Oxford University Press, 1999).

[135] Makal, *Beyaz Perdede ve Sahnede Nâzım Hikmet*, 92. On Behzad and Nâzım Hikmet, see Sülker, *Nâzım Hikmet'in Gerçek Yaşamı*, vol. 2, 134.

> Prisoner
>
> sounds on the floor
>
> electrify[136]

Behzad's style and themes were not so different from those of Nâzım, nor was his poetry's appearance on the page. While these rather superficial similarities by no means imply that the works of the two poets were equal in terms of their contributions, they do raise the question of how literary reputations are made.

Is it simply because Nâzım's poems were objectively so much better than everybody else's that we remember them today, while the careers of others, like Behzad Lav, have been forgotten? Or does Nâzım's ongoing literary reputation also have something to do with his engaging life story, or his comparatively large output?

Ercümend Behzad's life certainly differed from that of Nâzım, as did his level of literary production. After publishing *S.O.S.* and *Chaos*, Behzad married a woman named Muhattar and found a practical day job, setting up a career for himself in cultural administration. Talented with respect to both literature and music, Behzad began working for the Press Directorate in 1935, where he would remain for eight years. Later positions included a stint working as an administrator for the so-called "People's Houses" (*Halk Evleri*), and the Istanbul Municipal Theater.[137] From 1950 until his retirement in 1962, Lav was employed in the administration of the Istanbul Conservatory, where he was responsible for creating its theater and ballet branches.[138]

Ercümend Behzad Lav enjoyed a fine literary career. He published two books in the 1930s, two in the 1940s, and three more in the 1960s and 1970s before passing away in 1984. Nevertheless, no one today speaks of Ercümend Lav in the sort of terms reserved for Nâzım Hikmet. His work is known mainly by specialists.

Nâzım, by contrast, produced an absolutely dumbfounding amount of writing during these years. Between 1929 and 1937 he published eleven new volumes of poetry, three novels, four plays, and approximately 1,000 small columns, translations, and short stories. He was also involved in the production of at least seven films.[139] Some of Nâzım's cultural contributions were brilliant, while others were perhaps more valuable as a means of paying the bills, but all of them required time and energy.

Ercümend Behzad Lav would hold, in his later life, exactly the sort of high-level public positions in cultural administration that were impossible for Nâzım to obtain in Turkey. Precisely because a professional-bureaucratic future like this was blocked off to Nâzım he was free to—or rather, had to—devote himself entirely to writing.

---

[136] Doğan Hızlan (ed.), *Ercümend Behzad Lav: Bütün Eserleri* (İstanbul: Yapı Kredi Yayınlar, 2005), 53.

[137] The former Turkic Hearths had been absorbed into the CHP-controlled "People's Houses" in 1932. Shaw and Shaw, *History of the Ottoman Empire and Modern Turkey*, vol. II, 383.

[138] Hızlan, *Bütün Eserleri*, 45–46. On Lav, also see Eser Demirkan, *Ercümend Behzad Lav (Hayatı, Sanatı, Eserleri)* (Ankara: T.C. Kültür Bakanlığı, 2002), 3.

[139] Films that Nâzım worked on in some capacity following his release from prison in 1934 included: *Aysel Bataklı Damın Kızı* ("Aysel the Girl from the Hut in the Swamp") (1934), *Milyon Avcıları* ("The Hunters for the Million") (1934), *Leblebeci Horhor Ağa* ("The Chickpea Seller," 1934), and *Güneşe Doğru* ("Toward the Sun," 1937). Also see Makal, *Beyaz Perdede ve Sahnede Nâzım Hikmet*, 106–107; Ünser, "Nâzım Hikmet'in sinema çalışmaları," 24.

Whereas Ercümend Behzad Lav and other erstwhile border-crossers would eventually settle down, raise a family, and live in the same city for most of their adult lives, Nâzım never ceased crossing borders. And he never stopped writing.

Nâzım's published verse between the years 1934 and 1936 included *Portreler* ("Portraits"), *Taranta Babu'ya Mektuplar* ("Letters to Taranta Babu"), and *Simavne Kadısı Oğlu Şeyh Bedreddin Destanı* ("The Epic of Sheikh Bedreddin"). In *Portreler*, Nâzım's "portraits" were considerably more personal than his earlier Soviet-inspired works, through poems like "My Poetry," "Orhan Selim," and "Letter to My Wife."

In "Letter to My Wife," Nâzım's opening lines go as follows:

> My one and only!
> In your last letter:
> "My head aches
>                   my heart is dumbfounded"
>                                        you say;
> "If they hang you
>                   if I lose you";
>                        you say;
>                             "I cannot live!"

Here and elsewhere, the radicalism of his Moscow-based writing had gone, but the approach is still experimental. For Nâzım, bringing his family and himself into his poetry was, after all, something new. Whereas his Syllabist-era works had been more sentimental than truly personal, now Nâzım was telling stories that clearly meant something to him individually, anticipating the best-known examples of his later work.

"Letters to Taranta-Babu" and the Sheikh Bedreddin poems, on the other hand, were more abstract, impersonal, and overtly political. They were also both quite ambitious. "Letters to Taranta-Babu" was written in both prose and verse, and takes the form of a series of letters to one Taranta-Babu. The individual narrating the story, "Nâzım," had received the letters from a friend, who had found them in a boarding house in Rome, where they had been left behind by the previous tenant, an Ethiopian student. These poems openly criticized Mussolini's colonial project in Ethiopia, referring to "Il Duce" and other Italian politicians by name.[140]

"The Epic of Sheikh Bedreddin," meanwhile, tells the story of a prisoner reading late into the night, then "vividly imagining a fifteenth-century peasant uprising inspired by Sheikh Bedreddin."[141] Most of the work takes place in the medieval Ottoman Empire. It is told in a grand style, meant to bring to mind the tales of a traveling chronicler. Even more than "Letters to Taranta-Babu," this work is a fusion

---

[140] The translation of "Letters to Taranta-Babu" would also mark Nâzım's first publication in French, in 1936. Göksu and Timms, *Romantic Communist*, 126.

[141] Blasing, *Nâzım Hikmet*, 103. On "The Epic of Sheikh Bedreddin" also see Clark, *Eurasia Without Borders*, 75–80.

of poetry and prose. Two of the characters are named "Mustafa" and "Kemal," a choice that was bound to attract attention in Turkey.

Also during these years Nâzım continued to pseudonymously produce a large amount of writing in genres other than poetry. In 1936, he wrote a serialized novel called *Blood Doesn't Speak* ("Kan Konuşmaz"). In the same year, he published *Green Apples* ("Yeşil Elmalar), which was advertised as a tale of "love-desire-adventure-fear-excitement-horror," in the style of Vâlâ's pulp fiction.[142] Nâzım also wrote two new plays in the mid-1930s. The first, *This is a Dream* (*Bu Bir Rüyadır*), was written in 1934 but was never staged. The second, *The Forgotten Man* (*Unutulan Adam*), was published in 1935. It is unclear whether or not it was ever produced in Turkey.[143]

Despite the fact that the great majority of Nâzım's published works were in prose, he is today chiefly remembered as a poet. With the exception of his autobiographical novel *Life's Good, Brother*, Nâzım's biographers, translators, and readers tend to ignore most of his non-verse works. Even people who love Nâzım's poetry usually have little familiarity with, or affection for, the majority of his prose writings. Why is this?

Nâzım's poetry evinces his cosmopolitan life in a manner that his prose usually does not.[144] Whereas Nâzım's prose typically stays in one place, his poetry reflects his border-crossing experiences in a variety of ways. From the romanticism of his occupation-era works to the *türkü*s that Nâzım and Vâlâ had marched to in Anatolia, his style and influences had changed along with his locale and the circles in which he spent his time. This had also been the case when Nâzım wrote the epitaph for Suphi in Georgia, and when he had embraced the Futurism of revolutionary Moscow. In Istanbul in the 1930s, meanwhile, Nâzım had altered his poetic style yet again, retaining some elements of his Moscow days but jettisoning much of Futurism's more experimental features. Every time he crossed a border, Nâzım's poetry developed in some way.

Nâzım had mastered a variety of styles while spending time in a series of places. Only now, however, after traversing many frontiers, had he succeeded in developing verse that was unquestionably his own. The voice Nâzım had created was the offspring of his border-crossing.

*

On both sides of the Soviet–Turkish frontier, border-crossers faced more scrutiny and threats. The Bolshevik welcome that incoming communists could expect in the early 1920s was now a thing of the past, and those who remained in the USSR often faced a grim future. While in Turkey the level of state violence was much less than that of the Soviet Union, the doors were closing there, too, for border-crossers and the public at large.

---

[142] "Aşk-ihtiras-macera-korku-heyecan-ruh tahlili romanı." A third novel, *Yaşamak Hakkı*, was being serialized in the newspaper *Haber-Akşam Postası* in 1938. Following Nâzım's arrest and incarceration, the novel was never completed.

[143] See Makal, *Beyaz Perdede ve Sahnede Nâzım Hikmet*, 189–191. Sülker, *Nâzım Hikmet'in Gerçek Yaşamı*, vol. 3, 60–62.

[144] *Life's Good, Brother* is an exception in this regard which will be discussed later.

Would someone like Nâzım have survived the purges? Had Nâzım fled Turkey for the USSR in the manner of some other Turkish communists in the late 1930s and early 1940s, perhaps he would have found people like Galdzhian and İsmail Bilen ready to support his political rehabilitation. Then again, proximity to İsmail Bilen was hardly a guarantee of maintaining one's physical safety. As bad as life in Turkey was for Nâzım, living in the USSR at this time would almost assuredly have been a much more difficult experience, perhaps even a lethal one.

Getting arrested in Turkey may well have saved Nâzım Hikmet's life.

# 9

# Descending into Darkness

Toward the end of October 1937, Nâzım Hikmet was standing in the smoking section of the İpek Cinema in Taksim, looking around to see if he knew anyone in the audience. The cinema was showing one of the films that he had recently worked on, and Nâzım wanted to watch the upcoming newsreel. Looking up, he saw that he was being approached by a young, fit-looking adolescent with dark features. The boy greeted Nâzım politely.

"Thanks," responded the poet. "But who are you?"

The boy explained that he was a cadet at the War College. His name was Ömer Deniz, and he claimed to be a longtime fan of Nâzım's poetry. "At school," Ömer explained, "my friends and I read your works and engage in ideological discussions as a means of deepening our knowledge."

Nâzım did not like the direction this conversation was taking. Either this kid was just terribly naïve, or else he was a provocateur of some sort. Nâzım knew that prosecutors were looking for any excuse to put him back behind bars. And now a military cadet, of all people, was showing up one afternoon to tell him this? Nâzım smelled a rat.

"I'll say goodbye to you right now," Nâzım informed the boy tersely. "And don't you bother me again!"[1]

*

Nâzım had good reason to be feeling touchy about the cadet's possible intentions. Having already spent time in jail, he was simply trying to get on with his life.

But it was not to be. Whereas in 1929 Nâzım had sought out conflict, throughout the 1930s he was repeatedly put in the position of fending off attacks from others. Despite his efforts—most of the time—to keep a low profile and make a living from his writing, Nâzım well knew that he would likely be targeted again. The next strike against him was always lurking around the corner.

## The Example

After encountering the boy at the cinema, Nâzım was irate. He stormed out of the building and headed back up to the offices of İpek Films. From there he called the

---

[1] Sülker, *Nâzım Hikmet'in Gerçek Yaşamı*, vol. 4, 128–129. Sülker states that this encounter took place in 1936, but Göksu and Timms write that these events occurred in 1937. Göksu and Timms, *Romantic Communist*, 138–139. Blasing, citing Karaca, also notes this happened in 1937. *Nâzım Hikmet*, 111.

*Red Star over the Black Sea: Nâzım Hikmet and his Generation.* James H. Meyer, Oxford University Press. © James H. Meyer 2023.
DOI: 10.1093/oso/9780192871176.003.0011

police. According to Kemal Sülker, Nâzım wanted to file a complaint about their having sent a military cadet over to his workplace in an effort to entrap him. "All I'm trying to do is feed my family," Nâzım fumed. "But still the police are following and harassing me."[2]

But Ömer Deniz was not, it seems, a police plant. Rather, he was part of a cohort of leftist students at the Harbiye military academy in Ankara who idolized Nâzım. These students, all of them in their middle-to-late teens, formed a circle that dated back to their days at the high-school level Kuleli military academy in Istanbul. The friends—Ömer Deniz, A. Abdül Kadir, Orhan Alkaya, Necati Çelik, and Sadi Alkılıç—had first bonded over what they would later describe as late-night adolescent talk in their dormitory regarding literature and politics. They enjoyed reciting the works of Nâzım Hikmet and other leftist poets.

Ömer Deniz and his friends had been involved, over the years, in frequent run-ins with some rightist students that they knew from school. The bad blood between the two groups extended back to their earlier days in Istanbul. In 1937, when they were all still at Kuleli, a fight had broken out between the two sides. The next October, the rivals were re-united in Ankara at the Harbiye academy, where their mutual loathing had only metastasized.[3]

Ömer had not, it seems, been particularly put off by Nâzım's poor reaction to his appearance at the İpek Cinema. On December 3, 1937, he decided to try his luck once more, showing up unannounced at Nâzım and Piraye's home in Nişantaşı. It was a Friday night and the eve of the Ramadan holiday, a three-day feast marking the end of a month of daytime fasting. Nâzım and Piraye had been out shopping when Ömer Deniz arrived. Ömer had told Piraye's mother that he had an appointment to meet with Nâzım. When Nâzım got back home with Piraye and saw Ömer standing there inside his apartment, he "blew his stack."[4]

After settling down somewhat, Nâzım tried to reason with Deniz. "Listen my boy," Sülker quotes him as saying, "I don't know you, and I didn't invite you into my home. Somehow you found my address and got inside. You tricked my mother-in-law and waited for me. You need to stop following writers and poets like me…On top of everything, I work ten hours a day just to feed my family. I simply can't devote my time to just anybody who wants it. Do you understand?"

Ömer responded by asking Nâzım where he and his friends at school could learn about socialism. At this point, Nâzım's anger returned. Now feeling quite certain that he was being targeted, Nâzım coldly informed Ömer that for such questions he need not consult Nâzım, but rather simply look at an encyclopedia. Nâzım then tried to turn the tables on the boy. "Now I am going to ask you a question. Where did you learn that I live at this address…You got it from the police, didn't you?" Ömer denied the accusation and departed.

---

[2] Sülker, *Nâzım Hikmet'in Gerçek Yaşamı*, vol. 4, 129.
[3] Göksu and Timms, *Romantic Communist*, 139–140.
[4] Sülker, *Nâzım Hikmet'in Gerçek Yaşamı*, vol. 4, 131; Göksu and Timms, *Romantic Communist*, 141.

# 214 RED STAR OVER THE BLACK SEA

Upon returning to Ankara after the holiday, Ömer boasted to his friends about his encounter with their hero. Before long, members of the rival right-wing group at school had also learned about this meeting. The rightists, delighted by the opportunity to get their leftist classmates in trouble, sent a letter to the academy's Chief of Staff, denouncing Ömer for having spent time with a known communist. Shortly thereafter, the Harbiye's dormitories were searched by military police, who detained twenty-three students for questioning.[5]

Nâzım was arrested on January 17, 1938. The police searched the apartment where Nâzım, Piraye, and Memet Fuat were living in Nişantaşı. Another raid took place at Nâzım's office at İpek Films, where his manuscripts and other papers were confiscated.[6] In subsequent weeks, Nâzım would be charged on three main counts: "conspiring with more than one person to encourage acts of military insubordination," "inciting a revolt against army discipline," and "inciting a mutiny," a potentially capital offense.[7]

Why was Nâzım being charged? Clearly, he had done nothing illegal. The accusations were incredible, especially considering their source and the evidence. The boys at the academy had legally purchased Nâzım's books in bookstores. The point of the trial was to put Nâzım behind bars. The outcome was never really in doubt.

Nâzım's army trial took place at the Harbiye academy. The fact that this would be a military trial, rather than a civil one, marked an important distinction. After all, Nâzım had been arrested repeatedly in the 1930s, and in most cases had been acquitted by courts operating within a justice system that was still largely independent of political interference. In a military tribunal, however, the conditions surrounding Nâzım's trial would be quite different.

The proceedings began on March 1, 1938. Nâzım had been refused bail, and had thus spent the previous six weeks in jail. The presiding judge was Lieutenant Colonel Fahri. Alongside Nâzım, the court was also adjudicating the fates of twenty cadets from the academy, two high school students, one law student, and four other civilians. Throughout the legal process, Nâzım maintained that while he was a communist, he had not broken any laws and had certainly not given the students directives to revolt against their officers.

The trial lasted all of one week. On March 8, the court announced that Nâzım had been found guilty, sentencing him to fifteen years in prison. Ömer Deniz was given nine years, a punishment that was later reduced to seven and a half due to the fact that he was a minor. Among the other defendants, twenty-three were acquitted, while three others were sentenced to terms ranging between eleven and fourteen years.[8]

In his early letters back to Piraye, Nâzım's tone was optimistic. In a short note from the middle of March 1938, he mentioned that he had confidence in his new lawyer. "Polite, intelligent, young," effused Nâzım, the lawyer, named Saffet Nezihi, was

---

[5] Göksu and Simms, *Romantic Communist*, 141; Sülker, *Nâzım Hikmet'in Gerçek Yaşamı*, vol. 5, 23–25.
[6] Göksu and Timms, *Romantic Communist*, 142.    [7] Ibid., 145; Blasing, *Nâzım Hikmet*, 111–114.
[8] In these cases, too, sentences were reduced for those under twenty-one years of age. Also see Göksu and Timms, *Romantic Communist*, 147.

"ninety-nine percent sure" that he would be released soon.[9] As had been the case with his previous incarceration, Nâzım likely felt a responsibility to show a brave face to Piraye, but he also had good reason to feel confident of an early conclusion to this detention. Every time he had been imprisoned thus far, his sentence had either been shortened or vacated outright.

While Nâzım was still being held in a military prison in Ankara, a second trial against him began in Istanbul. On April 25, 1938, TKP member Dr. Hikmet Kıvılcımlı had been arrested as part of another round-up of communists in the days preceding May 1.[10] Kıvılcımlı's arrest had led to a police raid on a watchmaker's shop, where the owner's 19-year-old son was detained for possessing books by Nâzım Hikmet. One of the items found by the police was a photograph of the watchmaker's brother alongside a naval petty officer named Seyfi Tekdilek. Dozens of people were arrested as a result of this finding, despite the highly tenuous nature of the evidence. Nâzım now stood accused of trying to incite mutiny not only in the army, but also in the Turkish navy.

Nâzım's navy trial took place at sea. As was the case with the army trial, this was a military tribunal operating under the rules of its own legal system. It was every bit as much of a kangaroo-court style of injustice as that which was meted out in the USSR at this time.

The prisoners were held below deck on the battlecruiser *Yavuz* on the Marmara Sea, the inland body of water upon which Istanbul is located (Map 9.1). The ship was so crowded that prisoners were held in the corridors and machine rooms. There was no fresh air to be had. Trials were conducted literally as the ship sailed from one port to another, making it impossible for the accused to communicate regularly with their families and lawyers. Nâzım spent the summer on board this ship with his second trial beginning on August 10. It would last nineteen days.

On August 17, Nâzım sent a letter to Atatürk, appealing for clemency.

> I have been sentenced to fifteen years' imprisonment on the allegation of inciting the army to revolt. Now I am alleged to have incited the navy to revolt.
>
> I swear in the name of the Turkish revolution and in your name that I am innocent.[11]

No response was forthcoming. Within three months, Atatürk himself would be gone, dying of cirrhosis of the liver on November 10, 1938, at the age of fifty-seven.

On August 29, the verdicts for the navy trial were announced. Most of the accused were acquitted, while Kıvılcımlı was sentenced to fifteen years in prison. Incredibly, Nâzım was given a twenty-year sentence, with some deductions for time served and overlapping charges. With the merging of the respective terms from the army and navy trials, Nâzım was now facing a grand total of twenty-eight years and four

---

[9] *Piraye'ye Mektuplar*, 92. Letter # 73 from Nâzım to Piraye, March 16, 1938. He was in Ankara at this time.

[10] On Hikmet Kıvılcımlı, see Tarkan Tufan, *Hikmet Kıvılcımlı: Hayatı ve Eserleri* (İstanbul: Nokta Kitap, 2008).

[11] Göksu and Timms, *Romantic Communist*, 155–156. Also see Sülker, *Nâzım Hikmet'in Gerçek Yaşamı*, vol. 5, 156.

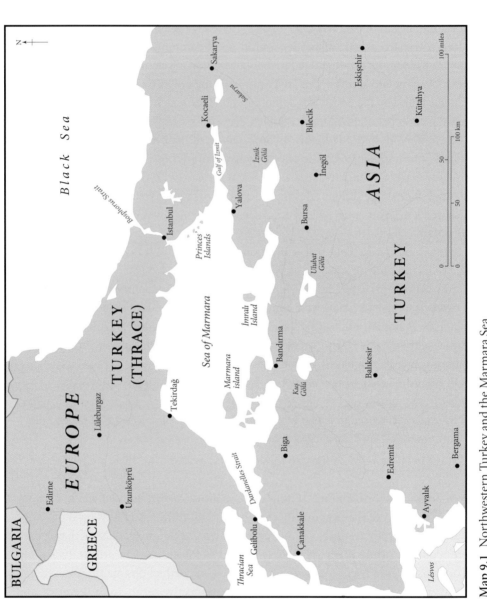

Map 9.1 Northwestern Turkey and the Marmara Sea

months behind bars. On August 31, 1938, he was remanded to Sultanahmet Prison in Istanbul.[12]

There was no monolithic "Turkish government" that was seeking to destroy Nâzım in a coordinated manner. In 1938, with Atatürk clearly dying, divisions between rightists and leftists were sharper than ever within Turkish state institutions.[13] Nâzım's persecution at the hands of the military was part of a broader campaign within the ranks to eradicate communism from the armed forces. The charges against Nâzım were absurd, Stalinesque fabrications, yet there was nothing to be done.

Nâzım had been found guilty of being Nâzım.

## Behind Bars

Shortly after the guilty verdicts were announced and the sentences read, Nâzım was sent to a prison in Çankırı, a small Anatolian town located about 85 miles northeast of Ankara.[14] In Çankırı Prison, Nâzım was joined by Kemal Tahir and Dr. Hikmet Kıvılcımlı, both of whom had, like Nâzım, been found guilty in the army sedition trial.[15]

Kemal Tahir, a former journalist who would later go on to become one of Turkey's best-known fiction writers, was eight years younger than Nâzım Hikmet. Like Nâzım, he had studied at Galatasaray high school. In the 1930s, Kemal Tahir and Nâzım had traveled in overlapping circles, as Tahir had worked as a writer, editor, and translator for a series of Istanbul dailies, including the Sertels' *Son Posta*.[16] Tahir had also gotten caught up in Nâzım's published polemics in the 1930s, reportedly going so far as to put out a pamphlet that attacked Peyami Safa, with whom Nâzım was publicly feuding at the time.[17] Kemal Tahir was a Marxist, but not, apparently, a member of the TKP. His communism was, by all accounts, a much more intellectual and independent variety, and it was along these lines that he found a companion in Nâzım Hikmet. Tahir had been sentenced to fifteen years in prison.

Hikmet Kıvılcımlı was a medical doctor by training, and had been a member of the TKP since 1929. In the 1930s, the bespectacled, wavy-haired doctor had already spent a number of short stints behind bars in Turkey. His paperwork from the Comintern archives notes that Kıvılcımlı was arrested in 1925, 1927, 1929, and 1934.[18] He had been removed from the Central Committee of the TKP in 1934 for "factionalism," but

---

[12] Today it is the Four Seasons Hotel. On Nâzım's sentencing, see Göksu and Timms, *Romantic Communist*, 152–158; Sülker, *Nâzım Hikmet'in Gerçek Yaşamı*, vol. 5, 146, 156.

[13] Göksu and Timms, *Romantic Communist*, 150.

[14] Çankırı had been the final outpost where Nâzım and Vâlâ had met up with Sadık Ahi and his friends in 1921, just prior to arriving in Ankara.

[15] Memet Fuat writes that Nâzım was sent to Çankırı in the middle of February 1940. *Gölgede Kalan Yıllar*, 336.

[16] The Sertels had been part of a group of journalists who founded *Son Posta* in 1930.

[17] Göksu and Timms, *Romantic Communist*, 121.

[18] See Belov's "spravka" about Kıvılcımlı from December 28, 1942. RGASPI, f. 495, op. 266, d. 193, ll. 7-7-ob.

had nevertheless remained a member of the party in good standing.[19] Prior to being sentenced to more than twenty-eight years in 1938, Kıvılcımlı had already spent a total of eight years in Turkish prisons.[20]

Piraye followed Nâzım to prison, spending two months in Çankırı. Renting a room in town, she visited Nâzım regularly during the first eight weeks of his incarceration. The prison had a courtyard with trees and benches, where Nâzım enjoyed sitting and talking to friends. There are numerous photographs from Nâzım's time in Çankırı showing him, Piraye, and others looking relaxed, even happy.[21] Such expressions were a reflection, perhaps, of a certain confidence that maybe, once again, Nâzım would find lenience with regard to his sentence.

At first, it didn't seem so bad. Shortly after arriving in Çankırı, Nâzım applied for medical leave from the prison. According to an interview that Piraye's son Memet Fuat gave in 1990, Nâzım had obtained a fellow prisoner's saliva sample as a means of tricking prison doctors into thinking that he was suffering from tuberculosis.[22] His ruse succeeded, and Nâzım was temporarily freed in April 1939. There was only one condition: he could not leave his home.

In what constituted another indication that Nâzım might not have been taking the prospect of serving many years behind bars very seriously, he soon began to flout the rules governing his release. One night, a group of naval officers spotted Nâzım out on the town and, knowing the conditions of his freedom, reported him to the police. Soon Nâzım was forced to undergo another medical examination with a different doctor. The test showed no sign of tuberculosis, and he was re-arrested and sent back to Çankırı prison in July 1939.[23]

He continued to hope that some kind of special treatment would come his way. In the relatively early years of his incarceration, Nâzım waxed optimistically, in his letters to Piraye, about his uncle Ali Fuat Cebesoy.[24] Perhaps, opined Nâzım, "Uncle Pasha" could be of some assistance in resolving his legal problems.[25]

In a letter written to Piraye in April 1940, Nâzım sounded confident that he would soon be freed, explaining that he did not care if this freedom came in the form of a successful legal appeal or via another channel:

> Uncle Pasha probably has some hope that I'll be let out soon. Is this hope strong? What is it all about?…Once I'm free again and with you, it matters not a bit to me whether this freedom is framed in gold or in tin.[26]

---

[19] According to one of Nâzım's biographies, Nâzım and Kemal Tahir had, in an effort to mitigate their sentences, written a letter to İnönü, distancing themselves from the dogmatic Marxism of the Kıvılcımlı fraction and expressing support for the state investment policies of the government. Göksu and Timms, *Romantic Communist*, 159.

[20] RGASPI, personal file of Hikmet Kıvılcımlı, f. 495, op. 266, d. 193, l. 9. "Spravka," March 7, 1938.

[21] Göksu and Timms, *Romantic Communist*, 161.

[22] Hikmet Kıvılcımlı had recently escaped to Syria while similarly out of prison due to medical issues, but was later re-captured.

[23] Göksu and Timms, *Romantic Communist*, 159.

[24] See *Piraye'ye Mektuplar*, 90 (# 71), 141–142 (# 125), 155 (# 132), 158 (# 134), 167 (# 138), 169 (# 141), 177 (# 144), 180 (# 146), 199 (# 154), 200–201 (# 155), 207 (# 162), 346 (# 261), 385 (# 290), 389 (# 294).

[25] See ibid., 179–181, letters # 145, # 146, and # 147, all from 1940.

[26] Ibid., 155. Letter # 132 from Nâzım to Piraye, April 7, 1940.

A week later, Nâzım wrote Piraye to tell her that he had heard from Semiha (Berksoy). "She met with Uncle Pasha," explained Nâzım. "In her letter, there is a sentence: 'You will soon be free in Çankırı.'"[27]

One day in August 1940, Nâzım received word that Ali Fuat Pasha was arranging to have him transferred to a prison in Bursa, which was closer to Istanbul than Çankırı and easier for Piraye and other visitors to get to. In a letter to Piraye telling her the news, Nâzım sounded vexed. "Where did this come from? I don't understand...I'd rather meet with you here, in the prison garden, even if it's intermittent, as opposed to sitting in the office of the warden or head of the prison guards." Despite his misgivings, Nâzım realized that Ali Fuat Pasha had his reasons. "If Uncle Pasha thinks that the conditions for you in Bursa when visiting me will be more favorable, then despite the fact that we've seen, from our own experience, that we can have that here...I'll pick up and go to Bursa right now."[28]

Ali Fuat Pasha also advised Nâzım to petition the prime minister in his quest for an early release. In describing the undertaking to Piraye, Nâzım again sounded a positive tone. "It's done," he announced triumphantly, telling her that he should be free "really soon." "All that's left is really a formality," he wrote in late 1940. "For sure I'm going to get out."[29] Meanwhile, with Ali Fuat's assistance, Nâzım began to receive certain privileges at the prison, such as a private room when he was in the infirmary.[30]

To what extent did Nâzım actually believe these rosy predictions of imminent freedom? The cheerful tone that he struck in his letters to Piraye may well have constituted an effort to reassure his wife. At the same time, Nâzım's experiences with the prison system in Turkey thus far had taught him to be optimistic. Had Nâzım not broken the rules and gotten himself re-arrested, he might have already found a face-saving way for the government to release him permanently.

## Scandal in the Comintern

Throughout the winter of 1939–40, Alexander Senkevich and Mara Kolarova endured increasingly harsh living conditions. In October 1940, a full year after he had initially contacted İsmail for assistance with his housing situation, Senkevich reported that he was occasionally spending his nights in railway stations, as his apartment was unlivable in the winter months. Thanks to the irregular nature of his nightly accommodations, Senkevich had started arriving late to work. For this reason, he had been repeatedly fined.[31]

---

[27] Ibid., 157. Letter # 133 from Nâzım to Piraye, April 15, 1940.

[28] Ibid., 177. Letter # 144 from Nâzım to Piraye, August 26, 1940.

[29] Ibid., 207. Letter # 162 from Nâzım to Piraye, December 13, 1940. On Nâzım's hopes for release during these early years, also see, for example, ibid., 95 (#7 6), 110 (# 94), 141 (# 125).

[30] Memet Fuat, *Gölgede Kalan Yıllar*, 534.

[31] RGASPI, f. 495, op. 266, d. 118, l. 94. Also see l. 95, message from Marat [İsmail Bilen] about Senkevich to the Cadres Department of the Comintern, October 31, 1940; ibid., l. 96, note on Senkevich, from Murav'ev to Iankovskii in the Cadres Department of the Comintern, October 26, 1940.

For Mara, meanwhile, citizenship was a growing concern amid a changing climate in the USSR for foreign residents. On March 5, 1940, the representative to the Comintern of the Bulgarian Communist Party stated that Mara Kolarova had visited him with "a request for receiving Soviet citizenship," noting that Kolarova's husband, Alexander Senkevich, was a citizen of the USSR.[32] Senkevich had, through his father and grandfather, been a subject of the Russian Empire, and therefore had become a citizen of the Soviet Union in a relatively straightforward manner.[33] However, a new Soviet law from 1938 had made it much more difficult for foreigners to obtain Soviet citizenship through marriage.[34]

Then, a potentially much more serious issue arose. In November 1940, Kolarova was reported to have visited the Bulgarian Embassy, allegedly in an effort to facilitate a return to her native country.[35] The government of Bulgaria was only a few months away from concluding a military alliance with Nazi Germany. If Kolarova really did go to the Bulgarian Embassy, she was taking a genuine risk, one that would not necessarily evaporate over time.

Sometimes Mara lived by herself, and at other times she shared a place with Senkevich. In a party autobiography written on May 23, 1941, Mara begged the Comintern for assistance, emphasizing the degree to which her poor accommodations in Moscow had exacerbated her illnesses.[36] She explained that her health problems had, in turn, prevented her from working for the past eighteen months. In June 1942, Kolarova started a new job working in a factory in the Volga-Ural city of Engels, but by the fall of that year she was back in Moscow, living again with Senkevich.[37]

Following Germany's attack on the Soviet Union on June 22, 1941, a number of TKP members living in the USSR would soon come to Moscow to work in Turkish-language publishing and broadcasting. Radio would constitute an increasingly important element of İsmail Bilen's activities in the Soviet capital, and Alexander Senkevich became a part of these operations. From the second half of 1941 onward, İsmail Bilen and Alexander Senkevich worked together closely for the first time since their days in Istanbul back in the early 1930s.[38]

Sometime in late 1941 or early 1942, Mara Kolarova and İsmail Bilen became lovers.[39] On December 17, 1942, Alexander Senkevich contacted Comintern general secretary Georgi Dimitrov, alleging that Bilen had abused his position as TKP representative in Moscow in initiating an intimate relationship with his wife.

---

[32] RGASPI, f. 495, op. 195, d. 303, ll. 66–68. Mara Kolarova personal file.

[33] RGASPI, f. 495, op. 266, d. 118, l. 92. Alexander Senkevich personal file.

[34] Studer, *Transnational World of the Cominternians*, 130. On changing citizenship regulations, see ibid., 141–142.

[35] RGASPI, f. 495, op. 195, d. 303, l. 63. Letter from the Representative of the Bulgarian Communist Party to the Comintern, November 30, 1940. The visit to the Bulgarian Embassy allegedly took place on November 26.

[36] RGASPI, f. 495, op. 195, d. 303, l. 56. "Autobiography," May 23, 1941.

[37] RGASPI, f. 495, op. 195, d. 303, l. 53. "Spravka" from June 11, 1942.

[38] Senkevich had begun working for the radio station when the war with Germany began in 1941. RGASPI, f. 495, op. 266, d. 118, l. 8.

[39] Senkevich would report that, starting in February 1942, he had begun hearing rumors from members of the Turkish community in Moscow that Masha was having an affair with Bilen. RGASPI, f. 495, op. 266, d. 118, ll. 24–25-ob, here 24. Letter from Senkevich to Ivanova, December 28, 1942.

Nowhere in Senkevich's letter is there any sense that Kolarova may have had some agency with regard to her relationship with Bilen. Instead, Senkevich charged that Bilen had "made use of a woman's weakness" to win Mara's affections, employing low-down tricks like "buying [Kolarova] different kinds of gifts, shoes, dresses, an overcoat, and so on" in his attempts to woo her.[40] Senkevich also complained that İsmail had provided Kolarova with clothes and other items belonging to Bilen's wife, who had been evacuated from Moscow not long after the start of the war.[41]

According to Senkevich's letter to Dimitrov, Bilen had approached him in October 1942 with an offer to join a mission to Syria. The plan, according to Senkevich, was for him to travel to Syria and then secretly cross the border into Turkey. There Senkevich would take up underground conspiratorial work on behalf of the party, or at least so İsmail had said. However, wrote Senkevich, the trip to Syria was nothing more than a pretext designed to send him out of town so that İsmail and Kolarova could be alone together.[42]

Living in a political and social system in which "the private was not considered a separate, autonomous sphere," Senkevich articulated his complaint to Dimitrov in both personal and party-related terms.[43] He stressed that he was "unmasking" Bilen not so much in the context of a cuckolded husband, but rather as a party member vigilantly battling against "anti-party behavior."[44] İsmail had abused his position, wrote Senkevich, by dangling the opportunity for political redemption before Kolarova, who had been expelled from the Bulgarian Communist Party prior to her arrival in the USSR. Bilen, alleged Senkevich, had hinted to Mara that she, too, might eventually be included on a future mission to Turkey. That was the explanation that İsmail had reportedly given for meeting privately with Kolarova and providing her with what he had claimed were "Turkish language lessons."[45]

Not long after Dimitrov received Senkevich's letter of complaint, a committee was formed in the Comintern to look into his accusations. Comrades Belov, Plyshevskii, and Ivanova from the Eastern Section of the Comintern interviewed the three principal figures in the final days of December 1942. During the course of these interviews, Senkevich was asked eleven questions, İsmail five, and Kolarova eighteen.

Senkevich's focus in these interviews was to present İsmail's transgression as a party-related offense, rather than simply a personal one. So, when the Belov–Plyshevskii–Ivanova *troika* asked Senkevich to tell them when he thought "intimate

---

[40] Owing to his position within the party, Bilen would have had more access to such goods than the average Soviet citizen, especially during wartime.

[41] RGASPI, f. 495, op. 266, d. 118, l. 28. Letter from Senkevich to Dimitrov, December 17, 1942.

[42] RGASPI, f. 495, op. 266, d. 118, ll. 28–29. Letter from Senkevich to Dimitrov, December 17, 1942. Also see l. 24, letter from Senkevich to Ivanova, December 28, 1942.

[43] Quotation from Studer, *Transnational World of the Cominternians*, 108–125, here 108. On the concept of a private life in the early decades of the Soviet Union, also see, cited in Studer: Vladimir Shlapentokh, *Public and Private Life of the Soviet People: Changing Values in Post-Stalin Russia* (New York: Oxford University Press, 1989); Marc Garcelon, "The Shadow of the Leviathan: Public and Private in Communist and Post-Communist Society," in *Public and Private in Thought and Practice: Perspectives on a Grand Dichotomy*, ed. Jeff Weintraub and Krishan Kumar (Chicago: University of Chicago Press, 1997), 303–332.

[44] RGASPI, f. 495, op. 266, d. 118, l. 28. Letter from Senkevich to Dimitrov, December 17, 1942.

[45] RGAPI, f. 495, op. 266, d. 118, l. 15. Report to Dimitrov from Belov, Plyshevskii, and Ivanova, February 1, 1943.

relations" had begun between his wife and İsmail, Senkevich pivoted toward a discussion of İsmail's party-related failures. İsmail, argued Senkevich, "knew that [Kolarova] had been expelled from the party," adding that it was "forbidden to talk to her about party business." This, in response to a question about when his wife had begun sleeping with İsmail.[46]

Bilen's defense, meanwhile, similarly focused upon party rules, and what he described as Senkevich's infractions of them. Senkevich was accused of "blabbing" about his upcoming mission to Syria, which İsmail insisted had been a genuine offer.[47] Bilen claimed that Kolarova knew all about the mission because Senkevich had told her—and that now, thanks to Sasha Senkevich's carelessness, everybody was "talking about this in the cafeteria of the Hotel Luxe."[48] Regarding his family situation, Bilen noted that he and his spouse "ha[d] not lived as husband-and-wife for a long time," and that he sent her 1,000 rubles per month to help support her expenses for the children. This sum equaled the combined total of Sasha and Mara's monthly salaries.[49]

In contrast to the more party-related conversations that the interviewers had undertaken with İsmail and Alexander, the first six questions asked of Mara focused upon personal matters—specifically, her relations with Senkevich and Bilen.[50] Only later did Belov, Plyshevskii, and Ivanova turn to the issue of who had said what to Kolarova about Senkevich's impending mission to Syria. Three times they asked her if Senkevich had mentioned anything to her about an upcoming trip abroad. On each occasion, Kolarova responded that Alexander had said nothing to her of the sort.[51]

Still, Mara indicated in no uncertain terms that she was fed up with Sasha personally, recounting the times that he had pleaded with her, "in tears," to not leave him. All she wanted now, she claimed, was for him to "leave me alone." Mara denied that there were any "intimate relations" between herself and Bilen. Instead, she stressed that she and İsmail were just friends, but that Senkevich had become jealous and agitated, "creat[ing] a huge scandal" within the Comintern.[52] Yes, İsmail had, out of generosity, given her some things that had belonged to his wife, but this did not mean they shared a sexual relationship. Instead, responded Kolarova, theirs had been a "comradely" friendship. She emphasized that only after she had realized that Bilen seemed to like her in a more personal way did she tell Senkevich to move out of the room they were sharing at the Luxe.[53]

---

[46] RGASPI, f. 495, op. 266, d. 118, ll. 16–19-ob, here 16. Notes from conversations between Belov, Plyshevskii, and Ivanova with comrades Senkevich, Kolarova, Marat, and Gregoriev. Gregoriev had been a witness to some of the events. Undated, but attached to previous document from February 1, 1943. The interviews took place on December 23, 1942.

[47] RGASPI, f. 495, op. 266, d. 118, ll. 3, 30. Note from Morozov to Dimitrov, December 8, 1942.

[48] This was from İsmail's interview with the Comintern *troika*. RGASPI, f. 495, op. 266, d. 118, l. 19.

[49] RGASPI, f. 495, op. 266, d. 118, l. 19. Alexander Senkevich noted in his interview with the *troika* that his monthly salary was 800 rubles per month, while Kolarova earned, "when she was working," 200 rubles per month. RGASPI, f. 495, op. 266, d. 118, l. 17-ob.

[50] Such as how her relations were currently with İsmail and Alexander, how intimate they were, what kind of gifts she had gotten from İsmail, and what Alexander thought about these gifts.

[51] RGASPI, f. 495, op. 266, d. 118, ll. 17–18-ob, here l. 18.

[52] RGASPI, f. 495, op. 266, d. 118, l. 17-ob.

[53] RGASPI, f. 495, op. 266, d. 118, ll. 17–18-ob. Here, 17-ob.

Shortly after giving these interviews, Kolarova and İsmail each wrote letters to Comrade Belov, amending their responses. Kolarova's letter, written on December 31, directly contradicted her previous answers to the *troika's* questions. Whereas she had thrice stated that Senkevich had never discussed his upcoming travels with her, now she claimed that he had. Senkevich, Kolarova explained, had asked her to keep it a secret, but now she "considered it [her] obligation" to report these conversations to the committee. She added that Senkevich was "weak" and "unreliable" and not the sort of person to be trusted with something so important as a mission like this, anyway.[54] Bilen's letter to Belov, written on January 3, likewise criticized Senkevich for telling party secrets. Continuing along the lines he had already established during his interview, Bilen sought to transform an investigation concerning his alleged abuses of power into one that examined Senkevich's lack of party discipline.[55]

On February 1, 1943, the Belov–Plyshevskii–Ivanova *troika* sent a report with recommendations to Comintern head Dimitrov. Both Bilen and Senkevich were issued "severe reprimands" for their actions. Senkevich was faulted for having allowed his "family squabbles" to affect his party work.[56] Kolarova was not punished.

Fault was articulated mainly in party terms. İsmail was criticized for having "used his party chairmanship" for personal advantage. His behavior, described in the committee's report as "obscene," led Bilen, in the words of the committee, to "[fall] into co-habitation with the wives of Turkish communists, in particular the wife of comrade Senkevich."[57] Nevertheless, three of the four recommendations that the *troika* made in their letter to Dimitrov related directly to Senkevich, and not Bilen.[58]

Just a few months after Bilen and Senkevich received their reprimands, the Comintern itself would be dismantled, allegedly at the behest of Moscow's new wartime ally Great Britain.[59] Many of the organization's former officials—individuals like Dimitrov, Galdzhian, and Belov—would find new employment within the International Section of the CPSU.

In the months to follow, İsmail and Mara each left their respective spouses and went on to create a new post-Comintern family of their own. İsmail, who had a daughter named Jale from his first wife, and Mara, whose only child had died, would later have two children together. A son, Erol, was born in 1947, and a daughter Natalia

---

[54] Letter from Mara Kolarova to Comrade Belov, December 31, 1942. RGASPI, f. 495, op. 266, d. 118, l. 21. Kolarova also claimed in this note that Senkevich had "dreamed of radio" as a means of evading the front lines.

[55] RGASPI, f. 495, op. 266, d. 119, ll. 20–20-ob. Letter from Marat [İsmail Bilen] to Comrade Belov, January 3, 1943.

[56] RGASPI, f. 495, op. 266, d. 118, l. 15-ob.

[57] RGASPI, f. 495, op. 266, d. 12, Part I, l. 62. April 2, 1943.

[58] The four recommendations were: (1) Reprimand for Bilen; (2) Reprimand for Senkevich; (3) "taking a signed statement from Senkevich, attesting that he will not disclose any of the party secrets he knows in connection with his preparations for party work abroad." The fourth recommendation was that the *troika* "consider[ed] it possible to employ Comrade Senkevich in his previous employment on the Radio Committee." RGASPI, f. 495, op. 266, d. 118, l. 15. Report to Comrade Dimitrov by Belov, Plyshevskii, Ivanova. February 1, 1943.

[59] The official announcement recommending the Comintern's dissolution was issued on May 15, 1943, with the formal end of the organization coming on June 10 of that same year. McDermott and Agnew, *The Comintern*, 204–211, here 205. On the dissolution of the Comintern, also see Studer, *Transnational World of the Cominternians*, 144.

followed in 1951.[60] Alexander Senkevich, meanwhile, would return to his previous position working for the radio committee—and for İsmail Bilen, who would continue to be Alexander's supervisor.[61]

Mara Kolarova's position within the Bulgarian Communist Party now changed for the better. In 1947, she was restored to the Bulgarian party's ranks, and the following year she began working as a translator for Moscow's Bulgarian-language radio broadcasting service.[62] With the expansion of Soviet political domination into Eastern Europe in the wake of World War II, İsmail Bilen and Mara Kolarova would soon begin their transformation into a Cold War-era Communist Party power couple.

Years later, Mara Kolarova-Bilen would remember her marriage to Alexander as one of convenience, at least insofar as she was concerned. About those early days at the Hotel Luxe and in Mariupol, she would unsentimentally recall, "he knew that I didn't love him."[63]

## Coming to Terms

As the years passed in Bursa Prison, Nâzım's talk of early release became less frequent. In December 1942 he mentioned, in a letter to Piraye, that Ali Fuat Pasha had sent him 100 liras, but noticeably absent from Nâzım's note was any hint of speculation regarding when his famous uncle would free him.[64]

He had grown more accepting of the conditions of his punishment. With the passage of time and a deepening understanding that he would remain behind bars for many years, Nâzım began to focus less upon winning his release. Now, he devoted more time and energy to mitigating the difficult circumstances in which he and his family were now living.

Nâzım also began to develop closer friendships with his fellow inmates, moving beyond the narrow circle of intellectual communists with whom he had initially congregated. One of his new friends was Mehmet Raşit Öğütçü, better known today by the pen name he would adopt in prison, "Orhan Kemal." Born in 1914 outside Adana, Öğütçü would later achieve fame as one of the greatest Turkish storytellers of the twentieth century. In 1938, however, while performing his military service, Öğütçü was denounced by fellow soldiers as a communist, apparently because he had been reading the works of Maxim Gorky and Nâzım Hikmet. A military tribunal sentenced Öğütçü to five years behind bars, and he had already begun serving his time in Bursa Prison when Nâzım arrived in December 1940. They would spend three and a half years together, sometimes occupying the same cell.

---

[60] RGASPI, f. 495, op. 195, d. 303, l. 3. "Spravka" from May 18, 1954. Personal file of Mara Kolarova. Also see RGASPI, f. 495, op. 266, d. 12, Part I, ll. 5, 13. Personal file of İsmail Bilen.

[61] Senkevich's name continued to appear on various Turkish radio-related documents for much of the decade. See, for example, RGASPI, f. 495, op. 266, d. 118. 15–15-ob. Also see f. 495, op. 266, d. 254, ll. 28, 30.

[62] RGASPI, f. 495, op. 195, d. 303, l. 7.      [63] Kolarova-Bilen, *Kanatlı Gençlik*, 59–60.

[64] *Piraye'ye Mektuplar*, 389. Letter # 294 from Nâzım to Piraye, December 28, 1942.

Even before meeting Nâzım, Öğütçü had long been a lover of literature. At first, he had written poetry. At Bursa Prison, Öğütçü endeavored to publish his verse in journals, but Nâzım advised his younger friend to give up this kind of writing. Nâzım, in Orhan Kemal's later recollection, declared the young Öğütçü's poetry to be "ghastly." Instead, Nâzım encouraged Öğütçü to focus upon writing short stories, which he declared to be a much more promising outlet for his younger friend.[65] In 1941, Öğütçü published his first story under the pen name "Orhan Reşit."

Bursa Prison could be a dangerous place. "Every day," wrote Orhan Kemal, "there was at least one stabbing."[66] In his memoirs, Kemal describes an environment in which conflicts were fueled by disputes over money, gambling, and drugs, with the prison hosting a flourishing market for both hashish and heroin. Enforcers bearing names like Scumbag Şevket, One-armed Hasan, and Mad Mehmet from Konya patrolled the cellblock.[67] Yet Nâzım, in Kemal's later reminiscences, was undeterred by this unsavory collection of individuals, and on his first day upon transferring to Bursa went around introducing himself to them. In fact, Nâzım already knew a number of his fellow inmates at Bursa, having met them earlier at Çankırı Prison.[68]

At around this time, Nâzım began to mentor another young prisoner by the name of İbrahim Balaban. Born in a village outside Bursa in 1921, Balaban resembled Öğütçü in that he was younger than Nâzım Hikmet and was the product of humble family origins. Balaban's parents were peasants who had removed him from school after the third grade. In 1937, the sixteen-year-old İbrahim was arrested for growing marijuana. Originally fined 16,000 liras and given a six-month prison term, Balaban's sentence was later extended by three years when he was unable to come up with the money to pay his fine. He would later describe his relationship with Nâzım as one of a master and apprentice, and even as a father and son. İbrahim had been eighteen years old when Nâzım, then almost forty, took him under his wing. Balaban called Nâzım "şair baba," the "poet father."[69]

In the early 1940s, Nâzım began to seek out a practical means of earning money through various types of labor. Nâzım was, like his mother, a talented amateur painter, and he began charging his fellow prisoners 2.5 liras to paint their portrait.[70] This is how Nâzım met Balaban, who as a child had developed an interest in drawing. Balaban asked Nâzım for painting lessons and the poet, who detected talent in the younger man, agreed to do so.[71] Eventually, the two of them began painting together.

In 1941, İbrahim Balaban completed his prison sentence and was released. Not long after getting back to his village, however, he discovered that his lover had married a rival while İbrahim had been incarcerated for the marijuana charge. İbrahim had then sought out the young man and murdered him. As a consequence of these

---

[65] Orhan Kemal (trans. Bengisu Rona), *In Jail with Nâzım Hikmet* (London: Saqi, 2010), 78.
[66] On Orhan Kemal and Nâzım also see Oral, *Nâzım Hikmet'in Yolculuğu*, 174–199.
[67] Kemal, *In Jail with Nâzım Hikmet*, 64–65, 92.    [68] Ibid., 70–71.
[69] See Balaban, *Hikmet'le Yedi Yıl*, 318. On Balaban more generally, see Göksu and Timms, *Romantic Communist*, 172–173.
[70] Göksu and Timms, *Romantic Communist*, 172.
[71] Balaban, *Nâzım Hikmet'le Yedi Yıl*, 21.

226   RED STAR OVER THE BLACK SEA

events, Balaban returned to Bursa Prison the following year, where he was re-united with Nâzım.[72]

One of Nâzım's most important sources of income at this time came from writing translations, and his friends provided him with as much work as possible.[73] The Sertels, in particular, had proven to be a lifeline for Nâzım and his family, repeatedly sending him advances for books that he would translate later.[74] Meanwhile, Nâzım's old friend Zeki Baştımar, who had by now returned from the Soviet Union and was living in Ankara, also came through with a job offer: translating *War and Peace* into Turkish. The work would pay a total of 1,000 liras, which Nâzım and Zeki agreed to divide evenly. Their client was none other than the Turkish Ministry of Education.[75]

How is it that Nâzım, a supposedly dangerous communist serving a more than 28-year prison sentence, was entrusted with translating Tolstoy's classic for the Ministry of Education? The answer lies with Zeki Baştımar. Zeki had known Nâzım since their days at KUTV in the 1920s. While Baştımar had been expelled from the TKP at the same time as Nâzım, he had eventually made his way back into the good graces of the party, moving to the USSR in 1934 to take up graduate studies at KUTV.

Upon completing his program of study in Moscow, Baştımar returned to Turkey in 1936. He initially found work as a Turkish-Russian translator, and then got the sort of job that the TKP leadership in Moscow must have considered almost too good to be true: working in the library of the Republic of Turkey's Council of Ministers (*Başvekâlet Murakabe Heyeti*).[76] While Baştımar never appears to have parlayed his position into an opportunity for espionage, he did at least end up getting a book contract.[77]

Another way that Nâzım earned money was from his work with İpek Films, which was owned by the İpekçi family. In the 1930s, Nâzım had been employed at the studio in a variety of capacities. Now, he pseudonymously wrote screenplays for İpek, including *Tosun Paşa* (1939), *Şehvet Kurbanı* ("The Sacrifice of Şehvet," 1940), *Kahveci Güzeli* ("The Beauty of the Coffeehouse," 1941), and *Kızılırmak Karakoyun* ("The Black Sheep of the Kızılırmak River," 1947).[78] In Nâzım's correspondence with Piraye, he makes frequent references to the various projects he was working on for the İpekçis during these years, sending his wife instructions regarding where and how she should collect his payments.[79]

---

[72] Göksu and Timms, *Romantic Communist*, 172–173.

[73] On Nâzım discussing his translations, see *Piraye'ye Mektuplar*, 231 (# 183), 513–514 (# 383), 577 (# 427), 608 (# 452), 610 (# 453), 622–623 (# 462), 641 (# 476).

[74] Sabiha Sertel also helped in other ways, such as finding work for Piraye. Ibid., 305. Letter # 237 from Nâzım to Piraye, May 11, 1942.

[75] Ibid., 605. Letter # 450 from Nâzım to Piraye. Undated, apparently from late 1945 or early 1946. From more on the translation project, also see ibid., 394, 403, 423, 570, 596, 597, 599, 653, 655.

[76] One party-related report from 1946 notes that "since 1936 and up to the present day [Baştımar] has been a member of the Central Committee of the TKP. At the same time he is working as the translator in the secretariat of the Prime Minister." RGASPI, f. 495, op. 266, d. 30, l. 145.

[77] *Piraye'ye Mektuplar*, 596. Letter # 442 from Nâzım to Piraye. Undated, but apparently from late 1945 or early 1946.

[78] Makal, *Beyaz Perdede ve Sahnede Nâzım Hikmet*, 108–112, 117–119, 256.

[79] See, for example, *Piraye'ye Mektuplar*, 104 (# 87), 105 (# 88), 501 (# 372), 687 (# 526), 696 (# 534), 699 (# 536), 707 (# 541).

In addition to painting and writing, Nâzım set up a number of small manufacturing enterprises while he was in prison. The idea for the first of these took root in May 1942 when Nâzım was in the infirmary, where he met an inmate by the name of Vehbi Ertuğrul. Vehbi mentioned to Nâzım that another prisoner, who had supported himself by running a weaving operation, was soon going to be released and was looking to sell his loom. Nâzım bought in, but quickly discovered that operating a weaving business was not such an easy task. His correspondence with Piraye from this time is filled with commentary about the enterprise, with Nâzım sharing the plans for how he and his partner would obtain the material they needed to make shirts, trousers, sheets, and other items. Nâzım wanted Piraye, in turn, to sell the items on the outside.

"Let's see," Nâzım wrote to Piraye in late 1947, "for the kilo of weaving silk, since it's six times the price of the raw silk thread, you'll be unloading them for at least ninety-five liras. As for the silk thread with the tied edges, those you can get rid of for 75 a kilo."[80] According to Orhan Kemal, Nâzım threw himself into this labor, with the other prisoners he had recruited into the business referring to him as "the Boss."[81] After two years, however, the enterprise went bankrupt and Nâzım sold off his equipment.[82]

Another operation was hand-made lampshades.[83] This business, too, went under, as Nâzım was not able to sell the finished product at a price that could compete with factory-made items.[84] Nevertheless, he continued to work on smaller handicraft products to sell, especially those which did not require expensive materials.[85]

The tone of Nâzım's letters to Piraye ranged dramatically during these years, shifting from drippy sentimentalism to chilly resentment. As had been the case during Nâzım's previous incarceration, he frequently complained about not getting enough mail from her. When a letter did come, Nâzım would often note that it was "short," or otherwise insufficient.[86]

When he wasn't chiding Piraye for the infrequency of her correspondence, Nâzım was begging her to visit him.[87] After finishing a job for the İpekçi brothers in the spring of 1944, Nâzım wrote to Piraye:

> Tomorrow morning, call İpek Cinema and make an appointment to meet İhsan. Go there the day that he says. They're going to give you 300 liras. The moment you get this money, you come here. No buts about it. Just give me some warning and I'll organize things for you at the hotel of your choice.[88]

---

[80] Ibid., 678. Letter # 517 from Nâzım to Piraye. Undated, but apparently from late 1947.
[81] Kemal, *In Jail with Nâzım Hikmet*, 209.  [82] Göksu and Timms, *Romantic Communist*, 179.
[83] On Nâzım's business ventures, also see Memet Fuat, *Gölgede Kalan Yıllar*, 543–546, 555.
[84] Göksu and Timms, *Romantic Communist*, 180.
[85] On Nâzım's handicraft operations, see *Piraye'ye Mektuplar*, 365 (# 274), 369 (# 277), 373 (# 280), 386–387 (# 291), 403–404 (# 305), 451 (# 333), 457 (# 337), 459–460 (# 338), 463 (# 341), 464 (# 342), 466 (# 343), 472 (# 348), 477 (# 352), 492 (# 364), 494 (# 365), 626 (# 465), 675 (# 512), 677 (# 516), 678 (# 517), 702–703 (# 538), 704 (# 540).
[86] Ibid., 103 (# 85), 235 (# 188), 241 (# 197), 328 (# 250), 355 (# 268), 374 (# 281), 496 (# 367), 556 (# 410), and elsewhere.
[87] Ibid., 238 (# 192), 239 (# 193).
[88] Ibid., 501. Letter # 372 from Nâzım to Piraye. Undated, but apparently from March–April 1944.

Nâzım was allowed, on occasion, to share conjugal visits with Piraye at a local hotel. However, Piraye reportedly felt self-conscious about this practice, concerned that the police guarding them might be somehow watching or listening in.[89] Nâzım persisted, however, complaining vociferously when she did not visit. Sending Piraye money he had earned from a screenplay in late May 1941, Nâzım told her to "come right away."[90] He emphasized how crucial her visits were to his mental health, writing that "if you weren't around, I would die."[91]

But the visits came infrequently. Nâzım complained that he only saw Piraye "once a year,"[92] while Orhan Kemal would later estimate that Piraye came to see Nâzım "twice a year, or three times at most."[93] Orhan Kemal also recalls an incident in which Piraye arrived in Bursa, but checked into a hotel that was not approved for conjugal visits. When Nâzım insisted that she change hotels, Piraye refused, leading Nâzım to tell her to go back to Istanbul.[94]

His incarceration notwithstanding, Nâzım may well have found other company at this time. The Turkish opera singer Semiha Berksoy would write, in the 1980s, that she and Nâzım had shared a hotel room when she visited him in Bursa in 1941. According to Berksoy, two guards were stationed outside the hotel's entrance but she and Nâzım were otherwise given adequate privacy.[95]

Perhaps as a means of justifying his physical infidelities, Nâzım repeatedly accused Piraye of spiritual duplicity. "Haven't you ever been in love?" asked Nâzım in an exasperated tone.[96] In another letter, he noted that Piraye had earlier written "these days I love you very, very much." Nâzım responded by telling her: "I don't just love you these days. From the first moment I saw you I have loved you very, so very much, even on those days when I was cheating on you."[97]

Because he had so frequently scolded Piraye for allegedly not saying "I love you" enough, Nâzım made a point of repeating these words to her all the time.[98] He buried Piraye with "I love yous," then berated her when she didn't take the hint and say the words he kept pressuring her to declare.

My Dear Wife,
I love you. I love you. I love you.
I'm looking forward to your letter. I'll send you a piece from *Landscapes*. Read it and tell me what you think.

---

[89] Blasing, *Nâzım Hikmet*, 174. Also see Memet Fuat, *Gölgede Kalan Yıllar*, 536.

[90] *Piraye'ye Mektuplar*, 232. Letter # 184 from Nâzım to Piraye. Undated, but apparently from late May or early June 1941.

[91] Ibid., 267. Letter # 210 from Nâzım to Piraye. Undated, but apparently from December 1941 or early January 1942.

[92] Ibid., 552. Letter # 406 from Nâzım to Piraye. Undated, but apparently from late 1944 or early 1945.

[93] Kemal, *In Jail with Nâzım Hikmet*, 126.      [94] Ibid., 128–129.

[95] Özbilgen, *Sana Tütün ve Tespih Yolluyorum*, 154. İbrahim Balaban also mentions Berksoy's visits. *Nâzım Hikmet'le Yedi Yıl*, 33–35.

[96] *Piraye'ye Mektuplar*, 373. Letter # 280 from Nâzım to Piraye. October 27, 1942.

[97] Ibid., 590. Letter # 437 from Nâzım to Piraye. Undated but apparently from late 1945. The Turkish verb "aldatmak" can also be translated as "deceive."

[98] Ibid., 429–430. Letter # 319 from Nâzım to Piraye. Undated but apparently from May or June 1943.

I love you, today, this hour, this minute I have no other words to say to you other than I love you.[99]

Nâzım was fond of invoking the theme of somehow outrunning time. He did so, however, in a manner that sounded like a warning that Piraye should not age. "We're gonna stay young together," he wrote one day in August 1943. "The day that I lose you, or even the day that you grow old, at that moment I'll wrinkle up like an emptied balloon and get old too."[100] On another occasion he wrote "Know that, and know it well, that there is no way you're going to grow old. If you feel for even one second that you've gotten old, for as long as I'm in your life, that one second will remain one second and you'll immediately get young again."[101]

All of this talk about staying young notwithstanding, Nâzım's health was suffering as a result of the years he had spent in prison. In 1946, a rotten tooth had become infected, causing him continuous and extensive pain. He was also diagnosed with kidney stones, leading to intense discomfort at times.[102] In late 1946 and early 1947, Nâzım began to feel pain in his liver, which doctors found to be swollen.[103] He spent still more time in the hospital infirmary.

Long gone were the days when Nâzım had dreamed of "Uncle Pasha" pulling strings on his behalf. Entering the second half of the 1940s, Nâzım hardly ever brought up his famous relative anymore. In March 1946, Nâzım mentioned him in a letter for the first time in years, albeit now in a rather jaded tone. "I got a letter from my uncle," wrote Nâzım. "He said he's really sorry about my situation, he'll do what he can, etc."[104] No longer would Nâzım parse his uncle's messages for clues regarding the possibilities for his impending freedom. Now the good news was that Ali Fuat Pasha thought that maybe he could help Nâzım obtain some thread.[105]

As Nâzım's term behind bars stretched into years beyond what he had ever previously served, or expected to serve, the awful truth began to sink in: they weren't going to release him early this time. The old practice of sentencing communists to a decade or more, and then commuting their sentence or declaring an amnesty, had apparently come to an end for him. Nâzım had gotten his warnings, received his amnesties, and been offered his last chances. And now he would sit in prison for a very long time, possibly until his sentence was set to expire in 1966.

## The Empire Builder

Following the dissolution of the Comintern, İsmail Bilen began requesting permission from the CPSU to return to Turkey. On May 15, 1944, he wrote a letter to former

---

[99] Ibid., 430. Letter # 320 from Nâzım to Piraye. Undated but apparently from May or June 1943.
[100] Ibid., 444. Letter # 328 from Nâzım to Piraye. Undated, but apparently from July or early August 1943.
[101] Ibid., 583. Letter # 430 from Nâzım to Piraye. Undated, but apparently from late 1945.
[102] Sülker, *Nâzım Hikmet'in Gerçek Yaşamı*, vol. 6, 6–7.    [103] Ibid., 10.
[104] *Piraye'ye Mektuplar*, 626. Letter # 465 from Nâzım to Piraye, March 19, 1946.
[105] Ibid.

Comintern head Georgi Dimitrov, who—like many former Comintern staff—had begun working in the International Section of the CPSU. In this letter, Bilen referred to a previous request he had made to leave the Soviet Union. "When you last communicated with me," Bilen wrote in reference to his efforts to leave the USSR, Dimitrov had promised to give him an answer "within 3–4 months." İsmail then added: "It has already been longer than that." Noting that "in recent years, many communists have been arrested" in Turkey, İsmail declared that he felt obliged to bolster their ranks. "I believe…that I am needed there," he wrote, "that I must be there."[106]

Why would İsmail have wanted to leave the USSR at this time? His official rebuke from the now-defunct Comintern notwithstanding, İsmail does not appear to have suffered any real consequences stemming from the affair with Kolarova. Moreover, his explanation that the TKP needed shoring up due to mass arrests in Turkey rings hollow. There had already been numerous waves of arrests that had taken place in previous years in Turkey without eliciting such a response from Bilen. By demanding to leave the USSR, İsmail may well have been looking to generate a vote of confidence of sorts from the party as a means of consolidating his position in Moscow, especially now that his old power base within the Comintern was no more.

Within a few weeks of receiving İsmail Bilen's most recent request to go back to Turkey, Georgi Dimitrov heard from Comrade Belov. Belov, who was also now working in the International Section of the CPSU, emphasized in a letter to Dimitrov the degree to which İsmail was overworked and needed more staff. Since 1941, İsmail Bilen had been providing Turkish-language commentary on the air for Radio Moscow, and he now headed a Turkish language "radio committee" that worked to expand Turkish-language services. Bilen was also involved in the Turkish-language publishing activities that had likewise developed in Moscow from 1941 onward.[107]

Bilen's enterprises required a growing staff to provide reporting, editing, and reading the news. In his June 1944 note to Dimitrov, Belov stressed that the handful of individuals working alongside Bilen "cannot replace" İsmail should he leave the Soviet Union for Turkey.[108] Soon after, Bilen would receive permission to further develop his operations, and his talk about wanting to return to Turkey came to an end.[109] Once again, İsmail had found a way to use the border to his advantage.

İsmail began to recruit new personnel to help him with the radio venture. Interestingly, most of these individuals had, like İsmail, first come to the USSR under irregular circumstances—i.e., either illegally or without party permission. Such was

---

[106] RGASPI, f. 495, op. 74, d. 495, ll. 3–4. Letter from "Marat" (İsmail Bilen) to Georgi Dimitrov, May 15, 1944.

[107] On Bilen's involvement with these activities, see RGASPI, f. 495, op. 266, d. 12, Part I, l. 3. Letter to the Central Committee of the CPSU from D. Shevliagin. April 1961.

[108] RGASPI, f. 495, op. 74, d. 495, ll. 1–2. Letter from Belov to Dimitrov. June 10, 1944.

[109] One of the individuals helping İsmail at this time was Nihat Nuri "the Electrician," who at this point was in ill health and planning on returning to Leningrad, where he had previously been employed as a Turkish language teacher at Leningrad State University. On the Electrician, see RGASPI, f. 495, op. 266, d. 86, esp. ll. 1, 3, 4, 26. Another individual working with İsmail at the radio station was Niko Asimov, an ethnic Greek. In Belov's estimation, however, Asimov was of limited value to İsmail because he "doesn't understand the situation in Turkey." RGASPI, f. 495, op. 74, d. 495, ll. 1–2. Letter from Belov to Dimitrov. June 10, 1944. On Asimov, see Akbulut and Tunçay (eds.), *İstanbul Komünist Grubu'ndan*, 393–394.

the case, for example, with Ali Haydar Kutlu.[110] Born in 1909 in a village in the province of Rize, Kutlu had first traveled to the Soviet Union in the late 1920s—not for political reasons, but rather to find work.[111] Altogether, Kutlu had spent eight years in the USSR, working as a laborer in Moscow, Rostov on Don, Samara, and Ryazan before returning to Turkey in 1935.

On October 12, 1937, Kutlu was arrested by Soviet authorities in Batumi for crossing the border illegally from Turkey. He was promptly remanded to a Soviet prison.[112] In May 1940, then-TKP Comintern representative İsmail Bilen had initiated a reconsideration of Kutlu's case, appealing to Belov, who took up the matter with Georgi Dimitrov. İsmail wrote a very positive profile of Kutlu, portraying him as a loyal communist who had "actively worked in the TKP and had connections with" Bilen and other TKP members.[113]

In March 1941, some three and a half years after he had first been detained at the border, Haydar Kutlu was finally released from prison. Upon getting out of jail, he was sent to Moscow to work for the Central Committee of the TKP.[114] In other words, his new boss would be İsmail Bilen.[115] In 1942, however, Haydar Kutlu returned to Turkey for reasons and by methods unknown. He does not appear to have ever gone back to the Soviet Union.[116]

Salih Hacıoğlu and his wife Sabiha Sünbül also arrived in Moscow at around this time.[117] One of the most venerable figures in Turkish communist history, Hacıoğlu, alongside Sünbül and their 13-year-old daughter, had immigrated to the Soviet Union in 1928.[118] Getting into trouble with the party leadership for the dual infractions of having shown up in the USSR without permission and bearing an unexpected letter from Şevket Süreyya, Salih had been expelled from the TKP. Nevertheless, he and his family had been allowed to stay on in the Soviet Union.

Working together, respectively, as a veterinarian and laboratory technician, Salih and Sabiha had initially settled in Kirov (today Ganje), in the west of Azerbaijan. In 1935, Hacıoğlu had received Soviet citizenship, and in 1939 a Comintern-based commission had cleared him of any wrongdoing with regard to his alleged misdeeds from

---

[110] Ali Haydar Kutlu was also known as Erol Bekiroğlu.

[111] This was during the era of the New Economic Policy, or NEP, when the Soviet government was encouraging foreign capital to invest in the USSR.

[112] RGASPI, f. 495, op. 266, d. 216, l. 33. Reference characterization ("*kharakteristika*") by Marat [İsmail Bilen] in relation to Ali Haydar Kutlu. May 15, 1940.

[113] Personal file of Ali Haydar Kutlu. RGASPI, f. 495, op. 266, d. 216, l. 32. Letter to Dimitrov from Belov. May 1940.

[114] RGASPI, f. 495, op. 266, d. 216, l. 2. "Spravka."

[115] Haydar was forgiving. A letter that he later sent to İsmail expressed his gratitude for the help İsmail Bilen had provided. "I was never angry at you," he wrote in reference to the nearly four years he had spent behind bars, "nor will I ever be angry at you for what happened." Letter to Marat [İsmail Bilen], May 24, 1941. RGASPI, f. 495, op. 266, d. 216, l. 14.

[116] RGASPI, f. 495, op. 266, d. 216, ll. 1–2, here 2. "Spravka" on Haydar Kutlu from October 20, 1948. In the 1970s, a Turkish communist named Nabi Yağcı would use the name Haydar Kutlu as an alias, but this was a different person.

[117] On Sünbül, see RGASPI, f. 495, op. 266, d. 98, ll. 1–2. "Spravka," 1959.

[118] RGASPI, f. 495, op. 74, d. 495, ll. 1–2. Letter from Belov to Dimitrov. June 10, 1944.

1928.[119] Redeemed in the eyes of the party, Salih was called to Moscow in 1941. There he too was drawn into Bilen's circle, working as a Turkish-Russian translator for a foreign language publishing house, apparently the same one as Bilen.[120]

Also coming to Moscow at this time was Sait Aliyev.[121] Like Ali Haydar Kutlu, Aliyev had crossed the Soviet border illegally from Turkey. "In the heat of the day on August 2," 1942, wrote Aliyev in a later letter to Georgi Dimitrov, "I, in my officer's uniform and aloft a horse, fled Turkey, country of putrefaction."[122] Despite Sait's apparent ardor for communism and the USSR, he was immediately arrested.[123]

Aliyev insisted to his Soviet captors that he had long been drawn to communism. Born in 1918 in Makhachkala—today the capital of the Russian Federated Republic of Dagestan—Sait and his parents had arrived as immigrants to Turkey when he was still an infant. Within the span of five years, however, his mother and father had both died, so Sait and his two younger siblings began living with an uncle in Ardahan. This uncle, claimed Sait, was Kahraman Araklı, a deputy in the Turkish parliament.[124]

Upon his arrest at the Soviet border, Sait explained that it was because he had been born "on the land that would later become Soviet" that he had first developed an interest in the USSR. In late adolescence, he had become a devoted communist. Upon finishing his studies at the Harbiye military academy in Ankara, he had endeavored to obtain a posting in Kars "because I very much wanted to cross over to the USSR."[125] And so he had, right into a Soviet jail.

Sait was, however, allowed to walk out of prison eight months later, on April 4, 1943.[126] In a form of work-release that resembled the arrangements made for Ali Haydar Kutlu, Aliyev was soon moved to Moscow. For about fourteen months he worked at the foreign-language literature publishing house, and then became a part of İsmail Bilen's radio staff in June 1944.[127]

The maintenance of Aliyev's life conditions largely depended upon Bilen. İsmail had, for example, been one of four individuals to sign off on Aliyev's work papers in 1944. In December 1945, meanwhile, Bilen had asked the Communist Party of the USSR for financial assistance on Aliyev's behalf. İsmail had also intervened to get Sait Aliyev a room to himself at the Hotel Luxe.[128]

When it came to Turkish communists living in the Soviet Union, it was always İsmail's choice. He could provide, and he could withhold, bestowing favors upon those

---

[119] RGASPI, f. 495, op. 266, d. 98, l. 7. Personal file of Salih Hacıoğlu. Also see "Spravka," ll. 65–70, May 20, 1939.

[120] RGASPI, f. 495, op. 266, d. 98, ll. 7–8, here 8. "Spravka" from January 18, 1957. Also see l. 16.

[121] According to a letter he later wrote to Nâzım Hikmet, Aliyev's actual name was Yusuf Araklı. RGASPI, f. 495, op. 266, d. 254, ll. 8–14, here 10.

[122] RGASPI, f. 495, op. 266, d. 254, l. 23. Letter from Sait Aliyev to Georgi Dimitrov. February 2, 1945.

[123] "Autobiography," RGASPI, f. 495, op. 266, d. 254, ll. 25–25-ob. February 12, 1945.

[124] Personal file of Sait Aliyev. RGASPI, f. 495, op. 266, d. 254, l. 23. Letter from Sait Aliyev to Dimitrov, February 2, 1945.

[125] RGASPI, f. 495, op. 266, d. 254, l. 23. Letter from Sait Aliyev to Georgi Dimitrov, February 2, 1945.

[126] Some documents report that Aliyev was released in January 1943. RGASPI, f. 495, op. 266, d. 254, ll. 17, 24.

[127] RGASPI, f. 495, op. 266, d. 254, ll. 23, 32–33. Letter from Sait Aliyev to Georgi Dimitrov, February 2, 1945, in which Aliyev mentions that he had been working for the radio station for eight months at the time of the letter's composition.

[128] RGASPI, f. 495, op. 266, d. 254, l. 18. Letter from P. Guliaev, December 7, 1945.

whom he wished to cultivate, and taking what he wanted from others. İsmail had succeeded in organizing the nucleus of a Turkish communist publishing and radio broadcasting team in Moscow, putting to work a group of border-crossers like himself. But
just as İsmail had collected these individuals, so too could he dispense with them.

## Blood from a Stone

Throughout his incarceration, Nâzım continued to write. The verse that he produced
during his years in Bursa Prison constitutes some of his most accomplished and beautiful work. None of it would be published in Turkey during his lifetime.

One of Nâzım's most popular poems from this period is "On Living" ("Yaşamaya
Dair"), which begins as follows:

> Living is no laughing matter:
>> you must live with great seriousness
>>> like a squirrel, for example—
> I mean, without looking for something beyond and above living,
>> I mean living must be your whole life.
> Living is no laughing matter:
>> you must take it seriously,
>> so much so and to such a degree
> that, for example, your hands tied behind your back,
>>> your back to the wall,
> or else in a laboratory
>> in your white coat and safety glasses,
>> you can die for people—
> even for people whose faces you've never seen,
> even though you know living
>> is the most real, the most beautiful thing.
> I mean, you must take living so seriously
>> that even at seventy, for example, you'll plant olive trees—
>> and not for your children, either,
>> but because although you fear death you don't believe it,
>> because living, I mean, weighs heavier.[129]

Most of the poems that Nâzım wrote in Bursa Prison had virtually no immediate
readership outside of himself, Piraye, and a few friends. With no public audience to
speak of, Nâzım's verse from the 1940s often reflects a simplicity that is not seen as
much in either his earlier or later works.

---

[129] "On Living: I." Translation from Blasing and Konuk, *Poems of Nâzım Hikmet*, 132. Blasing and Konuk note
that the book was written in 1948, but the Yapı Kredi edition lists it as from 1947.

In "My Lady's Eyes are Hazel but…" ("Hatunumun Gözleri Elâdır Da…") Nâzım alludes to a theme—how to avoid growing old—that was also part of his correspondence with Piraye.

> My lady's eyes are hazel but
> > inside them are watermarks of a deep, deep green:
> > deep green moiré on top of gold leaf.
> Brothers, what is this?
> > these nine years without her hand touching mine,
> > I've grown old here,
> > > she there.
> My girl with the thick, white neck that is wrinkling up,
> there's no way we can grow old,
> we need another term for sagging flesh,
> because growing old:
> > means to love no one but oneself.[130]

While many of Nâzım's individual poems from the 1940s were composed for a more intimate audience, he also developed larger projects that were conceived with a more official readership in mind. In 1939, when Nâzım was still housed in Istanbul's Sultanahmet Prison, he began working on *The Epic of the Nationalist Forces* ("Kuvây-i Milliye Destanı"). This major undertaking, which today comes out to just over 200 pages in most editions, recounts the Turkish War of Liberation. Based in part upon Mustafa Kemal Atatürk's own speeches, this was Nâzım's first work to be dedicated to the theme of war since his early adolescence.[131]

Was it purely a coincidence that Nâzım would return to this theme now? This was, after all, the great conflict that Nâzım and Vâlâ had missed. Could the choice of the War of Liberation as a subject of his poetry have constituted an effort by Nâzım to provide, at long last, his service to the war effort? Such an endeavor could, perhaps, lead to an amnesty.[132] Upon finishing *The Epic of the Nationalist Forces* in 1941, Nâzım had his mother give a copy to Ali Fuat Pasha, who then passed it on to İsmet İnönü, who had succeeded Atatürk as president.[133] But if winning an early release from prison had been on Nâzım's mind at this time, he would be disappointed. No changes were made to his sentence.

The writing of *The Epic of the Nationalist Forces* was deeply interwoven with that of another work that would eventually be published separately: *Human Landscapes from My Country* ("Memleketimden İnsan Manzaraları"). According to Mutlu Konuk Blasing, Nâzım completed *The Epic of the Nationalist Forces* in 1941 and sent the finished copy to Piraye, but then asked for the manuscript to be returned to him in

---

[130] Yapı Kredi edition of Nâzım Hikmet's collected works (*Şiirler* Vol. 4), 146.
[131] On this work, see Göksu and Timms, *Romantic Communist*, 220; Blasing, *Nâzım Hikmet*, 133–134.
[132] The twentieth anniversary of the Turkish Republic's establishment would be celebrated two years later.
[133] Göksu and Timms, *Romantic Communist*, 220–221.

1942.[134] At this point, *The Epic of the Nationalist Forces* was inserted into *Human Landscapes*.[135]

*Human Landscapes from My Country* is the enormous "epic novel in verse" that is today considered Nâzım Hikmet's masterpiece. Although the work would not be published until 1962, Nâzım first came up with the title and conceptual framework in the early 1940s. During these years he wrote the initial two books of an envisioned three-volume project, all of which would later be lost and rewritten.

*Human Landscapes* is a work of historical fiction resembling in its ambition the book Nâzım was translating into Turkish at this time, *War and Peace*. As Tolstoy does in his account of the Napoleonic Wars, Nâzım tells the story of the Turkish War of Liberation through the eyes of the ordinary foot soldiers, whom Nâzım placed at the project's thematic center.[136] In writing the work, Nâzım reportedly drew upon the experiences that some of his fellow prisoners had recounted to him.[137] In his later memoirs, Orhan Kemal observed that Nâzım frequently carried on long interviews with other inmates. Veterans like "Mehmet the Soup Maker," provided "a wealth of material" for his research.[138]

Nâzım frequently wrote to Piraye about *Human Landscapes*, occasionally sending sections of it for her to read. "Two days ago," wrote Nâzım to his wife in 1943, "I sent you one section of *Landscapes* and a small letter. Let me know if you got them."[139] In his next note to Piraye, he told her that he was sending along another part of the work.[140] In reference to *Human Landscapes*, Nâzım's tone toward Piraye could be as passive-aggressively belligerent as it was when he accused her of not writing him enough, or of failing to love him in the right way. "I can tell that *Human Landscapes* doesn't really grab you anymore. You don't like it. And I've decided to write a novel," he acidly reported in one letter from mid-1943. "Maybe you'll like this one, as long as I can hold your interest to the end."[141]

Some months later, in November 1943, Nâzım wrote about the work again to Piraye:

> For the last month I've been working like a madman on *Landscapes*. But I've changed the way that I work. Without having finished Book 2, I picked up the story again at the end of Book 3. That's what I'm going to send you. Hang on to it and stash it away in a place that I'll specify later. I'm pleased with myself that I started working again. If you're wondering why I started again with the end of Book 3, your curiosity will be satisfied once you read this piece. Because, after such a long break, in order to start

---

[134] Ibid., 221.

[135] Blasing, *Nâzım Hikmet*, 134. Later, however, all of these writings would be left behind in Istanbul. *The Epic of the Nationalist Forces* would be published in Turkey as a separate volume in 1968.

[136] Göksu and Timms similarly draw a connection to *War and Peace*, noting that "it is because both works so compellingly explore the nexus between the personal and the political." *Romantic Communist*, 237.

[137] When Nâzım had left jail following his previous imprisonment in 1933–34, he had reportedly told his cellmates that they would eventually see themselves in his writing. Ibid., 132.

[138] Kemal, *In Jail with Nâzım Hikmet*, 141.

[139] *Piraye'ye Mektuplar*, 433. Letter # 322 from Nâzım to Piraye. Undated, but apparently from 1943.

[140] Ibid., 434. Letter # 323 from Nâzım to Piraye. Undated.

[141] Ibid., 437. Letter # 324 from Nâzım to Piraye. Undated, but apparently from mid-1943. It is unclear what novel Nâzım is referring to here.

working again I needed your help. As always and everywhere, once again you came to my aid. You'll understand what I mean only upon reading what I've written.

My love, ah my love.[142]

Nâzım sometimes affectionately referred to the project as "Piraye's" work, such as when he wrote "These are the passages from the end of Book 3 from your *Human Landscapes from my Country*." He asked Piraye to "quickly tell me what you think."[143] In a letter he sent a couple of weeks later, Nâzım further reported on his progress by noting "I'm working at full speed. Your *Human Landscapes* is getting bigger and bigger."[144]

He sought out Piraye's views, but then chafed at her responses when they were not sufficiently glowing.

> For sure I'll (one day) write the kind of book you want, but even in these last sections of *Human Landscapes*—I haven't sent them to you yet—I saw what you were talking about. But I'm going to rewrite this in a manner that is stronger, more the way you would like it—make it really clean, without ornamentation, simple. But I also have a request for you: that you allow me to destroy your last two letters and be rid of your vulgar verse technique.[145]

Nâzım continued to send his work to Piraye throughout the 1940s, often noting his "impatience to learn" her opinion of his writing.[146] "If, for whatever reason, you don't immediately read these poems, I'll be angry," went a typical comment in his letters.[147] Yet the fact that she could not understand his writing in the manner that he craved ate away at him. Could the woman for whom he was destined really not understand his literary brilliance?

*

Even behind bars, Nâzım managed to lead a more interesting life than many people who walk the streets freely. In his first few years in prison, Nâzım still had a lot of fight. He sounded confident, in his letters to his wife and son, that release would arrive soon. Frequently, he had contacted his famous uncle to see if Ali Fuat Pasha could make any efforts on his behalf. As someone who had been arrested more than once in his life, Nâzım initially acted like he expected to be a free man again soon.

As the years passed, his attitude turned more cynical. He took out his frustrations on Piraye, emotionally blackmailing her for supposedly not loving him sufficiently, or

---

[142] Ibid., 468–469. Letter # 345 from Nâzım to Piraye. Undated, but apparently from late 1943.

[143] Ibid., 469. Letter # 346 from Nâzım to Piraye. Undated, but apparently from late 1943.

[144] Ibid., 481. Letter # 355 from Nâzım to Piraye. Undated, but apparently from December 1943 or January 1944. For other occasions when Nâzım refers to it as "her book," see ibid., 489, 520, 567, 623.

[145] Ibid., 559. Letter # 412 from Nâzım to Piraye. Undated, but apparently from March or April 1945.

[146] Ibid., 568. Letter # 420 from Nâzım to Piraye. Undated, but apparently from mid-1945.

[147] For other references to *Human Landscapes* in Nâzım's correspondence with Piraye, see ibid., 484 (# 357), 524 (# 392), 528 (# 394), 555 (# 409), 558 (# 412).

in the right way. In the years that followed, Nâzım began to focus more upon day-to-day survival. Like his father before him, he tried, and failed, at enterprises at which he had no experience, tasks for which he was not well-suited. Yet he gamely took them on because he felt that he had to try.

Most importantly, he continued to write. As he had done since adolescence, Nâzım responded to the tumult around him by putting pen to paper. He'd crossed another border, and sought to learn from the experience somehow.

# 10

## Desperate Measures

A crash rang out from the infirmary at Bursa Prison. It was the middle of the night in March 1949, and Vehbi Bey, a staff member watching over sick prisoners for the night, was awakened in the room next door. Running into the infirmary, he saw a body lying on the ground. Two empty bottles of sleeping pills lay nearby.

For the last several years, Nâzım Hikmet had periodically suffered from kidney stones, an affliction which had sent him, on occasion, to the Bursa Prison infirmary. He had complained of troubles sleeping, too. Recently, Nâzım had been given a bottle of pills to help him get through the nights more easily. While Vehbi Bey and the rest of the infirmary staff were asleep, however, Nâzım had apparently crept over to the medicine cabinet and taken a second bottle.

Vehbi Bey ran out of the room, looking for help. "Doctor, doctor!" he called out, "Come quickly, Nâzım Hikmet has killed himself!"[1]

*

Ten years. In January 1948, Nâzım marked his tenth year behind bars. While he had, earlier on during this incarceration, devoted considerable energy to fighting the charges that had been made against him, later his energies had been taken up with more prosaic tasks. Somewhere along the way, Nâzım had imperceptibly gotten used to this life.

The years 1948 to 1951, however, would mark a period of considerable turmoil for Nâzım. Having already labored through a decade of poor diet, menial labor, and painful incarceration for a crime he didn't commit, Nâzım wanted out. Whether or not the events transpiring in the prison infirmary in 1949 actually constituted a suicide attempt, from this point forward Nâzım began to display a renewed determination to change his life conditions. He began taking more risks, undertaking a series of gambles that, one after another, appeared to pay off.

### Turkey and the Cold War

In the years following the end of World War II, two far-reaching political developments were taking place in Ankara. The first was the emergence of real political competition in Turkey for the first time since the creation of the republic in 1923. Following the

---

[1] Sülker, *Nâzım Hikmet'in Gerçek Yaşamı*, vol. 6, 7–8. According to Sülker, Nâzım had threatened to kill himself in conversations he had with his mother. Ibid., 11. İbrahim Balaban also claims that Nâzım confided in him regarding his plans to commit suicide by overdose. *Nâzım Hikmet'le Yedi Yıl*, 194–195.

*Red Star over the Black Sea: Nâzım Hikmet and his Generation.* James H. Meyer, Oxford University Press. © James H. Meyer 2023.
DOI: 10.1093/oso/9780192871176.003.0012

Sheikh Sait rebellion in 1925, the only party that had been allowed to remain open was the Republican People's Party (CHP).[2] Within the CHP, however, there had always been some give-and-take with regard to various policies, and certain factions had emerged over time. Such was the case with the creation of the Democrat Party, whose earliest leaders had all been members of the CHP.[3]

"Westernization" under Atatürk had taken place primarily in the urban cultural sphere. Turkey's adoption of a European calendar, workweek, alphabet, clothing styles, and other aspects of social life constituted a major component of a top-down revolution designed to make city-dwelling Turks look more European. This set of policies did not, however, necessarily imply the adoption of democratic institutions. One could walk around in a suit and tie, Panama hat at the ready, and still crush political dissent. Such was the case in Turkey up through to the end of World War II.

An important political development taking place in postwar Turkey was the reintroduction of multi-party elections in 1946. Four years later, Adnan Menderes' opposition Democrat Party won a parliamentary majority, making Menderes Turkey's new prime minister. While the Democrats were a center-right party that was even more critical of communism than the CHP, the coming to power of Menderes' party in 1950 nevertheless fueled hopes in Nâzım's camp for an upcoming amnesty.

Another notable change occurring in Turkey during these years was the gradual abandonment of Atatürk's long-standing policy of neutrality. This shift in orientation had begun in 1945, when the Turkish government declared war against Japan. This had been a largely symbolic measure, at least insofar as the outcome of World War II was concerned, but it nevertheless opened the door in Ankara to becoming a founding member of the United Nations.

In June 1945, Moscow began making territorial demands upon Turkey. In exchange for the USSR signing a new peace treaty with Ankara, the Soviet government wanted Turkey to return the provinces of Kars and Ardahan.[4] These two districts, alongside Batumi, had previously been part of the Ottoman Empire for centuries, but were ceded to Russia at the conclusion of the Russian–Ottoman war of 1877–78. In 1918, the three provinces were returned to the Ottoman government in Istanbul as part of the Brest-Litovsk Treaty.[5] In exchange for gold and weapons from Moscow, however, the Ankara government had renounced its claims to Batumi as part of the Treaty of Moscow in 1921.[6] The other two provinces—Ardahan and Kars—had remained part of Turkey ever since.

The issue of neutrality was an important one. To many in Turkey, it had seemed a miracle that Ankara had managed to stay out of World War II. Mustafa Kemal Atatürk

---

[2] The Liberal Republican Party (*Serbest Cumhuriyet Fırkası*) was opened in 1930 but was closed later that year.

[3] The Demokrat Parti is typically called the "Democrat" party in English-language scholarship, a convention that I follow here.

[4] "Soviet Note Lists Demands on Turks," *The New York Times*, June 26, 1945, p. 1.

[5] Other demands included the opening of Soviet military bases on Turkish territory, readjusting Turkey's border with Bulgaria, and a revision of the Montreux convention regarding the Bosphorus and Dardanelle straits. See "Turks Said to Get 4 Soviet Demands," *The New York Times*, June 28, 1945, p. 7.

[6] This was the treaty that Nâzım's uncle Ali Fuat Pasha had signed.

and the Republican People's Party prime ministers who had led Turkey in the 1920s and 1930s had resisted all invitations to entangle themselves in a military alliance. The idea of signing up with a Western-based pact, especially one anchored by the United States, would have sounded laughable to most people in a position of power in Ankara during the republic's earlier days.

Desperate times, however, came with a call for drastic action as Moscow's aggressive attitude toward Ankara pushed Turkey into a postwar alliance with Washington.[7] The Turkish government sent emissaries to London and Washington to gauge Western support for defending Turkey in case of an attack by the USSR.[8] Ankara's postwar leaders—first the CHP, and then the Democrats—sought to integrate the country more fully into Western European and American-based international institutions. Turkey became an early member of the Council of Europe, joining in 1949 under the CHP.[9]

Following the Democrats' victory in 1950, Adnan Menderes' government pursued even closer relations with the West. In June 1950—one month after Menderes' Democrats had been swept into power—Turkey volunteered to send troops to Korea to fight on the side of the US-led UN coalition. After the United States, Turks would become the largest foreign contingent fighting on behalf of the south, dispatching nearly 15,000 soldiers, with more than 900 Turkish troops dying in the war.[10] By the time Turkey became a NATO member in 1952, Ankara's growing postwar entente with Washington had already become an established component of Turkish foreign policy.[11]

## Gasping for Air

Nâzım, meanwhile, was seeking out new alliances of his own. Frustrated with the state of his relationship with Piraye, he began pursuing a rekindled connection with his cousin, Münevver Andaç.

In 1945, 28-year-old Münevver Andaç had married Nurullah Berk, a Turkish painter and professor at the Academy of Fine Arts in Istanbul. The following year, she gave birth to a daughter named Renan. The family lived in a middle-class suburb in Kuzguncuk, on the Asian side of the Bosphorus.

---

[7] In December 1945, Moscow would demand from Turkey a 180-mile strip of territory, 75 miles deep, extending from Batumi to Giresun. See "Russians Demand Area of Turkey along Black Sea," *The New York Times*, December 21, 1945, p. 1.

[8] "Turkish Officials Awaited in London," *The New York Times*, June 29, 1945, p. 4; "Turks Talk War if Russia Presses, Prefer Vain Battle to Surrender," *The New York Times*, August 7, 1945, p. 1.

[9] Onur İşçi takes a different view, arguing that "ferocious hatreds and frantic fears," rather than Soviet aggression, were the source of "a new mindset in Turkey that was determined to rebuff Stalin's designs at all costs." *Turkey and the Soviet Union during World War II*, 173.

[10] On Turkish foreign policy more generally during these years, see Shaw and Shaw, *History of the Ottoman Empire and Modern Turkey*, vol. II, 429–430.

[11] In 1955, Turkey would also join the Baghdad Pact, which included Iran, Iraq, Pakistan, Turkey, and the United Kingdom. The organization never turned into a military alliance in the manner of NATO, and was primarily of diplomatic importance. It was dissolved in 1979, following the Islamic revolution in Iran.

Nâzım had not communicated with Münevver for ten years. Yet, there she was. In October 1948, Münevver, her cousin Ayşe Baştımar, and the novelist Peride Celâl visited Nâzım Hikmet in prison.[12] Ayşe was the wife of Zeki Baştımar, the TKP member who was Nâzım's friend and partner in translating *War and Peace*. According to the account that Münevver provided in an interview she gave in 1990, Nâzım's mother—and Münevver's paternal aunt—Celile had been the one to suggest to Münevver that she get in touch with Nâzım.[13] The other two women appear to have accompanied Münevver at least partly in order to act as chaperones. Münevver was, after all, a married woman.

Some of Nâzım's biographers have drawn a connection between Nâzım's reignited relationship with Münevver and his renewed friendship with Vâlâ Nureddin and his wife Müzehher. In the 1930s Nâzım and Vâlâ had experienced a falling out, and by the mid-1940s the two had not spoken for several years. Then, in the aftermath of a December 1945 dinner party where Nâzım had been a primary topic of conversation, Vâlâ's wife Müzehher had sent a care package to Nâzım at Bursa Prison.[14] From that point forward, Vâlâ and Müzehher began rebuilding their friendship with Nâzım, sending him money, books, and news throughout the latter half of the 1940s.[15] Vâlâ and Müzehher knew Münevver socially, and apparently encouraged her to visit the poet in prison.[16]

Nâzım was quickly taken, or re-taken, with his attractive younger cousin. While it is unclear what exactly took place during her visit to Bursa Prison, shortly thereafter Nâzım began writing love poems for her, including some quite sensual ones.

"The wine in my pot I have been keeping for you," Nâzım wrote in "Autumn" ("Sonbahar").

> The days are getting shorter,
> the rainy season is about to start,
> my doors were wide open, waiting for you,
> > what kept you so long?
> On my tables are green peppers, salt and bread,
> The wine in my pot I have been keeping for you
> I drank half of it on my own
> > waiting for you
> > > what kept you so long?
> But now the succulent fruits are hanging

---

[12] Balaban, *Nâzım Hikmet'le Yedi Yıl*, 136.

[13] Göksu and Timms conducted this interview, *Romantic Communist*, 191.

[14] Nâzım Hikmet, *Bursa Cezaevinden Vâ-Nû'lara Mektuplar* (3rd edition, İstanbul: Nâzım Hikmet Kültür ve Sanat Vakfı Yayınları, 1998), 7.

[15] For a collection of these letters, see *Bursa Cezaevinden Vâ-Nû'lara Mektuplar*. On Vâlâ and Müzehher sending money and other items to Nâzım, see ibid., 21, 52, 55, 63, and elsewhere.

[16] Göksu and Timms, *Romantic Communist*, 190–191; Blasing, *Nâzım Hikmet*, 174. For references to Münevver in Nâzım's correspondence with Vâlâ and Müzehher, see *Bursa Cezaevinden Vâ-Nû'lara Mektuplar*, 133, 189.

on their branches ripe and crunchy.
They were about to fall to the earth
if you had been delayed any longer.[17]

It must have felt intoxicating to have a young, pretty woman visit him in prison, especially a former lover.[18] Nâzım managed, however, to cover up his enthusiasm when he mentioned the episode to his wife. In a letter he wrote to Piraye from this time, Nâzım noted Ayşe and Münevver's arrival only in passing, recalling the visit alongside those of his sister and others who had come by recently. Münevver was, in this account, sandwiched among a list of relatives and friends, not to mention the Minister of Justice.

> Again no letters from you, it's been a long while. I guess one will arrive today or tomorrow. I have lots of news for you. All of a sudden over the last ten, fifteen days or so, there have been a great number of callers and seekers, people ringing at my door, as the saying goes. Samiye came, as did Vedat and Fehamet, as well as Aunty Sare's daughter Ayşe and Münevver. And then, most important of all, the Minister of Justice also paid me a visit. I was able to speak with him for twenty minutes.[19]

In some ways, life went on as usual. Nâzım was still sending Piraye money, asking after the kids, sending lines of verse, and making the occasional sweeping declaration. "I think about you all the time," Nâzım began one letter from 1949, "your health, your welfare, the fact that you're low on money. I think about the last eleven long years that you've spent, [a time] made up of longing and separation." At the end of the paragraph, Nâzım noted, almost as an aside, that "loving you has become for me a form of worship."[20]

Münevver's name once more appeared in a 1949 letter, again without fanfare. Piraye was sick, and most of the early part of Nâzım's note was spent asking after her health. He then briefly mentioned Münevver, before quickly changing the subject to money: "my cousin Münevver sent me 30 liras. In other words, I'm not broke, but when I think of the fact that you're broke I go nuts."[21]

But then, something happened. In his very next letter to Piraye, Nâzım had important news. From the letter's first lines, it was clear that a serious matter was afoot. Whereas virtually all of his letters, including the previous one, had begun with the words "My dear wife," this one started simply with "Piraye."

---

[17] Translation from Göksu and Timms, *Romantic Communist*, 193.
[18] Even if a chaste one. It is unclear whether or not their previous relationship included a physical dimension.
[19] *Piraye'ye Mektuplar*, 715, letter # 547. Undated, but apparently from early 1949.
[20] Ibid., 717, letter # 549. Undated, but apparently from late 1948 or early 1949. Nâzım's letters written between # 541 (July 29, 1948) and # 561 (May 2, 1949) are all undated.
[21] Ibid., 726, letter # 554. Undated, from late 1948 or early 1949.

Despite everything, we need to speak like two people who understand one another, who love one another, two people who respect one another. Our relationship has been the most honest, the cleanest, the most beautiful that two people can have, and it contains several facets. The fact that one of these has diminished changes nothing. We mustn't tell one another lies, we mustn't cheat on one another. I have too much respect for both you and myself to prefer to lose you by lying or by cheating on you.

With these words, Nâzım was declaring that he wanted his freedom from Piraye. Yet he hoped to remain friends. He hashed out a convoluted argument, emphasizing the fact that there were many different kinds of relationship other than those of a husband and wife.

With respect to physical relations, Nâzım was adamant, informing Piraye that they "need[ed] to end our husband-wife, woman-man relations" right away. "[W]e can't continue as husband and wife," he insisted, without further elaboration. On the bright side, however, Nâzım assured Piraye that she was "still the person closest to me, my closest friend and pal." "Your children are mine," he added. Regarding the prospects for their ongoing mutual affection, Nâzım observed, rather optimistically, that he was "of the belief that this will not change at all."[22]

Nâzım was vague about the details regarding his sudden desire to end what he euphemistically described as his "husband-wife" relations with Piraye. Nowhere in his letter did he explain that there was someone else in his life now. Instead, he entrusted his friend Rasih Güran to deliver the news to Piraye on his behalf.[23]

Even as Nâzım sought to end his marital relations, he expressed confidence that he and Piraye would continue to love each other in so many other ways—all of them sexless. "Goodbye for now," he wrote, addressing Piraye as "my girl, my mother, my sister, my friend, my comrade."[24]

The situation with Münevver, however, quickly turned uncertain. In late October 1948, Münevver's husband Nurullah Berk visited Nâzım in prison.[25] It is not known what exactly transpired between the two, but shortly thereafter Nâzım became more apprehensive in his dealings with both of the women in his life. He now began to insist that Münevver initiate divorce proceedings against Nurullah immediately. Münevver, however, responded by explaining that doing so could cut her off from her daughter, as Nurullah would likely receive full custody of Renan.

This development weighed heavily upon Nâzım's nerves. He became increasingly agitated by the possibility that he had thrown away one relationship without having secured a new one first.[26] In the spring of 1949, Nâzım's correspondence with Piraye

---

[22]  Ibid., 727–728, letter # 555. Undated, from late 1948 or early 1949.
[23]  Göksu and Timms, *Romantic Communist*, 194; Sülker, *Nâzım Hikmet'in Gerçek Yaşamı*, vol. 6, 82.
[24]  *Piraye'ye Mektuplar*, 729, letter # 556. Undated, from late 1948 or early 1949.
[25]  Balaban, *Nâzım Hikmet'le Yedi Yıl*, 160.
[26]  Also see Sülker, *Nâzım Hikmet'in Gerçek Yaşamı*, vol. 6, 12.

244 RED STAR OVER THE BLACK SEA

took a new turn—he wanted her back again. He no longer wished to "leave" Piraye. Instead, he pleaded with her to come see him in prison.[27]

Showing the remorse that had been missing in his earlier correspondence, Nâzım now acknowledged the pain he had caused her. "On the face of the Earth, no one has done anything worse to anybody than what I have done to you," he wrote. "But despite all of this, come." "Come," he implored, "and don't leave me alone again."[28] Nâzım's next letter was even more direct, consisting only of the words "Piraye, Come. I need you."[29]

Nâzım then sent a cryptic note to Memet Fuat, who was at this time twenty-two years old and studying English literature at Istanbul University. Lamenting that the "red haired big sister," a reference to Piraye, "might never come back to me," Nâzım shifted blame for the split onto her. He assured Memet that "as for us, we'll make it to Nanjing," a nudging reminder that Nâzım still hoped to remain buddies with his stepson.[30]

In Nâzım's subsequent letters to Piraye, he likewise portrayed her as the party responsible for their breakup, returning once more to the old theme that she had never loved him in the first place.

> You know, I was your husband, your father, your big brother, your friend, but at no time was I ever your beloved. I know this, and I also know that now you no longer see me as your husband, your child, your big brother, or your father. I know. But I have one last hope, maybe you can still count me as a friend. As a husband there were times when I cheated on you, and maybe even as a father or a big brother I have my flaws, but as a friend I never betrayed you.

His extramarital affairs were Piraye's fault. "If I could have been your beloved," he wrote, "perhaps I wouldn't have betrayed you as a husband."[31] His next letter continued in this vein, with Nâzım again pouting that "you were never in love with me." "Our 20-year life together," he wrote in the same letter, "despite the fact that you never loved me, was the brightest, most beautiful time of my life."[32] He begged for the connection to not be severed, even as he insisted that theirs had been a one-sided love all along.[33]

Nâzım would continue to go back and forth in his efforts with Piraye. He still pleaded with her to come see him, insisting that he loved and needed her. It was no use, however. Piraye was in no mood to re-start her relationship with Nâzım at this point. He chastised her some more for not responding to his letters.[34] Nâzım

---

[27] Göksu and Timms, *Romantic Communist*, 196–197. Also see Fish, *Nâzım'ın Çilesi*, 347; Memet Fuat, *Gölgede Kalan Yıllar*, 566.

[28] *Piraye'ye Mektuplar*, 732, letter # 558. Undated, but apparently from early 1949.

[29] Ibid., 733, letter # 560. Undated, but apparently from May 1949.

[30] Ibid., 735, letter # 560. Undated, but apparently from May 1949.

[31] Ibid., 737, letter # 562. Undated, but apparently from May 1949.

[32] Ibid., 740–741, letter # 564. Undated, apparently from May 1949. Also see Sülker, *Nâzım Hikmet'in Gerçek Yaşamı*, vol. 6, 81.

[33] Also see Sülker, *Nâzım Hikmet'in Gerçek Yaşamı*, vol. 6, 71.

[34] See, for example, *Piraye'ye Mektuplar*, letters # 565, # 566, # 567, and others.

continued writing to Piraye in this manner—of pleading mixed with vexation—up until the early months of 1950.[35]

At the same time, Nâzım had not given up his pursuit of Münevver. With respect to this relationship, too, Nâzım cast himself as the victim. In a letter he wrote to Vâlâ Nureddin in February 1949, Nâzım complained bitterly about Münevver's behavior.

> How could she do this to me? She was the first woman I ever loved unconditionally. While I was stabbing my closest, best, and most honest friend who never lied to me, I felt I was discovering love as if I were discovering a totally new universe. What did the other one discover while plunging a knife into me?[36]

In March 1949, not long after writing these lines, Nâzım entered the Bursa Prison infirmary, suffering from headaches, fever, and a toothache. Celile Hanım had come down to Bursa to visit her son, while Piraye stayed in Istanbul. The infirmary's medicine cabinet had apparently been left unlocked.[37]

## The International *Cause Célèbre*

Ahead of the national elections set to take place in Turkey on May 14, 1950, rumors had been circulating that an amnesty would soon be declared. Within Nâzım's circle of family, friends, and supporters, there was finally some hope that he might be released early. Thus began a pattern of activity in which Nâzım's hopes were repeatedly raised and then dashed.

Nâzım was growing desperate. He had been thirty-six when he had begun his sentence. If he served it in its entirety, he would be behind bars until he was sixty-four years old. With World War II over and a new government in place in Ankara, the time seemed right to bring his case forward again. Energized, perhaps, by the hope of beginning a new life with Münevver—with whom matters were still far from settled—Nâzım began to more forcefully exercise his legal options after a break of several years.

Shortly after Adnan Menderes' Democrat Party's overwhelming victory in 1950, an amnesty was declared in Turkey. It did not, however, include the crime for which Nâzım had been convicted—inciting mutiny—and therefore did nothing to lessen his sentence. Because he had been tried and found guilty in such a peculiar manner—through a Stalinesque kangaroo court run by the military—it was hard to free Nâzım as part of a larger cohort. Especially now that a general amnesty had already been declared, any law that could liberate Nâzım would likely have to be written for him specifically. This was something that most legislators in Turkey were not willing to do. So, in some ways, the Democrats' initial amnesty law did more to hurt Nâzım's case than help it.

---

[35] Ibid., 765, letter # 580, February 3, 1950.  [36] Göksu and Timms, *Romantic Communist*, 195.
[37] Sülker, *Nâzım Hikmet'in Gerçek Yaşamı*, vol. 6, 7–8.

246    RED STAR OVER THE BLACK SEA

The campaign to free Nâzım Hikmet developed out of a number of sources, but it originated with the actions of Ahmet Emin Yalman. Yalman was a journalist in Ankara who had worked, early in his career, for the Young Turk-oriented newspaper *Tanin*. Sometimes described as a "liberal," Yalman was also considered—at least by some individuals—as amenable to working with the Soviets in some manner.[38] Such was the view of a press attaché at the Soviet Embassy in Ankara by the name of I. M. Lavrov. Lavrov was quoted in a Soviet Embassy report from 1944, stating that Yalman was "desiring to get closer to us," and "not poorly disposed toward a relationship with us." "Without doubt he can be used," concluded Lavrov, "and there's no need to get in his face."[39]

Whether or not Yalman was being "used" by the Soviets at this time, he did begin to take a more active interest in reviving Nâzım's case. In 1947, Yalman sought to publish articles in *Vatan* arguing in favor of Nâzım's release from prison, but the newspaper's editorial board considered the topic too controversial. In August 1949, however, Yalman was given permission to go forward, and he went on to carry out an interview with Nâzım, conducted in prison, which was published in *Vatan* to considerable fanfare. Yalman also enlisted the support of Mehmet Ali Sebük, an attorney who worked as the legal counsel to *Vatan*, to look into Nâzım's options.[40]

With Ankara now seeking closer integration with Western democratic institutions, Nâzım's manifestly unjust trial and lengthy prison sentence constituted a genuine embarrassment to Turkey and its newfound friends in Europe and North America. The USSR and emerging Eastern Bloc, meanwhile, sought to raise the imprisoned poet's profile in order to draw attention to the hypocrisy surrounding his case.

After a period of decades in which Nâzım Hikmet's name had not appeared in the Soviet press, his fight to be released from prison attracted sympathetic attention from the Soviet and Eastern Bloc media.[41] In *Pravda*, the first of several articles relating to Nâzım's attempts to be released ran in September 1948, with similar pieces appearing in January, April, September, and November 1949.[42] *Literaturnaia Gazeta* likewise began running supportive articles about Nâzım Hikmet at this time, following a hiatus of some two decades in which his name had not once been mentioned in this newspaper.[43]

It was also at around this time that Nâzım's poetry came to be published once more in the USSR, again after two decades of silence. A collection of Nâzım's works was produced by the *Pravda* press in 1950 in Moscow, and soon thereafter publications of

---

[38] Christine Philliou describes Yalman as an advocate of an "American liberal agenda." *A Past against History*, 189.

[39] Literally "fall upon" or "crash down upon" (*obrushivat'sia*). Letter from Milogradov, RGASPI, f. 495, op. 74, d. 495, ll. 6–8. November 29, 1944.

[40] Sülker, *Nâzım Hikmet'in Gerçek Yaşamı*, vol. 6, 98–99.

[41] *Pravda* ran a TASS wire report about a demonstration in New York City on behalf of Nâzım Hikmet. "Save the Life of the Turkish Poet Nâzım Hikmet," May 3, 1950, p. 4.

[42] "Captive of Turkish Gendarmes," *Literaturnaia Gazeta*, 70, September 1, 1948. Prior to this, Nâzım had not been mentioned in the paper, which was owned by the Soviet Writers' Union, since 1932. Also see "V zashchitu Nazyma Khikmeta," *Pravda*, May 27, 1950, p. 2.

[43] January 29, 1949, p. 4; April 27, 1949; September 24, 1949, p. 4; November 19, 1949, p. 4; February 25, 1950, p. 4; April 19, 1950, p. 4; May 10, 1950, p. 1; May 20, 1950, p. 1, June 10, 1950, p. 1.

his work began to appear in the Eastern European "people's democracies" as well. A Hungarian-language anthology of his verse came out in Budapest in 1950.[44] A Czech translation of Nâzım's poetry was published the following year.[45]

An important new ally for Nâzım at this time came in the form of the World Peace Council (WPC). The WPC was a Moscow-supported "fellow-traveling" organization that sought to curb the American military presence in Western Europe by promoting, in the name of "peace," Soviet-backed disarmament proposals. The organization's creation can be traced back to meetings taking place in Wroclaw, Poland, in August 1948 and in Paris in April 1949.[46]

Connections with Moscow were vital to the WPC's early survival. In June 1949 the CPSU Central Committee voted to send "20,000 American dollars" to the WPC to help with the organization's initial set-up costs.[47] While 80 percent of the followers of the WPC lived in Soviet-occupied countries in Eastern Europe, the organization's leadership sought to present itself as an independent grass-roots movement. The WPC did have a genuine following in Italy and France, where local socialist and communist parties were part of the political mainstream. However, the WPC was expelled from Paris in 1950, after which point its headquarters moved to Czechoslovakia.[48]

In its early days, the WPC had attracted to its ranks a number of well-known Western intellectuals. These included the French physicist and Nobel Prize winner Frédéric Joliot-Curie, whose reputation added to the perceived political legitimacy of the WPC. In 1950, Nâzım Hikmet was honored with one of the organization's inaugural peace prizes, alongside Pablo Picasso, Pablo Neruda, and Paul Robeson. Later winners of WPC prizes would include Leonid Brezhnev and Nicolae Ceauşescu.

In Washington, views regarding Nâzım's case were still evolving. Until 1950, American diplomatic officials working on Turkey did not show much concern, or even familiarity, with Nâzım Hikmet's case. With Turkey growing increasingly important to early Cold War-era US foreign policymaking, however, Nâzım's ongoing imprisonment emerged as more of a cause for consideration.

In April 1950, Charles R. Moore of the Office of Greek, Turkish, and Iranian Affairs in the State Department met with the First Secretary of the Turkish Embassy in Washington, Melih Esenbel. Moore noted, in his account from their meeting that day, that "some weeks ago" he had let Esenbel know that a delegation headed by Eleanor Roosevelt, the Committee on Human Rights of the United Nations, had issued a request to review Nâzım Hikmet's case.

---

[44] *Izbrannye stikhi* (Moscow, 1950); *Versei* (Budapest: Révai Könyvkiadó Nemzeti Vállalat, 1950).

[45] *Zpěv za mřížemi* (Praha: Mladá fronta, 1951).

[46] In November 1950, the organization changed its name to the "World Peace Council." On the WPC, also see Milorad Popov, "The World Council of Peace," in *World Communism: A Handbook*, ed. W. S. Sworakowski (Stanford: Hoover Institution Press, 1973), 488–491.

[47] RGASPI, f. 17, op. 3, d. 1076, ll. 50–51. "On measures in connection to the Congress of Partisans for Peace." June 17, 1949.

[48] On most of WPC's "adherents" being from the Eastern Bloc, see Andrew G. Bone, "Russell and the Communist-Aligned Peace Movement in the Mid-1950s," *The Journal of Bertrand Russell Studies*, n.s. vol. 21 (Summer 2001), 31–57.

The news that the widowed First Lady had taken an interest in the jailed poet alarmed Esenbel. While he was quick to dismiss Nâzım Hikmet's champions as mere communist front organizations—which they often were—Esenbel also stressed that Nâzım would, in any event, soon be released. In reference to the amnesty bill that had been debated in the previous session of parliament, Esenbel had, according to Moore, emphasized that it "would be passed when the new Assembly met in May and that it would cover the category of prisoners in which Nâzım Hikmet falls." In closing, Esenbel had expressed his hope that:

> ...the above information could be passed along to Mrs. Roosevelt, as she enjoys the very high respect of Turkish Government officials who are anxious that she under-stand the real motivations of the petitioners in this particular case, as well as the sincere desire and intention of the Turkish Government to take appropriate action with respect to Nâzım Hikmet just as soon as feasible.[49]

On the ground in Turkey, American diplomats likewise sought to get a handle on the case. In a "despatch" issued on May 6, 1950, US Counselor of Embassy Warwick Perkins noted that Nâzım Hikmet was "still a subject of solicitude" in Turkey. Regarding the imprisoned poet, Perkins went on to observe:

> The release from imprisonment of Nâzım Hikmet, who is serving a long prison term for alleged Communist activity, has now been requested by a number of youth and student organizations. Pressure from sympathizers is growing, and there is a feeling among many observers that propaganda on behalf of Hikmet is now sufficiently strong to cause the Grand National Assembly to place the proposed amnesty law high on the legislative calendar for the next session.[50]

Meanwhile, Nâzım's legal team switched to a new tactic: campaigning for him to be released on health grounds. Nâzım's supporters emphasized the deteriorating nature of his physical condition over the course of the more than ten years that he had already spent behind bars. Also at this time, Nâzım began a hunger strike, further damaging his health and imperiling his life.

Nâzım's hunger strike was announced on the pages of *Vatan* on March 30. The following day, Ahmet Yalman wrote an open letter to Prime Minister Menderes, asking him to release Nâzım on account of his medical problems. Nâzım's lawyer Mehmet Ali Sebük then traveled to Ankara to lobby government officials and won an important concession: Nâzım would be transferred to a hospital in Istanbul while the government reviewed his case. Receiving this news, Nâzım decided to call off the hunger

---

[49] Charles R. Moore, US National Archives and Records Administration (henceforth, NARA), 782.00/4-650, p. 2. April 7, 1950.

[50] NARA, 782.001/5-650. Despatch from Ankara, May 6, 1950. The US Department of State uses the unorthodox spelling "despatch," rather than "dispatch," to refer to diplomatic correspondence which enters a foreign office.

strike, at least temporarily. Over the course of April 1950, he moved back and forth across Istanbul, shuttling between Cerrahpaşa Hospital, Paşakapı Prison in Üsküdar, and the infirmary of Sultanahmet Prison.

More than a month passed, however, without any progress in his case. Sensing, perhaps, that he could lose momentum if he did not follow up on his earlier activities, Nâzım pressed forward again with the hunger strike, which he re-started on May 2. Twelve days later, his health worsening, Nâzım was again transferred to Cerrahpaşa Hospital, where he was given a private room and allowed to receive visitors, including Münevver. However, this decision to resume the hunger strike in the middle of an election campaign turned out to be a tactical mistake, as the national press was preoccupied with other news. Concerned, Nâzım's friends, including Zekeriya Sertel, tried to convince Nâzım to call off the strike a second time, but Nâzım was determined to carry on.[51]

Another friend who was tending to Nâzım at this time was Abidin Dino. Born in Istanbul in 1913, Abidin had studied at the prestigious Robert College before leaving school to work on his own as an artist. Abidin had first met Nâzım in the early 1930s, when he did the artwork for some of Nâzım's publications.[52] Between 1934 and 1937, Dino had resided in Leningrad, working on set design alongside the Soviet film director Sergei Iutkevich.[53] He had even applied for Soviet citizenship, in 1937, but left the USSR before receiving a decision on this request.[54] Abidin Dino then traveled to London and Paris before returning to Turkey in 1939.

With Nâzım now refusing to call off the hunger strike, Abidin and Zekeriya found themselves caught between two immovable objects. They sought to simultaneously persuade Nâzım to give up the strike, while convincing the authorities to release him on health grounds. Meanwhile, petition campaigns and telegrams of support helped to draw still more attention to the movement calling for the poet-communist's freedom.[55] Even Nâzım's mother, Celile Hanım, became part of the media story, causing a stir by sitting down on the pavement of the Galata Bridge holding a sign that demanded justice for her son. On May 20, Nâzım gave up his hunger strike for the second time.

But by now, he was finally close to freedom. On July 14, as one of its final acts prior to recessing until November 1, the Turkish parliament approved a new amnesty bill. It constituted an interesting way of freeing Nâzım, commuting his remaining sentence in a manner that was not specific to him. The amnesty reduced the sentences of all long-term prisoners by two-thirds. As Nâzım had already served more than one-third of his term, he was eligible for immediate release. The bill went into effect the next day, on July 15. After more than twelve years behind bars, he was a free man again.

---

[51] Göksu and Timms, *Romantic Communist*, 215.

[52] Memet Fuat, *A'dan Z'ye Nâzım Hikmet*, 126–128. Also see Sülker, *Nâzım Hikmet'in Gerçek Yaşamı*, vol. 2, 54.

[53] RGASPI, f. 495, op. 266, d. 273, esp. ll. 7, 14. Also see Hirst, "Eurasia's Discontent," 44, 230, 233.

[54] Hirst, "Eurasia's Discontent," 44, 230, 233. Also see, from Hirst, RGASPI, f. 495, op. 266, d. 273, esp. ll. 7, 14. "Spravka" from the personal file of Abidin Dino.

[55] On telegraphs from Prague and Bulgaria in support of Nâzım, see, for example, BCA 30-1-0-0/5-24-8, "Protest telegrams from abroad in connection with Nâzım Hikmet's imprisonment," May 16, 1950.

The morning of the big day, *Cumhuriyet* sent a reporter down to Istanbul's Sultanahmet Prison to talk to newly-amnestied inmates and their happy families. The scene was a festive one. One Mürüvvet Aktaş, whose father was playing the *zurna* in celebration of his daughter's release, was rejoicing in her newfound freedom. "With one bullet I got rid of my husband," boasted Mürüvvet to the journalist interviewing her. Noting that her late spouse was an alcoholic who was also addicted to hashish, Mürüvvet displayed no remorse. "He got what he deserved."[56]

Just a few miles away, Nâzım Hikmet was similarly experiencing the sense of joy that newfound liberty can bring. A reporter from *Cumhuriyet* had come to cover this release as well, noting that Nâzım walked out of Cerrahpaşa Hospital at 2:15 p.m. "Nâzım Hikmet is going to rest for some time," concluded the piece that the newspaper ran the next day. "The poet has spent the last 13 years in prison."[57] Nâzım and Münevver then headed across the Bosphorus to Vâlâ and Müzehher Nureddin's home on the Anatolian side of Istanbul. There they would spend their first month of freedom.[58]

Hearing of Nâzım's release, Ankara Embassy First Secretary B. E. Kuniholm lamented that the Turkish government had not acted sooner. In Kuniholm's view, Nâzım's ongoing case had done nothing but provide a boon to a variety of communist front organizations. The poet's incarceration, he wrote, had served "as a principal foil for attacks against Turkey on the part of the communist press throughout the world." Thanks to misguided—albeit now corrected—policies in Ankara, Nâzım had been transformed into a "*cause célèbre*."[59]

## Suspicious Minds

Life in the USSR at this time was, for Turkish communists and other foreigners, still a fraught experience. The mass purges that had been commonplace in the Soviet Union in the late 1930s had ended with Germany's surprise attack on the USSR in June 1941. However, during the years following the conclusion of the Great Fatherland War—as World War II is known in the former Soviet world—there were signs that the purges would be revived. A well-known case of a postwar purge in the Soviet Union was the so-called "Doctors Plot" of 1951–53, in which a number of Jewish doctors were arrested in what appears to have been the opening salvo of a planned attack on Jewish communists.

Yet even before the "Doctors Plot," an investigation taking place within the ranks of Turkish radio broadcasting in Moscow similarly recalled the 1930s. In 1949—a time of prison camp revival in the USSR—one Comrade Raikhman ("Reichman") began

---

[56] *Cumhuriyet*, Sunday, July 16, 1950, p. 4.
[57] Ibid. Nâzım had actually been incarcerated for twelve years and six months in relation to the army and navy mutiny charges, including the three months he had spent under house arrest.
[58] Müzehher Vâ-Nû, *Bir Dönemin Tanıklığı* (İstanbul: Cem Yayınevi, 1987), 161–162.
[59] The term "*cause célèbre*" is from Kuniholm's report. NARA, 782.00/7-2050, p. 2.

digging into the pasts of several TKP members connected to İsmail Bilen.[60] Raikhman was the deputy head of the second chief directorate of the Ministry of State Security, or MGB, which was the successor to the NKVD and precursor to the KGB.[61] Of particular interest to Raikhman was a collection of Turks who had entered the USSR either illegally or without permission.

Two individuals who had caught Raikhman's attention were Salih Hacıoğlu and Sabiha Sünbül. Having redeemed his previous "mistakes" and been restored to the party's ranks, Salih Hacıoğlu had led a quiet existence in Azerbaijan with his family prior to moving up to Moscow in 1941. Life, however, had not been so easy for the couple. A son had committed suicide in 1938 while serving in the Soviet army in Vinnytsia, in west-central Ukraine.[62] In 1945, Sabiha and Salih's daughter had died.[63] According to her personal file, Sabiha had, the following year, sought permission from the Turkish Embassy to return to Turkey.[64] Meanwhile, a "spravka," from May 1948 noted ominously that Salih Hacıoğlu had been "a friend of the established Turkish intelligence agent Süleyman Nuri, who is currently located in Turkey."[65]

On March 10, 1949, Hacıoğlu and Sünbül were arrested on charges of having committed espionage on behalf of Ankara.[66] Sünbül's alleged visit to the Turkish Embassy was characterized as "engaging in anti-Soviet agitation." The fact that Hacıoğlu and Sünbül had, in 1928, entered the USSR irregularly—that is, without permission from the party—had been brought up several times over the years in Hacıoğlu's party file, which further claimed that he had once kept the company of "renegades" and "provocateurs," a reference to Nâzım Hikmet and Şevket Süreyya.[67]

In a report prepared by Raikhman in November 1950, Sabiha Sünbül is said to have confessed to having told officials at the Turkish Embassy "of her dissatisfaction with the living conditions in the USSR and had asked to return to Turkey." She then allegedly "admitted that she had given espionage information to the Turkish Embassy."[68] Fifty-three-year-old Sabiha Sünbül was sentenced to ten years in a labor camp in the

---

[60] Soviet prison camp survivor Eugenia Ginzburg described 1949 as the "twin brother" of 1937. *Within the Whirlwind* (London: Collins and Harvill Press, 1981), 279. From Tzouliadis, *The Forsaken*, 262.

[61] "Zam nachalnik vtorogo glavnogo upravleniia mgb." RGASPI, f. 495, op. 266, d. 98, l. 20.

[62] RGASPI, f. 495, op. 266, d. 98, l. 21, "Spravka" from May 28, 1948.

[63] RGASPI, f. 495, op. 266, d. 98, l. 9. "Spravka" from January 18, 1957. Another daughter was reportedly working in Azerbaijan in 1948. RGASPI, f. 495, op. 266, d. 98, l. 21, "Spravka" from May 28, 1948. Hayk Açıkgöz writes in his memoirs that a daughter of Hacıoğlu and Sünbül had died in a prison camp. *Anadolulu Bir Ermeni Komünistin Anıları*, 555.

[64] RGASPI, f. 495, op. 266, d. 98, l. 1-ob. Sait Aliyev also mentioned in his letter to Nâzım Hikmet that Sabiha Sünbül had wanted to return to Turkey. RGASPI, f. 495, op. 266, d. 254, ll. 8–14, here 13-ob. Undated, but apparently from August or September 1955.

[65] RGASPI, f. 495, op. 266, d. 98, ll. 21–21-ob, "Spravka," May 28, 1948.

[66] On accusations of Hacıoğlu mixing with "renegades," also see RGASPI, f. 495, op. 266, d. 98, ll. 65–70, May 20, 1939, here 68; ibid., ll. 59–61, October 23, 1940; ibid., ll. 42–43-ob, April 16, 1941. Şevket Süreyya is mentioned by name several times in Hacıoğlu's file as an unsavory contact. RGASPI, f. 495, op. 266, d. 98, ll. 42-ob, 59, 60, 67, 68, 76.

[67] On charges that Sabiha Sünbül made contact with the Turkish Embassy see RGASPI, f. 495, op. 266, d. 98, l. 10. This document is undated, but appears to be from the late 1950s. On Sünbül's alleged visit to the Turkish Embassy, also see Sertel, *Nâzım Hikmet ile Serteller*, 137.

[68] RGASPI, f. 495, op. 266, d. 98, l. 20.

252    RED STAR OVER THE BLACK SEA

district of Arkhangelsk Oblast, on the Arctic Ocean. Seventy-year-old Salih Hacıoğlu was likewise given a ten-year term, in a camp located in the Altay region of Siberia.[69]

Another illicit border-crosser caught in Comrade Raikhman's crosshairs was Sait Aliyev. Aliyev was the Dagestani-born Turkish military officer who had crossed illegally into the Soviet Union in 1942, only to be arrested immediately on the Soviet side of the frontier. The following year, Aliyev had been released from prison and sent to Moscow to work for İsmail Bilen. According to a later account by Aliyev, İsmail had told him that Salih's wife Sabiha was trying to return to Turkey and that she was therefore someone to be avoided. Despite what appears to have been an effort by İsmail to protect Sait, Aliyev would later blame Bilen for failing to provide help following his arrest, claiming that his old boss had "no conscience."[70] In March 1950, Aliyev was sentenced to fifteen years in a prison camp.[71]

Raikhman also looked into the file of Ali Haydar Kutlu, who had spent almost four years in prison after crossing the border illegally from Turkey in 1937. After his release in March 1941, Kutlu had lived for about one year in Moscow, where he worked for İsmail Bilen before somehow returning to Turkey in 1942. In Raikhman's estimation, Kutlu had likewise been "an agent of Turkish intelligence" and had come to the USSR in order to carry out espionage operations on behalf of Ankara.[72]

The common point connecting these four individuals was İsmail Bilen, whom Comrade Raikhman had also begun investigating. Sabiha Sünbül had, during her interrogation by Raikhman, allegedly "provided evidence relating to the nationalist disposition of Marat," in reference to İsmail.[73] While such a description may sound relatively innocuous to twenty-first century ears, being called a Turkish "nationalist" was not a good thing in Moscow at this time.

As frequently occurred with such investigations, Raikhman's case against İsmail was based primarily upon guilt by association. Bilen's ex-wife Sabiha Mesrure, who had disappeared from the ranks of the TKP in 1928, was dredged up as a means of imprecating Bilen's loyalty, with Raikhman describing her as "an agent of several foreign intelligence services."[74] Aziz Husametdin (Özdoğu), İsmail's friend from the 1920s and 1930s who had left the TKP in 1946 to help establish a legal socialist party in Turkey, was similarly presented by Raikhman as another one of Bilen's shady connections. It was the same with Aziz's sister, Sidika, who, Raikhman claimed, had shared "close relations" with a colonel in the Turkish police. Raikhman

---

[69]  RGASPI, f. 495, op. 266, d. 98, ll. 1, 8.
[70]  RGASPI, f. 495, op. 266, d. 254, ll. 8–14, letter from Sait Aliyev to Nâzım Hikmet, here l. 9.
[71]  RGASPI, f. 495, op. 266, d. 254, l. 5. Documents pertaining to Sait Aliyev, September 23. 1955.
[72]  RGASPI, f. 495, op. 266, d. 3, l. 46. "Report by Comrade Raikhman," November 3, 1950. On Kutlu leaving the USSR for Turkey, see RGASPI, f. 495, op. 266, d. 216, l. 3. A report from October 1948 states that Kutlu had left the USSR for Turkey in 1942.
[73]  RGASPI, f. 495, op. 266, d. 98, l. 20.
[74]  Personal file of (Aziz) Husametdin. RGASPI, f. 495, op. 266, d. 3, l. 46. "Report by Comrade Raikhman," November 3, 1950. Raikhman's report can be found in numerous personal files. See, for example, personal file of Salih Hacıoğlu, RGASPI, f. 495, op. 266, d. 98, ll. 19–20; personal file of Alexander Senkevich, f. 495, op. 266, d. 218, l. 9; personal file of Haydar Kutlu, f. 495, op. 266, d. 216, l. 1.

further accused İsmail of having maintained unsanctioned contacts with the Yugoslavian party.[75]

The main rationale behind investigating Bilen was that he—like Hacıoğlu, Sünbül, Aliyev, and Kutlu—had come to the USSR under irregular conditions. In the 1920s, border-crossers like these individuals had been welcome in the USSR. Now, however, such a background made one the object of official suspicion. For Bilen, hiring these people had constituted a means of putting at his disposal individuals who would be largely dependent upon him. In Raikhman's eyes, however, Bilen's empire-building was evidence that he was the ringleader of a network of spies working on Ankara's behalf.

Despite Raikhman's apparent determination to put Bilen behind bars, İsmail was not sent to a labor camp, nor was he arrested. As had been the case in 1937–38, people around Bilen were arrested and sent to camps, but nothing had happened to İsmail himself.

Had Nâzım known about the arrests of Hacıoğlu, Sünbül, and Sait Aliyev in 1949, it might have given him pause regarding the wisdom of returning to the Soviet Union at this particular moment. After all, the Turks whom Raikhman had targeted were all individuals who had arrived in the USSR from Turkey unexpectedly and via ad hoc means.

Just as Nâzım himself would set out to do in June 1951.

## Out of Jail

Nâzım was free again, or at least freer than he had been at any other point for the past twelve-and-a-half years. Even after he was released from prison, however, daily forms of harassment wore on. It was hard for Nâzım to find full-time work, as most potential employers were too frightened to offer him a job. He was still unable to publish under his own name.[76]

According to Memet Fuat, Nâzım and Piraye began divorce proceedings shortly after Nâzım's release from prison.[77] In March 1951, Münevver gave birth to a son they named Mehmet, and whom Nâzım would always refer to in writing as "Memet." The name marked an interesting choice, given that Piraye's son was named "Mehmet Fuat," and that Nâzım had likewise always used the same unconventional spelling in writing his name: "Memet."[78] It was almost as if Nâzım saw the new "Memet" as a replacement

---

[75] Aziz had helped to form the Turkish Socialist Party, a legal organization for which Aziz would become the Istanbul party secretary. RGASPI, f. 495, op. 266, d. 3, l. 44, personal file of Mamed (Aziz) Husametdin. On İsmail Bilen's alleged ties to Yugoslavia, see the collection of documents that was assembled about Nâzım and İsmail following Nâzım's return to the USSR in 1951, RGASPI, f. 82, op. 2, d. 1330, ll. 120–126, here 125–126.

[76] See Müzehher Vâ-Nû, "Önsöz" ("Foreword"), *Bursa Cezaevinden Vâ-Nû'lara Mektuplar*, 13.

[77] Memet Fuat, *Gölgede Kalan Yıllar*, 569.

[78] Memet Fuat's name was officially "Mehmet" Fuat and this is how Piraye referred to him. Ibid., 53, 78, 319.

**Figure 10.1** Nâzım and Münevver

child of sorts for his stepson, with whom Nâzım had enjoyed a close relationship (Figure 10.1).[79]

Shortly after Mehmet's birth, Nâzım received startling news: he was being drafted into the Turkish army as a private for a two-year term. When he received the news, Nâzım was forty-nine years old. The argument for conscription, from the army's perspective, was that Nâzım had never completed his military service.

This was hardly a randomly-selected form of harassment. The fact that Nâzım had traveled to Georgia in 1921 instead of to the front lines against the Greeks had always been something that Nâzım's detractors had held against him. As far as they were concerned, if Nâzım hadn't felt the urge to do his military service back when it was needed, he could at least do so now.

Fighting the conscription order, Nâzım won a temporary injunction while he sought the opinions of other doctors. This marked, however, a short-lived victory. No matter how many doctors wrote notes for Nâzım attesting to his physical unfitness to serve, military doctors deemed the poet healthy. Once again, the Turkish armed forces had successfully gotten to Nâzım, even as civilian state institutions had just released him.

---

[79] Nâzım and Münevver's son would go on to call himself "Mehmet Nâzım" and as an adult would never use the spelling "Memet," so I refer to him in this book as "Mehmet." Memet Fuat, meanwhile, would always employ the unconventional spelling when writing his name in later life, so I refer to him as "Memet."

Increasingly, he began to think about escape. At first, Nâzım would later tell his Eastern Bloc debriefers, he had considered crossing into Syria. The idea was to secretly traverse the border with smugglers, then make his way to the USSR from Damascus. This plan was later ruled out, however, as Nâzım came to the conclusion that "the Syrian government would have arrested me and sent me back to Turkey."[80] Nâzım then began to consider the possibility of fleeing by boat.

In order to escape via the Black Sea, all he needed was to get to Bulgaria. A Soviet ally, the People's Republic of Bulgaria was tantalizingly close. At the same time, the border between Bulgaria and Turkey had, in recent years, become a violent no-man's land. This tense situation along the Turkish–Bulgarian frontier was not simply a reflection of Cold War geopolitics, but was also a consequence of problems that were more local in origin.

The communist government in Bulgaria had been established in 1946, and its first prime minister was none other than former Comintern chief Georgi Dimitrov. In 1949, however, Dimitrov had died, and was replaced as prime minister and general secretary by Valko Chervenkov. Chervenkov's era as party leader in Sofia was characterized by Stalinist-style repression and purges. His policies vis-à-vis the country's Turkish population, moreover, were not only brutal, but also erratic. After initially relaxing exit visa restrictions in 1950, the Bulgarian government had begun forcing ethnic Turks to leave, sending a note to Ankara on August 10, 1950, demanding that Turkey accept 250,000 Turks from Bulgaria.[81] But then party authorities in Sofia changed course, now forbidding anyone from departing, even those who had already been issued an exit visa.[82]

Amid the more general air of tension between Sofia and Ankara, a series of violent incidents had recently taken place along their shared frontier. In early June 1950, *Cumhuriyet* correspondent Arif Necip Kaskatı was killed on the Bulgarian side of the border, his corpse later confiscated by Bulgarian frontier police.[83] A few months later, in October, Bulgarian soldiers opened fire on Turkish troops who had gone for water at a cistern in the border zone outside Edirne.[84]

On the Turkish–Soviet border as well, these years were marked by a tense mood and quick triggers. In August 1950, a Turkish *muhtar*, or village head, was shot by Soviet border guards as he attempted to divert the waters flowing into the river marking the Turkish–Soviet frontier.[85] In June 1951, there was an outcry in the Turkish media over reports that Ankara had turned over 156 "Turko-Tatar" refugees back to Soviet authorities. Şevket Mocan, a parliamentary deputy from Tekirdağı, submitted to the Grand National Assembly a request for information regarding the expulsion of

---

[80] "Nâzım Hikmet's Statement," June 26, 1951. Nâzım Hikmet personal file, Part I: RGASPI, f. 495, op. 266, d. 47, ll. 20–21.

[81] See "Deportation of Bulgarian Turks," December 19, 1950. Despatch from Ankara. NARA, 782.001/12-1950, p. 3; "Turkey Absorbing Mass of Refugees," *The New York Times*, April 15, 1951, p. 27.

[82] On these events, also see Göksu and Timms, *Romantic Communist*, 262–264.

[83] NARA, 782.00/6-1550. Despatch from Ankara, June 15, 1950.

[84] NARA, 782.001/1/11-1650. Despatch from Ankara, November 16, 1950, p. 2.

[85] NARA, 782.001/8-1150. Despatch from Ankara, August 11, 1950.

these individuals who, he charged, had already been granted asylum by Turkey. According to Mocan, the would-be migrants had been returned against their will to the USSR at the request of the Soviet Embassy.[86]

Even before the onset of the Cold War, Soviet authorities had begun to insist upon the return of Soviet citizens who had crossed the frontier illegally into Turkey. Ankara, for its part, endeavored to mollify Moscow in this regard. In May 1945, the Turkish Ministry of Defense had declared that "as is the case with Thrace, no refugees will be allowed into our borders from Syria or Soviet Russia." The policy, noted the ministry report, had been adopted at the behest of "neighboring governments."[87] Shortly thereafter, 243 Soviet citizens were returned to the Soviet Union despite their desire to stay in Turkey. According to the Governor of Yozgat, where most of the would-be emigrants were being held, a number of the detainees had been bound with handcuffs to prevent them from killing themselves.[88]

Such was the state of Turkey's frontiers with the emerging Eastern Bloc at the time that Nâzım was considering an escape. While he would be avoiding the treacherous terrain associated with crossing by land, traveling by water was hardly an easy matter. The Black Sea has strong currents that can develop suddenly, and the boat Nâzım planned to take was quite small. This was not a mission for the faint of heart.

Did Nâzım and Münevver tell themselves that this was only temporary?[89] It is unclear what future Nâzım imagined for his wife and son at this point. Perhaps he hoped that, after a few months, everything would blow over and his family would be allowed to quietly leave the country—assuming he survived the journey, of course, or was not arrested en route and sent back to prison in Turkey. Then again, Nâzım had left others behind on previous occasions, likely in the knowledge that he would probably never see them again. Dr. Lena had made it as far as Odessa before she was turned back. How far would Münevver get?

One can only imagine what Nâzım was thinking when he got up in the dead of night to exit his house for the last time. He made his way down to the shore of the Bosphorus, where he met up with Refik Erduran, the husband of Nâzım's half-sister.[90] In the boat, they traveled in the opposite direction for a while, heading southward toward the Marmara Sea just in case anyone was watching them. After a while, Refik turned the boat around and they started heading north toward the Black Sea.[91]

*

[86] NARA, 782.001/7-2351. Despatch from Ankara, July 23, 1951.

[87] BCA, 30-10-0-0/117-815-19. "On not accepting refugees crossing the border from Syria and Soviet Russia," May 15, 1945.

[88] BCA, 30-10-0-0/117-815-20. Note from Minister of Internal Affairs Hilmi Uran to Prime Minister Şükrü Saracoğlu, July 30, 1945.

[89] Zekeriya Sertel writes that he was in attendance on Nâzım's last night, "at Mühürdar Park in Kadıköy." *Nâzım Hikmet'in Son Yılları*, 12.

[90] Hikmet Bey's daughter, born to his second wife.

[91] Göksu and Timms, *Romantic Communist*, 250–252.

Nâzım had been rolling with a hot hand, and now he was upping the ante still further. His escape from Turkey is often presented as a new beginning, and in some ways it certainly was. But his flight was also a culmination of sorts, constituting only the most recent of a series of gambles that Nâzım had undertaken over the previous few years.

Having tasted freedom again, there was no way he would submit to conscription or spend more time in a Turkish prison. Nâzım was either going to get to the Eastern Bloc, or he would likely die trying.

# 11

# In Stalin's USSR

Some twelve days after setting out one early morning from his home on the Anatolian side of Istanbul, Nâzım had arrived in the Soviet Union by plane from Bucharest. It was June 29, 1951. He had come home once again to Moscow, the city of his youth (Figure 11.1).

It must have seemed like a good sign. Nâzım had been met at Moscow's Vnukovskii aerodrome by a flurry of representatives from various Soviet cultural institutions. The most important of these was the Soviet Writers' Union, the organization which had officially invited Nâzım to the USSR in the aftermath of his flight from Turkey. The Moscow dailies all wrote extensively about Nâzım's arrival, an event that was likewise broadcast throughout the official medias of the Eastern Bloc.

This was, after all, an important day for freedom.

In a warm editorial welcoming Nâzım to the Soviet Union, *Literaturnaia Gazeta* hailed the exiled poet as a "hero" and dedicated "fighter for peace." Appropriately, the paper greeted Nâzım with both a poem and a toast.

> Nâzım Hikmet! Our hearts burned with such bitter pain in the days when, together with all progressive humanity, we fought for the release from prison of the great son of the Turkish nation! How great was our joy when the walls of the prisons fell down![1]

It was time for Nâzım to sing for his supper. His public statements in Moscow during these early days were filled with denunciations of the Turkish and American governments, and especially Ankara's recent decision to become directly involved in the Korean War. In a letter that he published in *Literaturnaia Gazeta* shortly after his arrival in Moscow, Nâzım listed the calamities visited upon his homeland by US soldiers. "On the streets of Istanbul," Nâzım reported, "drunken officers stroll about, creating scandals. The Turkish people hate the American imperialists because they know that, at [the Americans'] command, Turkish fascists are shipping off Turkish youth to a likely death in Korea."

Nevertheless, noted Nâzım, there was still hope for humanity: Joseph Stalin. In an editorial otherwise devoted to castigating the American military presence in Turkey, Nâzım also found a way to laud the greatness of the Soviet leader. The poet-communist

---

[1] *Literaturnaia Gazeta*, "Nazym Khikmet v Moskve," June 30, 1951, p. 4.

*Red Star over the Black Sea: Nâzım Hikmet and his Generation*. James H. Meyer, Oxford University Press. © James H. Meyer 2023.
DOI: 10.1093/oso/9780192871176.003.0013

**Figure 11.1** All smiles for now: Nâzım arriving in Moscow, June 29, 1951

conjured an oleaginous image juxtaposing his wife, mother, and a certain Georgian dictator:

> During my most difficult days and hours in prison I never lost heart or certainty in my victory. Before me was the image (*obraz*) of Comrade Stalin. I always had a photograph of Comrade Stalin with me, which I faithfully saved alongside photographs of my mother and wife.[2]

\*

While Nâzım's biographers tend to assume that his communist credentials in Moscow were "almost impeccable" in 1951, this was far from being the case.[3] Practically no one in the Soviet Union, least of all a Turkish poet with an allegedly Trotskyite past, had an unimpeachable background at this time. While İsmail Bilen may have liked Nâzım, there was still a lot of unflattering material in the poet's party file. Moreover, being close to İsmail Bilen was hardly a guarantee that one could evade unjustified arrest and imprisonment—as Salih Hacıoğlu and others could attest. Although Nâzım was surely aware that his checkered past had been recorded in his party paperwork, he may not have understood the extent to which his reputation had been savaged in the 1930s.

---

[2] *Literaturnaia Gazeta*, "Amerikantsy v Turtsii," June 30, 1951.
[3] Göksu and Timms write: "Nâzım's credentials were almost impeccable: a dedicated Russian-speaking communist, educated in Moscow in the glorious days of Leninism, repeatedly imprisoned for his beliefs…" *Romantic Communist*, 259.

## Twelve Days in Romania

Nâzım left Istanbul in the early morning of June 17. By the end of the day, he had made it to Constanța, Romania. He did not, however, fly out of Bucharest until June 29. So, what was Nâzım doing during the course of these twelve days in Romania?

According to Zekeriya Sertel, who often met up with Nâzım in the 1950s, Nâzım was greeted in Constanța by a collection of writers, and then was personally ferried by car to Bucharest by Ana Pauker, Romania's Foreign Minister.[4] Arriving in the capital on June 19, Nâzım was installed at a Central Committee guesthouse located in a leafy neighborhood on A. A. Zhdanov Street, 32.[5] Nâzım's hosts in Bucharest brought him some new clothes, as he had still been wearing what had been on his back when he had left Istanbul.

His handlers in the Romanian capital kept him busy. On his first evening in Bucharest Nâzım was taken out to attend a performance of the ballet *The Red Poppy*, which he recalled having seen years earlier during his student days in Moscow. On June 20, a Wednesday, Nâzım was given a medical checkup, later visiting public exhibitions on Stalin and Romanian folkloric art. In the afternoon, he went to the offices of the Romanian branch of the World Peace Council, where he met with the Romanian media. As would be the case with nearly all of his public statements during this time in Bucharest, Nâzım said nothing about the actual reason why he had fled Turkey, preferring instead to focus upon the broader terms of Cold War politics.

Rather than tell his own story and underscore the inhumanity of conscripting a 49-year-old in weakened health, Nâzım criticized Ankara's developing relationship with the United States, declaring that Turkey had become "an American colony" under Menderes. The Turkish government, Nâzım charged, had transformed "the sons of Turkey into the murderers of the Korean people." The next day, he visited Radio Bucharest, where Nâzım made comments "almost exactly like" those from the day before at the WPC.[6]

Nâzım was making an audition of sorts to Soviet, Romanian, and other Eastern Bloc governments. He was demonstrating, in these early days, his potential value as a propagandizer, and he had ambitious plans about the role he could play in USSR-based TKP activities. In a report to Moscow from this time, party officials in Bucharest noted that Nâzım planned on asking the Communist Party of the USSR "to provide assistance for the strengthening" of the party. Nâzım, the report went on to say, was "constantly working on ideas about the need to reorganize the TKP and strengthen the moral support that it receives from the VKP (b) and the fraternal parties of the peoples' republics."[7]

On June 20, three days after the *Plekhanov* had plucked Nâzım out of the Black Sea, his arrival in Romania was announced internationally on Radio Bucharest. The next

---

[4] Zekeriya Sertel, *Nâzım Hikmet'in Son Yılları*, 16.　　[5] Today's Bulevardul Primăverii.
[6] RGASPI, f. 495, op. 266, d. 47, Part I, ll. 30–31. Personal file of Nâzım Hikmet, June 21, 1951.
[7] VKP (b) refers to the Communist Party of the Soviet Union. "Zametka," June 21, 1951. RGASPI, f. 495, op. 266, d. 47, Part I, ll. 30–31.

**Figure 11.2** Nâzım's arrival on the front page of *Scânteia*, June 21

day, the story was splashed across the front page of the Bucharest daily *Scânteia*.[8] Just below Nâzım's large photo, which was featured prominently above the newspaper's fold, was a handwritten message, in Turkish, from Nâzım to the Romanian people, again lauding Stalin (Figure 11.2):

> In the struggle between life and death, and between peace and war, life and peace will emerge victorious. This is because there are masses of people who rise to the defense of peace and life. And these masses of hundreds of millions are the free people of the Soviet Union and the peoples' republics. The hand that carries the flag of peace and life is Stalin's.[9]

In the Soviet press, meanwhile, nothing about Nâzım's arrival in Romania appeared until June 22, two days after the announcement on Radio Bucharest. The tone of this coverage, moreover, was noticeably understated in comparison with that of *Scânteia*. In *Pravda*, the news of Nâzım's escape was announced in a small item tucked away on page 3. The story was just a few paragraphs long and its headline was written in a noticeably smaller font than the two stories placed on either side of it (Figure 11.3).[10]

---

[8] This newspaper later adjusted the spelling of its name to *Scînteia*, following changes that were made to Romanian orthography.
[9] *Scânteia*, June 21, p. 1.   [10] *Pravda*, "Nazym Khikmet v Rumynii," June 22, 1951, p. 3.

Figure 11.3 Buried in the middle: the smaller print of Nâzım's page 3 arrival in *Pravda*

Titled "Nâzım Hikmet is in Romania," the article's contents were taken entirely from public statements that Nâzım had made to the Romanian media.[11] This would constitute the only comment that *Pravda* would make about Nâzım until June 27, the day after the Central Committee of the CPSU had made a decision on Nâzım's status.

On June 26, the Central Committee of the CPSU voted to admit Nâzım to the Soviet Union. The Deputy Chairman of the External Political Committee, Boris Ponomarev, sent a note to Stalin, Malenkov, Molotov, Beria, Mikoyan, Kaganovich, Bulganin, and Khrushchev regarding Nâzım's bid to re-locate from Bucharest to Moscow. Noting that Alexander Fadeyev, the Chairman of the Soviet Writers' Union, had "inquired with a request for permission to invite Nâzım Hikmet to the USSR as a guest" of the Writers' Union, Ponomarev forwarded a letter that Nâzım had written to Stalin and the rest of the Central Committee.[12] In this statement (*zaiavlenie*), Nâzım explained how he had gotten to the Eastern Bloc and what he hoped to do next.[13]

It is a remarkable document. According to Nâzım, the financing for his escape had come from the money that he had earned from his World Peace Council prize from the previous year. The Sertels, Nâzım claimed, had acted as go-betweens connecting Nâzım and the WPC. Nâzım stated that he had asked the WPC to give half of his peace prize money to Sabiha, and to deposit the other half in Nâzım's name into a Swiss bank account. Sabiha, who was living in Paris at this time, was not able to travel back to Turkey due to fear of arrest, so Zekeriya, Nâzım wrote, had brought the cash from France to Istanbul. "In this way," Nâzım claimed, "I had the money to organize

---

[11] Ibid. Meanwhile, no mention of Nâzım's escape appeared in *Literaturnaia Gazeta* until June 26.

[12] Fadeyev had also suggested finding Nâzım a three-room apartment in Moscow. Letter from Boris Ponomarev to Comrades Stalin, Malenkov, Molotov, Beria, Mikoyan, Kaganovich, Bulganin, and Khrushchev, June 23, 1951. RGASPI, f. 82, op. 2, d. 1330, ll. 62–63. While Ponomarev's letter was written on the 23rd, his suggestion was acted upon three days later.

[13] Note from Boris Ponomarev to comrades Stalin, Malenkov, Molotov, Beria, Mikoyan, Kaganovich, Bulganin, and Khrushchev, June 23, 1951. RGASPI, f. 82, op. 2, d. 1330, l. 62.

the escape. <u>The comrades from the party had permitted me</u>," Nâzım emphasized, "to organize my own escape" without the involvement of anyone else.[14]

This version of events that Nâzım sent to Stalin and the rest of the Central Committee conflicts with the usual story surrounding his escape, i.e., that it was Nâzım's brother-in-law, Refik Erduran, who had organized everything and captained the motorboat that Nâzım had taken from Istanbul. Born in 1928, Erduran was the husband of Nâzım's half-sister Melda, the daughter from Hikmet Bey's second marriage. Erduran had grown up in Istanbul as part of a well-off family—his father had worked as the legal advisor to a state-owned shipping company. After studying at Istanbul's Robert College and then in the US at Cornell University, Erduran had returned to Istanbul, marrying Melda in the fall of 1950.[15]

Erduran had recently begun his compulsory military service. In memoirs that he would publish in 1987, Erduran presents himself as the organizer of Nâzım's flight from Turkey.

> After weighing everything in my own mind and coming to a complete decision I spoke to Nâzım *Ağabey*.
>
> "You need to get away from Turkey for a while," I said.
>
> "But will they give me a passport?" he asked, grimacing with sorrow.
>
> I smiled along with him. In fact, I think I even laughed out loud...
>
> I took a deep breath. With the most persuasive possible tone of voice that I could hope for:
>
> "Go without a passport," I said.
>
> He didn't act so surprised. But he became all ears.
>
> "How?"
>
> "By sea. Going from the mouth of the Bosphorus to the Bulgarian border is like going from Istanbul to Tekirdağı. In calm weather with a fast boat you can get there quickly."[16]

According to Erduran's memoirs, he knew from first-hand experience that the Turkish Coast Guard did not regularly patrol the area of the Black Sea directly north of the mouth of the Bosphorus. Through an uncle who was the naval commander for the Northern Istanbul region, moreover, Erduran had learned that the Turkish navy did not have much of a presence in the region either. Nor did the customs service, which was "hopelessly ineffective," in the opinion of Erduran's uncle.

---

[14] "Some information regarding Nâzım Hikmet," June 26, 1951, from Pukhlov to V. G. Grigorian. From Nâzım Hikmet personal file, RGASPI, f. 495, op. 266, d. 47, Part I, ll. 17–23, here l. 20. Underlining in original.

[15] Göksu and Timms, *Romantic Communist*, 249–250.

[16] Erduran, *Gülerek*, 62.

264 RED STAR OVER THE BLACK SEA

In Erduran's account, the motorboat that he and Nâzım used that day came from Malik Yolaç. A wealthy young man who would go on to become a parliamentarian and publisher, Yolaç was also doing his military service at this time. In an interview he would later give to Turkish journalist Bilal Özcan, Yolaç confirmed that he had put the Chris-Craft motorboat up for sale, and that Erduran and a woman had shown up one day to look the boat over. They expressed interest in purchasing the vessel, but wanted to take it out for a test ride first. Erduran had later come by on his own, without the woman, to pick up the craft.[17]

The one-man escape story that Nâzım provided to Stalin and the rest of the Central Committee strains credulity.[18] There is no record of Nâzım Hikmet ever buying a motorboat, and no one has come forward to claim that they sold him one.[19] Nowhere, moreover, in the numerous books of memoirs about Nâzım that Zekeriya, Sabiha, and Yıldız Sertel would write in later years, is there any indication that either Zekeriya or Sabiha had any connection with Nâzım's flight.[20]

Why would Nâzım take the risk of telling lies to Stalin? By giving Soviet officials the impression that he had masterminded his own escape, Nâzım was likely trying to shield both his accomplices and himself from scrutiny. On the one hand, no good would come to Erduran or Yolaç if it were to become known in Turkey that they had helped him to flee. Even more important to Nâzım may well have been hiding, from Soviet officials, the fact that two Turkish military officers had been responsible for ferrying him out of Turkey.

Among the documents that Ponomarev forwarded to Stalin and the other members of the Central Committee on June 26 was a biographical reference-report ("spravka") about Nâzım that went back to his earliest years with the party. This paperwork indicated that Nâzım had previously been expelled from the TKP "due to his participation in a 'Trotskyite-Police' opposition." Interestingly, however, this note—which was likely written by İsmail Bilen—also went on to state that "the Politburo of the TKP reversed this decision in 1935," information that is not corroborated in any paperwork in Nâzım's file from the late 1930s or 1940s.[21] It may well have been the case that İsmail Bilen inserted this detail into Nâzım's file as a means of softening the blow of some of its more damning material.[22]

After reviewing Ponomarev's materials, the Central Committee voted to accept Fadeyev's proposal that the Writers' Union invite Nâzım to Moscow. An order was

---

[17] Göksu and Timms, *Romantic Communist*, 250.

[18] Yıldız Sertel notes how happily surprised her father had been to hear the news of Nâzım's escape, Yıldız Sertel, *Babam Zekeriya Sertel: Susmayan Adam* (İstanbul: Cumhuriyet Kitapları, 2002), 333.

[19] But there is evidence that Nâzım had a Swiss bank account. In her memoirs, Sevim Belli recalls unsuccessfully attempting to withdraw, with Nâzım's permission, money from a bank account in Switzerland to give to Münevver shortly after Nâzım had fled Turkey. *Boşuna mı Çiğnedik?*, 320.

[20] In Nâzım's letter to Stalin and the rest of the Central Committee, he notes that "the husband of my sister" piloted the boat, but neither mentions Erduran's name nor credits him with any other aspect of the escape. RGASPI, f. 495, op. 266, d. 47, Part I, ll. 12–23, here 20. From June 26, 1951.

[21] RGASPI, f. 82, op. 2, d. 1330, l. 64. "Spravka" on Nâzım Hikmet from June 1951 and a summary of materials relating to him from years past.

[22] Covering up Nâzım's expulsion altogether would have been unwise, given the great amount of paperwork pertaining to the incident that was still in existence.

then put through to find him a place to live, a "3–4 room apartment," which was expected to be ready for Nâzım "within 15 days."[23]

Living in a no man's land no longer, Nâzım caught a flight to Moscow for the final leg of his improbable journey.

## Early Days in Moscow

Once he had finally arrived in Moscow on June 29, Nâzım was given a hero's welcome. In contrast to the earlier Soviet press coverage regarding Nâzım's escape, the landing of his Aeroflot flight from Bucharest was a widely-covered media event. He was bombarded with congratulatory letters and telegrams: the National Writers' Committee in Paris, the Minister of Education and Culture of Czechoslovakia, and the Writers' Union of Vietnam all sent their best wishes. So too did representatives of student groups, trade unions, clubs, and other manifestations of top-down socialist civil society.[24]

At the aerodrome, Nâzım held a press conference alongside the group of Soviet writers who had come to meet him. After speaking for some time about his incarceration and answering queries about how people lived in Turkey, Nâzım suddenly paused and asked: "Perhaps it would interest you to hear about how they tortured us?" The Soviet poet Alexander Zharov responded by stating that he and the other writers "hadn't wanted to ask about this."[25]

"It was dark," began Nâzım. "There was little space." "They threw me into a room. The rain was dripping in because all of the windows had been broken; there were no windowpanes. In the room there was nowhere to sleep, I had only the clothes on my back. I spent six months like this," an apparent reference to his 1938 detention on the *Yavuz*. He told the assembled writers that he had been given just one glass of water a day. The stench was gut-wrenching, but Nâzım was able to get through it, he told the crowd assembled before him, by composing new poetry and singing revolutionary songs with his comrades.[26]

Nâzım's early schedule in the USSR was tightly organized, and every one of his first ten days in Moscow had two or three activities planned. Interestingly, the itinerary was heavily laden with touristic undertakings that would seemingly be more appropriate for a short-term visitor, rather than a potentially long-term exile. With the lion's share of Nâzım's early days spent strolling through museums, attending concerts, and inspecting Soviet accomplishments like the Moscow metro, there was little time left over for him to meet with state or party officials. Among the twenty-four activities listed for Nâzım during his first ten days in the capital, only two even hinted at a

---

[23] "Resolution of the Central Committee of the VKP (b). On admitting Nâzım Hikmet and providing him with accommodation." RGASPI, f. 82, op. 2, d. 1330, l. 73. June 29, 1951.

[24] "Telegrams to Nâzım Hikmet." RGALI, f. 631, op. 26, d. 168, ll. 1–50, here ll. 26, 28, 41.

[25] "Shorthand record of the poet Nâzım Hikmet's meeting with Soviet writers." RGALI, f. 631, op. 26, d. 5603, ll. 1–14, here ll. 3–4, June 30, 1951. This is the date the report was sent, not the date of the exchange, which was June 29 at the aerodrome, as is indicated in f. 631, op. 26, d. 5602, l. 1.

[26] "Shorthand record." RGALI, f. 631, op. 26, d. 5603, ll. 1–14, here ll. 8–10.

context other than the purely ceremonial. But even in these cases, the timing of Nâzım's visits seemed designed to emphasize a social, rather than political, connection: visiting the party secretariat on a Saturday (June 30), and going to the offices of *Literaturnaia Gazeta* on a Friday evening (July 6).[27]

He appeared frequently in the news that first month. In *Pravda* on July 1, there was a small story about his meeting with Soviet writers the day before.[28] A few days later, he was visiting Lenin's tomb in Red Square.[29] On July 11, a news item on *Pravda*'s page 2 reported that, the night before, Nâzım had held "a meeting with Muscovites" in the Great Hall of the Polytechnical Museum.[30] On July 24, one of Nâzım's poems, "After getting out of prison…" was published in Russian translation on the front page of *Literaturnaia Gazeta*.[31] Five days later, *Pravda* published a letter Nâzım wrote which denounced, once again, American–Turkish relations. In this open missive, Nâzım intoned that "the Turkish people have the ability to fight for their national independence. They can and will fight to deliver themselves from the subjugation of American imperialism."[32] Two days later, on August 1, Nâzım read poems at a rally for peace held in Moscow.[33]

Soon, however, he would be on the move again.

## Speaking Stalinist

A commonly told anecdote from Nâzım's first days back in Moscow relates to a speech that he supposedly gave at the Writers' Union. According to this story, Nâzım criticized Soviet theater in front of a large gathering of dignitaries who had come to a banquet in his honor. "I have seen ten plays in ten days," Nâzım is reported to have said. "Actually, it was the same play each time, with a different title—all of them in praise of Stalin."[34] Typically, this anecdote is presented as evidence that Nâzım was naïve about life in the Soviet Union in the early 1950s, unaware that criticizing this ubiquitous praise for Stalin could possibly land him in trouble.[35]

---

[27] "Plan for the Arrival in the Soviet Union of Turkish Writer Nâzım Hikmet." RGALI, f. 631, op. 26, d. 5602, ll. 1–2. Undated.

[28] On Nâzım meeting with the writers, see *Pravda*, "Nazym Khikmet v gostiakh u Sovetskikh pisatel'ei," July 1, 1951, p. 2.

[29] In this story, Nâzım is described as someone who was "staying" (*gostiashchii*) in Moscow. "Poseshchenie mavzoleia V.I. Lenina Nazymom Khikmetom," *Pravda*, July 5, 1951, p. 2.

[30] "Vstrecha Moskvichei s Nazymom Khikmetom," *Pravda*, July 11, 1951, p. 2.

[31] "Vyidia iz tiurmy," *Literaturnaia Gazeta*, July 24, 1951, p. 1.

[32] Nâzım Hikmet, "Reshenie, prodiktovannoe strakhom," *Pravda*, July 29, 1951, p. 4.

[33] "Iskusstvo i literatura v bor'be za mir," *Pravda*, August 2, 1951, p. 4.

[34] Göksu and Timms inexplicably use Refik Erduran as a source for this anecdote, *Romantic Communist*, 259–260.

[35] Individuals who have repeated this story include the famed Soviet poet Yevgeni Yevtushenko, who relates his version of the event from the perspective of a witness, although he would have been just eighteen at the time and unlikely to have been invited to such an affair. See Yevgeny Yevtushenko's preface "Great Actor—Pity about the Play!" in Göksu and Timms, *Romantic Communist*, xiii–xxiii. Also see Göksu and Timms, *Romantic Communist*, 260; Can Dündar, *Nâzım* (İstanbul: Can Sanat Yayınları, 2014), 24–26; Blasing, *Nâzım Hikmet*, 201.

Did this banquet ever take place, and did Nâzım actually say these things? As is the case with many stories relating to Nâzım, it is difficult to pin this incident down in terms of concrete detail. His early activities in Moscow were closely controlled, and there is no indication, in Nâzım's itinerary for his first ten days (and nights), of any banquet taking place at the Writers' Union.[36]

It also seems unlikely that Nâzım would have been so shocked by the Stalinist cult of personality. Even prior to arriving in Moscow, Nâzım had appeared to be quite fluent in "speaking Stalinist," i.e., invoking the leader's name when making public utterances.[37] While still in Bucharest Nâzım had dictated, by telephone, a "Letter to Moscow" to the literary newspaper *Literaturnaia Gazeta*, in which he was quoted as saying that he was "indebted to Comrade Stalin" for having taught him the "science" of Marxist-Leninist theory when Nâzım was a student in Moscow in the 1920s.[38]

On June 29, the day Nâzım arrived in Moscow, Ponomarev had sent a message to the Central Committee in which he quoted Nâzım as having said the following:

[T]he Turkish people, like all honest people that busy themselves with peaceful labor, want peace and fight for it under the sign of Stalin, the great friend and father of all progressive humanity. I speak of Stalin, because Stalin is the light of my eye...[39]

On June 30, meanwhile, Nâzım was quoted in *Pravda* as saying that, when he had come to Moscow for the first time at age nineteen, "I studied at a university which bore the name of Stalin, [and] listened to Stalin's lectures.[40] For me Stalin—the greatest person in all the world—is someone who taught me very much."[41]

Shortly thereafter, Nâzım published an opinion piece on page 3 of *Pravda*. Running under the title "The Peace and Life Front Will Win," it expanded upon the "peace and life" camp versus "death and war" theme that he had earlier introduced in Romania. Nâzım's note on the cover of *Scânteia* had identified Stalin as the "hand that carries the flag" of peace and life, and now he employed an even grander metaphor for praising the Soviet leader:

With each passing day, the ship of peace and life comes closer to the great illuminated port, sometimes sailing upon the glassy blue smoothness of the sea, sometimes along a stormy ocean. He sets his anchor down in this port, because this captain who

---

[36] The itinerary for his first ten days lists four nights at the theater. RGALI, f. 631, op. 26, d. 5602, ll. 1–2.

[37] Stephen Kotkin coined the term "Speaking Bolshevik" as a means of describing the discourses employed in the Soviet Union under Stalin and "the barometer of one's political allegiance to the cause." *Magnetic Mountain: Stalinism as a Civilization* (Berkeley, CA: University of California Press, 1997), 220. I, meanwhile, am simply referring to people invoking Stalin's name publicly.

[38] *Literaturnaia Gazeta*, "Pis'mo v Moskvu," June 26, 1951.

[39] RGASPI, f. 82, op. 2, d. 1330, l. 71. Letter to Stalin from B. Ponomarev, the Assistant Chairman of the External Committee, June 29, 1951.

[40] Following its opening, KUTV had been named after Stalin.

[41] *Pravda*, "Nazym Khikmet v Moskve," June 30, 1951. For the shorthand notes of the questions Nâzım was asked, see RGALI, f. 631, op. 26, d. 5603.

268 RED STAR OVER THE BLACK SEA

is standing at the helm is one of the greatest people to have ever been created by humanity. His name is Stalin.[42]

"Twenty-five thousand doves," began a poem Nâzım published in *Pravda* in August 1951, "are flying these days to the ends of the earth...The Anglo-American imperialists and their lackeys fear the flight of these doves...these doves carry on their wings peace, freedom, national independence, and in their hearts—love for Stalin."[43]

While Nâzım may indeed have criticized the plays praising Stalin in the manner that has frequently been attributed to him, doing so would have been completely out of character with how Nâzım was behaving in even his earliest days in Romania and the USSR. For as long as Stalin was still alive, and even after his death, Nâzım was very cautious with respect to his public utterances and written references regarding the Soviet leader.

He was not a naïve idealist by this time. If anything, Nâzım's early days in the Eastern Bloc reveal a far greater degree of calculation and planning than he has normally been given credit for. Far from blurting out that the emperor had no clothes, Nâzım knew well to be careful and measured. He had taken to speaking Stalinist as if it were his native tongue.

## Reunion with Bilen

Not long after getting to Moscow on June 29, Nâzım was back in touch with İsmail Bilen. Bilen was favorably inclined toward Nâzım, having defended him, in the late 1930s, at a time when no one else in the TKP or Comintern did. He was also one of Nâzım's few friends who knew anything about navigating the Soviet political world. İsmail was still very influential, even in the post-Comintern era. He was also savvy, a survivor who knew how to work the system.

Nâzım and İsmail soon formed a partnership of sorts. Just three weeks after Nâzım's arrival in the USSR, he and İsmail submitted to Stalin and the rest of the Central Committee a series of recommendations for the revitalization of the Turkish Communist Party. "Turkey," the proposal began, "is one of the military bases of American imperialism."[44] For this reason, "the necessary objective conditions have ripened for the creation of a broad and united national front in Turkey against American imperialism and its lackeys."

In particular, Nâzım and İsmail put forward three proposals:

1. Create organizations and committees in support of a united national front against the Americans.

---

[42] Nâzım Hikmet, "Front mira i zhizni pobedit!" *Pravda*, July 27, 1951, p. 3.
[43] *Pravda*, "Twenty-five thousand doves," August 20, 1951.
[44] RGASPI, f. 82, op. 2, d. 1330, ll. 82–86, here 82. Letter to the Central Committee CPSU from Marat (İsmail Bilen) and Nâzım Hikmet. July 23, 1951.

2. Establish a Foreign Bureau outside Turkey that would be a part of the Central Committee of the TKP.
3. Found an illegal organization inside Turkey that would collect information for the radio and press.

Why establish a "Foreign Bureau?" In Turkey, the TKP was much smaller and weaker than it had been in previous decades. In the 1920s and 1930s, the party's General Secretary in Istanbul and the TKP Representative to the Comintern in Moscow had served as "co-leaders" of a sort, each concerned with developments in their respective territory. As crossing the border between Turkey and the Soviet Union had become more difficult, however, and communications between the two branches of the party grew weaker, they began to function more independently of one another. By the late 1940s, there were few real links remaining between Moscow and the TKP in Turkey.

Creating a TKP Foreign Bureau in the Eastern Bloc would establish a Central Committee-like entity that would formally respect the illusion that the TKP in Turkey was still a fully functioning organization. Not coincidentally, forming an institution like this could additionally provide sinecures for the individuals who controlled it.[45]

Nâzım and İsmail also wanted to develop Turkish-language radio broadcasting and publishing services in the Eastern Bloc. As a means of upgrading these services, they made five principal recommendations:

1. Create a radio broadcasting organization by the name of "Radio Independent Turkey" that would operate as an organ of the united national front against imperialism and fascism.
2. Strengthen the Turkish-language services of radio broadcasting in Moscow and the people's republics.
3. Restore the publication of the central press organ of the TKP.
4. Create a new press organ that would circulate the ideas of peace and the independence front.
5. Translate, into Turkish, the classic works of Marxist-Leninism for the preparation and training of party cadres.

In order to carry out these plans, Nâzım and İsmail argued that it was necessary to import Turkish communists, illegally if necessary, from Turkey. The proposed list of individuals to be brought in included a number of Nâzım's close friends and associates, such as the Sertel family, the writer Fahri Erdinç, and Kemal Tahir, the novelist and old friend of Nâzım from Çankırı Prison.[46]

---

[45] On İsmail's move into publishing and broadcasting, also see "spravka" of İsmail Bilen, RGASPI, f. 495, op. 266, d. 12, Part I, l. April 3, 1961.

[46] Also on the list was Mehmet Ali Aybar, who was not only a well-known communist activist in Turkey, but also a famous athlete and relative of Nâzım Hikmet. Letter from Nâzım Hikmet and İsmail to the Central

On August 4, 1951, Nâzım and İsmail received word that the Central Committee had agreed to virtually every suggestion they had made. While the question of creating an illegal organization inside Turkey was left unaddressed, the Central Committee did pledge support for the establishment of a new radio broadcasting service beamed toward Turkey. They also agreed to bolster existing Turkish-language services at Radio Moscow. The committee even expressed support for bringing in Nâzım's friends to help work on broadcasting and publishing, although not all of the individuals that Nâzım and İsmail specified would end up living in the Eastern Bloc.[47] While in principle the idea of creating a "Foreign Bureau" was accepted by the Central Committee, in practice such an organization would only come into being several years later, in 1962.

The shadowy Bilen and the "romantic communist" Nâzım are often juxtaposed, in Nâzım's biographies, as stark contrasts to one another.[48] Without question, there were clear differences in style between the two comrades. When it came to their politics, however, Nâzım Hikmet and İsmail Bilen constituted two sides of the same coin.

## The Berlin Diaries

In early August 1951, Nâzım was asked to travel to East Germany to take part in the International Youth Festival. This was a massive, communist-organized get-together taking place every two years in Eastern European capitals. In 1947, the inaugural event had been held in Prague, and the festival took place in Budapest in 1949. Between August 5 and 19, the third festival would be staged in the Soviet-occupied sector of Berlin.[49]

But how to get there? Nâzım had no passport for foreign travel, and his Turkish citizenship had been rescinded by a vote in parliament shortly after his flight from the country. As he had not been given Soviet citizenship, Nâzım was now stateless. Instead of a passport, the Soviet Union had provided him with travel papers that could be used only if he crossed the border alongside a specified state representative.

Nâzım used to joke that this person was his "human passport."[50] The "human passport" may also have been the one sending dispatches back to Moscow detailing Nâzım's activities abroad. Writing under the name "F. Adılov," this individual addressed his reports to one Comrade Grigorian.[51] Grigorian worked for the

---

Committee of the Communist Party (b) of the Soviet Union, July 23, 1951. RGASPI, f. 82, op. 2, d. 1330, ll. 82–86. Erdinç was already living in Bulgaria, having crossed illegally from Turkey in 1949.

[47] The Central Committee's response can be found in RGASPI, f. 82, op. 2, d. 1330, ll. 90–92, August 4, 1951. Also see "Resolution regarding project recommended to Central Committee of the VKP (b) and answers to questions." RGASPI, f. 82, op. 2, d. 1330, ll. 109–111. September 7, 1951.

[48] See, for example, Göksu and Timms, *Romantic Communist*, 285, 319; Blasing, *Nâzım Hikmet*, 205.

[49] On Turks at the Berlin festival, also see Sayılgan, *Türkiye'de Sol Hareketler*, 291–292.

[50] On the "human passport," see Zekeriya Sertel, *Nâzım Hikmet'in Son Yılları*, 28–29, 70.

[51] For the report sent to Grigorian, see RGASPI, f. 495, op. 266, d. 47, Part II, ll. 158–163. August 27, 1951.

Cominform, an institution created to manage some of the former responsibilities of the Comintern.[52]

In his report from East Berlin, Adılov paid particularly close attention to Nâzım's interactions with other Turks. Such was the case, for example, with a young woman named Sevim Tarı. Tarı was born into an upper middle-class family in the Istanbul district of Beylerbey in 1925. She had studied in the United States, and then in France, developing an interest in communism in the early 1940s. According to her party paperwork, Sevim became a member of the TKP in 1945. She had gotten to know the Sertels' daughter Yıldız while studying medicine in Paris, and the two friends had worked together with the "Union of Progressive Young Turks," a Turkish communist organization that was based in France.[53] Regarding Sevim's meetings with Nâzım, Adılov had little to report, noting that "they immediately cut short their conversation" every time that he had come within eavesdropping range.[54]

In Berlin, Nâzım also met up with Sabiha Sertel. The Sertels had left Turkey before Nâzım.[55] According to party records in Moscow, Sabiha and Zekeriya had, in September 1950, first traveled to Italy, where their older daughter Sevim was living with her American journalist husband, Frank O'Brien. At the beginning of 1951, Sabiha and Zekeriya made their way to Paris, while their younger daughter, 27-year-old Yıldız, stayed behind in Italy with her older sister.[56] Also leaving Turkey at this time was Abidin Dino, who likewise had initially settled in Italy before moving on to Paris.[57]

According to Adılov's report, Sabiha Sertel arrived at the Berlin festival on the evening of August 13, having traveled there from Paris. Adılov noted that, as was the case with Sevim Tarı, Sertel did not speak much in front of him. However, Adılov did remark that Nâzım had conversed with him privately about Sertel, emphasizing the degree to which she had played a decisive role "in the organization of Nâzım's escape from Turkey."[58] This comment—which marked one of the few occasions on which he seemed eager to divulge information to Adılov—may well have constituted an effort by Nâzım to feed his handler—and the people to whom Adılov was reporting—his narrative regarding how he had escaped to the Eastern Bloc.[59]

---

[52] Grigorian is described as having been a "close associate of Lavrentii Beria" in Jerry F. Hough, "Soviet Policymaking toward Former Communists," *Studies in Comparative Communism*, vol. 15, no. 3 (Autumn 1982), 167–183, here 170. On the Cominform, see ibid., 168. On Grigorian also see, from Hough, Werner G. Hahn, *Postwar Soviet Politics: The Fall of Zhdanov and the Defeat of Moderation, 1946–53* (Ithaca and London: Cornell University Press, 1982), 77, 107, 220, fn. 18.

[53] *L'Union des jeunes turcs progressistes*. See Sevim Tarı's personal file, RGASPI, f. 495, op. 266, d. 271. Another member of the "Young Turks" that Nâzım met with in East Berlin was Doğan Aksoy, a 23-year-old Turk who was also studying in France at this time. On Doğan Aksoy, see RGASPI, f. 495, op. 266, d. 302, l. 3; Atay, *Serteller*, 296. On the Union of Progressive Young Turks, see Sayılgan, *Türkiye'de Sol Hareketler*, 286–291.

[54] RGASPI, f. 495, op. 266, d. 47, Part II, l. 159. For Sevim Tarı's account of her meeting in Berlin with Nâzım, see Belli, *Boşuna mı Çiğnedik?*, 316–321.

[55] Yıldız Sertel, *Babam Zekeriya Sertel*, 331.

[56] RGASPI, f. 495, op. 266, d. 23, l. 27. From a report on Sabiha Sertel filed on September 8, 1951. The Sertels had also sought asylum in the United States in 1945. See Ryan, "The Republic of Others," 208–209; Atay, *Serteller*, 280–283. On this period of the Sertels' lives, also see Yıldız Sertel, *Annem*, 235–237.

[57] He was later joined by his wife Güzin. On Dino, see RGASPI, f. 495, op. 266, d. 273, l. 14. "Spravka" on Abidin Dino from July 1953.

[58] RGASPI, f. 495, op. 266, d. 47, Part II, ll. 158–162. Here, ll. 160–161. August 27, 1951.

[59] I.e., that he had organized it himself with the money Sabiha had allegedly sent to him from Paris.

Nâzım appears to have understood that he was being surveilled. Commenting, for example, upon the general disinclination of Nâzım's interlocutors to speak in his presence, Adılov described an incident involving a physically handicapped Turkish student who had met with Nâzım in Berlin. Adılov, reporting to Moscow, wrote that "whenever Nâzım talked about this student with me, he simply called him 'the cripple' (*khromoi*). I felt that he didn't want me to learn his name." "It was clear," added Adılov, "that the student had been warned against mentioning his own name."[60] Adılov also noted that, in the face of the adulation he had been receiving in Berlin, Nâzım had tauntingly turned to him and said: "You see how they receive me. Talk about this to your comrades in Moscow!"[61]

After so many years of official harassment in Turkey, it must have felt nice to again be the object of public affection. At the same time, however, Adılov's account of Nâzım's reception may have given authorities in Moscow cause for concern:

> …at every meeting Nâzım was met with thunderous applause, especially among the delegates from eastern countries and from France. At a meeting of youth from colonial Arab countries, Nâzım was carried aloft in people's arms from his car to the place where the meeting was held—about 200 meters, amid the chants "Long live Nâzım Hikmet!" And many times they repeated the words: "Stalin," "Nâzım Hikmet!"[62]

Zekeriya Sertel, writing in the late 1970s, recalled that Nâzım had been "intoxicated" by the attention he had received at the festival.[63] Sertel was not the only one to notice this. "Based upon his conversations and behavior," recorded Adılov in a report to Moscow, "it is possible to conclude that [Nâzım] would really like to be not only a popular poet, but also a popular leader."[64]

According to Adılov, Nâzım had also met several times with Hasan Kudsi from the Syrian delegation. Nâzım, in Adılov's words, "told me that, through these meetings, he hoped to establish ties between the Communist Party of Turkey and the Communist Party of [Syria]. Hasan promised to help him with the sending of people [to Turkey] through Syria, and, if necessary, to provide support to those who cross the border into Syria from Turkey."[65]

Despite Hasan's pledges of support to Nâzım in Berlin, the young Syrian would later excoriate the poet-communist's conduct at the festival. In a letter he later sent to party offices in Bucharest, Hasan complained about Nâzım's propensity for loose talk.

---

[60] Report by F. Adılov on Nâzım's activities at the Berlin festival. RGASPI, f. 495, op. 266, d. 47, Part II, ll. 158–163, here l. 159. August 27, 1951.

[61] RGASPI, f. 495, op. 266, d. 47, Part II, ll. 158–163, here 162. Letter from Adılov to Grigorian.

[62] Nâzım Hikmet personal file, RGASPI, f. 495, op. 266, d. 47, Part II, l. 162. Report to V. G. Grigorian. August 27, 1951.

[63] Zekeriya Sertel, *Nâzım Hikmet'in Son Yılları*, 31. On meeting with Nâzım and the others in Berlin, also see Benderli, *Giderayak*, 40–44.

[64] Report by F. Adılov on Nâzım's activities at the Berlin festival. RGASPI, f. 495, op. 266, d. 47, Part II, l. 162. August 27, 1951.

[65] RGASPI, f. 495, op. 266, d. 47, Part II, l. 161. Adılov noted in his report that Nâzım had proposed a similar arrangement to the Israeli representative.

Writing that the poet "behaves carelessly," Hasan warned that Nâzım's approach to openly discussing politics "can be the cause of many very serious mistakes, including mistakes relating to conspiratorial work." Kudsi's complaint soon found its way to authorities in Moscow, where it was forwarded to Stalin himself in January 1952.[66]

## Other People's Doors

In September 1951, Nâzım undertook his second foreign visit on behalf of party authorities. This time, he was traveling to Bulgaria. The trip coincided with a period of considerable unrest within Bulgaria's Turkish minority communities. A botched attempt by Sofia at forcing ethnic Turks out of Bulgaria, followed by a reversal of this policy, had now metastasized into an uncontrollable flow of ethnic Turks toward the border with Turkey.

Most of the immigrants who had thus far crossed the border into Turkey were carrying legally issued exit visas from the Bulgarian government. Estimates from this time were that approximately 140,000 Turks had already left the country, out of what had once been a population of 700,000.[67] The government in Sofia had been the party chiefly responsible for initiating the exodus. Now realizing, however, that losing so many people would have a disastrous impact upon the country's agricultural and industrial development, Sofia had suddenly changed course again and begun employing force as a means of preventing ethnic Turks from leaving.

On August 7, 1951, Bulgarian premier Chervenkov sent a letter to Georgii Malenkov, a Central Committee member of the CPSU in Moscow, inviting Nâzım to Bulgaria.[68] The thinking behind this invitation was that Nâzım, a Turkish communist, would perhaps be more successful in convincing Bulgarian Turks to give up their efforts to leave the country. He arrived in Sofia on September 9.[69]

Nâzım would later recite the statistics from his two-week visit to Bulgaria with the numbers-oriented zeal of a collective farm director. He had, Nâzım noted, gone to fifteen cities and fourteen villages, given a total of twenty public talks, held nine closed discussions with party activists, conducted twelve forums with representatives of the Turkish population, and, in total, interacted with an estimated 130,000 people.[70]

Once again, Adılov accompanied Nâzım, keeping an eye on his charge and reporting on his activities. In an account that he filed with Grigorian on October 4, 1951, Adılov described Nâzım's first conversations with Bulgarian Premier Chervenkov

[66] On Hasan's comments regarding his meeting with Nâzım, see report to Stalin, Malenkov, Molotov, Beria, Bulganin, Mikoyan, Kaganovich, and Khrushchev. January 15, 1952. RGASPI, f. 82, op. 2, d. 1330, ll. 128–129.

[67] Ferdinand Kuhn, "Exodus of Bulgar Moslems Belies Talk of Red War Plans," *The Washington Post*, September 9, 1951, p. 2B.

[68] Letter to G. Malenkov from V. Chervenkov, August 7, 1951. Reproductions from the Bulgarian State Archive that were accessed at the TÜSTAV archive in Istanbul, f. 1, i.o. 7, a.e. 1659, ll. 1–2.

[69] RGASPI, f. 495, op. 266, d. 47, Part II, l. 153. Report from F. Adılov to V. G. Grigorian. October 4, 1951.

[70] Report by Nâzım Hikmet, filed in Sofia on July 2, 1952. Bulgarian State Archive (via TÜSTAV), f. 1, i.o. 32, a.e. 19, ll. 5–6.

upon arriving in Sofia. Nâzım had asked the Bulgarian leader why Turks were leaving the country. Chervenkov, according to Adılov's account, "responded that the [Bulgarian government's] biggest mistake was that they had allowed the emigration of Turks" in the first place. In Chervenkov's words, what they needed most now was "somehow to retain the remaining Turks."[71] Convincing Turks to stay and remain content in their villages became Nâzım's job.

In his dealings with Bulgarian officials, Nâzım focused mainly upon developing Turkish-language media, which, he claimed, was the best means of stabilizing the situation. Noting that the Bulgarian government relied upon Azeris for radio broadcasting in Turkish, Nâzım "emphasized that Turks did not understand Azeris." In talks with party officials in Bulgaria, reported Adılov, Nâzım "recommended they use political émigrés [from Turkey] for this task, as they know the Turkish language."[72] No one appears to have suggested employing Bulgarian Turks for these jobs.

While Adılov spent no time in his report detailing the complaints of Bulgarian Turks, he did describe the arguments that Nâzım made to them against emigration. "In Turkey," Adılov reported Nâzım as saying, "the rural population is starving. There are no schools or hospitals in the villages. Out of every five children born, three die. There is no freedom for the working people. In Turkey, the Americans are the bosses." Nâzım, in Adılov's account, also informed his audiences that "some of the people who left for Turkey have already been arrested and are sitting in prison."[73]

In the summer of 1952, Nâzım sent a report and suggestions for future action to the Central Committee of the Bulgarian Communist Party in Sofia. In this report, Nâzım demonstrated his skill at appropriating the discourses of Stalinist Moscow, placing the responsibility for the events in Bulgaria on the types of people who were typically held accountable for the regime's mistakes. It turned out, according to Nâzım, that "the mullahs, *kulaks*, wealthy middlemen and a portion of the nationalist and reactionary urban intelligentsia" had been causing all of the trouble.[74] In other words, the "most reactionary elements and wealthiest among the Turkish population," who had exploited the "simple people."[75]

Nâzım included, in his report, a list of recommendations for the Bulgarian government. As someone who had only recently risked his life in order to escape Turkey, and whose wife and son were currently trapped in Istanbul, Nâzım's suggestions were telling. The very first point he made was the most unequivocal—stop allowing Turks to emigrate.

"I think that this measure will by no means create dissatisfaction," Nâzım noted optimistically. "To the contrary, the majority of the peasants, even those who have

---

[71] "On the trip to Bulgaria with Nâzım Hikmet," see report from F. Adılov to V. G. Grigorian, October 4, 1951. RGASPI, f. 495, op. 266, d. 47, Part II, ll. 153–157, here l. 154.

[72] RGASPI, f. 495, op. 266, d. 47, Part II, ll. 153–157, see especially ll. 155–156.

[73] RGASPI, f. 495, op. 266, d. 47, Part II, ll. 153–157, here l. 155.

[74] *Kulak* was a term used in Stalinist Russia to describe wealthy peasants who were allegedly wrecking communist plans.

[75] Report by Nâzım Hikmet, received in Sofia on July 2, 1952. Bulgarian State Archive (via TÜSTAV), f. 1, i.o. 32, a.e. 19, l. 7.

a passport, will be pleased by this, as they themselves refer to emigration as an 'epidemic.'" "Don't allow even one Turk, even someone who has a visa, to leave for Turkey," he wrote. "It is necessary to close the door."[76]

By far the most detailed of Nâzım's suggestions were those that related to his favorite subject: Turkish-language publishing and broadcasting. His recommendations to the Bulgarian Communist Party echoed those which he and İsmail had made to the Soviet Central Committee the previous year. They included improving Turkish-language radio services, establishing a new Turkish-language journal that would "help with Marxist-Leninist preparation for party cadres," and publishing a newspaper aimed at Turkish youth in Bulgaria. Other suggestions included "making use of cinema," "installing loudspeakers" in villages to broadcast Turkish-language radio ("especially in cafés"), and publishing Turkish-language textbooks for schoolchildren. To carry out these duties, Nâzım recommended employing political émigrés from Turkey. Once again, the Turks of Bulgaria were left out of Nâzım's plans, except as potential consumers of content.[77]

Biographies of Nâzım tend to discuss his Bulgaria mission in rather idealized terms. Typically, they either pretend that Nâzım spoke truth to power in Bulgaria, or emphasize the degree to which he sought to better the life conditions of the country's Turks.[78] In fact, Nâzım exerted most of his energy on pitching his ideas for expanding state-run Turkish-language media services in Bulgaria, which he hoped would one day be run by his friends from Turkey. Otherwise, he had no suggestions for improving the lives of Bulgarian Turks.

Nâzım told the authorities in Sofia what they wanted to hear, echoing Chervenkov's own words in arguing that the real error had been to allow Turkish emigration in the first place. His overall diagnosis—that the mistake of allowing Turks to emigrate had been cynically manipulated by enemies of the regime—was typical blame-the-victim fiction of the sort that was standard fare in Stalin's USSR.

At least insofar as other people's doors were concerned, the border-crosser had become the border-guard.


## Raising Red Flags

No matter how much Nâzım sought to ingratiate himself in Moscow, he could not outrun his past. On September 8, 1951, Nâzım's checkered party history came back into view. In a party-initiated investigation into Nâzım's background which coincided with his trip to Bulgaria, archivists poring over Comintern and TKP paperwork uncovered unflattering material about him that went well beyond the scope of the

---

[76] Ibid.    [77] Ibid., ll. 12–14.
[78] See, for example, Göksu and Timms, *Romantic Communist*, 264; Zekeriya Sertel, *Nâzım Hikmet'in Son Yılları*, 35; Dündar, *Nâzım*, 38–40; Blasing, *Nâzım Hikmet*, 212.

details that had been disclosed earlier. Summaries of these documents were passed on to Stalin, as well as to other high-ranking Central Committee figures.[79]

It was not a good look. Nâzım was described in this paperwork as having led a group of "renegades," and "set[ting] up his own opposition group against the party leadership in 1929."[80] The report included quotations from nine documents produced between 1925 and 1939, all of which were damning in their assessment of Nâzım's behavior. These had been left out of the brief resume that had been produced back in June, when Nâzım was awaiting a decision on whether or not he would be allowed into the Soviet Union.

On September 21, with Nâzım still in Bulgaria, a second set of archival materials was sent to Stalin, Malenkov, Molotov, Beria, Mikoyan, Kaganovich, Bulganin, Khrushchev, and Suslov. If anything, these looked even worse than the first batch, and featured a relentless onslaught of accusations from years past. In these papers, Nâzım was called "a leader of the Trotsky-Police opposition," an "agent of Kemalism," and a "Trotskyite renegade."[81] While these accusations were not new—the term "Trotsky-Police opposition" had appeared in the "spravka" from June—the sheer force of repetition in these documents was impressive.[82]

Nâzım's behavior at times also invited suspicion, and reinforced whatever doubts Soviet leaders might have had about his loyalty. In October, Sevim Tarı, one of the young Turkish communists that Nâzım had met in Berlin, was arrested in Istanbul. The upshot of Tarı's detention was that sixty-seven people were taken into custody, one of the largest waves of communist arrests in Turkey since the 1930s. Before long, eyes turned to Nâzım.

In a party report sent to Stalin on January 15, 1952, Sevim Tarı was described as having traveled to Istanbul "on an errand for Nâzım Hikmet."[83] This was a reference to Adılov's earlier report from Berlin, which had stated that Tarı "is supposed to pass on messages to comrades in Turkey and return with two or three comrades."[84] Letters written about Nâzım by both Adılov and Hasan Kudsi were cited in this report, along with an analysis stating that some of the individuals that Nâzım had sent Sevim Tarı to meet had likely been agents of the Turkish police.[85]

---

[79] Including Malenkov, Molotov, Beria, Mikoyan, Kaganovich, Bulganin, and Khrushchev.

[80] "Spravka." RGASPI, f. 82, op. 2, d. 1330, l. 113, September 8, 1951.

[81] RGASPI, f. 82, op. 2, d. 1330, ll. 119–124, September 21, 1951.

[82] RGASPI, f. 82, op. 2, d. 1330, l. 64. The "Spravka" on Nâzım Hikmet from June 1951, which I discuss earlier, was quite gentle on Nâzım, claiming (perhaps falsely) that the decision to expel Nâzım from the party had been reversed in the 1930s.

[83] RGASPI, f. 82, op. 2, d. 1330, ll. 128–129, here 128. Report distributed to Stalin, Malenkov, Molotov, Beria, Bulganin, Mikoyan, Kaganovich, and Khrushchev. January 15, 1952.

[84] Nâzım Hikmet personal file, RGASPI, f. 495, op. 266, d. 47, Part II, ll. 158–163, here 159. Letter from Adılov to Grigorian. August 27, 1951. According to Belli's memoirs, Nâzım had asked Sevim to meet with Zeki Baştımar. Belli, *Boşuna mı Çiğnedik?*, 323–325.

[85] RGASPI, f. 82, op. 2, d. 1330, l. 128. Report to Stalin, January 15, 1952. For more on suspicions surrounding Nâzım at this time, see RGASPI, f. 495, op. 266, d. 47, Part II, ll. 158–163. Also see Sevim Tarı personal file, RGASPI, f. 495, op. 266, d. 271, l. 7.

Throughout the course of 1952, Nâzım's mail from Turkish communists was intercepted, opened, and translated into Russian.[86] In May, an envelope addressed to Nâzım from Jak İhmalyan and Hayk Açıkgözyan similarly ended up in the hands of party officials. İhmalyan and Açıkgözyan were Armenian communists from Turkey who had illegally crossed the border into Syria and were now living in Beirut. They hoped to immigrate to the Soviet Union along with their families. The two, alongside Jak's brother Vartan İhmalyan, were all eventually allowed, in 1955, to settle in the Eastern Bloc. Nevertheless, their letter to Nâzım, and a separate one that Açıkgözyan and İhmalyan had sent to the Soviet Embassy in Beirut, claimed that Nâzım had "guaranteed" them visas. This likely did little to enhance Nâzım's stature with party authorities in Moscow, who already had reason to distrust Nâzım's tendency to work independently.[87]

On June 2, 1952, Adılov wrote another report on Nâzım's activities, this time in connection to a writers' conference that they had attended in East Berlin. On this occasion, Adılov sent his report to both Grigorian and to the Central Committee directly.[88] According to Adılov, Sabiha Sertel—who again met with Nâzım at this time—wanted desperately to move to the Eastern Bloc. She was, in Adılov's view, expecting Nâzım to help her with this endeavor.[89] Sabiha, wrote Adılov, wanted to create an Eastern Bloc-based Turkish-language newspaper with a socialist theme. "And wouldn't it be better," Adılov quoted Sabiha as having said to Nâzım, "to invite Yıldız from Italy and, if possible, Zekeriya, too?"

"Be patient," Adılov quoted Nâzım as replying. "Do you think that I do nothing in Moscow, that I'm just running around with girls, and that I forgot about you? I've done everything that I can, but nothing has worked out yet. You need to be patient."[90]

## Turks Across the Danube

Two other Turkish communists that Nâzım had met at the Berlin festival were Gün Benderli Togay and her husband Necil.[91] They were younger than Nâzım's generation, both of them products of the early Turkish Republic, rather than the Ottoman Empire.

---

[86]  See Nâzım Hikmet personal file, RGASPI, f. 495, op. 266, d. 47, Part II, for letters from: "G," April 4, 1952, ll. 111–118; Doğan Aksoy, May 19, 1952, ll. 107–108; Zekeriya Sertel, August 21, 1952, l. 86; unidentified sender, October 13, 1952, ll. 78–79.

[87]  See personal file of Hayk Açıkgözyan, RGASPI, f. 495, op. 266, d. 41, ll. 23–28, here l. 24. Regarding Nâzım's alleged guarantee, see l. 24. For Hayk Açıkgözyan's letter to Nâzım Hikmet, see ll. 36–37. Also see letters from Jak İhmalyan to Nâzım Hikmet, personal file of Jak İhmalyan, RGASPI, f. 495, op. 266, d. 263, ll. 1–8 (undated letter); ll. 20–21 (letter from May 12, 1952).

[88]  RGASPI, f. 495, op. 266, d. 47, Part II, ll. 100–101. June 2, 1952.

[89]  At this time prior to the construction of the Berlin Wall, crossing the border between West and East Berlin was not as difficult as it would later become.

[90]  Report from F. Adılov to V. G. Grigorian, "Information about the trip with Nâzım Hikmet to Berlin for the Congress of German Writers," RGASPI, f. 495, op. 266, d. 47, Part II, l. 101. June 2, 1952. Regarding Yıldız Sertel, see RGASPI, f. 495, op. 266, d. 274.

[91]  On crossing the border into East Germany at this time, see Benderli, *Su Başında Durmuşuz*, 129–131.

Necil Togay was born in 1923 in Istanbul's Bakırköy district, and had studied at Işık Lisesi for high school, graduating in 1942.[92] Due to a traffic accident when he was fourteen, Necil was "unable to do normal work." His family did not hurt for money, however. In Necil's Communist Party autobiography, he noted that his father, a salesman, earned "a very good" salary.[93]

Gün was born on May 2, 1929. She was six years younger than Necil but, due to Necil's medical issues, only three years behind him at Işık, from which Gün had graduated in 1945. Her family was middle class and well-educated—Gün's father was a lawyer, and her mother a teacher. Gün had been in her final year at Işık when she started spending time with Necil Togay. As Gün would recount later, Necil spent nearly all of their first date talking about communism. Later, when a friend asked her what she and Necil had talked about, Gün confessed that she hadn't the slightest idea.[94]

Their courtship had a certain Romeo-and-Juliet quality to it, as Gün's parents did not approve of Necil. Nevertheless, the two were married in 1947. Shortly thereafter, the newlyweds left for France, where they would attend university in Grenoble. Over the next few years, Gün and Necil traveled back and forth between Europe and Istanbul.

Legal problems in Turkey, however, were beginning to follow the young couple abroad. According to party records, after the Turkish government found Gün guilty in absentia of being a member of an illegal communist organization, she would not be able to remain in France. Her choices were to either return to Turkey to face possible jail time, or else flee to an unknown freedom in the Eastern Bloc.[95]

Gün and Necil's arrival in the Eastern Bloc was in line with Nâzım and İsmail's ambitions to develop Turkish-language broadcasting. Young, educated communists from Turkey could certainly be of assistance in this endeavor. Traveling back from Berlin to Paris after meeting with Nâzım at the Youth Festival, the young couple looked forward to receiving word on where they would be going. Soon, Gün and Necil learned that their future would be in Budapest, even as visa-related difficulties in France forced them to temporarily relocate to Geneva.[96] By August 1952, their paperwork was ready.

Immigrating to the Eastern Bloc was a much more decisive act in 1952 than going to Russia had been for Nâzım's generation. For people like Nâzım who had first visited the USSR in the 1920s, there had been no reason to believe that they would not be allowed to later return to Turkey. By contrast, Gün Benderli Togay's generation of Cold War border-crossers had little expectation of ever going home again. For them, crossing the Iron Curtain was largely understood to be a one-way voyage.

The night before they left for Hungary, Gün sobbed for hours. It was forbidden for them to inform any of their friends or family about where they were going, so Gün

---

[92] A Turkish "lise" is a lycée, or high school.
[93] Gün Benderli Togay personal file. RGASPI, f. 495, op. 266, d. 275, l. 1. A smaller personal file of Gün can be found in RGASPI, f. 495, op. 266, d. 272, "Giun." According to NARA records, the US Consulate General in Istanbul had granted Necil Togay a non-immigrant visa in 1945. 782.001/10–2353. October 23, 1953.
[94] "Vallah bilmiyorum!" Conversation with the author, Budapest, June 1, 2018.
[95] RGASPI, f. 495, op. 266, d. 275, ll. 1–1-ob, September 2, 1954.
[96] Benderli, *Su Başında Durmuşuz*, 150–151.

had simply told her parents that she and Necil were heading to "Latin America." As far as Gün was concerned, she would never see them, or her younger sister, again.[97]

The next afternoon, Gün and Necil boarded a train for Hungary.[98] The young couple were met at Budapest's Keleti Pályaudvar station by party officials who took them to their residence. Peering out at this new land from the back seat of the car, Gün was shocked by the devastation that appeared before her. It was as if World War II had ended just the day before.[99]

The rather dismal appearance of Budapest notwithstanding, Gün and Necil were quite pleased by the accommodation that had been provided, an attractive villa that they had all to themselves. After the young couple had begun unpacking their things, however, the men who had picked them up at the station returned with bad news: they had made a mistake. The villa was not intended for Gün and Necil, but rather for another Turkish couple: Sabiha and Zekeriya Sertel.[100] The Sertels, and their daughter Yıldız, were quickly installed in the villa, while the Togays were evicted.

Gün and Necil's new accommodations were considerably less impressive: a room in a dormitory where, Gün would later recall, they shared a toilet with fifteen other students. Sometime not long thereafter, Necil went out of town and Gün, looking for a bit of pampering, moved into a hotel. She liked it so much, recalled Gün in a conversation with me in 2018, that when Necil returned to Budapest she informed him that she wouldn't leave the hotel until he came up with a better place for them to stay. Necil eventually found them a much nicer room in a guesthouse where a number of other foreigners were living.[101]

All of twenty-three years old, Gün had experienced her first victory in the Eastern Bloc.


## Socialist Unrealism


Nâzım's arrival in 1951 had helped to launch a multitude of new translations and editions of his poetry within the Soviet Union and the Eastern Bloc. His books, already experiencing a renaissance in the socialist world during the course of his 1949–50 hunger strikes in Turkey, were the subject of newfound interest.

During the years 1951–53 Nâzım did not write—or at least publish—many new poems. While Soviet publishing houses were busy producing multiple anthologies of his older verse, the most extensive collections of his complete works list just nine new poems written between Nâzım's flight to the Eastern Bloc in June 1951 and Stalin's

---

[97] Conversation with the author, Budapest. June 1, 2018. Benderli, *Su Başında Durmuşuz*, 181.

[98] Gün Benderli writes that they had boarded the train in either Bern or Zürich. *Su Başında Durmuşuz*, 183.

[99] Ibid., 187.

[100] In her party autobiography, Yıldız Sertel wrote that "with the permission of the party" she went to Berlin in order to work at the International Democratic Federation of Women, a pro-Moscow organization in the eastern sector. RGASPI, f. 495, op. 266, d. 274, ll. 1–3, here l. 3. September 2, 1954.

[101] Conversation with the author, Budapest. June 1, 2018.

death in March 1953.[102] This is in stark contrast to the jaw-dropping output of Nâzım's writing in Turkey in the 1930s, a time when he was harassed more or less continuously by various state and military authorities.

Nâzım's works from the early 1950s carry relatively simple political messages. "You're the field, I'm the tractor," written shortly after Nâzım's arrival in the USSR, marked an early attempt to fit into the socialist realist dictates of the Stalinist system.

> You're the field
> I'm the tractor,
> you're paper
> I'm a typewriter

This poem goes on to fantasize about the speaker rescuing a teenage girl.[103]

> You're China
> I'm Mao Zedong's army
> You're a 14-year-old Filipina
> I'm saving you
> > from the hand of an American sailor.[104]

Nâzım's other poems from his first two years back in the USSR were similarly political in rather obvious ways. "Korea *Türkü*" is a dirge-like piece from 1952 that repeats the line "go tell my mother, let my mother weep." "The Man with a Carnation" is a eulogy for the recently deceased Greek communist Nikos Beloyannis, while "The 23 Cent Soldier" refers to US Secretary of State John Foster Dulles, who was reported to have said that Turkish soldiers were "cheap" as they cost "only 23 cents a month" to feed.

In 1952, Nâzım wrote "I'm Thinking of You," which begins with these lines:

> Communist Party of Turkey
> > My TKP
> > > I'm thinking of you
> You're our yesterday, our today, our tomorrow
> our greatest masterpiece[105]

---

[102] The Yapı Kredi edition of Nâzım Hikmet's collected works (*Şiirler* Vol. 6) lists the following poems as having been written during these years: "Sen tarlasın, ben traktör" (1951), "Festivalin Kitabı" (1951), "Seni Düşünüyorum" (Moscow, October 9, 1951), "Ali'nin selamı var" (1952), "Kore Türküsü" (1952), "Çi-Çun-Tin" (Beijing, 1952), "Sözüm Sizedir Fransızlar" (Moscow, 1952), "Karanfilli Adam" (Moscow, May 26, 1952), "Mektup" (1952). The Bulgarian-published Narodna Prosveta edition of Nâzım's complete works also records nine poems from this time, but the list is slightly different: "Seni Düşünüyorum," "Festivalin Kitabı," "Çi-Çun-Tin," "Karanfilli Adam," "Sözüm Sizedir Fransızlar," "Mektup," "Lidya Ivanna," "Vasiyet," "23 Sentlik askere dair." Nâzım Hikmet, *Bütün Eserleri*, vol. 2.

[103] According to Zekeriya Sertel, Soviet censors initially cut out parts from this poem, believing them to sound too racy. *Nâzım Hikmet'in Son Yılları*, 24.

[104] Yapı Kredi edition of Nâzım Hikmet's collected works (*Şiirler* Vol. 6), 9.    [105] Ibid., 14.

This poem goes on to include easy-to-spot heroes and villains: the "American," paving over fields with concrete; "Rahmi the metal cutter," detained by the Turkish police for distributing communist literature; "the student girl," who "read one of my poems to me / your voice is still in my ear"; and other stock characters. Only toward the end does the poem get more personal:

> I'm thinking about you, Mom
> Has the curtain fallen completely before you?
> > Are you in the dark?
>
> I'm thinking of you, my dear wife.
> Has your milk dried out completely,
> Are you now unable to nurse my boy
> my Memet?
>
> Were you able to pay the rent this month?
> Do you think about me?

Not long after returning to the USSR, Nâzım wrote a play called *A Story about Turkey*. This work was published only once, in Russian, in 1952, and it is not included in his Turkish-language anthologies—not even in the Cold War-era Turkish-language edition of his complete works that was later published in Bulgaria.[106] The lone publication of this play was translated into Russian from the original Turkish by Ekber Babayev and Rady Fish, two Soviet Turkish-language specialists who befriended Nâzım in the 1950s.[107]

As Nâzım's biography constituted a large part of his propagandistic value, *A Story about Turkey* comes with a brief foreword, introducing Nâzım as "a laureate of the International Peace Prize," a reference to his WPC award. This introduction also notes that the play "was written on the land of our Russia, where for the first time in many years the poet can create freely."[108]

*A Story about Turkey* bears some resemblance to Nâzım's earlier play-writing from the 1930s, but there are also some significant differences. His earlier plays, like *Bir Ölü Evi* (*A House of Death*, 1932) or *Kafatası* (*The Skull*, 1932) were "realist" in a manner more befitting John Steinbeck than Socialist Realism.[109] *A Story about Turkey*, by contrast, brings a much heavier hand to its subject. The characters are one-dimensional: "good" and "bad" Turks who either resist, or collaborate with, the Americans who are occupying the country.

Despite the simplistic style of this work—or perhaps because of it—the publication of *A Story about Turkey* infuriated the Turkish government. Ankara swiftly

---

[106] *Bütün Eserleri* (Sofia: Narodna Prosveta, vol. 5, 1969).

[107] Fish was a Soviet-born Turkologist. Babayev was a native speaker of Russian and Azeri. On *A Story about Turkey*, see Babayev, *Nâzım Hikmet*, 351–352.

[108] Nazym Khikmet, *Rasskaz o Turtsii* (trans. from Turkish by A. Babayev and R. Fish) (Moscow: Izd-vo inostrannoi literatury, 1952), 3.

[109] On these plays, see Makal, *Beyaz Perdede ve Sahnede Nâzım Hikmet*, 184–187.

banned the play from ever being published, or even brought into Turkey in printed form.[110] *A Story about Turkey* should probably be read less as an example of Nâzım's best creative efforts, and more as something he likely felt he needed to produce in order to establish his Socialist Realist bona fides. The introduction to the play concludes with the observation that *A Story about Turkey* constitutes "a new step for the national poet along the path of Socialist Realism."[111]

Joseph Stalin died on March 5, 1953, following a stroke he had suffered the evening before. Tales abound of individuals—sitting alone at home, where no one else could see them—sobbing tears of genuine grief in response to the news of Stalin's death. The public outpouring of loss was enormous, and often a reflection of real pain and confusion.

Five days after Stalin's death, Nâzım Hikmet published a poem about the fallen leader in *Literaturnaia Gazeta*. Called "I Remember," the work offers a nostalgic and autobiographical perspective. The speaker recalls episodes from his youth—standing on Red Square in the middle of winter, working in the Turkish press in the 1930s, his prison years—and the presence of Lenin and Stalin at each of these moments. The poem ends with the observation that Stalin, like communism itself, is immortal.

> He is like the communism
> that his country embraced long ago;
> and communism
> is endless life
> endless youth
> and endless spring[112]

\*

In an account first published in the late 1970s, Zekeriya Sertel alleged that, during the Stalin years, there had been a government plot to murder Nâzım. Supposedly, Nâzım's chauffeur "Ivan" had been charged with faking a car accident and killing Nâzım in the process. The driver, however, in Zekeriya's telling, liked Nâzım so much that instead of killing him he resigned from his job and told Nâzım about the plot.[113]

This story, like most relating to Nâzım's life in the Eastern Bloc after 1951, originated with Nâzım himself, who in this case had told it to Zekeriya. Its veracity appears questionable. If the KGB had really wanted to kill Nâzım, it seems like this is something they could have eventually managed to pull off, regardless of the resignation of one individual. And why go to such complicated lengths to have someone killed, instead of simply arresting and executing him? It also seems unlikely that Soviet

---

[110] BCA 30-18-1-2/131-27-8, "On the prohibition of Nâzım Hikmet's play 'A Story about Turkey' and its translation in other languages," April 6, 1953.

[111] Khikmet, *Rasskaz o Turtsii*, 3.

[112] *Literaturnaia Gazeta*, March 10, 1953, p. 3.

[113] Zekeriya Sertel, *Nâzım Hikmet'in Son Yılları*, 192–193.

intelligence authorities would have subcontracted such a complicated job to a driver who did not, apparently, already work for them. And just because this driver changed his mind, why would the assassination be called off?

It's an odd story, but one that plays up the notion that Nâzım was somehow too outspoken for the Soviet Union. Nothing, however, could have been further from the truth. While in Turkey, Nâzım had publicly defended his right to believe what he wanted, and he had suffered bitter consequences for having done so. In the USSR, on the other hand, Nâzım was cautious and calculating, cognizant of what he needed to do in order to survive. He had already paid his dues, many times over. Turkey was his homeland, and for as long as he had lived there he had felt obliged to stand up and say what he thought.

In the Soviet Union, on the other hand, Nâzım was a guest. He did what he was asked and he tried his best to fit in.

# 12

# A Kind of Freedom

The letter was written in late 1956, and had been signed by a woman named Irina. In some ways, her note was typical of the sort of fan mail Nâzım received during these years. Irina lived in Moscow with her three-year-old daughter, Oksana—"Oksanochka," as Irina called her. "We live fine," explained Irina, who worked as a nurse in a polyclinic, "together with my parents."

"Everything is fine," Irina repeated, but there was, nevertheless, a problem: little Oksana did not have a father. "Of course, there is a father," her mom explained, "but Oksana was born outside of marriage and—even though [the father] isn't a bad guy, he doesn't want to know that he is a father." Opening up further to the poet she had never met yet somehow felt close to, Irina went on to remark that there had once been someone else in her life, a man with whom she had wanted to raise a family. But he had been killed in the war, leaving Irina to manage as best she could.

She had a question for Nâzım: "Would you be willing to become the girl's godfather?"[1]

*

Almost everyone who wrote to Nâzım now wanted something from him. He was, after all, in a position to give. A celebrity whose books were published everywhere in the socialist world, Nâzım regularly received fan mail from people who felt like they knew him. Fans from the Eastern Bloc asked for autographed copies of his books, while Turks in the USSR appealed to him for assistance. His wife Münevver would also begin corresponding with Nâzım at this time, and she too had needs to ask of him.

Nâzım may have been living the Soviet dream at this time, but in the words of the American poet Delmore Schwartz, "in dreams begin responsibilities."[2]

## Living the Soviet Dream

Materially, Nâzım was better off than he had ever been in his life. As he would mention three separate times during the course of an interview he gave on Radio Budapest in the early 1950s, Nâzım earned what any "well-known writer" made in the USSR.[3] He had been assigned a large apartment in a newly-developed Moscow neighborhood

---

[1] Letter from Irina to Nâzım Hikmet, RGALI, f. 2250, op. 1, d. 289, ll. 9–10. November 5, 1956.
[2] Delmore Schwartz, *In Dreams Begin Responsibilities and Other Stories* (New York: New Directions Paperbacks, 1978), 1–10.
[3] IISH Nâzım Hikmet CD 3: 274, Track 10.

*Red Star over the Black Sea: Nâzım Hikmet and his Generation.* James H. Meyer, Oxford University Press. © James H. Meyer 2023.
DOI: 10.1093/oso/9780192871176.003.0014

near the metro station Sokol, where numerous writers and artists were living. Before long, he was spending his weekends and summers at a dacha in Peredelkino, a leafy writers' colony to the west of Moscow, where his neighbors included Boris Pasternak.[4] In order to drive out to his dacha, Nâzım had been outfitted with a *Pobeda*, a four-door sedan. In the words of one Soviet writer, recalled Zekeriya Sertel in his later memoirs, "Nâzım was a proletarian in a bourgeois country, and in a proletarian country he became part of the bourgeoisie," an observation that I would agree with only halfway.[5]

Nâzım's work was now widely available in Russian, and new collections of his writing came out regularly. In what must have provided enormous satisfaction after years of frustration in Turkey, Nâzım would publish one or two volumes of poetry, plays, or other forms of literary or film production in almost every year of the 1950s.[6] His works were soon translated into several other languages of the USSR, including, early on, Azeri, Armenian, Ukrainian, and Uzbek. In the people's republics of Eastern Europe, his books appeared in Polish, Hungarian, and Bulgarian in 1952–53, with a Romanian edition coming out shortly thereafter. Translations into more than a dozen other languages would come over the course of the decade.

Outside of writing, Nâzım's main job from 1951 onward was to attend various types of meetings within the Soviet Union and internationally.[7] These conferences usually related to literature, culture, or other types of Eastern Bloc-sponsored soft-power diplomatic efforts.[8] Nâzım also took part in numerous congresses in connection with the Soviet-backed "peace" movement, and in particular the WPC. While the bulk of his border-crossing took the form of extended tours through Eastern Europe, in the early-to-mid-1950s Nâzım also visited China, Sweden, Finland, and Austria.

In late June 1952, while visiting Beijing to attend a meeting of Asian members of the WPC, Nâzım suffered a heart attack. Apparently, he was misdiagnosed in China, where doctors told him that he had an upset liver. Flying back to Moscow shortly thereafter, his condition deteriorated. Nâzım fell ill on the plane, then suffered another heart attack en route to the hospital after landing in Moscow. Somehow he survived, and was sent to recover at Barvikha, a sanatorium and health center west of Moscow that was used for treating the party elite.[9]

It was at Barvikha that Nâzım met Dr. Galina Kolesnikova, one of his caregivers.[10] In an interview she gave many years later, Galina described her initial interactions

---

[4] Nâzım did not own this property, but rather had the right to use it, a privilege granted to elite figures like himself.

[5] The second part. Zekeriya Sertel, *Nâzım Hikmet'in Son Yılları*, 63.

[6] The only year for which I could not find Russian-language Soviet publications of his works was 1959.

[7] For an exhaustive collection of published primary source material relating to Nâzım Hikmet and Azerbaijan, see Aslan Kavlak, *"Bakü'ye Gidiyorum Ay Balam." Nâzım Hikmet'in Azerbaycan'daki İzleri (1921–1963)* (2nd edition, İstanbul: Yapı Kredi Yayınları, 2009).

[8] On Nâzım's participation in these conferences, also see Djagalov, *From Internationalism to Postcolonialism*, 65, 72.

[9] Dursun Özden, *Galina'nın Nâzım'ı: Bilinmeyen Yönleriyle* (İstanbul: Kaynak Yayınları, 2007), 32–33. According to Zekeriya Sertel, Nâzım was convinced that he would not live another three years after the heart attack. *Hatırkladıklaırım*, 171.

[10] Özden, *Galina'nın Nâzım'ı*, 28.

with Nâzım in a rather matter-of-fact way. "I was a doctor at the Barvikha sanatorium," she said, "working as deputy director in the internal medicine section. Nâzım stayed there for three months.[11] All the girls aged from sixteen to twenty were falling in love with him, so why shouldn't I?"[12]

Nâzım and Galina—who, like Münevver, was born in 1917—would end up forming a close attachment to each other.[13] According to Galina's later recounting of her early days with the poet, Nâzım was so impressed by the attention she had given him at the sanatorium that he asked her to come and live with him as his personal physician.[14] Galina reported that her reasons for accepting the offer, at least initially, were quite simple: Nâzım gave her mother a "bag full of money," which the woman used to purchase a small home for herself in a village outside Moscow.[15]

The sexual nature of Nâzım and Galina's relationship started later, only after she had moved in with him. From Galina's perspective, Nâzım was difficult to resist, a charming and good-looking gentleman who smiled and complimented women, a breath of fresh air in dour Moscow. He led an exciting, globe-trotting life, traveling all over the USSR and the world. Galina, meanwhile, was single, from the provinces, and inexperienced. At the age of thirty-five she became Nâzım's personal doctor, traveling companion, and, eventually, his lover (Figure 12.1).

Galina understood that Nâzım was in love with Münevver, and not her, as Nâzım made no attempt to hide this fact from her. He would lie down next to Galina and read Münevver's letters aloud, translating them from Turkish to Russian as he went.[16] Because Galina knew that Nâzım was married, she made no claims upon him. As she was officially his personal physician, he was able to live and travel with her while still maintaining a public narrative as the devoted husband and father in exile.

She was good for him. Galina made sure that Nâzım lived in a healthy manner, and Nâzım would famously credit her with having saved his life on four occasions.[17] She helped him decorate his nearly-empty dacha in Peredelkino, bringing a gas heater from home and buying assorted items for the cottage.[18] Galina also possessed certain unexpected skills, such as the ability to knit socks, a hat, and an undershirt for Nâzım from the fur of his much-loved dog, Şeytan ("Devil").[19]

While she knew about Münevver and Mehmet, Galina clearly loved Nâzım. For as long as Nâzım was satisfied with sharing his life with a woman he was fond of, but not in love with, their relationship appears to have been quite stable. Nâzım took their connection seriously, making sure that Galina would be provided for in case anything happened to him. According to a will signed by Nâzım on August 25,

---

[11] Some of Nâzım's friends, such as Zekeriya Sertel, were certain that Galina was employed by the Soviet intelligence services to keep an eye on Nâzım. I have seen no evidence to support such a possibility. Zekeriya Sertel, *Nâzım Hikmet'in Son Yılları*, 184.

[12] Göksu and Timms, *Romantic Communist*, 313.　　[13] Memet Fuat, *A'dan Z'ye Nâzım Hikmet*, 191.

[14] Özden, *Galina'nın Nâzım'ı*, 34.　　[15] Ibid., 35.　　[16] Ibid., 43.

[17] Galina Kolesnikova, *Sem' Let s Nazymom Khikmetom* (Izhevsk: IPM UrO RAN), 3; Göksu and Timms, *Romantic Communist*, 314.

[18] Özden, *Galina'nın Nâzım'ı*, 36.　　[19] Ibid., 120.

**Figure 12.1** In Peredelkino with Galina, 1954

1956, in the event of his death all of his personal possessions, excluding money and books, would go to her.[20]

## Budapest Radio

After a period of transition, Hungary had started to feel like home. Upon arriving in Budapest, Gün and Necil had initially registered as full-time students, taking Hungarian language courses before moving on to more academic subjects. By

---

[20] According to this will, which would later be changed, Nâzım's future publishing royalties were, in the event of his death, to be divided equally between the TKP, on the one hand, and Münevver and Mehmet on the other. Nâzım's books were to be donated to the Lenin Library in Moscow, RGALI, f. 2250, op 1, d. 309, l. 1.

September 1954, they were both enrolled as students, Necil in the Faculty of Economics at Karl Marx University and Gün at the Institue of Marxism-Leninism. The two were also working for the Turkish-language section of Radio Budapest, the international short-wave radio service of the Hungarian People's Republic.[21]

It was an interesting life. Necil and Gün had given up their struggles with the Turkish police and criminal justice system, as well as the hassles they had encountered in applying for and maintaining their visas in France and Switzerland. The physical conditions associated with living in the Eastern Bloc in the early 1950s were at times quite shocking, but they felt like they were doing pretty well. Their stipends went far beyond what most other residents of Budapest were earning. There were also changes taking place with respect to their family life. In 1955, Gün gave birth to a son named Can.

Gün liked her job. Living in Budapest was interesting, and she was a part of a lively international cohort of young communists, a number of whom had become her close friends. Party files indicate that Gün attended student conferences in Prague, Bucharest, and Warsaw in 1953, with trips to Beijing and Moscow in 1954.[22] It is hard to imagine a position that Gün could have held at that time in Turkey that would have similarly taken her around the world in this manner. And, on top of everything else, she was doing all of this in the name of a cause in which she sincerely believed, as did her husband. Gün and Necil were convinced they were on the right side of history, and dug in deep behind the leadership of Stalin.

Also living in Budapest during these years were Sabiha and Zekeriya Sertel, who had arrived shortly after the Togays and appropriated their villa. Sabiha and Zekeriya formed part of the core group of Turkish communists working in Eastern Bloc-based broadcasting in the first half of the 1950s. Daughter Yıldız, who turned thirty in 1953, joined her parents in the Hungarian capital at around this time, describing herself as a journalist in a party autobiography from September 1954.[23]

More TKP members, meanwhile, were on their way. In September 1955, some three years after the letter that Hayk Açıkgözyan and Jak İhmalyan had written to Nâzım from Lebanon, Hayk and his wife Anjel were finally given the chance to immigrate. From Beirut, they traveled to Vienna via ship and rail. Crossing into the Soviet-controlled sector of the city, the two were met by Zekeriya Sertel, who helped them get onto a train to Budapest. At the Budapest train station, Hayk and Anjel were greeted by Nâzım Hikmet, Sabiha Sertel, and İsmail Bilen.[24]

---

[21] Necil was to write in a party autobiography from September 2, 1954, "I work in the Turkish section of Radio Budapest, [and] on the other hand I'm now continuing my studies in the Faculty of Economics at Karl Marx University." RGASPI, f. 495, op. 266, d. 276, ll. 1–3. Gün described her work and life in similar terms. "I've been in Budapest since August 1952," she wrote. "I'm studying in the Institute of Marxism-Leninism, in the second year. At the same time, I'm working in the Turkish section of Radio Budapest." RGASPI, f. 495, op. 266, d. 275, l. 1. September 2, 1954.

[22] Gün Benderli Togay's personal *fond*. RGASPI, f. 495, op. 266, d. 275, l. 1-ob. Party autobiography, September 2, 1954.

[23] Personal file of Yıldız Sertel. RGASPI, f. 495, op. 266, d. 274, l. 3.

[24] Açıkgözyan's memoirs were written under the name Açıkgöz. Açıkgöz, *Anadolulu Bir Ermeni*, 410–423. On Açıkgözyan, also see Güneş, *Suyun Şavkı*.

The Açıkgözyans would soon be sent to Warsaw, where they formed a team alongside Jak İhmalyan and his wife, who had themselves meanwhile arrived in the Eastern Bloc. The four began learning Polish, and then started work as Turkish-Polish wire news translators.[25] In 1956, Jak İhmalyan's brother Vartan, accompanied by his wife, likewise immigrated to the socialist world. Vartan soon began working in the Turkish broadcasting service at Radio Budapest, the latest link in an "eastward" bound chain migration from the "West," in the form of Turkey, to an "East" comprised of Warsaw and Budapest.[26]

In the first half of the 1950s, Nâzım visited Budapest frequently. When in town, he would usually sit down for radio interviews, often with Gün Togay asking the questions. Much of Nâzım's time on the air consisted of his reading poetry—both his own and that of others, such as Orhan Veli's *İstanbul'u dinliyorum* ("I'm Listening to Istanbul"), which Nâzım recited on one occasion.[27] Nâzım also answered what were presented as questions from the radio audience. He used this as an opportunity to explain to listeners why he had fled Turkey, pronouncing that "[i]f I hadn't left, I would have been killed. It's that simple."[28]

He claimed in one broadcast that what he wanted for Turkey was not yet communism, as he did not think it could come straightaway. Instead, said Nâzım, what he advocated for were just "the smallest rights," like the freedom to strike, create political parties that defend the workers' interests, undertake land reform, and "fight for Turkey's independence." On another occasion, Nâzım mentioned that he came to Budapest "a couple of times a year," and that the city reminded him a little bit of Istanbul.[29] Hungarians and Turks were "brother nations" he observed, noting their overlapping histories.[30]

Nâzım also dabbled in literary criticism on the airwaves, albeit of a largely uncritical variety. In 1951, İsmail Bilen published a book of fiction under the pseudonym "S. Üstüngel." Nâzım had authored the foreword to this book, which was called *Savaş Yolu* ("The Road to War"). On air, Nâzım said "I think that with *Savaş Yolu*, Üstüngel has entered Turkish literature in a great way...he has emerged as one of the most patriotic and masterful writers." Nâzım declined, however, the opportunity to read a selection from *Savaş Yolu* himself, turning over the honors to his interviewer.[31]

*Savaş Yolu* is a novel, yet it is told from the perspective of a character who bears a considerable resemblance to İsmail Bilen.[32] It is a heroic story, detailing the exploits and daily life of Turkish communists in prison and underground. *Savaş Yolu* would not be Bilen's last publication. Toward the end of the 1950s, he would publish *İnci Irmağı*

---

[25] Açıkgöz, *Anadolulu Bir Ermeni*, 430–433, esp. 424; Atay, *Serteller*, 335–337, 352–353.
[26] İhmalyan, *Bir Yaşam Öyküsü*, 144–145.
[27] On Nâzım reading Orhan Veli's poems, see IISH, CD 1: 272, Tracks 1–2.
[28] IISH, Nâzım interviews, CD 3: 274. Track 1.
[29] A reference, no doubt, to the fact that Budapest, like Istanbul, is divided by a beautiful waterway.
[30] IISH, Nâzım interviews, CD 3: 274. Track 1.      [31] Ibid.
[32] This book was originally published in Sofia in 1952. The copy that I consulted was the second edition, published in 1958. S. Üstüngel, *Savaş Yolu* (Sofia: Narodna Prosveta, 1958).

## 290 RED STAR OVER THE BLACK SEA

("Pearl River"), which was apparently inspired by İsmail Bilen's trip to China in 1956.[33] In later years, he would produce other books, likewise written in a biographical-fictional style, under the name İsmail Bilen.

Like many from his generation, İsmail had a strong sense of personal narrative. Could İsmail Bilen's literary ambitions, such as they were, have had anything to do with his apparent sympathy for Nâzım? At first glance, Bilen's championing of the poet-communist, especially in the 1930s, seems out of character for the no-nonsense Bolshevik. The fact that Bilen did speak in favor of Nâzım at a time when it was still politically incorrect to do so indicates that, at the very least, İsmail understood that the TKP could benefit from Nâzım's talents and reputation.

But perhaps there was more to it than that. Maybe, like Yevgraf Andreyevich in *Doctor Zhivago*, even a hard-boiled communist like İsmail Bilen could still have a soft spot for poets.

### Cigarettes and Radio Monte Carlo

Münevver Andaç lit another cigarette and took a break from the letter she was composing. She was trying to describe to Nâzım how she spent her days, but the words were not coming easily, not even for this language-oriented polyglot. "I read a lot of books," she jotted down in her small, tight cursive. "I listen to music, I work. I really like translating."[34] Life really wasn't so bad, she explained, especially now that she was allowed to communicate with Nâzım.

Münevver typically wrote her letters to him in the later evening, sometimes in the middle of the night, after Mehmet had gone to bed. Smoking one cigarette after another and sitting at a small table, she listened to Radio Monte Carlo while she wrote.[35] Münevver was professionally and personally isolated, and spoke to few people other than her infant son. To Nâzım, she poured out her frustrations, as well as her ambitions. He became Münevver's sounding board, an adult voice to talk to despite the fact that he was more than 1,300 miles to the north.

For four years, Nâzım and Münevver had not communicated with one another much, if at all.[36] Such were the circumstances when, in January 1955, Nâzım attended

---

[33] In a reflection of the ever-secretive Bilen, neither the book's place nor date of publication is listed in its opening pages, but it appears to have been published in or around 1959.

[34] Letter from Münevver Andaç to Nâzım Hikmet, RGALI, f. 2250, op. 1, d. 215, l. 5. Also see James H. Meyer, "Echoes across the Iron Curtain: The Letters of Münevver Andaç to Nâzım Hikmet," *Middle Eastern Studies*, vol. 56, no. 4 (2020), 664–679, here 667. The letter is undated but Münevver indicates that this was the second one she wrote to him, meaning that it was sent sometime in the middle of March 1955.

[35] Münevver often mentioned what was playing on Radio Monte Carlo while she wrote. See, for example, RGALI, f. 2250, op. 1, d. 215, ll. 5, 47; f. 2250, op. 1, d. 219, l. 2; f. 2250, op. 1, d. 26, l. 43; f. 2250, op. 1, d. 230, l. 35; f. 2250, op. 1, d. 239, l. 34.

[36] Göksu and Timms write that Nâzım and Münevver had managed to send letters via "a clandestine method of corresponding through third parties, sending letters via Paris or Rome." *Romantic Communist*, 312. However, Münevver notes in her letters to Nâzım that she and Nâzım had not communicated at all during this time. Letter # 3 (undated, but written in late March or early April 1951), RGALI, f. 2250, op. 1, d. 215, ll. 11–12. Zekeriya Sertel wrote that Nâzım and Münevver were not able to communicate with one another at all, and that they had only the vaguest understanding of what the other was doing. Zekeriya Sertel, *Nâzım Hikmet'in Son Yılları*, 123.

the World Peace Council's meeting in Vienna. There he met a Belgian delegate by the name of Isabelle Blume. While getting to know Blume, Nâzım had explained Münevver's plight to her. Blume had connections, and shortly after speaking to Nâzım she got in touch with the Belgian Foreign Minister, Paul-Henri Spaak, who was scheduled to visit Ankara shortly thereafter. Spaak was successful in convincing Turkish officials to lift the correspondence ban, and Nâzım and Münevver were given permission to send letters back and forth to one another directly.[37]

Münevver sent roughly 760 letters to Nâzım during the years 1955–60[38] and by my estimation she received approximately 400 letters and cards from him over this same period.[39] While most of Münevver's letters to Nâzım are located at the RGALI archive in Moscow, a smaller number of copies can be found the Aziz Nesin Archive in Istanbul.[40] Nâzım's letters to Münevver, meanwhile, are inaccessible and may no longer exist. In a June 1963 letter to the Soviet writer Konstantin Simonov, Münevver explained that she had been obliged to store everything that Nâzım had written to her "with comrades" prior to her own departure from Turkey.[41] No one has ever come forward to make this side of the correspondence public.[42]

In March 1955, Münevver's first letters began to arrive in Moscow. They describe a rather grim existence. She and Mehmet were living in the "attic," as she put it, in the house of her mother-in-law in Kadıköy. Celile Hanım spent the winters elsewhere, leaving the poorly-heated upper rooms to Münevver and Mehmet.[43] Translation was indeed an occupation that Münevver enjoyed, even if it didn't pay particularly well. In any case, her chances of getting a regular job outside the home were very slim, as most people were afraid to be associated with Nâzım Hikmet's wife.[44]

At times, the reality of her situation—Nâzım in Moscow, Münevver living an ostracized existence in Istanbul—would hit her with unexpected force. In the middle

---

[37] On the roles of Isabelle Blume and Paul-Henri Spaak in getting the correspondence ban lifted, see Göksu and Timms, *Romantic Communist*, 312; Zekeriya Sertel, *Nâzım Hikmet'in Son Yılları*, 124.

[38] In a letter Münevver wrote to Soviet writer Konstantin Simonov shortly after Nâzım's death, she estimated that she had written "more than 1000 letters to Nâzım" and that he had sent her "more than 700." However, these numbers appear to be incorrect. Münevver numbered most of her letters, and the last one at RGALI is # 549 (out of which approximately 400 are in the archive). For Münevver's letter to Konstantin Simonov, see RGALI, f. 2250, op. 1, 471, ll. 1–6, here ll. 3–4. June 11, 1963. Aziz Nesin estimated that Münevver sent Nâzım a total of 760 letters, a number that I agree with. See ANV file on Nâzım Hikmet, p. 126.

[39] Münevver would always mention in her letters the arrival of a card or letter from Nâzım, and appeared to receive about 4–8 letters and cards per month from him over a span of five and a half years.

[40] Aziz Nesin traveled to Moscow in 1965 and looked through these letters, apparently copying 88 of them into Arabic script Turkish, and taking two originals with him. See Meyer, "Echoes across the Iron Curtain," 665–666.

[41] RGALI, f. 2250, op. 1, 471, ll. 1–6, here l. 3. Letter from Münevver Borzecka (Münevver Andaç) to Konstantin Simonov, June 11, 1963, l. 4.

[42] If these letters were not lost altogether, they may have ended up in the hands of Münevver and Nâzım's son Mehmet Nâzım.

[43] On Münevver's difficulties with Nâzım's mother, see what appears to be letter # 5 (no letter number is written), RGALI, f. 2250, op. 1, d. 215, l. 14. Undated, but apparently from March 1955. Also see Meyer, "Echoes across the Iron Curtain," 667.

[44] Most of the individuals she reports meeting with during these years were Nâzım's friends, people who were considerably older than she was. In particular, Münevver spent a lot of time with Vâlâ and his wife Müzehher. In an early letter, Münevver writes that "other than 2-3 people, I don't see anybody. I don't visit anyone's home." RGALI, f. 2250, op. 266, d. 215, l. 14. This appears to be her fifth or sixth letter to him, likely from late March 1955.

of an early letter, Münevver abruptly stopped writing to note: "Ah, darling, isn't life a drag? Will I never see you again?"

"If we were a bit younger...," she began, and then stopped herself. She remembered that Nâzım used to say something to her about growing old.

> Just now it was as if I heard your voice. You'd say "We're still young, woman, what are you doing?" Your voice, your face, your walk, I haven't forgotten anything about you. But you've got a bad memory, you've probably forgotten all about me.[45]

Münevver was separated not only from Nâzım, but also from her older child Renan, whom she had not seen for three years.[46] Renan, Münevver's daughter from her first husband Nurullah Berk, was ten years old in 1955.[47] Because Münevver was on bad terms with her ex-husband, Nurullah had, apparently, forbidden his daughter from corresponding with her.[48]

Münevver's earliest letters reflect an instinct to reintroduce herself to Nâzım, as well as to explain to him why she no longer looked the way she used to. "I've really gotten old," she wrote in her fourth letter. "Probably the result of the bad life I've had over the past four years. My hair is practically white. I really wonder, if you're the sort of person that forgets a face, would you recognize me if you saw me?"[49]

Her re-introductory letters looked to both the past and the future in an effort, it appears, at rebuilding intimacy. Recalling the times that the two of them had spent together in Istanbul, Münevver remarked: "What sweet days they were."[50]

She quickly filled him in on the difficulties surrounding her current circumstances.

> I don't know if you've heard about this, but I'm living under incredible surveillance, a ridiculous and oppressive surveillance that is just incomprehensible. Outside my door—I mean, your mother's house—there's a jeep, and three police officers. Wherever I go, they follow me. Of course, everybody avoids me. Nobody comes to my door. And if this weren't enough, my financial state is a complete disaster. I don't pay rent, of course, but life has become so expensive...and I have no chance of finding a job. No one, of course, wants to hire a woman that's being followed by a jeep.[51]

---

[45] The theme of staying young forever was a recurring one in Nâzım's correspondence, as he made similar comments in his correspondence with Piraye, as well as with Memet Fuat. Blasing, *Nâzım Hikmet*, 15. Letter from Münevver Andaç to Nâzım Hikmet, RGALI, f. 2250, op. 1, d. 215, l. 5.

[46] This is what Münevver writes to Nâzım in her letter from late March 1955. RGALI, f. 2250, op. 1, d. 215. l. 15.

[47] RGALI, f. 2250, op. 1, d. 218, l. 27. In this undated note, Münevver indicated that this was letter # 67 to Nâzım, and it is classified as such at RGALI. However, judging from its content, the letter seems to actually be her 76th letter to Nâzım, written at some point in late December.

[48] RGALI, f. 2250, op, 1, d. 219, ll. 1–2, here l. 2. Letter from Münevver Andaç to Nâzım Hikmet. This letter is undated but was likely written in the final few days of December in 1955.

[49] Letter # 4, RGALI, f. 2250, op. 1, d. 215, l. 8. Letter from Münevver Andaç to Nâzım Hikmet, undated but probably from late March 1955.

[50] Ibid. Also see Meyer, "Echoes across the Iron Curtain," 667.

[51] RGALI, f. 2250, op. 1, d. 222, l. 48. Letter has no number but is likely around # 41. July 23, 1955. Münevver makes similar comments about being followed in letter # 4, RGALI, f. 2240, op. 1, d. 215, l. 14. Also see Meyer, "Echoes across the Iron Curtain," 668.

If these troubles were not enough, Münevver was also feuding with her mother-in-law, with whom she had a tense relationship. "Knowing that she's coming [in the summer] drives me out of my mind. You know your mother. It's difficult to get along with her, and when she gets angry she doesn't know what she's saying." The house where Münevver was living, moreover, was uncomfortable and decrepit. "It's hot in the summer, cold in the winter, and it's falling down all over the place. I don't have the strength to tell you about the house, but as the years pass it falls apart more and more. Moreover, it doesn't even have a garden. I have to send the child out into the streets to play!"[52]

Despite Münevver's frequent complaints about the state of her accommodation, she was conscious of the fact that she was living on charity. Münevver was, moreover, afraid of being forced out. "Samiye [Nâzım's younger sister] wants to tear down the house and put up an apartment building in its place. Hopefully she won't do this soon. I can still stand living here. Renting a place is so difficult, you know, [and] crazy expensive."[53]

The Turkish government's decision to allow Nâzım and Münevver to correspond with one another greatly changed the dynamics of their relationship. Now that they were permitted to write to each other, Münevver expected Nâzım to do so regularly and became cross when he failed to live up to her numbers. In a manner that resembled the sort of complaints that Nâzım had made about Piraye's correspondence when he had been imprisoned in Bursa, Münevver faulted Nâzım for not writing as much as she had.

After a year of corresponding with Nâzım, Münevver had this to say:

Given that you wrote me your first letter in the last days of March last year, it means that I've sent you about 100 letters in the span of one year. You have written less, in fact far less, to me. Let's not leap to conclusions, or else shall we just say that I love to write letters?

"I haven't heard from you in fifteen days," she continued. "At first I wasn't worried, because I assumed you were on the road. But now I'm feeling terribly worried. Why don't you write?"[54]

The worry and stress associated with trying to raise a child on her own often felt overwhelming. Münevver repeatedly mentioned, in her letters to Nâzım, that her nerves were at the breaking point.[55] She placed a lot of the credit, or blame, for her feelings on Nâzım's actions. "That's how my life goes," wrote Münevver to Nâzım in October 1957. "On those days when I get a letter from you, I'm happy. I feel okay

---

[52] Letter # 4, RGALI, f. 2250, op. 1, d. 215, l. 9. Also see Meyer, "Echoes across the Iron Curtain," 668.

[53] This is either the second or third sent from Münevver to Nâzım. It was written in either late March or early April 1955. RGALI, f. 2250, op. 1, d. 215, l. 6.

[54] Letter # 99, RGALI, f. 2250, op. 1, d. 220, l. 16. Undated, but apparently from March 1956.

[55] See, for example, RGALI, f. 2250, op. 1, d. 215, ll. 8, 18; f. 2250, op. 1, d. 222, l. 48; f. 2250, op. 1, d. 235, l. 23. Also see Meyer, "Echoes across the Iron Curtain," 668.

inside. But then one or two days pass and I start worrying."[56] These problems were exacerbated by the sleep-related issues she was experiencing at the time, which Münevver sought to counteract by taking sleeping pills.[57]

As a privileged traveling communist dignitary, Nâzım had access to shops selling high-quality goods. Münevver occasionally asked him to pick up certain items for her: a sweater-jacket suit for herself, or a bicycle for Mehmet. At times, Nâzım's ability to provide these items seemed to take on an importance to Münevver far beyond their monetary value, as she brought them up again and again with increasing vexation, reminding Nâzım of his pledges and responsibilities.[58]

In a manner not unlike Nâzım's prison-era efforts to make money via textile production or lampshade-making, Münevver sought to improve her miserable financial conditions through far-fetched entrepreneurial schemes that she wanted Nâzım to help her with. Early on, for example, she tried to convince him to buy her a car and ship it to her in Turkey.

> How would it work for you to send me a car? Don't laugh. On what basis is customs duty on a car paid? I wonder if it's done by the kilo or what? We need to learn this…if you send a nice big Czechoslovakian car it would be so great.[59]

Why get a car, let alone "a nice, big Czechoslovakian" one? Münevver explained that she saw it as a long-term investment. She could rent it out, for example, as a *dolmuş*, the shared taxis of Istanbul that carted up to twelve passengers at a time.[60] Münevver would continue to bring up this idea for two years, until it morphed into something bigger—a truck.[61] As was the case with the car, the reasoning here was to rent the truck out as a means of securing a steady income that she could rely upon for the years ahead.[62] Nâzım did not send Münevver a car or a truck, but he did begin to cable her money.[63] His financial assistance gradually became more regular, usually arriving in amounts of a few hundred dollars at a time.[64]

---

[56] Letter # 278, October 4, 1957, RGALI, f. 2250, op. 1, d. 228, l. 8.

[57] On Münevver's complaints of sleeplessness see, for example, letter # 67, RGALI, f. 2250, op. 1, d. 218, l. 25; letter # 89, RGALI, f. 2250, op. 1, d. 219, l. 39.

[58] On the suit and bike, see RGALI, f. 2250, op. 1, d. 231, l. 21, letter # 362, April 17, 1958; letter # 370, April 29, 1958; f. 2250, op. 1, d. 233, l. 26, letter # 390, May 31, 1958; f. 2250, op. 1, d. 239, ll. 6–8, letters # 514 and 515, March 1 and March 3, 1958. The customs dues for the bike were so high that Münevver ended up selling it.

[59] RGALI, f. 2250, op. 1, d. 216, letter # 24. Undated, but apparently from early July 1955. Also see Meyer, "Echoes across the Iron Curtain," 668.

[60] RGALI, f. 2250, op. 1, d. 216, l. 48, letter # 34, undated but apparently from mid-July 1955.

[61] Regarding the car idea, see RGALI, f. 2250, op. 1, d. 217, l. 8, letter # 43, undated but apparently from December 1955; RGALI, f. 2250, op. 1, d. 235, ll. 22–23, letter # 426, undated but apparently from late August 1958. Also see Meyer, "Echoes across the Iron Curtain," 668–669.

[62] Regarding Münevver's idea to buy a truck, see RGALI, f. 2250, op. 1, d. 225, l. 212, letter # 209, March 24, 1957; l. 9, letter # 213, late March 1957; l. 26, letter # 222; l. 38, letter # 232, and elsewhere; RGALI, f. 2250, op. 1, d. 235, ll. 22–23, letter # 426, undated but apparently from late August 1958.

[63] In February 1957, Münevver wrote to Nâzım to report that she had received 2,500 Czechoslovak crowns, which she had changed into 312 US dollars. RGALI, f. 2250, op. 1, d. 224, l. 22, letter # 195, February 23, 1957.

[64] RGALI, f. 2250, op. 1, d. 226, l. 6, letter # 236, June 12, 1957; f. 2250, op. 1, d. 228, l. 22, letter # 283, October 15, 1957; f. 2250, op. 1, d. 236, l. 48, letter # 463, November 15, 1958; f. 2250, op. 1, d. 239, letter # 532, April 7, 1959. Also see the Aziz Nesin Vakfı (henceforth, ANV), letter # 697, no date but number indicates it was written on or around March 13, 1960; ANV, letter # 740, June 18, 1960; ANV, letters # 728, 729, and 733, all of which

While Nâzım sent money and other items to Münevver, she passed on to him news of his son, family, and friends. Münevver also served as Nâzım's window onto Turkey, mailing him books in Turkish as well as postcards and photographs from Istanbul.[65] She filled him in on what was going on in the city and the West more generally, whether it was rock & roll ("nothing more than burning energy through dance"),[66] Brigitte Bardot ("the sexiest of sexy"), or James Dean ("he was a good actor, poor guy").[67] In later years, after Münevver had worked out a custody arrangement with Nurullah Berk, Münevver's daughter Renan began to live with her at times. Both kids wrote the occasional note to Moscow. Renan, who called Nâzım "uncle" (*dayı*), filled Nâzım in on the hula-hoop craze. Mehmet sent his dad some drawings.[68]

Münevver worked tirelessly on translations of Nâzım's poetry. From the very first weeks of their correspondence, her letters were replete with notes referring to poems of his that she had translated, asking for his feedback.[69] In April 1959, Münevver, with Nâzım's approval, sent eleven of her French translations of his work to Jean-Paul Sartre in the hope that he would publish them in Paris.[70] She also made suggestions, observing, for example, that she thought the end of "Henüz Vakit Varken Gülüm" ("While There's Still Time, My Rose") was good but not yet perfect. "I loved it…but I didn't like the end. I mean the last two lines. Should we get rid of them?"[71]

Even as Nâzım was living with one woman and common-law married to another, he fell in love with a third.[72] In the fall of 1955, some seven months after resuming his correspondence with Münevver, Nâzım met Vera Tulyakova, a young, attractive blonde Russian woman (Figure 12.2). Vera was then working for the design department of the Soiuz Multfilm Institute in Moscow.[73] She had contacted Nâzım to propose working together on an animation project relating to an Albanian folktale. Nâzım was immediately taken with her.

Nâzım began a determined pursuit of Tulyakova, but it wasn't going to be easy. She was thirty years younger than the 53-year-old poet, the married mother of a three-year-old daughter named Anna. Nevertheless, Nâzım didn't let up. He made a point of

---

were written in May 1960. According to Galina, Nâzım was only able to send money to Münevver from the USSR and Prague. Özden, *Galina'nın Nâzım'ı*, 43.

[65] RGALI, f. 2250, op. 1, d. 226, l. 29; d. 231, l. 25; d. 232, l. 6a.

[66] Münevver considered rock & roll's popularity a sign of a troubled world ("Bir dert varmış dünyada"). RGALI, f. 2250, op. 1, d. 226, l. 26, letter # 246. Undated, but its number suggests the letter is from July 1957.

[67] "Sexyinin sexyisi." RGALI, f. 2250, op. 1, d. 230, late January 1958, letter # 320. On James Dean, see letter from Münevver Andaç to Nâzım Hikmet, RGALI, f. 2250, op. 1, d. 235, l. 28, September 3, 1958 (misclassified in archive as 1959), letter # 430.

[68] RGALI, f. 2250, op. 1, d. 213, l. 3. Letter from Renan and Mehmet to Nâzım Hikmet, February 9, 1959.

[69] RGALI, f. 2250, op. 1, d. 226, l. 7. Letter # 237 from Münevver Andaç to Nâzım Hikmet, 15 June 1957.

[70] Nothing appears to have come of the efforts. On sending Nâzım's poems to Sartre, see RGALI, f. 2250, op. 1, d. 238, l. 32, letter # 498, 25 January 1959; f. 2250, op. 1, d. 239, l. 33, letter # 530, 3 April 1959. By the middle of May, she had still not heard back from Sartre regarding the 11 poems of Nâzım which Münevver had sent to Paris. RGALI, f. 2250, op. 1, d. 239, l. 43, letter # 537, 22 April 1959.

[71] The poem would later be known as "Henüz Vakit Varken Gülüm." RGALI, f. 2250, op. 1, d. 233, l. 18, letter # 382, May 1958. Also see Meyer, "Echoes across the Iron Curtain," 670.

[72] It does not appear that Nâzım and Münevver were ever officially married in Turkey.

[73] Vera Tulyakova writes that when Nâzım first met her he commented, in Turkish, to his (Azeri Turkish-speaking) friend Ekber Babayev, "Fena kız değil, ama göğüsleri biraz düz" ("Not a bad-looking girl, but she's a bit flat-chested"). She claims that she understood what Nâzım was saying because her family had been evacuated to the Volga-Ural region during World War II, where she had learned some Tatar. Tulyakova-Hikmet, *Bahtiyar Ol Nâzım*, 37; Göksu and Timms, *Romantic Communist*, 314.

**Figure 12.2** Nâzım and Vera

getting in touch with her, asking to meet up, ostensibly to discuss the film she wanted to produce. But even after the idea for the film was scrapped, Nâzım continued to phone Vera at work and attempt to schedule meetings with her.[74]

He sent her notes and postcards from abroad, offering glimpses of his glamorous international life. These came alongside simple messages redolent of adolescent puppy love. "My Dear Verochka!" he wrote from East Berlin in June 1958, "I kiss you. At last I'll be home again in Moscow at the end of July. I kiss you again."[75] From Warsaw, he informed her, "I heard your voice yesterday and was the happiest person in the world. I think of you all the time, of you and of me."[76]

From Stockholm Nâzım wrote to Vera:

> I think of you all the time
> I think of you all the time
> I think of you all the time
> I think of you all the time[77]

Writing in Russian, Nâzım implored Vera to "Write me, don't forget! Sometimes—in other words, every minute—think about me."[78]

---

[74] Göksu and Timms, *Romantic Communist*, 314–316.
[75] RGALI, f. 2250, op. 1, d. 159, l. 1. Letter from Nâzım Hikmet to Vera Tulyakova, June 5, 1958, from Berlin.
[76] RGALI, f. 2250, op. 1, d. 159, l. 6.
[77] RGALI, f. 2250, op. 1, d. 159, ll. 4–5, here l. 5. Letter from Nâzım Hikmet to Vera Tulyakova from Stockholm, undated.
[78] RGALI, f. 2250, op. 1, d. 159, l. 6. From Warsaw, June 14, 1959. Also see Meyer, "Echoes across the Iron Curtain," 671.

As he was writing these love-notes to Vera Tulyakova, Nâzım was also corresponding with Münevver and Galina. In a note from Prague dated July 18, 1958, Nâzım greeted the doctor by writing "Good afternoon, my darling! I kiss you and Prague…"[79] "Prague is great," noted Nâzım in another letter to Galina, "but still there's something that's missing, I'm guessing it's you. I send my kisses."[80] In a letter from March 21, 1960, Nâzım thanks Galina for having sent money to Münevver.[81]

Münevver, meanwhile, wrote to Nâzım about her daily challenges. A broken refrigerator that she couldn't get fixed, financial difficulties, issues with Mehmet, concerns about Renan—her life in letters became a litany of troubles large and small. She complained of fatigue during the day and sleeplessness at night, as well as continued problems with her nerves.[82] She felt tired, unhappy, and frequently spent time crying to herself.[83] "I feel no joy, Sweetheart," Münevver wrote in early April 1960. "There are so many reasons. Which ones should I list? I'm without joy, I'm tired."[84]

Did Nâzım ever hint at the fact that he was involved with two other women while he corresponded with Münevver? In a letter from February 22, 1959, Münevver wrote: "In your last letters, you keep hitting upon the same point, for some reason! 'I've ruined your life, etc. etc.' I have never felt toward you even the smallest grudge." Reassuring Nâzım, Münevver noted that "I've never even thought for a moment 'if it hadn't been like this,' 'if my life weren't this way.' I'm not saying this for the sake of providing comfort, either to you or to myself. We don't need that sort of thing, either of us." Instead, Münevver insisted, she honestly felt no regrets at all. Referring to her previous life with her now ex-husband Nurullah Berk, Münevver wrote "That life, in any case, could not have continued. That's different. Today it strikes me as a nightmare."[85]

Nâzım was not to blame, she insisted. But then again, Münevver did not know what Nâzım had been hiding from her.


## Transitions and Revolutions

It was not simply Stalin's death that rattled so many in the party, but rather his political burial. On February 26, 1956, Nikita Khrushchev gave his so-called "secret speech" at the 20th Communist Party Congress in Moscow. While Khrushchev had been a longtime henchman of Stalin, he now began to use the issue of de-Stalinization as a means of cudgeling the reputations of his would-be rivals for power, all the while burnishing his own credentials as the chief opponent of the cult of personality.

---

[79] Özden, *Galina'nın Nâzım'ı*, 96.    [80] Ibid., 97.    [81] Ibid., 99–100.

[82] On the broken refrigerator, see ANV, letter # 670, January 5, 1960, a problem that lasted at least until early March, when Münevver discusses the matter again in letter # 693, March 5, 1960. On Münevver's observations regarding the difficulty of raising two children on one's own, see ANV, letter # 688, February 24, 1960.

[83] On Münevver's discussions of her nerves and nervousness, also see ANV, letter # 688, February 24, 1960; letter # 691, February 28, 1960; letter # 674, January 11, 1960; letter # 675, January 1960; letter # 679, January 25, 1960; letter # 691, February 28, 1960; letter # 692, February 29, 1960; letter # 695, March 11, 1960; letter # 703, early March 1960, and numerous others.

[84] ANV, letter # 708, April 9, 1960. Also see Meyer, "Echoes across the Iron Curtain," 670.

[85] RGALI, f. 2250, op. 1, d. 239, ll. 3–4, letter # 511, February 22, 1959.

The combination of Stalin's death and Khrushchev's denunciation of him would reverberate far beyond Moscow, as Stalinist regimes in the Warsaw Pact were challenged one-by-one by reformers within the party. In April 1956, Valko Chervenkov, the Stalinist leader of Bulgaria who had initiated both the expulsion and the forced retention of Bulgarian Turks, was denounced at a party congress for his ties to the past and forced to retire. In March 1956, the Stalinist leader of Poland, Bolesław Bierut, died, and in October of that year a new reform-minded leadership came to power in Warsaw.

Also in October 1956, what is known as the "Hungarian revolution" began. On the heels of a summer of change in Eastern Europe, large crowds gathered in Budapest in late October, demanding reforms from Hungary's communist leaders. Outside the offices of Radio Budapest on October 23, Hungarian security forces shot into the crowd, and from this point forward matters escalated considerably. Ongoing protests begat increasing levels of state violence, which in turn contributed to the creation of still larger numbers of demonstrators. By October 24, order had largely broken down in the country, with both security forces and protesters experiencing heavy casualties. A few neighborhoods in Budapest constituted ground zero in the struggle over the country's future.

Within this increasingly dangerous environment, the Radio Budapest Turkish-language broadcasting team had stayed on at work. Soon, however, a decision was made to evacuate them by boat to Bratislava. Gün and her comrades were afraid that the people that she and the other Turkish communists had lived among for the past four years might turn on them. From the perspective of Gün and her TKP colleagues, the anti-government protesters were against communism, and probably opposed to foreign communists as well. The Togays and the Sertels tried hard not to give away their foreignness as they walked through the streets toward the boat's landing on the Danube.[86]

Finally reaching the river, the Togays and Sertels came upon a crush of humanity. Pushing their way through the crowds, Gün—according to her later retelling—began bellowing "Let us through! Let us through! We're Turks!" "From the embassy?" came a voice, which Gün and the others ignored as they charged through the opening which had been momentarily cleared for them. The ruse worked just long enough for them to force their way onboard. Arriving safely in Bratislava, Gün, Necil, Can, and the Sertels took an onward train to Prague, where they were soon joined by Nâzım.[87]

It was at this time that, according to Gün Togay's later recollection, Nâzım accused the Togays of a serious infraction of party discipline: communicating with individuals in Turkey. If true, such behavior could get one expelled from the party, at the very least. According to Gün's account, Nâzım took on the tone of an interrogator as he insisted that the Togays break off their alleged communications.

[86] On the events of that day, also see Yıldız Sertel, *Nâzım Hikmet ile Serteller*, 152; Benderli, *Giderayak*, 175–179.
[87] Yıldız Sertel, *Nâzım Hikmet ile Serteller*, 157.

"You're going to cut your ties with Turkey immediately!" [Nâzım] said.

In shock, [Gün] looked into his face

"What ties? We don't have any ties!"

"You've set up ties with Turkey. It's known that you've got a connection."

"You are going to immediately break off the relationship you've set up with Turkey. Don't waste your time trying to deny it! There are documents in hand showing the existence of this connection."[88]

Nothing seems to have come of this bizarre incident, however, and nowhere in Gün's party file is there any sign that she or Necil were suspected of having maintained connections with Turkey during these years. Perhaps, given the wrenching changes taking place within the Eastern Bloc at this time, Nâzım had felt obliged to play this role at someone else's request, possibly İsmail Bilen. The only permanent damage caused by this episode was that which had been done to the Togays' relationship with Nâzım. According to Gün Benderli, "The Nâzım that I saw in Prague really hurt me. Not hurt—disappointed."[89]

On November 4, the USSR and its Warsaw Pact partners invaded Hungary, crushing the fledgling resistance in less than a week. The reform communist Imre Nagy, who had assumed the role of Prime Minister early in the crisis, was arrested and later executed. Gün would not go back to Hungary for years. Nâzım, for his part, would never return.[90]

In the aftermath of the "secret speech," Moscow did not seem as welcoming as it once had to İsmail Bilen. One did not have to be a dyed-in-the-wool Stalinist to be made nervous by Khrushchev's attack on Stalinists and the socialist status quo. While the so-called "anti-Stalinist" purges which occurred under Khrushchev were, for the most part, bloodless, such an outcome was not necessarily obvious in February 1956. To an experienced old fox like İsmail Bilen, Khrushchev's anti-Stalinist tack may well have looked like the first step toward the sort of bloody political reckoning that had followed Lenin's passing in 1924.

In this age of de-Stalinization, after all, İsmail Bilen had a past to account for. Bilen's 1937 appointment as TKP representative in Moscow had coincided with the beginning of the purge of TKP members in the USSR. In 1949, Ismail Bilen had again stood by as those around him were arrested and sent to prison camps. He had held high-ranking positions in the party going back to the late 1920s, which meant that someone like Bilen was very much out of style in Moscow at this time.

The old leadership in Moscow was finally getting its comeuppance. Making oneself scarce, therefore, might not have seemed like a bad idea to İsmail, or to anyone close to him at this time. Starting in early 1954, Bilen had begun seeking permission to

---

[88] Benderli, *Giderayak*, 182–184.    [89] Ibid., 184–185.
[90] Although it does seem likely that Nâzım would have transited Hungary during his many peregrinations across Eastern Europe in the late 1950s. On Nâzım's never returning to Hungary, see Göksu and Timms, *Romantic Communist*, 273. On the situation in Poland after 1956, see Açıkgöz, *Anadolulu Bir Ermeni*, 446–454.

move to Bulgaria, citing his wife Mara Kolarova's desire to return to her homeland.[91] In 1957, the two of them, along with their two children, moved permanently to Sofia.[92]

Nâzım, who at this point was still taking his political cues from İsmail, likewise began spending most of his time outside of Moscow. While in the early 1950s Nâzım had already been a frequent traveler, in the aftermath of the "secret speech," he all but disappeared from the Soviet capital, staying away for most of the next two years. In April 1956, Nâzım traveled to Stockholm,[93] and from there made his way to Prague,[94] and then Warsaw.[95] While he spent July and August 1956 back in Russia, mainly at his dacha in Peredelkino, this was at a time when much of official Moscow would have been closed.

From October 1956 until mid-January 1957, Nâzım was in Czechoslovakia and Poland.[96] In March he was in Bucharest,[97] then Berlin and Dresden,[98] before heading down to the sandy Black Sea resort town of Varna, Bulgaria.[99] Nâzım then made his way back to Prague,[100] from which he eventually returned to Moscow at the end of July 1957. As had been the case with his previous visit to Moscow, this return to the capital occurred in the middle of summer, when few people in official positions would have been around.[101] Nâzım spent one month in Baku in the fall of 1957, leaving the country again with Galina in January 1958. They stayed in Warsaw until April, and then Nâzım visited Paris on his own. He returned to Moscow on August 31, 1958.[102]

Nâzım's absence from the Soviet capital in the years immediately following the "secret speech" is sometimes attributed to his lovesickness for Vera.[103] This could indeed have been the case, although the explanation seems rather odd, given Nâzım's aggressive courting of Vera Tulyakova at this time.

His departure from Moscow might have had more to do with his connection to İsmail Bilen. The two had worked closely together ever since Nâzım had arrived in the USSR in 1951. They had lobbied Khrushchev and others personally to expand Turkish radio broadcasting in the Eastern Bloc. In the eyes of the party, Nâzım Hikmet and

---

[91] According to paperwork in Mara Kolarova's personal file. RGASPI, f. 495, op. 195, d. 303, l. 4, February 12, 1954.

[92] RGASPI, f. 495, op. 266, d. 12, Part I, l. 5.

[93] Münevver reported receiving Nâzım's letter from Stockholm. Letter # 106, RGALI, f. 2250, op. 1. d. 220, l. 39, April 11, 1956.

[94] See letter #113 from Münevver to Nâzım, RGALI, f. 2250, op. 1, d. 221, l. 17, undated, but likely from late April 1956.

[95] See letter #120 from Münevver to Nâzım, RGALI, f. 2250, op. 1, d. 221, ll. 30–33.

[96] RGALI, f. 2250, op. 1. d. 223, l. 29, letter # 166. She mentions that the "end of year is near," so it is likely December 1956. Also see letter # 173, RGALI, f. 2250, op. 1, d. 223, l. 37. On Nâzım and Galina traveling together to Poland, see Göksu and Timms, *Romantic Communist*, 314.

[97] Letter # 198, RGALI, f. 2250, op. 1. d. 224, ll. 32–33, March 10, 1957.

[98] Letter # 209, RGALI, f. 2250, op. 1, d. 225, l. 4, late March 1957. Also see l. 10, letter # 214.

[99] Letter # 227, RGALI, f. 2250, op. 1, d. 225, ll. 11, 19, 26, 29, 31, from April 1957. Also see letter # 235, from Varna, RGALI, f. 2250, op. 1, d. 226, l. 1. Also see letter # 246, RGALI, f. 2250, op. 1, d. 226, l. 24, from early July 1957.

[100] Letter # 250, RGALI, f. 2250, op. 1, d. 226, l. 37.

[101] Göksu and Timms write that this took place on July 27, 1957. *Romantic Communist*, 317.

[102] Ibid., 318.     [103] Ibid., 316–317.

İsmail Bilen were closely bound to one another. If İsmail Bilen felt he had reason to worry about his political future in Moscow, perhaps Nâzım did as well.[104]

The year 1956 was a difficult one for Nâzım in several ways. His mother died, although it is unclear what, if anything, Nâzım knew about her passing.[105] A more immediate blow was the death of Nâzım's friend Alexander Fadeyev. Fadeyev had been the head of the Soviet Writers' Union when Nâzım had escaped from Turkey in 1951. He had been instrumental in welcoming Nâzım and helping him settle in the USSR. Like most of Nâzım's early friends in the Soviet Union, Fadeyev was a Stalinist insider.

Fadeyev's life was pulled out from under him in the wake of Stalin's death. He had been removed, in 1954, from his position as the General Secretary of the Writers' Union, but had stayed on as "board secretary." At the 20th Party Congress, however, Fadeyev was excoriated mercilessly, blamed personally for the deaths of Soviet writers during the Stalinist period. Removed from his position at the Writers' Union, Fadeyev fell into a deep depression. He then went to his dacha at Peredelkino, just a stone's throw away from Nâzım's own residence, and shot himself.[106]

During these years, Nâzım sought to end his statelessness and diversify his options within the Eastern Bloc. Party paperwork indicates that Nâzım applied for Polish citizenship in late 1955, prior to the death of Poland's Stalinist leader Bolesław Bierut in March 1956.[107] In June 1956, meanwhile, Nâzım officially requested to become a Soviet citizen.[108] Listing in his application his wife (Münevver) and two children— Mehmet and Renan—Nâzım obtained a letter of reference in favor of his application from Alexei Surkov, who had been appointed General Secretary of the Writers' Union in 1954.[109] One month later, in July 1956, Soviet Foreign Minister Dmitri Shepilov reported that party organizations in both Czechoslovakia and Poland were assisting Nâzım Hikmet in his efforts to obtain citizenship, a development which appears to have complicated matters regarding Nâzım's bid to receive a Soviet passport.[110]

Nâzım's reputation in Moscow was taking a hit at this time. A brief report written about Nâzım Hikmet on June 29, 1957, quoted one Comrade Tereshkin, who worked for the Central Committee of the CPSU, as stating:

---

[104] Even if Nâzım did not have anything to worry about politically, he may well have thought that he did.

[105] Celile's death is not mentioned in Münevver's correspondence with Nâzım from RGALI, but many of these letters are missing.

[106] On May 13, 1956. On Nâzım's friendship with Fadeyev, see Göksu and Timms, *Romantic Communist*, 281–282. In a suicide note sent by Fadeyev to the Central Committee of the CPSU, he wrote that, in signing the arrest lists of his fellow writers, "I thought I was guarding a temple, and it turned out to be a latrine." Tzouliadis, *The Forsaken*, 320.

[107] GARF, f. R7523-88-2216, Verkhovnyi Sovet SSSR, l. 1. On Nâzım becoming a citizen of Poland, also see Zekeriya Sertel, *Nâzım Hikmet'in Son Yılları*, 185. Gün Benderli writes that Nâzım applied on September 29, 1955. *Giderayak*, 191.

[108] GARF, f. R7523-88-2216, l. 1. Petition from Nâzım Hikmet to the presidium of the upper Soviet, June 7, 1956.

[109] Alexei Surkov's reference for Nâzım Hikmet, June 18, 1956. GARF, f. R7523-88-2216, l. 2.

[110] GARF, f. R7523-88-2216, l. 9.

Nâzım Hikmet, in Bulgaria, is expressing his dissatisfaction with his stay in the Soviet Union, with respect to what he describes as his poor treatment at the Kremlin Hospital, saying that they didn't even give him the correct diagnosis for his illness.[111]

In the same "spravka," Mikhail Apletin—the Vice-Chairman of the foreign section of the Soviet Writers' Union—is reported as saying that Nâzım had recently become a citizen of Poland.[112]

> About two years ago Hikmet received Polish citizenship and he holds a Polish passport. In response to Apletin's question [to Nâzım] regarding how he, living in the Soviet Union, did not acquire Soviet citizenship, but rather Polish citizenship, Nâzım Hikmet responded that his father was Polish. For this reason [Nâzım], in a meeting with (Polish Communist Party Secretary) Bolesław Bierut, asked to receive Polish citizenship, and as a result this was undertaken when Bierut was still alive.

"At the present moment," concluded the report, "Nâzım Hikmet is living in Bulgaria."[113]

Not long thereafter, on July 3, Apletin was quoted in another "spravka" relating to Nâzım Hikmet. In this one, Apletin reportedly stated that "for the time being it would not be entirely convenient, from our perspective, to decide the question of whether to accept N. Hikmet as a citizen of the USSR, taking into account his disposition." This was not, however, an outright rejection, and Apletin went on to argue that it would be best to extend a message to Nâzım stating that "our relationship with him has not changed, that we view him with complete respect." Nâzım's application was neither approved nor denied.[114]

The fact that Nâzım was tied in this report to the Stalinist Bierut is noteworthy. Göksu and Timms, citing Stalin's daughter Svetlana Alliluyeva, chalk up Nâzım's quest for Polish citizenship to his yearning for the "liberal communism" of Bierut successor Władysław Gomułka.[115] Yet it was actually during Bierut's Stalinist leadership, not that of Gomułka, when Nâzım drew closer to the regime in Warsaw. Throughout the mid-to-late 1950s, when governments across the Warsaw Pact were struggling with internal divisions between Stalinists and so-called "reform" communists, both İsmail Bilen and Nâzım Hikmet consistently preferred the company of the former.[116]

---

[111] GARF, f. R7523-88-2216, ll. 12–13. "Spravka," June 29, 1957.

[112] Apletin was, at the time, the vice-secretary of the Writers' Union's foreign commission. This paragraph was not written by Apletin, but rather by the report's author after interviewing Apletin. GARF, f. R7523-88-2216, Verkhovnyi Sovet SSSR, l. 12. June 29, 1957. "Spravka."

[113] GARF, f. R7523-88-2216, Verkhovnyi Sovet SSSR, l. 12.

[114] GARF, f. R7523-88-2216, Verkhovnyi Sovet SSSR, l. 10. From July 3, 1957. "Spravka."

[115] Göksu and Timms, *Romantic Communist*, 314. Also see Svetlana Alliluyeva, *Only One Year* (New York: Harper & Row Publishers, 1969), 246. At the time she published this book, Alliluyeva was a Soviet defector living in Princeton, NJ.

[116] The government of Czechoslovakia, the other country rumored to be interested in granting Nâzım citizenship, was likewise dominated by Stalinists at this time.

While Nâzım's biographers are fond of believing that he was a "democratic" communist who opposed Stalinism, in fact the opposite was the case.[117]

According to Zekeriya Sertel, the relationship between Nâzım and İsmail Bilen nevertheless started to cool in the late 1950s. In Sertel's account, Nâzım had wanted to attend the 20th Party Congress as a member of the TKP's delegation, but İsmail had not given him an invitation. According to Sertel, whose source for many of his Soviet-era stories about Nâzım was usually the poet-communist himself, İsmail did this because he saw Nâzım as a potential competitor for leadership within the TKP.[118]

This is a curious tale. To begin, it is very unlikely that İsmail would have considered Nâzım a rival for party leadership, although Zekeriya may well have gotten this impression from Nâzım. Moreover, given the way in which the 20th Party Congress unfolded—with not only Stalin, but also Stalinist-era elites like Nâzım's friend Fadeyev coming under attack—it may well have been the case that Bilen was trying to shield Nâzım from a potentially hostile environment.

In his memoirs, Zekeriya Sertel describes a luncheon in Prague that he and several others had attended with İsmail in 1957. Bilen informed everyone at the table that Nâzım had given an interview to an American journalist while traveling by train between Moscow and Warsaw. "Nâzım," intoned Bilen in Sertel's telling of the story, "is now spiritually dead to us." Following this lunch, wrote Sertel, he boarded the first plane to Sofia, where Nâzım was living at the time, to tell him what İsmail had said. According to Sertel's account, Nâzım traveled by train the next day to Bucharest, where he boarded a plane to Moscow in an effort to straighten out the situation. "I don't know what he did or who he spoke to," Sertel would write, "but what he feared didn't happen and the truth came out."[119]

During an interview she gave many years later, Galina Kolesnikova claimed that Nâzım attempted suicide in 1957. According to Galina's later account, she and Nâzım were staying in a hotel, and Galina had left their room to go to the market. When she returned, she found Nâzım "lying on the bed like a corpse" with "50 tablets of Nembutal," a barbiturate, "scattered across his bedside table."[120]

The seismic events that would follow Khrushchev's speech at the 20th Congress were difficult to predict and came at a time of personal turbulence for Nâzım. As someone who had been stateless since 1951, he was particularly vulnerable. Far from feeling liberated by the exciting changes that were taking place in Khrushchev's

---

[117] See, for example, Göksu and Timms, who uncritically present Nâzım as "anti-Stalinist" and "democratic" in his communism. *Romantic Communist*, esp. 80, 276, 285–286, 319. Also see Gündüz Vassaf's introduction to Zekeriya Sertel's *Mavi Gözlü Dev*, 15. Blasing claims, in reference to an earlier era, that at the time when Nâzım was expelled from the TKP he stood "pretty much alone in pressing for a national party with an independent, democratic organization." *Nâzım Hikmet*, 67. Also see ibid., 205. Can Dündar, citing the troubles Nâzım had in getting his play *Was there Really an Ivan Ivanovich?* produced, describes Nâzım as an "opponent of the regime." *Nâzım*, 71.

[118] Zekeriya Sertel, *Nâzım Hikmet'in Son Yılları*, 188–189.

[119] Ibid., 190–191. Hayk Açıkgöz tells a similar story. *Anadolulu Bir Ermeni*, 505. There is nothing in Nâzım's party file relating to any incident with an American journalist.

[120] Özden, *Galina'nın Nâzım'ı*, 153. Can Dündar writes that this occurred at a hotel in Moscow. *Nâzım*, 71. In a 1993 interview, Galina noted that "Nâzım was contemplating suicide" without apparently mentioning an actual attempt. Göksu and Timms, *Romantic Communist*, 314.

Moscow, Nâzım's response was to hit the road and seek out new protectors among the USSR's most politically conservative allies in Eastern Europe.[121]

But even as Nâzım was searching for support on his own behalf, others were looking to him for assistance.

## Letters to Nâzım

In a radio interview from 1962, Nâzım mentioned that, on average, he received "15 to 20" letters and cards per day from his fans, and Nâzım's personal *fond* at RGALI is overflowing with mail from a wide variety of individuals.[122] Well-known correspondents included Bertolt Brecht, who wrote a quick note to Nâzım in 1954 congratulating him on what Brecht described as Nâzım's "wonderful" play, *A Story about Turkey*.[123] Andreas Tietze, the celebrated Turkologist and professor at UCLA, sent a postcard bearing a photograph of his university campus and a brief message in Turkish.[124] The Turkish writer Yaşar Kemal wrote a number of letters to Nâzım from Cambridge, England, in the early months of 1963.[125]

Many of the letters that Nâzım received during his early years back in the Soviet Union had come from student associations and other expressions of Soviet-style "civil society." A pioneer troupe from the summer camp of Moscow State University wrote to Nâzım in July 1951 to compliment him on his "fight for peace," and welcome him to the USSR.[126] The young members of the literary society at the Feliks Dzerzhinsky High School in Yerevan, Armenia, respectfully invited Nâzım to visit them the next time he was in the Caucasus.[127] A literary circle at a school in Lutsk, Ukraine, wrote about their group's activities, and invited Nâzım to respond with a note about himself.[128] Thirty-three workers from Factory No. 426 signed a letter to Nâzım noting that they had been reading his works and, "knowing that you are in Moscow," invited him to come visit and talk about his life.[129] Turkish students from the *Şcoală elementară Turcă* in Cernavodă, Romania reported to Nâzım that "thanks to the Workers' Party," even the smallest of ethnic minorities "are free and live well."[130] Orphanages, Komsomol groups, an anti-fascist club in Baku, and other mostly top-down organizations contacted Nâzım frequently during this time.[131]

---

[121] I.e., those regimes still dominated by Stalinists.

[122] IISH, Nâzım Hikmet CD 3: 274, Track 10. Elsewhere in this interview, Nâzım is congratulated on his 60th birthday, indicating that it took place in 1962.

[123] Letter from Brecht to Nâzım Hikmet, March 10, 1954. RGALI, f. 2250, op. 1, d. 174. For a reproduction of this letter, see Güneş, *Hasretle*, 122–123.

[124] Postcard from Andras Tietze to Nâzım Hikmet, October 6, 1960. RGALI, f. 2250, op. 1, d. 252.

[125] RGALI, f. 2250, op. 1, d. 273. Letters from Yaşar Kemal to Nâzım Hikmet. For reproductions of several letters from Yaşar Kemal to Nâzım, see Güneş, *Hasretle*, 159–190.

[126] RGALI, f. 2250, op. 1, d. 285, ll. 2–4. July 29, 1951.      [127] RGALI, f. 2250, op. 1, d. 285, l. 54. Undated.

[128] RGALI, f. 2250, op. 285, ll. 5–6. October 26, 1953.

[129] RGALI, f. 2250, op. 1, d. 285, l. 15. No date, but most likely from the early 1950s.

[130] RGALI, f. 2250, op. 1, d. 286, l. 7. March 8, 1952.

[131] For letters from pioneers, factory workers, and other associative organizations, see RGALI, f. 2250, op. 1, dd. 284–285.

Other letters, meanwhile, stemmed more from personal initiative. People who liked Nâzım's poetry or who otherwise found his life story inspiring sent him a considerable amount of mail, with some identifying themselves as amateur poets. One woman, who signed her name simply as "V. R.," told Nâzım that she worked as a technician in a medical institute, where she had published a short poem about him in the workplace newsletter:

> Nâzım Hikmet
>
> Nâzım Hikmet is now in Moscow
> A national poet from Turkey
> In Turkey he sat in prison
> Tormented, but in good spirits[132]

Like fans all over the world, Nâzım's correspondents sought out some form of personal connection with him. Usually, this came in the form of asking Nâzım to send a postcard or a signed copy of one of his books. Other letter-writers, meanwhile, hinted at the possibility of future friendship, and perhaps even more. One V. I. Muratova, who lived in Kalinin (today's Tver), wrote to Nâzım the very day that his smiling photograph from Vnukovskii aerodrome had appeared on the front page of *Pravda*. She had sent the letter in care of the Writers' Union's offices in Moscow. "I don't know what your intentions are regarding where to stay long-term," began Muratova, "but I think…"—and here she began underlining her words—"<u>it would be great if you stayed with us in the USSR</u>." She then suggested that Nâzım consider making a trip out to Kalinin, double underlining the Russian word for "<u>come visit!</u>" at the bottom of the note.[133]

In the months and years following Stalin's death, personal letters like this one became more common. Friends and acquaintances from years past got in touch. A name from Nâzım's student days, Nihat Nuri "the Electrician," sent a warm letter to Nâzım in October 1953 wishing his former classmate health and happiness.[134] Charlotte Rosenthal, a comrade from the Egyptian Communist Party whom Nâzım had known in the 1920s, got in touch with Nâzım during the course of a visit she was making to a sanatorium outside Moscow.[135]

In two letters she sent him in January 1955, Charlotte reminisced about the good times the two of them had shared at KUTV. Remarking favorably upon the Soviet university students she had recently met, Charlotte observed that they reminded her a bit of her own long-past youth. "I look at them and it's like I'm seeing our club, at the 'Black Cat,'" noted Charlotte. "And among these kids…I often see your smile from

---

[132] Letter from V. R. to Nâzım Hikmet, RGALI, f. 2250, op. 1, d. 281, l. 7. 1952.

[133] Letter from V. I. Muratova to Nâzım Hikmet, RGALI, f. 2250, op. 1, d. 284, ll. 3–4. June 30, 1951.

[134] Letter from Nihat to Nâzım Hikmet, October 10, 1953, RGALI, f. 2250, op. 1, d. 277, l. 89.

[135] On Charlotte Rosenthal, also see Masha Kirasirova, "An Egyptian Communist Family Romance: Revolution and Gender in the Transnational Life of Charlotte Rosenthal," in *The Global Impacts of Russia's Great War and Revolution, Book 2: The Wider Arc of Revolution, Part 1*, ed. Choi Chatterjee, Steven G. Marks, Mary Neuburger, and Steven Sabol (Bloomington, IN: Slavica Publishers, 2019), 309–36.

times past when we were all so young and enthusiastic. You were blond…" Charlotte urged Nâzım to come visit her at the sanatorium ("it's one hour and ten minutes by commuter train from Leningrad Station") but there is no indication that he took her up on the offer.[136]

Another fan's letter began: "The person writing you is the woman you saw at the coat-check at the Academy of Medical Sciences." She had recognized Nâzım but apparently did not have the nerve to speak to him in person. Now, on the way back to her home in the provinces, Tamara Pavlovna Titova was writing Nâzım from the train. She gave him her address and encouraged him to get in touch.[137] Also writing to Nâzım was a young Turkish-speaking Hungarian woman named Klari, who had served as Nâzım's interpreter in Budapest. She sent him a friendly card in September 1955. "My sweet sir, my Sultan," she purred. "I love you very, very much, my rose."[138]

As the most famous Turk in the socialist world, Nâzım was contacted frequently by Turks and Turkophiles in the USSR and the Eastern Bloc. An ethnic Turk from Prizren, Kosovo, contacted Nâzım to tell him that "now my biggest desire is for your poems to be published in Yugoslavia."[139] A Hungarian man named Vallay K. Frigyes wrote Nâzım a letter in impeccable Turkish to tell him how much he enjoyed Nâzım's poetry. Frigyes explained that he had been held as a POW in Siberia during World War I and had first learned Turkish from his Ottoman campmates.[140]

Many had a favor to ask. In December 1956, one Behçet Özer wrote to Nâzım, explaining that he was a Turkish citizen who had been living in the Republic of Georgia for three years. Having recently moved to Moscow to continue his studies, Özer asked Nâzım to send him textbooks and a Russian–Turkish dictionary.[141] Two Turkish university students wrote Nâzım from Padova, Italy, explaining that they were interested in studying filmmaking in the USSR. They wanted to know if Nâzım had any advice regarding how they could do this without the Turkish government finding out. The would-be filmmakers passed on to the poet "some news from our country," copying out the headlines: "Sausage and salami is being produced from donkey meat…Liz and Fisher are getting a divorce…two people stabbed each other over the Cuba issue, Stevenson in Adana…Fenerbahçe 2-İzmirspor 0."[142]

Starting in the mid-1950s, some of the Turks who contacted Nâzım from inside the Soviet Union had darker tales to tell. A Turkish-born resident of the USSR named Hamit wrote a long and desperate-sounding letter to Nâzım in or around 1956,

---

[136] In the first of her letters, Charlotte mentions that, because she did not know Nâzım's address, she had sent her letter care of Alexander Senkevich. Charlotte would write Nâzım again in November 1959, when she was once again visiting Moscow. Letter from Charlotte to Nâzım Hikmet, January 15, 1955, RGALI, f. 2250, op. 1, d. 277, ll. 110–112-ob. For her 1959 letter, see l. 115.

[137] RGALI, f. 2250, op. 1, d. 288, l. 1. From March 8, 1954.

[138] Letter from Klari to Nâzım Hikmet, RGALI, f. 2250, op. 1, d. 293. September 3, 1955. For more on Klari, see Göksu and Timms, *Romantic Communist*, 272–273.

[139] RGALI, f. 2250, op. 1, d. 293, l. 17. Letter to Nâzım, 1957.

[140] Letter from Vallay K. Frigyes to Nâzım Hikmet, RGALI, f. 2250, op. 1, d. 286, l. 30. March 3, 1959. Frigyes is credited as a co-author of a book on comparative Sumerian grammar, *Összehasonlító Szumér Nyelvtan* (Budapest: Könyvkiadó Vállalat, 1977).

[141] Letter from Behçet Özer to Nâzım Hikmet, December 24, 1956. RGALI, f. 2250, op. 1, d. 289, l. 12.

[142] Letter to Nâzım Hikmet, November 2, 1962. RGALI, f. 2250, op. 1, d. 289, ll. 24–25.

outlining the bleak conditions of his existence. Hamit had been active in the TKP since 1948 and described the brutality he had suffered in Turkey prior to immigrating to the Soviet Union. Now he was living outside Leningrad with his wife and three children, but life hadn't gotten any better. The family was struggling, and Hamit said that he was out of work. His note took on a grimmer tone toward the end, with Hamit asking "if in the near future my children become orphans," Nâzım should please do something for him: "write a couple of lines" to Hamit's comrades in the TKP, and "let them know that I've committed suicide."[143]

Other letters told stories of arrest, exile to Siberia, and years ground out in labor camps. Abdülkadir Hacı Selimoğlu, a Turk by birth who had been arrested by the NKVD in 1938, wrote a letter to Nâzım in October 1956. Selimoğlu lamented that he had been imprisoned, "just because I'm Turkish" and despite the fact that he was "without guilt."[144] Writing to Nâzım in October 1956, Selimoğlu explained that he had recently been released from a prison camp and allowed to return to his place of residence in Gudauta, Abkhazia, on the Black Sea coast. During the course of Selimoğlu's absence, however, his home had been given to another family, and now he would have to pay for the house in order to get it back.[145] He was hoping for Nâzım to help him in some way.

In what may have been a coincidence, scam, or a reflection of practices in Abkhazia, two other individuals would soon contact Nâzım with nearly identical stories. Hüseyin Kara Ahmedoğlu wrote to Nâzım in late 1956 or early 1957, explaining that he was originally from Sürmene, in the province of Trabzon in the eastern Black Sea region. Having grown up crossing the Ottoman–Russian border in search of work, Ahmedoğlu had found himself in Russia when war between the two empires broke out in 1914. He was soon arrested as a civilian POW and sent to a camp in Kaluga, Russia. After the war was over, Ahmedoğlu had settled in Abkhazia. In 1948, however, he was jailed on charges of corruption and sent to a labor camp. He was released in 1955, but within a year was sent back to the camp after it was determined that he had been freed "by mistake." Having now been released a second time, he claimed to have lost his house. In addition to Nâzım, Ahmedoğlu noted, he was appealing for assistance in this matter from one other individual: Nikita Khrushchev.[146]

A third correspondent named S. Kadıoğlu had a similar complaint. Originally from the Ottoman Empire, Kadıoğlu had moved to the Russian Empire in 1911. He had remained in Russia throughout World War I, the revolutions of 1917, and the civil war before settling in Gagra, Abkhazia in 1929. In 1949—the same year that Raikhman was investigating Turkish communists in Moscow—Kadıoğlu was sent to a labor camp in Tomsk oblast'. The only reason this happened, he claimed, was "because I am a Turkish citizen." After his release in 1956, he had returned to Gagra to find that his

---

[143] RGALI, f. 2250, op. 1, d. 286, ll. 13–18, undated, but apparently from 1956.
[144] RGALI, f. 2250, op. 1, d. 288, ll. 3–5. October 1956.
[145] Letter from Selimoğlu to Nâzım Hikmet, October 1956. RGALI, f. 2250, op. 1, d. 288, ll. 5–12.
[146] Letter from Hüseyin Kara Ahmedoğlu to Nâzım Hikmet, late 1956 or early 1957. RGALI, f. 2250, op. 1, d. 288, ll. 22–34.

## 308    RED STAR OVER THE BLACK SEA

upstairs neighbor had obtained the rights to his apartment while Kadıoğlu had been away in prison.[147] He too, wanted help from Nâzım.

Sait Aliyev, the former Turkish military officer-turned-radio broadcaster who had been arrested alongside Salih Hacıoğlu and Sabiha Sünbül in 1949, likewise wrote to Nâzım at this time. Addressing Nâzım as "the great poet," Aliyev asked for Nâzım's assistance in securing his freedom. There was, he noted, no one else to come to his aid. At the bottom of the note, which was written from his prison camp in or around September 1955, Sait signed his name "*kimsesiz* Sait Aliyev," or "Sait the dispossessed."[148] It is unclear if Nâzım ever received this letter, which was intercepted by Soviet security officials before it reached him.[149] Aliyev was eventually freed in December 1957, and shortly thereafter immigrated to Romania.[150]

Salih Hacıoğlu was not so lucky. In April 1954, at the prison camp to which he had been sentenced for ten years, Hacıoğlu died of a heart attack at age 74. His wife Sabiha Sünbül, who had been given an identical sentence in a different camp, was released in March 1956, and shortly thereafter rehabilitated politically along with Salih. As compensation for her husband's wrongful conviction, needless suffering, and premature death, Sabiha was given two months of his former salary in December 1956. This worked out to a grand total of 1,650 rubles.[151]

## The Narrative of Exile

Personal biography constituted a much more important component of Nâzım's work than was the case for most other writers in the USSR. Even during Stalin's time, Nâzım could write about his family (in poems like "I'm Thinking of You") in a manner that was uncommon for Socialist Realism. His writing in Turkey had not typically been particularly autobiographical. Now, however, Nâzım's personal story was the prime reason behind his effectiveness as a tool of propaganda, and his poetry reflected this.[152]

In the advent of the cultural thaw which took place following Stalin's death, personal and biographical works became much more mainstream in Soviet literature and art.[153] Nâzım no longer had to balance his references to family members with invocations of farm machinery or American imperialism. Now he was free to

---

[147] Letter from S. Kadıoğlu to Nâzım Hikmet, undated but apparently from late 1956 or 1957. RGALI, f. 2250, op. 1, d. 288, l. 41.

[148] Or "Sait the orphan."

[149] Göksu and Timms write that Nâzım provided financial assistance to newly released prisoners, but supply no source for this information. *Romantic Communist*, 285.

[150] Letter from Sait Aliyev to Nâzım Hikmet, undated but apparently from August or September 1955. Sait Aliyev personal file, RGASPI, f. 495, op. 266, d. 254, ll. 8–14. Another Aliyev immigrating to Romania, see ibid., l. 2, "Spravka" from January 6, 1958.

[151] See personal file of Salih Hacıoğlu, RGASPI, f. 495, op. 266, d. 88, ll. 1, 8, 12, 17. On the payment of 1,650 rubles for Hacıoğlu's "posthumous political rehabilitation," see l. 17.

[152] On border-crossing narratives, also see Stephen F. Wolfe, "Some Cunning Passages in Border-Crossing Narratives: Seen and Unseen Migrants," in *Border Images, Border Narratives*, ed. Schimanski and Nyman, 168–186.

[153] Ilya Ehrenburg's novella *The Thaw* (1954) was published in *Novyi Mir* in 1954, and quickly came to serve as a metonym for the era more generally.

double-down upon the personal poet-as-subject style of writing that would become so common in his Soviet-era verse from the latter 1950s.

Münevver and "Memet," as Nâzım spelled the boy's name, were ever more frequently appearing characters in his writing.[154] In poems like "My Son Grows up in Photographs," "The Mailman," and "My Latest Letter to Memet," Nâzım alluded to the personal pain associated with his exile, a theme that would be a recurring feature in his work until 1960.

"Notes from Hungary," written in 1954, takes the form of a letter from Nâzım to Münevver. It begins with a jet-setting tone:

> We took the plane from Prague
> > and landed in Budapest.
> It's nice to be a bird
> > or even a cloud
> but I'm glad to be a person.

About one-third of the way through the poem, however, the speaker interrupts his description of children playing in the streets of Budapest to ask:

> My green-eyed one
> > Have you taught my Memet
> > who, when I left him behind
> > as a three-month-old in your lap
> > could barely laugh
> and who now speaks
> how to say "Daddy?"[155]

In "The Mailman," Nâzım similarly invokes his son as part of a work that reminds the reader once more of the drama surrounding the poet's life:

> Whether at dawn or in the middle of the night,
> I've carried people news
> —of other people, the world, and my country,
> of trees, the birds and the beasts—
> in the bag of my heart.
> I've been a poet,
> which is a kind of mailman.

---

[154] Münevver, meanwhile, wrote the boy's name as "Mehmet." See, for example, RGALI, f. 2250, op. 1, d. 215, ll. 7, 28, 29, 31; f. 2250, op. 1, d. 216, l. 16, and elsewhere. On Nâzım's poems about Mehmet and Münevver, also see Zekeriya Sertel, *Nâzım Hikmet'in Son Yılları*, 54–59, 65–67.

[155] "Notes from Hungary." Yapı Kredi edition of Nâzım Hikmet's collected works (*Şiirler* Vol. 6), 52–55. Also see "Lidi Vanna" (April 29, 1953), 31; "Letter from Poland (*Lehistan Mektubu*)" (1954), 44; "The Mailman" (May 1954), 50–52, "My Latest Letter to Memet," "I received a letter from Münevver, she says," "I wrote a letter to Münevver, I said," "Memet," and others.

Toward the end of the poem, which was written in May 1954, the poet homes in more specifically upon his personal story, and that of his son, while continuing to speak in the mailman's voice:

> Heaven is in my bag...
> One envelope
> writes:
> "Memet,
> Nâzım Hikmet's son,
>               Turkey."
> Back in Moscow I'll deliver the letters
> to their addresses one by one.
> Only Memet's letter I can't deliver
> or even send.
> Nâzım's son,
> highwaymen block the roads—
>               your letter can't get through.[156]

Another frequently appearing theme in Nâzım's verse from this time was border-crossing. For someone who was constantly traveling, the road had become Nâzım's closest companion. He had taken up the practice of recording, in print, where his poems were written, and many of his writings are peppered with the sort of colorful details embraced by tourists remarking upon the architecture, streets, and behavior of the locals. For this permanent foreigner, life abroad had come to mean life at home.

While Soviet writers like Ilya Ehrenburg had begun testing the limits of the post-Stalinist "thaw" as early as 1954, Nâzım's response to these changes was initially quite tepid. In contrast to many of his Soviet colleagues, Nâzım did not really know how to criticize the USSR, at least not in the genuine and straightforward manner with which he could discuss social problems in Turkey.

The poems that Nâzım wrote in the early months after the "secret speech" were tentative, and not representative of his most interesting work. In "A Couple of Words for Communists," written in 1956, Nâzım blandly invokes Lenin—a take that seems designed mostly to be inoffensive.

> Communists, I have a couple of words for you:
> whether you're the head of state, or in a dungeon
> a foot soldier, or party secretary
> Always and everywhere Lenin needs to be a part
> of your work, your home, your life
> just as if it were his work, his home, and his life.[157]

---

[156] Translation from Blasing and Konuk, *Poems of Nâzım Hikmet*, 160–161.
[157] Yapı Kredi edition of Nâzım Hikmet's collected works (*Şiirler* Vol. 6), 82.

In a similar vein, in "The Twentieth Congress," Nâzım imagines Lenin arriving at the congress, sitting down and taking notes. The poem emphasizes Lenin's humanity, in contradistinction to simply worshipping his statue.

> Lenin came to the Twentieth Congress,
> his blue, almond-shaped eyes were laughing.
> He came inside before the opening.
> He sat on a step at the foot of the rostrum.
> Even his statue did not notice.[158]

Yet this verse, too, which continues in a similar vein for two more stanzas, skirts the serious issues associated with the congress. Again, Nâzım appears to have mainly been trying to say something—to make some form of public comment regarding Khrushchev's momentous denunciation of Stalin—yet remain uncontroversial.

Another poem that touched upon the new politics facing the USSR was "Hacı oğlu Salih." This work, written a few months after the "secret speech," is a monument to Salih Hacıoğlu, who had died in a camp two years earlier. Nâzım and Salih had known each other in the 1920s, and it may well have been the case that the infamous letter from Şevket Süreyya that Hacıoğlu had allegedly brought with him in 1928 was in connection to Nâzım's bid for power in the TKP. This is significant because part of what had made Salih Hacıoğlu and his wife Sabiha Sünbül vulnerable to arrest in 1949 was the fact that Hacıoğlu's record already bore the black mark of having worked with "renegades."

"Hacı oğlu Salih" mourns the loss of Hacıoğlu while leaving out many of the details surrounding his murder-by-camp. Taking on a tone reminiscent of a "spravka," or biographical reference-report, the first half of this poem lists the late communist's accomplishments:

> He was a communist from the age of 19
> He struggled
> He landed in prison
> in Ankara, in Kırşehir
> then he came over here
> to his second homeland

Then, without much explanation, things suddenly take a turn for the worse:

> Later, in 49, in Moscow, on the night of the 10th of March
> he was sitting, reading Engels,
> they came for him, and took him away.[159]

---

[158] This is the first of three stanzas. Ibid., 81.     [159] Ibid., 83–84.

While "Hacı oğlu Salih" is sometimes described in biographical works of Nâzım as "outspoken," it needs to be remembered that this poem was published at a time when discussing Stalin's crimes and the "mistakes of the past" had already become the politically correct thing to do in the USSR.[160] Not only was Nâzım not being particularly daring in writing such a poem in 1956, he was actually following the party's new line.

Nâzım made another foray into the Soviet Union's new cultural landscape with a play called *Was there an Ivan Ivanovich?* In this work, a mysterious figure named "Ivan Ivanovich" devotes himself to tormenting a certain Petrov.[161] Why Ivan Ivanovich wishes to destroy Petrov "like a cancer" remains a mystery, but the manner in which he seeks to do so is through flattery: by festooning the town, where Petrov is a communist leader, with Petrov's portrait.[162] But was there ever really an "Ivan Ivanovich" in the first place, pulling the strings behind this cult of personality? Or was Ivan Ivanovich actually Petrov himself?[163]

The interrogative nature of the play's title hints at Nâzım's own uncertainty about how to talk about the Stalin years. Nevertheless, something about *Was there an Ivan Ivanovich?* invited the ire of officials in the Soviet Writers' Union. The play's message was so vague, it left others to come up with their own conclusions regarding what Nâzım's actual intentions were. In a report from June 1957, Mikhail Apletin of the Writers' Union referred to various difficulties surrounding this play which prevented its production.[164] Apletin explained that he had tried to convince Nâzım to make some changes to it but had been rebuffed.[165] The play would only be published in 1962.[166]

In Turkey, it had been easier for Nâzım to speak out in a convincing manner. He had seen problems and had talked about them in a way that almost anyone could understand. In the USSR, however, Nâzım had taken a starkly different approach to discussing social issues. Under Stalin, "politics" had appeared in Nâzım's writing only in the form of low-hanging fruit, castigating the Turkish and American governments. Nâzım's gift for social commentary had been left behind in Istanbul.

During the post-Stalin thaw, Nâzım struggled to find a critical voice. He generally kept his cards close to his chest. In his verse, he preferred to stick to relatively bland topics like the unifying power of Lenin, the scenery of the various places he was visiting, or the degree to which he missed Münevver and Mehmet. In his personal

---

[160] On this poem being "outspoken," see Göksu and Timms, *Romantic Communist*, 285. Can Dündar describes this work as a form of compensation for the fact that Nâzım did not speak out against the Soviet-led invasion of Hungary. *Nâzım*, 67–68.

[161] In Russian, the name "Ivan Ivanovich" is often used to impart a generic quality, a Slavic cousin to "John Doe." Perhaps not coincidentally, there was a popular singer in the Soviet Union in the 1950s by the name of Ivan Ivanovich Petrov.

[162] Göksu and Timms, *Romantic Communist*, 286–287.

[163] "İvan İvanoviç Var mıydı Yok muydu?" from the Yapı Kredi edition of Nâzım Hikmet's collected works (*Oyunlar* Vol. 3), here 262–263. On this play, also see Makal, *Beyaz Perdede ve Sahnede Nâzım Hikmet*, 215–226; Babayev, *Nâzım Hikmet*, 350.

[164] Göksu and Timms write that the play was staged five times in 1957. *Romantic Communist*, 289.

[165] GARF, F. R7523-88-2216, Verkhovnyi Sovet SSSR, l. 12. June 29, 1957.

[166] For Nâzım's contract with the publisher "Iskusstvo," see RGALI, f. 2250, op. 1, d. 315, l. 9.

conversations, he took to describing himself as a "foot soldier" (*sıra neferi*) for communism, even as he led a life of considerable privilege.[167]

Foot soldiers, after all, are not expected to lead.

*

By all appearances, Nâzım was living the Soviet dream. He had a nice apartment in a new and attractive part of Moscow, a dacha, car, remunerative salary, and plenty of opportunities to travel as a VIP within the Soviet Union and abroad. He had a lover and companion who, by all accounts, adored him. Most importantly, Nâzım was able to publish again, and widely.

But behind the scenes, not all was perfect. Carrying on relationships with three women simultaneously was hard on the heart in more ways than one. The death of Stalin and rise of anti-Stalinism in the Soviet Union posed further challenges for Nâzım. Having devoted his youth to honesty and truth in his writing and his politics, Nâzım had paid a horrific price in Turkey. Amid his present circumstances, however, he had no interest in being critical. He wanted to write, and get on with his life. He looked away as others were crushed, systematically, by the regimes that he served.

A certain form of second-world banality had crept into Nâzım's existence. He traveled the globe attending Soviet-backed peace colloquia, measuring out his life in forkfuls of national cuisine.[168] During his final years, a fear of death—indeed, an expectation—began to take root inside him. Nâzım's sense of legacy had become an urgent matter, and he grew increasingly preoccupied with tying up his complicated life's loose ends.

He had one last narrative remaining.

---

[167] Conversation with the author, June 19, 2018. She went on to say that a great artist like Nâzım could never be a "*sıra neferi*." On Nâzım's self-characterization in this fashion, also see Zekeriya Sertel, *Nâzım Hikmet'in Son Yılları*, 115.

[168] George F. Will refers to T. S. Eliot's "The Love Song of J. Alfred Prufrock" in observing that Richard Nixon "measured out his life in forkfuls of chicken à la king." *The Pursuit of Happiness and Other Sobering Thoughts* (New York: Harper Colophon Books, 1979), 50.

# 13

# Final Frontiers

On April 18, 1962, Süleyman Nuri sent a letter to his old comrade, Anastas Mikoyan. Mikoyan was an important Soviet politician, a member of the Politburo and a powerful ally of Nikita Khrushchev. Nuri, meanwhile, was the former Ottoman POW and early KUTV student who had been kicked out of the university in 1925. Having never accepted the liquidation of the Baku-based TKP, he had launched a rebellion within the TKP against Şefik Hüsnü, Nâzım Hikmet, and others whom Nuri had considered to be the leaders of the party at that time.

The road back from disgrace had been a long one. In 1927, Nuri had graduated from a technical institute in Leningrad, then moved to Baku to work as an engineer. According to Comintern records, he returned to Turkey in 1937, at around the same time that İsmail Bilen had come back from Turkey to the USSR. Two years later, Nuri was arrested in Turkey and sentenced to fifteen years in prison. In 1958—one year after İsmail Bilen had moved with his wife and children to Bulgaria—Nuri had finally made his return to the Soviet Union, an undertaking whose success Nuri credited at least in part to Mikoyan's intervention on his behalf.[1]

If anything, Süleyman Nuri's return to the USSR seems to have only aggravated his bitterness toward Nâzım Hikmet and İsmail Bilen. He began his letter to Mikoyan by noting that "after nine months," his application had finally been approved by the Party Control Commission, restoring his status as a member of the CPSU. Nevertheless, Nuri was not pleased. "My party business would have been settled much more easily," he noted sourly, "if the commission did not have a written denunciation of me from the chairman of the TKP."[2]

This comment was a reference to İsmail Bilen. In 1943, İsmail had provided, as representative of the TKP to the Comintern, a brief report ("spravka") regarding Nuri. In this document, Bilen alluded to Nuri's involvement in the opposition at KUTV in 1925, noting that Nuri "was against the party, [and] had connections with Trotskyites."[3] These comments had remained within Nuri's file ever since.[4]

Writing to Mikoyan, Nuri seemed less interested in taking on Bilen than in tearing down Nâzım Hikmet's reputation. In a writing style that resembled earlier letters

---

[1] Nuri wrote that "with your help I succeeded in returning to the USSR." RGALI, f. 495, op. 266, d. 117, ll. 2–7, here 2. Letter to Anastas Mikoyan, April 18, 1962. On the date of Nuri's return to the USSR, also see *Uyanan Esirler*, 6.

[2] RGALI, f. 495, op. 266, d. 117, l. 2.

[3] RGALI, f. 495, op. 266, d. 117, l. 46. "Spravka" signed by Marat, March 1943.

[4] Nuri had also been referred to as "an established Turkish intelligence agent" in Salih Hacıoğlu's file less than one year before Hacıoğlu and the others were arrested on espionage charges. RGASPI, f. 495, op. 266, d. 98, ll. 21–21-ob, "Spravka," May 28, 1948.

*Red Star over the Black Sea: Nâzim Hikmet and his Generation.* James H. Meyer, Oxford University Press. © James H. Meyer 2023.
DOI: 10.1093/oso/9780192871176.003.0015

denouncing Mustafa Suphi in 1920–21 and the TKP Central Committee in 1925, Nuri's April missive from 1962 began with a bland introduction that gave little immediate indication of where he was going. Reminding his old comrade Mikoyan of "how we carried out the battle against Turkish agents and pan-Turkists, all the way up to Enver and Nuri Pasha," Süleyman Nuri observed that four such individuals had nevertheless been allowed into the party. This was a reference to Nâzım, Vâlâ Nureddin, Şevket Süreyya, and Ahmet Cevat, who had all "turned out to be nationalists, pan-Turkists, and even spies."[5] And now, wrote Süleyman Nuri, one of these suspicious figures was back in the USSR.

Times sure had changed. Nuri, so far as he was concerned, had been right about Nâzım Hikmet all along. Hadn't the developments of 1929, when Nâzım had tried to set up his own Central Committee in Istanbul, proven once and for all that the bourgeois poet couldn't be trusted? And now, the fact that Nâzım had been transformed into some kind of communist hero was simply too much for Süleyman Nuri to take.

After almost forty years, Süleyman Nuri still couldn't let go of the humiliation he had suffered at KUTV. He had been roundly defeated in 1925, forced out of school and permanently damaged in communist circles. Instead of remaining in the USSR or leading the TKP, Süleyman Nuri had whiled away most of his adult life in and out of prison in Turkey. A photo taken of him in 1958 in front of the Kremlin and the Moscow River shows him wearing a dark overcoat and hat, his short hair and mustache greying with the years around an unsmiling mouth.

The passage of time, however, had done nothing to dim Nuri's sense of righteous indignation. How could so many communists have been duped, yet again, by an obvious fraud like Nâzım Hikmet?

Süleyman Nuri was determined to expose him.


## Radio Days

In the years following the crushing of the revolution in Hungary and the exodus from Budapest of the Turkish radio team, East Germany became the new center of Eastern Bloc Turkish-language broadcasting. In 1958, a Turkish-language radio station called Bizim Radyo ("Our Radio") was formed in Leipzig. Whereas there had previously been several Eastern Bloc stations with Turkish-language broadcasting segments, Bizim Radyo was created to be a full-time Turkish-language station.[6] İsmail Bilen, a longtime advocate for the expansion of Turkish-language publishing and broadcasting facilities, seems to have played a leading role in the station's creation. Not coincidentally, East German leader Walter Ulbricht was one of the last remaining Stalinist leaders in Eastern Europe at this time.

---

[5] RGASPI, f. 495, op. 266, d. 117, ll. 2–3. Letter from Süleyman Nuri to Anastas Mikoyan, April 18, 1962.
[6] On Bizim Radyo, also see Bülent Gökay, *Soviet Eastern Policy and Turkey, 1920–1991: Soviet Foreign Policy, Turkey and Communism* (New York: Routledge, 2006); Atay, *Serteller*, 311–318.

As a first step toward shoring up his new radio venture in Leipzig, İsmail had brought in the Sertels, Togays, Açıkgözyans, and İhmalyans. Nâzım Hikmet was closely involved with the operation, too, traveling frequently to Leipzig from 1958 onward to tape more than 100 sessions for the station.[7]

Dividing his time between Leipzig, Sofia, and Moscow, İsmail Bilen created several income streams in the Eastern Bloc, establishing himself and his wife in a comfortably international communist style. A 1961 audit into Bilen's finances by the Red Cross and Red Crescent society of the USSR noted that "Marat's Bulgarian friends have provided him with a furnished apartment for free" in Sofia.[8] He was also receiving a stipend of 3,500 leva per month in Bulgaria, in addition to getting paid for the work he was doing for Bizim Radyo. Bilen had further secured a pension from the Union of the Societies of the Red Cross and Red Crescent[9] and was reported to have received 16,500 rubles for seven months of party work in Moscow in 1960.[10]

Mara Kolarova had also benefited from her Eastern Bloc contacts. A party report from 1957 indicated that she had received government loans from the USSR totaling 13,100 rubles. These were canceled when she moved back to Bulgaria with İsmail.[11] This was at a time when a Soviet high school teacher with 25 years' experience was earning 935 rubles per month.[12] Kolarova's canceled loans worked out to roughly eight times the 1,650 rubles Sabiha Sünbül had received as compensation for her husband's death in a labor camp.[13]

Bizim Radyo's staff continued to grow. In November 1957, a 37-year-old communist by the name of Bilal Şen reached a legal agreement with the Turkish government, whereby he received a long-denied passport. This passport, however, was a very special one: good for only a single exit, preventing its bearer from ever returning to Turkey. The longtime communist took Ankara up on its offer, surrendering his Turkish citizenship and becoming a national of Bulgaria, his birthplace.[14] From Sofia, Şen made his way to Leipzig, where he was given a job at Bizim Radyo. Not long thereafter, Aram Pehlivanyan, an Armenian from Turkey who had crossed into the Soviet-controlled sector of Berlin in 1958, was also given a job at the station.[15]

In August 1961, a name from the distant past, Zeki Baştımar, likewise made his way to the socialist world.[16] Baştımar was an old friend of Nâzım from the 1920s, and the two had worked together on a Turkish translation of *War and Peace* when Nâzım was

---

[7] Including one in which Nâzım denounced Ahmet Emin Yalman, the *Vatan* writer who had championed Nâzım's release from prison in Turkey in 1949–50. See "American Agent Ahmet Emin Yalman," August 31, 1959, in Anjel Acıkgöz (ed.), *Bizim Radyoda Nâzım Hikmet* (İstanbul: TÜSTAV, 2002), 145–146. On Nâzım's times in Leipzig, also see Güneş, *Suyun Şavkı*, 32–46.

[8] RGASPI, f. 495, op. 266, d. 12, Part I, l. 3. Letter to the Central Committee from April 1961. Signed D. Shevliagin.

[9] RGASPI, f. 495, op. 266, d. 12, Part I, ll. 4–5. Spravkas from December 1960 and January 14, 1961.

[10] RGASPI, f. 495, op. 266, d. 12, Part I, l. 9. Letter to the Central Committee of the CPSU, June, 1960. Signed D. Shevliagin.

[11] RGASPI, f. 495, op. 195, d. 303, l. 1.

[12] George Z. F. Bereday and Ina Schlesinger, "Teacher Salaries in the Soviet Union," *Comparative Education Review*, vol. 6, no. 3 (1963), 200–208, here 201.

[13] RGASPI, f. 495, op. 266, d. 88, ll. 1, 8, 12, 17.     [14] He had come to Turkey from Bulgaria in 1944.

[15] On Pehlivanyan, see "spravka" from 1977, RGASPI, f. 495, op. 266, d. 307, l. 16.

[16] On Baştımar, also see Akbulut (ed.), *Zeki Baştımar*, 9–44, here esp. 10.

in prison. In 1951, Zeki had been arrested by Turkish authorities. Sentenced to ten years in prison for his supposed communist activities, he was released in 1959. Zeki Baştımar then left Turkey for good in 1961, heading to the Eastern Bloc via Berlin, and now he too began a new life in Leipzig.[17]

While Zeki had long-standing ties to Nâzım, his relationship with İsmail Bilen was less straightforward. Soon enough, Baştımar's arrival would contribute to the rise of certain tensions within the small colony of Turkish communists in East Germany.

## The End of Something

Münevver must have had her doubts. After all, she and Nâzım had already been apart for almost four years by the time they had begun corresponding with one another.[18] Nâzım was, at least in the socialist world, a genuinely famous individual who traveled extensively. He had plenty of opportunities for temptation.

There had been bad moments before. In her thirty-ninth letter to Nâzım, written in the second half of July 1955, Münevver had begun in an unusually formal tone before cutting to the chase. She had recently received a letter that Nâzım had sent her from Prague. In the envelope, Nâzım had accidentally included a shopping list that he had written out for himself and Galina. The list included nylons, as well as "velvet blouses, in blue and yellow, for Galina."

Münevver was not pleased. "Are you going to claim that these nylons and the velvet blouses are for yourself?" she asked.

> Who ordered these so that you would place so much importance on them and write this note? I don't like this one bit, you know. Would a guy buy such things for a woman he was not close to? And blouses, aren't these like [buying] a box of chocolates? Please don't think I'm joking, I'm really angry. Think what it would be like if I wrote you a letter and you found a note like this listing an "electric razor" or "men's underwear."

While Münevver temporarily managed to put her anger aside, she returned to the issue at the letter's conclusion. Her words reflected a mixture of longing, sadness, and anger. "What a bad thing loneliness is," she wrote, "what a difficult thing separation is, Sweetheart. Okay, Baby, that's all for now, I'll wait for your letter. Please provide an explanation for these blouses, don't forget! And don't think I'm joking. I take this business very seriously!"[19]

In a letter that appears to have been written approximately one week after her discovery of Nâzım's shopping list for Galina, Münevver's tone was despondent. Unique

---

[17] RGASPI, f. 495, op. 266, d. 30, ll. 101, 117, 121, 124, 145.   [18] In March 1955.
[19] Letter # 39 from Münevver to Nâzım. Undated, but apparently written in July 1955. RGALI, f. 2250, op. 1, d. 217, l. 1. Also see Meyer, "Echoes across the Iron Curtain," 670.

among her missives to Nâzım from these early months, this one had the date, July 23 [1955], written at the top.

> My darling, this separation has just destroyed me. I'm in such a bad state that while writing to you now I can't control myself, I've started to cry. Oh, sweetheart, am I never going to see you again, are you never going to see your child…I don't know where to start. I feel like I've just risen from the dead. It's really nice to be able to write you, but also painful…Sometimes I feel such fear inside me that all courage has left me, I think about dying and just being free of all of this sadness.
>
> I'm so lonely, darling. It's a loneliness that is enveloping. Why did our lives have to end up like this?[20]

Early on, Nâzım had a chance to level with Münevver. Instead, he kept his mouth shut, continuing to write to Münevver while sharing a bed with Galina and pursuing a relationship with Vera. Galina accepted Münevver as a fact of life, but Vera was not interested in sharing Nâzım with anyone. It would either be her or Münevver.

Nâzım's relationship with Vera Tulyakova entered a more serious phase in the early months of 1960. In a series of decisions that appear to have been negotiated over the course of months, Vera agreed to leave her husband and moved in with Nâzım in March. In order for this to take place, however, Nâzım first had to break off relations with Galina.[21]

Parting with his long-time live-in physician, traveling companion, and lover did not come cheap. Nâzım and Galina would end up signing, in January 1960, a formal agreement in which he handed over nearly all his belongings to her. Listed among the items Nâzım gave to Galina was a 1957 model Volga automobile, his writing table, two televisions, 1,500 books, 100 records, two record players, and all of the furniture in Peredelkino. The estimated total value of the settlement was almost 90,000 rubles.[22]

According to a will that Nâzım had signed four years earlier, in the event of his death Galina was slated to receive all of his possessions, other than his books and his money.[23] So, the agreement that Nâzım and Galina signed in 1960 differed from the preceding document only in that it also included Nâzım's books, which were valued at 5,000 rubles and no longer destined for the Lenin Library. Otherwise, as far as the terms of this agreement were concerned, it was as if Nâzım were already dead.[24]

---

[20] Letter from Münevver to Nâzım, July 23, [1955]. RGALI, f. 2250, op. 1, d. 222, ll. 48–49, here 49. Also see Meyer, "Echoes across the Iron Curtain," 671. This letter, which does not have a year written on it or a number, is classified in RGALI alongside letters from July 1956. However, the letter appears to actually be from July 1955, as it discusses the fact that Münevver was living in Celile's house, and Münevver had moved out of this house prior to July 1956.

[21] Göksu and Timms write "[i]n January 1960 they were finally united," without elaboration. *Romantic Communist*, 322. Nâzım and Vera would marry in November 1960.

[22] More precisely, 89,975 rubles.

[23] RGALI, f. 2250, op. 1, d. 309, l. 1. Copy of Nâzım's will, signed on August 25, 1956.

[24] RGALI, f. 2250, op. 1, d. 309, ll. 4–6. Agreement signed in Moscow between Nâzım Hikmet and Galina Kolesnikova, January 7, 1960.

Echoing this morbid finality was a letter Nâzım wrote to Galina at around this time, informing her that he had made payments on the car and the dacha in Peredelkino for the next nine months. "After that," promised Nâzım, he would continue to cover these costs, "if I am still alive."[25]

While carrying on his negotiations with Vera and Galina, Nâzım continued to write to Münevver. During these years of correspondence, Münevver had been working steadily on a new translation project: *Human Landscapes from My Country*.[26] This was the "novel in verse" that Nâzım had first begun composing while he was in prison in the 1940s. Rewriting the work in the Soviet Union, he sent sections of it piece-by-piece to Münevver. She, in turn, wrote out these parts in French and then sent them back to Nâzım for his inspection.

It was a never-ending project that became particularly intense in the early months of 1960, as parts of it began to near completion. "Tomorrow I'll work on the rest of *Human Landscapes*," Münevver wrote on June 18, 1960.[27] One week later, she added: "I'm waiting for news about the remaining parts of *Human Landscapes*."[28] Throughout the first half of the year, she asked him time and again to send her more selections from the work, notifying him of when they had arrived.[29] Once, many years earlier, Nâzım had written to Piraye from prison and had referred to this masterwork as "your" poem. Now, the work's legacy had passed on to Münevver.

Münevver also devoted considerable time and energy to getting selections of Nâzım's poetry translated into Italian. This opportunity had come about as a result of a June 1958 meeting of the World Peace Council in Stockholm, where Nâzım had made the acquaintance of a woman named Joyce Lussu.[30] Born in Florence on May 18, 1912, Lussu had joined the then-underground Italian Communist Party in 1930. Following the conclusion of World War II, she had become a leading figure in the Italian Socialist Party and the Italian branch of the WPC.[31] A wealthy woman who was accustomed to getting her own way, Lussu—who did not know Turkish and had no background in literature—announced to Nâzım in 1960 that she wished to translate his poetry from French into Italian.[32] Nâzım put her in touch with Münevver.

Lussu may have been a dilettante, but Münevver was convinced that the affluent socialist was a contact worth cultivating. "Don't forget," Münevver instructed Nâzım

---

[25] Göksu and Timms, *Romantic Communist*, 322.

[26] Working on *Human Landscapes* was an integral element of their correspondence going back to their earliest letters. See, for example, RGALI, f. 2250, op. 1, d. 215, l. 40, letter # 13, April 1955; d. 216, l. 28, letter # 28; l. 31, letter # 29; l. 37, letter # 31; l. 43, letter # 33.

[27] ANV, letter # 740, June 18, 1960. Also see Meyer, "Echoes across the Iron Curtain," 670.

[28] ANV, letter # 742, June 24, 1960.

[29] See, for example, letter # 665, December 27, 1959; letter # 668, January 1, 1960; letter # 669, January 3, 1960; letter # 670, January 5, 1960; letter # 671, January 7, 1960; letter # 676, January 18, 1960, letter # 687, February 17, 1960.

[30] Göksu and Timms, *Romantic Communist*, 326.

[31] Personal file of Joyce Lussu, RGASPI, f. 495, op. 221, d. 3508, esp. ll. 5, 7–8, 10–11, 15. Joyce Lussu's husband, Emilio Lussu, was a senator and a member of the Central Committee of the legal, and mainstream, Italian Communist Party. Personal file of Emilio Lussu, RGASPI, f. 495, op. 221, d. 3600. On the Lussus, also see Meyer, "Echoes across the Iron Curtain," 673.

[32] Lussu's previous involvement in publishing had consisted of editing a book relating to the lives of women in Italy called *Donne Come Te* (Milan: Roma Edizioni Avanti, 1957).

in mid-May 1960, "you write to her, too." "You finish your novel, and I'll translate it into French, *inşallah*."[33] On May 21, Münevver informed Nâzım that she had been contacted by Lussu. "The lady's husband is a senator, and she was apparently a sergeant in the army and got a medal. She sounds amazing."[34] After some false starts, Münevver and Joyce Lussu managed to develop an efficient and productive working relationship.[35] "We've become good friends," Münevver related to Nâzım on June 2, 1960.[36]

Eight days later, Münevver had more news to share about her new friend: Joyce Lussu would soon be visiting Turkey. "Our Italian translator *madame* is apparently coming to Istanbul rather soon. I'm happy. She's got to be shown around."[37] On Thursday, June 15, 1960, at 10 p.m., an exhausted Münevver finally found the time, as she explained in her letter's opening lines, to sit down and write Nâzım a proper note. Lussu and a friend had shown up in Istanbul on a yacht on Monday, and ever since then Münevver had been playing the role of tour guide. Lussu, Münevver explained, had wanted to see absolutely everything, and had questions about all topics related to Turkey. At night, Münevver partied with Joyce Lussu and her friends. "In the evenings, we were always invited out somewhere…Presto, presto, Münevver! We have much to do," Joyce and the others would say to her as they laid siege to the former Ottoman capital.[38]

In a letter from June 25, by which time Lussu and her friend appear to have departed, Münevver emphasized that she liked Joyce, the Italian communist's idiosyncrasies notwithstanding. "For example, when explaining to me how she met her husband she asked me a typical question: 'How long did you work,' she said, 'to get Nâzım to marry you?' I was shocked and didn't understand the meaning of what she was asking." Münevver felt that Lussu held some rather stereotyped views of Turks in other respects as well. "I explained that Turkish guys didn't like to rely on force" in their dealings with women, Münevver wrote. "I don't think she believed me."[39] Still, they had enjoyed their time together. "We laughed so much. Joyce has an island that she still hasn't visited," Münevver reported, somewhat overwhelmed by the unfathomable wealth of this Western European communist.

The strengthening nature of Nâzım and Münevver's literary collaboration notwithstanding, in late July 1960 their correspondence would largely come to an end. While the hasty demise of their relationship was mostly a result of Nâzım's deepening involvement with Vera Tulyakova in Moscow, the immediate cause of their breakup stemmed from revolutionary political developments taking place in Turkey.

---

[33] This was an apparent reference to the "novel-in-verse" *Human Landscapes*. ANV, letter # 729, May 14, 1960. *İnşallah* is typically translated as "God willing," but is used more like "hopefully."

[34] This is an apparent reference to Lussu's involvement in anti-fascist activities in Italy. ANV, letter # 731, May 21, 1960.

[35] After receiving copies of Lussu's early efforts, Münevver wrote to Nâzım and told him that Lussu was "ruining my translations." Münevver then sent detailed corrections to Lussu, and eventually the problems were worked out. ANV, letter # 735, June 2, 1960. Also see Meyer, "Echoes across the Iron Curtain," 673.

[36] ANV, letter # 735, June 2, 1960.     [37] ANV, letter # 738, June 10, 1960.

[38] ANV, Letter # 739, June 15, 1960. Also see Meyer, "Echoes across the Iron Curtain," 674.

[39] ANV, letter # 743, June 25, 1960.

The Democrat Party of Adnan Menderes was overthrown in a military coup on May 27, 1960.[40] The party's leadership, which was stridently anti-communist, had always been critical of Nâzım Hikmet, and had overseen Münevver's mistreatment since her husband's departure. Now that the Democrats were out of power, Münevver wanted to see if their downfall would lead to a change in state policy toward her. She decided to try her luck and apply for a passport in order to travel abroad.

She was optimistic. On July 1, 1960—more than three months after Vera had moved in with Nâzım—Münevver was cheerfully sending letter upon letter to him, informing Nâzım of the good news: the two of them may well be able to meet up again, and soon. All he had to do was write her a letter of invitation.

> According to the new passport law, we need a letter of invitation from a close relative…so go ahead and write that letter right away, Sweetheart…Just think—ten years. Ten years. That's no joke![41]

Three days later, on July 4, Münevver wrote to Nâzım again. She repeated the news in order to make sure he'd gotten it.

> Nâzım, this summer I'm finally going to see you. Can you believe it? What's it going to be like? I bet we won't even talk, how could someone talk after this many years, what words could there be? What can one do other than cry? I'm even crying right now.[42]

Over the next couple of weeks, she continued to write to Nâzım about this idea, reminding him in three subsequent letters that she needed his help in order to get the passport.

In a letter from July 19, 1960, Münevver's tone shifted abruptly. In a manner unlike all of her previous correspondence to Nâzım, she did not address him with the words "my darling" (Canım). Echoing Nâzım's breakup letter to Piraye from years earlier, Münevver simply called him by his name. She had received some bad, and apparently quite unexpected, news from him.

Her comments were made in response to an accusation by Nâzım that she had been the unfaithful one.[43] Münevver was furious.

> I haven't made love with anybody and am not doing so now. If something like that had occurred, I would have told you a long time ago. Don't worry—I wouldn't have been afraid that you would cut off support to me. The fact that you would write this

---

[40]  On Menderes's overthrow, see Zürcher, *Turkey: A Modern History*, 41–44. On Menderes's subsequent political rehabilitation, see James H. Meyer, "Memory and Political Symbolism in Post-September 12 Turkey: A History of the May 27th Debate," MA Thesis, Princeton University, Department of Near Eastern Studies, 2001.

[41]  ANV, letter # 747, July 1, 1960.

[42]  ANV, letter # 748, July 4, 1960. Also see Meyer, "Echoes across the Iron Curtain," 672.

[43]  According to Göksu and Timms, Nâzım had criticized Münevver for her friendship with Kemal Tahir, implying that the two had been carrying on an affair. *Romantic Communist*, 332–333.

right after I brought up getting a passport is not something that I can see in a good light. Several years ago, I received an unsigned letter telling me that you were living with some doctor lady. I wrote you about this and couldn't believe it, and above all never mentioned it to anybody.[44]

But if Nâzım thought Münevver was going to fade away quietly, he was wrong. Nâzım's attitude be damned, she was still determined to get a passport. And he was going to help her.

I've given this a lot of thought since getting your letter. I'm still going to get my passport, but I won't come stay with you. You've ruined the whole ten-year period.

She knew exactly what she wanted from him:

I'm going to get my passport and go to Italy with the kids. You're going to immediately fix Mehmet's legal situation, you'll recognize him [as your son], and then I don't want anything—and I mean anything—else from you.[45] If I can make a living in Italy, and I hope I can, I'll move there. Maybe I'll go to France, of course I don't know anything right now. But you are going to <u>immediately</u> send me an invitation and I'll request a passport.[46]

In addition to demanding Nâzım's assistance in getting a passport for herself and Mehmet, Münevver set out to make a couple of other points clear to Nâzım. In a letter written on October 8, 1960, she emphasized that she did not want to see any more invocations of herself or Mehmet in Nâzım's future writings. Münevver, the trilingual translator, was sensitive to language. She could recognize a narrative when she heard one.

From now on I don't want you using Mehmet in any sort of poem. Since the "distant lady" theme is finished, don't use the child theme...I don't want there to be even the slightest reference to me.[47]

Münevver didn't want to be his "distant lady" anymore, but it seems unlikely that Nâzım would have invoked her for much longer, anyway. He had, after all, found a new source of inspiration. About six weeks after Münevver sent this letter, Nâzım and Vera got married—on November 18, 1960—in Moscow.

---

[44] ANV, p. 130, July 19, 1960. Also see Meyer, "Echoes across the Iron Curtain," 672.

[45] Münevver had been periodically asking Nâzım to fill out a form acknowledging Mehmet as his son, apparently because he and Münevver had never been legally married.

[46] ANV, p. 130, July 19, 1960. Also see Meyer, "Echoes across the Iron Curtain," 673. Underlining in the original.

[47] ANV, October 9, 1960. This is one of the two original letters from Münevver in the ANV collection. After the July exchange, Münevver stopped numbering her letters. Also see Meyer, "Echoes across the Iron Curtain," 673.

Nâzım had come to depend upon the Iron Curtain to keep his worlds separate from one another. But now that the Menderes administration was out of power, his carefully compartmentalized personal life had begun to lose its coherence.

## Rebuilding the Party

The 1961 arrival of Zeki Baştımar in the Eastern Bloc created complications for İsmail Bilen. Unlike most of the Turks in the USSR and Eastern Europe in the late 1950s, Zeki Baştımar had some genuine heft within the TKP. Like İsmail, he had studied at KUTV in the 1920s, crossed between Turkey and the USSR multiple times, and spent years of his life in Turkish prisons. An articulate and quick-thinking intellectual, Baştımar also happened to be a longtime friend of Nâzım Hikmet.

Baştımar, notably, did not get along well with İsmail Bilen, while Bilen was likely not thrilled by the arrival from Turkey of this new, polypseudonymed rival.[48] It may have been relatively easy for İsmail to push around youngsters like the Togays or newcomers like the Açıkgözyans and İhmalyans, but Zeki Baştımar was practically a peer. He had been around the communist "bloc" a few times, and was not as easily intimidated by Bilen as some of the others.

In April 1962, a "conference" was held in Leipzig for Turkish communists. Twelve people were in attendance: Zeki Baştımar, İsmail Bilen, Nâzım Hikmet, Abidin Dino (who was living in Paris at this time), Bilal Şen, Sabiha Sertel, Yıldız Sertel, Aram Pehlivanyan, Vartan İhmalyan, Hayk Açıkgözyan, Fahri Erdinç (then living in Bulgaria), and Gün Benderli Togay.[49] This conference created a working Foreign Bureau for the TKP that would be organized and utilized mainly by the individuals attending this meeting. Of the six people elected to the bureau—İsmail Bilen, Zeki Baştımar, Nâzım Hikmet, Abidin Dino, Aram Pehlivanyan, and Gün Togay—all but Dino were directly tied to Leipzig-based Bizim Radyo.

The Foreign Bureau was, in theory, the East German-based "tail" of a party headquartered in Istanbul.[50] In reality, however, the Turkey-based TKP had long since ceased to operate as a viable organization with the means of coordinating with Moscow. While the Central Committee of the CPSU in Moscow had, in 1951, accepted the idea of creating a TKP Foreign Bureau, the organization was only now turned into a functioning party organ.[51]

The timing for this was likely not coincidental. In the aftermath of the military coup of 1960, a new liberal constitution had been adopted in Turkey, paving the way for the establishment of new leftist parties that cut into the TKP's remaining base of support.

---

[48] Like Bilen, Baştımar had several aliases, including Yakub Demir, Aydın, and Max Fiedler. RGASPI, f. 495, op. 266, d. 30, l. 1.

[49] *TKP MK Dış Bürosu 1962 Konferansı* (İstanbul: TÜSTAV, 2002), 9.

[50] On the creation of the Foreign Bureau see RGASPI, f. 495, op. 266, d. 12, Part II, l. 150, "spravka" on İsmail Bilen, June 1973, by Varakina; l. 192, "spravka" from April 30, 1963.

[51] See Erden Akbulut, "Sunu," *TKP MK Dış Bürosu 1962 Konferansı*, 7.

In 1961, the Turkish Workers' Party (TİP) was formed, a legal democratic socialist organization that attracted to its ranks a series of well-known leftist figures. These included Nâzım Hikmet's cousin, the lawyer and former Olympic athlete Mehmet Ali Aybar, who became leader of the party in 1962.[52]

Before long, the Leipzig-based TKP Foreign Bureau was being referred to in Moscow simply as "the TKP," dropping the polite fiction that there was still a viable party in Turkey.[53] Without ever admitting as much, İsmail Bilen and his Turkish comrades in the Eastern Bloc had staged a successful takeover of the TKP's "brand." Once again, İsmail Bilen would have the chance to play the role of a communist party leader, albeit in an organization with only a dozen active members.

It was not to be. Zeki Baştımar, rather than İsmail, was elected "First Secretary" of the Foreign Bureau.[54] Party paperwork from Moscow refers to a "compromise agreement" that Zeki Baştımar and İsmail Bilen hashed out "after many months of arguments."[55] According to the deal, "Nâzım Hikmet, Aram [Pehlivanyan], and Abidin Dino" would be placed on the Central Committee of the TKP.[56] This paperwork indicates that Bilen named Aram Pehlivanyan to the TKP Central Committee, while it was Zeki Baştımar who had nominated Nâzım Hikmet.[57]

For now, it looked as if İsmail Bilen had finally lost his hold over the TKP. But he was not the type to give up power so easily.


## Another Crossing

Was it during Joyce Lussu's visit to Istanbul that Münevver decided to escape? It seems likely. In memoirs that Lussu would write years later, she claimed that Nâzım knew that she was going to try to smuggle Münevver and the kids out of Turkey. Nâzım, Lussu later recalled, did not support the idea. He attempted to dissuade her, claiming it would be too dangerous.[58] Yet Joyce Lussu was not one to be dissuaded.

Neither was Münevver. In the wake of her breakup with Nâzım in July 1960, Münevver had drawn even closer to Joyce, who had taken an interest in the fortunes of Münevver and her children. Joyce was the only other person who knew about their relationship coming to an end. "I'm only writing Joyce, so that she can think about what kind of possibilities there might be for me in Rome. Who knows how surprised she'll be? If I can settle in Italy for at least a while, you'll be able to see your son from

---

[52] Aybar had competed for Turkey in track and field at the 1928 Olympics in Amsterdam.

[53] TKP and CPSU paperwork in the 1960s and early 1970s would use the terms "TKP Foreign Bureau" and "TKP" interchangeably.

[54] Akbulut (ed.), *Zeki Baştımar*, 41. Also see RGASPI, f. 495, op. 266, d. 30, l. 90; RGASPI, f. 495, op. 266, d. 12, Part II, l. 7. "Spravka" from August 15, 1983.

[55] RGASPI, f. 495, op. 266, d. 12, Part II, l. 150. "Spravka" from June 1973.

[56] "Spravka" on İsmail Bilen, written by Varakina, June 1973. RGASPI, f. 495, op. 266, d. 12, Part II, l. 150.

[57] RGASPI, f. 495, op. 266, d. 273, l. 1. "Spravka" from June 1973.

[58] Joyce Lussu, *Buluşma* (İstanbul: Açılım Yayınları, 1995), 23. On Münevver's escape, also see Zekeriya Sertel, *Nâzım Hikmet'in Son Yılları*, 222–226.

time to time."[59] In another note, written in October 1960, Münevver asked that Nâzım return to her all of the letters that she had written to him during their period of separation. "Put them all in a sturdy package and send them to Joyce Lussu in Rome."[60]

Toward the end of July 1961, Lussu again visited Istanbul. This time, she traveled with Münevver and her two children down to Ayvalık, a small city on Turkey's Aegean coast. There, they met up with Carlo Giullini, a friend of Joyce Lussu who also happened to own a Triton yacht.[61] The plan was to flee to the Greek island of Lesbos, located less than ten miles off Turkey's western coastline. Leaving in the evening, the group tried to appear as a typical collection of wealthy foreign tourists. En route to Greece, however, they experienced bad weather and the yacht began taking on water. Fearing for their lives, they fired off flares. The distressed vessel was spotted by Greek fishermen, who came to the party's rescue. Greek police officials showed up soon thereafter.

Thinking quickly, Münevver told the Greek authorities that she was a Polish citizen but had lost her passport amid all the confusion. The police then contacted the Polish Embassy in Athens, and the Embassy, upon learning that she was Nâzım Hikmet's wife, backed up Münevver's story and issued travel documents to her and the kids.[62]

In a hotel in Warsaw some ten days later, Nâzım would finally be reunited with Münevver and Mehmet after a decade of separation. It was, however, a rather short meeting, one that would be remembered bitterly by at least one of its attendees. In a brief and scathing interview-cum-memoir written in the early 1970s, Mehmet Nâzım, as Nâzım's son would later call himself, described a nervous Nâzım Hikmet making strained conversation with Münevver while absentmindedly glancing at "young women at nearby tables."[63]

In Warsaw, Nâzım found Münevver an apartment and a job teaching Turkish at a university.[64] He then quickly returned to Moscow and his new life with Vera Tulyakova.[65]

## A New Chapter

At age 58, Nâzım was a newlywed again, married to a woman less than half his age, someone with a small daughter of her own. Soviet and Turkish friends of Nâzım from this time have depicted Nâzım and Vera's marriage as a difficult one. Zekeriya Sertel observed years later that Vera would pick up and leave on occasion for one or two days.[66]

---

[59] ANV, letter from Münevver to Nâzım Hikmet, July 19, 1960. Following her break with Nâzım earlier in the month, Münevver stopped enumerating her letters.

[60] ANV, letter from Münevver to Nâzım Hikmet, October 9, 1960 (one of two original letters in the ANV collection). Also see Meyer, "Echoes across the Iron Curtain," 674.

[61] Also see Göksu and Timms, *Romantic Communist*, 329.

[62] Lussu, *Buluşma*, 30–31; Göksu and Timms, *Romantic Communist*, 329–331.

[63] Göksu and Timms, *Romantic Communist*, 332. [64] RGALI, f. 2250, op. 1, d. 320.

[65] On these events also see Açıkgöz, *Anadolulu bir Komünistin Anıları*, 512–513; Meyer, "Echoes across the Iron Curtain," 674.

[66] Zekeriya Sertel, *Nâzım Hikmet'in Son Yılları*, 214.

As her daughter Anna continued to live with her father, Vera would visit her ex-husband frequently.[67] This led to conflicts with Nâzım, who feared the worst from these meetings.[68] "As time passed," wrote Sertel, "their relationship as husband and wife began to change…husband and wife first went to separate beds, and then to separate rooms."[69]

For all his suspicions regarding his wife, Nâzım himself is alleged to have been carrying on an extramarital affair at this time. According to some sources, Nâzım's friend and translator Ekber Babayev introduced a young Azeri woman named Adile Hüseyinova to Nâzım in 1961. Hüseyinova had originally come to Moscow to study music and, at the time that she met Nâzım, was working at the Lenin Library. The relationship, according to Hüseyinova in interviews she would give years later, continued until the last days of Nâzım's life.[70]

Money had become a serious problem, even as Nâzım earned a very good living by Soviet standards. He had given away almost all of his belongings to Galina, and he could not rule out future expenses relating to Münevver and Mehmet—who were now in a much easier position to make financial claims upon him. Meanwhile, life with Nâzım's new bride was not inexpensive. Nâzım was spending considerable sums, such as when he and Vera spent forty days in Paris in April–May 1961.[71]

He signed publishing contracts at a frantic pace in an effort to balance his finances. Plays and films typically commanded the highest fees, but the royalties that Nâzım received varied from one project to another. In 1960, the publisher Iskusstvo agreed to pay Nâzım 3,000 rubles to write a script for a short animated film called *The Cloud that was in Love*.[72] That same year, he inked an agreement with Mosfilm Studios to write a screenplay for a film bearing the title *I am the God of Vengeance*, for which Nâzım would be paid 40,000 rubles.[73] At this time, a typical monthly salary for a physician in the USSR was between 850 and 1,000 rubles per month, with a skilled worker earning between 600 and 900 rubles.[74]

He sold off the rights to works that were old, new, and not yet written. Following the Soviet Union's adoption of a currency reform on January 1, 1961, whereby ten "old" (i.e., pre-1961) rubles were replaced by a single "new" ruble, all pre-1961 salaries and prices were cut by 90 percent. For this reason, the drop-off, in ruble terms, in royalties that Nâzım received at this time is not a reflection of an actual loss in compensation, as the "new" ruble had ten times more buying power than had been the case previously.[75]

---

[67] Dursun Özden, a Turkish poet who befriended Galina Kolesnikova in her final years, claims that Vera Tulyakova continued to carry on a physical relationship with her first husband. *Galina'nın Nâzım'ı*, 102.

[68] Göksu and Timms note Rady Fish's similarly critical take on this union. *Romantic Communist*, 338.

[69] Zekeriya Sertel, *Nâzım Hikmet'in Son Yılları*, 214.

[70] Remzi Öner Özkan, "Bir Nâzım Süprizi," *Radikal*, January 13, 2002; Özden, *Galina'nın Nâzım'ı*, 103.

[71] Following this time in Paris, Vera returned to Moscow on her own while Nâzım continued onward to Cuba. According to Göksu and Timms, Nâzım presented a "peace prize" to Fidel Castro in Havana during this trip. *Romantic Communist*, 326.

[72] RGALI, f. 2250, op. 1, d. 315, l. 2. Contract with Iskusstvo, September 28, 1960.

[73] RGALI, f. 2250, op. 1, d. 316, ll. 1–2. Contract with Mosfilm, June 13, 1960.

[74] Bereday and Schlesinger, "Teacher Salaries in the Soviet Union," 202.

[75] On the 1961 currency "reform," see Kristy Ironside, *A Full-Value Ruble: The Promise of Prosperity in the Postwar Soviet Union* (Cambridge, MA: Harvard University Press, 2021), especially 2, 22, 41–44, 187–189.

In January 1961, Nâzım agreed to a contract with the Mossovet Theater to receive 2,000 rubles (20,000 in "old" rubles) for the production of a play called *The Women's Mutiny*.[76] Later in the year, Nâzım signed an agreement with Iskusstvo to publish five of his plays, for which he would receive 300 rubles each for four of them and 180 rubles for the fifth.[77] The Soviet publisher Detskii Mir ("Children's World") signed a contract paying Nâzım 400 rubles to publish up to 50,000 copies of a book of short stories.[78] The Institute of Asian Peoples agreed to pay 800 rubles for a book of short stories in August 1961.[79]

Nâzım pursued a number of deals outside the USSR as well. On July 22, 1960, he signed a contract with the Romanian company Editura Tineretului, which brought him 8 percent royalties for a run of 8,000 copies for an anthology of his verse.[80] Also in 1960, he came to an agreement with the Czechoslovakian publisher Dilia to publish *The Sword of Damocles* in Slovakian, with 5.9 percent of the royalties for every book sold.[81] The following year Dilia agreed to print, in Czech, a selection of Nâzım's poetry, with a guaranteed minimum payment to Nâzım of 1,500 Czechoslovak crowns.[82]

Western European publishers had also begun to show interest in Nâzım's work. While the actual sums Nâzım received from Western Europe tended to be rather small, these deals nevertheless provided him with exposure in the West, and may have facilitated Nâzım and Vera's travels to Italy and France in the early 1960s. In April 1960, Nâzım signed a contract with the Italian publisher Opera, which gave him an advance of 150,000 Italian lire, as well as 10 percent royalties, for "the full collection of his essays and autobiography," an apparent reference to what would become *Life's Good, Brother*.[83] Another Italian company, Lerici Editori of Milan, agreed to publish Book III of *Human Landscapes*, with an advance of 100,000 lire and a royalty of 6 percent.[84] In 1961, Nâzım signed an agreement with the French label Le Chant du Monde to read four of his poems for a vinyl record they were producing, with a royalty of 5 percent.[85]

Nâzım would continue to be active in the selling of rights to his writings throughout 1962, mostly with respect to plays and films. A contract with Iskusstvo yielded 900 rubles to publish 15,000 copies of Nâzım's play *Was there Really an Ivan Ivanovich?*[86] For the production of a play called *The Cow*, Nâzım was due to receive 3,000 rubles from the Pushkin Theater in Moscow.[87] A contract from the Young Spectator Theater

---

[76] RGALI, f. 2250, op. 1, d. 316, ll. 3–6. January 17, 1961.

[77] RGALI, f. 2250, op. 1, d. 315, l. 5. July 14, 1961. On Nâzım's productions during the late 1950s and early 1960s, see Göksu and Timms, *Romantic Communist*, 291–299; Fevralski, *Nâzım'dan Anılar*.

[78] RGALI, f. 2250, op. 1, d. 315, ll. 3–4-ob. Contract with Detskii Mir. March 29, 1961.

[79] RGALI, f. 2250, op. 1, d. 315, ll. 6–7. Contract with Institute of Asian Peoples, August 1, 1961. The publisher Goslitizdat signed a contract to publish 10,000 copies of a collection of his poems in 1961, with a sliding scale of royalties based upon sales. RGALI, f. 2250, op. 1, d. 315, ll. 8–8-ob.

[80] RGALI, f. 2250, op. 1, d. 314, l. 3. July 22, 1960.

[81] RGALI, f. 2250, op. 1, d. 314, ll. 5–5-ob. March 24, 1960.

[82] RGALI, f. 2250, op. 1, d. 314, l. 7. February 10, 1961.

[83] Contract between Opera and Nâzım Hikmet, April 14, 1960, RGALI, f. 2250, op. 1, d. 314, ll. 1–2. In 1960, 150,000 Italian lire would have been worth about $240.

[84] RGALI, f. 2250, op. 1, d. 314, l. 4. December 21, 1960.

[85] RGALI, f. 2250, op. 1, d. 314, ll. 8–9. June 7, 1961.

[86] RGALI, f. 2250, op. 1, d. 315, ll. 12–13. December 13, 1962.

[87] RGALI, f. 2250, op. 1, d. 316, l. 10. May 23, 1962.

promised to pay 3,000 rubles for the rights to produce his play *The Blind Padishah*,[88] and for a play Nâzım was calling *The Old Place*, he was to receive 1,800 rubles from the Theater Romen.[89] A film company in the Soviet Republic of Tajikistan was paying Nâzım 4,000 rubles to tape a production of the ballet *Legend of Love*, for which Nâzım wrote the libretto.[90] A smaller deal with Goslitizdat brought 250 rubles for "Songs of True Love" and 135 rubles for "The Green Night," an indication of the less lucrative market for poetry in comparison to plays and film screenplays.[91]

According to Zekeriya Sertel, he and Nâzım discussed the latter's plays on a number of occasions. In Zekeriya's later account, he once wondered aloud to Nâzım why a great poet would invest so much time in the writing of plays that, in Zekeriya's estimation, were not nearly as good as his verse. "I have to," Zekeriya reported Nâzım as responding. "I have an enormous amount of expenses and need at least one thousand rubles per month. My poems can't bring me that. I don't want to have to ask anyone for money. I want to live independently in my own little corner. Only my plays can do that for me."[92]

The money Nâzım would earn from the contracts he signed in 1960–62 would come in handy. In November 1962, he and Vera set off again for Europe, this time taking an extended vacation through Milan, Florence, and Rome before moving on to France (Figure 13.1). The couple would stay in Paris until January 4, 1963, when they flew back to Moscow. Nâzım reportedly went on a "spending spree" during the course of their travels, "insist[ing] on buying expensive shoes and clothes for his glamorous young wife."[93]

## Settling Accounts

Süleyman Nuri's April 1962 letter to Mikoyan was bristling with accusation.[94] Yet it was also revealing. Nuri's attack on Nâzım appeared to border on obsession, and he seemed unable to stop repeating the poet-communist's name:

1. Nâzım Hikmet served up the heads of the TKP in İzmir and members of this organization were arrested.
2. Nâzım Hikmet organized in Istanbul an opposition against the leadership of the TKP.

---

[88] RGALI, f. 2250, op. 1, d. 316, ll. 11–13. May 28, 1962.
[89] RGALI, f. 2250, op. 1, d. 316, ll. 7–9. May 23, 1962.
[90] RGALI, f. 2250, op. 1, d. 316, ll. 14–15. October 31, 1962.
[91] On "Songs of True Love," see RGALI, f. 2250, op. 1, d. 315, ll. 10–10-ob. May 14, 1962. For "The Green Night," see ibid., ll. 11–11-ob. June 15, 1962.
[92] Zekeriya Sertel, *Nâzım Hikmet'in Son Yılları*, 107. Gün Benderli takes issue with this representation of Nâzım's plays. *Giderayak*, 118–119.
[93] Göksu and Timms, *Romantic Communist*, 341.
[94] Letter from Süleyman Nuri to Anastas Mikoyan, dated April 18, 1962. RGASPI, f. 495, op. 266, d. 117, ll. 2–7, esp. 4–5.

**Figure 13.1** Nâzım, Vera, and Abidin Dino in Paris, 1962

3. Nâzım Hikmet, in 1938, let's say due to his naïveté, gave up 15 people to the police.
4. Nâzım Hikmet has generals and marshals among his ancestors.
5. Nâzım Hikmet, for the second and last time in 1950, made off from Istanbul on a motorboat via the Bosphorus with a naval sergeant.
6. Nâzım Hikmet, from what I've heard and even read about in Turkey, may be a master of the Turkish language but in his works he extols a bourgeois and philistine life.
7. Nâzım Hikmet married here in Moscow for the second time... Not long ago his first wife came here from Istanbul with her beloved son Memet. He set her up in Warsaw. As far as I know, until recently Nâzım had a Polish passport.[95]

In a separate letter written the same day and addressed to the Central Committee of the TKP, Nuri continued this line of argument, attacking both İsmail Bilen and Nâzım,

---

[95] Letter from Süleyman Nuri to Anastas Mikoyan, April 18, 1962. RGASPI, f. 495, op. 266, d. 117, ll. 2–7, here 4–5. This list was enumerated in this form in Nuri's letter. This is a condensed version, including only the first line from each point. There are three to six sentences per point in the original document.

as well as long-forgotten figures like Ahmet Cevat. While taking care to use more moderate language than was the case in his letter to Mikoyan, Nuri could not resist venting his frustration about Nâzım once more. "It is incomprehensible," he complained, that "for a third time, Nâzım Hikmet would be so quickly accepted into the party."[96] At the same time, Nuri extolled his own credentials by reminding the committee of his long-standing ties to Mustafa Suphi—the man Nuri had repeatedly denounced as a thief in 1920–21—recalling their shared battles against the pan-Turkists.[97]

Nothing that Süleyman Nuri could say was going to have any impact upon the party's view of Nâzım. Indeed, Nuri's letter to the TKP was almost quaint with respect to its writer's faith in the party's ability, or even willingness, to mete out ideological justice. Having recently returned to the USSR after many years in Turkey, Nuri may not have fully understood the degree to which the TKP was now in the hands of people who liked Nâzım.[98] Neither the TKP nor Moscow was going to sanction Nâzım on the testimony of a nobody like Süleyman Nuri.

Nâzım, meanwhile, was seeking to settle some accounts of his own. During the final years of his life, he began to report to friends and others that he was experiencing strong premonitions of death. As a result, he explained, he was working hard to put his affairs in order. This took the form of a variety of tasks, such as writing a new will to replace the previous one he had signed in 1956. According to the new document, which was signed on September 10, 1959, in the event of Nâzım's death 75 percent of his future authorial royalties would go to Münevver and Mehmet, with the remaining 25 percent earmarked for the TKP.[99] It is unclear who else knew about this arrangement, but it may have served as an incentive for the Leipzig-based Turkish communists to formalize their "Foreign Bureau" three years later.

Another long-standing issue that Nâzım sought to resolve at this time was the matter of his citizenship. Even though Nâzım still had a Polish passport, he decided to try again to become a citizen of the USSR.[100] Back in 1957, Nâzım's application to become a Soviet national had been put on hold. Now, with a wife who was a Soviet citizen, he felt a responsibility to apply once more. On December 7, 1961, Nâzım took the unusual step of appealing directly to the General Secretary of the Communist Party, Nikita Khrushchev, to request assistance with this matter.

The tone of Nâzım's letter to Khrushchev is in some ways similar to that which was once used for the party autobiographies that Nâzım and other international communists had written back in the 1920s and 1930s.

---

[96] RGASPI, f. 495, op. 266, d. 117, ll. 30–36, here l. 35. It is unclear what Süleyman Nuri was referring to when he mentioned that Nâzım had been admitted to the party for a "third" time.

[97] On Nuri's references in this letter to Suphi, see RGASPI, f. 495, op. 266, d. 117, ll. 30–37, esp. ll. 30, 35. Letter from Süleyman Nuri to the TKP Central Committee, April 18, 1962.

[98] The episode must have created some kind of a sensation, as Vartan İhmalyan was able to recount parts of it in his memoirs. *Bir Yaşam Öyküsü*, 230–231.

[99] For a copy of this will, see RGALI, f. 2250, op. 1, d. 309, l. 2. September 10, 1959.

[100] On perceptions within the Eastern Bloc that the Polish government was more interested in maintaining connections with Western European countries, see Sheldon Anderson, *A Cold War in the Soviet Bloc: Polish-East German Relations, 1945–1962* (New York: Perseus, 2001), 245–246.

Dear Nikita Sergeyevich,

Since the age of 19, I have been connected with the Soviet Union not only with my heart and head, but also my personal biography.

I first applied to join the party of the Bolsheviks in Moscow in 1923, and then, in 1924, again in Moscow, I joined the Turkish Communist Party.

At the beginning of 1925 I finished KUTV in Moscow and went to Turkey on party work. At the end of 1925 I was sentenced in absentia to 15 years in prison due to the fact that I was working underground.

I returned again to Moscow. In 1928 I again went to Turkey on party work. From this point forward until 1950 I spent, in total, 17 years in prison, although I was sentenced to 56 years behind bars. I was freed from prison thanks to the battle undertaken by progressive people of many countries, the first among which being the Soviet peoples.

I—am one of the luckiest poet-communists. I had the opportunity to celebrate the 5th anniversary of the October Revolution in Moscow and write poems about this.

It's already been ten years that I've been living in Moscow. I have a family here. I've immersed myself into Soviet life, as well as with the whole of the Soviet people. Help me, Dear Nikita Sergeyevich. I want to become a Soviet citizen.

Wishing you the best.

With respect,
Nâzım Hikmet[101]

An interesting detail in this letter is the fact that Nâzım overstates both the number of years he was sentenced to prison after 1928 and the period of time he had actually served. In total, Nâzım had spent about fourteen and a half years in Turkish jails and prisons, and his post-1928 sentences had cumulatively totaled a little more than thirty years. These were significant periods of time in their own right, raising the question of why Nâzım felt the need to exaggerate.[102]

Is it possible that Nâzım simply forgot how many years he had served in prison, or what his sentences had been? Perhaps, but his hyperbole brings to mind earlier occasions on which Nâzım had likewise fibbed or fudged the truth in his dealings with Soviet officials. After having spent the better part of a decade telling his new Soviet friends often implausible stories about his life in Turkey and early years in the USSR, perhaps narrative and reality had become more difficult to separate from one another.

---

[101] RGALI, f. 2250, op. 1, d. 161, l. 4. Nâzım simply referred to the revolution as "October" in the letter. Letter from Nâzım Hikmet to Nikita Khrushchev, December 7, 1961. Melih Güneş provides a reproduction of this letter in *Hasretle*, 99.

[102] At the end of 1928, Nâzım and İsmail had spent roughly five months in jail for crossing the border illegally—the one occasion that Nâzım had been imprisoned for committing a non-political crime. In 1933, he had initially been sentenced to a term of five years, which was immediately shortened to two, with Nâzım ultimately serving fourteen months in prison. He had also spent up to three months in jail pending trial. In 1936–37, Nâzım spent four months in jail awaiting his proceedings. In the army and navy trials, Nâzım had been given a term of twenty-eight years and four months and served just under twelve years, plus six months of detention.

Or maybe, after ten years in the Soviet Union, this onetime truth-teller's instinct to obfuscate had simply become an automatic, unnoticed reflex.

Nâzım finally succeeded, in 1962, in becoming a Soviet citizen. While this development provided some relief to him, his mood concerning his own future only seemed to darken. On January 25, 1963, just three weeks after returning from Paris with Vera, Nâzım wrote a letter to the Communist Party of the Soviet Union that spoke of his impending death.

"I'm very sick," he began. "In a few days I'm set to fly to Tanganyika.[103] I have a presentiment that I won't return."

> I've never asked for anything for myself. But now I'm coming forward with a request. There are two people who are close two me: my wife Vera Tulyakova and my son Memet. I have no savings, and my honoraria will not be enough for them for long. It would be terrible for me to die thinking that in the event of my death they'll be left with nothing.

Nâzım wanted the party to provide for Vera and his son Mehmet after he died, repeating that this was something he felt he deserved. "I think," Nâzım wrote, "that I have the right to count on the help and support of my party, soldier that I have been my whole life."[104]

At first glance, he appeared to have everything—a successful and esteemed career, a comfortable and privileged life in the USSR, an attractive young wife on his arm as they wandered the streets of Paris and Rome. Yet more and more, Nâzım seemed unhappy and morose, focused upon preparations for his own demise. While Süleyman Nuri nursed a grudge for decades and tried to undo Nâzım's success by writing letters to Mikoyan and the TKP Central Committee, he needn't have bothered. For Nâzım, who had lived through multiple incarcerations in Turkey and the last years of Stalin, the most devastating wounds had almost always been self-inflicted ones.

## Late-Life Narratives

Nâzım's poetry had been growing increasingly autobiographical, especially in the years following Stalin's death. For much of the 1950s, Nâzım had frequently written about Münevver, Mehmet, and his life back in Turkey, presenting himself as an exiled family man pining for his homeland. In the last year of his life, however, Nâzım no longer wrote about Münevver or Mehmet. Nor did he produce many poems that were explicitly about Vera, who had often been the subject of his verse when he was

---

[103] Present-day Tanzania.
[104] RGALI, f. 2250, op. 1, d. 161, l. 6. Letter from Nâzım Hikmet to the CPSU, January 25, 1963. For a reproduction of this letter, see Güneş, *Hasretle*, 100–101.

courting her. Unable or unwilling to write about others, Nâzım composed more and more lines about himself.

In September 1961, he wrote what would become one of his better-known later works, "Autobiography." The title is a reference to the party autobiographies that Nâzım and so many others from his generation had composed. Stylistically, the poem also resembled a fun-house mirror image of Nâzım's recent petition to Khrushchev, in form if not in content.

> I was born in 1902
> I never once went back to my birthplace
> I don't like to turn back
> at three I served as a pasha's grandson in Aleppo
> at nineteen as a student at Moscow Communist University
> at forty-nine I was back in Moscow as the Cheka Party's guest
> and I've been a poet since I was fourteen
> some people know all about plants some about fish
> > I know separation
> some people know the names of the stars by heart
> > I recite absences[105]

"Autobiography" reflects a process of adding up the years, an occupation in which Nâzım was increasingly engaged at this time. The poem constituted a literary expression of a broader process of Nâzım's taking care of his end-of-life affairs. Through his efforts to establish future honoraria and royalty payments for his writings, receive Soviet citizenship, write a new will, and make sure that Vera and Mehmet would be provided for, Nâzım had been seeking to tie up his affairs financially. With "Autobiography" and Nâzım's final major work *Life's Good, Brother: A Novel*, Nâzım was likewise setting out to articulate his legacy.

As was the case with "Autobiography," *Life's Good, Brother* was part of a growing concern of Nâzım, in his final years, with consolidating certain narratives regarding his life story.[106] The fact that the word "novel" is embedded within the book's title is telling, as the protagonist of this prose work is someone who has led a life nearly—but not entirely—identical to that of Nâzım Hikmet.[107] The story's hero, "Ahmet," has done everything that Nâzım had done.[108] He traveled across Anatolia during the Turkish War of Liberation, lived in Georgia in the early 1920s, studied in Moscow, was chased by the police in Turkey, and experienced the sorts of travails and

---

[105] Translation from Randy Blasing and Mutlu Konuk, *Poems of Nâzım Hikmet*, 259–260.

[106] As did Atatürk with his famous *Nutuk* ("The Speech").

[107] During the final years of his life, Nâzım was in negotiations to sell a book he was describing as his "autobiography." RGALI, f. 2250, op. 266, d. 314, ll. 1–2.

[108] "Ahmet" was the pseudonym which Nâzım had used when he wrote for *Aydınlık* in 1925.

adventures that fans of Nâzım Hikmet would instantly recognize as having been taken from Nâzım's own biography.[109]

At the same time, *Life's Good, Brother* is nominally fiction. Precisely because the book is a "novel," Nâzım was free to say whatever he wanted about his life in a work that many readers—as well as some of Nâzım's later biographers—would read as a more straightforward memoir.[110] With *Life's Good, Brother*, Nâzım was deliberately flirting with the boundaries of fiction and autobiography in ways that bring to mind the novels of I. B. Singer and Philip Roth. Yet *Life's Good, Brother* also stands as Nâzım's most elaborate self-narrative ever, one that is by turns both self-serving and introspective.

As was the case with young Nâzım, for example, Ahmet has an uncle who is influential in wartime Ankara. Yet, in connecting with this historical fact, Nâzım avails himself of the opportunity to put his own spin on these events, such as when Ahmet recounts his alleged yearning to go to the front.[111]

> The most fertile soil of Anatolia, its most skilled cities, are in enemy hands: fifteen provinces and townships, nine big cities, seven lakes and eleven rivers, three seas and six railroads, and millions of people, our people, are in enemy hands.
>
> I saw my uncle: "I want to go to the front."
>
> "Impossible," he said.
>
> I insisted.
>
> "I'll see," he said.

The next day, Ahmet is heartbroken when he is told "you do not have permission to go to the front. They'll find you a job in the Press Office." "I did not try to fathom why I was not permitted to go to the front," he complains to the reader. But then, in a moment that resembles genuine reflection, the narrator asks: "Maybe I should have insisted on going, and maybe I would have been allowed, but I didn't."[112]

In another scene from *Life's Good*, the narrator—the book alternates between first- and third-person narration—describes walking from İnebolu with a group of former Ottoman prisoners of war.

"How old are you?" one of them asked.

"I just turned nineteen."

"We'll soon see you at the front," came the response.

---

[109] On *Life's Good* from a literary perspective, see Nergis Ertürk, "Nâzım Hikmet and the Prose of Communism," *Boundary 2: An International Journal of Literature and Culture*, vol. 47, no. 2 (2020), 153–180.

[110] Blasing, for example, cites *Life's Good* as a source for describing Nâzım's experiences in İzmir in 1925, as well as the criminal justice system in Bolu in 1921. *Nâzım Hikmet*, 59, 259, fn. 47. Sülker likewise employs *Life's Good* uncritically, taking the experiences of "Ahmet" as necessarily those of Nâzım. *Nâzım Hikmet'in Gerçek Yaşamı*, vol. 1, 106–107.

[111] Vâlâ's memoirs barely mention the fighting taking place in Anatolia, and never discuss the possibility of the boys going to the front.

[112] Nâzım Hikmet, *Life's Good, Brother*, 63. Citing no one but apparently getting the information from *Life's Good, Brother*, Blasing writes that "Nâzım was not allowed to go to the front. He had asked to be assigned to active duty, but he and Vâ-Nû were instead assigned jobs in the Press Office." *Nâzım Hikmet*, 44.

Later, they stop at an inn, where Ahmet sits down to a small feast of butter and honey served on steaming hot *lavash* bread. He looks up to see his traveling companions eating only the bread and cheese they had carried with them from İnebolu.

"Didn't they give you a travel allowance?"

"They did."

"How much?"

"Ten liras each."

Ahmet had been given one hundred liras. Embarrassed, he offers his food to the once and future soldiers. "Yes, no, it's embarrassing, and so on," wrote Nâzım in *Life's Good, Brother*. "[T]he innkeeper brought everyone butter, honey, lavash bread, and kefir. However, I felt an unbearable shame inside me. I'm like a prodigal heir spending his fortune wining and dining the poor."

But then, an epiphany of sorts. Nâzım's protagonist asks: "Damn it. Did I think all this back then? Or am I thinking it all up now?"[113]

*Life's Good, Brother* was published first in Russian, based on a translation from the original Turkish, in 1963. This edition was soon followed by French and Turkish versions—the latter published in Bulgaria—which came out later that year. The book first appeared in print in Turkey in 1967.[114] While Nâzım's other prose works—including his novels, plays, and films—have not been as well remembered as his poetry, *Life's Good, Brother* has, by contrast, stood out as perhaps the only well-known and well-liked work of Nâzım's non-verse.

One reason behind this work's relative popularity may have something to do with the fact that *Life's Good, Brother*, like Nâzım's poetry, crosses borders. It takes its readers through a facsimile of Nâzım's life, but follows a jagged itinerary, jumping between time periods, countries, and narrators. Whereas most of Nâzım's prose stays in one place, his best-known and most popular writing is that which reflects the border-crossing context in which Nâzım had led most of his life.

Now, however, Nâzım's border-crossing days were coming to an end.[115]

With one exception.

## One More Border to Cross

In April 1963, Nâzım wrote "My Funeral Service."

> Will my funeral start out from our courtyard?
> How will you get me down from the third floor?

---

[113] Nâzım Hikmet, *Life's Good, Brother*, 53.

[114] Mutlu Konuk Blasing, "Introduction," from Hikmet, *Life's Good, Brother*, xiii.

[115] Nâzım had retained his habit, begun in the early 1950s, of recording the place where he had composed each poem. Whereas in previous years his notes listed hundreds of works written during his relentless travels through Eastern Europe, in 1962–63 he appears to have made only one short trip to Bucharest (in June of 1962) and another to Berlin (in April of 1963), in addition to his February 1963 journey to Tanzania. See the Yapı Kredi edition of Nâzım Hikmet's collected works (*Şiirler*, Vol. 7), 143–145, 178–180.

My coffin won't fit in the elevator,
and the stairs are awfully narrow.

Maybe there'll be sun knee-deep in the yard, and pigeons,

maybe snow filled with children's laughter,
maybe rain with its wet asphalt.
And the trashcans will stand in the courtyard as always.

If, as is the custom here, I'm put in the truck open-faced,
a pigeon might drop something on my forehead: it's good luck.
Band or no band, kids will come up to me—
They're curious about the dead.

Our kitchen window will watch me leave.
Our balcony will see me off with the wash on the line.
In this yard I was happier than you'll ever know.
Neighbors, I wish you all long lives.[116]

Thoughts of death surrounded Nâzım during his final year. But what had so persuaded him, at this particular moment, that his life would soon come to an end?

On the morning of June 3, 1963, Nâzım Hikmet woke up early as usual, at around 7:30. He was in the habit of sleeping on the couch in the living room, and had apparently gotten up to get the newspaper.[117] Vera would later state that upon getting out of bed and leaving her room, she found Nâzım's dead body slumped up against the front door.[118]

In Vera's telling, she later found, in the days after Nâzım's death, the following poem on the back of a photograph of herself inside Nâzım's jacket:

Come, she said to me
stay, she said to me
laugh, she said to me
die, she said to me

I came
I stayed
I laughed
I died[119]

Could the words "I died" have really constituted the last line of verse that Nâzım ever wrote in his lifetime? Like so many of the anecdotes relating to Nâzım's life, this one sounds too perfect to be true. But was this just a fanciful story, a noteworthy coincidence, or a suicide note?

---

[116] Translation from Blasing and Konuk, *Poems of Nâzım Hikmet*, 269.
[117] Nesin, *Türkiye Şarkısı Nâzım*, 30.       [118] Göksu and Timms, *Romantic Communist*, 346.
[119] Tulyakova-Hikmet, *Bahtiyar Ol Nâzım*, 426.

According to a Turkish journalist's interview with Nâzım's alleged lover Adile Hüseyinova, Nâzım had shown up in a desperate state at her Moscow apartment in the spring of 1963. Nâzım, in Hüseyinova's account, felt absolutely devastated. "My heart is tired," Nâzım reportedly complained to her. "It hurts."

The cause of this misery was, according to Hüseyinova, Nâzım's wife Vera. In a call that Adile allegedly made to Ekber Babayev after Nâzım had left her apartment that day, Babayev told her that a major "scandal" had erupted between Nâzım and Vera. "Vera has been meeting up with her ex-husband, she's been cheating on [Nâzım]. Nâzım has learned this and is in terrible shape," Babayev reportedly told her. This news reminded Adile of something Nâzım had mentioned to her earlier that day. Referring to the suicide of Ernest Hemingway two years earlier, Nâzım had supposedly told Adile that Hemingway had "acted bravely in killing himself. If you can't do anything, you should go."[120]

On May 31, 1963, recalled Hüseyinova in her 2002 interview, Nâzım visited her apartment on Leningradskoe Shosse. Hüseyinova described him as looking as if he were about to collapse. "I'm like a leaf which has fallen from its tree," Nâzım reportedly told her. "I wander, I wander, and I don't know where I'm going to land. Most likely I won't end up in my native country." "The worst thing in life," she remembered him telling her, "the hardest thing, is being deceived. There's nothing harder than that."

"What can I do for you?" she asked him.

"Just cry with me, that's enough."

Nâzım, in Hüseyinova's later recollection, then kissed her eyes and said: "this means farewell."

The next day, however, Nâzım showed up again at Adile's door, his mood seemingly brightened. He was carrying his typewriter, which he had earlier promised to give her. According to Hüseyinova, "He had pulled himself together. His indecision had left him and he trusted himself. For the first time, he called me his darling (*sevgili*)." In Hüseyinova's account, Nâzım then told her that he had some important business to attend to, but that he would come back at noon on June 3, and from that point forward would be staying with her.[121] She never saw him again.

What to make of this story? Nâzım's cause of death has always been described as a heart attack, although the death announcements in the newspapers published the day after Nâzım's demise made no mention of the cause.[122] To be sure, the notion that Nâzım would have passed away in this manner hardly strains credulity. He had a long history of health problems and had almost died of a heart attack in 1952.

On the other hand, by most accounts Nâzım had become deeply depressed in the final years of his life. He had a history of depression, and on at least two occasions had overdosed on sleeping pills—intentionally, according to people who knew him at those times. In the last years of his life, moreover, Nâzım had worked hard to put his

---

[120] Özkan, "Bir Nâzım Süprizi"; Özden, *Galina'nın Nâzım'ı*, 46, 103–104.

[121] Özkan, "Bir Nâzım Süprizi"; Özden, *Galina'nın Nâzım'ı*, 46, 103–104.

[122] "Pamiati Nazyma Khikmeta," *Pravda*, June 4, 1963, p. 3; "Nazym Khikmet," *Literaturnaia Gazeta*, no. 66, June 4, 1963, p. 3.

affairs in order. He had given away nearly all of his belongings, including his books.[123] He spoke frequently of death, and was seemingly convinced that he would be dying soon. It does not seem unimaginable that he may have felt this way because he was planning to commit suicide.[124]

Nâzım had, moreover, reached what may have seemed to him a point of finality with respect to his literary career. The year before, he had completed his masterpiece *Human Landscapes from My Country*, a project that he had been working on for more than two decades. Nâzım had also just finished his fictionalized autobiography *Life's Good, Brother*, which would stand as his concluding testament regarding his life and experiences. Less monumental but still telling, he had composed one last short poem that literally ended with the words "I died."

\*

Like many from his time, Nâzım was skilled at producing self-narrative. He did so until the very end.

---

[123] And his typewriter, according to Hüseyinova.

[124] Whether or not Nâzım died of a heart attack, he appears to have been suicidal.

# Epilogue

## Afterlives

Gün Benderli Togay was looking out the window of her high-rise hotel in Sofia, Bulgaria, in September 1959. She had spent the last several days with her parents and younger sister, none of whom she had seen for the better part of a decade.[1]

It was a dream come true.

İsmail Bilen had organized the visit. As usual, he had been secretive about what, exactly, was going to happen. After all these years, he had still not abandoned his conspiratorial air, even when he was doing a comrade a favor.

Gün had traveled down to Bulgaria from Leipzig. She knew what was happening but wasn't sure how it was going to take place. She had been instructed to wait at a particular spot on a certain platform inside Sofia's dimly lit central train station. Young daughter in hand, Gün wondered if she would only get a chance to talk to her family for the fifteen minutes or so that their train would be in the station. Or perhaps she would travel with them on the train until they got to the border? She had no idea, but the promise of seeing her family, even if only for fifteen minutes, had erased all other thoughts from her mind.

When her family actually got off the train at the station, Gün was delighted. She, her daughter, parents, and younger sister would all be staying in neighboring rooms at a fancy, modern hotel in the Bulgarian capital. It was great news.

But Gün then noticed that her mother seemed to be eyeing her guardedly. Acting on a hunch, Gün pulled up her sleeve and showed off her birthmark. The elbow stain! Immediately, Gün's mother relaxed, certain at last that the young woman she was talking to on the platform was in fact her long-lost daughter.[2]

They never left the hotel. Instead, the long-separated family members sat in their rooms the whole time, chatting idly about the old days. When it came time for her parents and sister to go, Gün saw them off at the station. Back in her hotel room, Gün looked out the big glass windows and asked herself: "and if I were to jump from here right now…?"[3]

---

[1] Gün Benderli, conversation with the author, June 1, 2018. On meeting up with her parents in Sofia, also see Benderli, *Su Başında Durmuşuz*, 362–363. According to her party record, the last time Gün had been in Turkey was 1949. RGASPI, 495-266-275, ll. 1–1-ob. Party autobiography, Gün Togay, September 2, 1954.

[2] Gün Benderli, conversation with the author, June 1, 2018.

[3] Gün Benderli, conversation with the author, June 1, 2018.

*Red Star over the Black Sea: Nâzim Hikmet and his Generation.* James H. Meyer, Oxford University Press. © James H. Meyer 2023.
DOI: 10.1093/oso/9780192871176.003.0016

Gün had told me this story during the course of a conversation we had at her apartment in Budapest in June 2018. A few weeks later we met again, and I asked her to follow-up. Gün was quick to correct my interpretation. Looking out the window of the hotel, she said, she had been sad because she missed her family—and not, she assured me, as a result of any remorse regarding her decision to immigrate to the Eastern Bloc. To the contrary, Gün insisted that she regretted absolutely nothing about the choices she had made in her life.[4] Having given up so much for a cause, even one that had seemingly been so thoroughly discredited, Gün was adamant. Whatever people might think of the ideology today, she had done what she felt was right.

And Nâzım had never seriously wavered in his belief, either, at least in Gün's eyes. She noted that Nâzım was, in her estimation, "the greatest believer" that she had ever known.

"Believer in what?" I asked.

"He was the greatest believer I ever knew," she repeated, laughing. "But for the life of me I can't tell you what he believed in."[5]

## Life after Nâzım

Vâlâ Nureddin went on to establish a highly original writing career for himself, working as a journalist and becoming one of the most important early authors of Turkish pulp fiction. In the 1960s Vâlâ and his wife Müzehher collaborated on the production of a series of young adult novels under the pseudonym "Nihal Karamağaralı." Vâlâ died in 1967, and Müzehher in 2011. Şevket Süreyya would write sixteen books, all of them non-fiction, including biographies of Atatürk, İsmet İnönü, Enver Pasha, and Adnan Menderes. He died in 1976, with Leman Aydemir passing away in 2001. Ahmet Cevat Emre continued to publish frequently on subjects relating to Turkic and Turkish philology until his death in 1961.

Nüzhet Berkin eventually found the quiet life she had been looking for. She passed away in 1987. Dr. Lena Yurchenko, according to Vera Tulyakova, died tragically in a cholera epidemic.[6] Piraye went on living in Istanbul, refusing all interviews. She died in 1995. Her son Memet Fuat maintained a good relationship with Nâzım, albeit of a long-distance variety, and would go on to write and edit several books about him.[7] Memet Fuat died not long after Piraye, in 2002.

---

[4] Gün Benderli, conversations with the author, June 2 and June 19, 2018.

[5] Conversation with the author, June 19, 2018. Zekeriya Sertel similarly described Nâzım as having been "in need of believing." See *Nâzım Hikmet'in Son Yılları*, 187. Orhan Kemal likewise wrote that "Nâzım was a believer. He respected people who believe in a cause, whatever it might be." *In Jail with Nâzım Hikmet*, 98.

[6] Nâzım was the source of this information, but it is unclear how he came to know this. Tulyakova, *Bahtiyar Ol Nâzım*, 253.

[7] In a July 23, 1962 letter to Nâzım's friend Abidin Dino, Memet Fuat—who continued to spell his name the way Nâzım had first written it for him as a child—wrote warmly about Nâzım and expressed an interest in meeting up with him in East Germany if possible. RGALI, f. 2250, op. 1, d. 463. Letter from Memet Fuat Bengü to Abidin Dino.

Münevver would thrive professionally once she left Turkey. After living in Warsaw for several years, she married a French citizen of Russian origins by the name of Volkoff.[8] The two lived in France, but Münevver continued to visit Poland in the summers, in addition to making the occasional trip to Moscow.[9] She went on to become one of the most important twentieth-century translators of Turkish fiction and poetry. Turkish writers whose works Münevver Andaç helped introduce to readers of French include not only Nâzım Hikmet, but also Yaşar Kemal and Orhan Pamuk, the latter of whom was awarded the Nobel Prize for Literature in 2006.

In an August 1964 letter to Konstantin Simonov, who was the literary executor of Nâzım's estate, Münevver complained about the manner in which others were trying to gain from Nâzım. They were selling salacious stories, she said, commodifying him. "Nâzım has become some real merchandise. Everyone wants to profit from him."

> I've read the memoirs of his "friends." Mehmet said something quite right about them, he said that after reading these stories: "One would say that he led the life of an international playboy, some kind of Rubirosa." It's very true. Nothing but stories of women. I know well that he had many of them, but Nâzım all the same had another side, he was a great poet, a sincere communist, a generous man. People think of nothing other than money, and have commercialized their memories and their old friendship. I was asked for my memoirs, but I didn't respond. It's horrible, all of this.[10]

Münevver would outlive Nâzım by thirty-five years, passing away in France in 1998.[11] Their son Mehmet Nâzım would have a difficult time reconciling himself with his father's legacy. After the fallout stemming from the 1970 publication of an interview he gave about Nâzım, in which he was quite critical of his father, Mehmet refused to speak publicly of Nâzım again.[12] Mehmet Nâzım went on to become a painter, living out his years in Paris. He died in 2018.

Dr. Galina Kolesnikova, who would later re-settle in the Volga-Ural Republic of Udmurtia, does not appear to have ever married. Late in life, she gave interviews and wrote a book about her experiences with Nâzım. Photographs reveal Galina to have been living in a small house in the provinces that had been partially converted into a shrine dedicated to the late poet-communist. In 2014, Dr. Galina passed away at the age of 97.

Following Nâzım's death, Vera Tulyakova would go on to pursue a long academic career. In 1966, she began studying in the graduate program at the All-Union State Institute of Cinematography. After completing her degree, she received a position

---

[8] RGALI, f. 1814, op. 9, d. 1932, l. 11. Letter to Konstantin Simonov, 1971. Gün Benderli writes that Münevver had married "a rich and cultured" man of likely Slavic origins. *Giderayak*, 113.

[9] Münevver's last letters to Simonov were written in an elegant, handwritten Russian. See letters from Münevver Andaç-Volkoff to Konstantin Simonov, RGALI, f. 1814, op. 9, d. 1932, ll. 5–6, 11.

[10] Porfirio Rubirosa was a well-known international playboy of the 1950s. RGALI, f. 1814, op. 9, d. 1932, l. 1. Letter from Münevver Andaç to Konstantin Simonov, August 29, 1964.

[11] Most of the women in this story would outlive their male partners by decades.

[12] This was published in 1970 as *Mehmet Nâzım'ı Anlatıyor* (Ankara: Kardeş, 1970).

teaching at the same institute. In 1989, Vera published a book in which she described a "conversation" that she had with Nâzım starting "two–three weeks after his death."[13] It's a decidedly one-way discourse in which Vera, addressing Nâzım, recalls stories from their time together. She died in 2001 at the age of 69.

In November 1962, 67-year-old Sabiha Sertel was granted a pension from the International Department of the CPSU, and she and Zekeriya were given an apartment in Baku.[14] It was a time that Sabiha and Zekeriya's daughter Yıldız would later recall as one of disappointment for Sabiha. Coming from Leipzig, wrote Yıldız later, Sabiha found their living conditions appalling—in Azerbaijan more generally, and their apartment in particular. Yıldız Sertel, who was living with her parents at this time, would later describe the apartment as "third world."[15]

Living out her final years in the Azeri capital with Zekeriya and Yıldız, Sabiha wrote her memoirs, *Roman Gibi* ("Like a Novel"). As is the case with Zekeriya's published recollections, Sabiha's writing obfuscates as much as it explains, focusing mainly upon political issues in Turkey in the 1930s and 1940s, the Sertels' legal trials from those years, and the actions of the Turkish government in its crackdown on leftists. Like Zekeriya Sertel's *Hatırladıklarım* ("What I Remember"), Sabiha's memoirs end, frustratingly, with the couple's departure from Turkey in 1950. *Roman Gibi* was first published in Turkey in 1969, one year after Sabiha Sertel died of cancer in Baku. She is buried in Azerbaijan.

In the numerous books of memoirs that Sabiha and Zekeriya wrote, neither of them ever explicitly mentions that they were living in the Eastern Bloc. The closest that Zekeriya ever came to publicly discussing his life after 1950 took place in the form of the books he wrote about Nâzım. But even in these instances Zekeriya is a mysterious presence, suddenly meeting up with Nâzım in Vienna, for instance, but never revealing anything about his own circumstances. Within the Sertel family, too, information pertaining to Zekeriya, Sabiha, and Yıldız's whereabouts was kept close to the chest. Tia O'Brien, Sabiha and Zekeriya's American-born granddaughter, recalls that family pictures of her grandparents, images that Tia and her parents had thought were of Vienna, were actually taken in Budapest and Leipzig.[16]

Why would the Sertels have kept quiet about living in the Eastern Bloc? One possible reason, suggested to me by Gün Benderli, was that Zekeriya had long nursed hopes of returning to Turkey.[17] After Sabiha's death, Zekeriya left the Soviet Union, re-locating to Paris. He soon began lobbying the Turkish government for permission to visit. After years of staying away from Turkey because he had feared arrest, in 1977 Zekeriya

---

[13] Vera Tuliakova-Khikmet, *Poslednii razgovor s Nazymom* (Moscow: Vremia, 2009), 9. This was later published as *Bahtiyar Ol Nâzım*.

[14] She was given 120 rubles per month. RGASPI, f. 495, op. 266, d. 23, l. 31. Personal file of Sabiha Sertel. On these years, also see Atay, *Serteller*, 369–372, 375–392.

[15] Yıldız Sertel, *Annem*, 250.

[16] Tia O'Brien, personal conversation with the author, November 16, 2019. Also see Tia O'Brien, "Preface," Sabiha Sertel, *The Struggle for Modern Turkey*, xii–xiv; Atay, *Serteller*, 321–323.

[17] Gün Benderli, personal conversation with the author, Budapest, June 2, 2018. Also see Benderli, *Giderayak*, 74.

finally made a short trip to Istanbul. He then went back to Paris, where he died in May 1980.[18]

Zekeriya had never joined the Communist Party, either in Turkey or the USSR, and was typically listed as "non-party" in his TKP paperwork.[19] It was Sabiha who had been the party member—according to her Comintern file, she had joined the TKP in 1935.[20] Sabiha had been the true believer, the one who had led the family to East Berlin, Budapest, Leipzig, and Baku.

The books that Zekeriya would write in relation to Nâzım were critical of the Soviet Union and communism, sometimes quite bitterly so, and present Nâzım as naïve and credulous when it came to life in the Eastern Bloc. Years later, Zekeriya would repeat these critiques in a more obvious manner in *Olduğu Gibi: Rus Biçimi Sosyalizm* ("The Way It Is: Russian-Style Socialism"), which was published posthumously in 1993. Tia O'Brien recalls her grandfather Zekeriya Sertel telling her in 1978: "Communism is for fools."[21]

Yıldız Sertel lived with her parents in Baku until her mother's death, at which point she moved to Paris with her father. Between 1971 and 1989, she taught Ottoman and Middle Eastern History at the University of Paris. In 1991, Yıldız returned to Turkey, where she established a foundation for journalists and wrote books about her parents and herself. Yıldız Sertel died in Istanbul on December 17, 2009.

The file of Alexander Senkevich, one of the largest among the TKP membership at RGASPI, comes to an end almost immediately after the conclusion of the "scandal in the Comintern" in April 1943. Some reports indicate that Senkevich was arrested in the 1940s, and one source even states that he "died in a camp."[22] If Senkevich was indeed arrested or imprisoned, he appears to have survived the ordeal. Nâzım's old friend from the Egyptian Communist Party, Charlotte Rosenthal, who had written to Nâzım in 1955 from a sanatorium outside Moscow, mentioned that she had entrusted her letter to Senkevich because she did not know Nâzım's address.[23] Vartan İhmalyan also refers to Senkevich in his memoirs, in connection with developments transpiring in the 1950s and 1960s.[24]

Sevim Tarı became Sevim Belli after marrying fellow Turkish communist Mihri Belli. On the run from Turkish prosecutors, the two spent years in Algeria in the early 1960s. In 1964, Mihri and Sevim returned to Turkey, where they remained until the military takeover of September 12, 1980. The two later came back to Turkey following

---

[18] On Zekeriya Sertel's final years, also see Atay, *Serteller*, 393–421.

[19] See, for example, RGASPI, f. 495, op. 266, d. 48, "Mustafa Zekerriya Sertel" [Zekeriya Sertel], ll. 31, 35.

[20] RGASPI, f. 495, op. 266, d. 23, l. 2. "Spravka" from January 6, 1943. Written by Belov.

[21] O'Brien writes that, as of 1978, Zekeriya Sertel still "insists that if it hadn't been for Sabiha, he wouldn't have been forced to leave the country." O'Brien, *The Struggle for Modern Turkey*, xv.

[22] See Cemal Kıral's footnote to his translation of Kolarova-Bilen's memoirs *Kanatlı Gençlik*, 47, fn. 54. Kemal Sülker, a biographer of Nâzım Hikmet, mentions that "Niko" (one of Alexander's nicknames) Senkevich was among those arrested during the purges. *Nâzım Hikmet'in Gerçek Yaşamı*, vol. 2, 33.

[23] Letter from Charlotte to Nâzım Hikmet, January 15, 1955, RGALI, f. 2250, op. 1, d. 277, ll. 110–112-ob. Charlotte's note to Senkevich, thanking him for passing on the message to Nâzım, is included with her message to Nâzım. It is unclear whether or not Charlotte actually saw or spoke to Senkevich.

[24] Senkevich is listed as a signatory to a TKP document from April 13, 1965, in İhmalyan, *Bir Yaşam Öyküsü*, 234. Also see ibid., 244, 253–254.

the country's return to civilian rule. Mihri Belli passed away in Silivri, outside of Istanbul, in August 2011. Sevim Belli resides in Turkey.[25]

Gün Benderli has written three books about her life. She was kind enough to meet with me at her apartment in Budapest for three sets of conversations that took place in June 2018. In most cases, what Gün said to me in person about the past hewed closely to her written memoirs. Only on rare occasions, such as when she talked about jumping out of a tall building in Sofia, did Gün's in-person narrative diverge from what she had already put to paper. She remains intellectually engaged in sharing her stories about Nâzım Hikmet and her personal role in the history of the Cold War borderlands.[26]

One of the more unlikely survivors from Nâzım's generation was Şükrü Martel. The Turkish academic and writer İlhan Başgöz would write, years later, about having received a telephone call in his Moscow hotel room from Şükrü Martel sometime in the 1970s. Başgöz was, at that time, visiting Moscow in an official capacity on behalf of the Turkish government. On the phone, Martel explained to Başgöz that he was a Turk living in the USSR, and that he wanted to visit his hometown of Mersin. Martel had, apparently, received permission from Soviet authorities to go to Turkey, but the Turkish government would not grant him a visa. Could Başgöz help him out with this matter?

Başgöz relayed Martel's request to Turkish Prime Minister Bülent Ecevit. In Başgöz's rendering of the story, Martel received his visa for Turkey shortly thereafter.[27] Martel does appear to have spent some time in Turkey during the years to follow. He was the author of an article about Nâzım Hikmet that appeared in the Istanbul daily *Vatan* in 1976, although it is not clear where Martel was living at the time of this article's publication. Nail Çakırhan mentions in his memoirs that he had met up with Martel in Turkey in 1977 or 1978.[28] A column in *Cumhuriyet* from 1990 announcing Martel's death states that he had been living in the USSR and visited Turkey in the 1980s.[29]

The "nervous" outcast who had been sent to Moscow "by mistake" in the 1920s had, following his expulsion from KUTV, survived experiences that were not simply humiliating, but also exceedingly dangerous. He had been kicked out of the party repeatedly, arrested by the NKVD, and exiled to Siberia, yet somehow had managed to survive. Şükrü lived almost to the age of ninety, and up until his final years was still crossing borders.

---

[25] Sevim Belli's memoirs are called *Boşuna mı Çiğnedik?*

[26] I.e., the terrain where communist and anti-communist border-crossers resided. On Cold War-era border-crossers from East to West, see Susan L. Carruthers, *Cold War Captives: Imprisonment, Escape, and Brainwashing* (Berkeley: University of California Press, 2009). Also see Idem., "Between Camps: Eastern Bloc "Escapees" and Cold War Borderlands," *American Quarterly*, Vol. 57, No. 3, (September 2005), 911–942.

[27] İlhan Başgöz, "Yolu Bülent Ecevit'ten Geçen Anılar," *Radikal*, November 12, 2006. Also see İbrahim Dilek, "Türk Dünyası Edebiyatında Repressiya," *Türk Dünyası Dil ve Edebiyat Dergisi*, no. 48 (Autumn, 2019), 27–81, esp. 54–55.

[28] Çakırhan, *Anılar*, 100. On Martel's July 10, 1976 article in *Vatan*, see Göksu and Timms, *Romantic Communist*, 71. Also see Gündüz Vassaf, *Annem Belkıs* (İstanbul: İlestişim Yayınları, 2017).

[29] "Şükrü Martel Öldü," *Cumhuriyet*, March 18, 1990, p. 2.

## Grumpy Old Communists

The TKP Foreign Bureau was made up of a bickering bunch.[30] The divisions that had grown within the organization during the final years of Nâzım's life only intensified in the decade following his death. The months-long series of arguments between Zeki Baştımar and İsmail Bilen over the creation of the Foreign Bureau's Central Committee was only a prelude to the battles that the two would fight in the years to come. The metastasizing of these TKP leadership-related conflicts may have had something to do with the fact that the TKP was now, according to Nâzım's will, the beneficiary of 25 percent of his publishing royalties.[31] There was, it seems, money to be spent, but who would get to spend it?

The Foreign Bureau met about once a month in Leipzig. Members of the body's Central Committee did not receive a salary, but working for the party did come with some perks. Committee members were given road money to attend conferences and other meetings, in addition to receiving subsidized vacations to places like Sochi and Varna.[32] By November 1965, the Central Committee consisted of İsmail Bilen, Zeki Baştımar, Abidin Dino, Aram Pehlivanyan, Gün Togay, and Bilal Şen.[33] One "spravka" from the Soviet party's international division noted laconically that "the Central Committee of the TKP supposedly (*iakoby*) consists of 13 people."[34] Some of the individuals on this list, like Zekeriya Sertel, were not, in fact, even members of the party.[35] Yet even as the TKP's political imprint became increasingly inconsequential, the political battles within the party grew only more heated.[36]

İsmail Bilen was biding his time. He had survived not only Stalinism, but also the anti-Stalinism of Khrushchev's rule. Amid, however, the anti-anti-Stalinism of the early years of Leonid Brezhnev, who had led the coup ousting Nikita Khrushchev in October 1964, Bilen understood that he may have found yet another second chance.

Snubbed in favor of Zeki Baştımar with respect to the title of "First Secretary" of the Foreign Bureau, Bilen made life difficult for his adversary. Baştımar, for his part, felt obliged to respond to slights relating to Bilen and the question of who the real leader of the TKP was. In October 1971, Zeki Baştımar sent a letter to the Central Committee of the Bulgarian Communist Party to complain that Bilen had been introduced at a Bulgarian party meeting as the "Secretary general of the TKP."

---

[30] In particular, İsmail and Zeki Baştımar feuded bitterly over the TKP leadership in the early 1970s. RGASPI, f. 495, op. 266, d. 12, Part II, ll. 146, 150, 159; f. 495, op. 266, d. 273, l. 7. Also see Benderli, *Su Başında Durmuşuz*, 414–425; Açıkgöz, *Anadolulu bir Ermeni Komünistin Anıkları*, 539–51.

[31] It is unclear who receives this share of the royalty money today.

[32] Gün Benderli, conversation with the author, June 2. 2018.

[33] "Spravka" on Zeki Baştımar from June 28, 1966. RGASPI, f. 495, op. 266, d. 30, l. 116.

[34] "Spravka" from March 21, 1968. RGASPI, f. 495, op. 266, d. 30, l. 68.

[35] On Zekeriya Sertel not being in the TKP, see RGASPI, f. 495, op. 266, d. 48, l. 35. Included in the Central Committee were Zeki Baştımar, Zekeriya Sertel, Sabiha Sertel, Fahri Erdinç, Süreya Üstüngel (one of İsmail Bilen's many *noms de guerre*), as well as younger members such as Halis Okan, Ahmed Akenci, and Ahmed Saydam (Aram Pehlivanyan).

[36] On the various feuds taking place within the TKP at this time, see İhmalyan, *Bir Yaşam Öyküsü*, 256–300.

Apparently it wasn't the first time. "As we have already informed you," wrote Baştımar to the Bulgarian Communist Party, Bilen "is only a member of the politburo of the Central Committee of the TKP," and not the general secretary.[37] Baştımar had experienced a similar problem in Moscow in 1970, when İsmail Bilen had attended a meeting of "communist party leaders of European countries" and likewise had given the other attendees the impression that he was the TKP's leader.[38]

In November 1972, Zeki Baştımar began to suffer from internal bleeding, requiring his hospitalization in East Berlin. Six months later, in the last week of May 1973, Bilen struck at the prostrate Baştımar with everything he had. As the TKP leader lay in the hospital, İsmail disseminated what he claimed was Baştımar's medical report to the TKP Central Committee.

İsmail put it bluntly:

According to the March 28, 1973 report of the doctors at the hospital in the DDR, after suffering an apoplexy in November 1972, the health of Comrade Demir [Baştımar] has gotten even worse. In the report, it is made clear that Comrade Demir has aged prematurely due to general arteriosclerosis, coronasclerosis, and cerebral sclerosis. For this reason, he can't work with his head anymore.[39]

Bilen urged the Central Committee to take a vote on the party's leadership. It went against Baştımar, and he was replaced by İsmail Bilen.[40]

Zeki Baştımar was outraged. From his hospital bed, the ousted TKP leader dictated a bitter riposte, expressing his sense of shock at the committee's actions. He complained that "the so-called decision of the Foreign Bureau" was the result of "confusion" regarding the state of his health. Baştımar appealed for assistance from the international department of the Communist Party of the Soviet Union, arguing that he had been improperly replaced. The complaints fell on deaf ears, however, and Bilen was confirmed as the TKP's new leader.[41] Baştımar died in East Berlin on November 18, 1974.

As undisputed TKP leader from 1973 onward, İsmail Bilen finally came out of the shadows. Some fifty-one years after first traveling to Moscow to attend KUTV, he began to develop a more public personal profile. Based in Moscow, Sofia, and Leipzig, İsmail traveled the globe well into his seventies (Figure 14.1). As was the norm for party leaders in Brezhnev's USSR, he was festooned with awards and medals, like the "Friendship of Nations" prize, which he received in 1977.[42] On his eightieth birthday,

---

[37] RGASPI, f. 495, op. 266, d. 12, Part II, l. 159. Letter to the Central Committee of the Bulgarian Communist Party, October 28, 1971.

[38] RGASPI, f. 495, op. 266, d. 12, Part II, l. 161. On these events, also see Açıkgöz, *Anadolulu bir Ermeni Komünistin Anıları*, 601.

[39] RGASPI, f. 495, op. 266, d. 30, ll. 29–30. Letter from İsmail Bilen ["Marat"] and Aram Pehlivanyan to the Central Committee of the TKP. May 24, 1973.

[40] Akbulut, *Zeki Baştımar*, 10.    [41] RGASPI, f. 495, op. 266, d. 30, ll. 15–22, here esp. 19, 22.

[42] RGASPI, f. 495, op. 266, d. 12, Part II, l. 84. Article from *Pravda*, November 10, 1977.

**Figure 14.1** Meeting Fidel Castro in Cuba in 1978

in 1982, İsmail Bilen was awarded the Order of the October Revolution.[43] East German leader Erich Honecker presented him with the "Great Star of Friendship of Peoples" on November 5 of that same year.[44]

A communist who possessed a decidedly entrepreneurial streak, Bilen had somehow managed to keep himself employed for decades, receiving multiple stipends and paychecks from various organizations in different countries, often simultaneously. He'd come a long way since his days at the motorboat factory.

But time waits for no one. For some years, there had been concerns in Moscow about İsmail's advancing age. In December 1978, a report on the 76-year-old noted that "with each passing year there are more mistakes in his work as party leader."[45] Having lasted well into the Brezhnev era, when "stability among the cadres" was highly valorized in the Eastern Bloc, Bilen had managed to do the almost unthinkable: he had played a leading role in his party from the late 1920s all the way into the 1980s. That kind of staying power was virtually unparalleled in the communist world.

The time, however, had come to pass the baton. On November 15, 1983, more than sixty-one years after he had first shown up at KUTV's doorstep on Mokhovaia Street in Moscow, İsmail Bilen stepped down as leader of the TKP.

---

[43] RGASPI, f. 495, op. 266, d. 12, Part II, l. 20.   [44] RGASPI, f. 495, op. 266, d. 12, Part II, ll. 7, 18, 20.
[45] RGASPI, f. 495, op. 266, d. 12, Part II, l. 81. "Spravka," December 21, 1978.

Three days later, the 81-year-old Bilen died in East Berlin. Five years after that, Mara Kolarova-Bilen passed away in Sofia.

## Reconstructing the Idols

In the decades following his death, Nâzım Hikmet has undergone a considerable re-evaluation in both Turkey and the Soviet Union. In the USSR, his reputation lived on for as long as communism did. Until the 1990s, he was occasionally mentioned, usually on specific anniversaries relating to his life, in *Literaturnaia Gazeta* and *Pravda*.

Following the collapse of the Warsaw Pact in 1989 and the breakup of the USSR two years later, Nâzım's public profile in the former Eastern Bloc diminished considerably. His fame and significance in these countries had depended largely upon the continued existence of the Iron Curtain. With the end of the Cold War and state communism in Europe, Nâzım quickly disappeared from the pages of Russian newspapers and those of other post-socialist countries.[46] While Nâzım Hikmet still retains some faithful admirers in Russia and elsewhere in the formerly socialist world, to the public at large in these countries he is viewed primarily as a relic of communism, if indeed he is remembered at all.

In Turkey, the situation is quite different. The overthrow of Prime Minister Adnan Menderes in 1960 and the creation of a new constitution the following year marked the beginning of definitive changes with respect to the status of civil society in the country. For the first time in a Turkish constitution, genuine rights and freedoms were guaranteed unequivocally. This development impacted the manner in which Nâzım Hikmet could be discussed publicly in Turkey, as it became far more difficult for the Turkish state to ban the works of certain writers. In the mid-1960s, Nâzım's books began to be published in Turkey for the first time since the mid-1930s. In the 1970s and 1980s, Nâzım remained a controversial figure, at least for some people, but he was no longer outlawed.

With the end of the Cold War, a lot of the radioactivity surrounding Nâzım's reputation in Turkey evaporated, and he gradually has become a much more mainstream figure in public memory. Not everybody in Turkey likes Nâzım, but he is no longer the polarizing symbol that he once was. On January 5, 2009, the Turkish parliament—dominated by the rightist Justice and Development Party of Prime Minister Recep Tayyip Erdoğan—voted to annul the 1951 decision stripping Nâzım Hikmet of his Turkish citizenship.[47] Perhaps more than anything, the story of Nâzım's life—as well as his afterlife in Turkey—tells us that even the bitterest, most polarizing divisions can be overcome eventually.

---

[46] Searching through old editions of *Pravda*, I was able to find regular mentions of Nâzım—particularly on the anniversary of his death—until 1989. From that point forward, remembrance of Nâzım in the paper became much more sporadic, with occasional mentions occurring in 1995, 2002, 2004, 2011, 2012, and 2016.

[47] Although some politicians in Turkey denounced the move.

**Figure 14.2** Nâzım Hikmet's tomb in Moscow

As for Nâzım himself: our image of him has increasingly come to resemble his tomb in Moscow's Novodevichy Cemetery: as a heroic idol.[48] Nâzım the man has gradually been transformed into the mythical Nâzım, that of the tired, oft-repeated anecdote. This one-time rebel, who had once proposed "smashing the idols" of Turkey's literary elite, has stood for years as a monument constructed of stone and concrete (Figure 14.2). But maybe, like the Gioconda that Nâzım once conjured in his poetry, this statue, too, will take flight one day.

---

[48] Albeit one that nevertheless is meaningful to people, like my banker student Gökhan from this book's introduction.

Politicians in Ankara have, in recent years, called for bringing Nâzım Hikmet's remains "home" from Russia.[49] In my view, however, Nâzım's actual homeland is no more Turkey than it is Moscow. A child of trans-empire, Nâzım grew up in a time and place that would feel like ancient history to those demanding his repatriation today. Even before Nâzım's death, the border-crossing environment in which he had come of age had already long since disappeared. So too had the cosmopolitan era that so greatly affected his young life, and the lives of his generation.

## A Generation of Border-Crossers

What kind of a writer would Nâzım Hikmet have been had he never crossed a border? Nâzım came into his own as a poet only after he had begun traversing frontiers, and border-crossing is indelibly imprinted within his poetry's DNA. Had Nâzım never left Istanbul, his writing career would have been a very different one, and likely not nearly as memorable. More than any single factor beyond sheer talent, it was Nâzım's border-crossing that made his poetry great.

The women and men of Nâzım's generation had grown up during a time of flexible frontiers, but in their early middle age found themselves trapped on one side of the border or the other. From the late 1920s onward, the Turkish–Soviet frontier was increasingly difficult to cross, and would become ever more stringently controlled during the Cold War. Usually, the tightening of the border had the effect of limiting people's options. Others, however, would learn to benefit from the Iron Curtain's existence. İsmail Bilen was one such figure. Nâzım Hikmet was another.

We too are living in a time of closing doors. The revolutions taking place in the former Warsaw Pact in 1989 were symbolized by the tearing down of walls.[50] Today, voices calling for re-building those walls are, in much of the world, gaining ground. Looking increasingly inward, we attack ourselves.

There were many red stars that went over the Black Sea. The lives of the border-crossers discussed in this book contain stories of resilience, principle, and bravery, alongside banality, jealousy, and treachery. Many of these individuals found themselves in impossible situations, and just did their best to survive. Others would go on to produce narratives regarding their experiences and those of their generation.

The latter-day memoirs of communists who first traveled to the USSR in their early youth tend to focus upon ideology as the guiding force behind the choices they made. While ideology is something that was greatly valorized by this generation, its role in the decisions made by young communists—Turkish or otherwise—can be overstated. There were many reasons why Turks ended up in the USSR, and multiple paths to

---

[49] "We are willing to bring Nâzım Hikmet's remains to Turkey: Justice Minister," *Hürriyet Daily News*, January 16, 2017.

[50] And not only in Eastern Europe, but also through democratization movements in South Africa, South Korea, the Philippines, and Latin America, to name just a few.

communism. Ideological consistency, especially in the earliest years following the October Revolution, was often less important than practical expedience.

The transition from a time of porous frontiers to one of a nearly-sealed border did not occur in a vacuum. Changes on the frontier altered people's lives in myriad ways, whether or not they had crossed borders. While those who had traversed the frontier now felt the doors closing behind them, so too did the broader populations of Turkey and the Soviet Union. The shutting of the frontier took place in the broader context of an increasingly violent and autocratic regime developing in each country.

Nâzım Hikmet differed from most TKP members in the Eastern Bloc in that he had been well-known for years as a voice of political non-conformity prior to his emigration. For as long as he had lived in Turkey, Nâzım had demonstrated genuine courage in speaking up for what he believed in. He then went on to spend years of his life propagandizing on behalf of regimes that were exponentially more violent and systematically oppressive than the one he had fled in Turkey.

But Nâzım's flight was more personal than political. It wasn't systematic oppression that Nâzım had been fleeing, but rather a highly specific vendetta waged against him by individuals within the Turkish government and armed forces. Nâzım had not run to the Eastern Bloc due to some sort of naïve romantic communism, but rather because people in positions of power had made life intolerable for him in Turkey. Even as he had set out from Istanbul in June 1951, Nâzım knew that his interactions with Soviet and other Eastern Bloc authorities would not always be straightforward.

He devised strategies for his dealings with officialdom and realized early on that he needed help in maneuvering the Soviet political system, initially relying upon İsmail Bilen. Whatever he may or may not have known about crimes taking place under Stalin—and it seems likely that he knew something—Nâzım was no different from the vast majority of Soviet citizens and resident foreigners in rhetorically and enthusiastically toeing the line under Stalin and beyond.

As a veteran of many battles with state authorities in Turkey, Nâzım knew what a lost cause looked like. He wasn't going to risk his livelihood, or his life, speaking out in the USSR, whether it was under Stalin, Khrushchev, or anybody else. Nor would a life of emigration in France or Italy, countries where relatively few read his work, have likely seemed attractive to him. Where else could he publish his works to such a degree? Nâzım was in the Eastern Bloc to stay.

What did Nâzım Hikmet believe in? He would probably argue that everything he had done politically stemmed from his unwavering belief in communist ideology. For Nâzım, and many others, there was no inconsistency: he had supported communism in Turkey and did so in the Eastern Bloc as well. This, at least, is how he viewed his circumstances during his final years, when he was self-identifying as a "foot soldier" for communism. But perhaps what this aging "greatest believer" put his faith into most was not so much ideology, but rather the narratives about his life that he told himself and others.

Every death is singular. Nâzım's life was that of a generation.

*

Well past middle age, Nâzım Hikmet found a means of pushing his way back through a closing door. At a time of sealed frontiers, he still managed to traverse one. He had, once more, reached beyond his grasp.

Nâzım looked again at the motorboat, and then he climbed inside.

# Bibliography

## Archival and Manuscript Material

Russian Federation

Russian State Archive of Literature and Art (RGALI), Moscow

Fond 631: Union of Soviet Writers
Fond 634: Editorial Offices of *Literaturnaia Gazeta*
Fond 1814: Personal fond of Konstantin Mikhailovich Simonov
Fond 2250: Personal fond of Nâzım Hikmet

Russian State Archive of Social-Political History (RGASPI), Moscow

Fond 17: Central Committee of the KPSS (Communist Party of the Soviet Union)
Fond 82: Viacheslav Mikhailovich Molotov (1890–1986)
Fond 489: Second Congress of the Comintern (1920)
Fond 495: Comintern Executive Committee
Fond 529: Communist University for the National Minorities of the West (KUNMZ)
Fond 532: Scientific-Research Institute for National and Colonial Problems
Fond 544: First Meeting of the Peoples of the East and Council for Propaganda and Activities of the Peoples of the East (1920–22)

State Archive of the Russian Federation (GARF), Moscow

Fond R1318: People's Commissariat for affairs relating to nationalities of the RSFSR
Fond R3316: Executive Central Committee of the USSR
Fond R5446: Council of Ministers, USSR
Fond R7523: Supreme Soviet, USSR
Fond R9508: Personal fond of Mikhail Iakovlevich Apletin

Turkey
Aziz Nesin Vakfı (ANV), Çatalca, Istanbul, Turkey
Prime Ministry Ottoman Archive (BOA), Istanbul
Prime Ministry Republican Archive (BCA), Ankara (via BOA)
TÜSTAV archive, Istanbul, Turkey (reproductions from Bulgarian Central State Archives)

The Netherlands
International Institute of Social History (IISH), Amsterdam

Nâzım Hikmet CDs (interviews on Radio Budapest)
Personal papers of Kemal Sülker
RGASPI/IISH: Fond 495 Comintern Executive Committee (opis' 181)

The United States
US National Archives & Records Administration (NARA), Washington, DC
College Park (Maryland) Reading Room

511.82 US Cultural Relations with Turkey
561.82 Soviet Cultural Relations with Turkey
782.00 Internal Political Affairs of Turkey
782.001 Communism in Turkey
867.00B Despatches from US Embassy, Ankara

## Newspapers and Journals

*Akbaba*
*Akşam*
*Aydınlık*
*Cumhuriyet*
*Genç Kalemler*
*Literaturnaia Gazeta*
*Milliyet*
*Orak-Çekiç*
*Pravda*
*Resimli Ay*
*The New York Times*
*The Washington Post*
*Türk Yurdu*
*Vakit*

## Books by Nâzim Hikmet in Turkish and English

"Alman Faşizmi ve Irkçılığı." İstanbul: Kader Basımevi, 1936.

Blasing, Randy and Konuk, Mutlu. *Poems of Nâzım Hikmet: Revised and Expanded.* New York: Persea Books, 2002.

*Bursa Cezaevinden Vâ-Nû'lara Mektuplar* (3rd edition). İstanbul: Nâzım Hikmet Kültür ve Sanat Vakfı Yayınları, 1998.

*Bütün Eserleri* (ed. Ekber Babayev), 8 vols. Sofia: Narodna Prosveta, 1967–72.

*Kemal Tahir'e Mapusaneden Mektuplar* (2nd edition). İstanbul: Bilgi Yayınevi, 1975.

*Life's Good, Brother: A Novel* (trans. Mutlu Konuk Blasing). New York: Persea Books, 2013.

*Nâzım'ın Cep Defterlerinde Kavga, Aşk ve Şiir Notları (1937–1942).* İstanbul: Yapı Kredi Yayınları, 2018.

*Piraye'ye Mektuplar* (ed. Memet Fuat). İstanbul: Yapı Kredi Yayınevi, 2012.

"Sovyet Demokrasisi." İstanbul: Selamet Basımevi, 1936.

Yapı Kredi 3-volume collection of Nâzım Hikmet's novels. İstanbul: Yapı Kredi Yayınları, 2002. Cited as "Yapı Kredi edition of Nâzım Hikmet's collected works, *Romanlar.*"

Yapı Kredi 4-volume collection of Nâzım Hikmet's fables and stories. İstanbul: Yapı Kredi Yayınları, 2002. Cited as "Yapı Kredi edition of Nâzım Hikmet's collected works, *Masallar, Hikâyeler.*"

Yapı Kredi 5-volume collection of Nâzım Hikmet's plays. İstanbul: Yapı Kredi Yayınları, 2002. Cited as "Yapı Kredi edition of Nâzım Hikmet's collected works, *Oyunlar.*"

Yapı Kredi 6-volume collection of Nâzım Hikmet's prose writings. İstanbul: Yapı Kredi Yayınları, 2002. Cited as "Yapı Kredi edition of Nâzım Hikmet's collected works, *Yazılar.*"

Yapı Kredi 8-volume collection of Nâzım Hikmet's poetry (İstanbul: Yapı Kredi Yayınları, 2002). Cited as "Yapı Kredi edition of Nâzım Hikmet's collected works, *Şiirler.*"

*Yaşamak Güzel Şey Be Kardeşim* (13th edition). İstanbul: Yapı Kredi Yayınları, 2012.

## Published Sources and Dissertations

Açıkgöz, Anjel (ed.). *Bizim Radyoda Nâzım Hikmet.* İstanbul: TÜSTAV, 2002.

Açıkgöz, Hayk. *Anadolulu bir Ermeni Komünistin Anıları.* İstanbul: Belge Yayınları, 2006.

(Adıvar), Halide Edip. *House with Wisteria: Memoirs of Halide Edip* (ed. Sibel Erol). Charlottesville, VA: Leopolis Press, 2003.

(Adıvar), Halide Edip. *Yeni Turan.* İstanbul: Tanin Matbaası, 1912.

Aitken, Robbie. "From Cameroon to Germany and Back via Moscow and Paris: The Political Career of Joseph Bilé (1892–1959), Performer, 'Negerarbeiter' and Comintern Activist." *Journal of Contemporary History*, vol. 43, no. 4 (October 2008), 597–616.

Akal, Emel. *Moskova-Ankara-Londra Üçgeninde İştirakiyuncular, Komünistler ve Paşa Hazretleri*. İstanbul: İletişim, 2013.

Akal, Emel. *Mustafa Kemal, İttihat Terakki ve Bolşevizm*. İstanbul: İletişim, 2012.

Akbulut, Erden (ed.). *1929 TKP Davası*. İstanbul: TÜSTAV, 2005.

Akbulut, Erden (ed.). *Dr. Şefik Hüsnü Deymer: Yaşam Öyküsü, Vazife Yazıları*. İstanbul: TÜSTAV, 2010.

Akbulut, Erden (ed.). *Komintern Belgelerinde*. İstanbul: TÜSTAV, 2002.

Akbulut, Erden (ed.). *Milli Azadlık Savaşı Anıları*. İstanbul: TÜSTAV, 2006.

Akbulut, Erden (ed.). *Zeki Baştımar: Yaşam Öyküsü, Mektuplar, Yazılar*. İstanbul: TÜSTAV, 2009, second printing 2018.

Akbulut, Erden and Tunçay, Mete (eds.). *İstanbul Komünist Grubu'ndan (Aydınlık Çevresi) Türkiye Komünist Partisi'ne 1919–1926, I Cilt 1919–1923*. İstanbul: TÜSTAV, 2012.

Akgül, Hikmet. *Nâzım Hikmet Siyasi Biyografi*. İstanbul: Chiviyazilari Yayınevi, 2002.

Akgün, Seçil Karal and Uluğtekin, Murat. *Birinci Dünya Savaşı Sonunda İskandinavya'dan Sibirye'ya Hilal-i Ahmer Hizmetinde Akçuraoğlu Yusuf*. Ankara: Türkiye Kızılay Derneği Yayınları, 2009.

Alliluyeva, Svetlana. *Only One Year*. New York: Harper & Row, 1969.

Anderson, Sheldon. *A Cold War in the Soviet Bloc: Polish-East German Relations, 1945–1962*. New York: Perseus, 2001.

Applebaum, Rachel. *Empire of Friends: Soviet Power and Socialist Internationalism in Cold War Czechoslovakia*. Ithaca and London: Cornell University Press, 2019.

Arslan, Pelin. "1933–1950 Yılları Arasında Türkiye'ye Gelen Alman İktisatçılar: Gerhard Kessler'in Türkiye'de Sosyal Politikaların Gelişimine Katkıları." MA thesis, Maltepe University, 2019.

Ashby, Heather Winter. "Third World Activists and the Communist University of the Toilers of the East." Dissertation, University of Southern California, 2014.

Ataöv, Türkkaya. *Nâzım Hikmet'in Hasreti*. Istanbul: Literatür Yayıncılık, 2002.

Atay, Korhan. *Serteller*. İstanbul: İlestişim, 2021.

Ateş, Sabri. *Ottoman-Iranian Borderlands: Making a Boundary, 1843–1914*. Cambridge: Cambridge University Press, 2013.

Aydemir, Aydın. *Nâzım, Nâzım*. İstanbul: Broy Yayınları, 1986.

Aydemir, Şevket S. *Suyu Arayan Adam*. İstanbul: Remzi Kitabevi, 1987.

Aziz, Rüstem (trans.). *Georgi Dimitrov: Günlük 2*. İstanbul: TÜSTAV, 2004.

Babayev, Ekber. *Nâzım Hikmet: Yaşamı ve Yapıtları* (5th edition). İstanbul: Cumhuriyet Kitapları, 2011.

Babayev, Ekber. *Ustam ve Ağabeyim Nâzım Hikmet*. İstanbul: Milliyet, 1997.

Balaban, İbrahim. *Nâzım Hikmet'le Yedi Yıl*. İstanbul: Berfin Yayınları, 2003.

Başgöz, İlhan. "Yolu Bülent Ecevit'ten Geçen Anılar." *Radikal*, November 12, 2006.

Bayat, Ali Haydar. *Hüseyinzade Ali Bey*. Ankara: Atatürk Yüksek Kurumu, 1998.

Bayraktaroğlu, Arın Dilligil. *Nüzhet: Nâzım Hikmet'in "Minnacık" Kadını*. İstanbul: Remzi, 2022.

Belli, Sevim. *Boşuna mı Çiğnedik? Anılar*. İstanbul: Cadde Yayınları, 2006.

Belogurova, Anna. "The Civic World of International Communism: Taiwanese Communists and the Comintern (1921–1931)." *Modern Asian Studies*, vol. 46, no. 6 (November 2012), 1602–1632.

Benderli, Gün. *Giderayak: Anılarımdaki Nâzım Hikmet*. İstanbul: İletişim, 2020.

Benderli, Gün. *Su Başında Durmuşuz*. İstanbul: Belge Yayınları, 2003.

Bennigsen, Alexandre and Lemercier-Quelquejay, Chantal. *La Presse et le Mouvement Nationale chez les Musulmans de Russie avant 1920*. Paris: Mouton & Co., 1960.

Bereday, George Z. F. and Schlesinger, Ina. "Teacher Salaries in the Soviet Union." *Comparative Education Review*, vol. 6, no. 3 (1963), 200–208.

Beşikçi, Mehmet. *The Ottoman Mobilization of Manpower in the First World War: Between Voluntarism and Resistance*. Leiden: Brill, 2012.

Bezirci, Asım. "Toplumcu Şiirimiz içinde Nâzım Hikmet." *Gelecek* (May 1971), 36–41.

Bilen, İsmail. *TKP MK Genel Sekreteri İsmail Bilen Kısa Biyografi*. İstanbul: TÜSTAV, 2004.

Blasing, Mutlu Konuk. *Nâzım Hikmet: The Life and Times of Turkey's World Poet*. New York: Persea Books, 2013.

Blauvelt, Timothy. *Clientelism and Nationality in an Early Soviet Fiefdom: The Trials of Nestor Lakoba*. New York: Routledge, 2021.

Bone, Andrew G. "Russell and the Communist-Aligned Peace Movement in the Mid-1950s." *The Journal of Bertrand Russell Studies*, n.s. vol. 21 (Summer 2001), 31–57.

Can, Lâle. "Connecting People: A Central Asian Sufi Network in Turn-of-the-Century Istanbul." *Modern Asian Studies*, vol. 46, no. 2 (2012), 373–401.

Can, Lâle. *Spiritual Subjects: Central Asian Pilgrims and the Ottoman Hajj at the End of Empire*. Palo Alto, CA: Stanford University Press, 2020.

Can, Lâle. "The Protection Question: Central Asians and Extraterritoriality in the Late Ottoman Empire." *International Journal of Middle East Studies*, vol. 48, no. 4 (2016), 679–699.

Carr, E. H. *Twilight of the Comintern, 1930–1935*. New York: Pantheon Books, 1982.

Carruthers, Susan L. "Between Camps: Eastern Bloc "Escapees" and Cold War Borderlands," *American Quarterly,* vol. 57, no. 3 (2005), 911–942.

Carruthers, Susan L. *Cold War Captives: Imprisonment, Escape, and Brainwashing*. Berkeley: University of California Press (2009).

Cebesoy, Ali Fuat. *Moskova Hatıraları*. İstanbul: Vatan Neşriyatı, 1955.

Cinel, Dino. *The National Integration of Italian Return Migration, 1870–1929*. New York: Cambridge University Press, 1991.

Clark, Katerina. *Eurasia Without Borders: The Dream of a Leftist Literary Commons, 1919–1943*. Cambridge, MA: The Belknap Press of Harvard University Press, 2021.

Clark, Katerina. "European and Russian Cultural Interactions with Turkey: 1910s–1930s." *Comparative Studies of South Asia, Africa, and the Middle East*, vol. 33, no. 2 (2013), 201–213.

Crews, Robert. "Empire and the Confessional State: Islam and Religious Politics in Nineteenth Century Russia." *American Historical Review*, vol. 108, no. 1 (February 2003), 50–83.

Çakırhan, Nail. *Anılar*. İstanbul: TÜSTAV, 2008.

Çapa, Mesut. *Kızılay (Hilal-i Ahmer) Cemiyeti (1914–1925)*. Ankara: Türkiye Kızılay Derneği Yayınları, 2010.

Çatal, Barış. *Sabiha Sertel: Hayatı ve Entelektüel Mirası*. İstanbul: Tarih Vakfı Yurt Yayınları, 2022.

David-Fox, Michael. "The Iron Curtain as Semipermeable Membrane." In Patryk Babiracki and Kenyon Zimmer (eds.), *Cold War Crossings: International Travel and Exchange across the Soviet Bloc, 1940s–1960s*. College Station, TX: Texas A&M University Press, 2014, 14–39.

Demirkan, Eser. *Ercümend Behzad Lav (Hayatı, Sanatı, Eserleri)*. Ankara: T.C. Kültür Bakanlığı, 2002.

Demirkan, Tarık. *Macar Turancıları*. İstanbul: Tarih Vakfı, 2000.

Dervişoğlu, Sinan (trans.). *Türkiye Komünist Partisi 1926 Viyana Konferans*. İstanbul: TÜSTAV, 2004.

Dilek, İbrahim. "Türk Dünyası Edebiyatında Repressiya." *Türk Dünyası Dil ve Edebiyat Dergisi*, no. 48 (Autumn, 2019), 27–81.

Djagalov, Rossen. *From Internationalism to Postcolonialism: Literature and Cinema Between the Second and Third World*. Montreal: McGill-Queen's University Press, 2020.

Drachkovitch, Milorad M. and Lazic, Branko. *The Comintern*. Stanford, CA: Hoover Institution Publications, 1966.

Dumont, Paul. "Bolchevisme et Orient (Le parti communiste turc de Mustafa Suphi, 1918–1921)." *Cahiers du Monde russe et soviétique*, vol. 18, no. 4 (Octobre–Décembre 1977), 377–409.

Dumont, Paul. "La fascination du bolchevisme: Enver pacha et le parti des soviets populaires, 1919–1922." *Cahiers du Monde russe et soviétique*, vol. 16, no. 2 (April–June 1975), 141–166.

Dumont, Paul. "L'axe Moscou-Ankara. Les relations turco-soviétiques de 1919 à 1922." *Cahiers du Monde russe et soviétique*, vol. 18, no. 3 (July–September 1977), 165–193.

Dündar, Can. *Nâzım*. İstanbul: Can Sanat Yayınları, 2014.

Ellis, Matthew H. *Desert Borderland: The Making of Modern Egypt and Libya*. Stanford, CA: Stanford University Press, 2018.

Emre, Ahmet Cevat. "1920 Moskova'sında Türk Komünistler." Reprinted in Erden Akbulut (ed.), *Milli Azadlık Savaşı Anıları*. İstanbul: TÜSTAV, 2006, 45–78.

Erdem, Hamit. *Mustafa Suphi*. İstanbul: Sel, 3rd edition, revised and updated, 2010.

Erduran, Refik. *Gülerek: Gençlik Anıları*. İstanbul: Cem Yayınevi, 1987.

Ertuğrul, Muhsin. *Benden Sonra Tufan Olmasın*. İstanbul: Remzi Kitabevi, 2007.

Ertürk, Nergis. "Nâzım Hikmet and the Prose of Communism." *Boundary 2: An International Journal of Literature and Culture*, vol. 47, no. 2 (2020), 153–180.

Ertürk, Nergis. "Vâlâ Nureddin's Comic Materialism and the Sexual Revolution: Writing across Turkey and the Soviet Union." *Comparative Literature*, vol. 73, no. 3 (2021), 299–319.

Esin, Taylan. "Hilal-i Ahmer, Esirler ve Yusuf Akçura." *Toplumsal Tarih Dergisi*, no. 291 (March 2013), 22–29.

Faizrakhmanovich, Bulat. *Neizvestnyi Sultan Galiev*. Tatarskoe knizhnoe izd-vo, 2002.

Fernández, Sirio Rosado. *La democracia soviética*. Madrid: Asociación de Amigos de la Unión Soviética, 1938.

Fevralski, Aleksandr. *Nâzım'dan Anılar* (trans. Ataol Behramoğlu). İstanbul: Cem Yayınevi, 1979.

Feyzioğlu, Turhan. *Türk Ocağından Türk Komünist Parti'sine Mustafa Suphi*. İstanbul: Ozan Yayıncılık, 2007.

Filatova, Irina. "Indoctrination or Scholarship? Education of Africans at the Communist University of the Toilers of the East in the Soviet Union, 1923–1937." *Paedagogica Historica*, vol. 35, no. 1 (1999), 41–66.

Fish, Rady, *Nâzım'ın Çilesi* (trans. Güneş Bozkaya-Kollontay). İstanbul: Gün Yayınları, 1969.

Fisher, Alan. "Emigration of Muslims from the Russian Empire in the Years after the Crimean War." *Jahrbucher für Geschichte Osteuropas*, vol. 35, no. 3 (1987), 336–371.

Forestier-Peyrat, Étienne. "Dans les forêts d'Adjarie…: Franchir la frontière turco-soviétique, 1922–1937." *Diasporas*, vol. 23–24 (2014), 164–184.

Fortna, Benjamin. *Imperial Classroom: Islam, the State, and Education in the Late Ottoman Empire*. New York: Oxford University Press, 2002.

Fox, Michael David, *Revolution of the Mind: Higher Learning among the Bolsheviks, 1918–1929*. Ithaca, NY: Cornell University Press, 1999.

Garcelon, Marc. "The Shadow of the Leviathan: Public and Private in Communist and Post-Communist Society." In Jeff Weintraub and Krishan Kumar (eds.), *Public and Private in Thought and Practice: Perspectives on a Grand Dichotomy*. Chicago: University of Chicago Press, 1997, 303–332.

Garrard, John and Garrard, Carol. *Inside the Soviet Writers' Union*. New York: The Free Press, 1990.

Georgeon, François, *Aux Origines du Nationalisme Turc: Yusuf Akçura, 1876–1935*. Paris: ADPF, 1980.

Geraci, Robert P. *Window on the East: National and Imperial Identities in Late Tsarist Russia*. Ithaca: Cornell University Press, 2001.

Ginzburg, Eugenia. *Within the Whirlwind*. London: Collins and Harvill Press, 1981.

Göçek, Fatma Müge. *Rise of the Bourgeoisie, Demise of Empire: Ottoman Westernization and Social Change*. New York: Oxford University Press, 1996.

Gökay, Bülent. *Soviet Eastern Policy and Turkey, 1920–1991: Soviet Foreign Policy, Turkey and Communism*. New York: Routledge, 2006.

Göksu, Saime and Timms, Edward. *Romantic Communist: The Life and Work of Nâzım Hikmet* (2nd edition). London: Hurst & Co., 2006.

Göktürk, Halil İbrahim. *Bilinmeyen Yönleriyle Şevket Süreyya Aydemir*. İstanbul: Arı Matbaası, 1977.

Göze, Ergun. *Peyami Safa Nâzım Hikmet Kavgası*. Ankara: Selçuk Yayınları, 1981.

Guralnick, Peter. *Last Train to Memphis: The Rise of Elvis Presley*. Boston: Little, Brown, 1994.

Gutman, David. "Travel Documents, Mobility Control, and the Ottoman State in an Age of Global Migration, 1880–1915." *Journal of the Ottoman and Turkish Studies Association*, vol. 3, no. 2 (2016), 347–368.

Güneş, M. Melih. *Bu şehir güzelse senin yüzünden: Nâzım Hikmet'ten Vera Tulyakova'ya kartpostallar*. İstanbul: Yapı Kredi Yayınları, 2012.

Güneş, M. Melih. *Hasretle: Nâzım Hikmet Mektupları*. İstanbul: Yapı Kredi Yayınları, 2007.

Güneş, M. Melih. *Suyun Şavkı: Leipzig'de Bir Aile ve Nâzım Hikmet*. İstanbul: Yapı Kredi Yayımları, 2017.

Habiçoğlu, Bedri. *Kafkasya'dan Anadolu'ya Göçler ve İskanları*. İstanbul: Nart Yayıncılık, 1993.

## BIBLIOGRAPHY

Hahn, Werner G. *Postwar Soviet Politics: The Fall of Zhdanov and the Defeat of Moderation, 1946–53.* Ithaca and London: Cornell University Press, 1982.

Hallas, Duncan. *The Comintern: A History of the Third International.* Ann Arbor, MI: Chicago Haymarket Books, 2016.

Hanioğlu, Şükrü. *The Young Turks in Opposition.* New York: Oxford University Press, 1995.

Harris, George S. *The Communists and the Kadro Movement: Shaping Ideology in Ataturk's Turkey.* Piscataway, NJ: Gorgias Press, 2010.

Harris, George S. *The Origins of Communism in Turkey.* Stanford, CA: Hoover Institution Publications, 1967.

Hızlan, Doğan (ed.). *Ercümend Behzad Lav: Bütün Eserleri.* İstanbul: Yapı Kredi Yayınlar, 2005.

Hirst, Samuel J. "Anti-Westernism on the European Periphery: The Meaning of Soviet-Turkish Convergence in the 1930s." *Slavic Review*, vol. 72, no. 1 (2013), 32–53.

Hirst, Samuel J. "Comrades on Elephants: Economic Anti-Imperialism, Orientalism, and Soviet Diplomacy in Afghanistan." *Kritika*, vol. 22, no. 1 (2021), 13–40.

Hirst, Samuel J. "Eurasia's Discontent: Soviet and Turkish Anti-Westernism in the Interwar Period." PhD dissertation, Department of History, University of Pennsylvania, 2012.

Hirst, Samuel J. and İşçi, O. "Smokestacks and Pipelines: Russian-Turkish Relations and the Persistence of Economic Development." *Diplomatic History*, vol. 44, no. 5 (2020), 834–859.

Hook, Sidney. *Out of Step: An Unquiet Life in the 20th Century.* New York: Carroll & Graf, 1987.

Hough, Jerry F. "Soviet Policymaking toward Former Communists." *Studies in Comparative Communism*, vol. 15, no. 3 (Autumn 1982), 167–183.

Ironside, Kristy. *A Full-Value Ruble: The Promise of Prosperity in the Postwar Soviet Union.* Cambridge, MA: Harvard University Press, 2021.

İhmalyan, Vartan. *Bir Yaşam Öyküsü.* İstanbul: Cem Yayınevi. 2012.

İşçi, Onur. *Turkey and the Soviet Union during World War II.* London: I. B. Tauris, 2020.

İşlet, Banu and Moralıoğlu-Kesim, Cemile (eds.). *Haziran-Eylül 1920 Türkiye İştirakiyun Teşkilatı.* İstanbul: TÜSTAV, 2008.

Jangfeldt, Bengt. *Mayakovsky: A Biography.* Chicago: University of Chicago Press, 2014.

Kahramanoğlu, İnan. *Mustafa Suphi.* İstanbul: İleri Yayınları, 2008.

Kamphoefner, Walter D. "The Volume and Composition of German-American Return Migration." In Rudolph Vecoli and Suzanne M. Sinke (eds.), *A Century of European Migrations, 1830–1930.* Urbana, IL: University of Illinois Press, 1991, 293–314.

Kane, Eileen. *Russian Hajj: Empire and the Pilgrimage to Mecca.* Ithaca and London: Cornell University Press, 2015.

Kaplan, Sena, Pınar, Gül, Kaplan, Bekir, and Aslantekin, Fılız. "The Prevalence of Consanguineous Marriages and Affecting Factors in Turkey: A National Survey." *Journal of Biosocial Sciences*, vol. 48, no. 5 (September 2016), 616–630.

Kappeler, Andreas. *The Russian Empire: A Multiethnic History.* Harlow: Pearson, 2001.

Karaca, Emin. *Nâzım Hikmet'in Aşkları.* İstanbul: Gendaş, 1999.

Karaca, Emin. *Sevdalınız Komünisttir (Nâzım Hikmet'in Siyasal Yaşamı)* (5th edition). İstanbul: Destek Yayınevi, 2010.

Karaer, İsmail. *Türk Ocakları (1912–1931).* Ankara: Türk Yurdu Neşriyatı, 1992.

Karpat, Kemal. *Ottoman Population 1830–1914: Demographic and Social Characteristics.* Madison, WI: University of Wisconsin Press, 1985.

Karpat, Kemal. *The Politicization of Islam: Reconstructing Identity, State, Faith, and Community in the Late Ottoman State.* New York: Oxford University Press, 2001.

Karpat, Kemal. *The Turks of Bulgaria: The History, Culture and Political Fate of a Minority.* Istanbul: Isis Press, 1990.

Kashani-Sabet, Firoozeh. *Frontier Fictions: Shaping the Iranian Nation, 1804–1946.* Princeton, NJ: Princeton University Press, 1999.

Katz, Zev. "Party-Political Education in Soviet Russia 1918–1935." *Soviet Studies*, vol. 7, no. 3 (1956), 237–247.

Kavlak, Aslan. *"Bakü'ye Gidiyorum Ay Balam." Nâzım Hikmet'in Azerbaycan'daki İzleri (1921–1963)* (2nd edition). İstanbul: Yapı Kredi Yayımları, 2009.

Kayalı, Hasan. *Arabs and Young Turks: Ottomanism, Arabism, and Islamism in the Ottoman Empire, 1908–1918.* Berkeley, CA: University of California Press, 1997.

Kemal, Orhan. *In Jail with Nâzım Hikmet* (trans. Bengisu Rona). London: Saqi, 2010.

Khater, Fouad Akram. *Inventing Home: Emigration, Gender, and the Middle Class in Lebanon, 1870–1920.* Berkeley, CA University of California Press, 2001.

Khoury, Dina Rizk and Glebov, Sergey. "Citizenship, Subjecthood, and Difference in the late Ottoman and Russian Empires." *Ab Imperio*, vol. 18, no. 1 (2017), 45–58.

King, Charles. *Midnight at the Pera Palace: The Birth of Modern Istanbul.* New York and London: W. W. Norton, 2015.

Kirasirova, Masha. "An Egyptian Communist Family Romance: Revolution and Gender in the Transnational Life of Charlotte Rosenthal." In Choi Chatterjee, Steven G. Marks, Mary Neuburger, and Steven Sabol (eds.), *The Global Impacts of Russia's Great War and Revolution, Book 2: The Wider Arc of Revolution, Part 1.* Bloomington, IN: Slavica Publishers, 2019, 309–336.

Kirasirova, Masha. "The East as a Category of Bolshevik Ideology and Comintern Administration: The Arab Section of the Communist University of the Toilers of the East." *Kritika: Explorations in Russian and Eurasian History*, vol. 18, no. 1 (2017), 7–34.

Kirasirova, Masha. "The Eastern International: The 'Domestic East' and the 'Foreign East' in Soviet-Arab Relations, 1917–68." PhD Dissertation, New York University, Department of History and Department of Middle Eastern and Islam Studies, May 2014.

Kirişci, Kemal. "Disaggregating Turkish Citizenship and Immigration Practices." *Middle Eastern Studies*, vol. 36, no. 3 (July 2000), 1–22.

Kirschenbaum, Lisa. *International Communism and the Spanish Civil War: Solidarity and Suspicion.* Cambridge: Cambridge University Press, 2015.

Kolarova-Bilen, Mara. *Kanatlı Gençlik.* İstanbul: TÜSTAV, 2003.

Kolesnikova, Galina. *Sem' Let s Nazymom Khikmetom.* Izhevsk: IPM UrO RAN, 1999.

Kotkin, Stephen. *Magnetic Mountain: Stalinism as a Civilization.* Berkeley, CA: University of California Press, 1997.

Kotkin, Stephen. *Stalin: Volume I, Paradoxes of Power, 1878–1928.* New York: Penguin Press, 2014.

Kotkin, Stephen. *Stalin: Volume II, Waiting for Hitler, 1929–41.* New York: Penguin Press, 2017.

Landau, Jacob. *Pan-Turkism: From Irredentism to Cooperation.* Bloomington: Indiana University Press, 1995.

Lazzerini, Edward J. "İsmail Bey Gasprinskii and Muslim Modernism in Russia, 1878–1914." Dissertation, Department of History, The University of Washington, 1973.

Lewis, Bernard. *The Emergence of Modern Turkey.* London: Oxford University Press, 1961.

Lewis, Geoffrey. *The Turkish Language Reform: A Catastrophic Success.* Oxford: Oxford University Press, 1999.

Light, Matthew A. "What Does It Mean to Control Migration? Soviet Mobility Policies in Comparative Perspective." *Law & Social Inquiry*, vol. 37, no. 2 (Spring 2012), 395–429.

Lohr, Eric. "What Can Passports Tell Us about Putin's Intentions?" *The Washington Post*, March 4, 2014.

Low, Michael Christopher. "Unfurling the Flag of Extraterritoriality: Autonomy, Foreign Muslims, and the Capitulations in the Ottoman Hijaz." *Journal of the Ottoman and Turkish Studies Association*, vol. 3, no. 2 (2016), 293–323.

Lowry, Heath. *The Nature of the Early Ottoman State.* Albany: State University of New York Press, 2003.

Lussu, Joyce. *Buluşma* (trans. Engin Demiriz and Anna Lia Ergü). İstanbul: Açılım Yayınları, 1995.

MacIntyre, Ben. *Agent Sonya: Moscow's Most Daring Wartime Spy.* New York: Crown, 2020.

MacLeod, William Allister. "Şevket Süreyya Aydemir, Modern Turkish Biographer." PhD Dissertation, Department of Near Eastern Studies, University of Michigan, 1984.

McCarthy, Justin. *Death and Exile: The Ethnic Cleansing of Ottoman Muslims, 1821–1922.* Princeton, NJ: Darwin Press, 1995.

McClellan, Woodford. "Africans and Black Americans in the Comintern Schools, 1925–1934." *The International Journal of African Historical Studies*, vol. 26, no. 2 (1993), 371–390.

McDermott, Kevin and Agnew, Jeremy. *The Comintern: A History of International Communism from Lenin to Stalin.* New York: St. Martin's Press, 1997.

McGuire, Elizabeth. *Red at Heart: How Chinese Communists Fell in Love with the Russian Revolution.* New York: Oxford University Press, 2018.

McKenzie, Kermit Eubank. *Comintern and World Revolution, 1928–1943: The Shaping of Doctrine.* London: Columbia University Press, 1966.

Makal, Oğuz. *Beyaz Perdede ve Sahnede Nâzım Hikmet.* İstanbul: Kalkedon Yayımları, 2015.

Mango, Andrew. *Atatürk.* London: John Murray, 1999.

Martin, Terry. *The Affirmative Action Empire.* Ithaca: Cornell University Press, 2001.

Mazower, Mark. *Salonica: City of Ghosts.* New York: Vintage Books, 2004.

Mëhilli, Elidor. *From Stalin to Mao: Albania and the Socialist World.* Ithaca and London: Cornell University Press, 2017.

Memet Fuat (ed.). *A'dan Z'ye Nâzım Hikmet.* İstanbul: Yapı Kredi Yayınları, 2002.

Memet Fuat. *Gölgede Kalan Yıllar.* İstanbul: Adam Yayınları, 1997.

Memet Fuat. *Nâzım Hikmet: Yaşamı, Ruhsal Yapısı, Davaları, Tartışmaları, Dünya Görüşü, Şiirinin Gelişmeleri.* İstanbul: Yapı Kredi Yayınları, 2015.

Metin, Celal. "Yusuf Akçura ve I. Dünya Savaşında Rusya'daki Türk Esirleri." *Modern Türklük Araştırma Dergisi*, vol. 2, no. 3 (September 2005), 31–52.

Meyer, James H. "Children of Trans-Empire: Nâzım Hikmet and the First Generation of Turkish Students at Moscow's Communist University of the East." *Journal of the Ottoman and Turkish Studies Association*, vol. 5, no. 2 (Fall 2018), 195–218.

Meyer, James H. "Echoes across the Iron Curtain: The Letters of Münevver Andaç to Nâzım Hikmet." *Middle Eastern Studies*, vol. 56, no. 4 (2020), 664–679.

Meyer, James H. "Immigration, Return, and the Politics of Citizenship: Russian Muslims in the Ottoman Empire, 1860–1914." *International Journal of Middle East Studies*, vol. 39, no. 1 (2007), 9–26.

Meyer, James H. "Memory and Political Symbolism in Post-September 12 Turkey: A History of the May 27th Debate." MA Thesis, Department of Near Eastern Studies, Princeton University, 2001.

Meyer, James H. "The Economics of Muslim Cultural Reform: Money, Power, and Muslim Communities in Late Imperial Russia." In Uyama Tomohiko (ed.), *Asiatic Russia: Imperial Power in Regional and International Contexts.* London: Routledge, 2012, 252–270.

Meyer, James H. *Turks Across Empires: Marketing Muslim Identity in the Russian-Ottoman Borderlands, 1856–1914.* Oxford and New York: Oxford University Press, 2014.

Meyer, John W. *No Turning Back: On the Loose in China and Tibet.* Ann Arbor, MI: The Neither/Nor Press, 1991.

Molotov, Vyacheslav. *La démocratie soviétique.* Paris: Bureau d'éditions: les Amis de l'Union soviétique, 1935.

Morawska, Ewa. "Return Migrations: Theoretical and Research Agendas." In Rudolph Vecoli and Suzanne M. Sinke (eds.), *A Century of European Migrations, 1830–1930.* Urbana, IL: University of Illinois Press, 1991, 277–292.

Mouvafac, Nermine. "A Poet of the New Turkey." *The New Bookman*, vol. 74, no. 5 (1932), 508–515.

Navaro-Yashin, Yael. "The Market of Identities: Secularism, Islamism, Commodities." In Deniz Kandiyoti and Ayşe Saktanber (eds.), *Fragments of Culture: The Everyday of Modern Turkey.* New Brunswick, NJ: Rutgers University Press, 2002, 221–253.

Nesin, Aziz. *Türkiye Şarkısı Nâzım.* İstanbul: Nesin Yayıncılık, 2008.

Novikov, V. V. "On logichen v svoikh orientatsiyakh." *Kavkazskii sbornik*, vol. 8, no. 40 (2014), 288–325.

Nuri, Süleyman. *Çanakkale Siperlerinden TKP Yönetimine Uyanan Esirler.* İstanbul: TÜSTAV, 2002.

O'Keeffe, Brigid. *Esperanto and Languages of Internationalism in Revolutionary Russia.* London: Bloomsbury Academic, 2021.

Oral, Haluk. *Nâzım Hikmet'in Yolculuğu.* İstanbul: Türkiye İş Bankası Yayınları, 2019.

Özbilgen, Füsun, *Sana Tütün ve Tespih Yolluyorum: Semiha Berksoy'un Anıları Nâzım Hikmet ve Fikret Muallâ ile Mektuplaşmaları.* İstanbul: Broy Yayınları, 1985.

Özçelik, Ayfer. *Ali Fuat Cebesoy.* Ankara: Akçağ, 1993.

Özdemir, Ahmet. "Savaş Esirlerinin Milli Mücadele Yeri." *Ankara Üniversitesi Türk İnkılap Tarihi Enstitüsü Atatürk Yolu Dergisi*, vol. 2 (June 1990), 321–333.

Özden, Dursun. *Galina'nın Nâzım'ı: Bilinmeyen Yönleriyle.* İstanbul: Kaynak Yayınları, 2007.

Özkan, Remzi Öner. "Bir Nâzım Süprizi." *Radikal*, January 13, 2002.

Özlük, Nuran. *Siyasetten Edebiyata Türk Basınında Dergiler (1883–1957)*. İstanbul: Başlık Yayın Grubu, 2011.

Philliou, Christine M. *Turkey: A Past against History.* Oakland, CA: University of California Press, 2021.

Pinson, Mark. "Russian Policy and the Emigration of the Crimean Tatars to the Ottoman Empire, 1854–1862." *Güney-Doğu Araştırmaları Dergisi*, vol. 1 (1972), 38–41.

Pipes, Richard. *The Formation of the Soviet Union*. New York: Atheneum, 1974.

Popov, Milorad. "The World Council of Peace." In W. S. Sworakowski (ed.), *World Communism: A Handbook*. Stanford: Hoover Institution Press, 1973, 488–491.

Pujals, Sandra. "A 'Soviet Caribbean': The Comintern, New York's Immigrant Community, and the Forging of Caribbean Visions, 1931–1936." *Russian History*, vol. 41, no. 2 (2014), 255–268.

Ravandi-Fadai, Lana. "'Red Mecca'—The Communist University for Laborers of the East (KUTV): Iranian Scholars and Students in Moscow in the 1920s and 1930s." *Iranian Studies*, vol. 48, no. 5 (2015), 713–727.

Reynolds, Michael A. *Shattering Empires: The Clash and Collapse of the Ottoman and Russian Empires, 1908–1918*. New York: Cambridge University Press, 2010.

Riasanovsky, Nicholas V. and Steinberg, Mark D. *A History of Russia*. New York: Oxford University Press, 2011.

Ribard, André. *Les conquêtes de la démocratie soviétique*. Paris: Bureau d'éditions, 1937.

Riddell, John (ed.). *To See the Dawn: Baku, 1920 – First Congress of the Peoples of the East.* New York: Pathfinder Press, 1993.

Robarts, Andrew. *Migration and Disease in the Black Sea Region: Ottoman-Russian Relations in the Late Eighteenth and Early Nineteenth Centuries.* London: Bloomsbury Academic, 2016.

Rorlich, Azade-Ayşe. *The Volga Tatars: A Profile in National Resistance.* Stanford, CA: Hoover Institution Press, 1986.

Rothman, E. Nathalie. *Brokering Empire: Trans-Imperial Subjects between Venice and Istanbul.* Ithaca, NY: Cornell University Press, 2012.

Ryan, James D. "The Republic of Others: Opponents of Kemalism in Turkey's Single Party Era, 1919–1950." PhD dissertation, University of Pennsylvania, 2017.

Said, Edward. *Orientalism*. New York: Vintage Books, 1979.

Sarı, Mustafa. *Türkiye-Kafkasya İlişkilerinde Batum (1917–1921)*. Ankara: Türk Tarih Kurumu, 2014.

Sayılgan, Aclan. *Türkiye'de Sol Hareketler (1871–1972)*. İstanbul: Hareket Yayınları, 1972.

Schimanski, Johan and Nyman, Jopi (eds.). *Border Images, Border Narratives: The Political Aesthetics of Boundaries and Crossings.* Manchester: Manchester University Press, 2021.

Schlögel, Karl. *Moscow 1937*. Cambridge: Polity Press, 2012.

Schwartz, Delmore. *In Dreams Begin Responsibilities and Other Stories.* New York: New Directions Paperbacks, 1978.

Sertel, Sabiha. *Roman Gibi*. İstanbul: Can Sanat Yayınevi, 2015.

Sertel, Sabiha. *The Struggle for Modern Turkey: Justice, Activism and a Revolutionary Female Journalist* (trans. David Selim Sayers and Evrim Emir-Sayers, ed. Tia O'Brien and Nur Deriş). New York and London: I. B. Tauris, 2019.

Sertel, Yıldız. *Annem Sabiha Sertel Kimdi Neler Yazdı?* İstanbul: Yapı Kredi, 1993.

Sertel, Yıldız. *Babam Zekeriya Sertel: Susmayan Adam.* İstanbul: Cumhuriyet Kitapları, 2002.

Sertel, Yıldız. *Nâzım Hikmet ile Serteller: İdeolojileri, Yaşamlarında Bilinmeyenler.* İstanbul: Everest Yayınları, 2008.

Sertel, Zekeriya. *Hatırladıklarım*. İstanbul: Can Sanat Yayınları, 2015.

Sertel, Zekeriya. *Mavi Gözlü Dev*. İstanbul: Can Sanat Yayınları, 2015; first published 1968.

Sertel, Zekeriya. *Nâzım Hikmet'in Son Yılları* (3rd edition). İstanbul: Remzi Kitabevi, 2001.

Sertel, Zekeriya. *Olduğu Gibi: Rus Biçimi Sosyalizm.* İstanbul: İlesişim Yayınları, 1993.

Shapiro, Leonard. *Soviet Treaty Series, vol. I, 1917–1928.* Washington, DC: The Georgetown University Press, 1950.

Shaw, Stanford. *History of the Ottoman Empire and Modern Turkey*, vol. I. Cambridge: Cambridge University Press, 1976.

Shaw, Stanford and Shaw, Ezel Kural. *History of the Ottoman Empire and Modern Turkey*, vol. II. Cambridge: Cambridge University Press, 1977.

Shissler, Ada Holly. *Between Two Empires: Ahmet Ağaoğlu and the New Turkey*. London: I. B. Tauris, 2003.

Shlapentokh, Vladimir. *Love, Marriage, and Friendship in the Soviet Union: Ideals and Practices*. New York: Praeger, 1984.

Shlapentokh, Vladimir. *Public and Private Life of the Soviet People: Changing Values in Post-Stalin Russia*. New York: Oxford University Press, 1989.

Shlyakhter, Andrey Alexander. "Smuggler States: Poland, Latvia, Estonia, and Contraband Trade Across the Soviet Frontier, 1919–1924." PhD dissertation, Department of History, University of Chicago, December 2020.

Shore, Marci. *Caviar and Ashes: A Warsaw Generation's Life and Death in Marxism, 1918–1968*. New Haven, CT: Yale University Press, 2006.

Sloan, Pat. *Soviet Democracy*. London: Gollancz, 1937.

Smiley, Will. "Freeing 'The Enslaved People of Islam': The Changing Meaning of Ottoman Subjecthood for Captives in the Russian Empire." *Journal of the Ottoman and Turkish Studies Association*, vol. 3, no. 2 (2016), 235–254.

Smiley, Will. *From Slaves to Prisoners of War: The Ottoman Empire, Russia, and International Law*. New York: Oxford University Press, 2018.

Smiley, Will. "The Burdens of Subjecthood: The Ottoman State, Russian Fugitives, and Interimperial Law, 1774–1869." *International Journal of Middle East Studies*, vol. 46, no. 1 (2014), 73–93.

Stein, Sarah Abrevaya. *Extraterritorial Dreams: European Citizenship, Sephardi Jews, and the Ottoman Twentieth Century*. Chicago: University of Chicago Press, 2016.

Studer, Brigitte. *The Transnational World of the Cominternians*. New York: Palgrave Macmillan, 2015.

Sunderland, Willard. *The Baron's Cloak: A History of the Russian Empire in War and Revolution*. Ithaca and London: Cornell University Press, 2014.

Suny, Ronald Grigor. *The Soviet Experiment: Russia, the USSR, and the Successor States*. New York: Oxford University Press, 2011.

Sülker, Kemal. *Nâzım Hikmet Dosyası*. İstanbul: May Yayınları, 1967.

Sülker, Kemal. *Nâzım Hikmet'in Bilinmeyen İki Şiir Defteri*. İstanbul: Yazko, 1980.

Sülker, Kemal. *Nâzım Hikmet'in Gerçek Yaşamı*, 6 vols. İstanbul: Yalçın Yayınları, 1987–89.

Sülker, Kemal. *Nâzım Hikmet'in Sahte Dostları*. İstanbul: Matbaası, 1979.

Sülker, Kemal. *Nâzım'ın Polemikleri*. İstanbul: Ant Yayınları, 1968.

Svercheskaia, Antonina Karlovna. *Izvestnyi i neizvestnyi Nâzım: Materialy i biografii*. Moscow: Institut vostokovedenia RAN, 2001.

Şen, Bilal. *Anılar*. İstanbul: TÜSTAV, 2000.

Şimşir, Bilal. *The Turks of Bulgaria (1878–1985)*. London: K. Rustem & Brother, 1988.

Tairov, Nail. *Akchuriny*. Kazan: Tatarskoe knizhnoe izdatel'stvo, 2002.

Temuçin, Ertan. "Ahmet Cevat Emre ve Kemalizm'de Öncü Bir Dergi: *Muhit*." *Kebikeç*, vol. 5 (1997), 17–34.

Tufan, Tarkan. *Hikmet Kıvılcımlı: Hayatı ve Eserleri*. İstanbul: Nokta Kitap, 2008.

Tuliakova-Khikmet, Vera. *Poslednii razgovor s Nazymom*. Moscow: Vremia, 2009.

Tulyakova-Hikmet, Vera. *Bahtiyar Ol Nâzım*. İstanbul: Yapı Kredi Yayınları, 2007.

Tuncer, Hüseyin. *Türk Yurdu Bibliyografyası (1911–1992)*. İzmir: Akademi Kitabevi, 1993.

Tunçay, Mete. *Türkiye'de Sol Akımlar (1908–1925)*. Ankara: Bilgi Yayınevi, 1967.

Tzouliadis, Tim. *The Forsaken: An American Tragedy in Stalin's Russia*. New York: Penguin, 2008.

Uluğtekin, Murat and Uluğtekin, M. Gül. *Osmanlı'dan Cumhuriyet'e Hilal-i Ahmer İcraat Raporları, 1914–1928*. Ankara: Türk Kızılayı Derneği, 2013.

Usal, M. F. *Birinci, ikinci, ve üçüncü duma'da Müslüman deputatlar*. Kazan: Tipografiia I. N. Kharitonova, 1909.

Ünser, Orhan. "Nâzım Hikmet'in sinema çalışmaları: Ali Baba." *Antrakt*, vol. 33 (1996), 23–25.

Üstüngel, S. *Savaş Yolu* (2nd edition). Sofia: Narodna Prosveta, 1958.

Vâ-Nû, Müzehher. *Bir Dönemin Tanıklığı*. İstanbul: Cem Yayınevi, 1987.

Vâ-Nû (Vâlâ Nureddin). *Bu Dünyadan Nâzım Geçti*. İstanbul: Remzi Kitabevi, 1965.

Vassaf, Gündüz. *Annem Belkıs*. İstanbul: İlestişim Yayınları, 2017.

Wasti, Syed Tanvir. *An Introduction to Late Ottoman Turkish Poetry 1839–1922*. Berkeley, CA: Computers and Structures, Inc. 2012.

Wasti, Syed Tanvir. "The Political Aspirations of Indian Muslims and the Ottoman Nexus." *Middle Eastern Studies*, vol. 42, no. 5 (2006), 709–722.

White, Luise. *Speaking with Vampires: Rumor and History in Colonial Africa*. Berkeley, CA: University of California Press, 2000.

Will, George F. *The Pursuit of Happiness and Other Sobering Thoughts*. New York: Harper Colophon Books, 1979.

Wolfe, Stephen F. "Some Cunning Passages in Border-Crossing Narratives: Seen and Unseen Migrants." In Johan Schimanski and Jopi Nyman (eds.), *Border Images, Border Narratives: The Political Aesthetics of Boundaries and Crossings*. Manchester: Manchester University Press, 2021, 168–186.

Xiang, Alice. "Re-Worlding the *Mona Lisa*: Nâzım Hikmet's Modernist Diplomacy." *Journal of Modern Literature*, vol. 41, no. 2 (2018), 1–22.

Yanıkdağı, Yücel. *Healing the Nation: Prisoners of War, Medicine and Nationalism in Turkey 1914–1939*. Edinburgh: Edinburgh University Press, 2013.

Yılmaz, Seçil. "Threats to Public Order and Health: Mobile Men as Syphilis Vectors in Late Ottoman Medical Discourse and Practice." *Journal of Middle East Women's Studies*, vol. 13, no. 2 (2017), 222–243.

Young, Glennys. "To Russia with 'Spain': Spanish Exiles in the USSR and the *Longue Durée* of Soviet History." *Kritika: Explorations in Russian and Eurasian History*, vol. 15, no. 2 (Spring 2014), 395–419.

Yu, Miin-ling. "Sun Yat-sen University in Moscow, 1925–1930." PhD Dissertation, New York University, 1995.

Zekeria, M. "Solving Greco-Turkish Blood Feuds by Migration." *Current History*, vol. 17, no. 6 (1923), 939–942.

Zekeria, M. "The New Turkish Caliph." *Current History*, vol. 17, no. 4 (1923), 669–671.

Zekeria, M. "The Posthumous Memoirs of Mehmed Talat Pasha." *Current History*, vol. 15, no. 2 (1921), 287–295.

Zenkovsky, Serge. *Pan-Turkism and Islam in Russia*. Cambridge, MA: Harvard University Press, 1960.

Zürcher, Erik. *Turkey: A Modern History* (3rd edition). New York: I. B. Tauris, 2014.

Zürcher, Erik and Tunçay, Mete. *Socialism and Nationalism in the Ottoman Empire 1876–1923*. London: Bloomsbury Academic, 1994.

# Index

For the benefit of digital users, indexed terms that span two pages (e.g., 52–53) may, on occasion, appear on only one of those pages.

Abdülhak Hamit 170
Abdülhamid II 21–6, 29–31
Abkhazia 50–2, 115–16, 307–8
Açıkgözyan, Hayk 277, 288–9, 316, 323
Adılov, F. 270–4, 276–7
Adıvar, Adnan 47, 136
Adıvar, Halide Edip 26–7, 46–8, 58, 168
  in the *New York Times* 169
Ağaoğlu, Ahmet 44, 168
  background of 29
  and Pan-Turkism 30–1
  and Republic of Azerbaijan 62, 94
  and WWI 43
Ahmet Cevat, *see* Emre, Ahmet Cevat
Akçura, Yusuf 47–8, 50, 52, 168
  background of 27–8
  and İttifak 29
  and Ottoman POWs 43–5
  and Pan-Turkism 29
  and the Turkic Hearths 30
  and *Türk Yurdu* 30–1
Ali Fuat Pasha, *see* Cebesoy, Ali Fuat Pasha
Ali, Sabahattin 1–2
Alimov, Abid
  and Mustafa Suphi 71
Aliyev, Sait
  arrest of 1949 252–3
  defection to USSR 232
  immigration to Romania 308
  letter to Nâzım Hikmet 308
  in Moscow 232–3
Alliluyeva, Svetlana 302–3
Andaç, Münevver 10 11, 245, 286–7, 301, 326, 330
  background of 190–1
  breakup with Nâzım Hikmet 320–3
  correspondence with Nâzım Hikmet, 1955–60 284, 290–7, 317–23
  escape from Turkey 324–5
  after Nâzım Hikmet's death 341
  and *Human Landscapes from my Country* 319
  and Nâzım Hikmet in 1930s 190–1
  and Nâzım Hikmet, 1950–51 249–50, 253–4, 256

  and Nâzım Hikmet in Bursa Prison 240–2, 245
  as subject of Nâzım Hikmet's poetry 309, 312–13, 332–3
Apletin, Mikhail 302, 312
Atatürk, Mustafa Kemal 50, 55–7, 59, 65–6, 69–70, 117–18, 135–6, 140–1, 168–9, 173, 186–7, 234, 239–40
  and alleged assassination plot 125, 187
  commercialization of 5
  death of 215
  meeting Nâzım and Vâlâ 76–7
  and murder of Mustafa Suphi 72
  and Nâzım Hikmet's request for clemency 215
  and resistance movement in Ankara 21, 39, 46–7, 63, 73, 82–4
  as subject of biography 5
Aybar, Mehmet Ali 323–4
Aybek, Zafer Hasan 125
Aydemir, Leman 107, 198
  background of 99
  in Batumi 123
  death of 340
  at KUTV 116, 124
  marriage to Şevket Süreyya 99
  return to Turkey 138
  traveling from the Caucasus to Moscow 106
  in Udel'naia 107–8
Aydemir, Şevket Süreyya 251, 311, 315
  in Azerbaijan 97–9
  background of 41
  in Batumi 100
  and the Congress of Eastern Peoples 50, 66–7
  at KUTV 116, 120, 124, 147, 149–50, 195
  at the Hotel Luxe 106–8
  imprisonment in Turkey 141
  joining TKP 99
  later–life activities 340
  leaving TKP 196–7
  letter to the Comintern 161–4, 231
  marriage to Leman 99
  in postwar Istanbul and Edirne 45, 62–3

366 INDEX

Aydemir, Şevket Süreyya (*cont.*)
  and pan-Turkism 41
  traveling from the Caucasus to Moscow 106
  in Udel'naia 107–9
  in WWI 39–42
*Aydınlık* 136–8, 141–3, 148, 162
Aynühayat Voinova, *see* Voinova, Aynühayat
Aybar, Mehmet Ali 323–4
Azerbaijan
  Democratic Republic 30, 62–3, 94, 97–9,
    125, 197
  in imperial Russia 71
  Soviet Azerbaijan 49, 102, 113, 120, 146, 150,
    152, 157, 200, 231–2, 251, 342
Aziz, *see* Özdoğu, Mehmet Husametdin

Babayev, Ekber 22, 281, 326, 337
Baku Congress, *see* Congress of the Peoples of
    the East 49–52, 66–8, 94
Balaban, İbrahim
  background of 225
  with Nâzım Hikmet in prison 225–6
  and Nâzım Hikmet's alleged suicide
    attempt 238n. 1
Baraner, Reşat Fuat, aka Sidki 195–6
Barvikha 285–6
Bardot, Brigitte 295
Başgöz, İlhan 344
Baştımar, Zeki
  arrest in Turkey 165
  background of 122
  death of 346
  in Eastern Bloc 316–17, 323–4
  expulsion from TKP 163–4
  and İsmail Bilen 317, 323–4, 345–6
  at KUTV 122
  returning to TKP 165
  translating *War and Peace* with Nâzım
    Hikmet 226, 241
Benaroya, Abraam 25
Benderli, Gün 191–2, 277
  background of 278
  in Budapest 260–79, 287–8
  flight from Budapest, 1956 298–9
  later-life activities 344
  and Nâzım Hikmet 298–9, 309
  and the Sertels 342–3
  in Sofia 339–40
  and TKP organization in Leipzig 325, 345
Berk, Nurullah 240, 243, 292, 295, 297
Berkin, Nüzhet
  in Ankara 46, 73–4
  background of 73
  breaking up with Nâzım 139–41, 144
  in Georgia 79–80, 86–7, 90–1, 100

  later-life activities 340
  in Moscow 126–8
Berksoy, Semiha 189–90, 219, 228
Beyler Café 77–80
Bierut, Bolesław 298, 301–3
Bilen, İsmail, aka Marat
  and Alexander Senkevich 201–4, 220–4
  aliases of 192, 323
  death of 348
  and Gün Togay 191–2, 339
  introduction to communism 120–1
  at KUTV 121, 123, 145, 150–2
  and Mara Kolarova 220–4
  and Nâzım Hikmet 157–8, 204–6, 211, 259,
    264, 268–70, 289–90, 299–303, 350–1
  and radio broadcasting 229–33, 288–9,
    315–16
  and Raikhman investigation 250–3
  and the "secret speech," 300–3
  and Süleyman Nuri 314–15, 329–30
  as TKP representative to the Comintern
    194–6, 198–201
  and TKP politics in Leipzig 316, 323–4,
    345–7
  in Turkey in the 1930s 172–3, 191–4
  and Zeki Baştımar 317, 323–4, 345–6
Birgen, Muhittin 46
  in Ankara 73–5
  in Baku 127–8
  in Georgia 79, 86–7, 90–3, 100
Bolshevik eastern strategy 49, 66, 104
Border-crossers 11–16
Borzhenski, Constantine 20–1
Brecht, Bertolt 304
Brezhnev, Leonid 247, 345–7
Brikke, Semyon 133–5, 137, 147
Brown University 181
Bulgarian Turks, *see* Turks of Bulgaria

Ceauşescu, Nicolae 247
Cebesoy, Ali Fuat Pasha 21
  ambassador to Moscow 64, 67–8, 126
  in Ankara 46
  and Nâzım Hikmet's incarcerations 76,
    218–19
  political activity in Turkey after 1923 136,
    141, 161, 224, 229, 234, 236–7
Celile Hanım 18–23, 33, 35–7, 64, 82, 126, 139,
    142, 171–2, 190–1, 241, 245, 249, 291
Cemal Pasha 32, 34–5, 45, 63, 125–6
Chervenkov, Valko 255, 273–5, 298
Chicherin, Georgii 64
citizenship (or "subjecthood") 6, 10, 14–15,
    113, 116, 137, 189, 220, 231–2, 270,
    301–3, 307, 325, 330–3, 348

closing doors 12, 183, 210, 273–5, 350–1
  and increased state violence 187
Cominform 271
Comintern 7, 9–10, 16, 72, 107, 110, 113,
      120–1, 123, 130, 133–4, 137–9, 145–7,
      151–2, 156–7, 159, 162–4, 177,
      194–201, 204, 219–24, 229–30,
      270–1, 275–6
  dissolution of 229–30
Committee of Union and Progress (CUP) 23–4,
      26–7, 30, 32, 48
communist internationals 7, 16–17, 330
Communist University of the National Minorities
      of the West (KUNMZ) 109–12
  and Soviet "near abroad," 111
Communist University of the Toilers of the East
      (KUTV) 103, 105–7, 109–13, 156–7,
      185, 200–1
  and the offspring of Muslim emigrants from
      Russia 116–18
  and opposition movement among Turkish
      students 145–52, 199–201, 204
  and Ottoman POWs 114–15
  and the Ottoman-Russian borderlands 115
  and the Ottoman western borderlands 116
  other Turkish students 120–3
Congress of the Peoples of the East 49–52,
      66–7, 94
Crimean Tatars 13, 48, 50–1, 116–18, 149
Crimean War 12, 136
Cumhuriyet 158, 169, 250, 255, 344
Çamlıbel, Faruk Nafiz 36, 47, 54–7, 86

Damat Ferit Pasha 55–7
Dean, James 295
Demokrat ("Democrat") party, Turkey 238–40,
      245, 321
Deniz, Ömer 212–14
Detroit, Karl 20–1, 39
Detroit, Michigan 169
Deymer, Şefik Hüsnü 52–3, 104, 115, 119–21,
      123, 126–7, 137
  avoiding arrest in Istanbul, 1925 142
  background of 52
  establishment of Turkish Communist
      Party 72, 145–6
  establishment of Turkish Worker and Peasant
      Socialist Party 52
  and Nâzım Hikmet 135, 138–9, 141, 152,
      163, 195
  replaced by İsmail Bilen as TKP
      representative to the Comintern,
      1937 194–5, 198–9, 204–5
  and Turkish opposition at KUTV 145,
      148–51

Dimitrov, Georgi 197–8
  background of 198
  as head of the Comintern 198, 200–1, 220–1,
      223, 229–32
  as Prime Minister of Bulgaria 255
Dino, Abidin
  background of 249
  and Nâzım Hikmet's hunger strike 249
  in Paris 271, 323, 329
  and the TKP 323–4, 345
Dönmes
  and Celile Hanım's family 20–1
  and Sabiha Sertel 167–8
  and Şefik Hüsnü 52
Dr. Nâzım 125–6

Ecevit, Bülent 344
Ekk, Nikolai 153–4
Emre, Ahmet Cevat
  background of 93
  in Batumi 99–100
  departure from USSR 147
  and KUTV 103
  later–life activities 340
  in Moscow 106–9, 116, 130, 144, 146–7
  from pan–Turkism to communism
      94, 120
  and the "social family" in Batumi 100–3
  in Tbilisi with Nâzım Hikmet 94–6
  and TKP opposition at KUTV 148–50
  as a 'traitor' to the party 163–4, 195–6,
      314–15, 329–30
  and work on Turkish alphabet
      commission 197
Esenbel, Melih 247–8
Enver Pasha
  and 1913 coup 32
  and Bolsheviks 63–4, 67–8, 96–7, 125–6
  at Congress of Peoples of the East 66–7
  and the CUP "triumvirate," 32, 34–5, 45, 63,
      125–6, 168
  death of 68
  and flight from Ottoman Empire 45
  in WWI 41
Erduran, Refik 1–3, 256, 263
Ersoy, Mehmet Akif 84
Ertuğrul, Muhsin 154n. 109, 182–3, 207
Eshba, Efrem 50–1

Fadeyev, Alexander
  inviting Nâzım Hikmet to live in
      USSR 262, 264–5
  political disgrace and suicide of 301, 303
February Revolution, Russia 42n. 9, 44
Fevziye Habibova, see Habibova, Fevziye

368 INDEX

First Balkan War  31–2, 38, 52, 64, 136
Futurist poetry  128–9, 131, 142, 144, 152,
    179–80, 207, 210

Galatasaray High School  25, 32, 39, 47–8, 54,
    138, 217
Gasprinskii, İsmail
  and İttifak  28–9
  and Mustafa Suphi  48–9
"German" Turkish communists  53, 57–8,
    120, 138
Gomułka, Władysław  302–3
Gökalp, Ziya
  meeting Vâlâ Nureddin in Ankara  84
  and Turkism  26–7, 32–4, 58, 128

Habibova, Fevziye  117–18
Hacıoğlu, Salih  259, 308
  and Ankara-based TKP, 1920  65–6
  in Azerbaijan  231–2
  background of  65–6, 138
  death of  308
  in Moscow  231
  and Nâzım Hikmet's poem about
    Hacıoğlu  311–12
  and Raikhman's investigation, 1949  251–3
  and Şevket Süreyya's alleged letter to the
    Comintern  162
  Working on *Aydınlık* and *Orak-Çekiç*  138
Halide Edip, *see* Adıvar, Halide Edip
Harbiye, *see* War College
Hikmet Bey  21–3, 25, 36, 38, 139, 141, 145,
    160–1, 174
Hikmet, Nâzım, *see* Nâzım Hikmet
Hotel Luxe  106–9, 120, 124, 145, 147, 186,
    202–3, 222, 224, 232
Hula-hoops  295
*Human Landscapes from my Country*  143, 228,
    234–6, 319, 327, 337–8
Hungarian revolution  297–9
Husametdin, Aziz, *see* Özdoğu, Mehmet
    Husametdin, aka Aziz
Hüseyinzade, Ali  30–1, 43–4

Independence Tribunals, Turkey  140–1
International Lenin School (ILS)  109, 151
International Youth Festival, East Berlin
    270–3, 277–8
Iron Curtain  1, 278, 323, 348
İhmalyan, Jak  277, 288–9, 316, 323
İhmalyan, Vartan  277, 289, 323, 343
İnönü, İsmet  66, 234–5, 340
İpek Films  214, 226–7
İsmail Bilen, *see* Bilen, İsmail

İsmail Fazıl Pasha  21, 46, 76
İttifak  28–9

Kadirov, İsmail  71–2
Karabekir, Kâzım
  arrest and detention of  140–1
  correspondence with Mustafa Suphi  50, 68–9
  and political activities in Turkey after
    1923  136
Karaosmanoğlu, Yakup Kadri  171–2
Kayserili İsmail Hakkı  71, 95
Kemal, Orhan  224–5, 227–8, 235
Kemal, Yaşar  304, 341
Khrushchev, Nikita  262, 276, 300–1
  and de-Stalinization  297–9, 303–4, 307,
    311, 314
  Nâzım Hikmet's letter to  330–1, 333, 345, 351
Kıvılcımlı, Dr. Hikmet  215, 217
Kolarova, Mara (aka Stanka)
  and Alexander Senkevich  203–4, 219–22
  arrival in USSR  202–3
  background of  202–3
  and citizenship  220
  daughter of  203
  and housing problems in Moscow  203–4,
    219–20
  and İsmail Bilen  220–4, 299–300, 316, 348
Kolesnikova, Dr. Galina  285–7, 297, 299, 303,
    317–19, 341
  later-life activities  341
Korean War  240, 258–60, 280
Kuleli military academy  93–4, 213
Kutlu, Ali Haydar  230–2, 252
KUNMZ, *see* Communist University of the
    National Minorities of the West
KUTV, *see* Communist University of the Toilers
    of the East
Kuyulu Café  75–6, 84, 92

Lakoba, Nestor  50–3, 57–8, 70, 72, 74
Lav, Ercümend Behzad  207–9
Law for the Maintenance of Public Order,
    Turkey  140–1
Lenin, Vladimir  27, 44, 63–4, 71–2, 80–1, 145,
    184–5, 299
  in Nâzım Hikmet's writing  264, 310–13
Lussu, Joyce
  background of  319
  and Münevver Andaç  324–5
  and translating Nâzım's poetry  319–20

Mahmut Şevket Pasha  48
Manatov, Şerif  65–6, 95, 138
Marat, *see* Bilen, İsmail

Mariam, (wife of Mustafa Suphi) 69–71
Martel, Şükrü 116n. 58, 198–9, 344
  At KUTV 123
Mayakovsky, Vladimir 105, 128, 130, 142,
    174, 179
Mdivani, Polikarp "Budu," 84, 92–3
Mehmet Husametdin, see Özdoğu, Mehmet
    Husametdin, aka Aziz
Mehmet Nâzım (son of Nâzım Hikmet) 253–4,
    286–7, 290–1, 294–5, 297, 301,
    309n. 154, 313, 322–3, 325–6, 330,
    332–3, 341
Mehmet Nâzım Pasha 21–2
Melda (Nâzım Hikmet's sister) 1–2, 160, 263
Memet Fuat 175–6, 214, 218, 244, 340
Menderes, Adnan 239–40, 245, 248–9, 260,
    321, 323, 340, 348
Mesrure, Sabiha, aka "Rosa"
  and Alexander Senkevich 192–3
  background of 121
  and İsmail Bilen 121, 150, 252–3
  in Spetsgruppa 192–3
METLA 153–4
Mikoyan, Anastas 262, 276
  and Süleyman Nuri 314–15, 328–30
Moore, Charles R. 247–8
Mouvafac, Nermine 180–1
Muslim Bureau 65
Muslim Union of Russia, see İttifak
Mustafa Kemal Pasha, see Atatürk
Mustafa Suphi, see Suphi, Mustafa
Müsavat Party 49, 62–3, 94, 97, 125, 197

Nagy, Imre 299
NATO 240
Nâzım Hikmet
  and Adile Hüseyinova 326, 337
  and Ahmet Cevat (Emre) 93–7, 99–101,
      106–9, 116–17, 120, 130, 144, 147–50,
      163–4, 195–6, 314–15, 329–30
  in Ankara, 1921 73–7
  and archival holdings 9–11
  and Army-Navy trials 212–17
  background and early family life 18–23, 25
  and Berlin International Youth
      Festival 270–3
  biographies of 7–9
  in Bolu, 1921 77–81
  as a border-crosser 11–12
  on Budapest Radio 289–90
  in Bulgaria, 1951 273–5
  campaign for release from prison,
      1949–1950 245–50
  and Cemal Pasha 34–5, 125–6

citizenship of 6, 10, 270, 301–3, 330–3, 348
commonalities with Atatürk 5, 7n. 9
as a communist international 16–17
contracts signed in final years 326–8
death of 336–8
death preparations 330–2
divorce of parents 35–6
escape from Istanbul, 1921 39, 47, 53–4
escape from Istanbul, 1925 142
escape from Istanbul, 1951 1–3
fan letters to 284, 304–7
and film 182–3, 208, 212, 226, 326–8, 335
friends at KUTV 123–4, 126–8, 131, 135,
    137, 144–5
and Galina Kolesnikova 285–7, 297, 299,
    303, 317–19
in Georgia, 1921 88–97, 99–104
incarceration of, 1928 158
incarceration of, 1933–34 176–7
incarceration of, 1938–50 217–19, 224–9,
    233–8, 240–5
in Istanbul, 1924–25 135–42
in Istanbul, 1928–33 160–1
in Istanbul, 1934–38 189–91, 196–7
and İbrahim Balaban 225–6
and İsmail Bilen 193, 204–6, 268–70, 288–90,
    299–303, 323–4, 329–30, 350
in İzmir 141
joining TKP 97
journey to Ankara, 1921 54–61
journey to Georgia, 1921 81–7
and Khrushchev 262, 276, 300–1, 307,
    311, 330–2
in Moscow, 1922–24 105–8, 112, 116,
    120, 123–8
in Moscow, 1925–28 144–52
in Moscow, 1951–1963 258–9, 265–70,
    275–7, 284–7, 295–7, 304–13, 315,
    317–23, 325–38
and Münevver Andaç 190–1, 240–5, 253–4,
    256, 290–5, 297, 301, 309, 312–13,
    317–26, 330, 332–3
and Orhan Kemal 224–5
and Ömer Deniz 212–14
and Piraye 240, 253–4, 293, 319, 321
  makes the acquaintance of 175–6
  correspondence with 176–7, 218–19,
      227–9, 233–7, 242–5
prose versus poetry 210, 335
return to Istanbul, 1924 133–5
return to Istanbul, 1928 155–9
in Romania, 1951 3, 260–5
and Sadık Ahi 57–8, 61
after the "secret speech," 299–304, 310–13

Nâzım Hikmet (*cont.*)
and the Sertels  166–7, 226, 249, 260, 262–4, 269, 271–2, 277, 282, 284–5, 298, 303, 328
and "Smashing the Idols" series  170–2
and Şevket Süreyya Aydemir  100–1, 106–9, 116, 124, 147, 149–50, 162–4, 195–7, 251, 311, 314–15
and Stalin  205–6, 259–64, 266–8, 272–6, 280, 282, 302–3, 312
and Süleyman Nuri  145–52, 314–15, 328–30
and TKP in USSR, 1921–1928  93–7, 120, 145–52
and TKP in Istanbul, 1925–1928  137–43, 158–9
and TKP in Istanbul after 1929  161–5, 177, 181, 197, 206
and TKP in USSR and Eastern Bloc after 1951  260, 264, 268–70, 323–4, 328–32, 351
and the Togays  298–9
at Udel'naia  108–9
and Vâlâ Nureddin  34, 36, 38–9, 46–7, 53–61, 73–97, 99–109, 112, 116, 123–7, 131–5, 137, 144, 146–50, 155–6, 161, 163–8
and Vera Tulyakova  295–7, 300, 318, 320–1, 325–6
Writing, 1912–18  32–4
Writing, 1918–20  36–8
Writing, 1921–22, in Anatolia and the Caucasus  74, 101–2
Writing, 1922–24, Moscow  128–31
Writing, 1925, Istanbul  142–4
Writing, 1925–28, Moscow  152–5
Writing, 1928–33, Istanbul  178–83
Writing, 1934–38, Istanbul  208–10
Writing, 1938–50, prison  233–7
Writing, 1951–53, Moscow  279–82
Writing, 1954–59, Eastern Bloc  308–13
Writing, 1960–63, Moscow  332–6
near abroad, USSR  111
Nesin, Aziz  ix, 7, 11
Nevşirvanov, Zinetullah  94, 149
Nevşirvanova, Cemile  95, 117, 147
Nicholas II  24, 42
Nihat Nuri "the Electrician,"  53n. 59, 116n. 59, 230n. 109, 305
North Atlantic Treaty Organization, *see* NATO
Novodevichy Cemetery  4, 349
Nureddin, Müzehher (aka Müzehher Vâ-Nû)  241, 250, 340
Nureddin, Vâlâ (aka Vâ-Nû)
in Ankara  73–7, 82–4
background of  54

in Bolu  77–81
early friendship with Nâzım Hikmet  34, 36, 38
joining TKP  97
journeys to Ankara, 1921  39, 46–7, 53–61
in Georgia  88–97, 99–104
introducing Nâzım Hikmet to the Sertels  166
at KUTV  105–9, 112, 116, 120, 123–6, 131–5, 137, 144, 146–7, 149–51, 163–4
later–life activities  340
and Nâzım Hikmet  34, 36, 38–9, 46–7, 53–61, 73–97, 99–109, 112, 116, 123–7, 131–5, 137, 144, 146–50, 155–6, 161, 163–8
visiting Leningrad with Istanbul Chamber of Commerce  155
wife and child in Moscow  127, 144
Nuri, Süleyman
and Anastas Mikoyan  314–15, 328–30, 332
background of  51–2
denunciation of Mustafa Suphi  70–2
and Muhammad Ağa Shahtakhtinskii  122–3
and Nestor Lakoba  50–2
and rebellion against TKP "Central Committee,"  145–6, 149–52
and Salih Hacıoğlu  251
and the purging of his allies  200–1
Nüzhet, *see* Berkin, Nüzhet

*Orak–Çekiç*  138, 141–3, 162
Orbay, Rauf  44, 136
Ortaç, Yusuf Ziya  36, 47, 54–7, 143
"Orhan Selim,"  182, 189–90, 209
Özdoğu, Mehmet Husametdin, aka Aziz  121–2, 146, 150, 193, 252–3

pan-Turkism and pan-Turkists  13, 25–31, 41, 44, 127–8, 314–15, 329–30
and Turkish communists  25–6, 31, 41, 47–8, 53, 62, 65, 93–4, 97–9, 120, 168
Pauker, Ana  260
Pehlivanyan, Aram  316, 323–4, 345
Peyami Safa  189, 217
Piraye  176, 189–90, 213–14, 218, 224, 234–5, 253–4, 340
background of  175–6
correspondence with Nâzım Hikmet  160–77, 214–15, 218–19, 224, 226–9, 235–7, 242–5
*Plekhanov*  2–3, 260–1
Ponomarev, Boris  262, 264–5, 267
prisoners of war (POWs)  96, 119–20, 135, 137, 188
at KUTV  114–15
and the Ottoman government  43–5
and the TKP  49–50, 71

INDEX 371

Progressive Republican Party  136, 141
purges
    in the USSR in the late 1930s  125, 185–6,
        188, 198, 250
    in the USSR-based TKP, 1949  197–201,
        255, 299

Radek, Karl  63, 107, 186
Rahime Hakkı  95, 117, 149
Ran, Nâzım Hikmet, *see* Nâzım Hikmet
Red Crescent/Red Cross  44, 52, 316
Refugees  31–2, 41, 99, 106, 136nn. 14, 15,
    136–7, 184, 187, 255–6
Republican People's Party (CHP)  136,
    238–40
*Resimli Ay*  166–7, 169–70, 173, 175
    and the "Smashing the Idols" series
        170–2
Resulzade, Mehmet Emin  30, 62, 94
Rosenthal, Charlotte  305–6, 343
Russian Revolution of 1905  24, 27, 29, 80–1
Russian School of Istanbul  119

Sabiha Mesrure, aka Rosa  121, 150, 192–3,
    252–3
Sadık Ahi
    and Nestor Lakoba  53
    with Nâzım and Vâlâ  57–8, 75–6, 84–5, 89,
        92–3, 104
Salih Hacıoğlu, *see* Hacıoğlu, Salih
Salonica (Thessaloniki)  18, 20, 22–6, 31–2, 52,
    54, 64, 116, 167, 184
Samiye (Nâzım Hikmet's sister)  23, 35, 139,
    160, 175–6, 242, 293
Sarıdal, Vehbi  53, 57–8, 84, 92, 227
Sebük, Mehmet Ali  246, 248–9
Second Balkan War  31–2, 38, 64, 136, 184
Senkevich, Alexander
    background of  118–20
    and İsmail Bilen  192–3, 204, 219–24
    and Mara Kolarova  201–4, 219–24
    and Russian School of Istanbul  119
    party autobiography of, 1934  192–4
Sertel, Sabiha
    in Azerbaijan  342–3
    background of  167–8
    in Budapest  279, 288
    death of  342
    marriage to Zekeriya Sertel  167–8
    meets Nâzım Hikmet  166
    protesting Istanbul's occupation  46
    in the United States  168–9
    and *Resimli Ay*  169, 173
    with Nâzım Hikmet in East Berlin  271, 277

and Nâzım Hikmet's escape from Turkey
    262–4, 271
    in Leipzig  323
Sertel, Zekeriya
    in Azerbaijan  342–3
    background  167–8
    in Budapest  279, 288
    connections with Young Turks  167–8
    in the Eastern Bloc  323
    marriage to Sabiha Sertel  167–8
    and Nâzım Hikmet  166–7, 226, 249, 260,
        262–4, 269, 271–2, 277, 282, 284–5, 298,
        303, 328
    protesting Istanbul's occupation  46
    and *Resimli Ay*  169, 173
    in the United States  168–9
Sertel, Yıldız  264, 271, 277, 279, 288, 323, 342–3
Shahtakhtinskii, Muhammad Ağa  122–3
Sheikh Sait Rebellion  140–1, 169, 186–7,
    194, 238–9
Siao, Emi  124–5
    and Nâzım Hikmet's "Gioconda and
        Siao,"  178
Socialism in the Ottoman Empire  25–6, 31
    connections to Turkish communism  25–6
Soviet-Turkish relations, *see* Turkey, Republic of,
    relations with USSR
Spartakists  53, 57–8, 61, 74–6, 80, 82, 84, 88–9,
    92, 95, 107, 120, 138
*Spetsgruppa*  113, 121, 192–3
Stalin, Joseph  12, 17, 125, 145, 148, 185–6,
    205–6, 217, 255, 259–64, 266–8, 272–6,
    279–80, 282, 288, 297–9, 301–3, 305,
    308–13, 315, 332–3, 345, 351
Stalinism, *see* Stalin, Joseph
Stolypin, Pyotr  29, 122
subjecthood, *see* citizenship
Sun Yat-sen Communist University  109
Suphi, Mustafa  47–50, 64–73, 95, 101, 114,
    121, 150
    Background  47–9
    Correspondence with Kâzım Karabekir
        50, 68–9
    and İsmail Gasprinskii  48–9
    Murder of  69–70
Süleyman Nuri, *see* Nuri, Süleyman
Sülker, Kemal  8–9, 127, 139, 141, 174, 212–13
Sünbül, Sabiha  162, 231, 251–3, 308, 311, 316
Şefik Hüsnü, *see* Deymer, Şefik Hüsnü
Şevket Süreyya, *see* Aydemir, Şevket Süreyya
Şükrü Martel, *see* Martel, Şükrü

Tahir, Kemal  217, 269
Talat Pasha  32, 63, 125–6, 168

*Tanin* publishing group  26–7, 36, 48, 73, 246
Tanrıöver, Hamdullah Suphi  172
Taron, Gabrielle  190–1
Tek, Ahmet Ferit  28, 48
Tietze, Andreas  304
TKP, *see* Turkish Communist Party
Togay, Gün Benderli, *see* Benderli, Gün
Togay, Necil  277–9, 287–8, 298–9
Tör, Vedat Nedim  53, 138, 161, 164, 195
Treaty of Brest-Litovsk  67, 239
Treaty of Moscow (1921)  21, 64, 67–8, 70, 96
Treaty of Sèvres  46, 57
Tulyakova, Vera  297, 300, 318
  background  295–6
  following Nâzım Hikmet's death  340–2
  and Nâzım Hikmet  295–7, 300, 318–22,
    325–8, 332–3, 336–7
Turan  26–7, 62, 97–8
Turkey, Republic of
  establishment of  14, 18–21, 137
  relations with People's Republic of Bulgaria
    1–2, 255, 273–4
  relations with the United States  238–40
  relations with the USSR  135, 238–40
Turkic Hearths  30, 43, 172
  and future Turkish communists  53, 65,
    168, 170
Turkish Communist Party (TKP) based in Baku,
    1920–1921  8, 47–53, 64–73, 94–5, 97,
    99, 101, 114–15
Turkish Communist Party (TKP) based in
    Ankara, 1920  65–6
Turkish Communist Party (TKP), official, based
    in Ankara, 1920–21  65–6
Turkish Communist Party (TKP) in Moscow,
    1922–1951  105, 113, 115–20, 123,
    145–52, 156–7, 194–6, 198–201, 203–5,
    220, 231, 250–3
Turkish Communist Party (TKP) in Turkey,
    1922–onward  135–44, 156, 158, 161,
    163–5, 188, 191–4, 217–18
Turkish Communist Party (TKP) in USSR and
    Eastern Bloc after 1951  288, 290, 299,
    303, 306–7, 314, 323–4, 328–30
  and TKP "Foreign Bureau,"  345–8
Turkish students at KUTV, *see* Communist
    University of the Toilers of the East
Turkish War of Liberation  6, 21, 136, 140–1,
    161, 234–5, 333–4

Turkism and Turkists  25–7, 31, 33–4, 38, 48, 58,
    84, 93–4, 131, 168, 170, 188
  and Turkish communists  25–6, 31, 41, 47–8,
    53, 62, 65, 93–4, 97–9, 120, 168
Turks of Bulgaria  255, 273–5, 298
*Türk Ocakları*, *see* Turkic Hearths
*Türk Yurdu*  30, 43, 53, 62, 94

Uçuk, Cahit, aka Cahide Uçok  190
Udel'naia summer camp  107–9, 128, 144
United States  168–9, 181, 271
  Diplomatic attitudes regarding Nâzım
    Hikmet  247–8
  Relations with Turkey  239–40, 260

Vâlâ Nureddin, *see* Nureddin, Vâlâ
Voinova, Aynühayat  117, 149–51

War College (Harbiye)  27–8, 93–4,
    213–14, 232
War of Liberation, *see* Turkish War of
    Liberation
Warsaw Pact  298, 348, 350
  Invasion of Hungary, 1956  299, 302–3
Worker and Peasant Socialist Party of
    Turkey  52, 72, 104, 195n. 72
World Peace Council (WPC)  247, 260, 262–3,
    281, 285, 291, 319
World War I  12, 15–16, 26–7, 34–5, 37–8, 46,
    52, 64, 69, 94, 96, 98, 114–17, 121, 154,
    190–1, 306, 308
  And Ottoman manpower shortage  43–4

Yahya Kemal  35–6, 171–2
Yahya the boatman  69–70
Yalman, Ahmet Emin  246, 248–9
Young Turks, *see* Committee of Union and
    Progress
Young Turk Revolution (1908)  22, 24
Yurchenko, Yelena (Dr. Lena)  145, 157, 160–1,
    256, 340
Yurdakul, Mehmet Emin  33–4, 170, 172
Yusuf Akçura, *see* Akçura, Yusuf

Zafer Hasan, *see* Aybek, Zafer Hasan
Zedong, Mao  124, 280
Zinoviev, Grigory  71–2, 107, 148, 186
Ziya Hilmi  80–2, 85–6